AMERICAN CHRISTIANITY

1820–1960

American Christianity

AN
HISTORICAL INTERPRETATION
WITH
REPRESENTATIVE DOCUMENTS

by

H. SHELTON SMITH
ROBERT T. HANDY
LEFFERTS A. LOETSCHER

VOLUME II
1820–1960

CHARLES SCRIBNER'S SONS, NEW YORK

This book published simultaneously in the
United States of America and in Canada —
Copyright under the Berne Convention

1 3 5 7 9 11 13 15 17 19 B/C 20 18 16 14 12 10 8 6 4 2

Printed in the United States of America
Library of Congress Catalog Card Number 77-93739
ISBN 0-684-15745-4

TO OUR

THEOLOGICAL SEMINARY COLLEAGUES

AT

DUKE, PRINCETON, UNION

WITH

GRATITUDE AND AFFECTION

PREFACE

THE present volume continues the general structural pattern of the first: it organizes the contents according to major periods and combines within each period both interpretive exposition and original documents. As in the previous work, historical interpretation comprises roughly a third of the text and the remainder reproduces primary sources. There are slightly fewer documents in this volume than in the first, but they are of greater average length.

The years herein covered (1820–1960) witnessed remarkable growth in church membership among both Roman Catholics and Protestants. These years saw also vast social changes, changes provoked not only by the dynamic forces of urbanization and industrialization but by a convulsive North-South conflict and two world wars. Meanwhile the American mind encountered unprecedented developments in scientific, social, philosophic, and religious thought. Variant forms of radicalism, moderatism, and conservatism vigorously competed for the allegiance of men. Only as these sharp crosscurrents are explored in their full dimensions may one come to understand the moral and religious phenomena of modern American culture.

The present work, like its companion, grew out of an extended process of face-to-face dialogue; therefore, the final result represents the combined thinking of all three participants. Nevertheless, primary responsibility was divided as follows: Professor Handy, introduction to Period V and Chapters 12, 16, 21, 22; Professor Loetscher, introductions to Periods IV and VI and Chapters 13, 18, 19; Professor Smith, Chapters 14, 15, 17, 20.

Our three institutions—Duke, Princeton, Union—have generously shared in this two-volume enterprise by granting to us much extra time for research and by placing at our disposal, under competent guidance, their bountiful library collections. Union provided us with working space and living accommodations during joint sessions. Duke University, through its Research Council, made many financial grants to the chairman of the project. Dr. Doralyn Hickey, now assistant professor in the School of Library Science of the University of North Carolina, served as research assistant to the chairman while the second volume was passing through its most intensive period of preparation. She painstakingly proof-read the entire text in its final form and prepared the Index. Mr. William L. Savage, an enthusiastic sponsor of the project from the beginning, skilfully saved us from numerous technical pitfalls in the course of our labors. We extend our hearty thanks to these and all other helpers.

The chairman would be remiss if he did not add a personal word of gratitude to his esteemed colleagues, Professors Handy and Loetscher. From first to last, over a period of more than five years, they have been devoted co-laborers, always going the second mile to achieve a result which might be worthy of scholarly confidence and which might also stimulate others to undertake still further exploration in the history of American Christianity.

H. S. S.
R. T. H.
L. A. L.

January, 1963

CONTENTS

ix

LIST OF ILLUSTRATIONS

AMERICAN CHRISTIANITY

1820–1960

PERIOD IV
REFORM AND REACTION
1820–1865

INTRODUCTION

THE period 1820–65 was a time of unprecedented geographical expansion for both the American nation and its churches. The settlement of upstate New York was completed during these decades, and this dynamic new region became for a time a stronghold of revivalistic "new measures," denominational controversy and schism, perfectionism, and "ultraism" of various types. It was here, too, that Mormonism and modern spiritism emerged.[1] Population and churches also occupied the Lake Plains and Gulf Plains and pressed into the vast trans-Mississippi regions, including those acquired by the Oregon Treaty (1846) and by the Mexican Cession (1848).

The home missionary movement, which had come into being in the earlier period as settlements crossed the Appalachians, faced greatly expanded tasks with the rapid push westward. Home missions deeply affected the life and structure of the churches. Constituting a primary claim, this work necessarily diverted interest and resources from scholarship and theological thought, further increasing the already strong activism of Christianity in America. The nature of the ministerial office also was affected. The classical, churchly ideal of a minister, stationed in a parish and devoting long years to instructing his people in the church's heritage, was better suited to an old, settled civilization than to a new, highly mobile one. Thus, on the frontier, Baptists and Disciples with their nonprofessional farmer-preachers, and Methodists with their circuit riders who served many preaching points, often captured the new settlers before Presbyterians, Congregationalists, Lutherans, or Episcopalians were able to organize parishes and secure a pastor.[2] Churches clinging to the older parish ideal tried various procedures. (1) In an earlier period congregations sometimes had released their pastors for three to six months to do mission work in the new areas and then to return to their own churches. But after settlements extended beyond the Alleghenies, the greater distance made this impracticable. (2) Individuals from various denominations co-operated in the work of the American Home Missionary Society (organized in 1826).[3] (3) Most denominations, realizing that the distinctive tenets of their faith could not

[1] Whitney R. Cross, *The Burned-over District: The Social and Intellectual History of Enthusiastic Religion in Western New York, 1800–1850* (Ithaca, N.Y., 1950).

[2] Cf. William W. Sweet, *The Story of Religion in America* (N.Y., 1950), 205–21.

[3] The work of this society is treated in Colin B. Goodykoontz, *Home Missions on the American Frontier, with Particular Reference to the American Home Missionary Society* (Caldwell, Id., 1939). The Far West is dealt with in Harland E. Hogue, "A History of Religion in Southern California, 1846–1880" (typed Ph.D. dissertation, Columbia University, 1958).

be maintained in the new regions under this kind of nonecclesiastical control, organized purely denominational home missionary boards. For a time rivalry was sharp between the denominational and the nondenominational organizations, but it was characteristic of the increasing denominationalism of this period that in home and foreign missions and in religious education the purely denominational board became standard. The ecclesiastical machinery thus created became a major, and at times a decisive, force in the corporate life of the respective denominations.

The home missionary movement, as distinguished from the work of the local farmer-preachers and circuit riders in the frontier settlements, was dominated by the less democratically inclined denominations, and reflected the East's apprehensiveness of the exuberant and untamed West.[4] It is understandable that, previous to this period, antimission Baptists and antimission Disciples of Christ had tried for a time, but ultimately without success, to prevent the creation of home missions structures. They considered the missionary societies unbiblical and a threat to the autonomy of the local congregation.[5]

Eastern religious agencies, both nondenominational and denominational, circulated Bibles and religious literature throughout the West, and planted Sunday schools and churches. Some notable missionary work among Indians of the Far West was done by both Protestants and Catholics, educational aspects of this work sometimes receiving financial aid from the United States government.

In this period of expansion, many churchmen tried to give theological expression to the concept of American destiny. The early New England Puritans had seen their theocracies as God's new Israel, a "wilderness Zion," which occupied a central place in God's plan for mankind. In the era of the Revolution the theme had been renewed and brought up-to-date by patriotic clergymen. God, they then said, was bringing to birth a new nation to serve him. The idea was further developed during the nineteenth century. Perry Miller has suggested that between the Revolution and the Civil War the old ideal of a covenanted nation was replaced by the ideal of individual Christians and voluntaristic churches dedicated to the national purpose, religiously conceived.[6] God was expanding American power because the "Anglo-Saxons" were his chosen agents to bring blessing to the world. Many northern clergymen, especially New England Congregationalists, opposed the Mexican War as a scheme to expand slave territory, but after

---

[4] Cf., e.g., Horace Bushnell, *Barbarism the First Danger: A Discourse for Home Missions* (N.Y., 1847).

[5] William W. Sweet, *Religion on the American Frontier*, Vol. I: *The Baptists, 1783–1830* (N.Y., 1931), 58–76.

[6] "From the Covenant to the Revival," in James Ward Smith and A. Leland Jamison, eds., *Religion in American Life*, Vol. I: *The Shaping of American Religion* (Princeton, 1961), 355–68; cf. also James F. Maclear, " 'The True American Union' of Church and State: Reconstruction of the Theocratic Tradition," *Church History*, XXVIII (1959), 41–62.

the victory nearly all churchmen welcomed the opportunity for Protestant missions.[7] Home mission needs caused many clerical promoters to give renewed emphasis to America's great destiny under God. "If the Gospel is to form our character, and guide our power, we shall be a fountain of life to all nations," Charles Hodge declared in 1829.[8] The Mercersburg theologian, John W. Nevin, surveying the European revolutions of 1848, wrote: "All signs unite to show that a new order of world history is at hand, and that the way is to be prepared for it centrally in America." [9] Philip Schaff, Swiss-born church historian and American patriot, dared to tell his audience of Berlin theologians: "The Anglo-Saxon and Anglo-American, of all modern races, possess the strongest national character and the one best fitted for universal dominion, and that, too, not a dominion of despotism but one, which makes its subjects free citizens." Schaff saw America's grandiose world role based, not on any moral superiority on its part, but on God's inscrutable providence.[10] The idea of manifest destiny, which loomed so large in the general history of this period, was partly rooted in and supported by religious sanctions.

Immigration from abroad kept pace with the rapid geographical expansion of the country. Those entering America increased from 8,385 in 1820 to 427,833 in 1854. During the years 1848–57, more than three million came to the United States, mostly peasant farmers from southwestern Germany and from central and southern Ireland. Toward the end of the period the Scandinavian countries supplied many settlers to the Midwest. The Germans often became farmers in the East or in the Midwest, but many of the Irish, whose meager funds were consumed by the ship fare, settled in the new slums of the port cities, especially Boston and New York, where they performed unskilled work or provided cheap labor for the rising industries.[11]

Most of the Germans and nearly all of the Scandinavians were of Lutheran background. Thus American Lutheranism expanded rapidly, but remained divided by language and by differences of theological emphasis into numerous separate bodies until the twentieth century. Many of the Lutherans coming from Germany were reacting against rationalism and against the union which had taken place in Prussia and in other German states between the Lutheran and Reformed churches. These immigrants therefore brought victory to the more conservative forces which were already beginning to stir within American Lutheranism. In addition, they founded some

---

[7] Clayton S. Ellsworth, "The American Churches and the Mexican War," *American Historical Review*, XLV (1940), 301–26; John R. Bodo, *The Protestant Clergy and Public Issues, 1812–1848* (Princeton, 1954), 216–23.

[8] "Anniversary Address," *Home Missionary*, II (1829), 18.

[9] "The Year 1848," *Mercersburg Review*, I (1849), 33.

[10] Schaff, *America*, ed. Perry Miller (Cambridge, Mass., 1961), 47; cf. 16, 20.

[11] Oscar Handlin, *Boston's Immigrants: A Study in Acculturation* (rev. ed., Cambridge, Mass., 1959), analyzes the effects of Irish immigration in a strategic city.

strictly conservative new Lutheran bodies, notably the Missouri Synod.

Many of the Germans and almost all of the Irish were Roman Catholics. The statistics of Catholic growth speak for themselves:

1790—white population 3,172,006; Catholics 35,000.

1820—white population 7,866,797; Catholics 195,000.

1840—white population 14,195,805; Catholics 663,000.[12]

Thus, while the population of the United States during the half century, 1790–1840, increased by less than four and a half times, the Catholic population increased nearly nineteen times, and its rate of gain was accelerating rapidly. Inevitably this Catholic influx created fear and tension. The near monopoly of power and culture which American Protestantism had enjoyed throughout the colonial period was threatened by a church whose authoritarian government and persecuting policies in many Old World lands the colonial fathers had feared and hated. Emotions erupted in a "nativist" movement which expressed itself in hostile writings like Samuel F. B. Morse's *Foreign Conspiracy Against the Liberties of the United States* (1835), and even in such an overt act as the burning of a Catholic convent by a Charlestown, Massachusetts, mob in 1834.[13]

Less violent, but perhaps more dangerous for Catholics in the long run, was the continuous pressure on them of a predominantly Protestant culture.[14] To meet this peril in a positive way, Catholics built a costly parochial school system. Catholics in this period also faced acute internal problems. When some parishes adopted the system of lay trustees, which had spread rapidly among American Protestant churches after the Revolution, it threatened to undermine the canonical powers of the bishop until episcopal authority completely overthrew "trusteeism." Even the rapid increase in numbers was not an unmixed blessing, for the task of organizing the flood of newcomers diverted resources from the church's cultural and theological development, even as it was doing, to a less degree, among contemporary Protestants. The sudden influx of widely diverse nationalities created sharp tensions between people and priests of different national backgrounds, but these were gradually resolved by a broad policy of Americanization within the Catholic Church.

The economic life of the young nation, with its geographical mobility and quickened changes in status, stimulated equalitarianism and restlessness.[15] There was an optimism which had not been present, for example, in the period of the French and Indian War. It was in keeping with the democratic spirit of these years that many of the religiously devout turned toward

---

[12] Gerald Shaughnessy, *Has the Immigrant Kept the Faith?* (N.Y., 1925), 73, 117, 125.

[13] Ray A. Billington, *The Protestant Crusade, 1800–1860* (N.Y., 1938).

[14] For a leading bishop's anxiety over the Protestant influence of the public schools, cf. Hugh J. Nolan, *The Most Reverend Francis Patrick Kenrick, Third Bishop of Philadelphia, 1830–1851* (Washington, 1948), 293–5.

[15] Cf. Rowland Berthoff, "The American Social Order: A Conservative Hypothesis," *American Historical Review*, LXV (1960), 499–508.

more traditional forms of authority. For a time, revivalism was increasingly accepted even in denominations which previously had been quite outside the revivalistic tradition. Reflecting the newer democratic emphasis on man's initiative rather than on God's sovereignty, techniques were developed, under the leadership of men like Charles G. Finney, for working up revivals, to the consternation of strict Calvinists.[16]

Manufacturing, which had been stimulated by the War of 1812, developed in the years that followed. The entrepreneur rose steadily. As industry developed, workingmen became more class-conscious. Slum conditions began to appear in leading cities. But a predominantly rural and individualistic Protestantism did not seriously address itself to the emerging industrial and urban problems before the closing decades of the century. When churchmen did discuss poverty it was usually to exhort the poor to patience and virtue.[17] Christian social concern before the Civil War concentrated, rather, on such reforming crusades as antislavery, temperance, and peace.

In political life, sharply conflicting interests, which had not been evident during the earlier "era of good feeling," came fully to view under the presidency of Andrew Jackson (1829–37). Jackson and his party were symbols of a more radically democratic spirit than had previously governed America.[18] Churchmen were variously aligned in relation to the political parties. In the North, the well-educated and prosperous leaders of the religious voluntary societies, both lay and clerical, many of whom had a New England background, generally favored the more conservative and aristocratic Federalist-Whig tradition,[19] as did also the clergy of the more churchly Protestant bodies. On the other hand, Roman Catholics and the members of the more democratically inclined churches tended to support the new Jacksonian democracy.

The period was one of increasing sectionalism. Previously the chief sectional tension had been between East and West, but with the debate on the admission of Missouri (1818–20) and with the mounting abolitionism of the 1830's, a North-South cleavage on the slavery issue began to dominate American public life. Controversy over the annexation of Texas and the question of slavery in the Mexican Cession further aroused sectional feeling. Many hoped that the Compromise of 1850 would restore equilibrium, but the Kansas-Nebraska Act of 1854 opened old wounds. Divisions

[16] Charles G. Finney, *Lectures on Revivals of Religion*, ed. William G. McLoughlin (Cambridge, Mass., 1960).

[17] John R. Bodo, *The Protestant Clergy and Public Issues, 1812–1848*, 173–80; Glyndon G. Van Deusen, *The Jacksonian Era, 1828–1848* (N.Y., 1959), 8–10.

[18] For treatment of the era of Jackson, cf. Arthur M. Schlesinger, Jr., *The Age of Jackson* (Boston, 1945); Marvin Meyers, *The Jacksonian Persuasion: Politics and Belief* (Stanford, Calif., 1957).

[19] Clifford S. Griffin, "Religious Benevolence as Social Control, 1815–1860," *Mississippi Valley Historical Review*, XLIV (1957), 423–44.

within leading national church bodies reflected the sectionalism of the times.[20] When the Civil War came, church bodies on both sides of the line supported their respective governments and sought to minister to the spiritual needs of their fighting men.

Culture in America, like other aspects of life, was becoming more democratic in the decades following 1820. With the increasing wealth of the country and especially with the more radical democracy of the Jacksonian era, the "common man" became more interested in learning, and greater effort was put forth to make learning more interesting and more available to him. The churches contributed heavily to the diffusion of knowledge during this period. With a few exceptions, Protestants eagerly supported the expanding public schools, which were becoming more secular. Churches —especially the Congregational and Presbyterian—took the lead in founding numerous colleges, some of which proved to be very ephemeral.[21] Seminaries for the professional education of ministers multiplied.[22] Sunday-school and tract societies produced widely read literature. Religious periodicals increased greatly.[23]

The democratizing of culture was paralleled by a tendency to modify the Calvinistic theology inherited from more authoritarian days. Jonathan Edwards and Samuel Hopkins had sought to strengthen Calvinism by making it more defensible. Their heirs in the nineteenth century considerably modified it by their revised conception of original sin and by their increasing shift of emphasis away from God's sovereignty to man's initiative. By the end of this period the only major denomination adhering to strict Calvinism was the Old School Presbyterian Church.

At the same time that American culture was becoming more democratic, it was also, by a parallel process, becoming more national. Even though Americans began studying in Germany soon after the Napoleonic Wars, there was a greater tendency to adapt cultural importations to the conditions of American life. By mid-century the country was attaining a degree of cultural maturity.[24] These tendencies toward democracy and nationalism led the churches further away from authoritarian types of Christianity inherited from the Old World and from ideas of an historic universal church toward more individualistic forms of Christianity. At the same time, however, there were cultural currents which contributed to the resurgence of historic and more churchly conceptions of Christianity. In philosophy the

[20] On the historiography of the subject, cf. Kenneth M. Stampp, "The Historian and Southern Negro Slavery," *American Historical Review*, LVIII (1952), 613–24.

[21] Donald G. Tewksbury, *The Founding of American Colleges and Universities Before the Civil War . . .* (N.Y., 1932).

[22] H. Richard Niebuhr and Daniel D. Williams, eds., *The Ministry in Historical Perspective* (N.Y., 1956), 207–88.

[23] Frank L. Mott, *A History of American Magazines, 1741–1850* (Cambridge, Mass., 1930), 131–9, 369–74.

[24] F. O. Matthiessen, *American Renaissance: Art and Expression in the Age of Emerson and Whitman* (N.Y., 1941), vii.

Napoleonic Wars had isolated the United States from the European sources of deism, and the conservative reaction at home quite changed the intellectual climate. Americans meanwhile were appropriating more extensively the philosophy of Scottish common-sense realism, which John Witherspoon had been influential in promoting in the eighteenth century. This philosophy, because of its interesting blending of evangelicalism with many Enlightenment ideas, proved useful as a buttress to Calvinism—particularly to Calvinist scholasticism—and as a help to adherents of theological orthodoxy who desired to support laissez-faire economics. In this period there was also the quite different influence of philosophical idealism from Germany and England. This supplied the principal theoretical foundation for the American transcendental movement and other forms of religious liberalism. Philosophical idealism, together with a growing sense of history, also contributed during this period to the recovery of more churchly conceptions of Christianity.

The years under view were peculiarly important for the structure of American Christianity.[25] The last vestiges of the old church establishments disappeared in 1833. The American pattern of denominationalism had already begun to emerge in the eighteenth century,[26] but it was during the present period that it acquired the form which it still retained a century later.[27] A basic factor in giving distinctive character to this denominationalism was the churchly and orthodox reaction against revivalism and unionism.

[25] Cf. Richard C. Wolf, "The Middle Period 1800–1870, the Matrix of Modern American Christianity," *Religion in Life,* XXII (1952–53), 72–84.

[26] *American Christianity,* I, 231–4.

[27] Sidney E. Mead, "Denominationalism; the Shape of Protestantism in America," *Church History,* XXIII (1954), 291–320.

CHAPTER XII

Revivalism and Benevolence

THE first twenty years of the nineteenth century had seen the origin of many voluntary societies. These agencies channeled the energy released by the revivals into specific missionary, educational, and reform causes. Some of the benevolence societies were formed along denominational lines. But many of them were nondenominational in form, and drew support from the individual Christians of many denominations. Especially when the voluntary societies were designed for distributing religious literature, for planting educational institutions and Sunday schools, or for promoting humanitarian and reform causes, they crossed denominational lines.

By the late 1820's the control of these nondenominational societies was falling more and more into the hands of an "interlocking directorate" in which a group of Congregational and Presbyterian leaders were especially prominent. Conspicuous in the leadership of this "benevolent empire" were Arthur (1786–1865) and Lewis (1788–1873) Tappan, wealthy Presbyterian merchants. Many prominent ministers supported the societies and served as members of their boards.

A number of forces converged to give the movement its thrust and direction. First, the achievement of the British evangelical and reform societies served as an inspiration and as a pattern for American development. The British and Foreign Bible Society (1804) in particular provided a successful model in benevolence technique. Consciously, the American evangelicals sought to emulate the British "united front" in their benevolent efforts.[1]

Second, considerable humanitarian concern and effort had been created by the spirit of the Enlightenment. Serious interest in such great causes as peace and temperance had been aroused; genuine concern for the handicapped and the underprivileged had been stirred. The specific humanitarian movements that grew out of the influence of the Enlightenment were not flourishing in the early nineteenth century, but they had contributed to an atmosphere favorable to benevolence activity.

Third, certain changes in theology favored an emphasis on man's freedom and his use of that freedom to improve the human situation. Much of the leadership in the benevolence movement reposed in members of Congregational and Presbyterian churches, staunchly Calvinist in orientation. But a strong theological current was working in those denominations for a relaxation of such views of man's total depravity as minimized human

[1] Charles I. Foster, *An Errand of Mercy: The Evangelical United Front* (Chapel Hill, N.C., 1960), Part I.

effort for self-improvement. A strong center of such moderate views was New Haven, where Nathaniel W. Taylor (1786–1858), a Congregationalist, taught theology at Yale. Taylor claimed to be true to Calvinism, yet he so interpreted it as to make a larger place for man's freedom. He could insist that the "universal depravity of mankind is not inconsistent with the moral perfection of God," for he believed that all sin is voluntary in character. Man's created nature is the "occasion" for his sinning, but the possibility of the opposite result is not precluded. It is certain that man will sin, yet he has "power to the contrary." Taylor believed that man did not lose his free agency in the fall.[2] Such views encouraged men to use their freedom wisely, as in the evangelical and benevolent undertakings of the voluntary societies. These "New Haven" views had a large following in Presbyterianism as well as in Congregationalism. The influence of certain prominent preachers, such as Albert Barnes (1798–1870) at the historic First Church of Philadelphia, combined with the way the Plan of Union of 1801 sent former Congregationalists into Presbyterianism, contributed to the growth of the "New School" party in which support for the benevolence system was strong. While of course Protestants of differing viewpoints supported benevolence activity, its conspicuous leaders and advocates were often influenced by the liberalizing theological currents. Arthur Tappan, for example, worked with Lyman Beecher and Taylor in raising funds for the Yale Divinity School, and later bought a home in New Haven adjoining that of the theologian.[3]

Fourth, the general atmosphere of optimism and expectancy favored the activism of the benevolence movement. A new nation dedicated to liberty had been born. It was believed that the shackles of the past centuries had fallen, and that free man now had nothing to hinder him in his quest for the ideal. Alfred North Whitehead once observed that the America of the early nineteenth century had one great quality: "That quality was hope—not the hope of ignorance. The peculiar character of this central period was that wise men hoped, and that as yet no circumstance had arisen to throw doubt on the grounds of such hope."[4] In this atmosphere of hope, a high expectancy concerning American destiny flourished.[5] This was often given secular expression, as by Charles Sumner at the close of the Civil War. He wrote: "Give us peace, and population will increase beyond all experience; resources of all kinds will multiply infinitely; arts will embellish the land with immortal beauty; the name of the Republic will be exalted, until every neighbor, yielding to irresistible attraction, seeks new life in becoming part of the great whole; and the national example will be more puissant

[2] On Taylorism, see Sidney E. Mead, *Nathaniel William Taylor, 1786–1858, A Connecticut Liberal* (Chicago, 1942); H. Shelton Smith, *Changing Conceptions of Original Sin: A Study in American Theology Since 1750* (N.Y., 1955), Chaps. 5 and 6.

[3] Lewis Tappan, *The Life of Arthur Tappan* (N.Y., 1870), 256–7.

[4] *Essays in Science and Philosophy* (N.Y., 1947), 153.

[5] On this point, see *American Christianity*, I, 443.

than army or navy for the conquest of the world." [6] But Christians more often voiced their expectancies in terms of the coming millennium, which seemed very near in that time of progress. Early in the century it was not uncommon for preachers to put such sentences as these into their sermons: "May we not then yield ourselves to the confidence that Zion has seen her darkest hour, and that her light will henceforth continue to shine with increasing brightness to the perfect day?" [7] But Christians could speed the coming of the perfect day by helping to prepare the way of the Lord in the work of benevolence. As the success of the revivals seemed to be a sign of the approaching end, Christians were exhorted to work the harder toward the glorious day.

The fifth force which converged with the others to give the benevolence movement its power and purpose has just been mentioned—revivalism. An understanding of the way in which the power of the revivals was related to the benevolence thrust is important to the understanding of both. During the third and fourth decades of the century, the revival movements not only continued but reached new peaks. Gilbert Barnes has declared that "at the turn of the decade, in 1830, the revival burst all bounds and spread over the whole nation, the greatest of all modern revivals." [8]

The central figure in that revival was the Presbyterian awakener, Charles G. Finney (1792–1875). Under his preaching in the later 1820's, intense revivals swept through the "burned-over district" of New York State, so called because of the revival fires which burned back and forth across the area. Deeply in earnest, Finney studied how to get a revival going, and made full use of the methods that worked—"new measures," he called them. They were not exactly new, of course, but his method of organizing them into an ordered system was. Among the new measures were the following. Services were held at "unseasonable hours," oftentimes extended or "protracted" over a period of days so that a congregation might be "broken down." The evangelist uttered prayers which were highly emotional and which had an exhortatory intent. He invited women to pray aloud in mixed assemblies. He indulged in harsh, colloquial, and even irreverent language. He named specific individuals in prayer and sermon, thus heightening the emotional pressure on the man to be brought under conviction of sin. Prayer circles, inquiry meetings, and personal instruction under the direction of the revivalist and his helpers accompanied the revival effort, and had much to do with creating the proper atmosphere. Finally, there was the anxious bench, where those in deep anxiety about the state of their souls could be brought right under the revivalist's eye—and "never was man whose soul looked out through his face as his did."

[6] *Prophetic Voices Concerning America: A Monograph* (Boston, 1874), 175–6.
[7] Edward D. Griffin, sermon preached in Sandwich, Mass., Oct. 20, 1813, quoted in Oliver W. Elsbree, *The Rise of the Missionary Spirit in America, 1790–1815* (Williamsport, Pa., 1928), 130.
[8] *The Antislavery Impulse, 1830–1844* (N.Y., 1933), 16.

As the roll of Finney's converts lengthened, his fame increased. He received invitations to carry on his work in Philadelphia, New York, and other centers. Other revivalists adopted all or part of Finney's methods.[9] As the news of the new measures spread, eastern revivalists watched with timid fascination, fearful lest their Calvinism be undercut, anxious lest the excesses of the Great Awakening be repeated. Lyman Beecher, always one for glossing over differences and securing a united front, declared that a face to face meeting of eastern and western leaders was needed. A nine-day session was held at New Lebanon, New York, in 1827. The gulf was not bridged, however; the westerners thought that their brothers were too cold, too formal, while the easterners feared that the West was being deluded by wrong measures. Beecher gave Finney fair warning to keep out of his territory, saying (as he remembered it in later years!):

> Finney, I know your plan, and you know I do; you mean to come into Connecticut and carry a streak of fire to Boston. But if you attempt it, as the Lord liveth, I'll meet you at the State line, and call out all the artillerymen, and fight every inch of the way to Boston, and then I'll fight you there.[10]

That was in 1827. Four years later Beecher invited Finney to his Boston pulpit, and admitted that he did very well!

In part, the change in Beecher's attitude reflected the general lessening of prejudice against Finney, a change influenced not a little by the fabulous success of the Rochester revival of 1830–31. Hundreds were won at his meetings that winter, including many of the city's leading citizens. The life of the whole community was profoundly affected. The revival was intense enough, yet it lacked the emotional excesses that had given frontier revivalism its bad name. Finney's reputation was now established in the East, and though such a controversial man was always subject to criticism, the earlier opposition declined. At the end of 1830 a minister reported to the awakener that "Prejudices against Finneyism seem . . . to have almost wholly given way." [11] The Rochester revival allayed fears, and put the seal of success on the rising young revivalist.

There was another reason, however, for the change in attitude toward Finney. He had moved into the orbit of Protestantism's expanding system of benevolent action. The close relationship between "new measures" revivalism and benevolent enterprise strengthened. The leaders of the growing

[9] Men like Daniel Nash, Jedediah Burchard, James Boyle, and Luther Myrick were but the better-known names among the hosts of revivalists. Revivalists who were outside the new-measures circle, strictly defined, nevertheless reflected the trends. In Methodist circles such evangelists as Peter Cartwright and James Finley kept the force of revivalism fresh, while the Baptists were regularly revived by such men as Jabez Swan and Jacob Knapp.

[10] Charles Beecher, ed., *Autobiography, Correspondence, etc., of Lyman Beecher, D.D.* (2 vols., N.Y., 1864–65), II, 101.

[11] Quoted in Charles C. Cole, Jr., *The Social Ideas of the Northern Evangelists, 1826–1860* (N.Y., 1954), 89.

network of voluntary societies early sensed Finney's power, and on his several trips to New York in the late 1820's they exerted some modifying influence over him. He refined his methods a little, weaving strands from eastern revivalism into the pattern that had been so spectacular on the frontier. He came to see that the reform emphasis was indeed a useful addition and a legitimate complement to his stress on conversion. The success of the Rochester revival, in which Finney had paid considerable attention to the temperance crusade, dramatically illustrated the revival values of reformist emphases. With real insight, the *Rochester Observer* declared that temperance "was then a 'new measure' for the promotion of revivals," and a presbytery reported "that the Temperance Reformation and the Revivals of Religion have a peculiarly intimate relation and bearing upon each other." [12]

This "peculiarly intimate relation" was further intensified when Finney settled into a New York pastorate in 1832. His health had weakened, making it wise for him to moderate his itinerant habits. With the blessing of the Tappan group, he entered upon the pastorate of a Free Presbyterian Church in New York. Several years later he was called as pastor of the Broadway Tabernacle, which had been built around him with Tappan support, and became a Congregationalist. The union of revivalism and reform which he illustrated, but which was also evident in many others of more moderate stamp, contributed greatly to the growth of the benevolence movement. By 1834 the total annual receipts of the benevolence societies reached the then huge sum of nine million dollars. [13] The annual meetings of many of the societies were held during "Anniversary Week" in New York in May, with sessions arranged so that one could attend the gatherings of a number of societies. [14] Religious periodicals served to keep the movement fresh in men's minds, while revivals, society meetings, and May anniversaries periodically brought men into living touch with the vast enterprise.

Attention to the annual meetings of the societies tends to emphasize the importance of the controlling groups of the benevolent empire, in which Congregationalists and Presbyterians played a large role. But the benevolence movement was widespread throughout the churches of the land. In the South, for example, "Christian activity expressed itself chiefly in the creation of societies to support domestic and foreign missions, to encourage the distribution and reading of the Scriptures, to establish Sunday schools, to foster education in general, and to strive to bring about temperance, peace, and other desirable conditions." [15] The local benevolence societies of

[12] Quoted in Whitney R. Cross, *The Burned-over District: The Social and Intellectual History of Enthusiastic Religion in Western New York, 1800–1850* (Ithaca, N.Y., 1950), 169.

[13] Cole, *Social Ideas of the Northern Evangelists*, 103.

[14] Foster, *An Errand of Mercy*, 146–55. Some of the societies met later in May in Philadelphia during "Ecclesiastical Week," or at Boston in June.

[15] Charles S. Sydnor, *The Development of Southern Sectionalism, 1819–1848* (Baton Rouge, La., 1948), 57.

the South were ordinarily affiliated with the appropriate national organization, denominational or nondenominational. As the revivalism of the Presbyterian and Congregational bodies was coupled with benevolent action, so the intense revivalism of Baptists, Methodists, and Disciples was likewise related to evangelical and charitable purposes within and beyond denominational structures.[16]

The aim of the whole benevolence movement, as has been noted, was not only to evangelize individuals and plant churches, but also to remake society. Hence its supporters were not only concerned with encouraging revivals and promoting missions, but also with championing moral and social reform movements. The benevolence societies launched great crusades for temperance, prison reform, education, peace, and the abolition of slavery.[17] One of the greatest drives, for example, was for reform in drinking practices, spearheaded by the American Temperance Society (1826). Methods that had been perfected in winning converts were now employed to enlist them in the fight against intemperance. A long-lasting change in the drinking habits of the bulk of American Christians was effected, and a large body of opinion in favor of prohibition was won.

The benevolent empire also championed humanitarian movements for aiding the handicapped and the helpless. For example, there had been some efforts, largely under the influence of the Enlightenment, to improve the treatment accorded criminals, but not until the Rev. Louis Dwight (1793–1854), who had served as agent successively of American Tract, American Education, and American Bible societies, transferred the spirit and methods he had learned there to prison reform did that crusade enjoy success. As Alice Felt Tyler has said, "After 1815, in the renewed wave of revivalism and humanitarianism that swept the country, the cause of prison reform gained more adherents and new urgency."[18] So did movements for the education of the deaf and the blind, and for the care of the insane. In these latter crusades, humanitarians of Unitarian persuasion, steeped in the tradition of the Enlightenment, often joined with the evangelicals. Quakers also often associated themselves with these undertakings, exhibiting the concern for the unfortunate and the unjustly treated which had long been characteristic of them.

In most of the benevolence crusades, the British example served as guide and inspiration. In the cause of peace, however, the Americans took the initiative. In 1815 several state peace societies were organized; these actions helped to stimulate the forming of a peace society in London in 1816. In the United States a national organization, the American Peace Society, was formed in 1828. Many of the reformers played some part in the peace movement, which suffered internal tension between the extremists, who

---

[16] *Ibid.*, 57–9.

[17] On the organization of the national voluntary societies, see *American Christianity*, I, 522–5, 547–55.

[18] *Freedom's Ferment: Phases of American Social History to 1860* (Minneapolis, 1944), 274.

rejected all war under any circumstances, and the moderates. The peace movement had a somewhat more limited appeal than some of the other benevolence causes, but was a part of the general movement.

Education was another of the major concerns of the benevolence movement in the nineteenth century. It was generally believed by the supporters of the national voluntary societies that the growth in the number and quality of educational institutions would contribute to the cause of Christianizing the world. Home missionaries, for example, often devoted time and talents to the development of schools and colleges.[19] Protestants contributed significantly to the development of the public school systems of elementary and secondary education, but in this period they believed that the institutions of higher education should remain under private, particularly denominational, sponsorship. There was a strong drive on the part of the denominations to found colleges throughout the country; indeed, the years from 1800 to 1860 have been called the "denominational era in American higher education." [20] Voluntary societies, denominational and nondenominational, devoted considerable attention to the growth and development of the church colleges.

As the crusades gathered strength in the 1830's an extremist, "ultraist" party appeared in each. In part this grew out of the intensity of the revivalism that was yoked to the reform movement. The revivalists claimed that their work was done under the guidance and power of the Spirit. Hence they tended to identify rather uncritically their measures with God's measures. As Whitney Cross has put it, "The ultraist state of mind rose from an implicit, even occasionally an explicit, reliance upon the direct guidance of the Holy Ghost." [21] Their assurance was heightened by their expectancy that the millennium was at hand. Many of the societies suffered inner dissension between the absolutists and the moderates, as for example the temperance and the peace movements. The rise of perfectionism was one of the clearest expressions of the ultraist spirit. For in many places where revivalism had reached its emotional peaks there was the development of belief in the possibility that Christians could live perfect, wholly sanctified lives. There were different kinds of perfectionism. Some types were radical and moved in an antinomian direction. Others, such as that of Charles Finney himself, were considerably more cautiously stated and did not make such extravagant claims.

The crusade for the abolition of slavery won much of its support from the benevolence movement. The American Anti-Slavery Society (1833)

[19] Colin B. Goodykoontz, *Home Missions on the American Frontier: With Particular Reference to the American Home Missionary Society* (Caldwell, Id., 1939), 361–405.

[20] Donald G. Tewksbury, *The Founding of American Colleges and Universities Before the Civil War: With Particular Reference to the Religious Influences Bearing upon the College Movement* (N.Y., 1932), 55–132; see also Albea Godbold, *The Church College of the Old South* (Durham, N.C., 1944).

[21] *Burned-over District*, 198.

was formed as one of the major interlocking national benevolence societies. Abolitionism became the consuming concern of many reformers who had been trained in other benevolence efforts. The ultraist spirit was strongly felt in the antislavery movement, contributing to its inner turmoil. But that movement became distinctive in many ways; for example, though the South largely supported the benevolence movement in general, she not only rejected abolitionism but supported proslavery views. The movement was so important for the churches and for the country that it will be considered in detail in Chapter XV. But it is important here to remember the relationship between the general benevolence movement and abolitionism.

The rapid growth of the benevolent empire was checked in the late 1830's by a combination of both internal and external factors. The ultraist thrust had created tensions and dissatisfactions within the societies, leading to some schisms and loss of support. The financial panic of 1837 had wiped out the Tappan fortune and weakened the centralizing and controlling forces over the benevolence movement. By 1840, it became evident that the early bright hopes of the benevolence crusaders were not easily to be fulfilled. The appeal of the whole movement was no longer so confident or creative. Yet the basic pattern was not destroyed or even seriously shaken; it continued to be widely pervasive in American Protestantism for many years. Revivals continued to arouse interest in benevolence efforts. "There can be no doubt that the popularity of revival men and methods surged forward in the major segments of American religion between 1840 and 1860," writes Timothy L. Smith, on the basis of a study of the documents of that period. He adds that revival methods often continued to go hand in hand with humanitarian concern.[22]

The general acceptance of the revivalistic interpretation of the faith in the American churches is illustrated in part by the wide sweep and immense popularity of the great revival of 1857–58. The revival first attracted public notice in the United States when a noon-day prayer meeting in New York suddenly grew in size and power. The idea caught on, and the "prayer meeting revival" became a nationwide reality. In city after city, hugely attended prayer meetings, often held at noon on week-days, became a feature. The press devoted many columns to the exciting news. Lay leadership was conspicuous in the work. That the revival could spread so swiftly and so widely is good evidence that the revivalistic pattern had been carried far and had cut deep into American religious life. The new converts were urged to support the movements of Christian benevolence. The basic patterns which were so powerful in the 1830's continued strongly to shape Protestant thought and practice into the post-war period.

The revivalist system further stimulated the great emphasis on individualism then so prominent in American life. The evangelicals hoped to

[22] *Revivalism and Social Reform in Mid-Nineteenth Century America* (N.Y., 1957), 59 f. See especially Chap. 3, "The Resurgence of Revivalism, 1840–1857."

win by persuading the majority, but they could do little when minorities in their own midst broke away to move in new directions. Indeed, the whole revivalistic impulse tended to create an intense spiritual atmosphere out of which not only ultraist and perfectionist ideas could develop, but also new religious movements could rise. Sometimes such new movements were cut straight from the revivalistic pattern, and then new links in the evangelical chain were forged. The Disciples of Christ, formed by the merger of "Campbellite" and "Stoneite" groups in 1832, is an illustration.[23] Sometimes, however, the new movements took a distinctive course and became something of a threat to the major pattern.

One such distinctive movement which stemmed directly from revivalist emphases, but so overstressed one aspect of them that it produced a number of new church bodies, was adventism. Expectation of the coming millennium was strong in Protestant circles. The leading preachers and the most influential religious writers of the day often devoted much attention to the topic. Not only the frontier evangelists, but theologians like Hopkins and churchmen like Lyman Beecher dwelt on millennial themes. Thus the ground was prepared for an adventist harvest. William Miller (1782–1849) was a former deist who was converted in 1816 and joined a Baptist church. In the widely prevalent adventism he found the key which removed the difficulties in the Bible about which the deists had been so concerned. He came to the conclusion that the Lord would actually return in 1843–44. The assurance of the man, his knowledge of the Bible, and the impressiveness of his elaborate charts illustrating his position combined to win him followers. By the late 1830's the movement swelled into a crusade; other revivalists found the adventist emphasis a powerful instrument indeed. Millennial excitement prevailed in many churches; some adventists left their churches to move wholly in the amorphous adventist fellowships. Several dates for the return of Christ were set and passed. Finally all was staked on October 22, 1844. The faithful were disappointed, yet the fanciful legends of their gathering on hilltops in white robes, or the vicious rumors of their alleged immorality have been thoroughly disproved.[24] Most of the churches sought to hold on to the members of their flocks who had been carried away by the excitement, and probably the majority of the adventists either quietly went back to their churches, or discontinued church attendance entirely. But the deeply convinced could scarcely do either, and in 1845 an adventist general conference was held in Albany. The continuing movement suffered internal dissensions, and a number of adventist sects were crystallized. Some of the adventists adopted the seventh-day (Saturday) observance of the Sabbath from a Baptist group which held that view, and became Seventh Day Adventists. Smaller adventist bodies that developed were the Advent Chris-

---

[23] See *American Christianity*, I, 563, 576–86.
[24] See Francis D. Nichol, *The Midnight Cry* (Washington, 1944), 337–48; Cross, *Burned-over District*, 305–6.

tian Church, the Church of God (Adventist), and the Life and Advent Union. Such bodies on the whole continued essentially in the pattern of conservative, evangelistic Protestantism with their own distinctive twists, but some other movements, such as Mormonism, which arose out of the same general ferment, tended to move in much more radical directions.

The revivalistic Protestantism of the middle decades of the nineteenth century was strongly anti-Catholic, and the propaganda of the benevolence movement often identified "Romanism" as a chief enemy of Protestantism, peace, and progress. Preachers could deliver highly emotional sermons against Catholicism, and the religious periodicals called for the support of the various evangelical crusades as a way of checkmating Catholic advance. Alice Felt Tyler has noted that ". . . suspicion of the naturalized citizen and fear of the sinister designs of the Catholic church have never been entirely absent from the American mind, and outbreaks due to such fears have always accompanied periods of rapid increase in immigration. Between 1830 and 1860 such increase was remarkable, and the outbursts of opposition were frequent and violent." [25] The burning of several Catholic institutions, the organization of a number of societies to carry on the crusade against Catholicism, and the political nativism of the 1850's were directly related to this darker side of the Protestant crusading pattern.

In conclusion, it can be said that the new-measures, voluntary society system was not only a dominant influence in American religion in the middle third of the nineteenth century, but that it also exerted great influence over the cultural life of the nation. De Tocqueville found that "there is no country in the world where the Christian religion retains a greater influence over the souls of men than in America." [26] To a considerable extent this was a contribution of revivalism. Political thought also felt the stamp of evangelical Protestantism. In his perceptive analysis of the national faith in democracy, Ralph H. Gabriel finds that "the foundation of this democratic faith was a frank supernaturalism derived from Christianity. The twentieth-century student is often astonished at the extent to which supernaturalism permeated American thought of the nineteenth century." [27] Small wonder that many European travelers in the period found that the ideals of evangelical Protestantism seemed to dominate the culture of the country.

100. Baptism of the Holy Ghost

The ability of the leaders of the benevolence movement to tap the resources of enthusiasm and support released by revivalism was one of the

---

[25] *Freedom's Ferment,* 364. Pp. 358–95 provide a compact treatment of this negative side of the evangelical Protestantism of the time and its cultural and political results.

[26] *Democracy in America* (2 vols., N.Y., 1945), I, 303.

[27] *The Course of American Democratic Thought: An Intellectual History Since 1815* (N.Y., 1940), 14.

major reasons for the effectiveness of their crusades. The career of the leading revivalist of the time, Charles G. Finney (1792–1875), aptly illustrates how the conversion experience could resolve doubts and focus a person's interests and abilities around evangelical causes. Finney himself believed he had received a mighty baptism of the Holy Ghost, and devoted his life to bringing others to the same experience. Then he led them to serve the Lord in the movements to save men and bring Christian influence to bear on a nation's life.

Charles Finney was brought up on the frontier of upstate New York. After a period of service as schoolteacher, in 1816 he started work in a law office and read for admission to the bar. Though he was serving as a choir director in a Presbyterian church, he was still an "unconverted" man. The combined efforts of his fiancée and his pastor, George W. Gale (1789–1861), proved strong enough to enlist his interest. Study of the Bible paved the way for an intense conversion experience in 1821. He resolved immediately to devote himself to evangelistic work. He presently became an agent for the Utica Female Missionary Society, and was ordained by the Presbyterians in 1824.

Finney soon became a conspicuous awakener, as revival fires burst into flame when he crusaded through upstate New York. Equipped with a voice of great range and power, trained in the arts of persuasion, and skilled in the use of the idioms of the people, he was able to present the gospel in terms convincing to most of his hearers. But the man's intensity and certainty were major factors in his ability to bring others to conversion, and they were shaped in the crucible of his own conversion. Finney described the experience in his *Memoirs,* written in the seventy-fifth year of his long life, but he had lost none of his skill in forceful and colorful expression. His account tells much about the nature of the revivalistic Protestantism of the early nineteenth century, its stress on the conversion experience, its rootage in a Bible held to be literally inspired, and its power to redirect human lives. From the converts won by such revivalists as Finney came much of the support and enthusiasm that undergirded the benevolence crusades.

DOCUMENT

North of the village, and over a hill, lay a piece of woods, in which I was in the almost daily habit of walking, more or less, when it was pleasant weather. It was now October, and the time was past for my frequent walks there. Nevertheless, instead of going to the office, I turned and bent my course toward the woods, feeling that I must be alone, and away from all human eyes and ears, so that I could pour out my prayer to God. . . .

But when I attempted to pray I found that my heart would not pray. I had supposed that if I could only be where I could speak aloud, without being overheard, I could pray freely. But lo! when I came to try, I was dumb; that is, I had nothing to say to God; or at least I could say but a few words, and those without heart. In attempting to pray I would hear a rustling in the leaves, as I thought, and would stop and look up to see if somebody were not coming. This I did several times. . . .

The thought was pressing me of the rashness of my promise, that I would give my heart to God that day or die in the attempt. It seemed to me as if that was binding upon my soul; and yet I was going to break my vow. A great sinking and discouragement came over me, and I felt almost too weak to stand upon my knees.

Just at this moment I again thought I heard some one approach me, and I opened my eyes to see whether it were so. But right there the revelation of my pride of heart, as the great difficulty that stood in the way, was distinctly shown to me. An overwhelming sense of my wickedness in being ashamed to have a human being see me on my knees before God, took such powerful possession of me, that I cried at the top of my voice, and exclaimed that I would not leave that place if all the men on earth and all the devils in hell surrounded me. "What!" I said, "such a degraded sinner as I am, on my knees confessing my sins to the great and holy God; and ashamed to have any human being, and a sinner like myself, find me on my knees endeavoring to make my peace with my offended God!" The sin appeared awful, infinite. It broke me down before the Lord.

Just at that point this passage of Scripture seemed to drop into my mind with a flood of light: "Then shall ye go and pray unto me, and I will hearken unto you. Then shall ye seek me and find me, when ye shall search for me with all your heart." I instantly seized hold of this with my heart. I had intellectually believed the Bible before; but never had the truth been in my mind that faith was a voluntary trust instead of an intellectual state. I was as conscious as I was of my existence, of trusting at that moment in God's veracity. Somehow I knew that that was a passage of Scripture, though I do not think I had ever read it. I knew that it was God's word, and God's voice, as it were, that spoke to me. . . .

He then gave me many other promises, both from the Old and the New Testament, especially some most precious promises respecting our Lord Jesus Christ. I never can, in words, make any human being understand how precious and true those promises appeared to me. I took them one after the other as infallible truth, the assertions of God who could not lie. They did not seem so much to fall into my intellect as into my heart, to be put within the grasp of the voluntary powers of my mind; and I seized hold of them with the grasp of a drowning man. . . .

Just before evening the thought took possession of my mind, that as soon as I was left alone in the new office, I would try to pray again—that I was not going to abandon the subject of religion and give it up, at any rate; and therefore, although I no longer had any concern about my soul, still I would continue to pray.

By evening we got the books and furniture adjusted; and I made up, in an open fire-place, a good fire, hoping to spend the evening alone. Just at dark Squire W——, seeing that everything was adjusted, bade me good-night and went to his home. I had accompanied him to the door; and as I closed the door and turned around, my heart seemed to be liquid within me. All my feelings seemed to rise and flow out; and the utterance of my heart was, "I want to pour my whole soul out to God." The rising of my soul was so great that I rushed into the room back of the front office, to pray.

There was no fire, and no light, in the room; nevertheless it appeared to me as if it were perfectly light. As I went in and shut the door after me, it seemed as if I met the Lord Jesus Christ face to face. It did not occur to me then, nor did it for some time afterward, that it was wholly a mental state. On the contrary it seemed to me that I saw him as I would see any other man. He said nothing, but looked at me in such a manner as to break me right down at his feet. I have always since regarded this as a most remarkable state of mind; for it seemed to me a reality, that he stood before me, and I fell down at his feet and poured out my soul to him. I wept aloud like a child, and made such confessions as I could with my choked utterance. It seemed to me that I bathed his feet with my tears; and yet I had no distinct impression that I touched him, that I recollect.

I must have continued in this state for a good while; but my mind was too much absorbed with the interview to recollect anything that I said. But I know, as soon as my mind became calm enough to break off from the interview, I returned to the front office, and found that the fire that I had made of large wood was nearly burned out. But as I turned and was about to take a seat by the fire, I received a mighty baptism of the Holy Ghost. Without any expectation of it, without ever having the thought in my mind that I had ever heard the thing mentioned by any person in the world, the Holy Spirit descended upon me in a manner that seemed to go through me, body and soul. I could feel the impression, like a wave of electricity, going through and through me. Indeed it seemed to come in waves and waves of liquid love; for I could not express it in any other way. It seemed like the very breath of God. I can recollect distinctly that it seemed to fan me, like immense wings.

No words can express the wonderful love that was shed abroad in my heart. I wept aloud with joy and love; and I do not know but I should say, I literally bellowed out the unutterable gushings of my heart. These waves came over me, and over me, and over me, one after the other, until I recollect I cried out, "I shall die if these waves continue to pass over me." I said, "Lord, I cannot bear any more;" yet I had no fear of death.

How long I continued in this state, with this baptism continuing to roll over me and go through me, I do not know. But I know it was late in the evening when a member of my choir—for I was the leader of the choir —came into the office to see me. He was a member of the church. He found me in this state of loud weeping, and said to me, "Mr. Finney, what ails you?" I could make him no answer for some time. He then said, "Are you in pain?" I gathered myself up as best I could, and replied, "No, but so happy that I cannot live. . . ."

When I awoke in the morning the sun had risen, and was pouring a clear light into my room. Words cannot express the impression that this sunlight made upon me. Instantly the baptism that I had received the night before, returned upon me in the same manner. I arose upon my knees in the bed and wept aloud with joy, and remained for some time too much overwhelmed with the baptism of the Spirit to do anything but pour out my soul to God. It seemed as if this morning's baptism was accompanied with a gentle reproof, and the Spirit seemed to say to me, "Will you doubt?" I cried, "No! I will not doubt; I cannot doubt." He then cleared the subject up so much to my mind that it was in fact impossible for me to doubt that the Spirit of God had taken possession of my soul.

In this state I was taught the doctrine of justification by faith, as a present experience. That doctrine had never taken any such possession of my mind, that I had ever viewed it distinctly as a fundamental doctrine of the Gospel. Indeed, I did not know at all what it meant in the proper sense. But I could now see and understand what was meant by the passage, "Being justified by faith, we have peace with God through our Lord Jesus Christ." I could see that the moment I believed, while up in the woods, all sense of condemnation had entirely dropped out of my mind; and that from that moment I could not feel a sense of guilt or condemnation by any effort that I could make. My sense of guilt was gone; my sins were gone; and I do not think I felt any more sense of guilt than if I never had sinned.

This was just the revelation that I needed. I felt myself justified by faith; and, so far as I could see, I was in a state in which I did not sin. Instead of feeling that I was sinning all the time, my heart was so full of love that it overflowed. My cup ran over with blessing and with love; and I could not feel that I was sinning against God. Nor could I recover the least sense of guilt for my past sins. Of this experience I said nothing that I recollect, at the time, to anybody; that is, of this experience of justification. . . .

Soon after Mr. W—— had left the office, Deacon B—— came into the office and said to me, "Mr. Finney, do you recollect that my cause is to be tried at ten o'clock this morning? I suppose you are ready?" I had been retained to attend this suit as his attorney. I replied to him, "Deacon B——, I have a retainer from the Lord Jesus Christ to plead his cause, and I cannot plead yours." He looked at me with astonishment, and said, "What do you mean?" I told him, in a few words, that I had enlisted in the cause of Christ; and then repeated that I had a retainer from the Lord Jesus Christ to plead his cause, and that he must go and get somebody else to attend his law-suit; I could not do it. . . .

Soon after I was converted I called on my pastor, and had a long conversation with him on the atonement. He was a Princeton student, and of course held the limited view of the atonement—that it was made for the elect and available to none else. Our conversation lasted nearly half a day. He held that Jesus suffered for the elect the literal penalty of the Divine law; that he suffered just what was due to each of the elect on the score of retributive justice. I objected that this was absurd; as in that case he suffered the equivalent of endless misery multiplied by the whole number of the elect. He insisted that this was true. He affirmed that Jesus literally paid the debt of the elect, and fully satisfied retributive justice. On the contrary it seemed to me that Jesus only satisfied public justice, and that that was all that the government of God could require.

I was however but a child in theology. I was but a novice in religion and in Biblical learning; but I thought he did not sustain his views from the Bible, and told him so. I had read nothing on the subject except my Bible; and what I had there found upon the subject, I had interpreted as I would have understood the same or like passages in a law book. I thought he had evidently interpreted those texts in conformity with an established theory of the atonement. I had never heard him preach the views he maintained in that discussion. I was surprised in view of his positions, and withstood them as best I could.

SOURCE: *Memoirs of Rev. Charles G. Finney, Written by Himself* (N.Y., 1876), 14–7, 19–24, 42.

101. *"Fire in the Leaves"*

One of the clearest illustrations of the way in which support for the voluntary societies and their crusades was mustered at the parish level is provided by the career of colorful Lyman Beecher (1775–1863). Beecher entered Yale in 1793, and two years later fell under the influence of the new president, Timothy Dwight (1752–1817). He was ordained as pastor of a Presbyterian church on Long Island in 1799. He became widely known for a forceful sermon against dueling, and in 1810 was called as pastor of the Congregational Church at Litchfield, Connecticut. Here he served as "Pope" Dwight's lieutenant, and marshaled the Connecticut clergy against the forces threatening the Standing Order, namely infidelity and disestablishment.

During the second and third decades of the century, the emergence of Unitarianism posed a new threat to orthodoxy. Beecher quickly assumed leadership in vigorous counterattacks, and was effective in checking the spread of Unitarianism in New England. He had learned how to promote a revival, and how to direct its force against the enemies of true religion, as he saw it. "The Unitarians can not be killed by the pen, for they do not live by the pen," he declared. "They depend upon action, and by action only can they be effectively met." [28] Action they got from Beecher! His talents as revivalist were brought into full play when he was called to the pastorate of

[28] Charles Beecher, ed., *Autobiography, Correspondence, etc., of Lyman Beecher*, I, 552.

the newly organized Hanover Street Church in Boston in 1826. Here, where Unitarian sentiment was very strong, he soon succeeded in launching a significant revival among the more orthodox. His own account of it in his *Autobiography* is a classic description of the way a revival may be started and maintained. The reminiscences in the *Autobiography* cannot always be taken at face value, but they provide valuable insights into the movements of his day.

Beecher's organizational abilities were exhibited not only in promoting a revival but also in following it up. He organized voluntary societies which channeled the power generated by the revivals into mission and reform movements. His account of the Boston revivals closes with an explanation of the way in which the temperance movement, one of the major evangelical causes of the nineteenth century, was undergirded by the revivals.

DOCUMENT

When I commenced in Hanover Street, the first three Sabbaths the seats were free to all, and thronged above and below. Then they sold the pews, and the fourth Sabbath I preached to the Church and congregation specifically. The house was not thinned. There was a flood of young people of the middle classes that kept the congregation overflowing.

The Church numbered only thirty-seven; but there were many excellent young men in it, such as Lambert, Noyes, Palmer, Stone, Anderson, and others. Lambert was quick to take care of any thing in the house—quick as a cat to see. Noyes was a deliberate, deep, correct thinker. Then there was a fine set of women. There came in speedily a steady stream by letter, so that the house kept full.

The Church had had charge of their own affairs, property, etc., a year before I came, so that they were used to business; and, for fear it might fall into the hands of Unitarians, as other Church property had done, they had a trust deed, giving it entirely and forever to the Church. It was as finely organized a Church as ever trod shoe-leather. Extremely wise they were; I never knew them make a mistake. . . .

From the beginning my preaching was attended with interest. I could take hold. There was very earnest hearing in the congregation. I saw it was taking hold. Deep solemnity, not mere novelty. I felt in my own soul that the word went forth with power. It was a happy season, hopeful and auspicious. Not long after, Dr. Chaplin began to attend. He had been in the habit of listening to a dead, feeble fellow on the wrong side, but who didn't do much on any side. Shall never forget how Chaplin heard. He was of quick, strong feeling, and was wide awake to hearken. He made me think of a partridge on a dead limb, watching me when I was trying to get a shot at him. He began to bring over his family and his patients from Cambridgeport; and, as the seriousness increased, he came in with three or four carriages—some thirty persons—every Sabbath.

I kept watch from the first among my hearers. They told me of a young lady who had been awakened. I found her out, conversed with her, and she was converted. The next was Dea. P——'s daughter, and they kept dropping in. I tell this that you may know how to *begin* a revival. I always took it by word of mouth first, talking with single cases, and praying with them. Went on so till I found twelve, by watching and picking them out. I visited them, and explained what an inquiry meeting was, and engaged them, if one was appointed, to agree to come. I never would risk a blank attempt.

I began, early in this course, to intimate to the Church the probability of more interest. I grew in importunity, and roused the Church to take hold. At that time many ministers did not understand about this. I began to say to the Church, "I think there is a work begun. Fire in the leaves— not only among us, but in the community." I made no attack on Unitarians. I carried the state of warm revival feeling I had had in Litchfield for years. I carried it in my heart still with great success. They came to hear; there was a great deal of talk about me—great curiosity. They would hear, and then run me down—they would never go again. But they did come again, till they were snared and taken. Many that came to scoff remained to pray.

Finally, my soul rose to it, and I preached to the Church one afternoon, explained to them the state of interest and opposition, and what an inquiry meeting was, and that they must be ready, and gave out an invitation to a long list of persons, whom I described. There were fifteen the first week, twenty the second, thirty-five the third, and the fourth time three hundred. The vestry was filled. Lambert met me at the door, when I came to meeting, with his eyes staring:

"It's a mistake; they've misunderstood, and think it's a lecture. You must explain."

"No," said I, "it's not a mistake; it's the finger of God!"

But I made an explanation, and only one person left.

I parceled out the room to ten individuals, to see every person, and make inquiries of their state, and bring back to me the report. (Oh, that was glorious! It lasted all that winter.) They brought back reports of awakenings and conversions. I talked with forty or fifty myself; and if there were special cases, I went and visited. I said just a word, or a few—not many. I *struck* just according to character and state.

It was really almost amusing to see the rapid changes in language and manner I underwent as I passed from one class to another. A large portion, on being questioned, would reveal their state of mind easily, and being plain cases, would need only plain instruction. They believed the Bible, and they believed what I told them as if it was the Bible—as it was; and therefore the truth was made effectual by the Holy Spirit as well as if more conversation was had.

Another class would have difficulties. Could not see, realize, feel any thing. Did not know how to begin. To such a course of careful instruction was given.

Another class would plead inability—can not do any thing. Many of these told me their ministers told them so. Now I rose into the field of metaphysics, and, instead of being simple, I became the philosopher, and began to form my language for purposes of discrimination and power.

Next came the infidel and skeptical class, whom I received with courtesy and kindness; but, after a few suggestions calculated to conciliate, I told them the subject was one that could not be discussed among so many, but that I should be happy to see them at my house, and succeeded in that way many times. They had the idea that ministers scorned them, and that ministers were this, that, and the other. But it was necessary to go over with them, and trip up their arguments; for, until they were tripped up and crippled, logic was of little avail. So I put myself on the highest key with them, used the highest language and strongest arguments, and made them feel that somebody else knew something besides themselves; and then they came, meek as lambs, and were easily gained. Sometimes I had all these in a string. There were some pretty hard cases occasionally. There was ——, a vile fellow, who came. They used to have balls, and swap wives, and that sort of thing. I treated them politely, and they me, but I never made out any thing with them.

While I was in the inquiry meeting the Church held prayer meeting in a room near by, and, as conversions happened every night—ten, twenty, thirty—I went in and reported to them. That was blessed. They were waiting in hope and prayer, and I went in to carry glad tidings.

The Baptists came in to see what was going on, and pretty soon they began to revive. When I first set up evening meetings not a bell tingled; but, after a few weeks, not a bell that didn't tingle. The Unitarians at first scouted evening meetings; but Ware [29] found his people going, and set up a meeting. I used to laugh to hear the bells going all round.

In this thing of revivals, you would find all these things came by *showers*. Each shower would increase, increase, increase; and when I saw it was about used up by conversion, I would preach so as to make a new attack on mind and conscience, varying with circumstances, and calculated to strike home with reference to other classes, and bring a new shower. The work never stopped for five years. . . .

When the time came for admission of converts to the communion, some seventy at once, it produced no small excitement. Till then all had been the butt of ridicule. The enemy had kept whist, except a few outlaws, at first, although the higher classes—the Cambridge College folks—had their spies abroad to see what was going on.

But, as the work deepened, I told my Church one of two things would come: either the revival would burst out through all these churches, or else there would be an outbreak of assault upon us such as could not be conceived. It was the latter. In one day after the seventy joined, the press

[29] Henry Ware (1764–1845), Hollis Professor of Divinity at Harvard, was an important leader in the Unitarian movement.

belched and bellowed, and all the mud in the streets was flying at us. The upper class put mouth to ear, and hand to pocket, and said *St-boy!* There was an intense, malignant enragement for a time. Showers of lies were rained about us every day. The Unitarians, with all their principles of toleration, were as really a persecuting power while they had the ascendency as ever existed. Wives and daughters were forbidden to attend our meetings; and the whole weight of political, literary, and social influence was turned against us, and the lash of ridicule laid on without stint.

"Well," said I to the Church, "I have only one thing to say— Don't you let your fears be excited about *me*. God helping, I shall take care of myself. But watch your own hearts and pray; watch for the serious, and keep up a system of fervent, effectual prayer." And they did. . . .

When I revised and preached my six sermons on Intemperance,[30] they took strong hold, and made my audience even fuller. My young men were for having them printed. Marvin did it well, and a number of editions were sold. Then the Tract Society bought the copyright. They offered fifty dollars; but I said they ought to give a hundred, and they did. These sermons made a racket all around, more than I had any idea they would. They stirred up the drinkers and venders all over the city. There was a great ebullition of rage among a certain class. And from that commenced a series of efforts among my people and others in Boston to promote this reform.

> SOURCE: Charles Beecher, ed., *Autobiography, Correspondence, etc., of Lyman Beecher, D.D.* (2 vols., N.Y., 1864–65), II, 72–8.

102. Native Depravity and Free Will

The deliberate adoption of revivalistic methods by many Congregational clergymen under the leadership of Timothy Dwight and Lyman Beecher led them to modify certain of the tenets of Calvinism in a way which caused others to fear they were abandoning a sound position. The most crucial of the debated points was the doctrine of native depravity. Strict Calvinism had maintained that all men were by nature totally depraved and that the election of some to salvation and others to damnation was wholly the act of the sovereign God. Inasmuch as God is infinitely good and wise, so ran the argument, even the damnation of sinners serves ultimate purposes— the glory of God and the greatest good of being in general. Against this, the moderate Calvinists argued that sinners are punished because they have freely chosen evil. If the just and sovereign God punishes the sinner, they affirmed, then that indicates that the sinner indeed has free will.

Nathaniel W. Taylor (1786–1858) moved toward the moderate posi-

---

[30] Cf. Lyman Beecher, *Six Sermons on the Nature, Occasions, Signs, Evils, and Remedy of Intemperance* (N.Y., 1827).

tion fairly early in his career. He had been educated at Yale under Dwight, and assisted Beecher in his various campaigns. He served as pastor of the Center Church in New Haven from 1812 to 1822, when he became Dwight Professor of Didactic Theology at the newly organized Yale Divinity School. Because of the necessity of maintaining a united front of the Calvinists against their enemies (successively infidelity, disestablishment, Unitarianism), the widening internal differences among Calvinist leaders were deliberately kept beneath the surface. But the conservatives were troubled, and as the threat of Unitarianism was seen to have been largely contained, the deeper doctrinal issues emerged into the open. Professor Eleazer T. Fitch (1791–1871) of Yale endeavored to allay the rising doubts by stating the New Haven position forcefully in 1826. But he and the New Haven position were attacked vigorously in the conservative Calvinist press and pulpit.

In this crisis, Taylor contended that the best strategy was to affirm positively the correctness of the New Haven views. Before the Connecticut Congregational clergy, gathered at Yale chapel on September 10, 1828, he preached his famous sermon, *Concio ad Clerum* (Advice to the Clergy). His text was Ephesians 2:3, "And were by nature the children of wrath." He focused his attention directly upon the most crucial issue in Calvinist circles, native depravity. He sought to explain what moral depravity involved. It was man's own act, consisting in a free choice of some object rather than God, but it was "by nature" since it was consistent with his nature so to choose. The sermon had two major points. In the following selection, the first point is given in brief, but the second in full. The main body of the sermon was followed by a series of "Remarks" which related the view of moral depravity as defended to the theological controversies then raging; only the final such remark, forming the conclusion of the whole sermon, is included.

DOCUMENT

The Bible is a plain book. It speaks, especially on the subject of sin, directly to human consciousness; and tells us beyond mistake, what sin is, and why we sin. In the text, the Apostle asserts the fact of the moral depravity of mankind, and assigns its cause. To be "the children of wrath" is to possess the character which deserves punishment; in other words, it is to be sinners, or to be entirely depraved in respect to moral character. The text then teaches; THAT THE ENTIRE MORAL DEPRAVITY OF MANKIND IS BY NATURE.

In illustrating this position, I shall attempt to show, First, In what the moral depravity of man consists; and Secondly, That this depravity is by nature.

I. By the moral depravity of mankind I intend generally, the entire sinfulness of their moral character—that state of the mind or heart to which guilt and the desert of wrath pertain. . . .

The question then still recurs, what is this moral depravity for which man deserves the wrath of God? I answer—*it is man's own act, consisting in a free choice of some object rather than God, as his chief good;—or a free preference of the world and of worldly good, to the will and glory of God.* . . .

Having attempted to show in what the moral depravity of man consists, I now proceed to show

II. That this depravity is by nature. This I understand the Apostle to assert when he says, "and were by nature the children of wrath."

What then are we to understand, when it is said that mankind are depraved *by nature?*—I answer—*that such is their nature, that they will sin and only sin in all the appropriate circumstances of their being.*

To bring this part of the subject distinctly before the mind, it may be well to remark, that the question between the Calvinists and the Arminians on the point is this—whether the depravity or sinfulness of mankind is truly and properly ascribed to their *nature* or to their *circumstances of temptation?* And since, as it must be confessed, there can no more be sin without circumstances of temptation, than there can be sin without a nature to be tempted, why ascribe sin exclusively to nature?—I answer, it is truly and properly ascribed to *nature,* and *not* to circumstances, because all mankind sin in all the appropriate circumstances of their being. For all the world ascribe an effect to the nature of a thing, when no possible change in its appropriate circumstances will change the effect; or when the effect is uniformly the same in all its appropriate circumstances. To illustrate this by an example: Suppose a tree, which in one soil bears only bad fruit. Change its circumstances, transplant it to another soil, and it bears very good fruit. Now we say, and all would say, the fact that it bore bad fruit was owing to its situation,—to its circumstances; for by changing its circumstances, you have changed its fruit. Suppose now another tree, which bears bad fruit place it where you will;—change its situation from one soil to another, dig about it and dung it, cultivate it to perfection—do what you will, it still bears bad fruit only. Now every one says, the fact is owing to *the nature* of the tree,—the cause is in the tree, in its nature and *not* in its circumstances. So of mankind, change their circumstances as you may; place them where you will within the limits of their being; do what you will to prevent the consequence, you have one uniform result, entire moral depravity. No change of condition, no increase of light nor of motives, no instructions nor warnings, no any thing, within the appropriate circumstances of their being, changes the result. Unless there be some interposition, which is not included in these circumstances, unless something be done which is above nature, the case is hopeless. Place a human being any where within the appropriate limits and scenes of his immortal [mortal] existence, and such is his nature, that he will be a depraved sinner.

When therefore I say that mankind are entirely depraved *by nature,*

I do not mean that their nature is *itself* sinful, nor that their nature is the *physical* or *efficient* cause of their sinning; but I mean that their nature is the occasion, or reason of their sinning;—that *such is their nature, that in all the appropriate circumstances of their being, they will sin and only sin.*

Of this fact, I now proceed to offer some of the proofs.

1. I allege the text. It is here to be remarked, that the Apostle does not say, nor can he mean, that the nature of man is itself sinful. He is assigning the cause of all sin, and says it is *by nature.* If you say that he teaches that the *nature* itself is *sinful,* then as the cause must precede its effect, you charge him with the absurdity of asserting that there is sin, before sin.

The Apostle doubtless conforms his phraseology to common usage, and must mean just what every plain man, using the same language in any similar case would mean. His language too, must be understood with such restrictions as the nature of the subject and correct usage require. How then do we understand one another when using such language? We say the lion by nature eats flesh; the ox by nature eats grass; the tree by nature bears bad fruit; and so in a thousand cases. Now we mean by this, that the *nature* of the thing is such, that uniformly in all its circumstances, it will be the cause or occasion of that which we assert;—that the lion, for example, is of such a nature that he will eat flesh. So when the Apostle asserts, that mankind are by nature sinners, he must mean simply that such is their nature that uniformly in all the appropriate circumstances of their being, they will sin. He can no more mean that the nature itself is sinful, than we can mean in the example, that the nature of the lion is the same thing as the act of eating flesh, of which it is the cause. Still less can we suppose him to authorise the inference that the act of man in sinning, is not in some most important respects widely different from the act of a lion in eating flesh; so different that the one is sin, and the other not. This difference, the known nature of sin obliges us to suppose, it is intended not to deny, but to assume. The resemblance is simply in the *certainty* of the two things, and that which occasions this certainty; though in every other respect, especially in regard to the moral freedom and moral relations of man, the very nature of the acts spoken of, and the *mode* in which the certainty of them is occasioned, they are so diverse that the one is a moral act and has all the requisites of a moral act; the other cannot be a moral act. The Apostle then, using language as all other men use it, traces the universal depravity of men to *their nature,* and thus most explicitly teaches, contrary to the Arminian view, that it is *not* owing to circumstances. If this be not his meaning he uses language as no one else uses it, and the world, critics and all, may be safely challenged to tell what he does mean.

2. The Scriptures in many forms, teach the universal sinfulness of mankind in all the appropriate circumstances of their being.

First. They declare that "the imagination of man's heart is evil from his youth." And I need not cite passages from the word of God to show in how many forms it declares, that there is none that doeth good, no not one; that all have gone out of the way; that all depart from God and yield themselves to sin from the first moment of accountable action—sinning so early, that in the figurative language of the Scriptures they are said to "go astray as soon as they be born speaking lies." Thus God in his testimony, from the beginning to the end of it, asserts this appalling fact,—the absolute uniformity of human sinfulness, throughout the world and throughout all ages. Not a solitary exception occurs. Even those who become holy through grace are not noted as exceptions, and doubtless, because the object is to describe the character which without grace, is common to all. One character then, if God's record be true, prevails with absolute unvarying uniformity, from the fall in Eden till time shall be no longer. Let the circumstances of men be what they may, the eye of God sees and the voice of God declares that "there is no difference,—all are under sin." Now I ask, why is not the exception made—why, without intimating a single exempt case through favourable circumstances, or tracing sin in a single instance to adverse circumstances, why through all the tribes of men, is *all*—*all* sin— *all* depravity, in all the circumstances of their existence, according to God's testimony? If then the absolute uniformity of an event proves that it is *by nature,* then does this uniformity of human sinfulness prove that man is depraved by nature.

Secondly. The Scriptures teach the same thing, by asserting the universal necessity of regeneration by the Holy Spirit. "Except a man be born of water and of the Spirit, he cannot enter into the kingdom of God." Now I ask, how can the interposition of this Divine Agent be necessary to produce holiness in man, if light and truth and motives will do it? God send the Holy Ghost to perform a work, and declare the necessity of his mission for the purpose, when it might as well be done, were there no Holy Ghost? No, Brethren. Without the transforming grace of this Divine Agent, we are all "dead men" for eternity. It follows therefore that man is such a being, or has such a nature that he will sin in all circumstances of his being, if God does not interpose to save.

Thirdly. The *reason* assigned by our Lord for the necessity of the Spirit's agency, is equally decisive.—"That which is born of the flesh is flesh."— If the phrase "is flesh" is equivalent to the expression, *is sinful*, then this passage is a decisive testimony on the point under consideration. Be this however as it may, one thing is undeniable from this conversation of our Lord with Nicodemus, viz. that the first birth of a human being is an event, which involves the necessity of another birth by the divine spirit. —Say if you will, that what our Lord asserts in the passage cited is, that what is by natural birth is simply a man—a human being, thus intending to teach that none were the better for being born of Abraham; still our conclusion remains, viz. to be born once—to become a human being, is to come under the necessity of being born again of the Spirit. As then we can be at no loss, concerning what it is to be born of the Spirit, it follows that to be born once, involves the certainty of sin—to become a human being is to become a sinner, unless there be a second birth of the Spirit.

Fourthly, I add but one more out of many other scriptural testimonies, —the express declaration of the inefficiency of all truth and motives; or of all that is called *moral suasion.* Saith the Apostle "I have planted, Apollos watered, but God gave the increase; so then neither is he that planteth any thing, nor he that watereth, but God that giveth the increase."—But who are the men that can preach better than Paul and Apollos?—Who can make the arrows of conviction thrill in the conscience, and bring the terrors of guilt and of God into the soul, as did the great Apostle of the Gentiles? Who by telling of a Saviour's love, or of heavenly glories can do more to charm sin out of the human heart, than Apollos that "eloquent man and mighty in the Scriptures?" And yet Paul was nothing, and Apollos nothing, without God. Let then human eloquence do its best, (and it is not to be despised unless it be put in the place of the Holy Ghost)—let the powers of oratory to persuade, to allure, to awe be exhausted; such is the nature of man, that no accents of a Saviour's love, no lifting up of the everlasting doors, no rising smoke of torment, will save a human being from the character and the condemnation of a depraved sinner.

> The transformation of apostate man
> From fool to wise, from earthly to divine,
> Is work for Him that made him.

3. I appeal to human consciousness. In making this appeal, I am aware that some may think I am not warranted. They seem to imagine, that sin in its nature and its cause, is something quite mysterious, and hidden from human discovery or comprehension. But, is this so?—God charge *sin* upon a world of accountable subjects,—provide through the blood of his Son redemption from *sin,*—summon all on pain of his wrath to repent of and to forsake *sin,*—foretell a judgment of *sin,*—award to some eternal salvation from *sin,* and to others eternal perdition for *sin*—in a word, give a law by which *is* the *knowledge of sin,* and not a soul of them be able to know or tell what *sin* is, or why he commits it!!—God surely charges sin upon the world as an intelligible reality. He charges it, in the matter and the cause of it upon human consciousness, and human consciousness must respond to the charge in a judgment going beforehand to condemnation. And if men do not know what that is, of which, if the charge of God be true, they are conscious, I beg leave to ask what do they know? What then are they conscious of? They are conscious that in all sin, they do freely and voluntarily set their hearts, their supreme affections on the world, rather than on God; they are conscious that this supreme love of the world is the fountain and source of all their *other* sins.—They are also conscious, that they are led to set their hearts on the world by those propensities for worldly

good, which belong to their *nature*. They know this as well as they know why they eat when they are hungry, or drink when they are thirsty. A man choose the world as his chief good, fix his whole heart upon it, and pursue it as if God were unworthy of a thought, and not know why he does so? He knows he does so, for the good there is in it,—for the gratification of those natural propensities for this inferior good, which he ought to govern. He knows that it is not for want of knowledge; that it is not for want of motives to an opposite choice, that he thus makes light of God and everlasting glory. I say, he *knows* this, and I speak to the consciousness of all who hear me. All know, that propensities toward the good which the wealth or honour or pleasure of the world affords,—that desires of happiness from this world in some form, have led them to set their heart upon it, rather than on God. Yes, yes, we all know it and not a man of us dares deny it.

4. I appeal to facts. And here the question is, making the proper exception in respect to those whose character has been changed by grace, what is the moral history of man since the first apostacy? It begins with a brother's imbruing his hands in a brother's blood—it terminates in the character that qualifies for companionship with the devil and his angels. What (the grace of God excepted) has ever been adequate to restrain man from sin?—We pass by pagan nations, and merely glance at the utter inefficacy of even the miraculous interpositions of God to prevent sin and reclaim to duty. What was the character of men warned thus for a hundred and twenty years by Noah, God's commissioned servant? Its guilty millions swept to perdition by a deluge of waters, tell us. What the character of those under similar warnings, whom God destroyed by a storm of fire and brimstone on the cities of the plain? This emblem of the tempest of eternal fire, answers.—On mount Sinai God descended amid thunderings and lightnings, and with his own voice promulged his law to the hosts of Israel; and yet as it were, in this very sanctuary of his awful presence, they made a molten calf and said "these be thy Gods, O Israel." In their future history, what a course of apostacies, rebellions, idolatries, amid the warnings of indignant prophets, and a series of miracles by which God shook heaven and earth, at almost every step of his providence? When all else was in vain, when prophets and holy men had been stoned and murdered for their faithfulness in reclaiming men to allegiance to their Maker, see God sending his own Son! Him, though speaking as never man spake, doing the works of God, and proving that in him dwelt all the fulness of the Godhead—him, they nailed to the cross. Look at the persecutions that followed. See how religion doomed to the rack and the fire, stands lifting her streaming eyes to heaven, with none but God to help,—how kings and emperors like tigers, can feast as it were only on Christian blood.—See how every shrine is demolished where weakness can pray, and penitence can weep—how every thing is done, which human malice can invent, to blot out Christianity, name and me-

morial, from under heaven. And if you think that modern refinement and civilization have alleviated the picture, look at Paris in the French revolution —that city, the seat of art, of taste, of refinement, of every thing that can grace human nature short of religion, is converted as in a moment into a den of assassins, and her streets crowded with scaffolds raining blood on the gloomy processions of death, that pass beneath them.—But we need not look to other ages or other countries. In this land on which the Sun of Righteousness sheds his clearest, brightest day—here where the light of salvation, with all its motives, with all the love and grace of the Saviour, with the glories of heaven and terrors of hell, is concentred and poured burning and blazing upon the human heart,—here in this assembly, what do we find? Assassins and highwaymen, murderers of fathers and murderers of mothers? No. But we do find, despisers of the Lord that bought them. We find every one whom grace has not made to differ, an enemy of God. And when the veil of eternity shall be drawn, and the light of eternity reveal the results—when the sinner's place in hell shall be fixed and the measure of his woe be full, then shall he know what that depravity is, which now tramples under foot the Son of God, and does despite unto the Spirit of grace.—These are the stubborn things, called facts; facts which show how dreadful is the depravity of man under the most perfect efforts of God to prevent it; facts which show into what depths of guilt and woe, the creature man will plunge, if the arm of grace does not hold him back; facts which show that he is depraved, not for want of light or motives, but depraved *by nature.* Especially, what other account can be given of the depravity which prevails, amid the splendours of Gospel day? . . .

Finally, I cannot conclude without remarking, how fearful are the condition and prospects of the sinner. His sin is his own. He yields himself by his own free act, by his own choice, to those propensities of his nature, which under the weight of God's authority he *ought to govern.* The gratification of these he makes his chief good, immortal as he is. For this he lives and acts—this he puts in the place of God—and for this, and for nothing better he tramples on God's authority and incurs his wrath. Glad would he be, to escape the guilt of it. Oh—could he persuade himself that the fault is not his own,—this would wake up peace in his guilty bosom. Could he believe that God is bound to convert and save him; or even that he could make it certain that God will do it,—this would allay his fears,—this would stamp a bow on the cloud that thickens, and darkens, and thunders damnation on his guilty path. But his guilt is all his own, and a just God may leave him to his choice. He is going on to a wretched eternity, the self-made victim of its woes. Amid sabbaths and bibles, the intercessions of saints, the songs of angels, the intreaties of God's ambassadors, the accents of redeeming love, and the blood that speaketh peace, he presses on to death. God beseeching with tenderness and terror—Jesus telling him he died once and could die again to save him—mercy weeping over him day and night—

heaven lifting up its everlasting gates—hell burning, and sending up its smoke of torment, and the weeping and the wailing and the gnashing of teeth, within his hearing—and onward still he goes.—See the infatuated immortal!—Fellow sinner,—IT IS YOU.

Bowels of divine compassion—length, breadth, height, depth of Jesus' love—Spirit of all grace, save him—Oh save him—or he dies forever.

> SOURCE: Nathaniel W. Taylor, *Concio ad Clerum. A Sermon Delivered in the Chapel of Yale College, September 10, 1828* (New Haven, 1828), 5, 8, 13–22, 38.

103. The Temperance Campaign

The consumption of alcoholic beverages was a generally accepted practice in the early years of the nineteenth century, within as well as beyond church circles. Indeed, the drinking habit appeared to be on the increase; according to one estimate "the consumption of spirits in 1792 was two and a half gallons per person; in 1810, four and a half gallons; and in 1823, seven and a half gallons."[31] There were many voices lifted in protest, but until the crusade against intemperance was taken up by the Protestant evangelical forces as part of their benevolence movement, it had little effect. It was found that some of the other reform movements were hindered by the ill effects of intemperance. Revivalists soon found that their work went better when the temperance advocates had been at work. The cause was taken up by such crusading leaders as Lyman Beecher and Justin Edwards (1787–1853), Congregational pastor at Andover, Massachusetts. The movement developed rapidly with the organization of the American Society for the Promotion of Temperance in 1826. Edwards later became its corresponding secretary. The crusade was militantly and ably led. Revivalistic methods were effectively employed. Temperance enthusiasts were very certain that the best way to be "temperate" was to abstain totally from intoxicating beverages.

As the forces of evangelical Protestantism were marshaled into a great temperance drive in the 1830's, literally thousands of temperance sermons were preached and hundreds of temperance tracts were published. They were remarkably similar: they appealed to the same statistics, advanced the same arguments, and reached the same conclusion—the necessity for total abstinence. The following "Address to the Young Men of the United States on Temperance" is especially striking. It was prepared by the Rt. Rev. Charles P. McIlvaine on behalf of the New York Young Men's Temperance Society. That a bishop of the Protestant Episcopal Church should write such a temperance tract indicates that there was much support for the voluntary benevolence societies and their crusades within the evangelical wing

---

[31] Tyler, *Freedom's Ferment*, 312.

of that communion. Near the end of the bishop's twenty-page tract was the following appeal:

In order to exert ourselves with the best effect in the promotion of the several objects in this great cause to which young men should apply themselves, let us associate ourselves into *Temperance Societies*. We know the importance of associated exertions. We have often seen how a few instruments, severally weak, have become mighty when united. Every work, whether for evil or benevolent purposes, has felt the life, the spur, and power of co-operation. The whole progress of the temperance reformation, thus far, is owing to the influence of *societies;* to the coming together of the temperate, and the union of their resolutions, examples, and exertions, under the articles of temperance societies.

The first part of the tract (pp. 1–7), here reproduced, presents in strong terms the argument of the temperance leaders against any amount of drinking; for them complete avoidance of "ardent spirits" was the goal.

McIlvaine (1799–1873) was educated at Princeton, rose to early prominence as a member of the evangelical party in the Episcopal Church, and was consecrated Bishop of Ohio in 1832. The tract was not dated, but probably appeared in the middle 1830's. It was widely circulated by the American Tract Society.

DOCUMENT

In addressing the Young Men of the United States in regard to the great enterprise of promoting the universal prevalence of Temperance, we are not aware that any time need be occupied in apology. Our motives cannot be mistaken. The magnitude of the cause, and the importance of that co-operation in its behalf which this address is designed to promote, will vindicate the propriety of its respectful call upon the attention of those by whom it shall ever be received.

It is presumed that every reader is already aware of the extensive and energetic movements at present advancing in our country in behalf of Temperance. That an unprecedented interest in this work has been recently excited, and is still rapidly strengthening in thousands of districts; that talent, wisdom, experience, learning, and influence are now enlisted in its service, with a measure of zeal and harmony far surpassing what was ever witnessed before in such a cause; that great things have already been accomplished; that much greater are near at hand; and that the whole victory will be eventually won, if the temperate portion of society are not wanting to their solemn duty, must have been seen already by those living along the main channels of public thought and feeling. Elevated, as we now are, upon a high tide of general interest and zeal; a tide which may either go on increasing its flood till it has washed clean the very mountain tops, and drowned intemperance in its last den; or else subside, and leave the land infected with a plague, the more malignant and incurable from the dead remains of a partial inundation; it has become a question of universal application, which those who are now at the outset of their influence in society should especially consider, "What can *we* do, and what *ought* we to do in this cause?" For the settlement of this question we invite you to a brief view of the whole ground on which temperance measures are now proceeding.

It cannot be denied that our country is most horribly scourged by intemperance. In the strong language of Scripture, *it groaneth and travaileth in pain, to be delivered from the bondage of this corruption.* Our country is free! *with a great price obtained we this freedom.* We feel as if all the force of Europe could not get it from our embrace. Our shores would shake into the depth of the sea the invader who should presume to seek it. One solitary citizen—led away into captivity—scourged—chained by a foreign enemy, would rouse the oldest nerve in the land to indignant complaint, and league the whole nation in loud demand for redress. And yet it cannot be denied that our country is enslaved. Yes, we are groaning under a most desolating bondage. The land is trodden down under its polluting foot. Our families are continually dishonored, ravaged, and bereaved; thousands annually slain, and hundreds of thousands carried away into a loathsome slavery, to be ground to powder under its burdens, or broken upon the wheel of its tortures. What are the statistics of this traffic? Ask the records of madhouses, and they will answer, that one-third of all their wretched inmates were sent there by Intemperance. Ask the keepers of our prisons, and they will testify that, with scarcely an exception, their horrible population is from the schools of Intemperance. Ask the history of the 200,000 paupers now burdening the hands of public charity, and you will find that two-thirds of them have been the victims, directly or indirectly, of Intemperance. Inquire at the gates of death, and you will learn that no less than 30,000 souls are annually passed for the judgment-bar of God, driven there by Intemperance. How many slaves are at present among us? We ask not of slaves to man, but to Intemperance, in comparison with whose bondage the yoke of the tyrant is freedom. They are estimated at 480,000! And what does the nation pay for the honor and happiness of this whole system of ruin? *Five times as much, every year, as for the annual support of its whole system of government.* These are truths—so often published—so widely sanctioned—so generally received, and so little doubted, that we need not detail the particulars by which they are made out. What then is the whole amount of guilt and of wo which they exhibit? Ask Him *"unto whom all hearts are open, all desires known, and from whom no secrets are hid."* Ask *Eternity!*

The biographer of Napoleon, speaking of the loss sustained by England on the field of Waterloo, says: "Fifteen thousand men killed and wounded, threw half Britain into mourning. It required all the glory and all the solid advantages of that day to reconcile the mind to the high price at which it was purchased." But what mourning would fill *all* Britain if every year should behold another Waterloo? But what does every year repeat in our peaceful land? Ours is a carnage not exhibited only once in a single field, but going on continually, in every town and hamlet. Every eye sees its woes, every ear catches its groans. The wounded are too numerous to count. Who is not wounded by the intemperance of this nation? But of the dead, we count, year by year, more than double the number that filled half Britain with mourning. Ah! could we behold the many thousands whom our destroyer annually delivers over unto death, collected together upon one field of slaughter, for one funeral, and one deep and wide burial-place; could we behold a full assemblage of all the parents, widows, children, friends, whose hearts have been torn by their death, surrounding that awful grave, and loading the winds with tales of wo, the whole land would cry out at the spectacle. It would require something more than *"all the glory"* and *"all the solid advantages"* of Intemperance, *"to reconcile the mind to the high price at which they were purchased."*

But enough is known of the intemperance of this country to render it undeniable by the most ignorant inhabitant, that a horrible scourge is indeed upon us.

Another assertion is equally unquestionable. *The time has come when a great effort must be made to exterminate this unequalled destroyer.* It was high time this was done when the first drunkard entered eternity to receive the award of Him who has declared that no drunkard shall enter the kingdom of God. The demand for this effort has been growing in the peremptory tone of its call, as "the overflowing scourge" has passed with constantly extending sweep through the land. But a strange apathy has prevailed among us. . . . It seems as if some foul demon has taken his seat upon the breast of the nation, and was holding us down with the dead weight of a horrid nightmare, while he laughed at our calamity, and mocked at our fear—when our fear came as desolation, and our destruction as a whirlwind. Shall this state continue? Is not the desolation advancing? Have not facilities of intemperance—temptations to intemperance—examples to sanction intemperance, been fast increasing ever since this plague began? Without some effectual effort, is it not certain they will continue to increase, till intemperate men and their abettors will form the public opinion and consequently the public conscience and the public law of this land—till intemperance shall become like Leviathan of old, "king over all the children of pride," whose breath kindleth coals, and a "flame goeth out of his mouth"? Then what will effort of man avail? "Canst thou draw out Leviathan with a hook? His heart is as firm as a stone, yea, as hard as a piece of the nether millstone; he drinketh up a river, and hasteth not. When he raiseth up himself the mighty are afraid."

It is too late to put off any longer the effort for deliverance. It is granted by the common sense, and urged by the common interest; every feeling of humanity and every consideration of religion enforces the belief that the time has come when a great onset is imperiously demanded to drive out intemperance from the land.

This, to be great, *must be universal.* The whole country is enslaved; and the whole country must rise up at once, like an armed man, and determine to be free. Of what lasting avail would it be for one section of territory, here and there, to clear itself, while the surrounding regions should remain under the curse? The temperance reformation has no quarantine to fence out the infected. Geographical boundaries are no barriers against contagion. Rivers and mountains are easily crossed by corrupting example. Ardent spirits, like all other fluids, perpetually seek their level. In vain does the farmer eradicate from his fields the last vestige of the noisome thistle, while the neighboring grounds are given up to its dominion, and every wind scatters the seed where it listeth. The effort against intemperance, to be effective, *must be universal.*

Here, then, are three important points which we may safely assume as entirely unquestionable:—that *our country is horribly scourged by Intemperance;* that *the time has come when a great effort is demanded for the expulsion of this evil;* and that *no effort can be effectual without being universal.* Hence is deduced, undeniably, the conclusion that it is the duty, and the solemn duty of the people in every part of this country, to rise up at once, and act vigorously and unitedly in the furtherance of whatever measures are best calculated to promote reformation.

Here the question occurs; *what can be done? How can this wo be arrested?* The answer is plain. Nothing can be done, but in one of the three following ways. You must either suffer people to drink *immoderately;* or you must endeavor to promote *moderation* in drinking; or you must try to persuade them to drink *none at all.* One of these plans must be adopted. Which shall we chose? The first is condemned already. What say we to the second? It has unquestionably the sanction of high and ancient ancestry. It is precisely the plan on which intemperance has been wrestled with ever since it was first discovered that "wine is a mocker," and that "strong drink is raging." But hence comes its condemnation. Its long use is its death witness. Were it new, we might hope something from its adoption. But it is old enough to have been tried to the uttermost. The wisdom, the energy, the benevolence of centuries have made the best of it. The attempt to keep down intemperance by endeavoring to persuade people to indulge only moderately in strong drink, has been the world's favorite for ages; while every age has wondered that the vice increased so rapidly. At last we have been awakened to a fair estimate of the success of the plan. And what is it? So far from its having shown the least tendency to exterminate the evil, it is the mother of all its abominations. All who have attained the stature of full-grown intemperance were once children in this nursery—sucking at the breasts of this parent. All the "men of strength to mingle strong drink," who are now full graduates in the vice, and "masters in the arts" of drunkenness, began their education and served their apprenticeship under the discipline of moderate drinking. All that have learned to lie down in the streets, and carry terror into their families, and whom intemperance has conducted to the penitentiary and the mad-house, may look back to this as the beginning of their course—the author of their destiny. No man ever set out to use strong drink with the expectation of becoming eventually a drunkard. No man ever became a drunkard without having at first assured himself that he could keep a safe rein upon every disposition that might endanger his strict sobriety. *"I am in no danger while I only take a little,"* is the first principle in the doctrine of Intemperance. It is high time it were discarded. It has deluged the land with vice, and sunk the population into debasement. The same results will ensue again, just in proportion as the moderate use of ardent spirits continues to be encouraged. Let the multitude continue to drink a little, and still our hundreds of thousands will annually drink to death. It is settled, therefore, that to encourage moderate drinking is not the plan on which the temperance reformation can be successfully prosecuted. The faithful experiment of generation after generation, decides that it must be abandoned. A cloud of witnesses, illustrating its consequences in all the tender mercies of a drunkard's portion, demand that it should be abandoned. Its full time is come. Long enough have we refused to open our eyes to the evident deceitfulness of its pretensions. At last the country is awaking, and begins to realize the emptiness of this dream. Let it go as a dream, and only be remembered that we may wonder how it deceived, and lament how it injured us.

But, if this be discarded, what plan of reformation remains? If nothing is to be expected from endeavoring to promote a *moderate* use of ardent spirits, and stillness [still less] from an *immoderate* use, what can be done? There is but one possible answer. *Persuade people to use none at all. Total abstinence* is the only plan on which reformation can be hoped for. We are shut up to this. We have tried the consequences of encouraging people to venture but moderately into the atmosphere of infection; and we are now convinced that it was the very plan to feed its strength and extend its ravages. We are forced to the conclusion, that, to arrest the pestilence, we must starve it. All the healthy must abstain from its neighborhood. All those who are now temperate must give up the use of the means of intemperance. The deliverance of this land from its present degradation, and from the increasing woes attendant upon this vice, depends altogether upon the extent to which the principle of total abstinence shall be adopted by our citizens.

SOURCE: Charles P. McIlvaine, "Address to the Young Men of the United States on Temperance," *The Temperance Volume; Embracing the Temperance Tracts of the American Tract Society* (N.Y., n.d.), No. 244, 1-7.

104. Christian Perfection

There was an upsurge of perfectionist thought in the wake of the intense revivalism of the 1830's. One wing of perfectionism went to extremes. Some perfectionists claimed perfect holiness, moved in antinomian directions, and even lapsed into sexual promiscuity. The most conspicuous radical perfectionist leader to appear was John Humphrey Noyes (1811–86), the founder, in 1848, of the Oneida Community. Here, under communitarian discipline, a system of "plural marriages" was instituted and continued for three decades.[32]

A much more moderate version of Christian perfection was advocated by the Oberlin leaders, Charles G. Finney and Asa Mahan. At Oberlin, the doctrine of sanctification did not claim that the Christian could be absolutely perfect, but only that he could grow toward perfection. He should aim at being perfect, yet always recognize that holiness was the gift of faith. "Entire conformity of heart and life to all the known will of God" was possible, though the attainment of a spiritual peak would reveal visions of still greater heights beyond.[33] This view of perfection came very close to that which had long been advocated in Methodism; indeed, the Oberlin leaders were influenced by Wesley's writings on the subject. Conversely, the Oberlin views helped to stimulate new interest in holiness in American Methodism, where it had fallen into some neglect. In 1844, several bishops much concerned with a re-emphasis on perfectionist teaching were elected.[34]

President Mahan took the lead in shaping Oberlin perfectionism. In 1839, as Finney recorded it,

> One of our theological students arose, and put the inquiry, whether the Gospel did not provide for Christians all the conditions of an established faith, and hope, and love; whether there was not something better and higher than Christians had generally experienced; in short, whether sanctification was not attainable in this life; that is, sanctification in such a sense that Christians could have unbroken peace, and not come into condemnation, or have the feeling of condemnation or a consciousness of sin. Brother Mahan immediately answered, "Yes." [35]

He and Finney became ardent proponents of the controversial perfectionist position.

[32] John H. Noyes, *Salvation from Sin the End of Christian Faith* (Wallingford, Conn., 1869); Robert A. Parker, *A Yankee Saint: John Humphrey Noyes and the Oneida Community* (N.Y., 1935).

[33] For a discussion of the differences between radical and moderate perfectionist views, see Whitney R. Cross, *Burned-over District*, 238–51.

[34] John L. Peters, *Christian Perfection and American Methodism* (N.Y., 1956), 115–7.

[35] *Memoirs of Rev. Charles G. Finney, Written by Himself*, 350–1.

Asa Mahan (1799–1889) was born in Vernon, New York, and educated at Hamilton College and Andover Theological Seminary. He was ordained to the Congregational ministry in 1829, and participated in the revival movements of the day. Two years later he was called to the pastorate of the Sixth Presbyterian Church in Cincinnati. He was also a trustee at Lane Seminary, the only one who was in sympathy with the abolitionist students. He resigned to become the first president of Oberlin College, to which many of the Lane students migrated. He remained at Oberlin for fifteen years, teaching philosophy in addition to his presidential duties. Later years found him again alternating between pastoral and academic assignments, but still vigorously advocating the views on perfection which he had articulated so strongly in 1839 in his first book, *Scripture Doctrine of Christian Perfection.* The first chapter, an effort to define the nature of "perfection in holiness," is here reproduced; it is followed by a brief section from a later chapter ("Objections Answered") in which Mahan defended his views of holiness against the charge of "perfectionism" as exemplified by the radical groups with antinomian tendencies.

DOCUMENT

Be ye therefore perfect, even as your Father in heaven is perfect.—
Matt. v. 48

Two important features of this passage demand our special attention. 1. The command, "Be perfect." 2. The nature and extent of the command; "even as your Father in heaven is perfect." In other words, we are here required to be as perfect, as holy, as free from all sin, in our sphere as creatures, as God is in his as our Creator and our Sovereign.

My design in the present discourse is to answer this one question; *What is perfection in holiness?* In answering this inquiry, I would remark, that perfection in holiness implies a full and perfect discharge of our entire duty, of all existing obligations in respect to God and all other beings. It is perfect obedience to the moral law. It is "loving the Lord our God with all our heart, and with all our soul, and with all our strength, and our neighbor as ourselves." It implies the entire absence of all selfishness, and the perpetual presence and all-pervading influence of pure and perfect love. "Love is the fulfilling of the law."

In the Christian, perfection in holiness implies the consecration of his whole being to Christ—the subjection of all his powers and susceptibilities to the control of one principle—"faith on the Son of God." This is what the moral law demands of him in his circumstances. Were the Christian in that state in which he should "eat and drink, and do all that he does for the glory of God," in which his eye should be perfectly single to this one object; or in which the action of all his powers should be controlled by faith, which works by love, he would then, I suppose, have attained to a state of entire sanctification—his character would be "perfect and entire, wanting nothing." Every duty to every being in existence would be discharged.

It will readily be perceived, that perfect holiness, as above described, does not imply *perfect wisdom*, the exclusive attribute of God. The Scriptures, speaking of the human nature of Christ, affirm, that he "increased in wisdom." This surely does not imply that his holiness was less perfect at one time than at another. So of the Christian. His holiness may be perfect in *kind*, but *finite* in *degree*, and in this sense imperfect; because his wisdom and knowledge are limited, and in this sense imperfect.

Holiness, in a creature, may also be perfect, and yet progressive—progressive, not in its nature, but in degree. To be perfect, it must be progressive in the sense last mentioned, if the powers of the subject are progressive. He is perfect in holiness, whose love at each successive moment corresponds with the extent of his powers. "If there be first a willing mind, it is accepted according to that a man hath, and not according to that he hath not."

Hence I remark, that perfection in holiness does not imply, that we now love God with all the strength and intensity with which redeemed spirits in heaven love him. The depth and intensity of our love depend, under all circumstances, upon the vigor and reach of our powers, and the extent and distinctness of our vision of divine truth. "Here we see through a glass darkly; there face to face." Here our powers are comparatively weak; there they will be endowed with an immortal and tireless vigor. In each and every sphere, perfection in holiness implies a strength and intensity of love corresponding with the reach of our powers and the extent and distinctness of our vision of truth in that particular sphere. The child is perfect in holiness who perpetually exercises a filial and affectionate obedience to all the divine requisitions, and loves God with all the powers which it possesses as a child. The man is perfect in holiness who exercises the same supreme and affectionate obedience to all that God requires, and loves him to the full extent of his knowledge and strength as a man. The saint on earth is perfect, when he loves with all the strength and intensity rendered practicable by the extent of his knowledge and reach of his powers in his present sphere. The saint in heaven, will be favored with a seraph's vision, and a seraph's power. To be perfect there, he must love and adore with a seraph's vigor, and burn with a seraph's fire.

To present this subject in a somewhat more distinct and expanded form, the attention of the reader is now invited to a few remarks upon I Thes. v. 23. "And the very God of peace sanctify you wholly: and I pray God your whole spirit and soul and body be preserved blameless unto the coming of our Lord Jesus Christ." . . . In short, the prayer of the apostle is, that all the powers and susceptibilities of our being may not only be purified from all that is unholy, but wholly sanctified and devoted to Christ, and forever preserved in that state. Now, the powers and susceptibilities of our nature are all comprehended in the following enumeration: the will, the intellect, and our mental and physical susceptibilities and propensities. The question to which the special attention of the reader is invited is this: When are we in a perfectly sanctified and blameless state, in respect to the action of all these powers and susceptibilities?

1. That we be in a perfectly sanctified and blameless state in regard to our wills, implies, that the action of all our voluntary powers be in entire conformity to the will of God; that every choice, every preference, and every volition, be controlled by a filial regard to the divine requisitions. The perpetual language of the heart must be, "Lord, what wilt thou have me do?"

2. That we "be preserved blameless" in regard to our intellect, does not imply that we never think of what is evil. If this were so, Christ was not blameless, because he thought of the temptations of Satan. Nor could the Christian repel what is evil, as he is required to do. To repel evil, the evil itself must be before the mind, as an object of thought.

To be blameless in respect to the action of our intellectual powers, does imply, 1. That every thought of evil be instantly suppressed and repelled. 2. That they be constantly employed on the inquiry, what is the truth and will of God, and by what means we may best meet the demands of the great law of love. 3. That they be employed in the perpetual contemplation of "whatsoever things are true, whatsoever things are honest, whatsoever things are just, whatsoever things are pure, whatsoever things are lovely, whatsoever things are of good report; if there be any virtue, and if there be any praise," in thinking of these things also. When the intellectual powers are thus employed, they are certainly in a blameless state.

3. That our feelings and mental susceptibilities be preserved blameless, does not imply, that they are, at all times and circumstances, in the same intensity of excitement, or in the same identical state. This the powers and laws of our being forbid. Nor, in that case, could we obey the command, "Rejoice with those that do rejoice, and weep with those that weep." Nor does it imply that no feelings can exist in the mind, which, under the circumstances then present, it would be improper to indulge. A Christian, for example, may feel a very strong desire to speak for Christ under circumstances when it would be improper for him to speak. The feeling itself is proper. But we must be guided by wisdom from above in respect to the question, when and where we are to give utterance to our feelings.

That our feelings and mental susceptibilities be in a blameless state, does imply, 1. That they all be held in perfect and perpetual subjection to the will of God. 2. That they be in perfect and perpetual harmony with the truth and will of God as apprehended by the intellect, and thus constituting a spotless mirror, through which there shall be a perfect reflection of whatsoever things are "true," "honest," "just," "pure," "lovely," and of "good report."

4. That our "bodies be preserved blameless," does not, of course, imply that they are free from fatigue, disease, or death. Nor does it imply that no desire be excited through our physical propensities, which, under existing circumstances, it would be unlawful to indulge. The feeling of hunger in Christ, under circumstances in which indulgence was not proper, was not sinful. The consent of the will to gratify the feeling, and not the feeling itself, renders us sinners.

That we be preserved in a sanctified and blameless state in respect to our bodies, does imply, 1. That we endeavor to acquaint ourselves with all the laws of our physical constitution. 2. That in regard to food, drink, and dress, and in regard to the indulgence of all our appetites and physical propensities, there be a sacred and undeviating conformity to these laws. 3. That every unlawful desire be instantly suppressed, and that all our propensities be held in perfect subjection to the will of God. 4. That our bodies, with all our physical powers and propensities, be "presented to God as a living sacrifice, holy and acceptable," to be employed in his service.

Such is Christian Perfection. It is the consecration of our whole being to Christ, and the perpetual employment of all our powers in his service. It is the perfect assimilation of our entire character to that of Christ, having at all times, and under all circumstances, the "same mind that was also in Christ Jesus." It is, in the language of Mr. Wesley, "In one view, purity of intention, dedicating all the life to God. It is the giving God all the heart; it is one desire and design ruling all our tempers. It is devoting, not a part, but all our soul, body, and substance to God. In another view, it is all the mind that was in Christ Jesus, enabling us to walk as he walked. It is the circumcision of the heart from all filthiness, from all inward as well as outward pollution. It is the renewal of the heart in the whole image of God, the full likeness of him that created it. In yet another, it is loving God with all our heart, and our neighbor as ourselves." . . .[36]

I. This doctrine, it is said, is, or in its legitimate tendencies, leads to, Perfectionism. If any individual will point out any thing intrinsic, in the doctrine here maintained, at all allied to *that* error, I, for one, will be among the first to abandon the position which I am now endeavoring to sustain. Perfectionism, technically so called, is, in my judgment, in the native and necessary tendencies of its principles, worse than the worst form of infidelity. The doctrine of holiness, now under consideration, in all its essential features and elements, stands in direct opposition to Perfectionism. It has absolutely nothing in common with it, but a few terms derived from the Bible.

1. Perfectionism, for example, in its fundamental principles, is the abrogation of all law. The doctrine of holiness, as here maintained, is perfect

[36] "A Plain Account of Christian Perfection, as Believed and Taught by the Reverend Mr. John Wesley, from the Year 1725, to the Year 1777," *The Works of the Rev. John Wesley* (14 vols., London, 1829), XI, 444.

obedience to the precepts of the law. It is the "righteousness of the law ful-filled in us."

2. In abrogating the moral law, as a rule of duty, Perfectionism abrogates all obligation of every kind, and to all beings. The doctrine of holiness, as here maintained, contemplates the Christian as a "debtor to all men," to the full extent of his capacities, and consists in a perfect discharge of all these obligations—of every obligation to God and man.

3. Perfectionism is a "rest" which suspends all efforts and prayer, even, for the salvation of the world. The doctrine of holiness, as here maintained, consists in such a sympathy with the love of Christ, as constrains the subject to consecrate his entire being to the glory of Christ, in the salvation of men.

4. Perfectionism substitutes the direct teaching of the Spirit, falsely called, in the place of the "word." This expects such teachings only in the diligent study of the word, and tries every doctrine by the "law and the testimony," expounded in conformity with the legitimate laws of inter-pretation.

5. Perfectionism surrenders up the soul to blind impulse, assuming, that every existing desire or impulse is caused by the direct agency of the Spirit, and therefore to be gratified. The doctrine of holiness, as here maintained, consists in the subjection of all our powers and propensities to the revealed will of God.

6. Perfectionism abrogates the Sabbath, and all the ordinances of the gospel, and, in its legitimate tendencies, even marriage itself. The doctrine of holiness, as here maintained, is a state of perfect moral purity, induced and perpetuated by a careful observance of all these ordinances, together with subjection to other influences of the gospel, received by faith.

7. Perfectionism renders, in its fundamental principles, all perfection an impossibility. If, as this system maintains, the Christian is freed from all obligation, is bound by no law—in short, if there is no standard with which to compare his actions, (and there is none), if the moral law, as a rule of action, is abrogated—moral perfection can no more be predicated of the Christian than of the horse, the ox, or the ass. The doctrine of holiness, on the other hand, as here maintained, contemplates the moral law as the only rule and standard of the moral conduct, and consists in perfect conformity to the precepts of this law.

8. Perfectionism, in short, in its essential elements, is the perfection of licentiousness. The doctrine of holiness, as here maintained, is the perfect and perpetual harmony of the soul with "whatsoever things are true, what-soever things are honest," "just," "pure," "lovely," and of "good report," and if there be any virtue, "and if there be any praise," with these things also.

What agreement, then, has the doctrine of holiness, as here maintained, with Perfectionism? The same that light has with darkness. A man might, with the same propriety, affirm that I am a Unitarian, because I believe in one God, while I hang my whole eternity upon the doctrine of the Trinity, as to affirm that I am a Perfectionist, because I hold the doctrine of holiness as now presented.

> SOURCE: Asa Mahan, *Scripture Doctrine of Christian Perfection; With Other Kindred Subjects, Illustrated and Confirmed in a Series of Discourses Designed to Throw Light on the Way of Holiness* (4th ed., Boston, 1840), 7–13, 71–3.

105. A Plea for Western Colleges

Church colleges multiplied, especially in the West, under the pressure of denominational rivalry in the decades prior to the Civil War. Many of these institutions suffered from the lack of sound planning and adequate support, and did not long survive. In order that there might be better planning and financing in western college development, the familiar pattern of a national voluntary society was employed. In 1843, the Society for the Promotion of Collegiate and Theological Education at the West was formally organized in New York City. Five institutions—Western Reserve, Illinois, Wabash and Marietta colleges, and Lane Theological Seminary—were given assistance at the outset. A report on the origin of the society declared:

> These Colleges were all projected by religious men, most of whom were Home Missionaries—they were established upon religious principles—have grown up under religious influences, and have all been repeatedly blest with the converting influences of the Holy Spirit.
>
> In their infancy they were not only all approved and liberally aided by the Eastern churches—but the foundations of some of them were laid after very extensive consultation with leading benevolent minds in these churches.[37]

At first these colleges had fared well, but their financial condition became precarious during the period of national economic difficulty beginning in 1837. The new society largely consolidated the campaigns for the adequate financing of certain western colleges. Though the constitution of the society provided that anyone who contributed annually could be a member of it, actually the society was controlled by Congregationalists and New School Presbyterians, who were still co-operating in the Plan of Union. Colleges under Congregational and Presbyterian auspices were favored, but some assistance was given to other institutions, as to Wittenberg College, a Lutheran school.

[37] *The First Report of the Society for the Promotion of Collegiate and Theological Education at the West* (N.Y., 1844), 5.

Immediately after the founding of the society, a series of articles under the general title, "Plea for Western Colleges," appeared in the *New York Observer*. The "Plea" was deemed so graphic and powerful that the sponsors of the society had it reprinted as an appendix to their first report. The presentation was written by Truman Marcellus Post (1810–86), a professor at Illinois College in Jacksonville. Post had been born in Vermont, and was a graduate of Middlebury College. After a few months at Andover Seminary, he determined to enter the legal profession. Following a period of study in Washington, he resolved to set up his practice in the rapidly developing West, in St. Louis. But during a visit to a friend in Jacksonville in 1833, he was prevailed upon to become professor of ancient languages (and soon also professor of ancient history) at Illinois College. He served there for fourteen years, proving himself to be a stimulating teacher and a brilliant lecturer. He also became pastor of the Congregational Church in Jacksonville. In 1847 he left the college to take the pastorate of the Third Presbyterian (which later became the First Congregational) Church in St. Louis.

The five articles of his series stressed the need for eastern support of western colleges. The fourth article, reprinted herewith, sought to answer the question as to why colleges were so much needed in the West. The Protestant fear of Roman Catholicism, which he lists first, was a recurring theme in the literature of the society.

DOCUMENT

The considerations advanced in my last article go to show, that Colleges are a necessity of every extensive community, marked by nature as a social unity. We are now to look at some reasons why they are peculiarly needed at the West. First, then, we find such a reason in the fact that Rome is at this time making unprecedented efforts to garrison this valley with her seminaries of education. She claims already to have within it between fifteen and twenty colleges and theological schools; and this number is rapidly increasing. To these permanency is ensured by the steadfastness of her policy, the constancy of her receipts from Catholic Europe, yearly increasing under the stimulating reports of her missionaries, and by her exacting despotism, moral if not ecclesiastic, over the earnings of her poor in this country. They are among the enduring formative forces in western society; and the causes which sustain them, will constantly add to their number. These institutions, together with numerous grades, under the conduct of their Jesuits and various religious orders, are offering (what professes to be) education almost as a gratuity, in many places in the West. Whatever other qualities her education may lack, we may be sure it will not want a subtle and intense proselytism, addressing not the reason but the senses, the taste, the imagination, and the passions; applying itself diversely to the fears of the timid, the enthusiasm of the ardent, the credulity of the simple, the affections of the young, and to that trashy sentiment and mawkish charity to which all principles are the same. Now the policy of Rome in playing upon all these elements through her educational enginery, is steadfast and profoundly sagacious. Her aim, in effect, is at the whole educational interest. The college is naturally the heart of the whole. The lower departments necessarily draw life from that. If Rome then grasps the college in the system of Western education, she virtually grasps the common school; she distils out the heart of the whole, if not a putrid superstition, at least that covert infidelity of which she is still more prolific.

Now a system so deep and so persistent, must be met by a correspondent depth and persistency of policy. Protestantism can no more counteract it by temporary and spasmodic efforts, than she could stop the Mississippi with a whirlwind. She can encounter it only by a system of permanent and efficient Protestant colleges. And this for two reasons. First, the Catholic seminaries in this country seem to meet a great and deeply felt social want, and can be displaced only by a supply for this want from another quarter. And secondly, in the nature of things, a college alone can counteract a college. The college acts upon the public mind in a manner so peculiar, through such ages and classes, and through influences so various and subtle, so constant, noiseless and profound, that it can be successfully combated only by a similar institution. Place efficient Protestant colleges in the proximity of the Catholic, and the latter will wither. For all purposes of severe intellectual discipline or masculine reason, their education is soon found to be a sham. A spiritual despotism dare not, cannot, teach true history or a free and manly philosophy. Again, other facts, which constitute a peculiar necessity for colleges in the West, are found in the circumstances and character of its population. First, the West is in its formative state. Never will impressions be made so easily and so enduringly for good or evil. Never will it be so important that its architect-minds—its plastic forces— should be endued with a broad and liberal intelligence. According to the elements now thrown in, it will soon permanently crystalize into dark and unshapely forms, or into order and beauty.

Another peculiar demand for colleges, may be found in the immense rapidity of our growth, and in the character of that growth, being a representative of almost every clime, opinion, sect, language, and social institute, not only of this country but of Christian Europe. Never was a more intense power of intellectual and moral fusion requisite to prevent the utter disorganization of society. Never was a people put to such a perilous proof of its power of assimilation, or required to incorporate with itself so rapidly such vast masses. We have in this fact, as well as in that of the Catholic aggression, dangers and trials put upon us, which our fathers never knew. Society here is new yet vast, and with all its forces in insulation or antagonism. Never was a community in more urgent need of those institutions, whose province it is profoundly to penetrate a people with a burning intelligence that shall fuse it into a unity with those great principles which are the organic life and binding forces of all society.

Again, in consequence of the incoherency of this element in a population thus heterogeneous, and broken off from the fixtures of old communities, without time to form new ones, all the social forces are shifting and mutable, and yield like the particles of liquid to the last force impressed. This quality of western society, combined with the bold, prompt, energetic and adventurous temperament impressed generally on it by common influences in the life of the emigrant, exposes it to vehement and brief excitements, to epidemic delusion and agitation. Upon this sea of incoherent and vehement mind, every wind of opinion has been let loose, and is struggling for the mastery; and the mass heaves restlessly to and fro under the thousand different forces impressed. The West is, therefore, peculiarly perturbed with demagoguism and popular agitation, not only in politics, but in religion, and all social interests. Amid these shifting social elements, we want principles of stability, we want a system of permanent forces, we want deep, strong and constant influences, that shall take from the changefulness and excitability of the western mind, by giving it the tranquillity of depth, and shall protect it from delusive and fitful impulses, by enduing it with a calm, profound and pure reason.

Thus, while society with us has on the one hand to contend against a masked and political spiritual despotism entrenching itself in the educational interest, and on the other against a demagogic agitation, urged on too often by avarice, or ruffianism, or faction, or a sophistical but specious skepticism, or by fanatical or superstitious or shallow religionisms and socialisms of every hue, we find our defence against both to be the same, a thorough popular enlightenment and belief, anchored by permanent institutions gradually pervading the mass with great and tranquil and guardian truths, and adjusting the system to the fixed laws of intellectual and moral gravitation. It may perhaps be asked, "Why not, in such a community, immediately proceed by opposing to agitation for evil, agitation for good?" This may at times be expedient, but cannot be relied on permanently. First, because popular agitation, unless based on deep-wrought intellectual convictions, can only palliate, it cannot cure any evil. In the second place, in the germ of popular agitation, a freedom from the restraints of conscience and truth and honor, often gives a decisive advantage, and agitating movements springing forth immediately from the people to be moved, and possessing a quiet sympathy with its feeling, and a shrewd tact in dealing with its passions and prejudices, must ever out-general any countermovement originating from a different source. Especially, movements of this kind from abroad are liable to find themselves forestalled—the popular ear and mind preoccupied—arguments closed—opposing tracts already in the hands of the people—and the Bible itself, under their elected interpreters, made to preach another gospel.

The above exigencies of Western society cannot be met without colleges. I am far from undervaluing over [other?] movements of Christian philanthropy towards the country. I am most grateful for them. I bless God for his Word broad-cast by the American Bible Society amid this people; I am thankful for the interest the American Tract Society are directing hitherward, and hail with pleasure all the living truth and hallowed thought brought by it into contact with the popular mind. The attitude and history of the American Home Missionary Society in relation to the West, fill my mind with a sentiment of moral sublimity, and give it rank among the noblest and most sagacious schemes in the records of Christian benevolence. It will stand in history invested, to a great extent, with the moral grandeur of a civilizer and evangelizer of a new empire. But these are far from excluding the scheme of colleges. The permanency of their benefits can be grounded only on a thorough and liberal popular enlightenment. The educational interest, then, must underlie them all. But the only way in which the East can lay a controlling grasp on this, is by the establishment among us of permanent educational institutions. In a population, one tenth at least of which cannot read, it is plain that education is an essential prerequisite to bringing a large class—and that most necessary to be reached—within the influence of truth through the press. And no system of foreign supply of ministers, teachers or educated men, can obviate the necessity of institutions that shall constantly send forth those that shall be the educators of this people, in the school, the pulpit, the legislature, and the various departments of social life. Artificial irrigation cannot take the place of living waters. We are grateful for streams from abroad, but we feel there is need of opening fountains of life in the bosom of the people itself. The supplies from abroad we cannot rely on long. They are every day becoming more inadequate in numbers, and must to some extent be deficient in adaptation to our wants; a deficiency that often for years, sometimes for life, shuts one out from the people.

The common exigencies, then, of every extensive society, require colleges within itself. The peculiar evils to which that of the West is exposed, obviously cannot be permanently and successfully met by other means. The question then recurs in every aspect of this subject, Will the East assist the West in establishing a Protestant system of home education, or will she leave her to grapple single-handed with Romanism, and the other peculiar dangers to which she is exposed, in addition to the necessities that cluster around every infant community, or will she attempt by palliatives addressed to the symptoms, to heal a disease seated in the heart? A dangerous malady is on the patient. The peril is imminent and requires promptitude. Shall remedies be adapted to the disease or the symptoms? or, with such fearful chances against it, shall the patient be abandoned to the conflict betwixt nature and death? Let the East remember the life thus hazarded involves her own—it is to her the brand of Meleager.[38]

SOURCE: *The First Report of the Society for the Promotion of Collegiate and Theological Education at the West* (N.Y., 1844), 25-8.

106. Westward to Oregon

Much of the interest and activity of the benevolence movement was focused on missions. Conspicuous among the voluntary societies were those concerned with the sending of missionaries to the West and overseas. The origins of the American Board of Commissioners for Foreign Missions have already been traced.[39] In 1836, the American Board appointed a physician, Marcus Whitman, and a minister, Henry H. Spalding, and their wives as its first agents in the Oregon territory.

As a young man, Whitman (1803–47) had at one time considered the ministry, but for a boy who had lost his father the expense of the seven years of college and seminary education seemed prohibitive. Medical education was then much less expensive, so after "riding with a doctor" for experience, as well as serving as schoolteacher, Whitman entered Fairfield Medical College in the fall of 1825 and received a license to practice medicine the next spring.[40] After several years of practice in New York and in Canada, he studied for another term at Fairfield and received the degree of M.D. early in 1832. He then settled in Wheeler, New York, joined the Presbyterian church there, and offered himself to the American Board as a missionary physician. Before his departure for the West on a survey trip to determine the condition and character of Indian tribes, Whitman became engaged to Narcissa Prentiss (1808–47), a young lady of spirit and talent. They were married after his return to the East, and early in 1836 they left with the Spaldings for Oregon.

The Whitmans settled at Waiilatpu among the Cayuse Indians, while the Spaldings settled more than a hundred miles away at Lapwai among the Nez Percés. In 1838 the first Protestant church west of the Rockies was founded, with Spalding (1803–74) as pastor and Whitman as elder. It was provided that the church was to be governed on the Congregational plan, but be attached to the Bath Presbytery in New York. It was not untypical of many churches formed in the West in keeping with the Plan of Union. Served by a Presbyterian pastor, it was known as a Presbyterian church.[41]

[38] Meleager was a Greek legendary figure of whom it had been prophesied that his life would be preserved only so long as a certain brand remained unburnt.

[39] *American Christianity*, I, 547–52.

[40] Clifford M. Drury, *Marcus Whitman, M.D., Pioneer and Martyr* (Caldwell, Id., 1937), 39–43.

[41] Clifford M. Drury, *Henry Harmon Spalding* (Caldwell, Id., 1936), 188–9.

While Spalding focused on the spiritual aspects of the mission, Whitman devoted major attention to medical, agricultural, and educational efforts. The physician was much concerned with improving the state of civilization in Oregon, both by educating the Indians and by encouraging the westward migration of the whites. Indeed, the authorities of the American Board sometimes wondered if Whitman were not paying too much attention to such matters. The Rev. David Greene, Secretary of the Board, expressed this concern to Whitman in many letters. For example, on February 25, 1846, he wrote as follows:

> I fear from your account of what you have to do for the whites and the Indians, in respect to mills, fields and herds, that you will almost lose sight of the great spiritual object of your mission, and be too nearly satisfied with seeing the Indians advancing in industry, the arts of civilized life, and the means of comfortable living. Why should they not grow covetous and selfish, if their thoughts are mostly turned towards these things and they become habituated to regard them as the chief good and the great end of life and effort? It is highly important that your example and instructions should constrain them to see that, in your estimation, the great thing is to repent and believe the Gospel and become reconciled to God. In no other manner than by becoming heartily religious, can they be pre-pared to withstand the temptations and various influences which they must encounter, as the white population shall increase and press upon them more. Industry, and a settled mode of life, and the means of living comfortably are important, and even indispensable to their welfare and success in their new relations. But these will not do alone. We see no reason to doubt that your secular plans are wisely formed and carried into effect with energy and discretion. What we desire is that you should at the same time make your missionary character and object prominent. You are doing well—a most important work, we doubt not, for the temporal and social welfare of the Indians, and one nearly connected with, and perhaps indispensable to their full enjoyment of Christian privileges, or making rapid or great advances in Christian knowledge. But is as much done, comparatively, for their souls and their spiritual interests? [42]

As the letter that follows from Whitman's pen shows, he was indeed much interested in the development of civilization in Oregon, and saw the work of the missionary as an important part of that effort. Written to his brother-in-law, the letter reveals much about the attitude of the missionary mind

[42] Quoted in Archer B. Hulbert and Dorothy P. Hulbert, *Marcus Whitman, Crusader,* Part III, *1843 to 1847* (Denver, 1941), 162-3. On Whitman, see also Nard Jones, *The Great Command: The Story of Marcus and Narcissa Whitman and the Oregon Country Pioneers* (Boston, 1959).

of the time to some of the contemporary religious developments. Whitman was troubled because Perfectionism and Millerism detracted from the work of spreading Protestantism and civilization westward; this might have allowed Catholicism to take possession of the Northwest.

Slightly more than a year after he had written the letter, a rumor spread among the Cayuses that Whitman was responsible for a series of epidemics among them. This led to a vicious attack on the mission at Waiilatpu, and the massacre of fourteen persons, including the doctor and his wife. Thereupon the mission was closed, completing one of the most dramatic chapters in early Protestant mission history in the West.

The original of the letter reprinted below is at the Oregon Historical Society. In the interest of readability, the present text follows the version printed in the *Transactions* of the Oregon Pioneer Association, with certain corrections on the basis of a version conforming to the original which appears in A. B. and D. P. Hulbert, *Marcus Whitman*, III, 197–207.

DOCUMENT

Waiilatpu, Nov. 5th, 1846.

Rev. L. P. Judson, My Dear Brother:—I have a last moment to spare in writing, and I have resolved to write to you, inasmuch as you have given me the hint by the note you appended to a family letter from Mrs. Whitman's friends. I am going to write plainly to you, for we love you and do not like to see your influence and usefulness abridged. I have known you long and well—better perhaps than you me. I esteem you for your warm affections and ardent temperament, but although these are amiable qualities, they are like the health of an infant, of so high and excitable a nature that it is but a step between them and derangement or disease. Mental disease is not suspected by the person who is the subject of it. But do not be surprised at what I am intimating. There are but few who are possessed of perfectly balanced minds. I have felt and acted with you on points to which the public mind was not awake, nor ready for action. It is well to be awake on all important points of duty and truth, but it can do no good to be ultra on any of these points. Why part friends for an opinion only, and that, too, when nothing is to be gained for truth or principle, and much lost of confidence, love, usefulness, enjoyment and interest.

Why trouble those you cannot convince with any peculiarity of your own sentiment, especially if it is likely to debar you from the opportunity of usefulness to them. By one part of your own confession let me confute your ultra perfectionism; that is, you complain of not being perfect and pray for more sanctification. Now, brother, let that suffice that as long as you have to pray for sanctification you are not perfect, and that as long as you live you will pray for it and then conclude you will be perfect when "this mortal shall put on immortality and this corruption shall have put on incorruption," and not till then; and then let us cry, grace; grace unto it.

Do not think of being an ultra perfectionist until you could bear to hear a man say, I have already attained and am already perfect, and to use only thanksgiving to God for his having attained to and being perfect, instead [of] praying for more sanctification. If you could arrive at the point where you felt you were perfect, of course you would no longer pray for sanctification, and what would be your prayer after that? Let the thought awe you, for such cannot be the prayer of mortal in the flesh. Prayer becomes us, and we shall not be fitted in this life to join in the song of praise triumphant, of Moses and the Lamb.

And now for Millerism. I was in Boston when the famous time came for the end of the world, but I did not conclude that as the time was so short I would not concern myself to return to my family. But I did conclude that inasmuch as you had adopted such sentiments, you were not prepared for any work calling for time in its execution, and thinking the work of time so short with you that it would be in vain to call forth any principle to your mind that would involve length of time for its execution, I was contented to pass you in silence. For to my mind all my work and plans involved time and distance, and required confidence in the stability of God's government and purpose to give the heathen to his Son for an inheritance, and among them those uttermost parts of the earth for his possession.

I had adopted Oregon as my country, as well as the Indians for my field of labour, so that I must superintend the immigration of that year, which was to lay the foundation for the speedy settlement of the country if prosperously conducted and safely carried through; but if it failed and became disastrous, the reflex influence would be to discourage for a long time any further attempt to settle the country across the mountains, which would be to see it abandoned altogether. Now, mark the difference between the sentiments of you and me. Since that time you have allowed yourself to be laid aside from the ministry, and have parted with tried friends for an opinion only, and that opinion has done you nor no one else any good. Within the same time, I have returned to my field of labour, and in my return brought a large immigration of about one thousand individuals safely through the long and the last part of it an untried route to the western shores of the continent. Now that they were once safely conducted through, three successive immigrations have followed after them, and two routes for wagons are now open into the Willamette valley. Mark; had I been of your mind I should have slept, and now the Jesuit Papists would have been in quiet possession of this the only spot in the western horizon of America not before their own. They were fast fixing themselves here, and had we missionaries had no American population to come in to hold on and give stability, it would have been but a small work for them and the friends of English interests, which they had also fully avowed, to have routed us, and then the country might have slept in their hands forever.

Time is not so short yet but it is quite important that such a country as Oregon should not on the one hand fall into the exclusive hands of the Jesuits, nor on the other under the English government. In all the business of this world we require time. And now let us redeem it, and then we shall be ready, and our Lord will not come upon us unawares. Come, then, to Oregon, resume your former motto, which seemed to be onward and upward—that is in principle, action, duty and attainments, and in holiness. Dismiss all ultraism, and then you will be cooperative and happy in the society of acting and active Christians. I say again, come to Oregon; but do not bring principles of discord with you.

This is a country requiring devoted, pious labourers in the service of our Lord. There are many and great advantages offered to those who come at once. A mile square, or 640 acres of land such as you may select and that of the best of land, and in a near proximity to a vast ocean and in a mild climate where stock feed out all winter, is not a small boon. Nor should men of piety and principle leave it all to be taken by worldlings and worldly men.

A man of your stamp can do much by coming to this country, if you adopt correct principles and action. Should you come, the best way is to take a raft at Olean,[43] if you are near Cuba at the time of starting. You will need to bring bedding with you for the journey, so that you can come on a raft, and also take a deck passage on the steamboat if you wish to be saving of money. A piece of cloth painted suitable to spread under a bed will be most useful. Do not bring feathers, but let your bed be made of blankets, quilts, etc. If you want any goods after you get into the country, be sure and have them come around by water, if you do not like to trust the shippers in the country. A train of oxen will be the best with a light wagon; no loading except provisions. Good sheep are excellent stock to drive, and travel well. Some sheep we imported from the Sandwich Islands in 1838, have increased one hundred and twenty-five per cent in eight years. Think of what a few good men could do to come together into the country. On the way they could make a party of their own and so rest on the Sabbath. With 640 acres of land as bounty, they could, by mutual consent, set apart a portion for the maintenance of the gospel and for schools and learning in such form as they felt disposed.

A large country to the south as far as the California line is now open by the new wagon route made this fall. You have a good faculty to be a pioneer and lead out a colony; that is to start people to come. But when once on the way do not overpersuade the mind but remember that the best of men and women when fatigued and anxious by the way will be very jealous of all their rights and privileges and must be left to take their own way if possible. Restraint will not be borne under such circumstances.

As I do not know where to send to reach you, I will direct this to the

[43] Olean was situated on Olean Creek in southwestern New York. The creek flowed into the Allegheny River and provided a water route to the West.

care of Father Prentiss,[44] who will forward it to you, after reading it himself.

The Indians are doing very well we think in their way and their habits of civilization. A good attention is paid to religious instruction. Morning and evening worship is quite general in their lodges, and a blessing is strictly regarded as being a duty to be asked upon taking food.

I do not think you can be ignorant of the advantages of this country, nor of its disadvantages. I wrote a letter to Father Hotchkin,[45] which I hope was copied and sent to Father Prentiss, which you may have seen. That applies to this section and climate. The country best suited for settlement are the Willamette valley and the coast west. Then the valley of the Umpqua on the south, and still south the Klamath which takes you south to the California line.

North of the Columbia, you know, is in dispute between the British and the States; you may early learn the result. The greatest objection to the country west of the Cascade range is the rains in winter. But that is more than overbalanced by the exemption from the care and labour of feeding stock. It is not that so much rain falls, but that it rains a great many days from November to April or May. People that are settled do not find it so rainy as to be much of an objection. It is a climate much like England in that respect.

I hope you will excuse the freedom with which I have written. If we shall see each other, we can better bring our thoughts to harmonize.

Narcissa's health is on the gain, and is now pretty good. She joins me in love to yourself and wife, hoping to see you both in due time.

In the best of bonds,

Yours truly,

MARCUS WHITMAN

SOURCE: *Transactions of the Twenty-first Annual Reunion of the Oregon Pioneer Association* (Portland, Ore., 1894), 198–203.

107. Crusading for Peace

The roots of many of the benevolence movements of the nineteenth century may be traced back to pre-revolutionary times. The peace crusade is no exception. Quaker faith had inspired some to oppose war; William Penn and Anthony Benezet wrote forcefully on the theme of peace. The humanitarianism of the Enlightenment had encouraged others to lift their voices on behalf of the ideals of peace; Benjamin Franklin was perhaps the best

[44] Judge Stephen Prentiss was the father of Judson's wife, Mary Ann, Mrs. Whitman's sister.

[45] The Rev. James H. Hotchkin had been pastor to Narcissa Prentiss, later Mrs. Whitman, while he was minister of the Presbyterian church at Prattsburg, N.Y. Later he was Marcus Whitman's pastor at nearby Wheeler, and had assisted the doctor in securing his appointment as missionary by the American Board.

known of this group. The organized crusade for peace, however, developed during the second decade of the nineteenth century. In 1809, David Low Dodge (1774–1852), Presbyterian elder and New York merchant, issued *The Mediator's Kingdom not of this World,* a plea for universal peace on the basis of biblical and historical evidence. Three years later he published the more significant *War Inconsistent with the Religion of Jesus Christ,* in which he argued that war is inhuman, unwise, and criminal. In 1815, Dodge participated in the formation of the pioneer New York Peace Society, and was elected its president.

Meanwhile, reacting against the nation's participation in the War of 1812, Noah Worcester (1758–1837), a Congregational clergyman, had published in 1814 *The Solemn Review of the Custom of War.* It ran through five editions in two years, and became a classic in peace literature. In 1815, a few months after the organization of the New York Peace Society, the Massachusetts Peace Society was founded in the home of the Unitarian leader, William Ellery Channing. Worcester was chosen as corresponding secretary of this society, which soon became the most important of all the peace societies.

Though some substantial citizens supported the peace movement, it did not arouse much attention until a wealthy retired sea captain, William Ladd (1778–1841) devoted his life to its promotion. Won to the cause by Worcester's writings, Ladd joined the Massachusetts society in 1823. He became convinced of the need for a national society to unify the work of the various local and state units. At his instigation, the American Peace Society was founded in 1828 at Dodge's home in New York. Ladd traveled widely on behalf of the society, winning many of the reformers of the day to the peace movement. In 1840 he published a prophetic work, *Essay on a Congress of Nations.*[46]

Ladd sought to keep the American Peace Society broad enough to hold together men of differing views with respect to just war. The literature of the society reflects a vigorous debate between those who believed that defensive wars were justified under certain conditions and those who opposed all war. In 1837 a man who was to serve as the central influence in the society for many years became its secretary. George Cone Beckwith (1800–70) was a graduate of Middlebury College and Andover Seminary. He had served terms as seminary professor and as Congregational pastor. Beckwith sought to keep all the friends of peace, both the moderates and the extremists, within the fold, but a determined minority committed to complete nonresistance broke away, largely under the influence of abolitionist William Lloyd Garrison. Again in the 1840's a reform group opposed to defensive war arose within the American Peace Society, and challenged

---

[46] On these early peace crusaders, see David L. Dodge, *Memorial of Mr. David L. Dodge* (Boston, 1854); Henry Ware, *Memoirs of the Reverend Noah Worcester* (Boston, 1844); John Hemmenway, *Memoir of William Ladd, Apostle of Peace* (Boston, 1877).

Beckwith's leadership. Prominent in this group was Elihu Burritt (1810–79), the learned blacksmith. A self-educated man, master of many languages, he was an indefatigable writer and speaker. He led a second schismatic group out of the society, going on to become prominent as the organizer of a series of international peace congresses in Europe, 1848–56.[47]

Control of the American Peace Society was thus left in the hands of the moderates, with Beckwith as leader. In 1847, he published *The Peace Manual: or, War and Its Remedies*. Designed to supply the most important facts and arguments concerning peace, the book appealed to all good men to work for the abolition of war. The manual was divided into three parts: Physical Evils of War, Moral Evils of War, and Remedies for War. The selections which follow are from the second part; the first is from the chapter "War Viewed in the Light of Revelation," and the second from one entitled "Malign Moral Influences of War." The religious character of the reform drives of the day and the interrelation of the various benevolence movements are both illustrated in this widely circulated *Peace Manual*.

DOCUMENT

Let us put war and Christianity side by side, and see how far they agree. Christianity saves men; war destroys them. Christianity elevates men; war debases and degrades them. Christianity purifies men; war corrupts and defiles them. Christianity blesses men; war curses them. God says, thou shalt not kill; war says, thou *shalt* kill. God says, blessed are the peace-makers; war says, blessed are the war-makers. God says, love your enemies; war says, hate them. God says, forgive men their trespasses; war says, forgive them *not*. God enjoins forgiveness, and forbids revenge; while war scorns the former, and commands the latter. God says, resist not evil; war says, you may and must resist evil. God says, if any man smite thee on one cheek, turn to him the other also; war says, turn *not* the other cheek, but knock the smiter down. God says, bless those who curse you; bless, and curse not: war says, curse those who curse you; curse, and bless not. God says, pray for those who despitefully use you; war says, pray *against* them, and seek their destruction. God says, see that none render evil for evil unto any man; war says, be sure to render evil for evil unto all that injure you. God says, overcome evil with good; war says, overcome evil with evil. God says, if thine enemy hunger, feed him; if he thirst, give him drink: war says, if you do supply your enemies with food and clothing, you shall be shot as a traitor. God says, do good unto all men; war says, do as much evil as you can to your enemies. God says to all men, love one another; war says, hate and kill one another. God says, they that

[47] Concerning these internal dissensions, see Merle Curti, *The American Peace Crusade, 1815–1860* (Durham, N.C., 1929); on Burritt, see Charles Northend, ed., *Elihu Burritt: A Memorial Volume Containing a Sketch of His Life and Labors with Selections from his Writings and Lectures* (N.Y., 1879), and Merle Curti, *The Learned Blacksmith; the Letters and Journals of Elihu Burritt* (N.Y., 1937).

take the sword, shall *perish* by the sword; war says, they that take the sword, shall *be saved* by the sword. God says, blessed is he that trusteth in the Lord; war says, cursed is such a man, and blessed is he who trusteth in swords and guns. God says, beat your swords into ploughshares, your spears into pruning-hooks, and learn war no more; war says, make swords and spears still, and continue to learn war. . . .

INFLUENCE OF WAR UPON THE ENTERPRISES OF CHRISTIAN BENEVOLENCE.

The Church of Christ, after centuries of comparative slumber, has at length girded herself in earnest for the work of reclaiming the whole world to God, and has organized her Sabbath Schools, and her Peace and Temperance, Tract and Bible, Missionary and kindred Societies, as the special machinery wherewith to work out this grand and glorious result.

But war either stops or cripples all this machinery. It impedes every enterprise of Christian benevolence. Would you roll back the waves of intemperance? War would open its flood-gates wider than ever, and pour over the whole land its waves of liquid fire and death. It has ever been a hot-bed of this evil; nor could a war rage throughout our country, without putting back the cause of temperance a whole generation. Its fleets, its camps, and recruiting rendezvous, are all so many nurseries of drunkenness and kindred vices. So all experience, all observation, testify. The war-system even in peace is a most prolific source of intemperance; for its musters, its parades, and its military visits, and dinners, and balls, and other displays, are so many incentives to habits of intoxication.

Would you fain convert our seamen to God? Alas! war would soon carry them beyond your reach, on board those war-ships which warriors themselves have sometimes called "floating hells." This department of benevolence a vigorous naval war would almost entirely suspend, and leave at its close nearly our whole marine in a state of moral degeneracy, from which it would perhaps require a score of years fully to reclaim them.

Would you check the tide of impurity? War would multiply its reeking Sodoms all over the land. Would you follow hard upon the farthest wave of Western population, or thread the dark alleys and lanes of our cities, to gather the young into Sabbath schools, and there bring them under the power of God's truth? War would thwart you at every step, and either drive the children from you, or paralyze no small part of your efforts. Would you plant on the very confines of the wilderness, churches that shall one day make the moral desert there bud and blossom like the rose, and send back thence men, and money, and prayers for the world's evangelization? War would drive your home missionaries from their field, or well-nigh neutralize their power. The mere anticipation of a war in Canada once disbanded a whole presbytery of missionaries, and drove them out of the country; and, amid the whirlwind of war excitement that swept for a time down the great valley of the West, when our troops rushed to the Rio Grande, what could the best preachers in the world have done for the conversion of sinners, or the sanctification of Christians?

As a specimen of all the rest, however, take the great enterprise of evangelizing the world, and see how the custom of war bears upon this noblest form of benevolence. The providence of God pretty fully discloses his views of its influences in this respect. What time did he select for our Saviour's great mission from heaven? A time when the temple of Janus at Rome, in token of general peace and tranquillity, was shut more than twenty years; a longer period of rest from war than had then been known for ages. Review the history of his church from that day to this; and where will you find her eras of zealous, successful evangelization? Not in war, but in peace almost alone; and during the thirty years of general peace after the battle of Waterloo, more was done towards the world's conversion to God, than had been done for centuries before.

Peace fosters the spirit of missions. It was the spirit of peace that brought our Saviour from the bosom of his father; that breathed through his whole life, and drew from his cross the prayer, "Father, forgive them, for they know not what they do." The same spirit animated the martyr at the stake, and carried the apostles from continent to continent, through fire and blood, with their message of salvation to perishing men. Look at Brainerd in the Indian's wigwam; track the Moravian through the snows of Greenland; follow the footsteps of Schwartz across the burning plains of India, or of Martyn over the mountains of Persia; and you find in each case the same spirit that loves its enemies, turns the other cheek to the smiter, and seeks to overcome evil only with good. Such is the spirit of peace; nor can it exist without nourishing the disposition to bless the world with our religion of peace.

How unlike such a spirit is that of war! They are antagonistic, utterly incompatible. Could two neighbors, while fiercely panting each for the other's blood, seek one another's salvation? No more can two nations, while putting forth their utmost energies in vindictive, murderous strife, labor one for the spiritual good of the other. So of the world; and, if all its myriads were simultaneously engaged in war, the work of its Christianization must cease for the time, nor could ever begin again until the fires of war were quenched.

Peace is somewhat necessary, also, to secure God's blessing upon this enterprise. Why did he give to the fishermen of Galilee so much more success than he does to modern missionaries? There may be many other reasons; but we think a chief one is to be found in the war-degeneracy of the church. Even under the Jewish dispensation, God manifested his abhorrence of blood by forbidding David, expressly for this reason, to build the temple; and ever since the war-degeneracy of his followers, has the Prince of Peace shown his displeasure, by his diminished blessing on their efforts to spread his religion. How rapid its early progress! How signal, how glorious the success of its first missionaries! Without scrip or purse, with no diadem on her brow save a crown of thorns, and no weapon in her hand but the sword of the Spirit, the church went forth under God's smiles, from conquering to conquer. Paganism bowed or fled before her; and in less than three centuries did she fill the Roman Empire with her converts. At length she took the sword, and well-nigh perished by the sword. The Holy Spirit, the Dove of peace from heaven, fled before the vultures of war; and from that day the church lost the secret of her power, the mainspring of her progress, her simple reliance under God on moral means alone. For a thousand years she lost far more than she gained, and left nearly all the countries touching the Mediterranean on three continents, which had been the very centre of her primitive triumphs, in a condition less favorable to the religion of Jesus than they were at the hour of his crucifixion. Her whole war-period was at best a dead loss to the church; it merely embalmed in blood the trophies of her primitive purity and zeal. So with the Reformation; it won all its triumphs with the sword of the Spirit, and cut the sinews of its strength when it drew the sword of war; nor has it in the last two centuries gained so much as it once did in a single year.

Peace is, also, indispensable to secure the men and the money requisite for the world's conversion. It has been estimated, that 30,000 heralds of the cross would suffice for this purpose; but the wars of Europe alone sacrificed in twenty-two years three hundred times that number, and the war-system of Christendom employs for its support, even in peace, about one hundred times as many!

SOURCE: George C. Beckwith, *The Peace Manual: or, War and Its Remedies* (Boston, 1847), 139-40, 187-91.

LITERATURE

A number of useful works probe various aspects of the relationship between revivalism and the benevolence movements. Informative treatments dealing with certain of these aspects are by Charles C. Cole, Jr., *The Social Ideas of the Northern Evangelists 1826-60* (N.Y., 1954), and by Timothy L. Smith, *Revivalism and Social Reform in Mid-Nineteenth Century America* (N.Y., 1957). Cole deals especially with the relationship between the new measures and the reform crusades in the earlier part of the period, while Smith focuses on the continuing impact of revivalism and its social consequences for the 1850's. Both books have very useful bibliographies, which are recommended for further study in this area. Alice Felt Tyler's *Freedom's Ferment: Phases of American Social History to 1860* (Minneapolis, 1944) includes summary treatments of many of the moral and social reform movements of the period, together with a wealth of bibliographical material. Ralph H. Gabriel, *The Course of American Democratic Thought: An Intellectual History Since 1815* (N.Y., 1940), provides a stimulating interpretation of intellectual developments very useful for the understanding of the religious developments. Chapter 5 of Winthrop S. Hudson's *The Great Tradition of the American Churches* (N.Y., 1953), "The Great Century: The Voluntary Churches Demonstrate Their Strength and Effectiveness," traces the impact of evangelical Protestantism on the culture of the nation. Sidney E. Mead's useful chapter, "The Rise of the Evangelical Conception of the Ministry in America (1607–1850)," in *The Ministry in Historical Perspective,* ed. H. Richard Niebuhr and Daniel D. Williams (N.Y., 1956), traces to its climax in this period the course of an important aspect of American Protestant life. Mead's *Nathaniel William Taylor, 1786–1858, A Connecticut Liberal* (Chicago, 1942) is indispensable for understanding an important theologian whose work was utilized by leaders in the benevolence movement.

For a very useful work dealing with the shaping of the new measures revivals and their many consequences in upstate New York, see Whitney R. Cross, *The Burned-over District: The Social and Intellectual History of Enthusiastic Religion in Western New York, 1800–1850* (Ithaca, N.Y., 1950). This book provides a useful introduction to Finney, but the best way to approach him is through his own writings. *Lectures on Revivals of Religion* (N.Y., 1835), *Lectures to Professing Christians* (N.Y., 1837), *Lectures on Systematic Theology* (rev. ed.; London, 1851), and especially the *Memoirs of Rev. Charles G. Finney, Written by Himself* (N.Y., 1876), are recommended. In his *Modern Revivalism: Charles Grandison Finney to Billy Graham* (N.Y., 1959), William G. McLoughlin, Jr. devotes much attention to Finney, interpreting him as the real founder of modern revivalism. Bernard A. Weisberger's *They Gathered at the River: The Story of the Great Revivalists and Their Impact upon Religion in America* (Boston, 1958) has two long chapters on Finney and his times. On the revival of 1857–58, the first chapter of J. Edwin Orr's *The Second Evangelical Awakening in Britain* (London, 1949) provides a compact treatment with good bibliographical suggestions.

Some books on the history of the voluntary societies were mentioned in the first volume of this work (see I, 557–8). Consult also Colin B. Goodykoontz, *Home Missions on the American Frontier; With Particular Reference to the American Home Missionary Society* (Caldwell, Id., 1939). Good insights into the thought patterns that underlay the home missionary and church expansion drives can be found in Lyman Beecher, *A Plea for the West* (Cincinnati, 1835), and Horace Bushnell, *Barbarism the First Danger: A Discourse for Home Missions* (N.Y., 1847). Significant articles dealing with the Protestant thrust in this period are by Evarts B. Greene, "A Puritan Counter-Reformation," *Proceedings of the American Antiquarian Society,* New Series, XLII (1932), 17–46; Dixon Ryan Fox, "The Protestant Counter-Reformation," *New York History,* XVI (January, 1935), 19–35; and J. Orin Oliphant, "The American Missionary Spirit, 1828–1835," *Church History,* VII (1938), 125–37. Charles I. Foster, *An Errand of Mercy: The Evangelical United Front, 1790–1837* (Chapel Hill, N.C., 1960), and Clifford S. Griffin, *Their Brothers' Keepers: Moral Stewardship in the United States, 1800–1865* (New Brunswick, N.J., 1960), deal with important aspects of the benevolence society movement. Foster does not sufficiently emphasize the relationship between revivalism and reform in this period, while Griffin overstresses the view that the abolitionists were a group seeking to regain their influence after being undermined by social upstarts and new business classes. Donald

W. Tewksbury, *The Founding of American Colleges and Universities Before the Civil War, with Particular Rereference to the Religious Influences Bearing on the College Movement* (N.Y., 1932), ably deals with the way evangelical Protestantism dominated the college field in this period, utilizing the voluntary society approach in its thrust. Merle Curti's *The American Peace Crusade, 1815–1860* (Durham, N.C., 1929) is instructive; see also his fuller study, *Peace or War: The American Struggle, 1636–1936* (N.Y., 1936). There is a vast literature on the temperance crusade; such works as John A. Krout's *The Origins of Prohibition* (N.Y., 1925) and Ernest H. Cherrington's *The Evolution of Prohibition in the United States of America* (Westerville, O., 1920) provide useful introductions to the subject with extensive bibliographical help.

The anti-Catholic aspects of Protestant crusading are treated briefly in Gabriel, *Course of American Democratic Thought*, Chap. 5, and in Tyler, *Freedom's Ferment*, Chap. 14. A full scale treatment is by Ray A. Billington, *The Protestant Crusade, 1800–1860: A Study of the Origins of American Nativism* (rev. ed., N.Y., 1953).

On the Millerite Movement, a critical account has been written by Clara E. Sears, *Days of Delusion; A Strange Bit of History* (Boston, 1924). A favorable but careful restudy of the Millerite excitement has been done by Francis D. Nichol, *The Midnight Cry: A Defense of the Character and Conduct of William Miller and the Millerites* (Washington, 1944); see also Le Roy Edwin Froom, *The Prophetic Faith of Our Fathers: The Historical Development of Prophetic Interpretation*, Vol. IV: *New World Recovery and Consummation of Prophetic Interpretation* (Washington, 1954).

CHAPTER XIII

Resurgent Churchly Traditions

AMERICAN Christianity in the early nineteenth century faced the problem of the nature of the church. The times encouraged fresh thinking on this subject, and corporate action was needed which implied theories about it. The religious pluralism, revivalism, and Enlightenment of the eighteenth century had modified the various church traditions inherited from the Old World.[1] Americans had moved away from the European dichotomy of "established church" and "dissenting sect." The freedom of the frontier and the religious liberty that followed the American Revolution encouraged further religious experimentation. Rapid immigration was increasing the heterogeneity of American life to an alarming degree. The church faced pressing tasks of home and foreign missions, education, and social reform.

In the face of the needs and the general ferment of American life, how should the church conceive of itself, and how should it be structured? Three principal answers were offered. (1) Some said that the old European ecclesiastical traditions should be perpetuated unchanged. (2) Various "Christian Church" movements claimed to restore the true New Testament idea of the church, and sought to rally all Christians to it. (3) In the activistic American situation there was the possibility that inherited ecclesiastical and theological differences could be quietly ignored in a new kind of Christian unity in action.

For a time in the early nineteenth century, this third way, the way of Christian unity by action, gave promise of capturing the American field. It was a fresh and promising, even if thoroughly pragmatic, approach to the problem of Christian structure. A distinctive "American" type of Christianity began to emerge. It was built around a solid core of Puritanism,[2] especially as represented by Congregationalists and Presbyterians, but including also Baptists and Low Church Episcopalians, plus additions from the Reformed and Methodists, and even from the less closely related Lutherans. This was the "benevolent empire," in which individuals, but not church bodies, co-operated in voluntary societies for missionary, educational, and reforming activities.[3] Revivalism was its characteristic tool.[4] The doctrine

---

[1] Cf. *American Christianity*, I, 231–5.

[2] It is interesting that in opposing this new amalgam John W. Nevin repeatedly referred to it—by an anachronistic figure—as "Puritanism."

[3] Some of the principal activities of the benevolent empire are set forth in Chap. 12.

[4] It has been suggested that revivalism at this time was even a cohesive force within the culture as a whole. Cf. Perry Miller, "From the Covenant to the Revival," in James Ward Smith and A. Leland Jamison, eds., *Religion in American Life*, Vol. I: *The Shaping of American Religion* (Princeton, 1961), 354.

of the church which was implied in this benevolent empire borrowed heavily from Congregationalism. Congregationalism's doctrine of the invisible church, in which all true Christians are already one, greatly encouraged nondenominational co-operation, and Congregationalism's teaching that the term visible church was not applicable to denominational bodies, but only to local congregations or to universal Christendom, discouraged emphasis on denominations as such.[5] The voluntary society system was a Christian union of individuals, contractual and Lockean in character, organized for purely pragmatic purposes. It quietly by-passed the older, historical idea of a confessional church, and fostered a spirit of co-operation which reduced differences between the Protestant bodies to nonessentials.[6] Though borrowed from England,[7] the voluntary society pattern proved highly congenial to the American situation, and held the possibility of vast expansion by common consent until it would embrace within its unity, and even dominate, the group of closely related denominations which constituted the bulk of American Christianity.[8]

But American Protestantism proved unwilling to be restructured along these lines so early or so easily. Although there were obvious practical benefits to be derived from such co-operation, these were not sufficient to overcome the inertia of separateness. There was not yet enough unity in American society or in American religious life to provide a base for even the limited kind of unification toward which the voluntary society system was moving. And the rising sectional tension, stimulated by the slavery issue, was rapidly reducing what unity there was in society and in religious life.

An even more serious obstacle, however, to unity of the kind offered by the benevolent empire was that it quite ignored the historical roots of church life, at the very time when new interest in history and in the nature of the church was apparent in many parts of the Christian world. It is not surprising, therefore, that in the United States in the second quarter of the nineteenth century, spokesmen for all of the more churchly Protestant traditions—Lutheran, Reformed and Presbyterian, Anglican—arose to challenge the nondenominational unity which was forming. These critics were

---

[5] It is paradoxical that the Congregationalists, who of all the principal religious bodies were the least denominationally minded, were in process of transforming a major portion of American Christianity into a modified Congregationalism.

[6] Philip Schaff, who strongly desired a more catholic and theologically based unity, commented: "In the American Bible and Tract Societies and Sunday School Union, the various evangelical denominations work hand in hand and get along right well together, although their Catholicity is more of a negative character, not reconciling, but concealing their differences." Schaff, *America: A Sketch of Its Political, Social, and Religious Character*, ed. Perry Miller (Cambridge, Mass., 1961), 100.

[7] Charles I. Foster, *An Errand of Mercy: The Evangelical United Front, 1790–1837* (Chapel Hill, N.C., 1960), 3–118.

[8] Lyman Beecher, a principal leader of the benevolent empire, was quite conscious of it as "the great evangelical assimilation which is forming in the United States"; cited in William G. McLoughlin, Jr., *Modern Revivalism: Charles Grandison Finney to Billy Graham* (N.Y., 1959), 37.

alarmed by what they considered to be the increasing "subjectivism" of Protestantism and of American Protestantism in particular. They charged that the emphasis on the individual which the Reformation had offered as a corrective to medieval Catholicism was now being dangerously exaggerated, as seen in revivalism, rationalism, and sectarianism. Much of the Christian gospel was thus being lost. Such "subjectivism," these critics insisted, must be balanced and restrained by an emphasis on those "objective" aspects of Christianity which lie outside of and above the individual and are best preserved in the historic Christian church, with its divine origin and authority, its creed, its historical continuity, its "Catholic" or universal character, its ministry, and its sacraments. Furthermore, some of these critics said, the church should conduct its own educational and missionary enterprises, and not leave these tasks to nondenominational voluntary societies.

In challenging the dominant Puritan-revivalistic-unionistic movement, the challengers raised searching questions concerning the nature of the church. The early New England Puritans had been supremely concerned with this question, but their spiritual descendants who built the voluntary society system had largely ignored it. The immediate effect of the challenge was to give new vigor to denominationalism and to forces of division in American life. Paradoxically, the battle against "subjective" sectarianism stimulated an "objective" and churchly sectarianism and stifled the pragmatic unionism that was developing. But these advocates of churchliness were more positive in their long-range implications. Some of them were directly interested in Christian union on an historic and churchly basis. Many more of them, by emphasizing the universal and historic and creedal character of the church, were helping to preserve foundations which Americans, participating in the ecumenical movement of the twentieth century, would use.[9]

By the second quarter of the nineteenth century there were in America a number of general factors congenial to such more organic and authoritarian views about the nature of the church. Although states' rights were loudly championed, the kind of strong national union which Daniel Webster advocated was continually gaining ground. The ecclesiastical counterpart of this centralization was not a voluntary society, but a well-organized and self-conscious church that possessed authority. In culture, in spite of newer tendencies to democratize learning and to make it practical and popular, there were those who struggled to preserve the traditional Old World "genteel" traditions. Such traditions made easier the appeal to older, authoritarian conceptions of the church. So, too, did philosophic idealism,

---

[9] It has been customary to emphasize the conservative character of the voluntary society system as a kind of Puritan "Counter Reformation" against deism and against the Enlightenment. It is true, this "Evangelical united front" largely won the battle against deism, but the real core of historic conservatism in the Protestantism of the period is to be found in the churchly and denominational reaction against the Puritan-revivalistic-voluntary society system.

which entered American life from Germany and England before mid-century. Particularly in the form of romanticism, idealism stimulated interest in the past, especially the medieval past, and helped to open the minds of Protestants to more "Catholic" values in Christianity, though not to Roman Catholicism itself. Some, though not all, of the churchly movements viewed in the present chapter, adhered to philosophic idealism. The Gothic revival in architecture, which was introduced to the United States by Roman Catholics in 1805–06, stimulated High-Churchly tendencies.[10]

More important as an influence on the development of churchliness was the greatly increased interest in history, including American history. American political life, which like sectarian Christianity was poor in symbols, was during this period groping after more adequate national symbols.[11] Institutions loomed larger. Intellectuals now thought more in terms of continuity, process, and development. This suggested that Christianity was not merely an aggregation of individuals, but an organism, a living functioning community, continuous through the centuries. Interest in church history grew apace. Nearly four times as many church histories were published in America in the three decades after 1830 as in the three decades before, and most of these were denominational histories.[12] Such studies emphasized the distinctive features of each denominational heritage. All of the churchly groups made historical claims. Confessional Lutherans looked to the Lutheran Reformation and Old School Presbyterians to the Calvinistic. The Mercersburg movement in the German Reformed Church appealed to Reformation and pre-Reformation history. High Church Episcopalians and Roman Catholics looked back to pre-Reformation history. Old Landmark Baptists declared themselves heirs of an historic succession of congregations practicing believers' baptism by immersion continuously since apostolic days. Mormons appealed to an ancient, even if fictitious, pre-Reformation history.

A more churchly emphasis in America was stimulated, too, by the fact that in Europe all major branches of Christendom in the early nineteenth century were showing renewed interest in the nature of the church. This was true of important leaders of thought among the Eastern Orthodox, Roman Catholic, Lutheran, Reformed, and Anglican. In the reaction that followed the French Revolution and Napoleon, in the struggle against rationalism, in discussions with the Pietists, in facing the new biblical criticism, in the struggle for greater freedom for the church from state control, Europeans were re-examining the doctrine of the church. Among the Russian Orthodox, Khomiakov spoke for the Slavophiles in defining the

[10] Donald D. Egbert, "Religious Expression in American Architecture," in James Ward Smith and A. Leland Jamison, eds., *Religion in American Life,* Vol. II: *Religious Perspectives in American Culture* (Princeton, 1961), 388–90.

[11] Ralph H. Gabriel, *The Course of American Democratic Thought: An Intellectual History Since 1815* (N.Y., 1940), 88–100.

[12] Abdel R. Wentz, *The Lutheran Church in American History* (Phila., 1923), 129.

church over against Western Roman Catholicism and Protestantism. Roman Catholics, in the nineteenth-century resurgence of their faith, came to a clearer conception of their church as a united, world-wide, spiritual body headed by the pope. Lutheranism in Germany, over against the Evangelical union of Lutherans and Reformed, emphasized the Augsburg Confession as giving the church its distinctive character, and stressed also the sacraments, ministry, and state establishment. The Danish Lutheran, Grundtvig, gave high place to the sacraments and to the relation of the church to people and nation. The European Reformed Churches in the nineteenth century were particularly concerned with reaffirming the church's doctrines and with securing enough freedom from state domination to maintain vigorous spiritual life. Anglicanism, in the Oxford Movement, witnessed an important rebirth of High-Church convictions.[13] Churchly movements in America were a part of this world-wide phenomenon.

The churchly emphasis in the United States had a number of prominent characteristics. Not all of these were found in any one ecclesiastical body, but there were striking parallels. One of the most important characteristics of the churchly emphasis was a reaction against the widely popular revivalism. Revivalism stressed such "subjective" aspects of Christianity as the individual's reaction to the gospel and personal commitment to it, which made for great earnestness and zeal, but sometimes led to dangerous distortions and errors. Churchly critics insisted that much greater emphasis was needed on the "objective" aspects of Christianity—the church's heritage of doctrine, worship and church authority, which, antedating and standing above the individual, restrain and guide him. Some, like Samuel Miller, the Old School Presbyterian, merely warned against abuses in revivalism.[14] But others were more hostile. Bishop John Henry Hobart, leader of the Episcopal High-Church movement, publicly attacked a pietistic organization which his clergy had formed.[15] John W. Nevin early in life had received helpful influences from revivalism, but later, as he saw its effects among the German Reformed, revolted against its arbitrary subjectivism and its exaggerated emotionalism, preferring the broader and deeper representation of truth and experience in the historic Christian church.[16] Horace Bushnell, the Congregationalist, deprecated the way revivalism ignored a child's nurture and spiritual roots and made everything depend on a decision of the moment. Turning from this extreme individualism, Bushnell emphasized the organic nature of the family, and saw conversion and the Christian

---

[13] James H. Nichols, *History of Christianity, 1650–1950* (N.Y., 1956), 135–62, 204–16, 335–48.

[14] *Letters to Presbyterians on the Present Crisis in the Presbyterian Church in the United States* (Phila., 1833), 151–91.

[15] *A Pastoral Letter . . . on the Subject of an Association Styled The Protestant Episcopal Clerical Association of the City of New-York* (N.Y., 1829).

[16] Nevin's *The Anxious Bench* (Chambersburg, Pa., 1844) is a classic attack on revivalism, especially on Finney's widely discussed "new measures."

life not as something discontinuous and extraordinary, but as the normal working of God's grace through the appointed channels of home life and Christian instruction.[17] Even Southern Baptist Old Landmarkers turned attention away from the traditional Baptist emphasis on spiritual experience toward the historic and institutional church. Churches like the Episcopal, Lutheran, and Roman Catholic, which had less contact with American revivalism, criticized it as being chaotic, as giving a distorted conception of Christianity, and as impoverishing the Christian life by too slight a regard for the Christian church with its wealth of truth and experience.[18]

A second characteristic often found in the churchliness of the period was a central emphasis on creed as defining the church. Among Protestants, the Lutherans and Old School Presbyterians were the principal exponents of this view. The revivalism of the times tended increasingly to confine interest to those doctrines which were related to conversion and holiness. Unionistic tendencies concentrated on common tenets at the expense of distinctive beliefs. In neither case, so the argument ran, was the wholeness of Christian truth as a system emphasized for its own sake. Charles Hodge stated the case clearly when he said: "No such thing exists on the face of the earth as Christianity in the abstract. . . . Every man you see is either an Episcopalian or a Methodist, a Presbyterian or an Independent, an Arminian or a Calvinist, no one is a Christian in the general." Concerning an advocate of nondenominational missions, Hodge said further: "He is not a Congregationalist and he is not a Presbyterian. He is not an Episcopalian and he is not a Methodist. He is simply an anti-sectarian. He stands therefore alone, in violent opposition to the whole Christian world." [19] The emphasis on doctrine colored most of the other emphases of the churchly group. The theological poverty of revivalism was considered a chief cause of its inadequacy. The historical and institutional and sacramental character of the church was valued because of its role in transmitting and keeping alive Christian truth. The chief reason for supporting denominational boards was that they stood committed to the church's theological position. This creedal emphasis, contrary as it was to popular trends, was notably free from opportunism, but it tended to be intellectualistic, even scholastic. It was always in danger of defining Christianity in propositional terms, and at times fell short of adequate treatment of the Christian life of individuals or of the church. It consciously sacrificed immediate benefits of co-operation in the effort to preserve a larger portion of the Reformation and universal Catholic heritage.

A third characteristic sometimes found in the churchliness of the period

[17] *Discourses on Christian Nurture* (Boston, 1847).

[18] Cf. Martin J. Spaulding, *Sketches of the Early Catholic Missions of Kentucky* (Louisville, 1844), 82–3, 101, 104–6, in John T. Ellis, ed., *Documents of American Catholic History* (Milwaukee, 1956), 276–8.

[19] "The General Assembly of 1836," *Biblical Repertory and Theological Review*, VIII (1836), 430–2.

was the emphasis on institutional features as identifying the true church. Thus Roman Catholics attributed apostolic authority to their church on the basis of their claim that the pope and the bishops are the only lawful successors of Peter and the apostles. High-Church Anglicans claimed that the only true church is one which is governed by bishops in "apostolic succession." "Old Landmarkers" among the Baptists identified the one true church as that which had preserved believers' baptism by immersion, from apostolic times to the present. The ostensible "objectivity" of these claims was at the opposite pole from the subjectivity widely current in American religious life. Once the true church was thus identified by what appeared to be objective historical tests, it remained simply to receive Christian truth and life from her. In a day when many looked to their own feelings or to their own holiness for religious authority, with the uncertainty and diversity which that involved, it is not surprising that some found at this opposite extreme of "objectivity" peace and spiritual nurture.

A fourth characteristic found among some of the churchly was a sacramental conception of the church. This was characteristic of Roman Catholics and High-Church Episcopalians. Lutherans during the period began to recover their historic emphasis on the sacraments. Particularly interesting was the great concern of the Mercersburg theologians for the sacraments. Theirs was one of the most vigorous and original American theological movements of the century. John W. Nevin, influenced by idealistic philosophy and by current European theology, viewed the church as a great historical continuum. The church was instituted by God and within its fellowship flows divine life. Through the sacraments of the church this divine life is given to those who receive it by faith. Amid the prevailing revivalism and the preoccupation with subjective experiences, Nevin's view jarred some, but, though his doctrine included important innovating elements, it was essentially a repristination of the ideas of the Protestant reformers, especially of Calvin. The Mercersburg movement contrasted so sharply with the dominant mood of its day that it was destined to be more appreciated by the next century than by its own.

A fifth feature of the churchly movement was an emphasis on official ecclesiastical action and leadership. Among Roman Catholics this expressed itself in the restoration of the bishop's authority by the suppression of lay trusteeism and in the building of a school system under church authority which would nurture the faithful in a truly Catholic culture. Mormons created a highly theocratic system in which the church was the center of their society and of their culture. Bishops led not only the spiritual life of the early Mormon communities but also their economic and social life. An elaborate system of Mormon education was developed, from elementary schools through college, in order that thus the church itself might provide for its constituency a Mormon culture and world view.

Among Protestants this emphasis on ecclesiastical action found its most conspicuous expression in the idea that the church itself should conduct missionary and educational labors. The rapid expansion of Christian activities in the early nineteenth century created a major problem in the structuring of American Protestantism. Should these burgeoning enterprises be promoted and controlled by individual Christians co-operating in non-ecclesiastical organizations, or by the churches in their official capacity? If this work was to be done by voluntary societies, then a whole new system of super-church ecclesiastical government would develop. This would be controlled by wealthy laymen, with great loss not only of clerical power, but also of ecclesiastical and theological tradition. If on the other hand, the churches themselves assumed the new responsibilities, the function and even the conception of the nature of the church would be basically affected. The attention of church judicatories would then be diverted from their previous preoccupation with definition of doctrine and moral discipline and would be directed to the new overshadowing responsibility of raising budgets and placing and overseeing distant home and foreign missionaries. The new kind of church business would leave little time for the old. Advocates of the voluntary society system warned that denominational control of the new enterprises would "secularize" the churches.

But such possibilities did not deter High-Church Episcopalians and Old School Presbyterians from leading the way in insisting that the new enterprises were the responsibility not of individual Christians acting privately but of the Christian church in its corporate capacity. By so acting, they said, the church would faithfully bear witness to the particularities of gospel truth and would fulfill the commission which God gave to the church itself.[20] This pattern of ecclesiastical direction of the new missionary activities became the prevailing one in the United States. It opened the way to conceive of the church as a corporation chartered to do the Lord's business, and it later created pragmatic pressures to minimize doctrine and other aspects of the church's heritage in order effectively to promote and direct the enterprises. But it was this experience of corporate religious activity which gave to the developing denominations their chief *raison d'être* and which gave to many an American the only awareness he had of a universal church above the level of his local congregation.

In summary, it can be said that those who emphasized the church in early nineteenth-century America drew attention to some of the classic thought on the subject from the Reformation and earlier eras. There was much scholasticism in the thinking of many of them, and they did less justice to the great dynamic thrust of the Reformation than did some of their contemporaries whom they were denouncing as sectarian and sub-

[20] John Henry Hobart, *A Pastoral Letter . . . on the Bible and Common Prayer Book Societies* (N.Y., 1815); Hobart, *An Address to Episcopalians on the Subject of the American Bible Society* (N.Y., 1816); Calvin Colton, *Protestant Jesuitism* (N.Y., 1836), 105–38, charged the voluntary societies with a spiritual imperialism that supplanted the proper religious and moral functions of the churches.

jective. Nor did most of them seriously attempt to relate their important insights to distinctively American problems. Their social thinking was predominantly conservative. In a day in which radical individualism predominated, they failed to win any appreciable following to what was the central emphasis of most of them, the conception of the church as an historic and mystical body. Speaking, as they did, at a time of controversy and confusion, they were the major cause of the decline of nondenominational unity and of renewed emphasis on distinctively denominational tenets. A more ultimate and far more constructive consequence of their churchly emphasis was the preservation of the classical Reformation and pre-Reformation heritages for a day when Christian unity could be explored in its larger theological dimensions.

108. Episcopacy, Foundation of Truth and Unity

The Protestant Episcopal Church had suffered serious loss during the American Revolution, but in 1811 it entered upon a period of new expansion. In that year Alexander Viets Griswold (1766–1843), leader of the Evangelical party, and John Henry Hobart (1775–1830), leader of the High-Church party, were consecrated bishops.

Anglican Evangelicalism, in both England and America, had its roots in the preaching of the Wesleys, their more conservative followers remaining within the Anglican Church. In America, early Evangelicals were Devereux Jarratt (1733–1801) in Virginia [21] and Joseph Pilmoor in Philadelphia, the latter a Methodist itinerant who became an Episcopal rector. Bishop Griswold proved to be a zealous and moderate leader. The Evangelicals used the Prayer Book at Sunday morning service, but inclined toward many of the practices of the Wesleyan revival, such as emphasis on conversion, emotional preaching, and prayer meetings at which ministers and laymen offered extemporaneous prayers. They concentrated their attention on doctrines held in common with other Evangelical Protestants, rather than on the sacraments, ministry, and distinctive tenets of Anglicanism. They co-operated in nondenominational religious and reforming societies, and some participated in worship with other denominations. [22]

The roots of High-Church Anglicanism in America went back to colonial days. The Anglican missionary agency, The Society for the Propagation of the Gospel in Foreign Parts (founded in 1701), was dominated by High-Church principles, and the party in America properly dates from the conversion to it in 1722 of the three Congregationalists, Timothy Cutler, rector of Yale, Daniel Brown, tutor, and Samuel Johnson,

---

[21] Cf. *American Christianity*, I, 366–71.

[22] William W. Manross, *A History of the American Episcopal Church* (N.Y., 1935), 214–9; E. Clowes Chorley, *Men and Movements in the American Episcopal Church* (N.Y., 1946), 1–132.

minister at West Haven, Connecticut. The first American bishop, Samuel Seabury (1729–96), was an ardent High-Churchman. The High-Church party, because of its Tory inclinations, was particularly injured by the Revolution. John Henry Hobart not only rejuvenated High-Church Anglicanism in America, but led it forward to new gains. Favorite pupil of Bishop William White (1748–1836) of Philadelphia and graduate of the College of New Jersey (now Princeton University), he became assistant bishop of New York in 1811 and diocesan bishop five years later. He set his face against "sectarianism" outside of the Episcopal Church and against the Evangelical party within it. He was vigorous in controversy as seen in his charges to his diocesan convention, in pastoral letters, and in sermons and contributions to the press.[23] He thought that the chief weakness of American Protestantism in his day was a lack of churchly principles to give it authority and unity. He was deeply concerned to prevent Episcopal Evangelicals from co-operating with the voluntary societies, for he considered them permeated by a "liberalism" which placed all denominations on the same level and which regarded denominational differences as nonessential. In such an atmosphere, he warned, affirmation of distinctive Episcopal principles would seem discourteous and out of place. He thought that these societies were dominated by a Presbyterian spirit which imperceptibly would transform others into its own likeness.[24]

Hobart taught that the most important mark of the true church is possession of the threefold ministry of bishop, priest, and deacon. This is the guarantee of sound doctrine and of unity. He also extolled the Prayer Book as setting forth truth and worship according to the Word of God, although he was not a "ritualist" in the later sense of the term. Apart from these ideas, Hobart's doctrine of the church was nearer to the classical Reformed position than was the sectarianism of some who still considered themselves Calvinists. He emphasized the visible "Catholic" church: her ministry and sacraments and her authority. Such "evangelical" accents as sin, Christ's atonement, and justification by faith were prominent in his teaching. He was as vigorous in rejecting Roman Catholicism as he was in rejecting Protestant sectarianism.[25] Bishop Hobart brought to the American High-Church tradition of his day a new fervor, home missionary zeal, and organizing ability.[26]

DOCUMENT

God forbid, my Brethren, that I should say aught against the right of private judgment in matters of religion, when properly exercised. The doc-

---

[23] His ideal of a Christian bishop is seen in J. H. Hobart, *The Christian Bishop Approving Himself unto God* (Phila., 1827).

[24] Hobart, *An Address to Episcopalians on the Subject of the American Bible Society*, 8–9.

[25] *The Churchman* (N.Y., 1819).

[26] Chorley, *Men and Movements*, 133–67; George E. De Mille, *The Catholic Movement in the American Episcopal Church* (2nd ed., Phila., 1950), 1–39.

trine that every man being individually responsible to his Maker and Judge, must, in all those concerns that affect his spiritual and eternal welfare, act according to the dictates of his conscience, is that cardinal principle of the Protestant faith which should be most soundly guarded. But there is a wide difference between the unlimited and the restricted right of private judgment; between each individual forming his code of religious doctrine, without employing as lights amidst the innumerable and jarring opinions that perplex his researches, the faith of the universal Church, as far as he can ascertain it; and the same individual, while he claims the right, which no intelligent creature can surrender, of judging for himself, seeking with humility and with deference, that guidance which is to be found in the faith of the Church universal. He may, indeed, fail in his efforts; he must depend frequently on the learning and the information of others; and liability to error is inseparable from our present fallen state. But there is much less danger of error, when he follows the light, as far as it is disclosed to him, which has shone on the Church universal, than when he proudly violates that order of Providence by which, in the present world, the less informed must, in some measure, depend on those more enlightened; and takes for his guide, in matters of religion, his own judgment, taste, and fancy; disregarding entirely the faith of the great body of Christians in all places and at all times.

It is on this sound principle of human nature, as well as on those declarations of Scripture, which pronounce the Church to be "the pillar and ground of the truth," and which commands us to "hear the Church," that our Church declares in her articles, that "the Church is a witness and keeper of holy writ," and has "authority in controversies of faith." And by the Church she means, "a congregation of faithful men, in which the pure word of God is preached, and the sacraments duly administered according to Christ's ordinance." Those are authorised, as she declares, to minister the sacraments, "who are chosen and sent by men who have public authority given to them for this purpose." And we can be in no doubt whom she considers as having this public authority to call and send to the ministry, when we hear her declaring that Bishops, to whom she assigns this power as distinct from Presbyters and Deacons, "have been from the Apostles' times," and "instituted by God's Providence, and by his Holy Spirit."

Great, then, my Brethren of the Clergy, is the responsibility which rests upon us. According to the wise organization of our ecclesiastical government, the authority which the Church possesses in matters of faith, is exercised by all orders of men constituting her communion, her Bishops, Clergy, and Laity. But those who are especially commissioned to minister in sacred things, and to whom, as the stewards of the mysteries of God, it peculiarly appertains to dispense his sacred word, are particularly intrusted with the office of preserving Christian verity, and of guarding the fold of their Master from the assaults of heresy and schism. If we, then, of the Clergy, fail diligently to search for the old paths, and to continue therein, through that indolence which declines research; that timidity which withholds truth, because it may be odious; or that love of popularity which would rather bow to some modern idol which the multitude hath set up, than worship the God of our fathers in the faith and unity which distinguished the primitive ages of Christianity, but an attachment to which modern liberality may style bigotry and uncharitableness; we shall be answerable for the heresies and schisms which deform and distract the fold of the Redeemer, and for the guilt of those who, misled by us, err from the faith, and depart from the unity of Christ's body.

Connected with this extreme, to which the exercise of private judgment is carried in matters of religion, and arising indeed from it, is, the little regard which is paid to the Church as a divinely constituted society.

There was a period, when the authority of the Church was carried to an extreme, incompatible with the rights of conscience, and even with personal safety—when her Clergy, lording it over God's heritage, demanded implicit obedience to all their impositions; and forgetting that the kingdom of their Master was not of this world, employed to enforce their decrees the sanguinary weapons of secular power; thus deforming, by this unhallowed junction of the world and the Church, the spirituality of that holy society which its divine Head armed with no prerogatives but such as appeal to the understanding, the conscience, and the heart.

But in renouncing these despotic claims, is there not a contrary extreme, which appears in no small degree to characterize the mass of Protestant Christians? They seldom bring into view the divine institution of the Christian Church, and the divine origin of its powers. In their language, and in their practice, they reduce this sacred institution, which, founded by a divine hand, is animated and governed by him, to whom "all power is given in heaven and on earth," to a level with those associations which have no higher origin than human power, and no other object but human policy. Hence the duty of submission to its authoritative acts is made to rest not on its claims to a divine origin, but on the motives of mere expediency; and hence, the exercise of its discipline is not regarded as a duty demanded by the authority of its divine Head, and the purity of its sacred character, but as dictated merely by those considerations of policy which influence secular associations, and as left entirely to human discretion. Its discipline is thus relaxed; or, when exercised agreeably to established provisions, is secretly assailed, or openly opposed and disregarded. And the divine declaration, "Whatsoever ye shall bind on earth, shall be bound in heaven; and whatsoever ye shall loose on earth, shall be loosed in heaven;" which certainly, in the exercise of all the discipline necessary to her order, purity, and peace, assures to the Church the protection and support of the

Most High; is no more regarded than if it had proceeded from a frail mortal, and not from the lips of him who is Ruler of the inhabitants of the earth, and Lord of the armies of heaven. . . .

The Papal opinion of Church unity, that it consists in communion with the Bishop of Rome, as the visible head of the Catholic Church, has so little foundation in Scripture and in primitive practice, that it could not stand the test of that spirit of free inquiry which the Reformation excited. But many bodies of reformed Christians, who renounced the corruptions and usurpations of the Church of Rome, were not so happy as to carry with them that primitive Episcopacy which subsisted in the Church from which they separated, and which others of their brethren laid at the foundation of the external order of their churches. Such is the natural course of the human mind, through the gradations of error, that a departure from Episcopacy, the scriptural and primitive principle of Church unity, at first exercised on the plea of necessity, became afterwards wholly justified on the ground of right. The assumption of the Episcopal powers of ordination by Presbyters led to the usurpation of the powers both of Bishops and Presbyters by laymen. The separation of Episcopal Protestants from a Church which imposed sinful terms of communion, has been unwarrantably pleaded in evidence of the right of individual ministers and individual Christians, to establish communions as their judgment may dictate, wholly regardless of that primitive bond of Church unity, the ministry of Bishops. Thus we see the Protestant world divided into sects, the numbers or the tenets of which it is almost impossible to enumerate. And as the climax of this scale of error, we now hear the sentiments advanced and defended, on almost all occasions, in the writings of able divines, and in the language of Christian associations, which bid fair to obtain an unprecedented popularity, that all differences among Christians, except as to fundamental points of doctrine, are non-essential; and that separate communions without number, unless there is unsoundness in the faith, do not violate Church unity. But the unity of the Church is an obvious and fundamental doctrine of Scripture; and visible unity is entirely incompatible with distinct communions. Hence, the tenet of an invisible Church, of which all are covenanted members who exercise faith, threatens to subvert the doctrine, professed in the ancient creeds, of a visible Church, "one, Catholic, and Apostolic."

But, was it an invisible Church which our Saviour designates as "a city," "a kingdom," "a body?" Was it an invisible society, over which he set his Apostles as the instructors, the priests, and rulers, and of which they were to constitute officers, with similar powers, to the end of the world? Was it an invisible society, of which the Apostle declares, "Ye were all baptised by one spirit into one body?" Was it to an invisible Church that they were united, of whom it is said in the Acts of the Apostles, "the Lord added to the Church daily such as should be saved?" Was it an union only of faith and charity which distinguished those of whom, in the same inspired book, it is said, "they continued steadfastly in the Apostles' doctrine and fellowship, and in breaking of bread, and in prayers?" Was it an internal and invisible unity which the Apostle enjoined, when he said, "there should be no schism in the body?" Was it to the officers of an invisible Church that he commanded obedience—"Obey them that have the rule over you, and submit yourselves; for they watch for your souls, as they that must give account?" Was it an infraction only of an invisible unity which he reproved, when he said, "mark them which cause divisions" —"because there are divisions among you, ye are carnal—one saying, I am of Paul; and another, I am of Apollos?" Was it for a violation only of charity and internal unity, and not for a resistance to the priesthood in the Jewish Church, that Korah and his associates were punished, and that it is said of Christians, there are some who "perish in the gainsaying of Korah?" Were mutual love and soundness in the faith the only bond of unity in those ages, when the Church universal was indeed one fold, under the government of Bishops? Was this the unity of Ignatius, of Cyprian, of a host of Fathers, who, in almost every page of their writings, enforce a visible unity, maintained by the communion of Christians with the authorized orders of the ministry, Bishops, Priests, and Deacons? Was it for an invisible unity, that Jerome, the reputed champion of this modern error, contended, when, in the celebrated passage which is adduced in proof of it, he asserts, that at the very time when it was said, I am of Paul, and I am of Apollos, which was, undoubtedly, in the time of the Apostles, Bishops were constituted as superior to Presbyters, in order to be the bond of the visible order and unity of Christ's Church? When, indeed, was there any other bond, until, centuries after the first age of Christianity, the usurped precedence of the Bishop of Rome was constituted the principle of Church unity; and until the divisions of Protestants made this unity to consist solely in mutual affection and soundness in the faith, and, of course, compatible with any, and, indeed, with no form of the Christian ministry?

My Brethren, in opposing, under great, and, perhaps, if we may judge from the spirit of the age, increasing odium, those prevalent errors, which, if I know my own heart, a profound sense of duty alone has induced me to endeavour to expose and refute; and in maintaining and enforcing correct views of the constitution of the Christian Church, and of the principles of Church unity, we must be consoled and supported by the consideration that we are maintaining the principles of the saints of the primitive ages, and for which, sooner than relinquish them, they would have shed their blood.

SOURCE: John Henry Hobart, *The Corruptions of the Church of Rome Contrasted with Certain Protestant Errors* (N.Y., 1818), 8–13, 22–7.

109. New Light from Heaven

The dynamism of early nineteenth-century religion sometimes directly stimulated a reaction in the direction of greater authority and control. This occurred, for example, in the case of Mormonism, in upstate New York, a region noted for its uninhibited religious experimentation. Joseph Smith (1805–44) at the age of ten was brought by his parents from New England to the vicinity of Palmyra, New York. Like many others, he was caught up in the contemporary waves of revivalism, different members of his family joining different denominations. The antagonisms and uncertainties created by the intense denominational rivalries caused him to distrust all existing denominations and to search for a surer and more ultimate authority. It was in 1822, according to his claim, that he found his answer in a new revelation from God by means of the golden plates of the Book of Mormon. In 1830 he organized a church which four years afterwards adopted its present official title, The Church of Jesus Christ of Latter-day Saints. Smith claimed other revelations later, which are to be found in the Doctrine and Covenants. The Doctrine and Covenants, together with the Bible, the Book of Mormon, and the Pearl of Great Price, constitute the authoritative standards of Mormonism.

There was thus offered to the faithful a unity and spiritual security based directly on divine authority, but the doctrine of continuing revelation was itself so dynamic as to open the door to division and confusion. This danger, however, was obviated by the doctrine that only the president of the Mormon Church could receive revelations binding on the whole church. Presently a very powerful, centralized church organization developed under a First Presidency and a Quorum of Twelve Apostles.[27] At Smith's death, Brigham Young (1801–77), a remarkably strong and able man, succeeded Smith in the leadership of the movement. Under him the authority of the church increased, and its influence was dominant in the social and cultural as well as the religious life of Mormons. The growth which he fostered continued until in 1960 the church numbered 1,486,887 members.

In Mormonism, sons of New England[28] brought to birth a strange new theocracy just as the last vestiges of the old New England theocracies were disappearing. Somewhat inconsistently, like their Puritan forebears, the Mormons aspired to be both a separated covenant community and a theocracy, never fully resolving the antinomy. Abolishing a professional ministry, they practiced the universal priesthood of believers in a radically democratic way, while at the same time creating a centralized church or-

[27] Cf. *The Doctrine and Covenants of the Church of Jesus Christ of Latter-day Saints* (Salt Lake City, 1911), 121–9, 383–7.

[28] Cf. David B. Davis, "The New England Origins of Mormonism," *New England Quarterly*, XXVI (1953), 147–63.

ganization of great power. Mormonism developed a high view of the authority of the church over the total life of its members, at first attempting to control even political and economic affairs, and continuing to exercise wide influence over the cultural and social life of its constituents. In its theological tenets Mormonism diverged radically from traditional orthodoxy.[29]

In the document here presented Joseph Smith described the anguish that preceded his visions, his first visions themselves, and his discovery of the golden plates.

DOCUMENT

My mind at different times was greatly excited, the cry and tumult was so great and incessant. The Presbyterians were most decided against the Baptists and Methodists, and used all their powers of either reason or sophistry to prove their errors, or, at least, to make the people think they were in error. On the other hand the Baptists and Methodists, in their turn, were equally zealous to establish their own tenets, and disprove all others.

In the midst of this war of words and tumult of opinions, I often said to myself, what is to be done? Who of all these parties are right? or, are they all wrong together? If any one of them be right, which is it, and how shall I know it?

While I was labouring under the extreme difficulties, caused by the contests of these parties of religionists, I was one day reading the Epistle of James, first chapter and fifth verse, which reads, "If any of you lack wisdom, let him ask of God, that giveth unto all men liberally and upbraideth not, and it shall be given him." Never did any passage of scripture come with more power to the heart of man than this did at this time to mine. It seemed to enter with great force into every feeling of my heart. I reflected on it again and again, knowing that if any person needed wisdom from God, I did; for how to act I did not know, and unless I could get more wisdom than I then had, would never know; for the teachers of religion of the different sects understood the same passage so differently as to destroy all confidence in settling the question by an appeal to the Bible. At length I came to the conclusion that I must either remain in darkness and confusion, or else I must do as James directs, that is, ask of God. I at length came to the determination to "ask of God," concluding that if he gave wisdom to them that lacked wisdom, and would give liberally and not upbraid, I might venture. So, in accordance with this my determination to ask of God, I retired to the woods to make the attempt. It was on the morning of a beautiful clear day, early in the spring of eighteen hundred and twenty. It was the first time in my life that I had made such an attempt,

[29] On Mormon churchliness, cf. Thomas F. O'Dea, *The Mormons* (Chicago, 1957), 155–85; on Joseph Smith, cf. Fawn M. Brodie, *No Man Knows My History* (N.Y., 1945).

for amidst all my anxieties I had never as yet made the attempt to pray vocally.

After I had retired into the place where I had previously designed to go, having looked around me and finding myself alone, I kneeled down and began to offer up the desires of my heart to God. I had scarcely done so, when immediately I was seized upon by some power which entirely overcame me, and had such astonishing influence over me as to bind my tongue so that I could not speak. Thick darkness gathered around me, and it seemed to me for a time as if I were doomed to sudden destruction. But exerting all my powers to call upon God to deliver me out of the power of this enemy which had seized upon me, and at the very moment when I was ready to sink into despair and abandon myself to destruction, not to an imaginary ruin, but to the power of some actual being from the unseen world, who had such a marvelous power as I had never before felt in any being. Just at this moment of great alarm, I saw a pillar of light exactly over my head, above the brightness of the Sun, which descended gradually until it fell upon me. It no sooner appeared than I found myself delivered from the enemy which held me bound. When the light rested upon me, I saw two personages, whose brightness and glory defy all description, standing above me in the air. One of them spake unto me, calling me by name, and said (pointing to the other) "THIS IS MY BELOVED SON, HEAR HIM."

My object in going to enquire of the Lord was to know which of all the sects was right, that I might know which to join. No sooner therefore did I get possession of myself, so as to be able to speak, than I asked the personages who stood above me in the light, which of all the sects was right (for at this time it had never entered into my heart that all were wrong), and which I should join. I was answered that I must join none of them, for they were all wrong, and the personage who addressed me said "that all their creeds were an abomination in his sight; that those professors were all corrupt, they draw near to me with their lips, but their hearts are far from me; they teach for doctrine the commandments of men, having a form of godliness, but they deny the power thereof."

He again forbade me to join with any of them; and many other things did he say unto me which I cannot write at this time. When I came to myself again, I found myself lying on my back, looking up into heaven. . . .

I often felt condemned for my weakness and imperfections; when on the evening of the above mentioned twenty-first of September, after I had retired to my bed for the night, I betook myself to prayer and supplication to Almighty God, for forgiveness of all my sins and follies, and also for a manifestation to me, that I might know of my state and standing before him; for I had full confidence in obtaining a divine manifestation, as I had previously had one.

While I was thus in the act of calling upon God, I discovered a light appearing in the room, which continued to increase until the room was lighter than at noonday, when immediately a personage appeared at my bedside, standing in the air, for his feet did not touch the floor. He had on a loose robe of most exquisite whiteness. It was a whiteness beyond anything earthly I had ever seen; nor do I believe that any earthly thing could be made to appear so exceedingly white and brilliant; his hands were naked, and his arms also, a little above the wrist; so, also, were his feet naked, as were his legs, a little above the ankles. His head and neck were also bare. I could discover that he had no other clothing on but this robe, as it was open, so that I could see into his bosom.

Not only was his robe exceedingly white, but his whole person was glorious beyond description, and his countenance truly like lightning. The room was exceedingly light, but not so very bright as immediately around his person. When I first looked upon him I was afraid, but the fear soon left me. He called me by name and said unto me, that he was a messenger sent from the presence of God to me, and that his name was Nephi.[30] That God had a work for me to do, and that my name should be had for good and evil among all nations, kindreds, and tongues; or that it should be both good and evil spoken of among all people. He said there was a book deposited, written upon gold plates, giving an account of the former inhabitants of this continent, and the source from whence they sprang. He also said that, the fulness of the everlasting gospel was contained in it, as delivered by the Saviour to the ancient inhabitants. Also, that there were two stones in silver bows (and these stones, fastened to a breastplate, constituted what is called the Urim and Thummim) deposited with the plates, and the possession and use of these stones was what constituted Seers in ancient or former times, and that God had prepared them for the purpose of translating the book. . . .

I . . . went to the place where the messenger had told me the plates were deposited, and owing to the distinctness of the vision which I had had concerning it, I knew the place the instant that I arrived there. Convenient to the village of Manchester, Ontario county, New York, stands a hill of considerable size, and the most elevated of any in the neighbourhood. On the west side of this hill, not far from the top, under a stone of considerable size, lay the plates deposited in a stone box; this stone was thick and rounding in the middle on the upper side, and thinner towards the edges, so that the middle part of it was visible above the ground, but the edge all round was covered with earth. Having removed the earth and obtained a lever which I got fixed under the edge of the stone, and with a little exertion raised it up; I looked in, and there indeed did I behold the plates, the Urim and Thummim, and the breast-plate, as stated by the messenger. The box in which they lay was formed by laying stones together in some kind of cement. In the bottom of the box were laid two stones crossways of the

[30] Later editions read "Moroni."

box, and on these stones lay the plates and the other things with them. I made an attempt to take them out, but was forbidden by the messenger, and was again informed that the time for bringing them forth had not yet arrived, neither would until four years from that time. . . .

At length the time arrived for obtaining the Plates, the Urim and Thummim, and the Breast-plate. On the 22nd day of September, 1827, having gone, as usual, at the end of another year, to the place where they were deposited; the same heavenly messenger delivered them up to me with this charge, that I should be responsible for them; that if I should let them go carelessly or through any neglect of mine, I should be cut off; but that if I would use all my endeavours to preserve them, until he, the messenger, should call for them, they should be protected.

I soon found out the reason why I had received such strict charges to keep them safe, and why it was that the messenger had said, that when I had done what was required at my hand, he would call for them; for no sooner was it known that I had them, than the most strenuous exertions were used to get them from me; every stratagem that could be invented was resorted to for that purpose; the persecution became more bitter and severe than before, and multitudes were on the alert continually to get them from me if possible; but by the wisdom of God they remained safe in my hands, until I had accomplished by them what was required at my hand; when, according to arrangements, the messenger called for them, I delivered them up to him, and he has them in his charge until this day, being the 2nd day of May, 1838.

> SOURCE: *The Pearl of Great Price: Being a Choice Selection from the Revelations, Translations, and Narrations of Joseph Smith, First Prophet, Seer, and Revelator to the Church of Jesus Christ of Latter-day Saints* (Liverpool, 1851), 37-9, 40-1, 43-4.

110. Bishop Kenrick Combats Trusteeism

If American Catholics shared in any degree the "sectarian" conceptions of the church which were widespread in American Christianity in the early nineteenth century, these are to be found in Catholic "trusteeism." In the democratic and Protestant atmosphere of the times, many Catholic laymen thought that boards of trustees should have the right to call and dismiss pastors, and even to nominate and request the removal of bishops. This was utterly un-Catholic, for in the Roman Catholic Church God gives his authority to the church, not through the laity, but through the pope and hierarchy, and government is by the clergy alone. State laws providing for the incorporation of churches and for the vesting of title to church property in boards of trustees paved the way for this democratic innovation of trusteeism. These legal provisions did not in themselves contravene Catholic principles, but they readily lent themselves to radical democratic innovations. The issue was often complicated by being combined with prejudices of people, priests, and bishops toward each other arising from their different national origins. The fact that until 1790 American Catholics had not had any bishop was also a factor in the delayed acceptance by many Catholic laymen of the full implications of episcopal authority.

The churchly character and authority of Roman Catholicism were directly challenged and would be undermined if trusteeism were allowed to prevail. The hierarchy therefore opposed it vigorously. While Father John Carroll was still prefect-apostolic, the trustees of the New York church in December, 1785, had tried to oust their pastor. Carroll had protested: *"If ever the principles there laid down should become predominant, the unity and catholicity of our Church would be at an end:* and it would be formed into distinct and independent societies, nearly in the same manner as the congregational Presbyterians of our neighboring New England States." [31] Archbishop Maréchal of Baltimore in 1818 had seen in trusteeism a strong influence from Protestantism. In spite of resistance by Catholic authorities, manifestations of trusteeism were widespread until the middle of the nineteenth century. Then, as hierarchical authority became stronger, and as state laws provided for Catholic churches the right of "corporation sole," with the bishop holding title to church property, trusteeism declined.[32]

The document here presented was called forth by the Hogan schism in Philadelphia, one of the most famous cases of trusteeism. In 1819 the Rev. William Hogan, a native Irishman leaving his country for his country's good, arrived in Philadelphia. The trustees of St. Mary's Church, as was often being done at the time, engaged him as their pastor. The next year the aged Henry Conwell (1745?–1842) arrived from Ireland as bishop of Philadelphia. Efforts of the new bishop to assert his authority over Hogan and over the trustees who supported him proved unsuccessful, and the parish became sharply divided between bishop and trustees. Civil and ecclesiastical litigation failed to settle the matter. An agreement drafted in 1826 was disallowed by the Sacred Congregation in Rome as impairing proper hierarchical authority. The struggle dragged on until the First Provincial Council of Baltimore, meeting in 1829, petitioned that the able young secretary of the Council, Francis Patrick Kenrick (1796–1863), be appointed coadjutor of Bishop Conwell with full power of administration. This was done, and Kenrick entered upon his duties the next year. Kenrick, also a native Irishman, had been seminary professor and college lecturer at Bardstown, Kentucky, where he also preached. In 1851 he became archbishop of Baltimore, and during his life produced many scholarly writings. In Philadelphia, Kenrick met the continued resistance of the trustees by the resolute exercise

---

[31] Peter Guilday, *The Life and Times of John Carroll* (N.Y., 1922), 265. Italics are Carroll's.
[32] R. F. McNamara, "Trusteeism in the Atlantic States, 1785-1863," *Catholic Historical Review*, XXX (1944), 135-54.

of his full episcopal powers, and on April 14, 1831, threatened suspension to any clergymen conducting sacred functions in St. Mary's. Eight days later he followed this with the pastoral address here reprinted. The next month the trustees yielded to his authority.[33] The conflicts over trusteeism in Philadelphia and elsewhere brought into clear light the great ecclesiastical authority possessed by Roman Catholic bishops.

DOCUMENT

Beloved Children in Christ:

With much anguish of heart, we have, through the deepest sense of duty, ordered the cessation from all sacred functions in the Church and Cemeteries of St. Mary's, under penalty of the Ecclesiastical censure of suspension, to be incurred by any clergyman attempting the exercise of any such function. Of the cause which led to the adoption of this painful measure, you are already apprised; yet we deem it expedient to state the events that led to it, clearly and distinctly, lest any amongst you should imagine that we had in any degree ceased to cherish that tender affection and zeal for your happiness and salvation, which from our first coming amongst you, we invariably manifested. Though discharging the duties of the sublime office originally committed to the Apostles of Christ, we became little ones in the midst of you, as a nurse should cherish her children. So desirous of you, we would gladly have imparted to you not only the gospel of God, but also our own souls, because you were become most dear to us.

At an early period after we had made the Episcopal visitation of the Diocese, and promulgated the Jubilee throughout the Churches of the city, namely, on the 27th day of December last, we resolved to devote ourselves to the discharge of the pastoral duties amongst you, and we officially communicated to the Board of Trustees our determination, which sprang only from the sincerest zeal for your spiritual welfare. To our astonishment and affliction the Lay-Trustees made the communication a matter of deliberation, instead of simply recording it on their books, and even expressed to us their dissatisfaction, though the Charter of Incorporation gives them no right whatever of interference under any shape or form in pastoral appointments, and though the discipline of the Catholic Church does not allow such interference. Having complained in a solemn and paternal manner, nowise unworthy the sanctity of the Pulpit, or the meekness of the Prelacy, of this attempt to impede the conscientious exercise of our Episcopal authority, we received from the Lay-Trustees a letter dated the 12th of January, wherein, in terms not usually employed by the faithful to the Bishops of the Church, they expressed their determination to persevere in their resistance. We patiently bore their opposition, in the hope that our untiring efforts for the instruction and sanctification of our flock would

[33] F. E. Tourscher, *The Hogan Schism and Trustee Troubles in St. Mary's Church Philadelphia, 1820–1829* (Phila., 1930); Joseph L. J. Kirlin, *Catholicity in Philadelphia . .* (Phila., 1909), 210–74.

convince them of the justice of our views, and induce them spontaneously to desist from a course directly opposed to the principles of Church government, and the provisions of the Charter; and we carefully abstained from all attempts to influence the election, avowing nevertheless publicly in our pastoral address our unchangeable resolution to maintain, at every risk and sacrifice, the spiritual rights with whose guardianship we have been entrusted. More than three months having passed, and the Lay-Trustees after their re-election having proved their determination to persist in disregarding our corporate rights as Chief Pastor, by assembling a Board without our participation, though the Charter declares the three Pastors of St. Mary's Members of the Board by their office, we could no longer tolerate this violation of our chartered rights which implied manifestly the denial of our Pastoral office. We therefore in a Circular Letter of the 12th of April, apprised the Pewholders of the illegal course of the Lay-Trustees, and of the penalty decreed by the Provincial Council and Apostolic See against such interference in Pastoral Appointments. On the 15th we received a letter signed by seven of their number, the other having refused to persevere with them in their resistance to the Episcopal authority. In this communication they denied having assumed or asserted the right of choosing their own Pastors; but they did not venture to deny that they had indirectly, (as we had charged them in our Circular) asserted and assumed it, by rejecting the Pastors duly appointed, and especially by violating our corporate rights as chief Pastor. We called on them for a formal and explicit disclaimer of all right of interfering, directly or indirectly, in the appointment, rejection, or dismissal of Pastors, and for a pledge that they would henceforward act according to the provisions of the Charter; but they explicitly declined that disclaimer and pledge, and six of them merely offered to subscribe a memorandum declaring that they agreed to recognize us, and the Rev. Jeremiah Keilly, as clerical members of the Board of Trustees. Such an agreement, so far from being a practical proof of their adherence to the Catholic principles of church government, and of their respect for the provisions of the charter, was a measure calculated to confirm and establish the assumed right of agreeing to or dissenting from the Episcopal appointments. The letter which accompanied the memorandum contained still further evidence, that the Lay-Trustees claimed and attempted to exercise in our regard this power, since they grounded their assent to our future exercise of the pastoral office, on the actual want of another Pastor; thereby intimating, that though we had since the 27th of December declared our determination to act thenceforward as chief pastor of St. Mary's, and though we had since that time constantly performed all the duties of that office, yet we were not in reality chief pastor hitherto, because the Lay-Trustees had withheld their assent and approbation.

Under such circumstances we could not consistently with our attachment to Catholic principles and the rights of our office, recall the order for the cessation from sacred functions in St. Mary's Church and Cemeteries, which we had on the preceding evening issued, when the receipt of the letter of the seven Trustees had convinced us of their determination to persevere in eluding Episcopal authority. We did indeed abstain from issuing the more solemn sentence of Interdict, which the provincial Council authorizes us to pronounce, though we well knew that the evil which called for this severity was not of recent growth, but had originated and been matured in times of schism and confusion, and had long since defied every mild remedy.

We still hope that the speedy acknowledgment of the Catholic principles of church government, may enable us not only to abstain from any more painful exercise of authority, but even to restore to our beloved children in Christ, the consolation of worshipping in the splendid edifice in which you and your fathers worshipped, and which your and their generous piety erected, and the legislative authority of this State secured for the exercise of the Roman Catholic religion. We willingly persuade ourselves, that those who have hitherto resisted the conscientious and mild exercise of Episcopal authority, acted under misconception; and we indulge the hope, that they will soon render us that rational and Christian obedience and subjection, which the Apostle requires of the faithful to the Prelates of the Church, whom the Holy Ghost has placed Bishops to rule the Church of God purchased with His blood. We shall hail with joy and thanksgiving to God, their return to duty, and endeavor by all the exhibitions of paternal tenderness and affection, to obliterate from their minds, and from yours, the remembrance of these days of affliction, wherein the Church sits solitary that was full of people.

May the God of peace crush Satan speedily under your feet. The grace of our Lord Jesus Christ be with you.

Given at Philadelphia, this 22nd day of April, 1831, in the first year of our Episcopacy.

FRANCIS PATRICK,
Bishop of Arath, and Coadjutor of Phila.

By Order John Hughes, *Sec'y.*

> SOURCE: Joseph L. J. Kirlin, *Catholicity in Philadelphia: From the Earliest Missionaries down to the Present Time* (Phila., 1909), 270–3.

111. Church Boards Versus Voluntary Societies

Presbyterianism, from its early days in America, had experienced an inner tension between two heritages. The Scotch and Scotch-Irish element held to a more authoritarian ideal of strong church courts and of a rigid theology. The New England Puritan element held a more dynamic view of theology and a more decentralized conception of church government. Under the Plan of Union of 1801 between Congregationalists and Presbyterians, many emigrating from New England to New York and the Midwest became Presbyterians, reinvigorating within the church the New England heritage.

The New England tradition in the church, known in the nineteenth century as New School, was much influenced by the Edwardean theology which was teaching milder views of original sin and attributing to man greater powers of initiative. The teaching, for example, of Nathaniel W. Taylor was finding acceptance in New School quarters. The New School, with its New England traditions, was more favorable to the antislavery movement than was the Old School. Church government as practiced by the New School gave less authority to local church sessions and to presbyteries. New School men generally supported the voluntary societies, including the American Home Missionary Society, founded in 1826.

The Old School, or Scotch-Irish, tradition was deeply concerned about the growing influence of the New England theology in the church. The reducing of the authority of the church judicatories weakened a chief protector of orthodoxy. If in addition to this, the voluntary societies, which were not under any control by church judicatories, were to take over the educational and missionary work of the church, the floodgates would be open. In 1802 the Presbyterian General Assembly had created a Standing Committee of Missions which was succeeded in 1816 by a Board of Missions under the Assembly's control.[34] Old School men urged Presbyterians to support the Assembly's Board rather than the American Home Missionary Society.[35] In 1837, the growing tension over theological, organizational, and slavery issues divided the Presbyterian Church into two almost equal parts.

In the year of the division, Charles Hodge (1797–1878) argued in favor of denominational boards for educational and missionary work as against voluntary societies. Hodge, a graduate of the College of New Jersey and of Princeton Seminary, had studied in Germany under Tholuck, Hengstenberg, and Neander. As professor at Princeton Seminary he founded the distinguished *Biblical Repertory and Princeton Review* in 1825. Though a strict Calvinist, he favored moderation almost to the moment of the division of 1837. In old age he unsuccessfully opposed the Presbyterian Reunion of 1869. His magnum opus, *Systematic Theology*,[36] was widely used as a textbook. By the time of his death he was one of the most influential ex-

---

[34] Clifford M. Drury, *Presbyterian Panorama: One Hundred Years of National Missions History* (Phila., 1952), 21–90.

[35] Cf. Joshua L. Wilson, *Four Propositions Sustained Against the Claims of the American Home Missionary Society* (Phila., 1831).

[36] 3 vols., N.Y., 1871–72.

ponents of old Calvinism in the English-speaking world.[37] Hodge's argument in favor of church boards, here presented, emphasized the importance of denominational boards for safeguarding the church's theology.

DOCUMENT

We have always readily admitted that there are purposes for which voluntary societies, embracing members of different religious denominations, are greatly to be preferred to separate ecclesiastical organizations. And in our number for July 1836, p. 429,[38] we stated at least one principle by which such cases may be easily distinguished. Wherever the field of operation is common to different denominations, and the proper means for its cultivation are also the same for all, there is an obvious reason why all should unite. These conditions meet with regard to the Bible and Tract Societies, and in many important respects in regard to Sunday School Unions. There are other cases in which voluntary societies of a denominational character may be either indispensable or highly desirable. On the other hand there are cases for which ecclesiastical organizations appear to us to be entitled to decided preference. To this class belong the work of educating ministers of the gospel, and that of missions. We shall proceed to state very briefly some of the grounds of this opinion.

In the first place, the object of these societies is strictly ecclesiastical as well as denominational. Every church has its peculiar system of opinions and form of government, which it is bound to preserve and extend. And in order to effect this object it is necessary that it should have under its own direction the means employed for its accomplishment. Of these means beyond all comparison the most important are the education of ministers, and the organization and support of churches. The men who decide where and how the rising ministry are to be educated, and who determine where they are to go when their education is completed, have the destiny of the church in their hands. This being the case, is it wonderful that each denomination should wish not only to have this matter under their own control, but confided to persons of its own selection? Is it wonderful that Presbyterians and Episcopalians should decline committing their candidates to the care of Congregationalists or Baptists? Or that they should be uneasy at seeing their churches supplied with ministers by a society in which some other denomination than their own, has an equal or controlling influence? On the contrary, would not indifference on these points argue a strange and criminal unconcern about what they profess to regard as the truth and order of God? We consider, therefore, the extension of the principle of united action by voluntary societies to cases affecting the vital inter-

---

[37] A. A. Hodge, *The Life of Charles Hodge, D.D., LL.D., Professor in the Theological Seminary, Princeton, N.J.* (N.Y., 1880).

[38] [Charles Hodge,] "The General Assembly of 1836," *Biblical Repertory and Theological Review*, VIII (1836), 429.

ests of separate denominations as fraught with evil. Even if these sects ought to be indifferent to their respective peculiarities, they are not, and the attempt to deal with them as though they were, must excite ill-will and strife.

The answer to this objection, that the Education and Missionary Societies do nothing but provide and sustain men to be examined and installed by the judicatories of the several denominations, is very far from being satisfactory. The mere right to examine before Presbytery the candidates for ordination is not the only security which the church needs for the fidelity of her ministers. She wishes that by their previous training they should be made acquainted with her doctrines, and become attached to her order. Reason and experience alike demonstrate that the perfunctory examination before an ecclesiastical body is altogether an inadequate barrier to the admission of improper men into the ministry, and that by far the most important security lies in the education and selection of the ministers themselves. If these matters are committed to other hands, every thing is given up.

Again, the office assumed by these societies involves an encroachment on the rights and duties of ecclesiastical courts. This may be inferred from what has already been said. One of the most important duties of the church in her organized capacity is the preservation of the truth. It is her business to see that faithful men are introduced into the ministry and set over her congregations. To discharge this duty properly, she must do more than merely examine men prepared and sent forth by other hands. She must herself see to their education and mission. These are in a great measure strictly ecclesiastical functions, which, to say the least, it is incongruous for societies composed for the most part of laymen, and without any ecclesiastical appointment or supervision to perform. Indeed it is one of the anomalies of the times, that laymen should be the great directors and controllers of theological education and domestic missions.

We have already remarked that there are in the work of missions two distinct functions, the one ecclesiastical, the other secular. The one *must* be performed by church courts; the other *may* be performed by others. To the former belong the ordination, mission, direction, and supervision of evangelists; to the latter the mere provision of the ways and means, and the administration of them. There is a great difference between theory and practice on this subject. According to theory the committee of the Home Missionary Society may be the mere almoners of the churches' bounty. They may profess simply to stand at the door of the treasury to receive applications from feeble congregations and presbyteries. This is all very well. But if in practice they go much farther than this, and assume the direction of ecclesiastical persons, deciding where they are to labour, instructing them as to the discharge of their official duties, and requiring their missionaries to report to them on all these points, then do they assume the rights and privileges of an ecclesiastical court; they usurp an authority and power which do not belong to them, and which they have no right to exercise. People may cry out against all this as high churchism. It is Presbyterianism. And if they dislike it, let them renounce it and the name; but do not let them under the guise of presbyterians undermine the whole fabric. There can be no doubt that, according to the system of our church, the control of ecclesiastical persons rests with ecclesiastical courts. Every licentiate and minister is under the direction of his own presbytery, and is bound to go where they send him, and to stay where they place him. It is to them he is responsible for the right discharge of his official duties, and to them he is bound to report. For any set of men to assume this direction, supervision and control of such licentiates and ministers, is a direct interference with the rights of presbyteries. If then, the Home Missionary Society practically assumes the direction and supervision of its four or six hundred missionaries, if it regards them as its missionaries, sent by it, determined directly or indirectly as to the place or character of their labours by its authority or influence, and demanding accountability to that society or its committee, whatever be the theory of the matter, it is a practical subversion of the whole system of our church.

> SOURCE: [Charles Hodge,] Article reviewing *A Plea for Voluntary Societies* . . . (N.Y., 1837) in *Biblical Repertory and Princeton Review,* IX (1837), 112–4.

112. The Real Presence

One of the most significant of the American Protestant churchly movements in the early nineteenth century was the Mercersburg theology, developed in the theological seminary of the German Reformed Church at Mercersburg, Pennsylvania.

The Continental Reformed Churches in America from the beginning had more churchly ideals than had those churches coming out of English Puritanism. In addition, their use of foreign languages for a time had reduced the impact on them of American sectarianism. From early days the German Reformed had spoken of themselves and their German Lutheran neighbors as "church people" in contrast to the German sectaries whom they characterized as "sect people." Though many German Reformed in the early nineteenth century co-operated with the voluntary societies, others of their number were averse to these nondenominational co-operative organizations.

The names of three men stand out in the Mercersburg movement. Frederick Augustus Rauch (1806–41), German born and educated, came to Mercersburg in 1832 as principal of the classical department and professor of biblical literature. His lectures on philosophical idealism, romantic poetry, and contemporary German theology opened new vistas to his students. His strongly Hegelian *Psychology* contributed to Nevin's later emphasis on the living presence of Christ in the Lord's Supper.[39] He was, however, more a forerunner than an actual developer of the Mercersburg theology.[40] Philip Schaff (1819–93), a native Swiss educated at the universities of Tübingen, Halle, and Berlin, taught at Mercersburg (1843–63) and later at Union Seminary (1870–93). He brought to Mercersburg thorough familiarity with contemporary German religious thought. His inaugural address, "The Principle of Protestantism," delivered in 1844, viewed the Christian church genetically, and gave a much more favorable interpretation to medieval Christianity and to the Roman Catholicism of his day than was customary in America, which at the moment was being swept by anti-Catholic nativism.[41]

John Williamson Nevin (1803–86), the principal leader of the movement, was of Scotch-Irish Presbyterian ancestry. After graduating from Union College, Schenectady, New York, and Princeton Theological Seminary, he taught two years at Princeton Seminary and ten years at Western Seminary in Allegheny, now Pittsburgh, Pennsylvania. He was professor in the German Reformed seminary at Mercersburg, Pennsylvania (1840–53), lecturer at Franklin and Marshall College (1861–66), and president of the college (1866–76).[42]

The Mercersburg movement had its start in Nevin's reaction against revivalism. As a student at Union College he was converted in a revival led by the Calvinist, Asahel Nettleton, whose more orthodox methods contrasted sharply with Finney's "new measures." Later, when Nevin was on the faculty at Mercersburg, he made some dampening remarks in the midst of a local revival, which led to lectures and to the publication in 1843 of his booklet, *The Anxious Bench*. This was a classic attack on the revivalistic "new measures" of Finney and others, criticizing their pragmatism and externality and what he considered to be their irrelevance to a true, deep spirituality.

Nevin's thought centered in the doctrine of the church. His sermon on "Catholic Unity," preached in 1844; his greatest work, *The Mystical Presence* in 1846; and numerous articles published in the *Mercersburg Review* developed this theme. Nevin had read extensively in German theology and was deeply influenced by the historical spirit, by the biographical interest of the German church historian, Neander, and by

[39] *Psychology, or a View of the Human Soul, Including Anthropology* (N.Y., 1840); James H. Nichols, *Romanticism in American Theology: Nevin and Schaff at Mercersburg* (Chicago, 1961), 47–8, 104.

[40] Howard J. B. Ziegler, *Frederick Augustus Rauch, American Hegelian* (Lancaster, Pa., 1953).

[41] David S. Schaff, *The Life of Philip Schaff* (N.Y., 1897); Philip Schaff, *The Principle of Protestantism, as Related to the Present State of the Church* (Chambersburg, Pa., 1845); reviewed by Charles Hodge in *The Biblical Repertory and Princeton Review*, XVII (1845), 626–36.

[42] Theodore Appel, *The Life and Work of John Williamson Nevin* (Phila., 1889).

Schleiermacher, both of whom led him to view Christianity as life. Idealistic philosophy caused Nevin to think that the universal precedes the particular, and that the church precedes the individual believer. Thus unity is of the essence of the church.

Nevin emphasized the living Christ as constituting the very center of the church's life. He regarded the sacraments, viewed in a much "higher" way than the Calvinistic churches of the day were accustomed to view them, as the high point of the church's life, for in them the church experiences fellowship with the living Christ. Unlike most professed Calvinists of his day, he did not regard the Lord's Supper as primarily a memorial of Christ's atoning death, but rather, like Calvin himself, he emphasized that in the Supper the believer receives the "spiritual real presence" of Christ. Charles Hodge challenged this view. In the debate with Hodge and others, which ensued, it became evident that Nevin was nearer to German Protestantism and to most of Christendom than were his American critics. Nevin's doctrine of the Lord's Supper was the chief factor in leading him to a more organic conception of the church.[43] Thus for the individualistic, and what he considered forced, spirituality of revivalism Nevin and the Mercersburg movement sought to substitute the organic and more historical and biblical mystical experience to be found in the corporate life of the church as a whole.

Nevin's book, *The Mystical Presence,* a selection from which is here reproduced, was one of the ablest American theological writings of this period. It is interesting to observe that some of Nevin's strictures coincided with criticisms of American Protestantism which High-Church Episcopalians and even Roman Catholics were making, while at the same time Nevin vigorously re-asserted evangelical Protestant values in balance with the more Catholic values which he was seeking to recover. In some respects Nevin anticipated criticisms of Protestant scholasticism which have been made by twentieth-century neo-orthodoxy; and the ideal, which he developed elsewhere, of Christian unity based on the historic church, foreshadowed aspects of the twentieth-century ecumenical movement.

DOCUMENT

It cannot be denied that the view generally entertained of the Lord's Supper at the present time, in the Protestant Church, involves a wide departure from the faith of the sixteenth century with regard to the same subject. The fact must be at once clear to every one at all familiar with the religious world as it now exists, as soon as he is made to understand in any measure the actual form in which the sacramental doctrine was held in the period just mentioned.

[43] Nichols, *Romanticism in American Theology,* 84–106; George W. Richards, *History of the Theological Seminary of the Reformed Church in the United States, 1825–1934, Evangelical and Reformed Church, 1934–1952* (Lancaster, Pa., 1952), 213–94.

This falling away from the creed of the Reformation is not confined to any particular country or religious confession. It has been most broadly displayed among the continental churches of Europe, in the form of that open, rampant rationalism, which has there to so great an extent triumphed over the old orthodoxy at so many other points. But it is found widely prevalent also in Great Britain and in this country. It is especially striking, of course, as has been already remarked, in the case of the Lutheran Church, which was distinguished from the other Protestant confession, in the beginning, mainly by its high view of the Lord's Supper, and the zeal it showed in opposition to what it stigmatized reproachfully as sacramentarian error. In this respect, it can hardly be recognized indeed as the same communion. The original name remains, but the original distinctive character is gone. Particularly is this the case, with a large part at least, of the Lutheran Church in our own country. We cannot say of it simply, that it has been led to moderate the old sacramental doctrine of the church, as exhibited in the *Form of Concord;* it has abandoned the doctrine altogether. Not only is the true Lutheran position, as occupied so violently against the Calvinists in the sixteenth century, openly and fully renounced; but the Calvinistic ground itself, then shunned with so much horror as the very threshold of infidelity, has come to be considered as also in unsafe contiguity with Rome. With no denomination do we find the anti-mystical tendency, usually charged upon the Reformed Church, more decidedly developed. Methodism itself can hardly be said to make less account of the sacraments, practically or theoretically. A strange contradiction surely, which, we may trust, is not destined always to endure. For it is not to be imagined that such an utter abandonment of the Lutheran principle in the case of the Lord's Supper, can be confined to this single point. Central as the doctrine of the sacrament is to the whole Christian system, (so felt to be especially by Luther,) such a change necessarily implies a change that extends much farther. The whole life of the Church, in these circumstances, must be brought into contradiction to its own proper principle. It cannot be true to itself. This of course we regard as a fit subject for lamentation. Never was there a time when it was more important, that this Church should understand and fulfil her own mission; and in no part of the world perhaps is this more needed than just here in America, where the tendency to undervalue all that is sacramental and objective in religion, has become unhappily so strong.

But it is not the Lutheran Church only, which has fallen away from its original creed, in the case of the Lord's Supper. Though the defection may not be so immediately palpable and open to all observation, it exists with equal certainty, as was said before, on the part of the Reformed Church. It does so for the most part in Europe; and in this country the case is, to say the least, no better. Our sect system must be considered, in its very nature, unfavourable to all proper respect for the sacraments. This may be taken, indeed, as a just criterion of the spirit of *sect,* as distinguished from the true spirit of the Christian church. In proportion as the sect character prevails, it will be found that Baptism and the Lord's Supper are looked upon as mere outward signs, in the case of which all proper efficacy is supposed to be previously at hand in the inward state of the subject by whom they are received. It is this feeling which leads so generally to the rejection of infant baptism, on the part of those who affect to improve our Christianity in the way of new schisms. It is particularly significant, moreover, in the aspect now considered, that the *Baptist* body, as such, is numerically stronger than any other denomination in the country. But the *baptistic principle* prevails more extensively still; for it is very plain that all true sense of the sacramental value of baptism is wanting, in large portions of the church, where the ordinance is still retained; and the consequence is, that it is employed to the same extent as a merely outward and traditional form. Along with this, of course, must prevail an unsacramental feeling generally, by which the Lord's Supper also is shorn of all its significance and power. Methodism, in this way, may be said to wrong the sacraments, (as also the entire idea of the *Church,*) almost as seriously as the Baptist system itself. The general evil, however, reaches still farther. Even those denominations among us which represent the Reformed Church by true and legitimate descent, such as the Presbyterian in its different branches, and the Reformed Dutch, show plainly that they have fallen away, to some extent, from the original faith of the church, in the same direction. Remains of it indeed may still be found in the private piety of many, the result, in part, of their special advantage in the way of early traditional education, and in part the product of their own religious life itself; but, so far as the general reigning belief is concerned, the old doctrine may be said to be fairly suppressed by one of a different character. It is so theoretically, to a great extent, in our systems of theology, biblical expositions, sermons, and religious teaching generally, so far as the sacramental question is concerned. It is so practically, to an equal extent, in the corresponding views and feelings with which the use of the sacraments is maintained on the part of professing Christians. Not only is the old doctrine rejected, but it has become almost lost even to the knowledge of the Church. When it is brought into view, it is not believed, perhaps, that the Reformed Church ever held or taught, in fact, any doctrine of the sort; or if it be yielded at length, that Calvin and some others maintained some such view, it is set down summarily as one of those instances in which the work of the Reformation appears still clogged with a measure of Popish superstition, brought over from that state of darkness and bondage which had just been left behind. In this view, the doctrine is considered to be of no force whatever for the Church, in her present condition of gospel light and liberty. It is unintelligible and absurd; savors of transubstantiation; exalts the flesh at the expense of the spirit. A real presence of the whole

Christ in the Lord's Supper, under any form, is counted a hard saying, not to be endured by human reason, and contrary to God's word. Thus it stands with our churches generally. Even in the Episcopal Church, with all the account it professes to make of the sacraments, few are willing to receive in full such representations of the eucharistic presence, as are made either by Hooker or Calvin. . . .

The triumph of Rationalism, during the eighteenth century, in Germany and throughout Europe generally, brought with it of course a still more extensive degradation of religious views. It is not necessary here to trace the rise of this apostacy and its connection with the previous state of Protestantism. Enough to say, that it grew out of a tendency involved in the very nature of Protestantism from the beginning; the opposite exactly of that by which the Catholic Church previously had been carried into an equally false extreme, on the other side. As Romanism had sacrificed the rights of the individual to the authority of the general,—the claims of the subjective to the overwhelming weight of the objective; so the tendency of Protestantism may be said to have been from the very start, to assert these same rights and claims in the way of violent reaction, at the cost of the opposite interest. In the age of the Reformation itself, deeply imbued as it was with the positive life of truth and faith, this tendency was powerfully held within limits. With Luther, and Calvin, and the Reformers generally, the principle of freedom was still held in check by the principle of authority, and the reason of the individual was required to bend to the idea of a divine revelation as something broader and more sure than itself. It came not however in all this, it must be confessed, to a true inward reconciliation of these polar forces. The old orthodoxy, it is now generally allowed, particularly under the form it carried in the Lutheran Church, involved in itself accordingly the necessity of such a process of inward conflict and dissolution, as it has since been called to pass through; in order that the contradiction which was lodged in its bosom, might come fairly into view, and the way be opened thus for its reconstruction, under a form at once more perfect and more true to its own nature. The characteristic tendency of Protestantism already mentioned, burst finally through all the counteracting force, with which it had been restrained in the beginning. Religion ran out into sheer subjectivity; first in the form of Pietism, and afterwards in the overflowing desolation of Rationalism, reducing all to the character of the most flat natural morality. The eighteenth century was characteristically infidel. As an age, it seemed to have no organ for the supernatural. All was made to shrink to the dimensions of the mere human spirit, in its isolated character. Theology of course was robbed of all its higher life. Even the supernaturalism of the period was rationalistic; and occupying as it did in fact a false position with regard to the truth, by which a measure of right was given to the rival interest, it proved altogether incompetent to maintain its ground against the reigning spirit. The views of rationalism may be said to infect the whole theology of this period, and also of the first part of the present century, openly heretical and professedly orthodox alike.

In the nature of the case, this may be expected to show itself in low views of the sacraments, Baptism and the Lord's Supper. Rationalism is too *spiritual,* to make much account of outward forms and services of any sort in religion. All must be resolved into the exercises of the worshipper's own mind. The subjective is every thing; the objective next to nothing. Hence the supernatural itself is made to sink into the form of the simply moral. The sacraments of course become signs, and signs *only.* Any power they may have is not to be found in *them,* but altogether in such use merely as a pious soul may be able to make of them, as *occasions* for quickening its own devout thought and feelings. . . .

Parallel to a great extent with the development of the subjective principle in the false form now noticed [i.e., "rationalism"], runs the revelation also of the same tendency in the equally false form of Sectarism and schism. No one can study attentively the character of either, without being led to see that the two tendencies are but different phases of one and the same spiritual obliquity. No one, in reading the history of the Church, can well fail to be struck with the many points of correspondence, which are found universally to hold between the two forms of life, in spite of the broad difference by which they might seem to be separated, in many cases, on a superficial view. The spirit of sect is characteristically full of religious pretension; and professing to make supreme account of religion as something personal and experimental, it assumes always a more than ordinarily spiritual character, and moves in the element of restless excitement and action. Hence it is often, generally indeed at the start, fanatical and wild; especially in the way of opposition to outward forms and the existing order of the Church generally. And yet how invariably it falls in with the rationalistic way of thinking, as far as it may *think* at all, from the very beginning; and how certainly its principles and views, when carried out subsequently to their legitimate results, are found to involve in the end the worst errors of Rationalism itself. Both systems are antagonistic to the idea of the *Church.* Both are disposed to trample under foot the authority of *history.* Both make the *objective* to be nothing, and the *subjective* to be all in all. Both undervalue the *outward,* in favour of what they conceive to be the *inward.* Both despise *forms,* under pretence of exalting the *spirit.* Both of course sink the *sacraments* to the character of mere outward rites; or possibly deny their necessity altogether. Both affect to make much of the *bible;* at least in the beginning; though sometimes indeed it is made to yield, with Sectarism, to the imagination of some superior inward light more directly from God; and in all cases, it is forced to submit, to the tyranny of mere private interpretation, as the only proper measure of its sense. With both forms of thinking, the idea of Christianity, as a permanent order of life, a real supernatural constitution unfolding itself historically in the world, is we may say wanting altogether. All at last is flesh, the natural life of man as such; exalted it may be in its own order, but never of course transcending itself so as to become *spirit*. The sect principle may indeed affect to move in the highest sphere of the heavenly and divine; carrying it possibly to an absolute rupture even with all that belongs to the present world. But in this case it begins in the spirit, only to end the more certainly in the flesh. Hyper-spiritualism is ever fleshly pseudo-spiritualism; that is sure to fall back sooner or later impotent and self-exhausted, into the low element from which it has vainly pretended to make its escape. Anabaptism finds its legitimate, natural end in the excesses of Munster; as Mormonism in the like excesses of Nauvoo. What a difference apparently between the inspiration of George Fox, and the cold infidelity of Elias Hicks. And yet the last is the true spiritual descendant of the first. The inward light of the one, and the light of reason as held by the other, come to the same thing at last. Both contradict the true conception of religion. Both are supremely subjective, and in this view supremely rationalistic at the same time. . . .

It must at all events be regarded as a presumption against the modern Puritan view of the Lord's Supper, that, in departing from the doctrine of the Reformation, it is found to fall in so strikingly with what may be styled the apostacy of Rationalism in the same direction. It might seem sufficiently startling to be sundered, in such a case, from the general faith of Christendom as it has stood from the beginning. But still more startling, certainly, is the thought of such separation in *such* company. This much is clear. The Reformation included in its original and proper constitution, two different elements or tendencies; and it was felt that it could be true to itself, only by acknowledging the authority of both, as mutually necessary each for the perfection and proper support of the other. In the nature of the case, however, there was a powerful liability in the movement to become ultraistic and extreme, on that side which seemed to carry the most direct *protest* against the errors of the Church, as it stood before. In the course of time, undeniably, this became, as we have already seen, its general character. The simply Protestant tendency was gradually sundered, in a great measure, from its true Catholic complement and counterpoise; and in this abstract character it has run out into theoretical and practical rationalism, to a fearful extent, in all parts of the Church. The low view of the sacraments, which we have now under consideration, came in with this unfortunate obliquity. It belongs historically and constitutionally to the bastard form, under which the original life of Protestantism has become so widely caricatured in the way of heresy and schism. Its inward affinity with the spirit of Rationalism, in one direction, and the spirit of Sect in another, (two different phases only of the same modern Antichrist,) is too clear to be for one moment called in question. In this character, it forms most certainly, like the whole system with which it is associated, a departure from the faith, not only of the Lutheran, but of the Reformed Church also, as it stood in the sixteenth century. It involves in this respect, what would have been counted, at that time, not only a perversion, but a very serious perversion of the true Protestant doctrine. Now, with this neological and sectarian view, we find the modern Puritan theory of the Lord's Supper to be in full agreement. Both sink its objective virtue wholly out of sight. Both do this, on the principle of making the service spiritual and rational, instead of simply *ritual*. Both, in this way, wrong the claims of Christianity as a supernatural *life*, in favour of its claims as a divine doctrine. Both proceed on the same false abstraction, by which soul and body, outward and inward, are made to be absolutely different, and in some sense really antagonistic, spheres of existence. Both show the same utter disregard to the authority of all previous history, and affect to construct the whole theory of the Church, doctrine, sacraments, and all, in the way of independent private judgment, from the Bible and common sense. Both, in all this, involve a like defection, and substantially to the same extent, from the creed of the Reformation; and would have been regarded accordingly, not only by Luther, but by Calvin also, and Beza, and Ursinus, and the fathers of the Reformed Church generally, as alike treasonable to the interest, which has become identified with their great names.

> SOURCE: John W. Nevin, *The Mystical Presence. A Vindication of the Reformed or Calvinistic Doctrine of the Holy Eucharist* (Phila., 1846), 105–9, 141–2, 147–8, 152–3.

113. Confessionalism Revived

Lutherans in the Reformation era laid great stress upon the church and sacraments, and it might have been expected that in early nineteenth-century America they would have been a bulwark against the strong tides of more individualistic Christianity. But such was not at first the case.

Among early Lutherans in Pennsylvania there had been strong tendencies to unionism under the influence of the Moravian, Count Nikolaus Ludwig von Zinzendorf (1700–60). Henry M. Mühlenberg (1711–78), who was sent from Halle to plant churches and to counteract these unionistic tendencies, had himself received pietistic influences and fraternized with Christians of other denominations.[44] Rationalistic tendencies among Lutherans at the end of the eighteenth century further disinclined them to exclusive emphasis on their Augsburg Confession.[45] It is not surprising, therefore, that the early nineteenth century saw many Lutherans adopting revivalistic methods,[46] co-operating in the voluntary societies, and accepting

[44] *American Christianity*, I, 280–7.

[45] Vergilius Ferm, *The Crisis in American Lutheran Theology: A Study of the Issue between American Lutheranism and Old Lutheranism* (N.Y., 1927), 3–70.

[46] Sydney E. Ahlstrom, "The Lutheran Church and American Culture: A Tercentenary Retrospect," *Lutheran Quarterly*, IX (1957), 332–3.

the current—but quite un-Lutheran—conceptions of individual ethics and social reform. Because these religious and reforming movements were dominated by the heirs of Calvinism, there was real danger that Lutheranism would lose its distinctive character and be swept along in the stream.

But a new interest in the church and in distinctive Lutheran beliefs began to appear in America about 1820. This was soon greatly strengthened by large immigration from Germany. In Germany, following the Napoleonic Wars and stimulated by the twin solvents of dogma—pietism and rationalism—there was in 1817 an effort to unite the Lutheran and Reformed Churches in Germany. Many Lutherans protested, some fleeing to the United States where they gave real vitality in the General Synod to a new emphasis on distinctively Lutheran beliefs. In the United States others of these newcomers organized the strongly conservative Synods of Buffalo, Ohio, and Missouri. Many of those who came were also reacting against the theological innovations that were being proposed by the great philosophers and theologians of nineteenth-century Germany, and were taking refuge in a traditionalistic confessionalism.

The earlier tendencies to adapt Lutheranism to its non-Lutheran American environment did not surrender meekly to the confessionalism which the new immigrants were importing from Germany, but found vigorous and able leadership in Samuel S. Schmucker (1799–1873) and his "American Lutheranism." In 1838 Schmucker's strong desire for Christian unity expressed itself in the publication of his *Fraternal Appeal to the American Churches, with a Plan for Catholic Union on Apostolic Principles,* which contained a creed that he had compiled from generally acceptable portions of various denominational creeds. More important and far more controversial was the "Definite Synodical Platform" which he and two others circulated in 1855. It proposed a revision of the revered Augsburg Confession which would eliminate the Lutheran doctrines of baptismal regeneration and of the "real presence" of Christ's body and blood in the Communion, and would also revise certain other Lutheran doctrines. Schmucker favored eliminating or reducing many distinctive elements of Lutheranism and encouraged closer relations with the other American denominations. But the tide had already turned. The General Synod vigorously repudiated Schmucker's program of "American Lutheranism," and leaders and policies committed to strict construction of distinctively Lutheran beliefs came into control. Central in this new confessional program was emphasis on the Lutheran doctrine of the church and the sacraments.[47]

A prominent spokesman for confessionalism was Charles Philip Krauth (1792–1867). Krauth was largely self-educated. After serving pastorates (1819–33) he became the first president of Pennsylvania College, and professor in Gettysburg Theological Seminary (1850–67). His son, Charles

[47] Vergilius Ferm, *The Crisis in American Lutheran Theology;* Carl Mauelshagen, *American Lutheranism Surrenders to Forces of Conservatism* (Athens, Ga., 1926).

Porterfield Krauth (1823–83), became the foremost leader of confessionalist forces in the church.[48]

The father, while in favor of tightening confessional restraints, was moderate in spirit, and avoided taking an extreme position, repeatedly urging harmony. He criticized "extreme subjectivity" and "leaning to the emotional in religion" into which American Lutherans had fallen, but noted with satisfaction that the denomination's earlier history was now being studied for the light it cast on the heritage of faith. Lutherans should not close their minds to sacramental or other doctrines which they wrongly ascribe to a particular party within the church. The Augsburg Confession should be the norm of the church's faith. Subscription to it should be required of every minister, and should be construed more strictly than at present. Borrowing from other denominational heritages must cease. With some degree of self-restraint, Krauth sought to point his fellow Lutherans to the wealth of Christian heritage that was theirs, particularly as epitomized in their Augsburg Confession. He believed that their church occupied middle ground within Christianity as a whole; was large and satisfying in its conceptions; and, while emphasizing true spirituality, was free from the excessive subjectivism which was harassing contemporary American life. The selection here given is from the address which Charles Philip Krauth delivered as president of the Lutheran General Synod in 1850.

DOCUMENT

The time has, perhaps, arrived, in which it becomes the duty of the Lutheran Church in the United States to examine its position, and to determine its future course. It cannot be denied that at this moment the state of things amongst us is peculiar, and that necessity exists for definite views in regard to our duty, in these circumstances, deserving to be called critical.

The Lutheran Church in this country traces its origin to the Lutheran Church in Germany. It is an integral part of the great Lutheran family which is spread so extensively over Germany, and other Germanic countries. Coeval with the Reformation, and established upon the doctrinal system of Luther, as expressed in the Augsburg Confession, its Apology, the Smalcald Articles and the Catechism of Luther, as developed and explained in the Formula Concordiæ, its history has been rendered illustrious by great intellectual and moral achievements. Unfolding its banner in this Western hemisphere, it marshalled its soldiers to no other service and aimed by no new weapons to accomplish its victories. It did not, in other words, profess to be any thing but Lutheran. Its first ministers, educated in the schools of sound Lutheran theology, designed to transfer the same to this country. They followed their countrymen who had emigrated to

---

[48] The standard biography by Adolph Spaeth, *Charles Porterfield Krauth* (2 vols., N.Y., 1898–1909), devotes the first chapter to the father, Charles Philip.

America and brought with them the faith in which they had been nurtured. That the orthodoxy of the olden time was gradually lost sight of, that the Confessions were practically superseded, that formal subscription was entirely abandoned, are facts which admit of no controversy. It is true, since the commencement of the era, as it has been called, of the General Synod, the Augsburg Confession has again been brought into notice, and a limited subscription to it enforced; but it cannot be regarded as any thing more than an approximate return to the ancient landmarks. . . .

The church is divided on some points. Although some minor shades of opinion might be referred to, we direct attention to one point as alone material. In the Augustan Confession, the 10th Article, on the Lord's Supper, reads thus: "Concerning the Lord's Supper they teach, that the body and blood of Christ are truly present, and are administered to the communicants, and they condemn those who teach otherwise." The doctrine of the real bodily presence, here presented to the view, and, certainly, a part of its primitive faith, is that about which there is not uniformity amongst us. All admit that Christ is present, but all do not explain that presence in the same way. That the older view has advocates is a matter of notoriety; that their number has increased by emigration from abroad, is likewise well known; that these views are finding favor amongst men whose training predisposed them to reject them, it would be useless to conceal. On the other hand, a large part of the church asserts its inability to comprehend and to receive this doctrine. . . .

The Lutheran church in this country is in a state of reaction. She has passed, in some parts, through an extreme subjectivity, an extreme leaning to the emotional in religion; she permitted herself, to some extent, to be carried away by the surges of animal feeling, and lost much of her ancient propriety. She is now retracing her steps, acknowledging her error, seeking release from crude views and objectionable measures. She is hunting amongst the records of the past for the faith of former days, and endeavoring to learn what she was in her earliest form. . . .

We believe that there has been too much looseness, in our church, in regard to the necessity and utility of creeds, in general. The change from the original ground occupied by the church, the disuse of the symbols, the latitudinarianism about them, were calculated to be productive of much evil. That this has not occurred, may be said to be happy for the church. We believe that the evils to be dreaded from the neglect of the symbols, have not followed in a very great degree, yet they have in some. That orthodoxy which we retain, strongly tinctured as it is with Lutheranism, has various phases, never running perhaps into Calvinism, on the one hand, or Pelagianism on the other, but sometimes passing almost into the region of the one, and at others hardly steering clear of the other.

Now we suppose that this requires a remedy, and we can suggest no other, in the present state of our church, than the use of the Augustan

Confession as a creed, and requiring the subscription of it, within certain limits, by every minister of Jesus Christ who serves at our altars. It may be said, that it has been used, that it has received the sanction of the General Synod of our church, and that it is subscribed by the ministers of those synods which are connected with the General Synod. This is true, but we object to the liberty allowed in that subscription. Thus far, it has been without serious injury, but it is liable to very great abuse. The terms of the subscription are such as to admit of the rejection of any doctrine or doctrines which the subscriber may not receive. It is subscribed or assented to as containing the doctrines of the word of God substantially; they are set forth in substance, the understanding is that there are some doctrines in it, not contained in the word of God, but there is no specification concerning them. Every one could omit from his assent whatever he did not believe. The subscription did not preclude this. It is at once evident that a creed thus presented is no creed, that it is anything or nothing, that its subscription is a solemn farce. It is true, that the views of subscribers were ascertained in advance of their subscription, and the dangers were avoided which otherwise might have ensued; but then they were ascertained under no circumstances of special solemnity, under none that bind the conscience as does an oath of subscription to a creed, and consequently nothing was gained, or if there was a previous conviction as to the soundness of the candidate, the subscription was superseded as entirely supererogatory. To set aside this great, this venerated symbol, would meet with no favor in the church, an *ex animo* subscription is not possible to all. What then is to be done? We insist upon a creed, we consider it a *sine qua non;* the church cannot operate harmoniously, efficiently without it, the only course that we can devise is to give it normative authority. It may be subscribed *ex animo* by all who can do so; it may be subscribed by others, with the privilege of dissenting from certain doctrines, which shall be stated or specified. The doctrines from which there may be dissent, cannot be any that are essential to the orthodox system, cannot be any which, if received and rejected in the same church, would tend to confusion. Different views may be allowed in regard to the power of the sacraments, but not as to their validity, not as to their subjects.—Different views may be allowed in regard to our relation to the first man, and the manner in which we became involved in his sin, but not in regard to the sinfulness of man, original sin, and the necessity of regeneration. Different views may be entertained as respects the *communicatio idiomatum* in the natures of Christ, but not in regard to those natures. Carefully must we exclude every form of Arianism high and low, Socinianism and rationalism, and anti-trinitarianism of all kinds. . . .

It is our duty to exert a conservative influence. The true position of the Lutheran church is conservative. It should hold fast the form of sound words which it has received, and display its doctrinal and ritual moderation.

Occupying a middle position between prelatical Episcopacy and *jure divino congregationalism;* extreme neither in the one direction nor the other; conceding to utility all that it can ask, without detriment to order; avoiding in doctrine the errors of Calvinism, and those of low Arminianism and Pelagianism; repudiating a mere animal religion whilst it shows no countenance to a morality cold and religionless—these its true position, its very essence and form, adapt it to exert an influence favorable to doctrinal soundness and religious purity. We do not claim for it too much, when we ascribe to it a capacity to uphold a true living system of christianity, when we regard it as adapted to exert an influence opposed to extremes in the one direction or the other. It might appear invidious to ascribe such a power to the Lutheran church exclusively. This we do not do, but at the same time, we think that in no other is their capacity to do so much, and upon so extensive a scale. No other church occupies, we think, so nearly the central point between Roman Catholic and Protestant extremes. No other so central a point between the high Churchism of Protestantism and the extremes of Protestantism, and therefore we suppose that no other can more fairly regard itself as summoned to act a conservative part—conservative not only by upholding a moderate orthodoxy in doctrine—ecclesiastical government and ceremonies—but by preventing extremes, either on the one hand subversive of human liberty, or on the other of the grace of God.

> SOURCE: Charles Philip Krauth, "The Lutheran Church in the United States," *The Evangelical Review,* II (July, 1850), 1-2, 5-6, 9, 11-5.

114. Parochial Schools Advocated

As a minority group in a culture which had been formed by Protestants, American Catholics faced acute problems. When immigration rapidly swelled their numbers, they encountered not only persecution and the problem of assimilating their heterogeneous newcomers, but also the task of creating cultural organs which would adequately express their faith. On the level of higher education, the early American tradition had been every group for itself, so that Catholics there had a clear field, and their task was simply to put forth the necessary effort to build their own colleges. On the level of elementary education, however, the problem was more difficult, because of the tax-supported public school system which was then rapidly developing. Pressures of financial interest and public opinion were strong on Catholics to incorporate themselves in the common educational enterprise. But this they could not conscientiously do, for the whole atmosphere in which this education was conducted was non-Catholic, and at times even anti-Catholic. Catholicism, with its deep-rooted churchly traditions, had a strong sense of the obligation of the church to indoctrinate its constituents in the full Catholic heritage of the centuries. The ideal involved not only giving instruction in specifically religious matters, but orienting the whole educational process to the Catholic world view. Parochial schools were designed for this specific end. It was difficult for non-Catholics to understand this viewpoint, or, understanding it, to accept during a fervently nationalistic and even nativistic era the permanent cultural bifurcation which this meant for American life.

Francis Patrick Kenrick (1796–1863), bishop of Philadelphia (1830–51), was a leader in developing Catholic parochial schools, securing one in nearly every church of his diocese. He was also concerned about the five thousand Catholic children still in the Philadelphia public schools, and in 1842 wrote to the Board of Comptrollers of Public Schools protesting against the Protestant translation of the Bible, Protestant worship, and anti-Catholic textbooks in the public schools.[49] The letter provoked widespread hostility and was even a prelude to the anti-Catholic riots of 1844 in Philadelphia. Bishop, later Archbishop, John Hughes of New York also actively promoted parochial schools in his diocese. He charged that the Public School Society in New York City, to which the state was giving financial aid, was really a Protestant organization, and demanded an apportionment for the Catholic schools. The legislature refused Bishop Hughes' request, and forbade state aid to all religious schools. Meanwhile the hierarchy as a whole was becoming increasingly concerned about elementary education. A decree of the First Provincial Council of Baltimore in 1829 indicated the need of founding a Catholic parochial school system, and the pastoral letter of the Second Provincial Council of Baltimore in 1833 urged the support of Catholic schools.[50] It remained, however, for the First Plenary Council of Baltimore in 1852 to make the parochial school "an integral part of the Church's organization in this country." [51] Francis Patrick Kenrick had become archbishop of Baltimore two years before, and presided over the council by appointment of the pope. Catholic education was one of the two principal themes of the council's pastoral letter. A decree of the council urged all of the bishops to organize parochial schools in the parishes of their dioceses, and a plan for supporting these schools was instituted. The Second Plenary Council in 1866 reaffirmed this policy. But inevitably there was inertia, and the financial burden to the parishes was severe. The Sacred Congregation of Propaganda at Rome, therefore, in response to certain midwestern bishops, on November 24, 1875, found it necessary to re-emphasize the importance of parochial schools.[52] The portion of the pastoral letter of the First Plenary Council (1852) on the subject of "Catholic Schools" is here given in its entirety.

[49] Text of the letter is in Hugh J. Nolan, *The Most Reverend Francis Patrick Kenrick, Third Bishop of Philadelphia, 1830–1851* (Washington, 1948), 293–5.

[50] Peter Guilday, *The National Pastorals of the American Hierarchy (1792–1919)* (Washington, 1923), 19, 74.

[51] Peter Guilday, *The Life and Times of John England, First Bishop of Charleston, 1786–1842* (2 vols., N.Y., 1927), II, 518.

[52] John T. Ellis, ed., *Documents of American Catholic History*, 416–20.

DOCUMENT

No portion of our charge fills us with greater solicitude than that which our Divine Master, by word and example, has taught us to regard with more than ordinary sentiments of affection—the younger members of our flock. If our youth grow up in ignorance of their religious duties or unpractised in their consoling fulfilment; if, instead of the words of eternal life, which find so full and sweet an echo in the heart of innocence, the principles of error, unbelief or indifferentism, are imparted to them; if the natural repugnance, even in the happiest period of life, to bend under the yoke of discipline, be increased by the example of those whose relation to them gives them influence or authority,—what are we to expect but the disappointment of all hopes which cause the Church to rejoice in the multiplication of her children! We therefore address you brethren, in the language of affectionate warning and solemn exhortation. Guard carefully those little ones of Christ; "suffer them to approach Him, and prevent them not, for of such is the kingdom of heaven." To you, Christian parents, God has committed these His children, whom He permits you to regard as yours; and your natural affection towards whom must ever be subordinate to the will of Him "from whom all paternity in heaven and on earth is named." Remember that if for them you are the representatives of God, the source of their existence, you are to be for them depositaries of His authority, teachers of His law, and models by imitating which they may be perfect, even as their Father in heaven is perfect. You are to watch over the purity of their faith and morals with jealous vigilance, and to instil into their young hearts principles of virtue and perfection. What shall be the anguish of the parent's heart,—what terrible expectation of judgment that will fill his soul, should his children perish through his criminal neglect, or his obstinate refusal to be guided in the discharge of his paternal duties, by the authority of God's Church. To avert this evil give your children a Christian education, that is an education based on religious principles, accompanied by religious practices and always subordinate to religious influence. Be not led astray by the false and delusive theories wh[i]ch are so prevalent, and which leave youth without religion, and, consequently, without anything to control the passions, promote the real happiness of the individual, and make society find in the increase of its members, a source of security and prosperity. Listen not to those who would persuade you that religion can be separated from secular instruction. If your children, while they advance in human sciences, are not taught the science of the saints, their minds will be filled with every error, their hearts will be receptacles of every vice, and that very learning which they have acquired, in itself so good and so necessary, deprived of all that could shed on it the light of heaven, will be an additional means of destroying the happiness of the child, embittering still more the chalice of parental disappointment, and weakening the foundations of social order. Listen to our voice, which tells you to walk in the ancient paths; to bring up your children as you yourselves were brought up by your pious parents; to make religion the foundation of the happiness you wish to secure for those whom you love so tenderly, and the promotion of whose interests is the motive of all your efforts, the solace which sustains you in all your fatigues and privations. Encourage the establishment and support of Catholic schools; make every sacrifice which may be necessary for this object: spare our hearts the pain of beholding the youth whom, after the example of our Master, we so much love, involved in all the evils of an uncatholic education, evils too multiplied and too obvious to require that we should do more than raise our voices in solemn protest against the system from which they spring. In urging on you the discharge of this duty, we are acting on the suggestion of the Sovereign Pontiff, who in an encyclical letter, dated 21 November, 1851, calls on all the Bishops of the Catholic world, to provide for the religious education of youth. We are following the example of the Irish Hierarchy, who are courageously opposing the introduction of a system based on the principle which we condemn, and who are now endeavoring to unite religious with secular instruction of the highest order, by the institution of a Catholic University,—an undertaking in the success of which we necessarily feel a deep interest, and which, as having been suggested by the Sovereign Pontiff, powerfully appeals to the sympathies of the whole Catholic world.

> SOURCE: Peter Guilday, *The National Pastorals of the American Hierarchy (1792–1919)* (Washington, 1923), 189–91.

115. Old Landmarkism

The multiplicity of denominations and efforts to have fellowship indiscriminately across denominational lines evoked among Southern Baptists a kind of "High-Church" movement known as Old Landmarkism. "Which of the existing sects, is the Kingdom of Christ, is a question worthy the serious attention of every candid christian," said the Rev. James R. Graves (1820–93), father of the movement and editor of the *Tennessee Baptist*.[53] Amid the confusing pluralism, Old Landmarkers reasserted—with some unconscious shifts of emphasis—distinctive Baptist tenets. Among Baptists, denominational consciousness was already stronger in the South than in the North, as evidenced by the fact that when southern Baptists organized separately in 1845 they created a denominational Convention which conducted both home and foreign missions and tended increasingly to be a denominational bond of union among the churches. Northern Baptists did not have a comparable consolidating tie until 1907, preferring to support their home and foreign missions through two separate missionary societies.

Within six years of the founding of the Southern Baptist Convention,

[53] *Communion: or, the Distinction Between Christian and Church Fellowship* (n.p., n.d.), 8.

Landmarkism was seeking to define Baptist principles more precisely. At a meeting in Cotton Grove, Tennessee, in 1851, Landmarkism made its first formal stand by means of five questions presented by Graves. Implying a negative answer, the questions asked whether Baptists could properly recognize other denominations ("societies") as "the Church of Christ" or could officially acknowledge their ministers as gospel ministers by inviting them into Baptist pulpits.[54] Landmarkism, starting with the traditional Baptist emphasis on the local church, gave new significance to institutional aspects of the local congregation. A true church, wrote Graves, must be "a voluntary association"; it must have "no temporal head, as bishops, conferences, or Assemblies"; it must be "an executive body only"; it must have preserved "that form of doctrine, and the ordinances, once delivered"; it must "never have shed the blood of . . . human beings for conscience sake"; and one or more of such churches must have "existed from the days of the apostles until now." [55]

Landmarkism, along with its extremely "Low-Church" evangelical piety, thus claimed a "High-Church" apostolic succession of its own, not through a line of bishops, but through an unbroken succession of true "New Testament" churches from apostolic times to the present. Graves viewed this succession as outside of and paralleling medieval Catholicism, and was very critical of Protestants for deriving their heritage from Catholicism, an error which resulted in their retention of many Catholic corruptions and crippled their defense against Catholic expansion in contemporary America.[56]

Such sharpened emphasis on the true church necessarily raised questions about the ministry. Only one who had received true baptism from one who had himself been properly baptized could have a valid ministry. Questions of church and ministry led to refusal to exchange pulpits—"pulpit affiliation"—with those who baptized infants, pedobaptists. This issue was discussed in the Southern Baptist Convention for the first time in 1855. "Alien immersion"—that is, immersion by pedobaptists—was also rejected. The Landmarkers' great emphasis on the autonomy and discipline of the local church led them to the view that "the members of no one church have a right to come to the [Communion] table spread in another church, though of the same faith and order." [57] Jealousy for the local church caused Landmarkers to question the right of the mission boards to exercise centralized authority over mission churches. Again emphasizing the local church, Landmarkers thought that representation in the Southern Convention

[54] Text of the questions in William W. Barnes, *The Southern Baptist Convention, 1845–1953* (Nashville, 1954), 104.

[55] Graves, *Communion*, 7.

[56] Graves, *The Great Iron Wheel: or, Republicanism Backward, and Christianity Reversed* (Nashville, 1855), 253–61.

[57] Graves in *Tennessee Baptist*, Sept. 1, 1855, cited by Barnes, *The Southern Baptist Convention*, 107.

should be on the basis of local churches rather than on the basis of gifts to missions, a proposal which would greatly increase the organic unity of the denomination. A large group of Landmarkers withdrew from this Southern Baptist Convention in 1905, but their principles had a lasting influence on the parent body, greatly stimulating its denominational consciousness and commitment to Baptist principles.[58]

The movement received its name from a tract written by James M. Pendleton (1811–91) and published by Graves in 1854 under the title *An Old Landmark Reset.* Born in Virginia, Pendleton was pastor at Bowling Green, Kentucky, where he wrote this pamphlet. At the outbreak of the war, he left the South because of his antislavery and pro-Union views and served pastorates in Ohio and Pennsylvania. He did not develop Landmark principles as fully as did Graves, confining his attention mostly to opposing pulpit affiliation, as seen in the accompanying selection from *An Old Landmark Reset.*

DOCUMENT

The question, Ought Baptists to recognize Pedobaptist preachers as gospel ministers?—must receive either an affirmative or negative answer. It does not admit an ambiguous response. The truth is in the affirmation or negation. And the writer will aim to show that truth requires the question to be answered negatively. . . .

The unwarranted substitution of sprinkling for baptism of itself invalidates the claim of Pedobaptist Societies to be considered churches of Christ. But there is another fact which renders that claim utterly worthless. It is the element of infant membership in those societies. Why is the distinctive epithet Pedobaptist applied to them? Because they practice what is called infant baptism. They seem, in the judgment of Baptists, at least, to make a specific effort to subvert the foundation principles of New Testament church organization. They introduce unconscious infants into their churches falsely so called—thus practically superseding the necessity of personal repentance, faith and regeneration in order to membership. . . .

If Pedobaptists fail to exemplify the precepts of the New Testament in reference to the subjects and the action of baptism, they have no churches of Christ among them. They have their organizations, but they are not gospel organizations. It will be said that there are good, pious men among Pedobaptists. This is cheerfully conceded, but it proves nothing as to the evangelical nature of those organizations. There are good, pious men in Masonic Lodges, Bible Societies, Temperance Societies, and Colonization

[58] On Landmarkism, cf. also James E. Tull, "A Study of Southern Baptist Landmarkism in the Light of Historical Baptist Ecclesiology" (typed Ph.D. dissertation, Columbia University, 1960); Robert G. Torbet, "Landmarkism," in Winthrop S. Hudson, ed., *Baptist Concepts of the Church* (Phila., 1959), 170–95; John E. Steely, "The Landmark Movement in the Southern Baptist Convention," in Duke K. McCall, ed., *What Is the Church? A Symposium of Baptist Thought* (Nashville, 1958), 134–47.

Societies; but Masonic Lodges, Bible Societies, Temperance Societies and Colonization Societies are not churches of Christ. Nor are Pedobaptist Societies.

In this day of spurious liberality and false charity much is said about *evangelical* denominations and *evangelical* churches. What is an evangelical denomination? A denomination whose faith and practice correspond with the gospel. What is an evangelical church? A church formed according to the New Testament model. Pedobaptist denominations, therefore, are not evangelical. Pedobaptist churches, as they are called, are not evangelical. . . .

If Pedobaptist Societies are not churches of Christ, whence do their ministers derive their authority to preach? Is there any scriptural authority to preach which does not come through a church of Christ? And if Pedobaptist ministers are not in christian churches, have they any right to preach? That is to say, have they any authority *according to the gospel?* They are doubtless authorized by the forms and regulations of their respective societies. But do they act under evangelical authority? It is perfectly evident to the writer that they do not. . . .

Now, if Pedobaptist preachers do not belong to the church of Christ, they ought not to be recognized as ministers of Christ. But they are so recognized whenever Baptist ministers invite them to preach or exchange pulpits with them. . . .

We have reason "to thank God and take courage" that our number in the United States is nearly a million of members, and that it is constantly increasing. But would we not have been much more numerous than we are if we had had no more religious intercourse with Pedobaptists than in the days of persecution in Virginia and Massachusetts? There cannot be a rational doubt of it. All compromises with Pedobaptists have been disadvantageous to Baptists, and they will always be. These dishonorable compromises have ever involved an implied understanding that Baptists were not to preach the whole truth on the subject of baptism. Look for an illustration of this doctrine of compromises to a union protracted meeting. Different denominations combine their efforts. But it would be considered altogether out of place for any thing to be said about baptism. The teachings of the New Testament on this subject are held in abeyance. No man, it is true, can preach the whole gospel and leave baptism out; but in these Union Meetings it is thought best to leave it out for the sake of a harmonious co-operation. It is to be hoped that the day of these Union Meetings is passing away, never to return. It is time for it to be understood that Baptists and Pedobaptists cannot "walk together," because they are not "agreed." . . .

It is often said by Pedobaptists that Baptists act inconsistently in inviting *their* ministers to preach with them, while they fail to bid them welcome at the Lord's table. I acknowledge the inconsistency. It is a flagrant inconsistency. No one ought to deny it. . . .

Our refusal to commune with Pedobaptists grows out of the fact that they are unbaptized, and out of the church. We say they have no right to commune as unbaptized persons. Pedobaptists, however, have as much right to commune unbaptized as they have to preach unbaptized. That is to say, they have no right to do either. The Baptist argument on "Communion" possesses great power, but it is paralyzed whenever Pedobaptists can say, "You invite our ministers into your pulpits, but you do not invite us to commune with you." Let Baptists repudiate the inconsistency that most of them have been guilty of for half a century, and then their Defence of Close Communion will be perfectly triumphant. It will stand, a tower of strength, against which Pedobaptists will vainly turn their impotent artillery. . . .

And another thing follows: The official acts of Pedobaptist preachers have no validity in them. Their falsely so-called baptisms are a nullity—their ordinations are a nullity. Immersions administered by them ought to be repudiated by Baptists. How is it? Pedobaptist ministers are not in the visible kingdom of Christ. How then can they induct others into it by baptism? Can they introduce others where they have not gone themselves?

SOURCE: J. M. Pendleton, *An Old Landmark Reset* (Nashville, 1854), 4, 7–17.

116. The Syllabus of Errors

Roman Catholic political and cultural conservatism was vigorously championed by Pius IX (pope, 1846–78) in the Syllabus of Errors (1864). In his first two years Pius had seemed ready to go along with the rising tide of democratic liberalism that was sweeping across Europe. But in 1848 Italian nationalists, fighting to unite Italy, drove him from Rome, to which he was restored only by the French soldiers of Napoleon III. He now dedicated the remainder of his long papal reign to reasserting older Catholic political and cultural ideals. This seemed the more necessary in view of the fact that some within the church, especially in Germany, France, and Belgium, had embraced modern theological scholarship and democratic principles of government.

But the pope could count on a powerful Ultramontane party to support high views of papal authority and to suppress liberalism. For ten years the idea was being considered of a careful listing and condemning of the most dangerous errors of the day. Finally, on December 8, 1864, Pius issued an encyclical, *Quanta cura,* along with a Syllabus of Errors. The Syllabus under ten headings listed eighty errors in propositions excerpted from earlier deliverances of Pius. The Syllabus attacked some things like atheism, infidelity, and rationalism which all Christians reject, but it also condemned religious liberty, education by the state, civil marriage, the amenability of clergy to civil courts, and many other practices which lie at the foundation of modern democratic society. The last thesis repudiated the idea that "the Roman Pontiff can and should reconcile and adapt himself to progress, liberalism, and the modern civilization." The Syllabus sometimes had double negatives, because things listed as condemned were themselves negative. Presumably the pope had no expectation of strictly enforcing the theses of the Syllabus, but was rather raising a standard around which conservative forces could rally.[59]

The Syllabus created embarrassment for liberal Catholics in Europe and America. They sought to interpret the excerpts in relation to their original contexts and also to restrict the ideas as much as possible to the European political situation existing in 1864. Ultramontane conservatives, however, held out for a literal interpretation of the theses.[60] Sections V, VII, and X of the Syllabus are here reproduced in full.

DOCUMENT

§ V.

Errors concerning the Church and her rights.

19. The Church is not a true and perfect Society, entirely free; nor is she endowed with proper and perpetual rights of her own, conferred upon her by her Divine Founder; but it appertains to the civil power to define what are the rights of the Church, and the limits within which she may exercise those rights.

20. The ecclesiastical power ought not to exercise its authority without the permission and assent of the Civil Government.

21. The Church has not the power of defining dogmatically that the religion of the Catholic Church is the only true religion.

22. The obligation by which Catholic teachers and authors are strictly bound, is confined to those things only which are proposed to universal belief as dogmas of Faith by the infallible judgment of the Church.

23. Roman Pontiffs and Œcumenical Councils have wandered outside the limits of their powers, have usurped the rights of princes, and have even erred in defining matters of faith and morals.

24. The Church has not the power of using force, nor has she any temporal power, direct or indirect.

25. Beside the power inherent in the Episcopate, other temporal power has been attributed to it by the civil authority, granted either expressly or tacitly, which on that account is revocable by the civil authority whenever it thinks fit.

---

[59] J. B. Bury, *History of the Papacy in the 19th Century (1864–1878)*, ed. R. H. Murray (London, 1930), 43.

[60] Cf. James H. Nichols, *History of Christianity, 1650–1950: Secularization of the West* (N.Y., 1956), 209–16; Fredrik Nielsen, *The History of the Papacy in the XIXth Century*, II (London, 1906), 258–70; James MacCaffrey, *History of the Catholic Church in the Nineteenth Century (1789–1908)*, I (Dublin, 1910), 438–41.

26. The Church has no innate and legitimate right of acquiring and possessing property.

27. The sacred ministers of the Church and the Roman Pontiff are to be absolutely excluded from every charge and dominion over temporal affairs.

28. It is not lawful for bishops to publish even Letters Apostolic without the permission of Government.

29. Favours granted by the Roman Pontiff ought to be considered null, unless they have been sought for through the civil government.

30. The immunity of the Church and of ecclesiastical persons derived its origin from civil law.

31. The ecclesiastical Forum or tribunal for the temporal causes, whether civil or criminal, of clerics, ought by all means to be abolished, even without consulting and against the protest of, the Holy See.

32. The personal immunity by which clerics are exonerated from Military Conscription and service in the Army may be abolished without violation either of natural right or of equity. Its abolition is called for by civil progress, especially in a society framed on the model of a liberal government.

33. It does not appertain exclusively to the power of ecclesiastical jurisdiction by right, proper and innate, to direct the teaching of theological questions.

34. The teaching of those who compare the Sovereign Pontiff to a Prince, free, and acting in the universal Church, is a doctrine which prevailed in the middle ages.

35. There is nothing to prevent the decree of a General Council, or the act of all peoples, from transferring the Supreme Pontificate from the Bishop and City of Rome to another bishop and another city.

36. The definition of a National Council does not admit of any subsequent discussion, and the civil authority can assume this principle as the basis of its acts.

37. National Churches, withdrawn from the authority of the Roman Pontiff and altogether separated, can be established.

38. The Roman Pontiffs have, by their too arbitrary conduct, contributed to the division of the Church into Eastern and Western.

§ VII.

Errors concerning Natural and Christian Ethics.

56. Moral laws do not stand in need of the Divine sanction, and it is not at all necessary that human laws should be made conformable to the laws of nature, and receive their power of binding from God.

57. The science of philosophical things and morals, and also civil laws,

may and ought to keep aloof from Divine and ecclesiastical authority.

58. No other forces are to be recognized except those which reside in matter, and all the rectitude and excellence of morality ought to be placed in the accumulation and increase of riches by every possible means, and the gratification of pleasure.

59. Right consists in the material fact. All human duties are an empty word, and all human facts have the force of right.

60. Authority is nothing else but numbers and the sum total of material forces.

61. The injustice of an act when successful, inflicts no injury upon the sanctity of right.

62. The principle of non-intervention, as it is called, ought to be proclaimed and observed.

63. It is lawful to refuse obedience to legitimate princes, and even to rebel against them.

64. The violation of any solemn oath, as well as any wicked and flagitious action repugnant to the eternal law, is not only not blameable, but is altogether lawful and worthy of the highest praise, when done through love of country.

§ X.

Errors having reference to Modern Liberalism.

77. In the present day it is no longer expedient that the Catholic religion should be held as the only religion of the State, to the exclusion of all other forms of worship.

78. Hence it has been wisely provided by law, in some Catholic countries, that persons coming to reside therein shall enjoy the public exercise of their own peculiar worship.

79. Moreover it is false that the civil liberty of every form of worship, and the full power, given to all, of overtly and publicly manifesting any opinions whatsoever and thoughts, conduce more easily to corrupt the morals and minds of the people, and to propagate the pest of indifferentism.

80. The Roman Pontiff can, and ought, to reconcile himself, and come to terms with progress, liberalism, and modern civilization.

SOURCE: *The Syllabus for the People: A Review of the Propositions Condemned by His Holiness Pope Pius IX with Text of the Condemned List.* By a Monk of St. Augustine's, Ramsgate (N.Y., 1875), 13–5, 19–20, 22–3. (References to the various previous Acts of Pius IX from which the respective articles of the Syllabus were excerpted have been omitted in the present reproduction.)

LITERATURE

The importance of this period as a formative one for the American churches is suggested by Richard C. Wolf, "The Middle Period, 1800-1870, The Matrix of Modern American Christianity," *Religion in Life*, XXII (1952-53), 72-84; Sidney E. Mead, "Denominationalism: The Shape of Protestantism in America," *Church History*, XXIII (1954), 291-320; and Martha L. Edwards, "Religious Forces in the United States, 1815-1830," *Mississippi Valley Historical Review*, V (1919), 434-49. The increased social mobility which underlay the churchly reaction is discussed by Rowland Berthoff, "The American Social Order: A Conservative Hypothesis," *American Historical Review*, LXV (1960), 495-514. John R. Bodo, *The Protestant Clergy and Public Issues, 1812-1848* (Princeton, 1954) is particularly concerned with "theocratic" traditions; and Wilson Smith, *Professors & Public Ethics: Studies of Northern Moral Philosophers before the Civil War* (Ithaca, N.Y., 1956), deals with types of social ethics, some of them rooted in right-wing Protestantism. William W. Sweet, *Religion in the Development of American Culture, 1765-1840* (N.Y., 1952), has much information on denominationalism in the early part of the period. Illuminating contemporary comment will be found in Philip Schaff's *America: A Sketch of Its Political, Social and Religious Character*, ed. Perry Miller (Cambridge, Mass., 1961).

George E. DeMille, *The Catholic Movement in the American Episcopal Church* (rev. ed., Phila., 1950), deals with the Episcopal High Church movement, as does also E. Clowes Chorley, *Men and Movements in the American Episcopal Church* (N.Y., 1946), 133-283, 315-92, while William W. Manross, *A History of the American Episcopal Church* (N.Y., 1935), supplies useful denominational context. Samuel Wilberforce, the English bishop, was sharply critical of unchurchly tendencies among American Episcopalians in *A History of the Protestant Episcopal Church in America* (London, 1844; N.Y., 1849). A lengthy biography of Hobart and his published works are available: John McVickar, *The Early Life and Professional Years of Bishop Hobart* (Oxford, England, 1838); *The Posthumous Works of the Late Rt. Rev. John Henry Hobart, with a Memoir of his Life by the Rev. William Berrian, D.D.* (3 vols., N.Y., 1832-33); *The Correspondence of John Henry Hobart* (6 vols., N.Y., 1911-12). Many of Hobart's most important addresses and pastoral letters were published at the time in pamphlet form.

Perhaps the best introduction to Mormonism is Thomas F. O'Dea, *The Mormons* (Chicago, 1957). With careful scholarship and fairness of spirit the author discusses Mormon sacred writings, history, beliefs, organization, and relation to the surrounding society and culture. Compact and informing is Charles S. Braden, *These Also Believe: A Study of Modern American Cults & Minority Religious Movements* (N.Y., 1950), 421-52. Whitney R. Cross, *The Burned-over District: The Social and Intellectual History of Enthusiastic Religion in Western New York, 1800-1850* (Ithaca, N.Y., 1950), 138-50, offers suggestive comments on the origins of Mormonism. Ray B. West, *Kingdom of the Saints: the Story of Brigham Young and the Mormons* (N.Y., 1957), 365-71, contains a helpful bibliography. Colorful representative documents are to be found in William Mulder and A. Russell Mortensen, eds., *Among the Mormons: Historic*

Accounts by Contemporary Observers (N.Y., 1958). Mormon modernists, Austin and Alta Fife, treat Mormon legends poetically in *Saints of Sage and Saddle: Folklore among the Mormons* (Bloomington, Ind., 1956). The New York State origin of the Book of Mormon was established by Walter F. Prince, "Psychological Tests for the Authorship of the Book of Mormon," *American Journal of Psychology,* XXVII (1917), 373–95. Theocratic aspects of Mormonism are dealt with in Leonard J. Arrington, *Great Basin Kingdom: An Economic History of the Latter-Day Saints, 1830–1900* (Cambridge, Mass., 1958), and in Norman F. Furniss, *The Morman Conflict, 1850–1859* (New Haven, 1960). The best biography of Joseph Smith is Fawn Brodie, *No Man Knows My History: the Life of Joseph Smith, the Mormon Prophet* (N.Y., 1946). Donald D. Egbert and Stow Persons, eds., *Socialism and American Life,* II (Princeton, 1952), 121–4, provide a bibliography of Mormon communitarianism. Numerous doctoral dissertations on economic and sociological aspects of Mormonism have appeared in recent years.

Maurice W. Armstrong, Lefferts A. Loetscher, and Charles A. Anderson, *The Presbyterian Enterprise: Sources of American Presbyterian History* (Phila., 1956), 146–71, provide documents and editorial comment on the Presbyterian Old School-New School controversy. Older comprehensive histories treating the Presbyterian disruption are E. H. Gillett, *History of the Presbyterian Church in the United States of America,* II (rev. ed., Phila., 1864), 443–574, and Robert E. Thompson, *A History of the Presbyterian Church in the United States* (N.Y., 1895), 102–49. Lewis Cheeseman, *Differences between Old and New School Presbyterians* (Rochester, N.Y., 1848), is written from the Old School viewpoint, while Zebulon Crocker, *The Catastrophe of the Presbyterian Church in 1837* (New Haven, 1838) and George Duffield, "Doctrines of the New-School Presbyterian Church," *Bibliotheca Sacra and Biblical Repository,* XX (1863), 561–635, represent the New School viewpoint. Issues of the *Biblical Repertory,* especially for the years 1836–38, set forth the Old School doctrine of the church. The Joshua L. Wilson Papers are in the Library of the University of Chicago. Calvin Colton, *Protestant Jesuitism* (N.Y., 1837), is a poorly written but suggestive "churchly" criticism of the voluntary societies by a Presbyterian who became an Episcopalian.

A perceptive study of the Mercersburg movement is James H. Nichols, *Romanticism in American Theology: Nevin and Schaff at Mercersburg* (Chicago, 1961). Three writings by George W. Richards shed much light on the Mercersburg movement: "The Mercersburg Theology Historically Considered," *Papers of the American Society of Church History,* 2nd Series, III (1912), 119–49; "The Mercersburg Theology—Its Purpose and Principles," *Church History,* XX (1951), 42–55; and *History of the Theological Seminary of the Reformed Church in the United States, 1825–1934, Evangelical and Reformed Church, 1934–1952* (Lancaster, Pa., 1952), 225–93. A recent treatment is by Kenneth M. Plummer, "The Theology of John Williamson Nevin in the Mercersburg Period, 1840–1852" (Chicago, Department of Photoduplication, University of Chicago Library, 1958). Luther J. Binkley, *The Mercersburg Theology* (Manheim, Pa., 1953), offers a sketch of the movement. There are biographies of the three principal figures in the movement: Howard J. B. Ziegler, *Frederick Augustus Rauch: American Hegelian* (Lancaster, Pa., 1953); Theodore Appel, *The Life and Work of John Williamson Nevin* (Phila., 1889); David S. Schaff, *The Life of Philip Schaff* (N.Y., 1897). Philip Schaff, *The Principle of Protestantism* (Chambersburg, Pa., 1845), was a masterful attack on pietism and rationalism based on an organic historical conception of the universal Christian church.

The confessional revival in Lutheranism is interpreted unfavorably by Vergilius Ferm, *The Crisis in American Lutheran Theology: A Study of the Issue between American Lutheranism and Old Lutheranism* (N.Y., 1927) and by Carl Mauelshagen, *American Lutheranism Surrenders to Forces of Conservatism* (Athens, Ga., 1936); and is interpreted favorably by J. A. Brown, *The New Theology: Its Abettors and Defenders* (Phila., 1857) and Frederick Bente, *American Lutheranism* (2 vols., St. Louis, 1919). Articles in the *Evangelical Review,* which was founded in 1849, championed confessionalism. Bibliographical data on Charles Philip Krauth will be found in the biography of his son, *Charles Porterfield Krauth* (2 vols., N.Y., 1898–1909), by Adolph Spaeth, and in Abdel R. Wentz, *History of the Gettysburg Theological Seminary* (Phila., 1926). *The Life and Times of Rev. S. S. Schmucker, D.D.* (York, Pa., 1896) should also be consulted. Informing general histories of American Lutheranism are Abdel R. Wentz, *A Basic History of Lutheranism in America* (Phila., 1955), and J. L. Neve, *History of the Lutheran Church in America* (Burlington, Ia., 1934).

On Roman Catholicism, two general works by John T. Ellis are valuable: *Documents of American Catholic History* (Milwaukee, 1956), and *American Catholicism* (Chicago, 1956). Thomas T. McAvoy discusses "The Formation of the Catholic Minority in the United States, 1820–1860," *Review of Politics,* X (1948), 13–34. Two studies by Peter Guilday deal with activities of the hierarchy: *The National Pastorals of the American Hierarchy* (1792–1919) (Washington, 1923), and *History of the Councils of Baltimore, 1791–1884* (N.Y., 1932). "Trusteeism in Philadelphia and New York" is discussed by Peter Guilday in *Historical Records and Studies,* XVIII (1928), 7–74. The work of the Leopoldine Society is summarized in Benjamin J. Blied, *Austrian Aid to American Catholics, 1830–1860* (Milwaukee, 1944). *The Works of the Right Reverend John England* have been edited by Sebastian Messmer *et al.* (7 vols., Cleveland, 1908), and *The Life and Times of John England* has been presented by Peter Guilday (2 vols., N.Y., 1927). Catholic parochial schools before and after 1840, respectively, are treated in two volumes by James A. Burns: *The Catholic School System in the United States* (N.Y., 1908), and *The Growth and Development of the Catholic School System in the United States* (N.Y., 1912). Bishop Kenrick's life can be studied in Hugh Joseph Nolan, *The Most Rev. Francis Patrick Kenrick, Third Bishop of Philadelphia, 1830–1851* (Washington, 1948), and in *The Kenrick-Frenaye Correspondence,* ed. Francis E. Tourscher (Phila., 1920). Light is cast on Bishop McQuaid by Frederick J. Zwierlein, "Bishop McQuaid of Rochester," *Catholic Historical Review,* V (1919–20), 42–54, 311–52, and *Letters of Archbishop Corrigan to Bishop McQuaid, and Allied Documents* (Rochester, N.Y., 1946).

CHAPTER XIV

The Transcendental Pattern of Religious Liberalism

WHAT seems liberal to one generation often appears conservative to the next. This difference in perspective was strikingly illustrated in the early theological thought of Unitarianism. The American Unitarian movement had emerged from within New England Congregationalism in the early years of the nineteenth century under the leadership of ministers who were markedly liberal for their day.[1] Yet even before most of those pioneers had passed from the stage of action, they became targets of criticism within their own communion. Their critics were a small group of younger churchmen who had become dissatisfied with what they regarded as an outmoded type of liberalism. Thus they sometimes called themselves "the new school," or "the movement party," terms which clearly implied the static outlook of their elder brethren. These new theological rebels were, in return, dubbed "transcendentalists"; and that tongue-twisting epithet, though disliked, could not be shaken off.

The rise of a more radical liberalism was foreshadowed in a letter written by young Ralph Waldo Emerson to his former Harvard College classmate, John Boynton Hill. "When I have been to Cambridge and studied Divinity," he wrote in January of 1823, "I will tell you whether I can make out for myself any better system than Luther or Calvin, or the *liberal besoms* of modern days. I have spoken thus because I am tired and disgusted with the preaching which I have been accustomed to hear."[2] One would like to know when Emerson first began to question the views of these old-line liberals. It could have been during his undergraduate years, for he was then studying Scottish thinkers, especially Dugald Stewart, who impressed him with the value of the "moral sense" as an intuitional faculty.[3] About the same time he was also reading Richard Price, who likewise led him to ponder the adequacy of Locke's epistemology. In March of 1821 he made a

---

[1] *American Christianity*, I, 481–5, 493–507.

[2] Letter to John Boynton Hill, Jan. 2, 1823, in Ralph L. Rusk, ed., *Letters of Ralph Waldo Emerson* (6 vols., N.Y., 1939), I, 128. Italics in original. Emerson's criticism evidently did not apply to William Ellery Channing, since in Oct. of 1823 he wrote to his Aunt Mary Moody Emerson, saying, "Dr. Channing is preaching sublime sermons every Sunday morning in Federal Street." James E. Cabot, *A Memoir of Ralph Waldo Emerson* (2 vols., Boston, 1887), I, 105.

[3] Merrell R. Davis, "Emerson's 'Reason' and the Scottish Philosophers," *New England Quarterly*, XVII (1944), 209–28. See also Edgeley W. Todd, "Philosophical Ideas at Harvard College, 1817–1837," *New England Quarterly*, XVI (1943), 63–90.

very significant entry in his *Journal:* "Price says that right and wrong are not determined by any reasoning or deduction, but by the ultimate perception of the human mind." [4]

When, in February of 1825, Emerson entered the Divinity School, he found it theologically dominated by two distinguished "liberal besoms": Henry Ware, Sr. (1764–1845), Hollis Professor of Divinity, and Andrews Norton (1786–1853), Dexter Professor of Sacred Literature. Owing to poor health, he never finished the required work for a degree; but even if he had taken every course in the curriculum, his nascent heresy would not have been encouraged, since the faculty was well satisfied with the traditional tenets of rational Christianity.

Nevertheless, young Emerson persisted in his quest for what he regarded as a more vital faith than that of the "liberal besoms." Fortunately he has left us a record of the transcendental cast of his mind when he embarked upon his vocational career. In October of 1826 he went before the Middlesex Association of Ministers with the request that he be formally approbated or licensed to preach the gospel. Following the practice of all candidates, he preached a trial sermon on that occasion, using as his text St. Paul's exhortation, "Pray without ceasing" (I Thess. 5:17).[5] The general introduction is especially significant in that it adumbrated two basic philosophic ideas which were to characterize Emerson's mature religious thought: (1) the primacy of spirit over matter, and (2) the immediacy of God to the human soul. These ideas were at first nourished on Platonic and Neo-Platonic thought, but in later years they were reinforced or modified by other influences, notably by German idealism as mediated through Carlyle and Coleridge.[6]

Although Emerson pioneered in the new religious liberalism, other young churchmen soon emerged with a similar interest, including William H. Furness (1802–96), George Ripley (1803–80), Orestes A. Brownson (1803–76), Frederic Henry Hedge (1805–90), James Freeman Clarke (1810–88), Theodore Parker (1810–60),[7] and William Henry Channing (1810–84),[8] all of whom, except Brownson, had grown up under Unitarian influence and had attended both Harvard College and its Divinity School.

[4] Edward Waldo Emerson and Waldo Emerson Forbes, eds., *The Journals of Ralph Waldo Emerson* (10 vols., Boston, 1909–14), I (March 14, 1821), 78. See also Alexander Kern, "The Rise of Transcendentalism, 1815–1860," in Harry Hayden Clark, ed., *Transitions in American Literary History* (Durham, N.C., 1953), 264–6.

[5] For the full text of the sermon, see Arthur C. McGiffert, Jr., ed., *Young Emerson Speaks* (Boston, 1938), 1–21.

[6] Henry A. Pochmann, *German Culture in America: Philosophical and Literary Influences, 1600–1900* (Madison, Wis., 1957), 153–207.

[7] John Edward Dirks has argued that Parker was not a transcendentalist (*The Critical Theology of Theodore Parker* [N.Y., 1948], 136); but for an opposite view, see H. Shelton Smith, "Was Theodore Parker a Transcendentalist?" *New England Quarterly*, XXXIII (1950), 351–64.

[8] For a comprehensive list of transcendentalists, see Kern, "The Rise of Transcendentalism," in Clark, ed., *Transitions in American Literary History*, 249.

When they began their pastoral ministry, most of them were already budding transcendentalists. Almost to a man they then took a dim view of Lockean philosophy, to which older Unitarianism was committed, because they had discovered in Coleridge, among others, hints of something better than Locke. Clarke's pilgrimage may be regarded as somewhat typical of that of the whole clan. While a senior in college he read Coleridge's *Aids to Reflection* (in the Marsh edition of 1829) and found that he "was born a transcendentalist." [9]

Much research has been undertaken to identify and evaluate the philosophical and theological influences which helped to shape the new-school mind. This has not been easy, for, as René Wellek observed, the transcendentalists gathered suggestions from "almost the whole intellectual history of mankind." [10] Nevertheless, the general idealistic tradition—Platonic, Neo-Platonic, Kantian, and post-Kantian—furnished the main stimulus to their thinking. [11] Even more narrowly, German idealism directly or indirectly provided the preponderant impact. There is therefore much evidence to support Henry D. Gray's thesis that transcendentalism "was produced by the deliberate importing of certain imperfectly understood elements of German idealism into American Unitarianism." [12] In their religious thought, the leading new-school divines were surely more inspired by German biblical and theological liberalism than by any other single tradition. Churchmen like Clarke, Ripley, Hedge, and Parker were thoroughly familiar with Schleiermacher and kindred German theologians, and they frequently reviewed German treatises in the *Christian Examiner* and other journals. Their chief interest in men like Coleridge and Cousin lay in the fact that they were mediators of important elements of German philosophy and theology.

When these young anti-Lockean liberals became aggressive in propagating their views, Norton and other old-line Unitarians openly charged them with infidelity. Emerson, Ripley, and Parker became special targets of criticism. Since these historic episodes need no reiteration here, [13] the present chapter will focus its attention on the theological and ethical patterns which characterized transcendental thought. In the beginning it is doubtless well to observe that the transcendentalists, like many other groups,

[9] Edward Everett Hale, ed., *James Freeman Clarke: Autobiography, Diary and Correspondence* (Boston, 1891), 39. The thing that most impressed Clarke was Coleridge's distinction between the Reason and the Understanding.

[10] "The Minor Transcendentalists and German Philosophy," *New England Quarterly,* XV (1942), 661–2.

[11] Kern, "The Rise of Transcendentalism, 1815–1860," in Clark, ed., *Transitions in American Literary History,* 270–5; Pochmann, *German Culture in America,* 153–242.

[12] *Emerson: A Statement of New England Transcendentalism as Expressed in the Philosophy of its Chief Exponent* (Palo Alto, Calif., 1917), 14.

[13] The basic documents are available in Perry Miller, *The Transcendentalists: An Anthology* (Cambridge, Mass., 1950). For an authoritative general treatment of the religious aspects of transcendentalism, see William R. Hutchison, *The Transcendentalist Ministers: Church Reform in the New England Renaissance* (New Haven, 1959).

contained within their ranks radicals like Parker and conservatives like Clarke, with Ripley and others occupying a more or less intermediate position. Though alike in much of their religious thought, they nonetheless diverged at significant points.

We may, then, begin with theology's supreme question: what is the nature of ultimate Reality? Emerson gave the lead answer in his Middlesex sermon when he observed that while man belongs to two worlds, the world of matter and the world of spirit, the latter "is more certain and stable than the material universe." When man's intellect is invigorated, said he, nature seems at times "to ebb from him, like a sea, and leave nothing permanent but thought." [14] The same idea appeared ten years later in *Nature* (1836), where the world of matter was viewed as "a perpetual effect" of spirit. In his "The American Scholar" (1837) he called nature the "web of God." Parker attached more stability to the world of nature than did the early Emerson, but he also grounded the whole created order in Cosmic Mind or Spirit. Thus what he called "natural religion" must not be confused with modern brands of naturalistic or nontheistic religion. Similarly all the other transcendentalist ministers, including Ripley, Clarke, and Hedge, held to an idealistic metaphysics which rooted the created world in Spirit.

When it came to defining the nature of the Divine Spirit, the transcendentalists were often vague. Nor did they agree in their definitions. During his ministry at Second Church in Boston (1829–32), Emerson may have held to the personality of God,[15] but certainly his religious thought in later years was essentially pantheistic.[16] Parker considered it fruitless to speculate as to whether God was personal or impersonal; [17] nonetheless, his theological thought as a whole indicates that he held to a personalistic theism. Hedge is not easily placed, and yet there is much in his major theological treatise that at least borders on pantheism.[18] James Freeman Clarke, on the other hand, held firmly to the personal being of God, and he explicitly repudiated pantheism.[19] Ripley, at least while he remained in the ministry, likewise held to the personality of the Deity.[20]

In their interpretation of the nature of God, the transcendentalists agreed with traditional Unitarianism in two basic respects. First, they uniformly affirmed the oneness of God and opposed trinitarianism. When men like Clarke and Hedge used the terms Father, Son, and Holy Ghost, they did not thereby signify their belief in an ontological trinity. Second, transcendentalists strongly accented the benevolent character of God. Especially

[14] McGiffert, ed., *Young Emerson Speaks*, 1–2.   [15] *Ibid.*, xxxiii.
[16] Gray, *Emerson*, 67.
[17] *A Discourse of Matters Pertaining to Religion*, ed. Thomas W. Higginson (Boston, 1907), 141–50.
[18] *Reason in Religion* (Boston, 1865), 71–82.
[19] "A True Theology the Basis of Human Progress," in Henry W. Bellows, et al., *Christianity and Modern Thought* (Boston, 1873), 41–2.
[20] *Discourses on the Philosophy of Religion* (Boston, 1836).

dear to Parker was his doctrine of "the infinite perfection of God," a doctrine which constituted "the corner-stone" of his theological structure.[21] Of all the divine attributes, the "all-lovingness" of God seemed to impress Parker most; and to bring out the full tenderness of that attribute, he often referred to God as "Mother." [22]

The God of the transcendentalist sustained an intimate relation to the world of nature and of man. The new-school divines generally predicated a God who, as Creator, transcended the phenomenal order, but they were more concerned with a God who immanently vitalized the whole cosmos, and especially the human soul. This concern is evident in all of Emerson's ethical and religious thought. In 1830 he declared, "God is the substratum of all souls." [23] Returning to this idea a little later, he observed that "the soul is the kingdom of God: the abode of love, of truth, of virtue." [24] During this period Emerson was preaching sermons at Second Church in which he often developed the same theme.[25] Thus long before he published his classic essays, "Self-Reliance" and "The Over-Soul," Emerson had fully accepted the doctrine of divine immanence. That doctrine was no less basic in Parker's theological thought, and he expounded it in numerous books and sermons.[26] The less radical transcendentalists, such as Frederic Henry Hedge, also held that doctrine in high esteem.[27]

The idea of divine immanence underlay some of the transcendentalist's most fundamental theological conclusions. For one thing, it led him to deny the sharp antithesis which the old-line Unitarians drew between the natural and supernatural. Thus Emerson and Parker rejected the interventionist theory of miracle for which Andrews Norton so strenuously contended in the 1830's. As Parker put it, "God, ever present, never intervenes; acting ever by law a miracle becomes needless, and also impossible." [28] In the second place, belief in an immanent God prompted the transcendentalist to erase the old distinction between natural and revealed religion, a distinction so dear to the heart of Henry Ware, Sr., and other Paleyans at Harvard. "There is no difference but of words," said Parker, "between *revealed* religion and *natural* religion, for all actual religion is revealed in us, or it could not be felt, and all revealed religion is natural or it would be of no use to us." [29] Similarly Hedge disavowed the validity of the distinction,

---

[21] Parker, "Experience as a Minister," in Rufus Leighton, ed., *Autobiography, Poems and Prayers* (Boston, 1911), 330.
[22] *Ibid.*, 57, 59, 430–1.   [23] *Journals*, II (Dec. 10, 1830), 323.
[24] *Journals*, II (March 13, 1831), 361.
[25] McGiffert, ed., *Young Emerson Speaks*, 99–111, 180–90.
[26] See, for example, *A Discourse of Matters Pertaining to Religion*, 151–6; *The World of Matter and the Spirit of Man*, ed. George W. Cooke (Boston, 1907), 250–85.
[27] *Reason in Religion*, 77–82.
[28] "God's Revelation in Matter and Mind," in George W. Cooke, ed., *The World of Matter and the Spirit of Man*, 305. See also W. H. Furness, *Jesus and His Biographers; or the Remarks on the Four Gospels* (rev. ed., Phila., 1838), 237–314.
[29] *A Discourse of Matters Pertaining to Religion*, 32.

contending that all religion involved revelation and that also all religion was natural to human nature.[30] In the third place, belief in divine immanence led the transcendentalist to abandon the sharp antithesis between Christianity and the ethnic religions. Since the same God had been actively disclosing himself to some degree in all religious traditions, the non-Christian faiths could not be regarded as entirely erroneous. Hence, it was only logical that the transcendentalists should have been the chief American pioneers in exhibiting the positive values of Oriental religion.

The new-school theologians also fashioned a distinctive doctrine of man. Fundamental with the whole group was a belief in man's native capacity to apprehend spiritual truth directly in terms of perceptive intuition. They became literally infatuated with a distinction which Coleridge had made between the role of the Understanding and that of the Reason. The Understanding, they argued, was dependable in sensory perception, but only by the Reason could one perceive supersensory realities. Thus while acknowledging value in the Lockean epistemology, which derived all knowledge from sense data, the new-school churchmen insisted that if the theologian depended upon "sensational" epistemology alone he would be logically doomed to religious skepticism.

As an alternative to ultimate skepticism, the transcendentalist fervently embraced the intuitionist doctrine. Theodore Parker is a good illustration of its saving potency. While attending Harvard Divinity School (1834–36), he sank into deep despair mainly because he had lost faith in the reliability of the Bible and could not trust Lockean philosophy to "legitimate" his "religious instincts." He finally rescued himself, as he later testified, only by becoming convinced of a threefold intuition: the intuition of God, of the moral law, and of immortality.[31]

These three "primal intuitions" undergirded all of Parker's preaching and writing. Although he constantly appealed to natural phenomena and to history in confirmation of his intuitions, he always insisted that without an antecedent intuitive perception one could never really prove the existence of God. It was upon this basis that Parker and the other new-school theologians downgraded the value of Paley's design argument for the existence of God. Hedge, for example, explicitly rejected that argument, holding that it was "worthless" as a positive proof of the existence of God. "It only proves, that if there be a God, and that God the maker of the world, he has wrought with consummate skill." [32] According to Hedge, the only real proof of God is "our own consciousness, our moral instincts." [33]

---

[30] "Natural Religion," *Christian Examiner*, LII (1852), 118–23.

[31] *Autobiography, Poems and Prayers*, 301–2. In achieving his intuitive faith, Parker said that he "found most help in the works of Immanuel Kant." That help must have been indirect, since God, freedom, and immortality were for Kant postulates of the practical reason, not realities of cognitive verification. Parker doubtless received more direct guidance from Coleridge, and especially from Cousin.

[32] "Natural Religion," *Christian Examiner*, LII (1852), 130.   [33] *Ibid.*, 133.

This faith in the virtual infallibility of human intuition was the feature which gave the transcendentalists their distinctive name. "These are called Transcendentalists," said George Ripley in 1840, "because they believe in an order of truths which transcends the sphere of the external senses." [34] Transcendentalists, he then observed, "maintain that the truth of religion does not depend on tradition, nor historical facts, but has an unerring witness in the soul." [35] Taking direct issue with Andrews Norton, who had denied the possibility of an intuitive perception of the truth of Christianity,[36] Orestes Brownson rejoined, "We may know that God exists as positively, as certainly, as we may know that we feel hunger and thirst, joy and grief." [37]

Owing to their complete confidence in the intuitive capacity of the soul, the left-wing transcendentalists refused to bow to any external authority, be it church, book, or person. Theodore Parker, who was noted for his candor, declared, "I take not the Bible for my Master, nor yet the Church; nor even Jesus of Nazareth for my master." [38] In his Divinity School Address, Emerson was no less radical. He rejected not only the external evidence of miracle; he also denied the final authority of Jesus, an authority which Norton had endeavored to defend by appealing to miracle. "The soul knows no persons," blurted out Emerson.

Only the ultraistic believers in the soul, however, went along with Emerson and Parker at this point. Moderates like Clarke and Hedge certainly placed a much higher value upon Jesus, the church, and the Scriptures; and their appreciation of historical Christianity apparently grew in their later ministry.[39] At no time did they fall into the kind of *"ego-theism"* that William Ellery Channing feared.[40]

Along with their abounding faith in human intuition, the new liberals also entertained a high opinion of man's moral estate and potentiality. In this respect they resembled the older Unitarians, most of whom had emphasized the essential divinity of man in contrast to the Calvinist doctrine of human depravity.[41] The new-school leaders, however, carried this tendency much farther than was acceptable to Unitarian conservatives like Nathaniel L. Frothingham, minister at First Church in Boston. In a doctrinal sermon

[34] Quoted in O. B. Frothingham, *George Ripley* (Boston, 1882), 84. See also Cyrus A. Bartol, *Radical Problems* (3rd ed., Boston, 1873), 84.

[35] Quoted in Frothingham, *George Ripley,* 84–5.

[36] "A Discourse on the Latest Form of Infidelity," in Perry Miller, *The Transcendentalists,* 211–2.

[37] "Two Articles from the Princeton Review," *Boston Quarterly Review,* III (1840), 275.

[38] *Autobiography, Poems and Prayers,* 62.

[39] Clarke, *Theodore Parker, and His Theology: A Discourse Delivered in the Music Hall, Boston, Sunday, Sept. 25, 1859* (Boston, 1859); Hedge, "Antisupernaturalism in the Pulpit: An Address Delivered to the Graduating Class of the Divinity School, Cambridge, July 17, 1864," *Christian Examiner,* LXXVII (1864), 145–59.

[40] Elizabeth Peabody, *Reminiscences of William Ellery Channing* (Boston, 1880), 365.

[41] H. Shelton Smith, *Changing Conceptions of Original Sin: A Study in American Theology Since 1750* (N.Y., 1955), Chap. 4.

of 1843, entitled "The Believer's Rest," Frothingham warned: "The present era seems to be that of the apotheosis of human nature. Human nature is exalted into the 'heavenly places' to acknowledge nothing above its own height. Man, who started into his first deviation from the truth by the worship of the surrounding universe, appears approaching, as his last delusion, to the worship of himself. Ah, poor worm!" [42]

Nothing provoked Theodore Parker to sharper invective than this "poor worm" view of human nature. Though he fought wickedness in every form, especially slavery, he held a philosophy of history which postulated the ephemeral character of evil. Said he: "All the evil of the world is something incident to man's development, and no more permanent than the stumbling of a child who learns to walk. . . . It will be outgrown, and not a particle of it or its consequences shall cleave permanent[ly] to mankind. This is true of the individual wrongs which you and I commit; and likewise of such vast wickedness as war, political oppression, and the hypocrisy of priesthoods." [43]

James Freeman Clarke, however, did not share Parker's sunny view of human nature. During Parker's terminal illness, Clarke preached a sermon at the Music Hall in which he frankly exposed his friend's theological shortcomings. Parker, he contended, did not take the full dimension of sin in that he viewed it as merely ignorance, weakness, or wilfulness. "But sin as disease,—this profound depravity which has taken hold of the soul itself; . . . of this experience I see no recognition in his writings." [44] Elaborating his own view of sin a few years later, Clarke conceded that orthodoxy was "substantially right in its views of sin as being a deep and radical disease," a disease which had been transmitted by natural descent since the time of "the historical Adam." [45] Yet it must be said that Clarke also held an optimistic view of history which tended to cancel his seemingly realistic conception of sin.[46]

The transcendentalist's view of human nature necessarily affected his doctrine of salvation. According to Theodore Parker, "Religion will not be a regeneration, being born again, a change of nature, . . . but a development of nature, what the blossom is to the bud, what growth to manhood or womanhood is to girl or boy." [47] Hedge reached a similar conclusion. Holding that the work of nature and the work of grace were one and the

[42] Quoted in O. B. Frothingham, *Boston Unitarianism, 1820–1850: A Study of the Life and Work of Nathaniel Langdon Frothingham* (Boston, 1890), 44–5. Cf. a similar view of human nature in Orville Dewey, "The Unitarian Belief," *Works* (3 vols., N.Y., 1848–52), III, 16–9.

[43] "The Natural and Philosophical Idea of God," in George W. Cooke, ed., *The World of Matter and the Spirit of Man*, 162.

[44] *Theodore Parker, and His Theology*, 18.

[45] *Orthodoxy: Its Truths and Errors* (Boston, 1866), 134.

[46] Cf. Arthur S. Bolster, Jr., *James Freeman Clarke: Disciple of Advancing Truth* (Boston, 1954), 352–3.

[47] "False and True Theology," in George W. Cooke, ed., *The Transient and Permanent in Christianity* (Boston, 1908), 359.

same, he declared: "The operation of God's spirit in the regeneration of a human heart but unfolds a life-germ inborn in the heart, and is therefore a natural process, as much as the growth of an apple or an apple-tree." [48] George Ripley likened regeneration of the soul to the growth of a plant. "In both cases," he said, "no new properties are imparted, by the operation of external causes, but only the inward tendencies are called into action and clothed with strength." [49]

In this context it is relevant to consider the transcendentalist's view of the role of Jesus in the process of human regeneration. In one important respect the new liberals agreed with the old-line Unitarians. They opposed all ideas of the atonement which assumed that God must be reconciled to man. Christ's only mission, therefore, was to lead men into ever fuller fellowship with the Father.[50] Jesus performed this mission by actualizing the full potentiality of his being, not by becoming a substitute for the sinner. James Freeman Clarke emphasized the death of Christ more than most transcendentalists, but for him the saving efficacy of that death lay in its manifestation of love, not in its expiational character. "God saves us," he said, "by pouring into us his own life, which is love. When Christian love is formed within us, it has killed the roots of sin in the soul, and fitted us to be forgiven, and to enter the presence of God." [51]

Who, then, was the Christ who saved by pouring love into the life of the sinner? The answer of the new liberals was often vague, but some spoke with clarity. Parker, for example, left no doubt as to his position. According to him, Jesus of Nazareth was the world's best teacher of "absolute religion"—love to God and love to man—but he was strictly a human being. He was indeed a religious genius and the model of religious excellence, but still only a man.[52] Therefore, the church "should aim to have its members Christians as Jesus was the Christ;—sons of man as he was;—sons of God as much as he." [53] In his later thought, at least, William H. Furness took a Christological position which was essentially the same as Parker's. His favorite phrase was "the Man of Nazareth," and by it he meant to indicate that Jesus belonged solely to the human category, albeit he was the very best human who ever trod the earth.[54]

Emerson is perplexingly vague, but while in the ministry he gave some broad hints of his view of the person of Jesus. The greatness of Jesus, he

---

[48] *Reason in Religion*, 27–8. Cf. 138–9.

[49] *Discourses on the Philosophy of Religion*, 42.

[50] Hedge, *Reason in Religion*, 310–1; Clarke, *Orthodoxy: Its Truths and Errors*, Chap. 10.

[51] *Orthodoxy: Its Truths and Errors*, 264.

[52] "The Relation of Jesus to His Age," in George W. Cooke, ed., *The Transient and Permanent in Christianity*, 40–57.

[53] Parker, *The Idea of a Christian Church; A Discourse at the Installation of Theodore Parker as Minister of the Twenty-Eighth Congregational Church in Boston, January 4, 1846; Delivered by Himself* (Boston, 1846), 7.

[54] *Thoughts on the Life and Character of Jesus of Nazareth* (Boston, 1859), 28, 47. The seeds of Furness' humanitarian view of Jesus seem to be latent in his *Jesus and His Biographers*, published in 1838.

thought, lay in the fact that he embodied "living moral truth." It was the incarnation of moral truth, not the appointment to an "office" which made him the Messiah.[55] This moral truth "is not confined to the pure and benevolent Founder of Christianity but may and must belong to all his disciples in that measure in which they possess themselves of the truth which was in him." [56] The disciple should therefore "scorn to *imitate* any being, knowing that if he uses his own share of God's goodness to the uttermost, it will lead him on to a perfection which has no type yet in the universe, save only in the Divine Mind." [57] Thus before leaving the Second Church, Emerson had already abandoned Arian Christology, to which most of the Unitarian clergy then adhered, and was well on the way to a strictly humanitarian view of Jesus. By the later years of his pastoral ministry George Ripley had also rejected Arianism. He lauded Jesus as "the brightest type of the divine excellence" which had yet appeared on earth, but he did not say that Jesus was God's final type. Furthermore, the quality of Jesus' divinity, according to Ripley, derived not from his ontological status but from the degree of his God-consciousness. Jesus was "filled and penetrated with the consciousness of God within his soul." [58] William Henry Channing expressed his view of Jesus in rather peculiar and mystical terms; nevertheless, it is clear that he took essentially a humanitarian view of Jesus. Jesus was only the head of the race and the unifying center of humanity; he was not one in substance with the Father. The divinity revealed in him is possible for all men who become fully one with the Father. The divinity which filled and transfigured Jesus "reveals itself as that inspiration which visits all who are pure in heart." [59]

The Christological thought of Clarke and Hedge was more conservative than that of the radical transcendentalists. Explicitly taking issue with Parker, Clarke declared: "There is something in Christ not found in Nature, nor known through the intuitions of Reason, but absolutely necessary for the peace of the soul and the progress of the race." While he spoke of Jesus as "the central figure of the Human Race" and "the type of Humanity," he also added that Jesus was "the perfect manifestation of a personal God." [60] According to Hedge, the Christian church would stand or fall with "the confession of Christ as divinely Human Master and Head." [61] On the other hand, said he, Jesus "nowhere assumes to be an incarnation of God." [62] Thus although both Clarke and Hedge apparently ascribed a higher dignity to Jesus than did Emerson and Parker, they still fell short of classical Christology. Neither, for example, could accept a

[55] McGiffert, ed., *Young Emerson Speaks*, 96.   [56] *Ibid.*, 97.
[57] *Ibid.*, 108. Italics in original.
[58] *Discourses on the Philosophy of Religion*, 43–7. At this point Ripley reflects the influence of Schleiermacher, with whose writings he was well acquainted.
[59] O. B. Frothingham, *Memoir of William Henry Channing* (Boston, 1886), 188, 190.
[60] *Theodore Parker, and His Theology*, 17.   [61] *Reason in Religion*, 218.
[62] *Ibid.*, 229.

truly immanent Trinity as the foundation of their faith in Jesus and in the finality of Christianity.

The transcendentalists were not only advanced in their theological thinking; they also as a group stood to the left of the conservative Unitarians in their social doctrines. It is important to recognize the religious basis of their radical social ethic. Emerson identified it quite accurately when in 1834 he made this entry in his *Journal:* "Democracy, Freedom, has its roots in the sacred truth that every man hath in him the divine Reason." [63] Likewise Brownson declared, "It is only on the reality of this inner Light [Reason], and on the fact, that it is universal, in all men, and in every man, that you can found a democracy, which shall have a firm basis." [64] Emerson and Brownson were here articulating a universal conviction of the transcendental churchmen. They all believed that since the Divine Reason or the Moral Sentiment is immanent within every human soul, every person must be free to realize his fullest potentialities. They also believed, with William Henry Channing, "that the promise of a HEAVEN UPON EARTH, which was the first and last word of Jesus, is in time to be realized." [65]

Believing profoundly in universal divine immanence and in social progress, the transcendentalists were necessarily reformers. They sought reform in the church itself, and to this end Brownson and others engaged in experimental ventures designed to type "the church of the future." [66] They also demanded reform in society; and even those who, like Emerson, were constitutionally unfitted for crusading, ardently affirmed the principles and ideals of social reform.[67] War, capitalism, intemperance, slavery— these and other social evils found some of their greatest enemies in the camp of the transcendentalists.

Such, then, was the prevailing theological and ethical pattern of transcendentalism. As our analysis has indicated, the new liberalism bore continuity with the old liberalism in some important respects; for example, (1) it accented the divine benevolence; (2) it denounced traditional trinitarianism; (3) it affirmed the essential divinity of man; (4) it rejected the classical theories of the atonement. On the other hand, the new liberalism advanced beyond the older Unitarian liberalism at crucial points, most importantly in (1) its doctrine of divine immanence; (2) its reliance upon intuitive perception; (3) its rejection of external authority; and (4) its radical social ethic.

Tension between the old-school and the new-school mind was logically inevitable, and it is unrealistic to assume that any amount of mere good will could have avoided it. The conservatives justifiably felt that radicals

---

[63] *Journals,* III, 474.

[64] "Norton on the Evidences of Christianity," *Boston Quarterly Review,* II (1839), 111.

[65] *The Christian Church and Social Reform* (Boston, 1848), 6.

[66] Cf. Hutchison, *The Transcendentalist Ministers,* Chap. 3.

[67] Cf. Emerson, "Man the Reformer," *The Complete Works of Ralph Waldo Emerson,* I (Boston, 1903), 228.

like Emerson and Parker were a serious threat to historic Christian faith. They should have been all the more concerned when Noah Porter of Yale argued, with considerable validity, that the germs of Parker's "monstrous theories" could be detected in the thought of William Ellery Channing and other old-line Unitarians.[68] Although they denied Porter's claim, they felt constrained, in self-defense, to proclaim what amounted to a creed, despite their long-standing opposition to creed-makers.[69] As one way of demonstrating their loyalty to the older liberalism, the Boston Association of (Unitarian) Ministers earnestly importuned Parker to withdraw from that body. When he refused to budge, some of their number were for expelling him; and this step was probably ruled out largely because the Unitarians thereby would have convicted themselves of practicing the same sort of exclusiveness for which they had always castigated the Calvinists.

The new liberalism met with stout resistance for many years; nevertheless, it steadily leavened the Unitarian community, including the Harvard Divinity School, to which Hedge and Clarke were finally admitted as teachers.[70] Since Hedge and Clarke were conservative and irenic transcendentalists, they became influential mediators between the more extreme factions within the Unitarian family. Furthermore, by allying themselves with such churchmen as the powerful Henry W. Bellows of New York, they were able to restrain (at least temporarily) the radicalism of some who had gone even beyond Emerson and Parker.[71] Yet while the mediators helped to make the transition more gradual and less painful, they did not prevent the ultimate victory of the more radical form of transcendentalism. As symbolizing the complete triumph of the new liberalism, the two greatest transcendentalist mavericks, Emerson and Parker, were by the middle 1860's exalted to a lasting place in the Harvard pantheon of the great.

117. Beyond the World of the Senses

An early member of "the movement party" was George Ripley (1802–80), and in his house the Transcendental Club held its initial meeting on

[68] "Theodore Parker and Liberal Christianity," *New Englander*, II (1844), 528–59. See also C. H. Faust, "The Background of the Unitarian Opposition to Transcendentalism," *Modern Philology*, XXXV (1937–38), 313–8.

[69] Cf. "Report of Executive Committee," *The Twenty-Eighth Report of the American Unitarian Association, with the Addresses at the Anniversary, May 24, 1853* (Boston, 1853), 22–3; and Theodore Parker, *A Friendly Letter to the Executive Committee of the Unitarian Association Touching Their New Unitarian Creed or General Proclamation of Unitarian Views* (Boston, 1853). See also Orville Dewey, "The Unitarian Belief," *Works*, III, 3–26.

[70] Sydney Ahlstrom, "The Middle Period (1840–80)," in George H. Williams, ed., *The Harvard Divinity School* (Boston, 1954), 130–45; Hutchison, *The Transcendentalist Ministers*, Chap. 6.

[71] Cf. Henry W. Bellows, *The Suspense of Faith: An Address to the Alumni of the Divinity School of Harvard University, Cambridge, Mass., Given July 19, 1859* (N.Y., 1859); Bellows, *A Sequel to "The Suspense of Faith"* (N.Y., 1859); Hedge, "Antisupernaturalism in the Pulpit," *Christian Examiner*, LXXVII (1864), 145–59; Clarke, *Sermon Preached Before the Delegates to the National Unitarian Convention, New York, Tuesday Evening, April 4, 1865* (Boston, 1865).

September 19, 1836. A gifted thinker, he graduated from Harvard College at the head of his class. Shortly after finishing his work at Harvard Divinity School, he became pastor of the newly organized church on Purchase Street in Boston. Despite the young minister's vigilance, the church did not flourish. One reason for this was the unwise location of the church, but another was the increasing coolness shown by the congregation to Ripley's advanced social and theological doctrines.

Finally becoming weary, Ripley in the fall of 1840 wrote a long letter to the officials of the church laying out his troubles.[72] Among other things, he confessed that his new-school views were not of recent origin; that in fact he had preached transcendentalism from the beginning of his pastorate in 1826. He also reaffirmed his conviction that it was the business of Christianity to overthrow every form of social evil.

Since he received no encouraging reactions to the letter, he offered his resignation in January of 1841. This marked the end of his ministerial career. With vigor Ripley then turned to the establishment of Brook Farm, an educational and agricultural experiment located on a two-hundred acre estate in West Roxbury. As the founder explained to Emerson, the object was to unite the thinker and the manual worker under noncompetitive conditions, and to open the benefits of education and the profits of labor to all. "If not the sunrise, it will be the morning star," prophesied Ripley.

The "morning star," however, soon lost its luster. The Brook Farmers were better social dreamers than farmers, and their enterprise flagged under chronic indebtedness. In the spring of 1845 the Farm was reorganized into a Phalanx in accord with Fourierism, and a promotional journal, *The Harbinger*, was established. Since the Phalanx failed to rejuvenate the enterprise, the social experiment soon collapsed. Disillusioned, the founder turned to journalism in New York City and never again actively engaged in social reform.

The discourse from which the following document is extracted was preached by Ripley toward the close of his Purchase Street ministry and published in 1836.

DOCUMENT

"For he endured, as seeing him who is invisible."

HEBREWS XI.27

These words are applied by the writer of the Epistle to the Hebrews, to the ancient lawgiver of their nation, as descriptive of the principle of faith which formed a prominent element in his character. They may be regarded as describing with no less justice and force the peculiar character of every truly religious man. For there is nothing which more strongly marks the believer in religious truth, than his firm conviction of the reality of a vast range of subjects, which do not come under the cognizance of any

[72] The letter is printed in full in O. B. Frothingham, *George Ripley*, 63–91.

of the senses. His thoughts are not confined to the contemplation of facts, which are presented to the notice of the outward eye. His mind is not limited to the gross and material objects, with which he is now surrounded, but passing over the boundaries of space and time, is conversant with truths, which bear the stamp of Infinity and Eternity. He is conscious of an inward nature, which is the source of more important and comprehensive ideas, than any which the external senses suggest, and he follows the decision of these ideas as the inspiring voice of God, with none the less confidence, because they lead him into the region of the Infinite and Invisible. . . .

He reposes as firm faith in those ideas, which are made known to him by his Reason,[73] as in those facts, which are presented to his notice by the senses. He has no belief that human nature is so shackled and hemmed in, even in its present imperfect state, as to be confined to the objects made known by the eye of sense, which is given us merely for the purposes of our temporal existence, and incapable of ascending to those higher spheres of thought and reality, to which the eternal elements of our being belong.

But, allowing this, it by no means follows, that the religious man is a visionary, in any just sense of that word, because, in the first place, he need not neglect the objects, with which he is at all times surrounded, and which are appropriate to the province of sense, and in the second place, the invisible objects, with which he is conversant, have no less truth and reality, than those which are seen.

The religious man need not see less, in the sphere of the senses, than any other man. There is nothing in his faith in the Invisible, which should blind him to any perceptions, within the sphere of the visible. Indeed, he ought to give his understanding a generous culture, that it may be acute and ready to decide on all objects, that come within its province. One part of his nature is not to be educated at the expense of another. One portion of his existence is not to be sacrificed to the claims of another. The present, with its duties, its enjoyments, and its dangers, is not to be forgotten, amid the hopes and prospects of the future. It is a most pernicious mistake, which leads men to suppose, that they must give up the interests of this world in order to prepare for another, instead of making their preparation for another, to consist in a faithful discharge of all the claims and trusts of this. . . .

But, again, the invisible objects, with which the religious man is conversant, possess as much reality, as those within the sphere of the outward senses. Do not call him a visionary, until you have proved that he is dealing with visions. What if the objects of his attention should be found to have a more substantial existence than any thing which we now see? Do not deem him a man of a fantastic mind, until you have proved that he is fol-

[73] The word Reason is used here and throughout these Discourses, not as the power of reasoning, of evolving derivative truth from admitted premises; but in its highest philosophical sense, as the faculty of perceiving primitive, spiritual truth. I am justified in this use of the term by the authority of some of the older English writers, and by a similar use of the corresponding term in the philosophical literature of Europe. [George Ripley]

lowing phantoms. What if the things that are not seen, should turn out to be enduring realities, while the things that appear, are only transitory appearances? It may be that this is the case. We have great reason to hold that it is probable. Nay, we have the words of inspiration, declaring that it is a fact. "For the things which are seen are temporal, but those which are unseen are eternal." What then are the unseen realities, to which the Christian gives his faith, and on which he acts, with as much confidence and hope, as if they had passed within the boundaries of his earthly vision?

I. The Christian is conversant, I answer, with an invisible God. The Mighty Being, upon whom he depends and whom he worships, is infinite, and of course, incomprehensible. He, who sees all things, is himself unseen. His existence is of a spiritual nature, and of course, not perceptible to the eye of sense. The very idea of God, as that of the Primeval Spirit,—from whom all things proceed and by whom they are sustained, who is present in every part of his creation, to receive the homage of the intellect and the heart,—precludes the supposition, that he can be seen by the outward eye. That is formed for a different purpose, organized with different powers, and called to a different service. It is designed to place us in connexion with the various forms of matter, to reveal to our souls the beauty of the external universe, and to make us acquainted with the properties and laws of created Nature. If it were possible for God to be seen by the eye, he would be no longer the Being that he is. He would be deprived of the attributes, which make him worthy of our highest adoration and praise. He would no longer be infinite but finite, for our finite senses comprehend only the latter, and ceasing to be infinite, he would cease to be God. The Creator of the universe, if capable of being seen by the bodily eye, would be reduced to a level with nature, would become a material object, and of course no longer God, since God is a Spirit, and only by the pure in heart can he be spiritually discerned. But I would ask, if the fact, that God is invisible, and from his very nature ever must be so, takes aught from the reality of his presence, or from our convictions of his existence? Is he any the less near to the heart of the good man, than if he could be apprehended with the eye of sense? Do we not repose as firm a faith in the Being of God, as we do in the objects of nature, which reveal his wisdom and his love? It is impossible for the enlightened Reason to avoid this. Though the eye cannot see God, the soul perceives him. It does as great a wrong and injustice to its own nature, when it doubts the inward convictions of a Maker and Governor of the world, as if it were to refuse evidence to the testimony of the senses, with regard to the outward universe. The decisions of Reason, which may be regarded as the very essence of the soul, compel us to admit the existence of God, as the ground of our own existence, of an Infinite Being, as the first cause of finite nature, of an invisible spirit, as the origin and support of the visible universe. . . .

II. Again, the Christian cherishes communion with an invisible Saviour.

Next to the God and Father of our Lord Jesus Christ, it is Jesus himself who is the dearest object of his gratitude, his sympathy, and his love. No subject makes a deeper impression on his heart than the character of his blessed Lord. No remembrance touches more powerfully the springs of his best feelings than the remembrance of the love of Christ, who laid down his life, that we might live. He sees in him the manifestation of the Father's glory, the express image of the Divine Perfections. All that we most love and adore in God,—his holiness, his justice, his benevolence and his truth,— is displayed in the person of his Son, and by the spiritual contemplation of that, we obtain the best idea of the Father himself. But here is nothing presented to the senses. None of us ever saw the Saviour of men. We did not know him after the flesh. No material representation could convey to our souls a just impression of his character. Indeed, we obtain so much clearer a perception of him, by bringing his actions in review before the mental eye, that there can scarcely be a material representation, intended to represent the features of his character, which does not fall far short of the conceptions which we had previously formed. Every thing here is addressed to the soul. It is the inward eye, that beholds the glory of Christ. It is to the principle of faith, that his spiritual presence is revealed,—and who can say that it does not make him conversant with a noble object? Who can deny that the recollection of such a being as our Saviour was, calls forth our highest faculties, and introduces us into a region of thought, in which it well befits a man to expatiate? Is the Christian the sport of a vain and idle fancy, when he communes with an unseen Saviour? Is he giving way to a visionary delusion, when he calls up the remembrance of him who became a man of sorrows, that we might be partakers of joy; who tasted the bitter cup of death, that we might drink the waters of life, and opened to us the gates of Heaven, by his own agony on the cross? Is this communion with an invisible Saviour, the delusion of an enthusiast? All the better feelings of our nature declare that it is not. All the homage that is paid at the tomb of departed worth, all the gratitude that is lavished on the benefactors of our race, all the reverence that is accorded to glorious specimens of moral perfection declare that it is not.

III. Again, the Christian is conversant with the invisible powers of his own nature. He is in a state of constant communion with feelings and faculties, that he has never seen. He takes counsel of Reason. He inquires at the oracles of Conscience. He communes with his own heart. He is conscious that he is the possessor of a living soul—of a soul which is to live for ever. He has no more doubt of the existence of his soul, than he has of the existence of his senses. He believes in his Reason as much, nay more, than he does in his eyes. But it is all invisible. Nobody has ever seen the inward nature of man. The researches of the anatomist stop short of it. It cannot be laid open with the knife. It cannot be exhibited for inspection. It is the object of no one of the senses. It is as invisible as the Creator himself. But does any one doubt, on that account, the reality of his inward nature? Can the Christian be charged with folly or with prejudice, because it is his aim to submit the senses to the soul? Can we call in question the existence of the Reason, of the Conscience, of the feeling of moral obligation, because we have never seen them? If we are not aware of their existence, it is because we have never felt their power; and if we have never felt their power, what does it prove with regard to ourselves? If the Christian is guilty of folly, in paying reverence to unseen powers, give me his folly rather than the wisdom of one, who by his own confession, is a stranger to Reason, to Conscience, to a sense of obligation, to the noblest attributes and faculties of man.

IV. Once more, the Christian is conversant with an invisible world. He believes in the existence of a state of being which he has not seen, with as much confidence as in the reality of the world which he now occupies. He has obtained too deep and correct an insight into his own nature, to admit the idea for a moment, that the "be-all and end-all" of man is with the present state. He is conscious of undeveloped powers, which demand an Eternity for their expansion, and he feels sure that God will grant the opportunity, where he has given the capacity. The future world then rises before him, as his final home. His thoughts often dwell upon it, with the deepest interest. There he hopes for brighter manifestations of God. There he expects more intimate communion with his Saviour. There he trusts to enjoy the acquaintance of kindred minds, who have lived in past ages and distant lands, and who in Heaven have become one through Christ Jesus. . . . Who would deny him the privilege of indulging in those anticipations, which are demanded by his feelings and sanctioned by his Reason, because they are not laid open to the eye of sense? He cannot tell, indeed, by any cold deductions of the understanding, how the dead are raised up, or with what body they do come, but he believes that the same God, who raised up Christ, will also raise him from this mortal life on earth, to a higher life in Heaven. The nature of that life he cannot fully describe. Its pursuits, he does not know. Its connexion with space and with time, he does not comprehend. But he feels his intimate connexion with it. He knows, that compared with it, this life is but a dream—a vapor. He is sure, that it cannot be far off. Soon will he enter upon its amazing scenes. Soon will its mysteries be disclosed to his waiting faith, and a higher consciousness of existence commence. He does not see that world, but he expects to meet there beings like himself. How many have gone before him! How many will be there to receive him! Angel voices call him from on high. Angel-hands are stretched forth for his aid. The dead, who have gone, are living still. The angel-friends who have vanished from earth are angel-spirits in the presence of God. They speak to his heart, when it is open to the voices of Eternity. Their spiritual presence is revealed, as the shadows of earth disappear and the glories of Heaven draw nigh. And will you say, that the Christian should not often commune with invisible realities like these? Will you tell him that because the prospects of Eternity are shut out from his sight, they should also be shut out from his heart? Speak, thou faithful disciple of Christ! Speak, ye, who look up for rest in Heaven! Speak, pilgrim of earth, as ye behold in the distance the shining walls of the city of God! Speak, heart of man, that yearns, with desires that cannot be expressed, for a closer union with the Infinite and the Eternal! Speak! and ye will say, that there is no worthy object for the Everlasting Soul, but the things that are unseen—no source of illimitable joy, but the Infinite Presence of God!

> SOURCE: George Ripley, "On Faith in the Invisible," *Discourses on the Philosophy of Religion Addressed to Doubters Who Wish to Believe* (Boston, 1836), 9–20.

118. The Manifesto of 1838

The most widely known transcendentalist was Ralph Waldo Emerson (1803–82), whom Orestes Brownson called "the sovereign pontiff" of the clan. The son of a leading Unitarian minister of Boston, Emerson followed the traditional groove in going to Harvard College and to its Divinity School, although he did not graduate from the latter. His only pastoral charge was the Second Church in Boston, from which he resigned in October of 1832. For some time thereafter, however, he preached occasionally. By January of 1839 he had delivered a total of 885 sermons.[74]

The best explanation of why Emerson left the ministry is to be found in his celebrated Manifesto, delivered at Divinity Hall on July 15, 1838, to a graduating class of seven prospective clergymen. It has been said that his scathing message on this occasion was due largely to the lifeless preaching of his pastor, Barzillai Frost (1804–58).[75] Emerson's *Journal* does indeed indicate that he was often annoyed at the lame effort of Frost, but he was not the type of man to waste this all-important opportunity on the obscure junior minister at Concord. Instead, the ex-minister was speaking from his observation of the whole Unitarian communion, which he had come to believe was generally suffering from spiritual dry rot.

According to Emerson, the root of Unitarian decay lay in the fact that the ministers, despite their avowed liberalism, were tied hand and foot to an authoritarian type of religion. They had made a monster of miracle, for example, because they had failed to recognize the soul as the fountain of religious creativity. It is not surprising that the courageous Address, which is reproduced in substance in the following document, blew up the worst

[74] For Emerson's "Preaching Record," see A. C. McGiffert, Jr., ed., *Young Emerson Speaks*, 263–71.

[75] Conrad Wright, "Emerson, Barzillai Frost, and the Divinity School Address," *Harvard Theological Review*, XLIX (1956), 19–43.

controversial storm in New England since Channing's Baltimore sermon of 1819.

DOCUMENT

Truly speaking, it is not instruction, but provocation, that I can receive from another soul. What he announces, I must find true in me, or reject; and on his word, or as his second, be he who he may, I can accept nothing. On the contrary, the absence of this primary faith is the presence of degradation. As is the flood, so is the ebb. Let this faith depart, and the very words it spake and the things it made become false and hurtful. Then falls the church, the state, art, letters, life. The doctrine of the divine nature being forgotten, a sickness infects and dwarfs the constitution. Once man was all; now he is an appendage, a nuisance. And because the indwelling Supreme Spirit cannot wholly be got rid of, the doctrine of it suffers this perversion, that the divine nature is attributed to one or two persons, and denied to all the rest, and denied with fury. The doctrine of inspiration is lost; the base doctrine of the majority of voices usurps the place of the doctrine of the soul. Miracles, prophecy, poetry, the ideal life, the holy life, exist as ancient history merely; they are not in the belief, nor in the aspiration of society; but, when suggested, seem ridiculous. Life is comic or pitiful as soon as the high ends of being fade out of sight, and man becomes near-sighted, and can only attend to what addresses the senses. . . .

Jesus Christ belonged to the true race of prophets. He saw with open eye the mystery of the soul. Drawn by its severe harmony, ravished with its beauty, he lived in it, and had his being there. Alone in all history he estimated the greatness of man. One man was true to what is in you and me. He saw that God incarnates himself in man, and evermore goes forth anew to take possession of his World. He said, in this jubilee of sublime emotion, 'I am divine. Through me, God acts; through me, speaks. Would you see God, see me; or see thee, when thou also thinkest as I now think.' But what a distortion did his doctrine and memory suffer in the same, in the next, and the following ages! There is no doctrine of the Reason which will bear to be taught by the Understanding. The understanding caught this high chant from the poet's lips, and said, in the next age, 'This was Jehovah come down out of heaven. I will kill you, if you say he was a man." The idioms of his language and the figures of his rhetoric have usurped the place of his truth; and churches are not built on his principles, but on his tropes. Christianity became a Mythus, as the poetic teaching of Greece and of Egypt, before. He spoke of miracles; for he felt that man's life was a miracle, and all that man doth, and he knew that this daily miracle shines as the character ascends. But the word Miracle, as pronounced by Christian churches, gives a false impression; it is Monster. It is not one with the blowing clover and the falling rain.

He felt respect for Moses and the prophets, but no unfit tenderness at postponing their initial revelations to the hour and the man that now is; to the eternal revelation in the heart. Thus was he a true man. Having seen that the law in us is commanding, he would not suffer it to be commanded. Boldly, with hand, and heart, and life, he declared it was God. Thus is he, as I think, the only soul in history who has appreciated the worth of man.

1. In this point of view we become sensible of the first defect of historical Christianity. Historical Christianity has fallen into the error that corrupts all attempts to communicate religion. As it appears to us, and as it has appeared for ages, it is not the doctrine of the soul, but an exaggeration of the personal, the positive, the ritual. It has dwelt, it dwells, with noxious exaggeration about the *person* of Jesus. The soul knows no persons. It invites every man to expand to the full circle of the universe, and will have no preferences but those of spontaneous love. . . .

That is always best which gives me to myself. The sublime is excited in me by the great stoical doctrine, Obey thyself. That which shows God in me, fortifies me. That which shows God out of me, makes me a wart and a wen. There is no longer a necessary reason for my being. Already the long shadows of untimely oblivion creep over me, and I shall decease forever. . . .

2. The second defect of the traditionary and limited way of using the mind of Christ is a consequence of the first; this, namely; that the Moral Nature, that Law of laws whose revelations introduce greatness—yea, God himself—into the open soul, is not explored as the fountain of the established teaching in society. Men have come to speak of the revelation as somewhat long ago given and done, as if God were dead. The injury to faith throttles the preacher; and the goodliest of institutions becomes an uncertain and inarticulate voice. . . .

The man on whom the soul descends, through whom the soul speaks, alone can teach. Courage, piety, love, wisdom, can teach; and every man can open his door to these angels, and they shall bring him the gift of tongues. But the man who aims to speak as books enable, as synods use, as the fashion guides, and as interest commands, babbles. Let him hush.

To this holy office you propose to devote yourselves. I wish you may feel your call in throbs of desire and hope. The office is the first in the world. It is of that reality that it cannot suffer the deduction of any falsehood. And it is my duty to say to you that the need was never greater of new revelation than now. From the views I have already expressed, you will infer the sad conviction, which I share, I believe, with numbers, of the universal decay and now almost death of faith in society. The soul is not preached. The Church seems to totter to its fall, almost all life extinct. . . .

My friends, in these two errors, I think, I find the causes of a decaying church and a wasting unbelief. And what greater calamity can fall upon a nation than the loss of worship? Then all things go to decay. Genius leaves the temple to haunt the senate or the market. Literature becomes frivolous. Science is cold. The eye of youth is not lighted by the hope of other worlds, and age is without honor. Society lives to trifles, and when men die we do not mention them.

And now, my brothers, you will ask, What in these desponding days can be done by us? The remedy is already declared in the ground of our complaint of the Church. We have contrasted the Church with the Soul. In the soul then let the redemption be sought. Wherever a man comes, there comes revolution. The old is for slaves. When a man comes, all books are legible, all things transparent, all religions are forms. He is religious. Man is the wonderworker. He is seen amid miracles. All men bless and curse. He saith yea and nay, only. The stationariness of religion; the assumption that the age of inspiration is past, that the Bible is closed; the fear of degrading the character of Jesus by representing him as a man;—indicate with sufficient clearness the falsehood of our theology. It is the office of a true teacher to show us that God is, not was; that He speaketh, not spake. The true Christianity,—a faith like Christ's in the infinitude of man,— is lost. None believeth in the soul of man, but only in some man or person old and departed. Ah me! no man goeth alone. All men go in flocks to this saint or that poet, avoiding the God who seeth in secret. . . . Once leave your own knowledge of God, your own sentiment, and take secondary knowledge, as St. Paul's, or George Fox's, or Swedenborg's, and you get wide from God with every year this secondary form lasts, and if, as now, for centuries,—the chasm yawns to that breadth, that men can scarcely be convinced there is in them anything divine.

Let me admonish you, first of all, to go alone; to refuse the good models, even those which are sacred in the imagination of men, and dare to love God without mediator or veil. Friends enough you shall find who will hold up to your emulation Wesleys and Oberlins, Saints and Prophets. Thank God for these good men, but say, 'I also am a man.' Imitation cannot go above its model. The imitator dooms himself to hopeless mediocrity. The inventor did it because it was natural to him, and so in him it has a charm. In the imitator something else is natural, and he bereaves himself of his own beauty, to come short of another man's.

Yourself a newborn bard of the Holy Ghost, cast behind you all conformity, and acquaint men at first hand with Deity. Look to it first and only, that fashion, custom, authority, pleasure, and money, are nothing to you,—are not bandages over your eyes, that you cannot see,—but live with the privilege of the immeasurable mind. . . . By trusting your own heart, you shall gain more confidence in other men. For all our penny-wisdom, for all our soul-destroying slavery to habit, it is not to be doubted that all men have sublime thoughts; that all men value the few real hours of life; they love to be heard; they love to be caught up into the vision of principles. We mark with light in the memory the few interviews we have had, in the dreary years of routine and of sin, with souls that made our souls wiser;

that spoke what we thought; that told us what we knew; that gave us leave to be what we inly were. Discharge to men the priestly office, and, present or absent, you shall be followed with their love as by an angel. . . .

And now let us do what we can to rekindle the smouldering, nigh quenched fire on the altar. The evils of the church that now is are manifest. The question returns, What shall we do? I confess, all attempts to project and establish a Cultus with new rites and forms, seem to me vain. Faith makes us, and not we it, and faith makes its own forms. All attempts to contrive a system are as cold as the new worship introduced by the French to the goddess of Reason,—to-day, pasteboard and filigree, and ending to-morrow in madness and murder. Rather let the breath of new life be breathed by you through the forms already existing. For if once you are alive, you shall find they shall become plastic and new. The remedy to their deformity is first, soul, and second, soul, and evermore, soul. A whole pope-dom of forms one pulsation of virtue can uplift and vivify. . . .

I look for the hour when that supreme Beauty which ravished the souls of those Eastern men, and chiefly of those Hebrews, and through their lips spoke oracles to all time, shall speak in the West also. The Hebrew and Greek Scriptures contain immortal sentences, that have been bread of life to millions. But they have no epical integrity; are fragmentary; are not shown in their order to the intellect. I look for the new Teacher that shall follow so far those shining laws that he shall see them come full circle; shall see their rounding complete grace; shall see the world to be the mirror of the soul; shall see the identity of the law of gravitation with purity of heart; and shall show that the Ought, that Duty, is one thing with Science, with Beauty, and with Joy.

> SOURCE: Ralph Waldo Emerson, "An Address Delivered Before the Senior Class in Divinity College, Cambridge, Sunday Evening, July 15, 1838," in Edward Waldo Emerson, ed., *The Complete Works of Ralph Waldo Emerson* (12 vols., Boston, 1903–04), I, 127–32, 134–5, 143–7, 149–51.

119. The Transient and Permanent

Theodore Parker (1810–60), unlike Emerson, stuck to the ministry. Stemming from generations of farmers, he grew up in the village of Lexington where his grandfather, Captain John Parker, had led a handful of raw militiamen against the British Regulars on April 19, 1775. As a nonresident student at Harvard he met all the academic requirements for his A.B., but the degree was never awarded because he could not pay the required fees. After an interval of teaching in several common schools, Parker studied also at the Harvard Divinity School, graduating in 1836.

Parker's first pastoral charge was the Unitarian church on Spring Street in West Roxbury, Mass., where he began preaching in June of 1837. Being

Nathaniel W. Taylor, Metaphysician
and Theologian

Joseph Smith, Founding Father of the
Mormons

John W. Nevin, Theologian of the
"Mercersburg Movement"

The Rt. Rev. John England, First Bishop of
the Catholic Diocese of Charleston (embracing the Carolinas and Georgia)

Three Famed Beechers: Lyman, with his daughter Harriet and his son Henry Ward

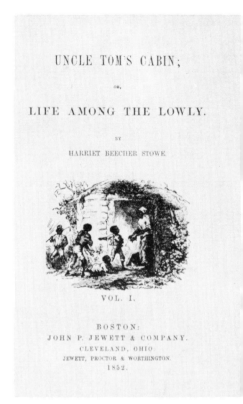

UNCLE TOM'S CABIN;

OR,

LIFE AMONG THE LOWLY.

BY

HARRIET BEECHER STOWE.

VOL. I.

BOSTON:
JOHN P. JEWETT & COMPANY.
CLEVELAND, OHIO:
JEWETT, PROCTOR & WORTHINGTON.
1852.

America's most influential Antislavery Trac

Above: Theodore Dwight Weld, Antislavery Crusader

Right: Theodore Parker, Preacher of Transcendentalism

a small parish, with only about sixty families, it afforded the young minister plenty of time to read widely in those fields which were then of special interest to transcendentalists.[76] Thus when in 1838 Parker heard Emerson's lecture in Divinity Hall, its main effect was not to give him any new ideas but rather to inspire him to express more openly his own similar convictions.[77] Some of those convictions were revealed in his Levi Blodgett Letter of 1840, but it was his South Boston sermon—"The Transient and Permanent in Christianity"—of 1841 which disclosed the large sweep of his radicalism. The Unitarian outcry was so loud that most of his ministerial brethren soon refused to exchange pulpits with him.[78]

During the next winter the young heretic aired his views in a series of five lectures, delivered at the Masonic Temple in Boston to large and enthusiastic audiences. In 1842 the lectures were published in amplified form under the title, *A Discourse of Matters Pertaining to Religion.* Instead of calming the theological waters, the *Discourse* actually whipped them into new heights.

When the Boston Unitarian clergy managed, by a thinly-veiled stratagem, to render it impossible for Parker ever again to give the historic Thursday Lecture, a few irate local laymen held a conference (Jan. 22, 1845) and resolved to give the Roxbury minister an opportunity to be heard in their city. Accordingly, on February 16, 1845, Parker, then thirty-four years of age, preached his first sermon at the Melodeon. Within a year the Twenty-Eighth Congregational Church (Unitarian) was organized, and to it Parker preached with great success until his death in 1860.

The document below contains a substantial part of Parker's famed sermon, "The Transient and Permanent in Christianity." This discourse ranks in importance with William Ellery Channing's Baltimore sermon of 1819 and Emerson's Cambridge address of 1838.

DOCUMENT

In actual Christianity—that is, in that portion of Christianity which is preached and believed—there seems to have been, ever since the time of its earthly founder, two elements, the one transient, the other permanent. The one is the thought, the folly, the uncertain wisdom, the theological notions, the impiety of man; the other, the eternal truth of God. These two bear, perhaps, the same relation to each other that the phenomena of outward nature, such as sunshine and cloud, growth, decay, and reproduction, bear to the great law of nature, which underlies and supports them all. As in that case more attention is commonly paid to the particular phenomena than to the general law, so in this case more is generally given to the transient in Christianity than to the permanent therein. . . .

[76] John Weiss, *Life and Correspondence of Theodore Parker* (2 vols., N.Y., 1864), I, 100.
[77] *Ibid.,* 113.
[78] Parker, *A Letter to the Boston Association of Congregational Ministers* (Boston, 1845), 3–7.

The stream of Christianity, as men receive it, has caught a stain from every soil it has filtered through, so that now it is not the pure water from the well of life which is offered to our lips, but streams troubled and polluted by man with mire and dirt. If Paul and Jesus could read our books of theological doctrines, would they accept as their teaching what men have vented in their name? Never till the letters of Paul had faded out of his memory; never till the words of Jesus had been torn out from the book of life. It is their notions about Christianity men have taught as the only living word of God. They have piled their own rubbish against the temple of truth where piety comes up to worship; what wonder the pile seems unshapely and like to fall? But these theological doctrines are fleeting as the leaves on the trees. . . .

Like the clouds of the sky, they are here to-day; tomorrow, all swept off and vanished, while Christianity itself, like the heaven above, with its sun, and moon, and uncounted stars, is always over our head, though the cloud sometimes debars us of the needed light. It must of necessity be the case that our reasonings, and therefore our theological doctrines, are imperfect, and so perishing. It is only gradually that we approach to the true system of nature by observation and reasoning, and work out our philosophy and theology by the toil of the brain. But meantime, if we are faithful, the great truths of morality and religion, the deep sentiment of love to man and love to God, are perceived intuitively, and by instinct, as it were, though our theology be imperfect and miserable. The theological notions of Abraham, to take the story as it stands, were exceedingly gross, yet a greater than Abraham has told us Abraham desired to see my day, saw it, and was glad. Since these notions are so fleeting, why need we accept the commandment of men as the doctrine of God?

This transitoriness of doctrines appears in many instances, of which two may be selected for a more attentive consideration. First, the doctrine respecting the origin and authority of the Old and New Testament. There has been a time when men were burned for asserting doctrines of natural philosophy which rested on evidence the most incontestable, because those doctrines conflicted with sentences in the Old Testament. Every word of that Jewish record was regarded as miraculously inspired, and therefore as infallibly true. It was believed that the Christian religion itself rested thereon, and must stand or fall with the immaculate Hebrew text. He was deemed no small sinner who found mistakes in the manuscripts. . . .

The history of opinions on the New Testament is quite similar. It has been assumed at the outset, it would seem with no sufficient reason, without the smallest pretence on its writers' part, that all of its authors were infallibly and miraculously inspired, so that they could commit no error of doctrine or fact. Men have been bid to close their eyes at the obvious difference between Luke and John—the serious disagreement between Paul and Peter; to believe, on the smallest evidence, accounts which shock the moral sense and revolt the reason, and tend to place Jesus in the same series with Hercules, and Apollonius of Tyana; accounts which Paul in the Epistles never mentions, though he also had a vein of the miraculous running quite through him. Men have been told that all these things must be taken as part of Christianity, and if they accepted the religion, they must take all these accessories along with it; that the living spirit could not be had without the killing letter. All the books which caprice or accident had brought together between the lids of the Bible were declared to be the infallible word of God, the only certain rule of religious faith and practice. Thus the Bible was made not a single channel, but the *only* certain rule of religious faith and practice. To disbelieve any of its statements, or even the common interpretation put upon those statements by the particular age or church in which the man belonged, was held to be infidelity, if not atheism. . . .

Another instance of the transitoriness of doctrines taught as Christian is found in those which relate to the nature and authority of Christ. One ancient party has told us that he is the infinite God; another, that he is both God and man; a third, that he was a man, the son of Joseph and Mary —born as we are, tempted like ourselves, inspired, as we may be, if we will pay the price. Each of the former parties believed its doctrine on this head was infallibly true, and formed the very substance of Christianity, and was one of the essential conditions of salvation, though scarce any two distinguished teachers, of ancient or modern times, agree in their expression of this truth.

Almost every sect that has ever been makes Christianity rest on the personal authority of Jesus, and not the immutable truth of the doctrines themselves, or the authority of God, who sent him into the world. Yet it seems difficult to conceive any reason why moral and religious truths should rest for their support on the personal authority of their revealer, any more than the truths of science on that of him who makes them known first or most clearly. It is hard to see why the great truths of Christianity rest on the personal authority of Jesus, more than the axioms of geometry rest on the personal authority of Euclid or Archimedes. The authority of Jesus, as of all teachers, one would naturally think, must rest on the truth of his words, and not their truth on his authority. . . .

Now it seems clear, that the notion men form about the origin and nature of the scriptures, respecting the nature and authority of Christ, have [sic] nothing to do with Christianity except as its aids or its adversaries; they are not the foundation of its truths. These are theological questions, not religious questions. Their connection with Christianity appears accidental: for if Jesus had taught at Athens, and not at Jerusalem; if he had wrought no miracle, and none but the human nature had ever been ascribed to him; if the Old Testament had for ever perished at his birth, Christianity would still have been the word of God; it would have lost none of its truths. It would be just as true, just as beautiful, just as lasting, as now it is; though we should have lost so many a blessed word, and the work of Christianity itself would have been, perhaps, a long time retarded. . . .

To turn away from the disputes of the Catholics and the Protestants, of the Unitarian and the Trinitarian, of old school and new school, and come to the plain words of Jesus of Nazareth, Christianity is a simple thing, very simple. It is absolute, pure morality; absolute, pure religion; the love of man; the love of God acting without let or hindrance. The only creed it lays down is the great truth which springs up spontaneous in the holy heart —there is a God. Its watchword is, Be perfect as your Father in heaven. The only form it demands is a divine life; doing the best thing in the best way, from the highest motives; perfect obedience to the great law of God. Its sanction is the voice of God in your heart; the perpetual presence of him who made us and the stars over our head; Christ and the Father abiding within us. All this is very simple—a little child can understand it; very beautiful—the loftiest mind can find nothing so lovely. Try it by reason, conscience, and faith—things highest in man's nature—we see no re-dundance, we feel no deficiency. Examine the particular duties it enjoins— humility, reverence, sobriety, gentleness, charity, forgiveness, fortitude, resignation, faith, and active love; try the whole extent of Christianity, so well summed up in the command, "Thou shalt love the Lord thy God with all thy heart, and with all thy soul, and with all thy mind—thou shalt love thy neighbor as thyself"; and is there anything therein that can perish? No, the very opponents of Christianity have rarely found fault with the teachings of Jesus. The end of Christianity seems to be to make all men one with God as Christ was one with him; to bring them to such a state of obedience and goodness that we shall think divine thoughts and feel divine sentiments, and so keep the law of God by living a life of truth and love. Its means are purity and prayer; getting strength from God, and using it for our fellow-men as well as ourselves. It allows perfect freedom. It does not demand all men to *think* alike, but to think uprightly, and get as near as possible at truth; not all men to *live* alike, but to live holy, and get as near as possible to a life perfectly divine. Christ set up no pillars of Hercules, beyond which men must not sail the sea in quest of truth. . . .

In an age of corruption, as all ages are, Jesus stood and looked up to God. There was nothing between him and the Father of all; no old world, be it of Moses or Esaias, of a living rabbi, or sanhedrim of rabbis; no sin or perverseness of the finite will. As the result of this virgin purity of soul and perfect obedience, the light of God shone down into the very depths of his soul, bringing all of the Godhead which flesh can receive. He would have us do the same; worship with nothing between us and God; act, think, feel, live, in perfect obedience to him; and we never are *Christians* as he was the *Christ,* until we worship, as Jesus did, with no mediator, with nothing between us and the Father of all. He felt that God's word was in him; that he was one with God. He told what he saw, the truth; he lived what he felt, a life of love. The truth he brought to light must have been always the same before the eyes of all-seeing God, nineteen centuries before Christ, or nineteen centuries after him. A life supported by the principle and quickened by the sentiment of religion, if true to both, is always the same thing in Nazareth or New England. Now that divine man received these truths from God, was illumined more clearly by "the light that lighteneth every man," combined or involved all the truths of religion and morality in his doctrine, and made them manifest in his life. Then his words and example passed into the world, and can no more perish than the stars be wiped out of the sky. The truths he taught; his doctrines respecting man and God; the relation between man and man, and man and God, with the duties that grow out of that relation—are always the same, and can never change till man ceases to be man, and creation vanishes into nothing. No; forms and opinions change and perish, but the word of God cannot fail. The form religion takes, the doctrines wherewith she is girded, can never be the same in any two centuries or two men; for since the sum of religious doctrines is both the result and the measure of a man's total growth in wisdom, virtue, and piety, and since men will always differ in these respects, so religious *doctrines* and *forms* will always differ, always be transient, as Christianity goes forth and scatters the seed she bears in her hand. But the *Christianity holy men feel in the heart,* the Christ that is born within us, is always the same thing to each soul that feels it. This differs only in degree, and not in kind, from age to age, and man to man. There is something in Christianity which no sect, from the "Ebionites" to the "Latter-Day Saints," ever entirely overlooked. This is that common Christianity which burns in the hearts of pious men.

Real Christianity gives men new life. It is the growth and perfect action of the holy spirit God puts into the sons of men. It makes us outgrow any form or any system of doctrines we have devised, and approach still closer to the truth. It would lead us to take what help we can find. It would make the Bible our servant, not our master. It would teach us to profit by the wisdom and piety of David and Solomon, but not to sin their sins, nor bow to their idols. It would make us revere the holy words spoken by "godly men of old," but revere still more the word of God spoken through conscience, reason, and faith, as the holiest of all. It would not make Christ the despot of the soul, but the brother of all men. It would not tell us that even he had exhausted the fulness of God, so that he could create none greater; for with him "all things are possible," and neither Old Testament nor New Testament ever hints that creation exhausts the creator. Still less would it tell us the wisdom, the piety, the love, the manly excellence of Jesus was the result of miraculous agency alone, but that it was won, like the excellence of humbler men, by faithful obedience to him who gave his son such ample heritage. It would point to him as our brother, who went before, like the good shepherd, to charm us with the music of his words, and with the beauty of his life to tempt us up the steeps of mortal toil, within the gate of heaven. It would have us make the kingdom of God on earth, and enter more fittingly the kingdom on high. It would lead us to form Christ in the heart, on which Paul laid such stress, and work out our salvation by this. For it is not so much by the Christ who lived so blameless and beautiful eighteen centuries ago that we are saved directly, but by the Christ we form in our hearts and live out in our daily life, that we save ourselves, God working with us both to will and to do.

Compare the simpleness of Christianity, as Christ sets it forth on the mount, with what is sometimes taught and accepted in that honored name; and what a difference! One is of God; one is of man. There is something in Christianity which sects have not reached; something that will not be won, we fear, by theological battles, or the quarrels of pious men; still we may rejoice that Christ is preached in any way. The Christianity of sects, of the pulpit, of society, is ephemeral—a transitory fly. It will pass off and be forgot. Some new form will take its place, suited to the aspect of the changing times. Each will represent something of truth, but no one the whole. It seems the whole race of man is needed to do justice to the whole of truth, as "the whole church to preach the whole gospel." Truth is intrusted for the time to a perishable ark of human contrivance. Though often shipwrecked, she always comes safe to land, and is not changed by her mishap. That pure ideal religion which Jesus saw on the mount of his vision, and lived out in the lowly life of a Galilean peasant; which transforms his cross into an emblem of all that is holiest on earth; which makes sacred the ground he trod, and is dearest to the best of men, most true to what is truest in them—cannot pass away. Let men improve never so far in civilization, or soar never so high on the wings of religion and love, they can never outgo the flight of truth and Christianity. It will always be above them. It is as if we were to fly towards a star, which becomes larger and more bright the nearer we approach, till we enter and are absorbed in its glory. . . .

Such, then, is the transient and such the permanent in Christianity. What is of absolute value never changes; we may cling round it and grow to it for ever. No one can say his notions shall stand. But we may all say, the truth as it is in Jesus shall never pass away. Yet there are always some, even religious men, who do not see the permanent element, so they rely on the fleeting, and, what is also an evil, condemn others for not doing the same. They mistake a defence of the truth for an attack upon the holy of holies, the removal of a theological error for the destruction of all religion. Already men of the same sect eye one another with suspicion, and lowering brows that indicate a storm, and, like children who have fallen out in their play, call hard names. Now, as always, there is a collision between these two elements. The question puts itself to each man, "Will you cling to what is perishing, or embrace what is eternal?" This question each must answer for himself.

> SOURCE: Theodore Parker, "The Transient and Permanent in Christianity," in George Willis Cooke, ed., *The Transient and Permanent in Christianity* (Boston, 1908), 6, 11-3, 15-9, 28-36.

120. The Creed of a Transcendentalist

The new-school liberals generally condemned creed making, and yet a striking creed was prepared by one of them, William Henry Channing (1810–84), nephew and protégé of William Ellery Channing.

Young Henry had a rich religious heritage and a good Harvard education, but he experienced difficulty in finding his vocational niche; indeed, he wandered to and fro much of his life, trying first one experiment and then another. His first venture was to start a chapel for the poor in New York City, but he abandoned it after a few months. Next he held a short Unitarian pastorate in Cincinnati, Ohio, from which he resigned in the spring of 1841 because of a loss of faith in Jesus. On recovering faith, he began services in a Brooklyn school house in the fall of 1842. Removing to New York City, he organized in April of 1843 the Christian Union, where he preached a form of Christian socialism which bore the tinge of Pierre Leroux and Charles Fourier. In order to spread his ideas the more widely he established in the fall of 1843 a monthly, *The Present,* but it was discontinued in the following April. The Union was also given up in the fall of 1845.

Still romantic and visionary, despite his many failures, Channing next tried a social experiment in Boston, where in January of 1847 he founded the Religious Union of Associationists, a Fourierist inspired project. The thirty-three charter members, including George Ripley and Albert Brisbane, affirmed their faith in Universal Unity and in the earthly realization of the Kingdom of God.[79] In July of 1849 the reformer sought to augment the Boston experiment with a weekly, *The Spirit of the Age,* but it died in less than a year. The Religious Union also soon experienced the same fate.

Channing conducted no more social experiments, but he remained a reformer at heart to the end of his days, preaching against slavery and other social evils wherever he had an opportunity. From 1854 until the advent

[79] O. B. Frothingham, *Memoir of William Henry Channing,* 221.

of the Civil War he preached to the Unitarians in Liverpool, England. During the North-South conflict he served the Unitarian Church in Washington, giving his full support to the Union. After the Union victory he returned to England, where he preached and lectured until his death in 1884.

Channing launched *The Present* with "A Confession of Faith," a creed that represents the finest summary of his romantic theology. That document is here reproduced in its entirety.

DOCUMENT

To publish a Credo, may well seem to imply pretension or dullness; for the guesses of a creature whose existence is bounded to a speck, limited to a moment, must be folly. Such a publication, too, subjects one to the charge of cant on some sides and heresy on others, and has this difficulty attending it, that no selection of words and phrases can make a meaning so plain as not to be misapprehended. And yet in these Babel times of various *isms,* it is but fair and courteous, that every one who offers himself in any sense as a guide, should point out the direction in which he aims to lead. Pledging myself, then, to no other consistency than conviction, and hoping, year by year, month by month, and day by day, to gain juster views, I am ready to confess that, briefly sketched, and without completeness or scientific accuracy, my present faith is as follows:

I. The Divine Being, Nature, Spirits.

I believe,

1. That the Infinite, Eternal, all-blessed Being, who alone is God, from essential love, through ideas of truth, puts forth benign and beautiful creative power from everlasting to everlasting;

2. That, in harmonious series of existences, endless in numbers and varieties, and sublimely related by successive growths, mutual dependence and analogy, he manifests his perfections in forever brighter glory;

3. That, through systems on systems, and worlds on worlds, he crowns his creations by giving birth to hosts of spirits, destined originally, through revelations, for ever brightening, to grow up in his likeness, and, by interchanges of good, to be united into families of immortal children, imaging in the heavens their holy Father;

4. That these spirits are born in races, the individuals of which are organised by transmitted qualities into living wholes, and occupy, upon the globes where they find their school, the position of mediators between the temporal and eternal worlds—through animal natures which concentrate the excellencies of lower creations, communing with the harmonies of the universe—through souls receiving inspiration of love and truth and beauty, from God—through powers of rational volition, and in intercourse with fellow-spirits recombining these influences, and diffusing them for the formation of society and the perfecting of nature; and, by this alternate action and reaction, assimilating life in perpetual new-birth.

II. The Human Race.

I believe,

1. That the human race, upon this earth, thus constituted of nations and men, thus placed between God's inspiration and nature's limited forms of good, thus endowed with free intelligence, is led by Providence through a discipline, of which the past is the history and the present the experience, filled as it is with prophecy of a future, which, in the fullness of time, shall actualize its ideal;

2. That, in the process of this destined growth from instinctive harmonies to conscious and chosen conformity to God and good spirits, and the union thence ensuing, which is immortality, mankind have, through causes acting from past ages, and originating in themselves, yielded too much to the impressions of nature; allowed the excessive development of the animal passions; exaggerated the element of self; confused the judgments, weakened the power of the spiritual faculties; broken true society; in various degrees become incapable of receiving life from heaven; and so interrupted the divine order, and introduced depraved social tendencies, diseases, and natural confusions, which react to multiply evil;

3. That the Eternal Father, in whom disinterestedness and rectitude, mercy and justice, are one in unbroken peace, whose action is the unlimited diffusion of good, has never left men to themselves; but has sorrowed in their failures, rejoiced in their successes, forborne with their perverseness, suffered with their sufferings, and, through every means, not violating their reason and prudence—through the beautiful harmonies contrasted with the dread convulsions of nature, through lovely relations amidst monstrous social struggles, through remembrances and anticipations of higher joys, breaking in upon the stern miseries of their self-imposed condition—has infused foreshadows of perfect union in perfect bliss;

4. That the worships and legislations, wars and alliances, colonizations and empires of all ages, have been the steps of this progressive conquest of good over evil, by which mankind have been at once redeemed and educated, and that saints and sages, prophets and poets, heroes of high and humble spheres, martyrs of many grades, the gracious and lovely of all people, are the ministering servants of Providence in this grand work of salvation.

III. The Jewish Tribes and Jesus Christ.

I believe,

1. That, in this ministry of reconciliation, this establishment of religion, in which all families of the race conspire, the Jewish tribes, who combined in singular intenseness high aspiration, stubborn wilfulness, and coarse sensuality, have been used as a centre of spiritual influence, as they were a centre in physical position;

2. That, carefully guarding the purest traditions, profoundly conscious

of God's inspiring presence, sternly announcing the divine law, illustrating in their fortunes his government, even amidst deepest degradation and guilt declaring his promises in glowing visions, they have revealed, as in a symbol, the progress of the human race, from Adam once blessed in Eden, through the woes of selfish division, to the far more blessed reunion of all nations in the city of peace, where God shall dwell with men and be their God;

3. That in the fullness of time, when the civilization of East and West had borne their fruits and were falling into decay, when floods of untamed, vigorous tribes were gathering to oversweep and cover with fresh soil the exhausted nations, when universal man stood watching in mournfulness and longing, was born Jesus; conceived in holiness by a devout mother, cradled in her solemn aspirations, nurtured on the prophetic hopes of his nation and age, filled, in his human nature, with the fullness of a superhuman life, a son of man transfigured by goodness, and made a Son of God —a divine man;

4. That he was commissioned and anointed to be the image of the Father, the Adam of a spiritualized and reunited race, the prophecy of redeemed humanity, the desire of all nations, the way, the truth, the life; and that, by his life and death of perfect self-sacrifice, by his words of inspired wisdom, by his purely disinterested deeds, in the joy of oneness with God and man and nature, he had the glory of founding upon the new commandment, love, the kingdom of Heaven on earth.

IV. The Kingdom of Heaven.

I believe,

1. That the reign of Him, who alone is good, the King of Kings and Lord of Lords, shall be universal, and shall organize the now warring and scattered nations into one holy society, where justice, wisdom, joy, shall harmonize the external world, and crowd it with countless varieties of beautiful productions;

2. That the central power of this kingdom of Heaven is holiness, the indwelling spirit of God, which ever more brightly reveals its presence in the growing spirituality and humanity of the free, brave, and generous tribes, whom Providence appointed to diffuse this life; ever more visibly organizes their policies and legislations, their philosophies and ethics, their literatures and arts, their modes of social and private action; and is now hastening to mould mankind into communities of devout and loving, wise and earnest, healthful and happy beings, where the ideal of heavenly order may be worthily imaged, and God shall be all in all;

3. That, in the establishment of this heavenly order upon earth, the churches of Christendom have been instrumental as depositories, amid an unreconciled world, of the gospel of peace, as professors and partial practisers of godliness, as imperfect symbols of that society, truly one, holy, and

universal, which, in God's own time and way, shall be visibly organized; but that they have all, in various degrees, been guilty of the great heresy of giving preference to what is of only secondary importance, of substituting speculations for faith, human fallibility for heavenly inspiration, a priesthood of man's ordination for the ministry of God's anointing, creeds for charity, prayers for self-sacrifice, rituals for rectitude, and a service of days, places, and forms, for the perpetual worship of souls, becoming united to God, their fellow-spirits, and the universe, through goodness, wisdom, and beauty, continually received and diffused;

4. That the schisms and infidelities, which have resulted as necessary reactions against this heresy, the divisions between church and state, science and revelation, piety and industry, duty and joy, ending as they do in hypocritical asceticism and worldly materialism, and augmenting, as they have and will, the jealousies between man and man, class and class, nation and nation, will never cease till Christians abandon sophistical polemics and sentimental or formal piety, and manifest, in practical affairs, their faith by their works; till, acknowledging God as sovereign and his law of goodness as supreme, they reform their constitutions and treaties, their intercourse and trade, their modes of producing and distributing wealth, their plans of education, their rewards and privileges, their means of elevation and pleasure, their homes and all relations, their characters and lives, after the models of divine righteousness.

V. The United States a Member of Christendom.

I believe,

1. That, as a member of the confederacy of Christendom, these United States have peculiar opportunities and duties; that consecrated by the devout faithfulness of forefathers, whom Providence led to this new-found land —planted at the very season when the vital elements of Europe, Christian love and German freedom, were casting off the oppressions of outgrown usages, and prompting men to seek a more earnest piety and a purer virtue —guided onward through a discipline of toil and poverty and simple habits, through unexampled experiences in social government, and the gradual growth of untried institutions—forced by necessities of condition, by slow-formed convictions, and the tendencies of a whole age, to a declaration of principles, which is the clearest announcement of universal rights, though, unfortunately, not of universal duties, ever made by any people—permitted to expand through an unobstructed, unexhausted, healthful, fertile, and most beautiful country—wondrously composed of representatives from every European state, who bring hither the varied experiences, convictions, manners, tastes, of the whole civilized world, to fuse and blend anew—this nation is manifestly summoned to prove the reality of human brotherhood, and of a worship of the heavenly Father, varied as the relations, grand as the destinies of present existence;

2. That, acknowledging, as we do, our providential mission to fulfil the law of love, and professing, as we do, to encourage each and every member of our communities in the exercise of their inalienable rights, we stand before the face of God and fellow-nations, as guilty of hypocrisy and of a breach of trust;

3. That we deserve the retributions, losses, disgraces, which our savage robberies of the Indians, our cruel and wanton oppressions of the Africans, our unjust habits of white serfdom, our grasping national ambition, our eagerness for wealth, our deceitful modes of external and internal trade, our jealous competitions between different professions and callings, our aping of aristocratic distinctions, our licentiousness and sensuality, our profligate expenditures, public and private, have brought, and will continue to bring upon us;

4. That it behoves our religious bodies, our political parties, our statesmen and philosophers, our scholars and patriots, and all who desire a growing life for themselves or their race, to put aside questions of minor importance, and concentrate their energies upon measures which may remove inhumanity utterly from our land;

5. That our duties will not be done, our ideal will not be fulfilled, till we solve the problem of UNITED INTERESTS, now pressing upon all Christendom; till, within our own borders, we secure for every individual man, woman, child, full culture, under healthy, pure, and holy influences; free exercise of their faculties, for the glory of God and the good of man; recompense for all services that shall be just; such stations of honorable usefulness as their virtues merit, and access to all sources of refinement and happiness which our communities can command—till, in intercourse with other lands, we strive honestly and bountifully to share the blessings which the universal Father gives, and so aid to reunite all nations in one family of the children of God, where his will shall be done on earth as it is in heaven.

SOURCE: William Henry Channing, "A Confession of Faith," *The Present,* I (September, 1843), 6–9.

121. The Class Struggle

Like William Henry Channing, Orestes A. Brownson (1803–76) was one of the new school's prominent social reformers, but his social insights as well as his philosophical powers were far more acute than Channing's.

Brownson's remarkable pilgrimage from Calvinism to Catholicism must be seen in terms of his unusual experience. Born in the small frontier settlement of Stockbridge, Vermont, he saw little of culture and as a child knew only the most rigid type of Protestant orthodoxy. At the age of fourteen he and his mother moved to the little upstate New York community of Ballston Spa, where he learned the printer's trade and where he briefly attended an academy, with which his formal education ended. At nineteen he became a Presbyterian, but within two years joined the Universalists, and finally became one of their ministers. His social and theological liberalism soon carried him beyond the pale of his denomination, and for a short interval he allied himself with Frances Wright's socialist enterprises and supported the Working Men's Party of New York. After a brief experience of infidelity, he resumed preaching on an independent basis, but in 1832 united with the Unitarians and accepted a pastorate at Walpole, New Hampshire. While there he met many Boston liberals, and soon became so friendly with George Ripley that they often exchanged books. When, in May of 1834, Brownson became pastor of the church at Canton, Massachusetts, Ripley preached his installation sermon.

By this time Brownson was a zealous crusader for the working man, especially the industrial laborer; and he insisted that unless the church of the future engaged in radical social reform it would lose its creative leadership. With the encouragement of his friends, he began in May of 1836 independent services in the Lyceum Hall in Boston, and presently founded the Society for Christian Union and Progress. The principles underlying the Society were fully expounded in Brownson's *New Views of Christianity, Society and the Church* (1836), a book which owed much to Saint-Simon's *Nouveau Christianisme*. After three years the Society seems to have declined, but in its more active period its normal weekly attendance has been estimated at about three hundred.[80] The cause of the laborer was kept before the congregation, and the Kingdom of God was presented as an ideal social order to be progressively realized on earth.[81]

In the midst of his ministry to the Society, Brownson founded in January of 1838 the *Boston Quarterly Review,* one of the most brilliant journals of its time. Though ceasing as an independent journal in 1841, it promoted "the progress of Humanity" on all fronts while it lasted. Although the editor aligned himself with the transcendental movement, he was always critical of its more mystical stargazers.[82] His supreme commitment, as already observed, was to the industrial proletarian, whom he considered to be no better off than the Negro slave. Thus in 1840, at the peak of his social radicalism, he published his most celebrated essay, "The Laboring Classes."[83] As a means of improving the economic condition of the proletarian, he therein recommended the abolition of hereditary property. Even his liberal friends recoiled from this drastic idea, and of course the capitalists were outraged by it. Yet, far from bowing to the clamor, Brownson used

[80] William R. Hutchison, *The Transcendentalist Ministers,* 158.

[81] In this period of his religious thought, Brownson foreshadowed much of what was to be known as the social gospel in the late 1890's and early 1900's. See his "The Kingdom of God," *Boston Quarterly Review,* II (1839), 326–50.

[82] For a good analysis of the *Review*'s contribution to social and religious thought, see Clarence L. F. Gohdes, *The Periodicals of American Transcendentalism* (Durham, N.C., 1931), 38–82.

[83] *Boston Quarterly Review,* III (1840), 358–96.

ninety pages in the very next issue of the *Review* in further defense of his views.[84] Since the author was a prominent Democrat, his radicalism greatly embarrassed the party in its effort in 1840 to win the presidency for Van Buren against the Whig, Harrison. In order to further their "hard cider" cause, the Whigs only needed to tar Van Buren with Brownson's socialistic brush. With much truth Brownson has been called Karl Marx's "nearest forerunner in America." [85]

Almost immediately Brownson began a rapid retreat from his radical social and religious positions—a retreat which finally ended in his becoming (October, 1844) a Roman Catholic.[86] Like most converts, he was at first doubly zealous in defending his new faith and in condemning his former views. After the middle 1850's, however, he gradually recovered something of his earlier mental independence, and indeed went so far as to present ideas, such as the absolute separation of church and state and the need for a modern Catholic apologetic, which rendered him suspect within his own church.[87] Thus when in 1864 Pius IX issued the Syllabus of Errors, the convert, believing himself included among those condemned, at once discontinued *Brownson's Quarterly Review,* a journal which had existed for twenty years. Near the end of his life, however, Brownson revived the *Review.*

The present document is extracted from Brownson's first article on "The Laboring Classes."

DOCUMENT

No one can observe the signs of the times with much care, without perceiving that a crisis as to the relation of wealth and labor is approaching. It is useless to shut our eyes to the fact, and like the ostrich fancy ourselves secure because we have so concealed our heads that we see not the danger. We or our children will have to meet this crisis. The old war between the King and the Barons is well nigh ended, and so is that between the Barons and the Merchants and Manufacturers,—landed capital and commercial capital. The business man has become the peer of my Lord. And now commences the new struggle between the operative and his employer, between wealth and labor. . . .

In regard to labor two systems obtain; one that of slave labor, the other that of free labor. Of the two, the first is, in our judgment, except so far as the feelings are concerned, decidedly the least oppressive. If the slave

[84] "The Laboring Classes," *Boston Quarterly Review,* III (1840), 420–510.

[85] Arthur M. Schlesinger, Jr., *Orestes A. Brownson: A Pilgrim's Progress* (Boston, 1939), 100.

[86] Brownson, "The Convert," in Alvan S. Ryan, ed., *The Brownson Reader* (N.Y., 1955), 287–303. See also Theodore Maynard, *Orestes Brownson: Yankee, Radical, Catholic* (N.Y., 1943), Chap. 8.

[87] Brownson, "Catholic Polemics," in Ryan, ed., *Brownson Reader,* 331–40; "Civil and Religious Freedom," *ibid.,* 349–56.

has never been a free man, we think, as a general rule, his sufferings are less than those of the free laborer at wages. As to actual freedom one has just about as much as the other. The laborer at wages has all the disadvantages of freedom and none of its blessings, while the slave, if denied the blessings, is freed from the disadvantages. We are no advocates of slavery, we are as heartily opposed to it as any modern abolitionist can be; but we say frankly that, if there must always be a laboring population distinct from proprietors and employers, we regard the slave system as decidedly preferable to the system at wages. . . .

We know no sadder sight on earth than one of our factory villages presents, when the bell at break of day, or at the hour of breakfast, or dinner, calls out its hundreds or thousands of operatives. We stand and look at these hard working men and women hurrying in all directions, and ask ourselves, where go the proceeds of their labors? The man who employs them, and for whom they are toiling as so many slaves, is one of our city nabobs, revelling in luxury; or he is a member of our legislature, enacting laws to put money in his own pocket; or he is a member of Congress, contending for a high Tariff to tax the poor for the benefit of the rich; or in these times he is shedding crocodile tears over the deplorable condition of the poor laborer, while he docks his wages twenty-five per cent.; building miniature log cabins, shouting Harrison and "hard cider." And this man too would fain pass for a Christian and a republican. He shouts for liberty, stickles for equality, and is horrified at a Southern planter who keeps slaves.

One thing is certain; that of the amount actually produced by the operative, he retains a less proportion than it costs the master to feed, clothe, and lodge his slave. Wages is a cunning device of the devil, for the benefit of tender consciences, who would retain all the advantages of the slave system, without the expense, trouble, and odium of being slave-holders. . . .

We really believe our Northern system of labor is more oppressive, and even more mischievous to morals, than the Southern. We, however, war against both. We have no toleration for either system. We would see the slave a man, but a free man, not a mere operative at wages. This he would not be were he now emancipated. Could the abolitionists effect all they propose, they would do the slave no service. Should emancipation work as well as they say, still it would do the slave no good. He would be a slave still, although with the title and cares of a freeman. If then we had no constitutional objections to abolitionism, we could not, for the reason here implied, be abolitionists. . . .

Now the great work for this age and the coming, is to raise up the laborer, and to realize in our own social arrangements and in the actual condition of all men, that equality between man and man, which God has established between the rights of one and those of another. In other words, our business is to emancipate the proletaries, as the past has emancipated the slaves. This is our work. There must be no class of our fellow men doomed to toil through life as mere workmen at wages. If wages are tolerated it must be, in the case of the individual operative, only under such conditions that by the time he is of a proper age to settle in life, he shall have accumulated enough to be an independent laborer on his own capital,—on his own farm or in his own shop. Here is our work. How is it to be done?

Reformers in general answer this question, or what they deem its equivalent, in a manner which we cannot but regard as very unsatisfactory. They would have all men wise, good, and happy; but in order to make them so, they tell us that we want not external changes, but internal; and therefore instead of declaiming against society and seeking to disurb [sic] existing social arrangements, we should confine ourselves to the individual reason and conscience; seek merely to lead the individual to repentance, and to reformation of life; make the individual a practical, a truly religious man, and all evils will either disappear, or be sanctified to the spiritual growth of the soul. . . .

This theory, however, is exposed to one slight objection, that of being condemned by something like six thousand years' experience. For six thousand years its beauty has been extolled, its praises sung, and its blessings sought, under every advantage which learning, fashion, wealth, and power can secure; and yet under its practical operations, we are assured, that mankind, though totally depraved at first, have been growing worse and worse ever since. . . .

The truth is, the evil we have pointed out is not merely individual in its character. It is not, in the case of any single individual, of any one man's procuring, nor can the efforts of any one man, directed solely to his own moral and religious perfection, do aught to remove it. What is purely individual in its nature, efforts of individuals to perfect themselves, may remove. But the evil we speak of is inherent in all our social arrangements, and cannot be cured without a radical change of those arrangements. Could we convert all men to Christianity in both theory and practice, as held by the most enlightened sect of Christians among us, the evils of the social state would remain untouched. Continue our present system of trade, and all its present evil consequences will follow, whether it be carried on by your best men or your worst. . . .

But whence has this evil originated? How comes it that all over the world the working classes are depressed, are the low and vulgar, and virtually the slaves of the non-working classes? This is an inquiry which has not yet received the attention it deserves. It is not enough to answer, that it has originated entirely in the inferiority by nature of the working classes; that they have less skill and foresight, and are less able than the upper classes, to provide for themselves, or less susceptible of the highest moral and intellectual cultivation. Nor is it sufficient for our purpose to be told, that

Providence has decreed that some shall be poor and wretched, ignorant and vulgar; and that others shall be rich and vicious, learned and polite, oppressive and miserable. We do not choose to charge this matter to the will of God. "The foolishness of man perverteth his way, and his heart fretteth against the Lord." God has made of one blood all the nations of men to dwell on all the face of the earth, and to dwell there as brothers, as members of one and the same family; and although he has made them with a diversity of powers, it would perhaps, after all, be a bold assertion to say that he has made them with an inequality of powers. There is nothing in the actual difference of the powers of individuals, which accounts for the striking inequalities we everywhere discover in their condition. The child of the plebeian, if placed early in the proper circumstances, grows up not less beautiful, active, intelligent, and refined, than the child of the patrician; and the child of the patrician may become as coarse, as brutish as the child of any slave. So far as observation on the original capacities of individuals goes, nothing is discovered to throw much light on social inequalities. . . .

For our part we are disposed to seek the cause of the inequality of conditions of which we speak, in religion, and to charge it to the priesthood. . . .

Man is naturally a religious being, and disposed to stand in awe of invisible powers. . . . Can their anger be appeased? Can their favor be secured? Thus he asks himself. Unable to answer, he goes to the more aged and experienced of his tribe, and asks them the same questions. They answer as best they can. What is done by one is done by another, and what is done once is done again. The necessity of instruction, which each one feels in consequence of his own feebleness and inexperience, renders the recurrence to those best capable of giving it, or supposed to be the best capable of giving it, frequent and uniform. Hence the priest. . . . Once thus distinguished, he becomes an object of envy. His condition is looked upon as superior to that of the mass. Hence a multitude aspire to possess themselves of it. When once the class has become somewhat numerous, it labors to secure to itself the distinction it has received, its honors and its emoluments, and to increase them. Hence the establishment of priesthoods or sacerdotal corporations, such as the Egyptian, the Braminical, the Ethiopian, the Jewish, the Scandinavian, the Druidical, the Mexican, and Peruvian. . . .

But, having traced the inequality we complain of to its origin, we proceed to ask again what is the remedy? The remedy is first to be sought in the destruction of the priest. We are not mere destructives. We delight not in pulling down; but the bad must be removed before the good can be introduced. Conviction and repentance precede regeneration. Moreover we are Christians, and it is only by following out the Christian law, and the example of the early Christians, that we can hope to effect anything. Christianity is the sublimest protest against the priesthood ever uttered, and a protest uttered by both God and man; for he who uttered it was

God-Man. In the person of Jesus both God and Man protest against the priesthood. What was the mission of Jesus but a solemn summons of every priesthood on earth to judgment, and of the human race to freedom? He discomfited the learned doctors, and with whips of small cords drove the priests, degenerated into mere money changers, from the temple of God. He instituted himself no priesthood, no form of religious worship. He recognized no priest but a holy life, and commanded the construction of no temple but that of the pure heart. He preached no formal religion, enjoined no creed, set apart no day for religious worship. He preached fraternal love, peace on earth, and good will to men. . . .

We object not to religious instruction; we object not to the gathering together of the people on one day in seven, to sing and pray, and listen to a discourse from a religious teacher; but we object to everything like an outward, visible church; to everything that in the remotest degree partakes of the priest. A priest is one who stands as a sort of mediator between God and man; but we have one mediator, Jesus Christ, who gave himself a ransom for all, and that is enough. It may be supposed that we, protestants, have no priests; but for ourselves we know no fundamental difference between a catholic priest and a protestant clergyman, as we know no difference of any magnitude, in relation to the principles on which they are based, between a protestant church and the catholic church. Both are based on the principle of authority; both deny in fact, however it may be in manner, the authority of reason, and war against freedom of mind; both substitute dead works for true righteousness, a vain show for the reality of piety, and are sustained as the means of reconciling us to God without requiring us to become godlike. Both therefore ought to go by the board. . . .

The next step in this work of elevating the working classes will be to resuscitate the Christianity of Christ. The Christianity of the Church has done its work. We have had enough of that Christianity. It is powerless for good, but by no means powerless for evil. It now unmans us and hinders the growth of God's kingdom. The moral energy which is awakened it misdirects, and makes its deluded disciples believe that they have done their duty to God when they have joined the church, offered a prayer, sung a psalm, and contributed of their means to send out a missionary to preach unintelligible dogmas to the poor heathen, who, God knows, have unintelligible dogmas enough already, and more than enough. All this must be abandoned, and Christianity, as it came from Christ, be taken up, and preached, and preached in simplicity and in power.

According to the Christianity of Christ no man can enter the kingdom of God, who does not labor with all zeal and diligence to establish the kingdom of God on the earth; who does not labor to bring down the high, and bring up the low; to break the fetters of the bound and set the captive free; to destroy all oppression, establish the reign of justice, which is the reign of equality, between man and man; to introduce new heavens and a new earth, wherein dwelleth righteousness, wherein all shall be as brothers, loving one another, and no one possessing what another lacketh. . . .

Having, by breaking down the power of the priesthood and the Christianity of the priests, obtained an open field and freedom for our operations, and by preaching the true Gospel of Jesus, directed all minds to the great social reform needed, and quickened in all souls the moral power to live for it or to die for it; our next resort must be to government, to legislative enactments. Government is instituted to be the agent of society, or more properly the organ through which society may perform its legitimate functions. It is not the master of society; its business is not to control society, but to be the organ through which society effects its will. Society has never to petition government; government is its servant, and subject to its commands. . . .

But what shall government do? Its first doing must be an *undoing*. There has been thus far quite too much government, as well as government of the wrong kind. The first act of government we want, is a still further limitation of itself. It must begin by circumscribing within narrower limits its powers. And then it must proceed to repeal all laws which bear against the laboring classes, and then to enact such laws as are necessary to enable them to maintain their equality. We have no faith in those systems of elevating the working classes, which propose to elevate them without calling in the aid of the government. We must have government, and legislation expressly directed to this end.

But again what legislation do we want so far as this country is concerned? We want first the legislation which shall free the government, whether State or Federal, from the control of the Banks. The Banks represent the interest of the employer, and therefore of necessity interests adverse to those of the employed; that is, they represent the interests of the business community in opposition to the laboring community. So long as the government remains under the control of the Banks, so long it must be in the hands of the natural enemies of the laboring classes, and may be made, nay, will be made, an instrument of depressing them yet lower. . . .

Following the distruction [sic] of the Banks, must come that of all monopolies, of all PRIVILEGE. There are many of these. We cannot specify them all; we therefore select only one, the greatest of them all, the privilege which some have of being born rich while others are born poor. It will be seen at once that we allude to the hereditary descent of property, an anomaly in our American system, which must be removed, or the system itself will be destroyed. . . . A man shall have all he honestly acquires, so long as he himself belongs to the world in which he acquires it. But his power over his property must cease with his life, and his property must then become the property of the state, to be disposed of by some equitable law for the use of the generation which takes his place. Here is the principle without any of its details, and this is the grand legislative measure to which we look forward. We see no means of elevating the laboring classes which can be effectual without this. And is this a measure to be easily carried? Not at all. It will cost infinitely more than it cost to abolish either hereditary monarchy or hereditary nobility. It is a great measure, and a startling. The rich, the business community, will never voluntarily consent to it, and we think we know too much of human nature to believe that it will ever be effected peaceably. It will be effected only by the strong arm of physical force. It will come, if it ever come at all, only at the conclusion of war, the like of which the world as yet has never witnessed, and from which, however inevitable it may seem to the eye of philosophy, the heart of Humanity recoils with horror.

We are not ready for this measure yet. There is much previous work to be done, and we should be the last to bring it before the legislature. The time, however, has come for its free and full discussion. It must be canvassed in the public mind, and society prepared for acting on it. No doubt they who broach it, and especially they who support it, will experience a due share of contumely and abuse.

> SOURCE: Orestes A. Brownson, "The Laboring Classes," *Boston Quarterly Review*, III (1840), 366, 368, 370–1, 373–80, 384–6, 388, 391–5.

122. Truth in Oriental Religions

One of the first Americans to devote extensive scholarly theological and philosophical study to the non-Christian religions was a transcendentalist, James Freeman Clarke (1810–88).[88]

Until ten years of age, Clarke was largely under the tutelage of his step-grandfather, James Freeman, famed minister of King's Chapel in Boston. He was educated at Boston Latin School, Harvard College, and Harvard Divinity School. While in the Divinity School, he mastered German and read, in the original, Goethe, Schiller, and Schleiermacher.[89]

Ordained in July of 1833, Clarke began his ministry in a small Unitarian church at Louisville, Kentucky. In 1835 he helped to establish the pioneer periodical of American transcendentalism, *The Western Messenger*, of which he was editor from 1836 to 1839.

The young transcendentalist was not at home on the frontier; indeed, he often longed for the cultured East. Hence, in June of 1840 he offered his resignation, although he had nothing else in sight. Going to Boston,

---

[88] Before Clarke's investigations there had, of course, been considerable research in the field of the Oriental languages. To promote this interest the American Oriental Society was founded in 1842.

[89] John W. Thomas, *James Freeman Clarke: Apostle of German Culture in America* (Boston, 1949), 25–6. A partner in reading German was his warm friend, Margaret Fuller, later editor of the *Dial*.

he began preaching to a group of Unitarians who were dissatisfied with the conventional type of church service. Out of this grew the Church of the Disciples, which was organized in April of 1841.[90] The forty-eight charter members subscribed to the following Declaration: "Our faith is in Jesus, as the Christ, the Son of God; and we hereby form ourselves into a Church of the Disciples, that we may cooperate together in the study and practice of Christianity." [91]

Clarke began some new features. For example, he discontinued the old New England dual plan of having both a "church" and a "society" (the latter existing only to transact business), and formed just one body, the church. Also, he abolished the pew-owning and pew-renting system and handled the budget on a voluntary basis. Again, he had the members of the church undertake special study and service during the week. Finally, he provided for lay participation in the Sunday service of worship.[92]

These innovations, plus Clarke's vital preaching, soon made the Disciples a thriving and influential body. Meanwhile, the minister grew in popular esteem and was showered with many public honors. For example, he served on the State Board of Education and was an overseer at Harvard. For a time he was also a nonresident professor in the Divinity School. His greatest influence, however, was probably wielded by his writing, which was prolific.

By mid-century Clarke became deeply engrossed in the study of the non-Christian faiths, and he familiarized himself with the best British and Continental scholarship in this field. Thus in the year 1857 he published a prophetic article in the *Christian Examiner* in which he contended that the Oriental religions were not, as viewed by most Christians, wholly untrue. He did not place the ethnic religions on a par with Christianity, yet he viewed them as stepping stones to the higher truth in Christ.

The heart of the essay in the *Christian Examiner* is contained in the following document. Although the author later expanded his thought in two large volumes, *Ten Great Religions* (1870, 1883), he did not add anything essentially new to the position taken in 1857.

DOCUMENT

According to the old way of regarding the religions of the world, they were divided into two classes, the true and the false. Judaism and Christianity were the true religions; all the other religions of the world were false. In the true religions there was nothing false; in the false religions, nothing true. Wherever in false religions there was any trace of truth, it was so darkened and perverted as to be little better than error. The belief in one God had degenerated into polytheism, spiritual worship had sunk into

[90] Clarke, *A Sermon on the Principles and Methods of the Church of the Disciples. . . . Dec. 7, 1845* (Boston, 1846), 30.
[91] *Ibid.*, 4.   [92] *Ibid.*, 4–18.

idolatry, the belief in immortality and retribution had become feeble and inefficient. As the doctrines of heathenism were thus corrupt, so its worship was superstitious and formal. Unmeaning ceremonies took the place of gratitude, reverence, and prayer. The influence, therefore, of these religions tended to make men worse, and not better, producing sensuality, cruelty, and universal degradation. Such religions as these could not be believed to come from God, nor even from the better part of the nature of man. They are therefore supposed to have been the invention of priestcraft, and a deliberate imposition on the people. This is the dark picture of heathen religions which we have all been taught in our childhood, and which is set up as a gloomy background to give relief and prominence to revelation. A supernatural revelation had become necessary, so it was argued, because the religions of the world were so utterly corrupt and corrupting. . . .

Now, when we look at this theory of the heathen world, there is much about it quite unsatisfactory. Let us consider it.

To ascribe the vast phenomena of religion, in all their variety and complexity, to man as their author, and to suppose the whole a mere work of human will, is not a satisfactory solution of these phenomena. That priests, working on human ignorance and fear, should be able to build up such a great mass of opinion, sentiment, and act, is like supposing a cathedral to be built on a quicksand.

How happens it, if the people are so ignorant, that the priests are so wise? If the people are so credulous, why are not the priests credulous also? Among so many nations, and through so many centuries, why has no priest betrayed the secret of the imposition? Apply a similar theory to other human pursuits, and how easily we discover its absurdity. . . . We say, therefore, that the foundation of these religions is not priestcraft, but some permanent need of the human soul. They are founded, not on man's will, but on man's nature. Their source is not pure fraud, but the feeling of dependence, the sense of accountability, the need of worship, and the instinct which makes us recognize the presence of the spiritual in the midst of material things.

Nor can it be believed by one who believes in Providence that God has left himself without a witness in the world in ancient times except among the Hebrews, and in modern times except among the Christians. This narrow creed excludes God from communion with the great majority of human beings. It teaches that he has forgotten to be gracious except in the land of Palestine, that he only makes himself known to Abraham and his descendants, and leaves the rest of mankind orphaned. Is this the Being without whom not a sparrow falls to the ground,—the Being who never puts an insect into the air, or a polype into the water, without providing it with some appropriate food, so that it may live and grow? Does he leave men, made with religious appetencies of reverence, conscience, hope, with no corresponding nutriment of truth? This view tends to atheism; for if the presence of adaptation everywhere is the legitimate proof of the being of God, the absence of these adaptations in so large and important a sphere of existence tends in so far to overthrow that evidence.

This view, also, which we are opposing, contradicts that law of progress which alone gives unity and meaning to history. It teaches, instead of progress, degeneracy and failure. The world is a mistake, a badly made machine, which has to be stopped and mended. The real God of the world is Satan, and from nine tenths of the world he has expelled its Creator. We cannot sing the psalm, "The Lord reigneth, let the earth rejoice"; for disorder and confusion reign. But everywhere else we see progress, not recession. Geology shows us higher forms of life succeeding to the lower. Botany shows us the lichens and mosses preparing a soil for higher forms of vegetation. Civil history shows the savage state giving way to the semi-civilized, and that to the civilized. Everywhere else the lower form prepares for the next and higher which succeeds it. If heathen religions are preparations for Christ, then we can see a progress, and an order, and understand why Christ's coming was delayed, and why he came when he did. But otherwise, the law of the world is disorder; that is, *not* law, but caprice and accident; that is, *no* God present in it, for God is Order. Disorder and atheism are the rule, order and the presence of God the exception.

Nor do the facts which we observe in the religions of the world confirm the popular view. In their essence they are not superstitions, but religions. Their doctrines as a whole convey truth rather than falsehood. Their moral tendency, in the main, is good rather than evil. And instead of degenerating towards that which is worse, their movement is upward toward something better. . . .

This view, which does justice to heathenism, will do justice also to Christianity. Recognizing the truths in heathenism, it can demonstrate that they are all partial and incomplete, that a universal religion is also needed to fulfil and harmonize them, and that this universal religion can be nothing but Christianity. The religion of Jesus, of which Judaism is the root, and Islam a Judaizing sect, is shown by this new science to be the only possible religion for the human race. Every ethnic religion is a preparation for it; and Christianity, supplying the deficiencies of each, brings it into harmony with the rest. A life rather than a creed, it has the power of admitting into itself every good thing out of every creed. It has within itself a spiritualism as profound as that of the Vedas, and more vital; it recognizes, like Buddhism, the progress of the soul through the laws of nature; like the system of Confucius, it sees a divine order in the relations of human life; like Zoroaster, it places man between good and evil, and tells him to choose between them; with the Egyptian, it can recognize something divine even in the lowest forms of animal existence; with the Greek, it can reverence the ideals of human nature; with the Roman, hear the voice of God in the voice of the nation; and, lastly, with the Scandinavian, find the true worship of God in the stern conflicts of human life. Thus is the genius of the Gospel catholic enough to receive all ethnic creeds into itself; but it could not do this unless it had something to impart in which they are all deficient. This something, which is the catholic principle in Christianity, is the knowledge of God as Father, and so of man as brother. No ethnic religion has this knowledge; it is the life-principle in Christianity,—perfect life, because perfect love. Our new science is therefore a confutation of all Deism, just as it was a confutation of all Atheism.

Observe also what will be the practical results of this view. How changed will be the aspect of missions! Protestant missions have been hitherto conducted in a contemptuous ignorance of the condition of the soul which was to be enlightened. "He is a poor, benighted heathen—give him light,"—has been the whole prescription. . . .

Different from the hitherto Jesuit and Protestant methods would be the form of missionary action resulting from the new view of heathenism. The missionary in a heathen country will say, "Amid all this error there is a grain of God's truth, amid all this evil there is a seed of God's good." This belief will be seen in all his intercourse with the heathen, and will disarm their hostility. They will see that the object to be accomplished is not the overthrow of their system, but its improvement and purification.

> SOURCE: James Freeman Clarke, "Comparative Theology of Heathen Religions," *Christian Examiner,* LXII (1857), 183, 185-7, 194-6.

LITERATURE

Perry Miller's *The Transcendentalists: An Anthology* (Cambridge, Mass., 1950) contains an indispensable body of primary materials. The best single essay on origins is Alexander Kern's "The Rise of Transcendentalism, 1815-1860," in Harry Hayden Clark, ed., *Transitions in American Literary History* (Durham, N.C., 1953), 247-314. Transcendentalism is viewed as "the flowering of the Enlightenment" in Herbert W. Schneider's *A History of American Philosophy* (N.Y., 1946), 261-318. An instructive specialized work is Clarence L. F. Gohdes' *The Periodicals of American Transcendentalism* (Durham, N.C., 1931).

For the extra-American sources of transcendentalism, see Arthur E. Christy, *The Orient in American Transcendentalism: A Study of Emerson, Thoreau, and Alcott* (N.Y., 1932); Henry A. Pochmann, *German Culture in America: Philosophical and Literary Influences, 1600-1900* (Madison, Wis., 1957); René Wellek, "The Minor Transcendentalists and German Philosophy," *New England Quarterly,* XVI (1943), 41-62; E. W. Todd, "Philosophical Ideas at Harvard College, 1817-1837," *New England Quarterly,* XVI (1943), 63-90; Sydney E. Ahlstrom, "The Scottish Philosophy and American Theology," *Church History,* XXIV (1955), 257-72; Noah Porter, "Coleridge and His American Disciples," *Bibliotheca Sacra and Theological Review,* IV (1847), 117-71; Marjorie H.

Nicholson, "James Marsh and the Vermont Transcendentalists," *Philosophical Review*, XXXIV (1925), 28–50.

Transcendentalism in its religious expression is excellently treated in William R. Hutchison's *The Transcendentalist Ministers: Church Reform in the New England Renaissance* (New Haven, 1959), which also provides a valuable classified bibliography. For accounts of the older Unitarian doctrines against which the transcendentalists revolted, see O. B. Frothingham, *Boston Unitarianism, 1820–1850* (Boston, 1890); Clarence H. Faust, "The Background of the Unitarian Opposition to Transcendentalism," *Modern Philology*, XXXV (1938), 297–324; and Conrad Wright, "The Early Period (1811–40)," in George H. Williams, ed., *The Harvard Divinity School* (Boston, 1954), 21–77.

William E. Channing's ideological relationship to the transcendental movement has been frequently discussed. Some light is thrown upon this in Elizabeth Peabody's *Reminiscences of Rev. Wm. Ellery Channing* (Boston, 1877). For two somewhat divergent viewpoints, see Herbert W. Schneider, "The Intellectual Background of William Ellery Channing," *Church History*, VII (1938), 3–23, and Arthur I. Ladu, "Channing and Transcendentalism," *American Literature*, XI (1939), 129–37.

Much of the more precise work on the religious aspects of transcendentalism has been done in connection with individual members of the movement. Indispensable to an understanding of Emerson's early theological views is *Young Emerson Speaks*, ed. Arthur C. McGiffert, Jr. (Boston, 1938). James E. Cabot's *A Memoir of Ralph Waldo Emerson* (2 vols., Boston, 1887) remains a work of great value. A more recent study is Ralph L. Rusk's *The Life of Ralph Waldo Emerson* (N.Y., 1949). Extra-American sources of Emerson's thoughts are discussed in Frederic I. Carpenter, *Emerson and Asia* (Cambridge, Mass., 1930); Frank T. Thompson, "Emerson's Indebtedness to Coleridge," *Studies in Philology*, XXIII (1926), 55–76; Merrell R. Davis, "Emerson's 'Reason' and the Scottish Philosophers," *New England Quarterly*, XVII (1944), 209–28; and Stewart G. Brown, "Emerson's Platonism," *New England Quarterly*, XVIII (1945), 325–45. The question of Puritanism's relationship to transcendentalism is treated in Perry Miller, "From Edwards to Emerson," *New England Quarterly*, XIII (1940), 589–617. On Emerson's manifesto of 1838, see Clarence L. F. Gohdes, "Some Remarks on Emerson's Divinity School Address," *American Literature*, I (1929), 27–31, and Conrad Wright, "Emerson, Barzillai Frost, and the Divinity School Address," *Harvard Theological Review*, XLIX (1956), 19–43.

O. B. Frothingham's *George Ripley* (Boston, 1882), though old, remains helpful. For an account of Ripley's social experiment, see Lindsay Swift, *Brook Farm: Its Members, Scholars, and Visitors* (N.Y., 1900). Ripley's religious views are examined briefly in Arthur R. Schultz and Henry A. Pochmann, "George Ripley: Unitarian, Transcendentalist, or Infidel?" *American Literature*, XIV (1942), 1–19. Further light on Ripley may be found in Jeter A. and Elizabeth Isely, "A Note on George Ripley and the Beginnings of New England Transcendentalism," *Proceedings of the Unitarian Historical Society*, XIII (1961), 62–74.

A standard work on Parker, containing valuable primary material, is John Weiss' *Life and Correspondence of Theodore Parker* (2 vols., N.Y., 1864). Henry S. Commager's *Theodore Parker* (Boston, 1936; 2nd ed., 1947) is a lively account, but some of its generalizations should be checked against such older works as John W. Chadwick's *Theodore Parker* (Boston, 1900). All of Vol. XIII, Part I (1960) of the *Proceedings of the Unitarian Historical Society* is devoted to a "Theodore Parker Centennial" series of instructive articles. Parker's religious thought is treated perceptively in J. Edward Dirks' *The Critical Theology of Theodore Parker* (N.Y., 1948). For somewhat different interpretations, see George F. Newbrough's "Reason and Understanding in the Works of Theodore Parker," *South Atlantic Quarterly*, XLVII (1948), 64–75; Hutchison's *Transcendentalist Ministers;* and H. Shelton Smith's "Was Theodore Parker a Transcendentalist?" *New England Quarterly*, XXIII (1950), 351–64. Perry Miller's "Theodore Parker: Apostasy Within Liberalism," *Harvard Theological Review*, LIV (1961), 274–95, judiciously reviews recent efforts to upgrade Parker's contemporary critics.

For a stimulating account of Brownson's social and political ideas, see Arthur Schlesinger, Jr., *Orestes A. Brownson: A Pilgrim's Progress* (Boston, 1939). A supplementary work is Theodore Maynard's *Orestes Brownson: Yankee, Radical, Catholic* (N.Y., 1943), which emphasizes Brownson's Catholic period. A useful older work is Henry F. Brownson's *Orestes Brownson's Early Life, Middle Life, and Later Life* (3 vols., Detroit, Mich., 1898–1900). For a short anthology, see Alvan S. Ryan, ed., *The Brownson Reader* (N.Y., 1955). A. R. Caponigri's "Brownson and Emerson: Nature and History," *New England Quarterly*, XVIII (1945), 368–90, is stimulating.

O. B. Frothingham's *Memoir of William Henry Channing* (Boston, 1886) is especially valuable for its primary materials, but a fresh study is needed. The most satisfying religious analysis is in Hutchison's *Transcendentalist Ministers*, 169–77. For illuminating surveys of the contents of the two periodicals which were edited by Channing, see Gohdes, *The Periodicals of American Transcendentalism*, Chaps. 4 and 6.

A highly readable work on Clarke is Arthur S. Bolster's *James Freeman Clarke: Disciple of Advancing Truth* (Boston, 1954), but unfortunately it is not documented. A necessary older work is *James Freeman Clarke: Autobiography, Diary and Correspondence*, ed. Edward E. Hale (N.Y., 1891). For additional light on Clarke, see John Wesley Thomas, *James Freeman Clarke: Apostle of German Culture to America* (Boston, 1949), and *The Letters of James Freeman Clarke to Margaret Fuller*, ed. John Wesley Thomas (Hamburg, Germany, 1957).

The religious thought of Frederic Henry Hedge is perceptively explored in Ronald V. Wells' *Three Christian Transcendentalists* (N.Y., 1943), Chap. 4. The religious ideas of James Marsh and Caleb Sprague Henry are analyzed in the same volume. Two other instructive studies are Orie W. Long, *Frederic Henry Hedge: A Cosmopolitan Scholar* (Portland, Me., 1940), and George H. Williams, *Rethinking the Unitarian Relationship with Protestantism: An Examination of the Thought of Frederic Henry Hedge* (Boston, 1949).

A minor figure of some importance in relation to the new religious trends is illuminated in Odell Shepard's *Pedlar's Progress: The Life of Bronson Alcott* (Boston, 1937). The Pedlar's social experiment is discussed in Clara E. Sears' *Bronson Alcott's Fruitlands* (Boston, 1915).

CHAPTER XV

The Irrepressible Question of Slavery

No question has ever agitated the American mind more than did that of Negro slavery. Time and again just when men began to hope that the vexatious issue had been buried for good, it would return with even greater urgency until the Union finally exploded in bloody violence. Two factors were especially potent in keeping the question alive. One was the swelling tide of humanitarian reform,[1] which revealed the radical contradiction between human bondage and the professed creed of American democracy. The other factor was the westward expansion of the nation, a process which periodically forced the American people to determine how far slavery should be allowed to extend itself. From the Missouri controversy to the Kansas-Nebraska debate this was the crucial question. And every time that question emerged it involved not merely economic and political elements, but moral ones as well.

In the early part of this century many historians were so strongly influenced by an economic interpretation of history that they tended to minimize the moral aspect of the slavery question. Thus in 1927 two able historians declared: "Slavery was but one element, and if the number of abolitionists is any evidence, a minor element, in the sweep of political and economic forces that occupied the attention of statesmen throughout the middle period and finally brought on the irrepressible conflict."[2] Recent critical scholarship makes that statement appear decidedly one-sided. According to many present-day historians, the slavery question was crucially involved in the making of the Civil War.[3]

It is often forgotten that during the first third of the nineteenth century the South was quite as critical of slavery as the North. Indeed, Alice Dana Adams has argued that from 1808 to 1831 "the South was indubitably the leader, and the larger force in the antislavery movement."[4] There is considerable evidence to support her claim. First, the southern antislavery forces were, in that period, better organized than were those in the North. For example, Kentucky formed a state antislavery society in 1808; Tennessee, in 1815; North Carolina, in 1816; and Maryland in 1825. Many active

---

[1] See *supra*, Chap. 12.

[2] Charles R. and Mary Beard, *The Rise of American Civilization* (2 vols., N.Y., 1927), I, 710.

[3] Gilbert H. Barnes, *The Antislavery Impulse, 1830–1844* (N.Y., 1933); Dwight L. Dumond, *Antislavery Origins of the Civil War in the United States* (Ann Arbor, Mich., 1939), and *Antislavery: The Crusade for Freedom in America* (Ann Arbor, Mich., 1961); Kenneth M. Stampp, *The Peculiar Institution: Slavery in the Ante-Bellum South* (N.Y., 1956); Louis Filler, *The Crusade Against Slavery, 1830–1860* (N.Y., 1960).

[4] *The Neglected Period of Anti-Slavery in America, 1808–1831* (N.Y., 1908), 249.

auxiliaries also existed in these states. North Carolina led in 1826 with forty-five such local societies.[5] According to Benjamin Lundy, the South's antislavery societies vastly outnumbered those in the North even as late as 1827.[6] Second, the South was then better served with antislavery newspapers than any other section. The first exclusively antislavery paper in America was begun by Elihu Embree in 1819 at Jonesboro, Tennessee, under the name of the *Manumission Intelligencer.*[7] Lundy's *Genius of Universal Emancipation* (1821–39), the best of all such journals, had its widest circulation in the slave states. In 1822 the *Abolition Intelligencer and Missionary Magazine* was begun as the organ of the Kentucky Abolition Society, with the Rev. John Finley Crowe as editor. Third, the South in this period produced a majority of the foremost antislavery figures in the nation, including such men as Levi Coffin, Charles Osborn, David Barrow, Samuel Doak, James Duncan, John D. Paxton, James H. Dickey, and John Rankin. They wrote many of the most influential antislavery tracts of their generation.[8] Many of them spent their later years in the Midwest, where they pioneered in lighting the antislavery torch.[9]

Without doubt, then, the southern antislavery movement revealed much vitality during the first third of the nineteenth century. Unfortunately, that vitality did not continue. Why? In trying to answer that question, one must first of all recognize an important fact: the antislavery movement, even in its heyday, was confined geographically to a very small part of the South. It never did take significant root in the lower South; and even in the upper South, it showed little strength outside of central North Carolina, the western part of Virginia, eastern Tennessee, and certain pockets in Kentucky. The North Carolina Manumission Society was the strongest of all the state agencies, and yet it had no basic support except among the Quakers. The local branches mostly centered in three counties: Guilford, Randolph, and Chatham, where Quakerism was strongest. The Society declined rapidly after 1828, and expired altogether in 1834. The movement also declined in other southern areas about the same time.[10]

No single factor will account for the ultimate failure of the southern antislavery movement. The fear of servile uprising was one factor, though probably not a major one. Another was the bitter attack made upon the

[5] H. M. Wagstaff, ed., *Minutes of the North Carolina Manumission Society, 1816–1834* (Chapel Hill, N.C., 1934), 122–4.

[6] *The Life, Travels and Opinions of Benjamin Lundy* (Phila., 1847), 218.

[7] Thomas E. Drake, *Quakers and Slavery* (New Haven, 1950), 127. The name was soon changed to the *Emancipator.*

[8] See Gordon E. Finnie, "The Antislavery Movement in the South, 1787–1836: Its Rise and Decline and Its Contribution to Abolitionism in the West" (typed Ph.D. dissertation, Duke University, 1962), Chap. 4.

[9] *Ibid.*, Chaps. 5–6.

[10] Some small pockets of antislavery persisted in western Virginia and Kentucky until the Civil War, but no aggressive action could be taken. Cf. Kenneth Stampp, "The Fate of the Southern Antislavery Movement," *Journal of Negro History*, XXVIII (1943), 18–22.

South by northern and western radical abolitionists. A third was the loss to the region, either by death or migration, of its bravest antislavery leaders. Still another seems to have been the South's anxiety over its growing minority status in the Union.

Yet more influential than all those factors put together was the South's conviction that its economy was fundamentally dependent upon slave labor. Owing to technological progress, the British and New England textile mills were rapidly increasing their demands for cotton fiber in the early decades of the nineteenth century. Eli Whitney's gin (1793), vast rich soil in the Black Belt, and abundance of Negro slaves enabled the southern planter to furnish that fiber in increasing volume at a generally fair and sometimes lucrative profit. Consequently cotton production in the United States rose from 731,452 bales in 1830 to 4,541,285 in 1859.[11]

Of the almost four million slaves in 1860, some three-fourths of that number were employed in cotton growing, predominantly in the lower South. Thus Georgia and Mississippi together produced 1,483,478 bales in 1859. The slaves, who outnumbered the whites in both states, totaled 898,831 in 1860.[12] In that year Mississippi had 30,943 slaveholders, and Georgia 41,084. In the former state, almost fifty per cent of the white population either owned slaves or belonged to slaveholding families.[13]

Of great importance was the fact that the major molders of public opinion generally had a direct economic stake in perpetuating slavery. This was true not only of educators, doctors, and politicians, but of preachers as well. Prominent churchmen in all denominations held slaves, such as Richard Furman (Baptist), William Capers (Methodist), Robert L. Dabney (Presbyterian), and Leonidas Polk (Episcopalian). Numerous less well-known preachers likewise had a vested interest. An estimated two-fifths of all the Baptist clergymen in South Carolian owned slaves.[14] In 1844 some two hundred traveling Methodist preachers owned a total of 1,600 slaves, while a thousand local preachers owned 10,000.[15]

Is it not reasonable, therefore, to conclude that the economic motive played a major role in binding the South to its "peculiar institution"? In all ages the beneficiaries of power have generally opposed measures which would destroy their vested interests. Southerners were no exception to this rule.

Of fateful import was the fact that just when antislavery sentiment was drying up in the land of cotton, it was taking on new vitality north of the Mason-Dixon line. William Lloyd Garrison (1805–79) claimed that when he entered upon his antislavery crusade, almost no American "dared to

---

[11] Charles S. Sydnor, *Slavery in Mississippi* (N.Y., 1933), 183–4.

[12] Ralph Flanders, *Plantation Slavery in Georgia* (Chapel Hill, N.C., 1933), 66, 82; Sydnor, *Slavery in Mississippi*, 186, 192.

[13] Sydnor, *Slavery in Mississippi*, 193.

[14] Robert G. Torbet, *A History of the Baptists* (Phila., 1950), 300.

[15] William Warren Sweet, *Methodism in American History* (N.Y., 1933), 273.

peep or mutter on the subject of slavery," [16] but he was quite mistaken. As a matter of fact, the South still had a few antislavery prophets crying in the wilderness, and in other regions many (including southern exiles) were sounding the antislavery alarm long before he took to the hustings.[17]

Still, it is true that not until the decade of the 1830's was there a massive organized assault upon slavery. On January 1, 1831, Garrison launched the *Liberator,* the most vitriolic antislavery paper ever published. In December of that same year he organized the New England Anti-Slavery Society. Following the lead given in Elizabeth Heyrich's famed English tract, *Immediate, Not Gradual Abolition* (1824), both agencies adopted the slogan of immediate emancipation.

Meanwhile, two prominent merchants in New York City, Arthur and Lewis Tappan, had been promoting various humanitarian reforms, including the antislavery movement. With their financial and moral support, two militant agencies came into being in 1833: the Anti-Slavery Society of New York, formed on October 3; and the American Anti-Slavery Society, organized on December 4 in Philadelphia. Garrison played an important role in establishing the latter.[18] Arthur Tappan (1786–1870) was elected president of both organizations, a fact indicating his vital role in the antislavery cause.[19] Like the New England Society, both bodies adopted the principle of immediate emancipation, although they defined it to mean merely the immediate beginning of a process which would gradually abolish slavery.

These new abolitionist societies necessarily clashed with the American Colonization Society (1817), since the latter's sole purpose was to settle, with their consent, free Negroes in Africa. The Tappans, Gerrit Smith, Garrison, and other radical antislavery men had at first endorsed the Society, but they quickly realized that it was no real enemy of slavery. Thus in 1833 Arthur Tappan sent a letter to the secretary of the Society, Ralph R. Gurley (1797–1872), explicitly charging that colonization was "a device of Satan" with a "single motive to perpetuate slavery." [20] Even in terms of its own limited objective, the Society had failed. For example, by the close of 1830 it had sent to Liberia only 1,420 Negroes, and all those except 244 came from Maryland, Virginia, and North Carolina.[21] The

[16] Wendell P. and Francis J. Garrison, *William Lloyd Garrison, 1805–1879* (4 vols., N.Y., 1885–89), I, 458.

[17] Leonard Bacon, *Anti-Slavery Before Garrison* (New Haven, 1903); Adams, *The Neglected Period of Anti-Slavery in America,* Chaps. 6–8; W. W. Sweet, *Religion on the American Frontier: The Baptists,* Chap. 5; Dwight L. Dumond, *Antislavery,* Chap. 15; Filler, *The Crusade Against Slavery,* Chap. 2.

[18] Both Barnes (*The Antislavery Impulse*) and Dumond (*Antislavery,* Chap. 19) tend to minimize the role of Garrison in the antislavery movement and to magnify that of the Finneyites. For a more balanced perspective, see Louis Filler, *The Crusade Against Slavery.*

[19] Lewis Tappan, *The Life of Arthur Tappan* (N.Y., 1870), 174–5.

[20] Quoted in Early Lee Fox, *The American Colonization Society, 1817–1840* (Baltimore, 1919), 140.

[21] *Ibid.,* 89.

Society never did much better; indeed, by the end of the Civil War it had colonized altogether only 12,000 Negroes.[22]

The story of the American Anti-Slavery Society was entirely different; within a single decade it proved to be the greatest organized enemy of slavery in existence. It issued tons of tracts, formed hundreds of local societies, and blanketed the free states with mass conventions. It carried its message to the grass roots through a band of antislavery agents as brave as they come, many of them being converts of Charles Grandison Finney.

One of the most valiant Finneyites was Theodore Dwight Weld (1803–95).[23] Weld grew up in Hampton, Connecticut, where his father ministered to the Congregational church for thirty years. Later the family moved to Fabius, New York. In 1825 Weld was converted under the preaching of Finney, and immediately joined the evangelist's "holy band" of lay workers. About this time he became deeply attached to a retired British army officer, Charles Stuart, who was not only an enthusiastic Finneyite but also an abolitionist in full sympathy with England's effort to outlaw slavery in the West Indies. When Weld entered Oneida Institute to prepare for the ministry, Stuart met his expenses. In 1829 Stuart returned to England to lecture and write against slavery. From there he plied Weld with antislavery tracts designed to win him to abolitionism.[24]

Meanwhile the Tappan brothers were also seeking to enlist Weld in some type of social reform. They became so impressed with Oneida's manual-labor plan of education, according to which students combined work and study, that in 1831 they formed the Society for Promoting Manual Labor in Literary Institutions. Weld consented to become its general agent. One of his tasks was to locate a suitable site in the West for a theological seminary to be set up on the manual-labor pattern. It was understood that the Tappans would give generously toward the enterprise.

Weld moved westward in the fall of 1831, lecturing on both temperance and manual-labor education. After some time in the West, he traveled southward as far as Huntsville, Alabama, where in June of 1832 he and James G. Birney, a prominent lawyer and planter, exchanged views on slavery. In October of that same year he visited Western Reserve College (Ohio), meeting there three believers in immediate emancipation: the president, Charles B. Storrs, and professors Beriah Green and Elizur Wright, Jr.[25] These evangelical churchmen were destined to serve valiantly in the antislavery crusade.

[22] Dumond, *Antislavery*, 129.

[23] For a lively biography, see Benjamin P. Thomas, *Theodore Weld: Crusader for Freedom* (New Brunswick, N.J., 1950).

[24] Gilbert H. Barnes and Dwight L. Dumond, eds., *Letters of Theodore Dwight Weld, Angelina Grimké Weld, and Sarah Grimké, 1822–1844* (2 vols., N.Y., 1934), I, 48–9. Hereafter cited as *Weld-Grimké Letters*.

[25] Gilbert Barnes (*The Antislavery Impulse*, 46, 55) credited Weld with winning Storrs, Green, and Wright to radical abolitionism; but these men were already converted to this viewpoint. If therefore anyone needed conversion, it was Weld himself, not they. Cf. Thomas, *Theodore Weld*, 36–7.

About this time the newly formed Lane Seminary (Cincinnati), to which Weld had given his approval, secured the famed Lyman Beecher as its president, a trophy due largely to the influence of the Tappans. Since Weld had not yet finished his theological education, he gave up his manual-labor agency to enter Lane in the fall of 1833. During his first year there he led a radical assault upon slavery and converted Lane into a hotbed of abolitionism. Thenceforth he was to outstrip all other Finneyites as an anti-slavery crusader. Among other services, he wrote two of abolitionism's most powerful tracts: *The Bible Against Slavery* (1837), and *Slavery As It Is* (1839). The massive data in the latter were gathered from more than twenty thousand southern newspapers. According to Angelina Grimké Weld (wife of Theodore Weld), Harriet Beecher Stowe lived with *Slavery As It Is* day and night "till its facts crystalized into Uncle Tom's Cabin." [26]

Meanwhile another militant antislavery leader, James G. Birney, was emerging as Weld's western ally.[27] Shortly after Weld's Huntsville visit, Birney became a full-time agent for the American Colonization Society, with duty in the Southwest. Yet in about a year he had become so discouraged over the apathy of the lower South that he decided to surrender his agency. In November of 1833, therefore, he returned to his native state of Kentucky and settled on a farm near Danville. Early in the next December he took a leading part in forming the Kentucky Society for the Gradual Relief of the State from Slavery.[28] The constitution, written by Birney, opened membership to any white citizen of the state who would agree "to emancipate any slave which may be born his or her property *thereafter*—when such slaves may have attained the age of 25 years, and if a female, her offspring with her." [29] The address to the public, also prepared by Birney, declared the aim of the Society to be *"the total abolition of slavery throughout the Commonwealth."* However, opposition was expressed to "immediate emancipation" unless the slaves had been first prepared for their freedom. Thus the Society advocated "immediate preparation for *future* emancipation." [30]

Clearly Birney now stood on the very threshold of the radical doctrine of the American Anti-Slavery Society, and within a few weeks he had become an enthusiastic convert to immediate abolitionism. In token of his new position, he cut all ties with both the Colonization Society and the newly formed Kentucky Society, and he took immediate steps to manumit the rest of his slaves.[31] Soon thereafter he also became an agent for the American Anti-Slavery Society, with the focus of his activity in Kentucky. Thus began

[26] Barnes, *The Antislavery Impulse*, 231.
[27] For an excellent biography, see Betty Fladeland, *James Gillespie Birney: Slaveholder to Abolitionist* (N.Y., 1955).
[28] Birney to Ralph R. Gurley, Dec. 11, 1833, in Dwight L. Dumond, ed., *Letters of James Gillespie Birney, 1831–1857* (2 vols., N.Y., 1938), 98–9. Hereafter cited as *Birney Letters*.
[29] *Ibid.*, 99. Italics in original.   [30] *Ibid.*, 104. Italics in original.
[31] Fladeland, *James Gillespie Birney*, 82.

The Mother Church of Christian Science (Boston)

Charles W. Eliot, former President of Harvard and forecaster of "The Religion of the Future"

Above: Riverside Church in New York, erected during the ministry of Harry Emerson Fosdick

Right: William Newton Clarke, first major American systematizer of Christocentric Liberalism

a Weld-Birney crusade which was destined to light the fires of abolitionism across the whole western frontier.[32]

It would be an illusion, however, to think that the abolitionist movement anywhere in the free states made headway easily. On the contrary, the anti-slavery men of the Weld-Tappan-Birney type were terrorized almost everywhere during the crucial decade of the 1830's. From the first, the American Anti-Slavery Society was considered fanatical and subversive. When, therefore, the Society tried to hold a public meeting in New York City on July 4, 1834, rioters broke up the assembly and started a wave of violence which lasted almost two weeks.[33] The churches and parsonages of abolitionist clergymen were damaged and numerous Negro homes wrecked. Arthur Tappan's store was showered with brickbats, and barely escaped complete destruction. A mob broke into Lewis Tappan's home, smashed the glassware, threw the furniture into the street, and fired the dwelling with the bed mattresses. With only one or two exceptions, the city papers berated the abolitionists and laid the blame for the whole trouble upon the shoulders of the Tappan brothers.

Agents of the American Anti-Slavery Society were victims of frequent mob action. Gangster tactics were routinely applied to Weld. Reporting his experience at Troy, New York, he noted that a city official was one of the leaders of his attackers. "Twice a rush was made up the aisles to drag me from the pulpit. Stones, pieces of bricks, eggs, . . . were thrown at me while speaking." [34] John Rankin reportedly suffered one hundred mobbings, while Henry B. Stanton received the same treatment one hundred and fifty times before 1840.

Abolitionist editors were often persecuted. When Birney tried to launch the *Philanthropist* at Danville, the outcry of the community forced him to make a start in Cincinnati; but there also he ran into serious trouble. On the night of July 12, 1836, a mob raided his printing shop, destroyed a week's issue of the paper, and made off with parts of the press. A second press was set up, but on the night of July 30 a mob returned and cast it into the Ohio River. Afterwards the rioters made shambles of numerous Negro homes in the city.

About this same time editor Elijah P. Lovejoy came off worse than Birney. He had formerly published a paper in St. Louis, but was forced to leave there because he had condemned the local judge for condoning the action of mobmen who had forcibly taken a Negro from jail and burned him. Relocating at Alton, Illinois, he started the *Alton Observer,* an anti-slavery paper which, among other things, advocated the organization of a state abolitionist society. The community felt outraged, and a lawless element proceeded to wreck his press. Finally, on November 5, 1837, Lovejoy

---

[32] Dumond, *Antislavery Origins of the Civil War in the United States,* 21–36.

[33] Tappan, *The Life of Arthur Tappan,* 203–24.

[34] Weld to the Rev. Ray Potter, June 11, 1836, *Weld-Grimké Letters,* I, 309.

was shot to death while trying to save his third press with a gun. According to Edward Beecher, president of Illinois College, he was "the first martyr in America to the great principle of the freedom of speech and of the press." [35]

Nor did abolitionism fare much better among northern churchmen in the 1830's. Highly placed leaders in all communions except the Friends were, at best, only moderates on the slavery question; that is to say, they generally deplored slavery but hesitated to engage in any decisive or concerted action to liquidate it. Their sympathies were clearly with the colonizationists, not with the immediate emancipationists. This was true of such influential denominationalists as Wilbur Fisk (Methodist), Francis Wayland (Baptist), Charles Hodge (Presbyterian), Leonard Bacon (Congregationalist), and Henry W. Bellows (Unitarian), all of whom scathingly condemned abolitionists. Even the renowned Horace Bushnell (Congregationalist) went so far as to oppose the formation of antislavery societies in the free states.[36]

Vehement hostility toward abolitionism was displayed by the General Conference of the Methodist Episcopal Church when it met at Cincinnati, Ohio, in May of 1836. On discovering that two of its delegates—Revs. George Storrs and Samuel Norris, of the New Hampshire Conference—had on May 10 addressed the Cincinnati Anti-Slavery Society, the Conference became so enraged that it spent two days in tempestuous discussion,[37] the final outcome of which was the almost unanimous adoption of resolutions which not only censured the two delegates, but expressed unqualified opposition to "modern abolitionism." [38] In their Pastoral Address, the bishops solemnly warned Methodist preachers "to abstain from all abolition movements and associations, and to refrain from patronizing any of their publications." [39]

If the other major denominations had taken collective action during this period, there is good reason to believe that their sentiments would also have been overwhelmingly anti-abolitionist. In fact, those communions with a strong churchly tradition were probably even more solidly opposed to abolitionism than was Methodism. The American hierarchy of the Roman

[35] *Narrative of Riots at Alton: In Connection with the Death of Elijah P. Lovejoy* (Alton, Ill., 1838), 5.

[36] Charles C. Cole, Jr., "Horace Bushnell and the Slavery Question," *New England Quarterly,* XXIII (1950), 24–5.

[37] For a summary of the fireworks, as reported by James G. Birney, see Lucius C. Matlack, *The History of American Slavery and Methodism, from 1780 to 1849: and History of the Wesleyan Methodist Connection of America* (N.Y., 1849), 118–40.

[38] *Journals of the General Conference of the Methodist Episcopal Church,* Vol. I, *1796–1836* (N.Y., 1855), 447. Only fourteen of the conference delegates were abolitionists, and they were easily smothered despite the forensic powers of their leader, Orange Scott.

[39] "Pastoral Address," *Christian Advocate and Journal* (June 17, 1836), 171. See also Lucius C. Matlack, *The Life of Orange Scott* (N.Y., 1848), 146.

Catholic Church, for example, never did pronounce slavery an inherent evil.[40]

But although the odds were strongly against them, the immediate emancipationists never lost hope. Even during the controversial 1830's they steadily made converts, many of whom were former colonizationists. The Presbyterians offered unusually fertile soil for propaganda, owing largely to the early groundwork which had been done in the West by such pioneer southern exiles as John Rankin and James Dickey.[41] Under their leadership, the Chillicothe Presbytery (Ohio), for example, had become a veritable hotbed of abolitionism more than ten years before the Lane rebels began their western campaign. Thus when Weld attended the General Assembly of the Presbyterian Church in 1835 as an observer and lobbyist, he estimated that a fourth of its commissioners were immediate abolitionists.[42]

Presbyterians were in the antislavery vanguard, but other denominations were also catching the abolitionist spirit. Even before the General Conference of the Methodist Church met at Cincinnati, the New Hampshire and New England Conferences had been thoroughly honeycombed by abolitionism, despite the stout opposition of the episcopacy. Decisive evidence of this lay in the fact that all the delegates from those conferencecs to the General Conference of 1836 were outright abolitionists. Thriving antislavery societies, moreover, had been organized in both conferences in 1835. By the end of the decade antislavery leaven was also spreading among Maine Baptists.[43] Prominent figures like John G. Fee, Pardee Butler, and Nathaniel Field were evidence that the Disciples of Christ likewise were being infiltrated by abolitionism. Elder Field's radicalism was made evident when he wrote in 1834 that he had "resolved not to *break the loaf* with slaveholders or in any way to countenance them, as Christians." [44] In 1837 a vigorous antislavery faction within Lutheranism resulted in the forming of the Franckean Synod in central New York, comprising twenty-one congregations and ten ministers. The Synod, branding slavery a sin, was closed to any slaveholding pastor or even one who sanctioned the principle of slavery.[45]

These few examples indicate that many Protestant communions in the East and West were by the middle 1830's producing significant antislavery

[40] Cf. Madeline Hook Rice, *American Catholic Opinion in the Slavery Controversy* (N.Y., 1944), 90.

[41] Recent research indicates that the initial impulse toward antislavery in the West among all denominations was furnished overwhelmingly by southern exiles, most of whom fled their native region as a result of their strong antipathy toward the institution of slavery. See Gordon E. Finnie, "The Antislavery Movement in the South, 1787–1836: Its Rise and Decline and Its Contribution to Abolitionism in the West," Chaps. 5–6.

[42] Weld to Elizur Wright, Jr., June 6, 1835, *Weld-Grimké Letters*, I, 224.

[43] Mary B. Putnam, *The Baptists and Slavery: 1840–1845* (Ann Arbor, Mich., 1913).

[44] Quoted in David E. Harrell, "The Sectional Pattern," *Discipliana*, XXI (March, 1961), 8.

[45] Robert Fortenbaugh, "American Lutheran Synods and Slavery, 1830–60," *Journal of Religion*, XIII (1933), 75–7; Charles W. Heathcote, *The Lutheran Church and the Civil War* (N.Y., 1913), 54–8.

remnants of a decidedly militant temper. They were destined to grow until, by the end of the 1840's, the tide would turn decisively in their favor.

Meanwhile the people below the Potomac, well aware of the changing sentiment in the free states, lost no opportunity to tighten their grip upon the slave. Indicative of this fact was the Great Debate staged in 1832 by the Virginia Legislature against the background of the Nat Turner uprising.[46] The crucial contest was largely between the Tidewater and the Piedmont, the former section being the stronghold of the planter class. The Piedmont legislators, with a few others, fought hard to outlaw human bondage, but finally lost by a small margin.

Shortly thereafter, the debate was exhaustively analyzed by Thomas Roderick Dew (1802–46), political economist at William and Mary College.[47] The professor's supreme purpose was to demolish the antislavery argument. Actually he added nothing essentially new to the proslavery argument, but he stated his case brilliantly. In sum, he contended: (1) that slavery, which had existed from earliest times, had been the chief means of improving civilization; (2) that slavery fostered equality between white people and therefore did not contradict the republican spirit; (3) that the plans currently offered for emancipation (with or without deportation) were visionary and impracticable; and (4) that slavery had been established by divine authority.[48]

These sweeping claims were to be repeated *ad nauseam* over the next thirty years. Among southern statesmen who were deeply impressed by Dew's defense of the peculiar institution was the formidable John C. Calhoun (1782–1850). The statesman from South Carolina warmly welcomed Dew's view of slavery as a positive good, and in 1838 he championed the same doctrine in the Senate. "Many in the South," said he, "once believed that it [slavery] was a moral and political evil. That folly and delusion are gone. We see it now in its true light, and regard it as the most safe and stable basis for free institutions in the world." [49]

As the century wore on, Southerners more and more acclaimed the virtues of a slavocratic order. An extreme example in the 1850's was the son of a Virginia planter, George Fitzhugh (1806–81), distant kinsman of two militant abolitionists, Gerrit Smith and James G. Birney.[50] The fervent propagandist unfolded his astonishing notions in two books: *Sociology for the South, or the Failure of Free Society* (1854), and *Cannibals All! or, Slaves Without Masters* (1857), both of which portrayed the South as the Garden of Eden and the North as the land of industrial slavery. He ex-

[46] Joseph C. Robert, *Road from Monticello: A Study of the Virginia Slavery Debate of 1832* (Durham, N.C., 1941).

[47] [Thomas R. Dew,] "Debate in the Virginia Legislature of 1831–32, on the Abolition of Slavery," *American Quarterly Review*, XII (1832), 189–265.

[48] Dew, *An Essay on Slavery* (2nd ed., Richmond, Va., 1840), 13, 24, 40–9, 99.

[49] Richard K. Cralle, ed., *The Works of John C. Calhoun* (6 vols., N.Y., 1851–56), III, 179–80.

[50] For an illuminating biography, see Harvey Wish, *George Fitzhugh, Propagandist of the Old South* (Baton Rouge, La., 1943).

plicitly condemned the Declaration of Independence and the Virginia Bill of Rights as having sprung out of the very same infidel philosophy which had bred abolitionism.

The southern clergy were no less zealous in their defense of a slave-based social order. They were especially infuriated by the abolitionist charge that slavery was in principle sinful. Ministers of a philosophical bent denied that indictment on social and political grounds. A notable apology from this standpoint was presented by the president of Randolph-Macon College, William A. Smith. Predicating inequality as the law of nature and the will of God, he argued that since the Negro was intellectually and socially inferior to the white man, he was properly enslaved by the latter. Hence slavery was not sinful *per se,* and could only become sinful by perversion. Smith, like Fitzhugh, arraigned the natural rights philosophy, notably its belief that "all men are born free and equal." [51]

In general, however, the clergy preferred to measure the morality of slavery by the Bible. The astute Presbyterian theologian, Robert Lewis Dabney, held that the only sure way to rout the abolitionist and align northern Christians with the South was to take one's stand solely on the Bible, not on any philosophical platform.[52] This strategy would force the enemies of slavery to reveal their true infidel colors. "Here is our policy then," wrote Dabney in 1851, "to push the Bible argument continually, to drive Abolitionism to the wall, to compel it to assume an anti-Christian position." [53] James Henley Thornwell apparently operated on the same principle. In a report on slavery, written by him and adopted unanimously by the Presbyterian Synod of South Carolina in 1851, Thornwell observed that the church's "only argument is *Thus it is written.*" [54] Then appealing to the Word, he declared, "The Scriptures not only fail to condemn Slavery, they as distinctly sanction it as any other social condition of man. The Church was formally organized in the family of a slaveholder; the relation was divinely regulated among the chosen people of God; and the peculiar duties of the parties are inculcated under the Christian economy." [55] Consequently, to call slavery sinful was in effect to reject the Bible in favor of some rationalistic mode of thought. "Opposition to slavery has never been the offspring of the Bible," said the proslavery theologian.[56]

In the end, then, southern Christian moralists narrowed down the issue between themselves and the abolitionists to the point where the latter either had to agree with the South's position on slavery or be charged with infidelity to the biblical revelation. This was precisely the dilemma into which

---

[51] *Lectures on the Philosophy and Practice of Slavery* (Nashville, 1856), Lecs. 2–3.

[52] Frank Bell Lewis, "Robert Lewis Dabney: Southern Presbyterian Apologist" (typed Ph.D. dissertation, Duke University, 1946), 42–3.

[53] Quoted from Dabney's letter in *ibid.,* 43.

[54] "Relation of the Church to Slavery," in John B. Adger and John L. Girardeau, eds., *The Collected Writings of James Henley Thornwell, D.D., LL.D.* (4 vols., Richmond, Va., 1871–73), IV, 384. Italics in original.

[55] *Ibid.,* 385.   [56] *Ibid.,* 393.

Dabney had wanted to drive the abolitionist, with the hope that then the North could not unite against the South.

Dabney's hope, however, proved in vain; for the Christian abolitionist focused his attention primarily upon the spirit and teaching of Jesus Christ, especially upon the Law of Love and the Golden Rule, not upon the patriarchal ethic of the Old Testament. Meanwhile he was also aided by a growing tendency, in northern liberal circles, to interpret the Scriptures in terms of a progressive revelation which gave greater weight to the New Testament. Thus when the southern moralist endeavored to stigmatize the abolitionist as an infidel or an atheist, the charge failed to stick.

Nevertheless, the southern churchman unflinchingly insisted that to condemn slavery as inherently sinful was necessarily to reject the Word of God. Thus Christians of the two sections finally found themselves in an unresolvable predicament, with one party insisting that Negro slavery was divinely ordained and the other contending that it was contrary to the Christian gospel. Caught in this tragic quandary, Christian community broke down. The two largest denominations, the Methodists and the Baptists, severed their ecclesiastical bonds in 1844 and 1845 respectively. New-School Presbyterians split in 1857, and Old-School Presbyterians did the same in 1861. Lutherans and Episcopalians took a like course at the eleventh hour. The Roman Catholics survived schism, but at the price of excluding the slavery question from hierarchical discussion.

Ecclesiastical division not only foreshadowed political disunion, but actually prepared the moral ground for it. Some distinguished clergymen in the South advised secession as the only right and honorable course which could be taken. A vigorous proponent of this solution was Benjamin Morgan Palmer, minister of the First Presbyterian Church in New Orleans. Shortly after Lincoln was elected to the presidency, Palmer delivered an eloquent Thanksgiving sermon in which he argued that the South held a providential trust *"to conserve and to perpetuate the institution of domestic slavery* as now existing." [57] In order to fulfill this trust the South must, he urged, take immediate steps toward full independence. Said he:

> Let the people in all the Southern states, in solemn council assemble, reclaim the powers they have delegated. . . . Let them pledge each other in sacred covenant, to uphold and perpetuate what they cannot resign without dishonor and palpable ruin. Let them further, take all the necessary steps looking to separate and independent existence; and initiate measures for framing a new and homogeneous confederacy. Thus, prepared for every contingency, let the crisis come.[58]

Should the crisis come, the South could be sure that *"we defend the cause of God and religion,"* since "the abolition spirit is undeniably atheistic." [59]

---

[57] *The South: Her Peril and Her Duty; A Sermon Preached at First Presbyterian Church, New Orleans, on Thursday, Nov. 29, 1860* (New Orleans, 1860), 6. Italics in the original.
[58] *Ibid.,* 15.   [59] *Ibid.,* 10. Italics in original.

The crisis was indeed already at hand. In December of 1860 South Carolina took the revolutionary step of secession, and was later followed by ten other southern states, which together formed the Confederate States of America, with Jefferson Davis as president. Firing on Fort Sumter on April 12, 1861, the Confederacy opened an apocalyptic conflict which was to last four years and in the end wipe out the morally outdated system of human bondage.

123. A United Indictment of Slavery

As already observed, many churchmen in both the North and the South at one time agreed that slavery contradicted the Christian gospel and should be abolished. This fact was forcefully revealed in a report which was adopted by the General Assembly of the Presbyterian Church in the United States of America, when it met at Philadelphia in May of 1818. That report is reproduced in full below.

The action of the Assembly is impressive from two standpoints. First, the institution of slavery was condemned in most scathing terms; in fact, no future Assembly would ever take a stronger Christian stand on this question. Second, the report was adopted unanimously, despite the fact that many commissioners were from the South.[60]

The reader will observe that the report incorporated the antislavery resolution which had been adopted in 1787 by the Synod of New York and Philadelphia.

DOCUMENT

The General Assembly of the Presbyterian Church, having taken into consideration the subject of SLAVERY, think proper to make known their sentiments upon it to the churches and people under their care.

We consider the voluntary enslaving of one part of the human race by another, as a gross violation of the most precious and sacred rights of human nature; as utterly inconsistent with the law of God, which requires us to love our neighbour as ourselves; and as totally irreconcilable with the spirit and principles of the Gospel of Christ, which enjoin that, "all things whatsoever ye would that men should do to you, do ye even so to them." Slavery creates a paradox in the moral system—it exhibits rational, accountable, and immortal beings, in such circumstances as scarcely to leave them the power of moral action. It exhibits them as dependent on the will of others, whether they shall receive religious instruction; whether they shall know and worship the true God; whether they shall enjoy the ordinances of the

---

[60] According to Professor Clifton Olmstead (*History of Religion in the United States* [N.Y., 1960], 366), the southern commissioners "retired, leaving the floor to the opponents of slavery, who promptly proceeded to pass the resolution." But the Minutes of the Assembly explicitly say that the report was unanimously adopted. If this highly important report had been adopted merely by a northern faction, the Minutes surely would have made this fact clear. Indeed, the Southerners themselves would have demanded this clarification in their own interest.

Gospel; whether they shall perform the duties and cherish the endearments of husbands and wives, parents and children, neighbours and friends; whether they shall preserve their chastity and purity, or regard the dictates of justice and humanity. Such are some of the consequences of Slavery—consequences not imaginary—but which connect themselves with its very existence. The evils to which the slave is *always* exposed, often take place in fact, and in their very worst degree and form: and where all of them do not take place, as we rejoice to say that in many instances, through the influence of the principles of humanity and religion on the minds of masters, they do not—still the slave is deprived of his natural right, degraded as a human being, and exposed to the danger of passing into the hands of a master who may inflict upon him all the hardships and injuries which inhumanity and avarice may suggest.

From this view of the consequences resulting from the practice into which christian people have most inconsistently fallen, of enslaving a portion of their *brethren* of mankind—for "God hath made of one blood all nations of men to dwell on the face of the earth"—it is manifestly the duty of all christians who enjoy the light of the present day, when the inconsistency of slavery, both with the dictates of humanity and religion, has been demonstrated, and is generally seen and acknowledged, to use their honest, earnest, and unwearied endeavours, to correct the errors of former times, and as speedily as possible to efface this blot on our holy religion, and to obtain the complete abolition of slavery throughout christendom, and if possible throughout the world.

We rejoice that the church to which we belong commenced, as early as any other in this country, the good work of endeavouring to put an end to slavery,[61] and that in the same work, many of its members have ever since been, and now are, among the most active, vigorous, and efficient labourers. We do, indeed, tenderly sympathize with those portions of our church and our country, where the evil of slavery has been entailed upon them; where a *great,* and *the most virtuous part* of the *community* abhor

[61] In the minutes of the Synod of New York and Philadelphia, for the year 1787, before the General Assembly was constituted, we find the following, viz.

"The Synod of New York and Philadelphia, do highly approve of the general principles, in favor of universal liberty, that prevail in America; and of the interest which many of the states have taken in promoting the abolition of slavery: yet, inasmuch as men, introduced from a servile state to a participation of all the privileges of civil society, without a proper education, and without previous habits of industry, may be, in many respects, dangerous to the community: Therefore, they earnestly recommend it to all the members belonging to their communion, to give those persons who are, at present, held in servitude, such good education as may prepare them for the better enjoyment of freedom. And they, moreover, recommend, that masters, whenever they find servants disposed to make a proper improvement of the privilege, would give them some share of property to begin with; or grant them sufficient time and sufficient means of procuring, by industry, their own liberty, at a moderate rate; that they may, thereby, be brought into society with those habits of industry, that may render them useful citizens:—And finally, they recommend it to all the people under their care, to use the most prudent measures consistent with the interest and the state of civil society, in the parts where they live, to procure, eventually, the final abolition of slavery in America." [The Minutes]

slavery, and wish its extermination, as sincerely as any others—but where the number of slaves, their ignorance, and their vicious habits generally, render an immediate and universal emancipation inconsistent, alike, with the safety and happiness of the master and the slave. With those who are thus circumstanced, we repeat that we tenderly sympathize.—At the same time, we earnestly exhort them to continue, and, if possible, to increase their exertions to effect a total abolition of slavery.—We exhort them to suffer no greater delay to take place in this most interesting concern, than a regard to the public welfare *truly* and *indispensably* demands.

As our country has inflicted a most grievous injury on the unhappy Africans, by bringing them into slavery, we cannot, indeed, urge that we should add a second injury to the first, by emancipating them in such manner as that they will be likely to destroy themselves or others. But we do think, that our country ought to be governed in this matter, by no other consideration than an honest and impartial regard to the happiness of the injured party; uninfluenced by the expense or inconvenience which such a regard may involve. We therefore warn all who belong to our denomination of christians, against unduly extending this plea of necessity; against making it a cover for the love and practice of slavery, or a pretence for not using efforts that are lawful and practicable, to extinguish the evil.

And we, at the same time, exhort others to forbear harsh censures, and uncharitable reflections on their brethren, who unhappily live among slaves, whom they cannot immediately set free; but who, at the same time, are really using all their influence, and all their endeavours, to bring them into a state of freedom, as soon as a door for it can be safely opened.

Having thus expressed our views of slavery, and of the duty indispensably incumbent on all christians to labour for its complete extinction, we proceed to recommend—(and we do it with all the earnestness and solemnity which this momentous subject demands)—a particular attention to the following points.

[1.] We recommend to all our people to patronize and encourage the Society, lately formed, for colonizing in Africa, the land of their ancestors, the free people of colour in our country. We hope that much good may result from the plans and efforts of this Society. And while we exceedingly rejoice to have witnessed its origin and organization among the *holders of slaves,* as giving an unequivocal pledge of their desire to deliver themselves and their country from the calamity of slavery; we hope that those portions of the American Union, whose inhabitants are by a gracious Providence, more favourably circumstanced, will cordially, and liberally, and earnestly co-operate with their brethren, in bringing about the great end contemplated.

2. We recommend to all the members of our religious denomination, not only to permit, but to facilitate and encourage the instruction of their slaves, in the principles and duties of the christian religion; by granting

them liberty to attend on the preaching of the gospel, when they have the opportunity; by favouring the instruction of them in Sabbath-Schools, wherever those Schools can be formed; and by giving them all other proper advantages for acquiring the knowledge of their duty both to God and man. We are perfectly satisfied, that as it is incumbent on all christians to communicate religious instruction to those who are under their authority, so that the doing of this in the case before us, so far from operating, as some have apprehended that it might, as an excitement to insubordination and insurrection would, on the contrary, operate as the most powerful means for the prevention of those evils.

3. We enjoin it on all Church Sessions and Presbyteries, under the care of this Assembly, to discountenance, and, as far as possible, to prevent, all cruelty of whatever kind in the treatment of slaves; especially the cruelty of separating husband and wife, parents and children, and that which consists in selling slaves to those who will either themselves deprive these unhappy people of the blessings of the Gospel, or who will transport them to places where the Gospel is not proclaimed, or where it is forbidden to slaves to attend upon its institutions.—The manifest violation or disregard of the injunction here given, in its true spirit and intention, ought to be considered as just ground for the discipline and censures of the church.—And if it shall ever happen that a christian professor, in our communion, shall sell a slave who is also in communion and good standing with our church, contrary to his or her will, and inclination, it ought immediately to claim the particular attention of the proper church judicature; and unless there be such peculiar circumstances attending the case as can but seldom happen, it ought to be followed, without delay, by a suspension of the offender from all the privileges of the church, till he repent, and make all the reparation in his power, to the injured party.

> SOURCE: *Extracts from the Minutes of the General Assembly of the Presbyterian Church, in the United States of America: A. D. 1818* (Phila., 1818), 28–33.

124. A Fateful New Trend

Long before the rise of northern abolitionism, the lower South was becoming more militant in its defense of Negro slavery. Even the conservative American Colonization Society had never made much appeal to the chief cotton-growing states. Georgia and South Carolina were always cold toward the Society, and Mississippi's spurt of interest in it soon declined.[62]

The rising proslavery spirit is clearly reflected in a paper written in 1822 by Richard Furman (1755–1825). Shortly after Richard was born, the family left New York City and settled in Charleston, South Carolina. Later, in 1770, the family moved to High Hills, where young Furman

---

[62] Sydnor, *Slavery in Mississippi.* Chap. 9.

underwent conversion and joined the local Baptist church. He began preaching almost immediately, and was ordained in 1774. An ardent patriot during the Revolution, he served as a member of the state constitutional convention. When the Baptist Triennial Convention was organized (1814), Furman was elected as its first president. Likewise, he became president of the South Carolina Baptist State Convention as soon as it was organized in 1821. The declaration on slavery was issued while he held the latter office.

The social climate giving rise to the Furman paper was created chiefly by the debate over the Missouri Question and by the Denmark Vesey episode of 1822 in Charleston. Vesey, a slave, won a lottery prize of $1,500, out of which he purchased his freedom for $600. In May of 1822 news spread that a Negro uprising was being planned. Vesey, the alleged leader, and some 131 other suspects were jailed. Finally, the leader and thirty-four other Negroes were hanged, and thirty-seven more were banished from Charleston.[63]

The exciting Vesey affair did more than anything else to move South Carolina Baptists to declare their views on domestic slavery. Their inevitable spokesman was Richard Furman. Although written by Furman, the declaration came before the public as an expression of the sentiments of the entire Baptist constituency of the state. The slavocracy could not have wanted firmer support from the church. Furman insisted that slavery was thoroughly biblical and therefore truly Christian. Furthermore, he explicitly warned the bondmen that unless they were obedient to their masters, they "could neither be the faithful servants of God, nor be held as regular members of the Christian Church."

Governor Wilson, to whom the message was officially addressed, had good reason to tell Furman "that such doctrines, from such a source, will produce the best of consequences in our mixed population, and tend to make our servants not only more contented with their lot, but more useful to their owners."

The Baptist declaration of 1822 is historically significant in that it marked an early stage of the emerging doctrine of slavery as a positive good. The following document contains the essential elements of the declaration.

DOCUMENT

On the lawfulness of holding slaves, considering it in a moral and religious view, the Convention think it their duty to exhibit their sentiments, on the present occasion, before your Excellency, because they consider their duty to God, the peace of the State, the satisfaction of scrupulous consciences, and the welfare of the slaves themselves, as intimately connected with a right view of the subject. The rather, because certain writers on politics, morals and religion, and some of them highly respectable, have

---

[63] James Hamilton, *An Account of the Late Intended Insurrection Among a Portion of the Blacks of this City* (2nd ed., Charleston, S.C., 1822).

advanced positions, and inculcated sentiments, very unfriendly to the principle and practice of holding slaves; and by some these sentiments have been advanced among us, tending in their nature, *directly* to disturb the domestic peace of the State, to produce insubordination and rebellion among the slaves, and to infringe the rights of our citizens; and *indirectly,* to deprive the slaves of religious privileges, by awakening in the minds of their masters a fear, that acquaintance with the Scriptures, and the enjoyment of these privileges would naturally produce the aforementioned effects; because the sentiments in opposition to the holding of slaves have been attributed, by their advocates, to the Holy Scriptures, and to the genius of Christianity. These sentiments, the Convention, on whose behalf I address your Excellency, cannot think just, or well founded: for the right of holding slaves is clearly established in the Holy Scriptures, both by precept and example. In the Old Testament, the Israelites were directed to purchase their bond-men and bond-maids of the Heathen nations; except they were of the Canaanites, for these were to be destroyed. And it is declared, that the persons purchased were to be their "bond-men forever;" and an "inheritance for them and their children." They were not to go out free in the year of jubilee, as the Hebrews, who had been purchased, were; the line being clearly drawn between them.[64]. . .

In the New Testament, the Gospel History, or representation of facts, presents us with a view correspondent with that, which is furnished by other authentic ancient histories of the state of the world at the commencement of Christianity. The powerful Romans, had succeeded in empire, the polished Greeks; and, under both empires, the countries they possessed and governed were full of slaves. Many of these with their masters, were converted to the Christian Faith, and received, together with them into the Christian Church, while it was yet under the ministry of the inspired Apostles. In things purely spiritual, they appear to have enjoyed privileges; but their relationship, as masters and slaves, was not dissolved. Their respective duties are strictly enjoined. The masters are not required to emancipate their slaves; but to give them the things that are just and equal, forbearing threatening; and to remember, they also have a master in Heaven. The "servants under the yoke" [65] (bond-servants or slaves) mentioned by Paul to Timothy, as having "believing masters," are not authorized by him to demand of them emancipation, or to employ violent means to obtain it; but are directed to "account their masters worthy of all honour," and "not to despise them, because they were brethren" in religion; "but the rather to do them service, because they were faithful and beloved partakers of the Christian benefit." Similar directions are given by him in other places, and by other Apostles. And it gives great weight to the argument, that in this

---

[64] See LEVITICUS, xxv. 44. 45. 46. &c. [Furman]

[65] *Upo zugon Douloi;* bond-servants, or slaves. *Doulos,* is the proper term for slaves; it is here in the plural and rendered more expressive by being connected with yoke—UNDER THE YOKE. [Furman]

place, Paul follows his directions concerning servants with a charge to Timothy, as an Evangelist, to teach and exhort men to observe this doctrine.

Had the holding of slaves been a moral evil, it cannot be supposed, that the inspired Apostles, who feared not the faces of men, and were ready to lay down their lives in the cause of their God, would have tolerated it, for a moment, in the Christian Church. If they had done so on a principle of accommodation, in cases where the masters remained heathen, to avoid offences and civil commotion; yet, surely, where both master and servant were Christian, as in the case before us, they would have enforced the law of Christ, and required, that the master should liberate his slave in the first instance. But, instead of this, they let the relationship remain untouched, as being lawful and right, and insist on the relative duties.

In proving this subject justifiable by Scriptural authority, its morality is also proved; for the Divine Law never sanctions immoral actions.

The Christian golden rule, of doing to others, as we would they should do to us, has been urged as an unanswerable argument against holding slaves. But surely this rule is never to be urged against that order of things, which the Divine government has established; nor do our desires become a standard to us, under this rule, unless they have a due regard to justice, propriety and the general good. . . .

If the holding of slaves is lawful, or according to the Scriptures; then this Scriptural rule can be considered as requiring no more of the master, in respect of justice (whatever it may do in point of generosity) than what he, if a slave, could, consistently, wish to be done to himself, while the relationship between master and servant should be still continued.

In this argument, the advocates for emancipation blend the ideas of injustice and cruelty with those, which respect the existence of slavery, and consider them as inseparable. But, surely, they may be separated. A bond-servant may be treated with justice and humanity as a servant; and a master may, in an important sense, be the guardian and even father of his slaves. . . .

And here I am brought to a part of the general subject, which, I confess to your Excellency, the Convention, from a sense of their duty, as a body of men, to whom important concerns of Religion are confided, have particularly at heart, and wish it may be seriously considered by all our Citizens: This is the religious interests of the Negroes. For though they are slaves, they are also men; and are with ourselves accountable creatures; having immortal souls, and being destined to future eternal award. Their religious interests claim a regard from their masters of the most serious nature; and it is indispensable. Nor can the community at large, in a right estimate of their duty and happiness, be indifferent on this subject. To the truly benevolent it must be pleasing to know, that a number of masters, as well as ministers and pious individuals, of various Christian denominations among us, do conscientiously regard this duty; but there is great reason to believe, that it is neglected and disregarded by many.

The Convention are particularly unhappy in considering, that an idea of the Bible's teaching the doctrine of emancipation as necessary, and tending to make servants insubordinate to proper authority, has obtained access to any mind; both on account of its direct influence on those, who admit it; and the fear it excites in others, producing the effects before noticed. But it is hoped, it has been evinced, that the idea is an erroneous one; and, that it will be seen, that the influence of a right acquaintance with that Holy Book tends directly and powerfully, by promoting the fear and love of God, together with just and peaceful sentiments toward men, to produce one of the best securities to the public, for the internal and domestic peace of the state.

SOURCE: *Rev. Dr. Richard Furman's Exposition of the Views of the Baptists, Relative to the Coloured Population of the United States, in a Communication to the Governor of South-Carolina* (Charleston, S.C., 1823), 7–10, 15–6.

125. A Militant Declaration

In 1833, when the American Anti-Slavery Society was organized, two important papers were adopted: (1) the Constitution; and (2) the Declaration of Sentiments. The latter is here reproduced in full.

The Declaration was prepared under the auspices of a committee of ten, including Elizur Wright, Jr., Samuel J. May, John Greenleaf Whittier, and William Lloyd Garrison. It was written, however, by the editor of the *Liberator*.[66] Garrison was then enjoying special antislavery prestige because of his recent triumphant visit to England.

The original draft of the Declaration, on which Garrison had labored all night, was searchingly scrutinized by the whole committee for three hours. As a result, his long diatribe against the American Colonization Society was deleted. The remainder, with minor changes, was approved. When the document came before the whole convention, it was again subjected to detailed examination before adoption. Members of the convention personally signed the historic paper in a spirit of complete dedication to the antislavery movement.

The Declaration may be regarded as the Magna Charta of American abolitionism. It contains the cardinal doctrines of all the great abolitionists. It also sounds the same militant note and breathes the same confidence in victory as Thomas Paine's famous *Rights of Man*.

DOCUMENT

The Convention, assembled in the city of Philadelphia, to organize a National Anti-Slavery Society, promptly seize the opportunity to promul-

---

[66] Wendell P. and Francis J. Garrison, *William Lloyd Garrison, 1805–1879*, I, 399–400.

gate the following DECLARATION OF SENTIMENTS, as cherished by them in relation to the enslavement of one-sixth portion of the American people.

More than fifty-seven years have elapsed since a band of patriots convened in this place, to devise measures for the deliverance of this country from a foreign yoke. The corner stone upon which they founded the TEMPLE OF FREEDOM was broadly this—"that all men are created equal; and they are endowed by their Creator, with certain inalienable rights; that among these are life, LIBERTY, and the pursuit of happiness." At the sound of their trumpet-call three millions of people rose up as from the sleep of death, and rushed to the strife of blood; deeming it more glorious to die instantly as freemen, than desirable to live one hour as slaves. They were few in number—poor in resources; but the honest conviction that TRUTH, JUSTICE and RIGHT, were on their side, made them invincible.

We have met together for the achievement of an enterprise, without which that of our fathers is incomplete; and which, for its magnitude, solemnity, and probable results upon the destiny of the world, as far transcends theirs as moral truth does physical force.

In purity of motive, in earnestness of zeal, in decision of purpose, in intrepidity of action, in steadfastness of faith, in sincerity of spirit, we would not be inferior to them.

Their principles led them to wage war against their oppressors, and to spill human blood like water, in order to be free. *Ours* forbid the doing of evil that good may come, and lead us to reject, and to entreat the oppressed to reject, the use of all carnal weapons for deliverance from bondage; relying solely upon those which are spiritual, and mighty through God to the pulling down of strong holds.

Their measures were physical resistance—the marshalling in arms—the hostile array—the mortal encounter. *Ours* shall be such as only the opposition of moral purity to moral corruption—the destruction of error by the potency of truth—the overthrow of prejudice by the power of love—and the abolition of slavery by the spirit of repentance.

Their grievances, great as they were, were trifling in comparison with the wrongs and sufferings of those for whom we plead. Our fathers were never slaves—never bought and sold like cattle—never shut out from the light of knowledge and religion—never subjected to the lash of brutal task-masters.

But those for whose emancipation we are striving—constituting at the present time at least one-sixth part of our countrymen—are recognized by the law, and treated by their fellow beings, as marketable commodities, as goods and chattels, as brute beasts; are plundered daily of the fruits of their toil without redress; really enjoying no constitutional nor legal protection from licentious and murderous outrages upon their persons; are ruthlessly torn asunder—the tender babe from the arms of its frantic mother—the heart-broken wife from her weeping husband—at the caprice or pleasure of irresponsible tyrants. For the crime of having a dark complexion, they suffer the pangs of hunger, the infliction of stripes, and the ignominy of brutal servitude. They are kept in heathenish darkness by laws expressly enacted to make their instruction a criminal offence.

These are the prominent circumstances in the condition of more than two millions of our people, the proof of which may be found in thousands of indisputable facts, and in the laws of the slaveholding states.

Hence we maintain,—that in view of the civil and religious privileges of this nation, the guilt of its oppression is unequalled by any other on the face of the earth; and, therefore,

That it is bound to repent instantly, to undo the heavy burden, to break every yoke, and to let the oppressed go free.

We further maintain,—that no man has a right to enslave or imbrute his brother—to hold or acknowledge him, for one moment, as a piece of merchandise—to keep back his hire by fraud—or to brutalize his mind by denying him the means of intellectual, social, and moral improvement.

The right to enjoy liberty is inalienable. To invade it, is to usurp the prerogative of Jehovah. Every man has a right to his own body—to the products of his own labor—to the protection of law, and to the common advantages of society. It is piracy to buy or steal a native African, and subject him to servitude. Surely the sin is as great to enslave an AMERICAN as an AFRICAN.

Therefore we believe and affirm—That there is no difference, *in principle,* between the African slave trade and American slavery:

That every American citizen who retains a human being in involuntary bondage as his property, is [according to scripture] [67] a MAN STEALER:

That the slaves ought instantly to be set free, and brought under the protection of law:

That if they had lived from the time of Pharoah down to the present period, and had been entailed through successive generations, their right to be free could never have been alienated, but their claims would have constantly risen in solemnity:

That all those laws which are now in force, admitting the right of slavery, are therefore before God utterly null and void; being an audacious usurpation of the Divine prerogative, a daring infringement on the law of nature, a base overthrow of the very foundations of the social compact, a complete extinction of all the relations, endearments, and obligations of mankind, and a presumptuous transgression of all the holy commandments —and that therefore they ought instantly to be abrogated.

We further believe and affirm—That all persons of color who possess the qualifications which are demanded of others, ought to be admitted forthwith to the enjoyment of the same privileges, and the exercise of the same prerogatives, as others; and that the paths of preferment, of wealth,

[67] Ex. xxi. 16. [The Declaration]

and of intelligence, should be opened as widely to them as to persons of a white complexion.

We maintain that no compensation should be given to the planters emancipating their slaves,

Because it would be a surrender of the great fundamental principle, that man cannot hold property in man;

Because SLAVERY IS A CRIME, AND THEREFORE IS NOT AN ARTICLE TO BE SOLD;

Because the holders of slaves are not the just proprietors of what they claim; freeing the slaves is not depriving them of property, but restoring it to its rightful owners; it is not wronging the master, but righting the slave—restoring him to himself;

Because immediate and general emancipation would only destroy nominal, not real property; it would not amputate a limb or break a bone of the slaves, but by infusing motives into their breasts, would make them doubly valuable to the masters as free laborers; and

Because, if compensation is to be given at all, it should be given to the outraged and guiltless slaves, and not to those who have plundered and abused them.

We regard as delusive, cruel, and dangerous, any scheme of expatriation which pretends to aid, either directly or indirectly, in the emancipation of the slaves, or to be a substitute for the immediate and total abolition of slavery.

We fully and unanimously recognize the sovereignty of each state, to legislate exclusively on the subject of the slavery which is tolerated within its limits; we concede that Congress, *under the present national compact,* has no right to interfere with any of the slave states, in relation to this momentous subject:

But we maintain that Congress has a right, and is solemnly bound, to suppress the domestic slave trade between the several states, and to abolish slavery in those portions of our territory which the Constitution has placed under its exclusive jurisdiction.

We also maintain that there are, at the present time, the highest obligations resting upon the people of the free states, to remove slavery by moral and political action, as prescribed in the Constitution of the United States. They are now living under a pledge of their tremendous physical force, to fasten the galling fetters of tyranny upon the limbs of millions in the southern states; they are liable to be called at any moment to suppress a general insurrection of the slaves; they authorize the slave owner to vote on three-fifths of his slaves as property, and thus enable him to perpetuate his oppression; they support a standing army at the south for its protection; and they seize the slave who has escaped into their territories, and send him back to be tortured by an enraged master or a brutal driver. This relation to slavery is criminal and full of danger: IT MUST BE BROKEN UP.

These are our views and principles—these our designs and measures. With entire confidence in the overruling justice of God, we plant ourselves upon the Declaration of our Independence and the truths of divine revelation as upon the Everlasting Rock.

We shall organize Anti-Slavery Societies, if possible, in every city, town and village, in our land.

We shall send forth agents to lift up the voice of remonstrance, of warning, of entreaty, and rebuke.

We shall circulate, unsparingly and extensively, antislavery tracts and periodicals.

We shall enlist the pulpit and the press in the cause of the suffering and the dumb.

We shall aim at a purification of the churches from all participation in the guilt of slavery.

We shall encourage the labor of freemen rather than that of slaves, by giving a preference to their productions: and

We shall spare no exertions nor means to bring the whole nation to speedy repentance.

Our trust for victory is solely in God. *We* may be personally defeated, but our principles never. TRUTH, JUSTICE, REASON, HUMANITY, must and will gloriously triumph. Already a host is coming up to the help of the Lord against the mighty, and the prospect before us is full of encouragement.

Submitting this DECLARATION to the candid examination of the people of this country, and of the friends of liberty throughout the world, we hereby affix our signatures to it; pledging ourselves that, under the guidance and by the help of Almighty God we will do all that in us lies, consistently with this Declaration of our principles, to overthrow the most execrable system of slavery that has ever been witnessed upon earth—to deliver our land from its deadliest curse—to wipe out the foulest stain which rests upon our national escutcheon—and to secure to the colored population of the United States all the rights and privileges which belong to them as men, and as Americans—come what may to our persons, our interests, or our reputation—whether we live to witness the triumph of LIBERTY, JUSTICE, and HUMANITY, or perish untimely as martyrs in this great, benevolent, and holy cause.

Done at Philadelphia, the sixth day of December, A.D. 1833.

SOURCE: *The Declaration of Sentiments and Constitution of the American Anti-Slavery Society* (N.Y., 1837), 3–6.

126. The Lane Debate

When Lyman Beecher assumed his presidential duties at Lane Theological Seminary, in the fall of 1833, little did he expect that before the first academic year had ended he would have to guide that institution through a major crisis. Yet that was his fate. From the opening of the academic year, student opinion diverged on the slavery question. Some, like Theodore Weld, were outright abolitionists, but the majority were far less radical. This situation naturally provoked an exchange of views. Early in February the two groups decided to debate the issues publicly. Despite discouragement from the faculty, the debate was scheduled. The eighteen-night forensic marathon ended in overwhelming victory for the abolitionists. The upshot was the organization, on March 10, of a vigorous Lane antislavery society.

The young abolitionists did not confine their labors to the campus; they conducted classes for the free Negroes in Cincinnati, and even socialized with them in their homes. The social mixing raised a loud outcry in the community. Lane officials warned the students against such mingling, but to no avail. Finally, while Beecher was in the East, the Executive Committee of the Board of Trustees found it necessary to impose restraint upon the Lane enthusiasts. The committee abolished the newly formed antislavery society, severely curtailed student discussion of the slavery question, and banned all public pronouncements except those officially approved.[68] When the full Board met, the actions of the Executive Committee were approved by all members except Asa Mahan.

After it became evident that the Board meant to hold firmly to its position, fifty-one students, including Weld, bolted the Seminary. Many of them later entered the newly founded Oberlin College, which agreed not only to call Asa Mahan as president but to admit Negroes. John Morgan, the one teacher at Lane who had favored the rebels, joined the Oberlin faculty. Arthur Tappan cut off his gifts to Lane and bestowed them upon Oberlin. The great Finney was persuaded to join the faculty as instructor in theology. Thus Lane's loss was an enormous gain for Oberlin, which rose into academic prominence over night. Within a short time Oberlin had become America's greatest academic center for the promotion of abolitionism.

The document which follows gives a remarkable account of the Lane debate by an inside observer, Henry B. Stanton. Stanton's letter first appeared in the *New York Evangelist,* of which Joshua Leavitt was the editor.

DOCUMENT

BROTHER LEAVITT—Many of your readers are undoubtedly interested in whatever concerns this rising institution. Therefore, I send you the following. Slavery and its proposed remedies—immediate abolition and colonization, have been subjects of occasional remark among the students, since the commencement of the late term (June). A flourishing Colonization Society has existed among us almost from the foundation of the institution. Our

[68] Thomas, *Theodore Weld,* 75-7, 82.

interest in these topics increased gradually until about the first of February, when it was resolved that we discuss publicly the merits of the colonization and abolition schemes. At this time, there were but few decided abolitionists in the Seminary. The two following questions were discussed, separately:

1st. *"Ought the people of the Slaveholding States to abolish Slavery immediately?"*

2d. *"Are the doctrines, tendencies, and measures of the American Colonization Society, and the influence of its principal supporters, such as render it worthy of the patronage of the Christian public?"*

Our respected faculty, fearing the effect the discussion would have upon the prosperity of the Seminary, formally *advised,* that it should be postponed indefinitely. But the students, feeling great anxiety that it should proceed, and being persuaded from the state of feeling among them, that it would be conducted in a manner becoming young men looking forward to the ministry of the gospel of reconciliation, resolved to go on. The President, and the members of the faculty, with one exception, were present during parts of the discussion.

Each question was debated nine evenings of two hours and a half each; making forty-five hours of solid debate. We possessed some facilities for discussing both these questions intelligently. We are situated within one mile of a slaveholding State; eleven of our number were born and brought up in slave States, seven of whom were sons of slaveholders, and one of them was himself a slaveholder, till recently; one of us had been a slave, and had bought his freedom, "with a great sum," which his own hands had earned; ten others had lived more or less in slave States, besides several who had travelled in the midst of slavery, making inquiries and searching after truth. We possessed all the numbers of the African Repository, from its commencement, nearly all the Annual Reports of the Colonization Society, and the prominent documents of the Anti-Slavery Society. In addition to the above, our kind friends in the city, furnished us with Colonization pamphlets in profusion. Dr. Shane, a young gentleman of Cincinnati, who had been out to Liberia, with a load of emigrants, as an agent of the Colonization Society, furnished us with a long statement concerning the colony; and a distinguished instructress, recently of Hartford, Connecticut, now of Cincinnati, sent us a communication from her hand, which attempted to prove, that Colonizationists and Abolitionists ought to unite their efforts, and not contend against one another.—These were our materials. And, sir, it was emphatically a discussion of *facts,* FACTS, FACTS.

The first speaker occupied nearly two evenings, in presenting facts concerning slavery and immediate emancipation, gathered from various authentic documents. Conclusions and inferences were then drawn from these facts, and arguments founded upon them favourable to immediate abolition, during the two next evenings. Nearly four of the remaining five evenings were devoted to the recital of facts, in regard to slavery, slaves, and slaveholders, gathered, not from written documents, but from careful personal observation and experience. Nearly half of the seventeen speakers, on the evenings last alluded to, were the sons of slaveholders; one had been a slaveholder himself; one had till recently been a slave; and the residue were residents of, or had recently travelled or lived in slave States. From their testimony, the following facts and premises were established, to wit: That slaves long for freedom; that it is a subject of very frequent conversation among them; that they know their masters have no right to hold them in slavery; that they keenly feel the wrong, the insult and the degradation which are heaped upon them by the whites; they feel no interest comparatively in their master's affairs, because they know he is their oppressor; they are indolent, because nothing they can earn is their own; they pretend to be more ignorant and stupid than they really are, so as to avoid responsibility, and to shun the lash for any real or alleged disobedience to orders; when inspired with a promise of freedom, they will toil with incredible alacrity and faithfulness; they tell their masters and drivers they are contented with their lot, merely through fear of greater cruelty if they tell the truth; no matter how kind their master is, they are dissatisfied, and would rather be his hired servants than his slaves; the slave-drivers are generally low, brutal, debauched men, distinguished only for their cruelty and licentiousness; they generally have the despotic control of the slaves; the best side of slavery is seen; its darker features being known only to slaves, masters and drivers; [upon this point, horrid facts, in regard to the whipping and *murdering* of slaves, were developed. God sparing my life, they shall be given to the public.] The state of morals among slaves, especially in regard to licentiousness, is sickening! This condition is attributable to the treatment they receive from their masters; they being huddled together from their infancy in small apartments without discrimination of sex; and oftentimes being compelled to steal or starve; the influence of slavery upon the physical condition, and mental and moral character of the whites, is decidedly and lamentably pernicious; the internal slave trade is increasing, and is carried on by men distinguished, even among slave-drivers, for their cruelty and brutality! No class in the country have stronger social affections, than slaves; nevertheless, the ties of parent and child, husband and wife, brother and sister, are torn asunder by this bloody traffic. A husband has been known to cut his throat deliberately, because this damnable traffic was about to separate him from a wife whom he tenderly loved. The horrid character of Louisiana slavery, was developed in some degree by one who had resided there. The planters in that State, when sugar commands a high price, do not hesitate to kill a few of their negroes by overworking, if by that means they can bring more sugar into a favourable market; in consequence of this, one of the usual prayers of the poor negro is, *that sugar may be cheap*. Multitudes of slaves are being carried into that State from other slave States; blacks are kidnapped from this State, (Ohio,) and sold into slavery; slaves are decidedly hostile to Liberia, and only consent to go there to escape from slavery; masters are generally opposed to their negroes being educated; *that the blacks are abundantly able to take care of, and provide for themselves; and that they would be kind and docile if immediately emancipated.* These points, with many others equally important, were established, so far as a multitude of facts could establish them. On the two last points, the following was interesting and decisive.

James Bradley, the emancipated slave above alluded to, addressed us nearly two hours; and I wish his speech could have been heard by every opponent of immediate emancipation, to wit: first, that "it would be unsafe to the community;" second, that "the condition of the emancipated negroes would be worse than it now is; that they are incompetent to provide for themselves; that they would become paupers and vagrants, and would rather steal than work for wages." This shrewd and intelligent black, cut up these *white objections* by the roots, and withered and scorched them under the sun of sarcastic argumentation, for nearly an hour, to which the assembly responded in repeated and spontaneous roars of laughter, which were heartily joined in by both Colonizationists and Abolitionists. Do not understand me as saying, that his speech was devoid of *argument.* No. It contained sound logic, enforced by apt illustrations. I wish the slanderers of negro intellect could have witnessed this unpremeditated effort. I will give you a sketch of this man's history. He was stolen from Africa when an infant, and sold into slavery. His master, who resided in Arkansas, died, leaving him to his widow. He was then about eighteen years of age. For some years, *he managed the plantation for his mistress.* Finally, he purchased his time by the year, and began to earn money to buy his freedom. After five years of toil, having paid his owners $655, besides supporting himself during the time, he received his "free papers," and emigrated to a free State with more than $200 in his pocket. Every cent of this money, $855, he earned by labour and trading. He is now a beloved and respected member of this institution.

Now, Mr. Editor, can slaves take care of themselves if emancipated? I answer the question in the language employed by brother Bradley, on the above occasion. "They have to take care of, and support themselves *now, and their master, and his family into the bargain;* and this being so, it would be strange if they could not provide for themselves, *when disencumbered from this load.*" He said the great desire of the slaves was *"liberty and education."* And shall this heaven-born desire be trampled in the dust by a free and Christian nation?

At the close of the ninth evening, the vote was taken on the first question, *when every individual voted in the affirmative except four or five,* who excused themselves from voting at all, on the ground that they had not made up their opinion. Every friend of the cause rendered a hearty tribute of thanksgiving to God, for the glorious issue.

At the next evening, we entered upon the discussion of the second question. Here, there was a much greater diversity of sentiment. But we entered upon the debate not like blinded partizans, but like men whose polar star was facts and truth, whose needle was conscience, whose chart the Bible.

The witnesses summoned to the stand, were the documents of the Colonization Society. They were examined at great length and in great numbers. We judged it out of its own mouth. There was no paucity of testimony; for, as I before observed, we had all its "Repositories," and nearly all its Reports and Addresses, in addition to which, we were benevolently furnished by friends with numerous collated witnesses, whom we of course had the privilege of cross-examining. Notwithstanding the length of this part of the discussion, but two individuals spoke, one on each side, and another read some testimony in favour of the Colony. Several individuals at the opening of the debate, intended to speak on the affirmative, but before it was closed, they became warmly attached to the other side. Others were induced to espouse the cause of anti-Colonizationism, by examining the documents of the Colonization Society, for the purpose of preparing to speak in the affirmative. *Most of the Colonizationists who expressed any opinion on the subject, declared their ignorance of the doctrines and measures of the Society until this debate.* They cannot find words to express their astonishment that they should have been so duped into the support of this Society, as a scheme of benevolence towards the free blacks, and a remedy for slavery. They now repudiate it with all their hearts. Is it not the "immediate" duty of such men (benevolent, and scrupulously honest, no doubt,) to examine this subject?

I will state a fact. A member of this Institution was a member of the Oneida Institute, during the Colonization debate held there last summer, and took an active part in that discussion.[69] An anti-Slavery and a Colonization Society were the offspring of this debate. My worthy brother was placed at the head of the latter Society. He was a sincere friend of the negro, and what is quite as rare, was a consistent and practical man. About five months since, he left Oneida, and came to Lane Seminary. On his way hither, he took great pains to converse with every negro he could find about emigrating to Liberia. He talked with some thirty or forty, all of whom except one, were incorrigible in their preference to remain in their native land, rather than to emigrate "home" to a foreign shore. This shook his faith in the entire practicability of the scheme. Still he arrived here, the warm friend of the Society; and so continued, until this debate, in which he intended to have taken an active part. But before he had an opportunity to take the floor, facts pressed upon him, (he was always open to conviction,) he changed his views, became the decided opponent of the Society, has left the Institution for the purpose of commencing a school for the education of the people of colour in Cincinnati, and has devoted himself to the elevation of the free blacks on our own soil, and to the making up of a public sentiment favourable to the abolition of slavery without ex-

[69] Augustus Wattles (1807–83), who later became an agent of the American Anti-Slavery Society, and devoted much attention to the education of free Negroes in the North.

patriation. I would give you his name were it not that he is about to present to the public some interesting facts, bearing upon slavery and emancipation, which he has collected within a few weeks among the free people of colour, in Cincinnati, in the course of which he will probably allude to the facts stated above by me. This, sir, is what I call practical anti-colonizationism.

At the close of the debate, the question was taken by ayes and noes, and decided in the negative with only one dissenting voice. Four or five who did not regularly attend the discussion, declined voting. Two or three others were absent from the Seminary.—When the debate commenced, I had fears that there might be some unpleasant excitement, particularly as slaveholders, and prospective heirs to slave property, were to participate in it. But the kindest feelings prevailed. There was no crimination, no denunciation, no impeachment of motives. And the result has convinced me that prejudice is vincible, that colonization is vulnerable, and that immediate abolition is not only right, and practicable, but is *"expedient."*

The result has convinced me of another thing, which I hail as the bright bow of promise to this holy cause. It is that southern minds, trained and educated amidst all the prejudices of a slaveholding community, can, with the blessing of God, be reached and influenced by *facts and arguments, as easy as any other class of our citizens.* To be sure, they will not endure *blind* and *unintelligent* denunciation; and what *rational* being will? But after being thoroughly aroused by facts, they will receive rebuke, remonstrance, and entreaty, if kindly offered, with that frankness and honesty which have ever marked the southern character. And when thoroughly converted, they manifest an ardor in behalf of the deeply injured black, which astonishes while it delights. Almost all of our southern brethren are engaged in colored Sabbath schools and Bible classes. Some of them have devoted their lives in doing good to that oppressed race. Let me state one or two facts on this point. The son of a slaveholder has just left the institution on account of ill-health, with a determination that he will not cease his efforts until his parent is induced to liberate his slaves. Another said, until this debate, he had ever considered slaveholding right, but now, being convinced it was wrong, he should exert an influence accordingly. Another entered this institution last spring the owner of two slaves. Having been taught to look upon slavery as a necessary evil and not a sin, he hired out his slaves where they would receive kind treatment, intending that the proceeds of their labor should aid him in his preparations for the ministry. Towards the close of the last session, facts were pressed upon his conscience, his duty was pointed out, he saw it, returned home to Kentucky, liberated his slaves—and now, instead of their working to educate *him,* he is working and studying, and educating *them.* I need not add, that, on this occasion, he took the side of immediate abolition, and anti-colonization. This, sir, is what I call *practical* "immediate emancipation."

It is the decided opinion of our brethren from the slave states, that if the plan of abolition proposed by the friends of that measure, could be kindly spread out before the southern community, and the entire practicability of the scheme illustrated and enforced by existing facts, slaveholders would embrace it as the only rational remedy for slavery, and would come over to the cause of immediate emancipation in crowds. They have somehow gotten the opinion that *abolition* is an infuriated monster, with a thousand heads and ten thousand horns, panting after blood, and ready to gore to death every slaveholder in the Union. And is it wonderful that they should receive this impression, when we consider the tone of the Colonization journals of the north? Our southern fellow-citizens should be disabused on this vitally interesting subject. Depend upon it, the *people,* (I speak not of *politicians,*) the *people* of the south are not devoid of reason. *I know* that facts and reasoning *have* prevailed with them: and until truth loses its power, they *will continue* to prevail, overcoming prejudice, reaching the conscience, and changing the mind. I am acquainted with intelligent gentlemen residing in this country, not professing Christians, who are intimately acquainted with slavery in all its details, having lived many years in slaveholding states, who *on principles of political economy,* are the decided advocates of immediate emancipation. Look at the facts as they exist in this seminary. Every member of this institution who was born and brought up in the midst of slavery, or who now resides in a slave state, with one exception, is the advocate of immediate abolition without expatriation. . . . There has been no necromancy employed in this work. *Prayer, the Bible, the condition of the slave, and the documents of the Colonization Society,* have been the instruments. When a brother resolved to use these means faithfully, we had no anxiety as to the result. Would not the use of these measures by every Christian in the land work wonders in the American church? Alas! how few Christians have prayed over, and talked about, and examined a system which crushes into the dust two millions of their brethren and sisters, and consigns them over to oppression, to caprice, to lust, to brutality, to ignorance, to degradation, to death, to damnation. I thank God that the night of torpor is past in this institution; that prejudice has been buried in a dishonored grave, and that the persecuted blacks, bond and free, have a place in our sympathies, our prayers, and our labors. . . .

This evening [March 10, 1834], we formed an Anti-Slavery Society.

Yours in the gospel,

H. B. STANTON.

SOURCE: *Debate at the Lane Seminary, Cincinnati. Speech of James A. Thome, of Kentucky, . . . Letter of the Rev. Dr. Samuel H. Cox, against the American Colonization Society* (Boston, 1834), 3-7.

127. *Irrepressible Abolitionism*

After the Methodist General Conference of 1836 had denounced "modern abolitionism," the annual conferences redoubled their efforts to safeguard themselves against abolitionist taint. For example, the Philadelphia Conference for some ten years operated under a rule whereby any known abolitionist ministerial candidate was refused membership. In 1837, and again in 1838, Lucius C. Matlack was rejected under this rule.[70]

The bishops ardently supported this anti-abolitionist campaign. When, for example, Orange Scott refused to cease his abolitionist activities, Bishop Hedding removed him from the post of presiding elder and assigned him to a local charge.[71] As presiding officer over annual conferences, the bishop often used his prerogative to prevent the slavery question from being discussed on the conference floor.[72]

This frustrating situation gave birth to Methodist antislavery conventions, which were open to laymen as well as to clergymen. One of the earliest of these conventions met at Lynn, Massachusetts, in October of 1837. The "call" was signed by 700 preachers and laymen from four annual conferences.[73] The main business of these popular gatherings was to provide inspirational speeches, formulate stirring resolutions, and devise strategies by which to abolitionize the masses.

The following document represents the gist of the resolutions which grew out of the Methodist antislavery convention held at Boston on January 18, 1843. As these resolutions indicate, Methodist abolitionists agreed with the Declaration of Sentiments of the American Anti-Slavery Society that slavery was "a sin under all circumstances." Since slaveholders belonged to the Methodist Church, the only alternative for Methodists was "reformation or division."

As a matter of fact, a division within Methodism was already under way in the East. In 1842 Orange Scott had announced his decision to break with the mother church. At a convention held at Utica, New York, on May 31, 1843, he and other prominent abolitionists organized the Wesleyan Methodist Connection of America. All slaveholders were excluded from the new denomination. This schism foreshadowed a much greater division which would take place at the 1844 session of the General Conference of the Methodist Church.

DOCUMENT

1. *Resolved,* That the holding or treating human beings as property, or claiming the right to hold or treat them as property, is a flagrant violation

---

[70] Matlack, *The Antislavery Struggle and Triumph in the Methodist Episcopal Church* (N.Y., 1881), 117.

[71] Matlack, *History of American Slavery and Methodism,* 157.

[72] *Ibid.,* 169–71.   [73] *Ibid.,* 165.

of the law of God: it is sin in itself: a sin in the abstract, and in the concrete: a sin under all circumstances, and in every person claiming such right; and no apology whatever can be admitted to justify the perpetration.

2. *Resolved,* That as the unanimity and harmony of feeling which should ever characterize the people of God, can not exist so long as slavery continues in the Church, we feel it our imperative duty to use all such means as become Christians, in seeking its immediate and entire abolition from the Church of which we are members.

3. *Resolved,* That the Methodist Episcopal Church, being a unit in its doctrine and Discipline, in its legislative and judicial departments, and almost one in its executive operations, is, as a body, responsible for the existence of slavery in its pale, but more especially the ministry, with whom the legislative, judicial, and executive duties rest, and who have the power to purge the Church of this shocking abomination.

4. *Resolved,* That slavery being a sin, and this sin in the Methodist Episcopal Church, and the Church a unit as above, nothing short of a speedy and entire separation of slavery from the Church can satisfy the consciences of honest and faithful abolitionists; and, therefore, reformation or division is the only alternative.

5. *Resolved,* That we all unitedly and solemnly pledge to God and each other, our zealous and unceasing efforts, while there is hope, to purge the Methodist Episcopal Church and the land from slavery.

Whereas, all slaveholding, that is, all claim of the right of property in human beings, is essentially a sin against God; and whereas, every slave-holder is, per consequence, a sinner; therefore,

6. *Resolved,* That we do not and will not fellowship a person claiming the above right, or holding slaves, as a Christian; nor ought he to be admitted to the pulpit or the communion.

7. *Resolved,* That while we do all we can in the several relations we sustain to the Church, to extirpate the great sin of slavery from her pale, we do not, by remaining members, either countenance or fellowship the slaveholder. . . .

11. *Resolved,* That the Methodist Episcopal Church being governed by a majority of the General conference, and as the north have a majority in the legislative, judicial, and executive branches of the Church, the sin of slavery in the Methodist Episcopal Church is emphatically a sin of the north, as it exists by their consent, and could be abolished from the Church by their votes at any time.

12. *Resolved,* That as our bishops and presiding elders have most authority as judicial and executive officers of the Methodist Episcopal Church, they can do more in the intervals of the General conference than any other portion of the Church, for the overthrow of slavery in it, and therefore are more responsible in the premises, and are hereby earnestly requested to coöperate with us for its removal. . . .

14. *Resolved,* That the passage of the resolution at our late General conference, by which the colored members of our Church in such states as reject their testimony in courts of law, are denied the right of bearing testimony against white persons in Church trials, is an alarming and arbitrary exercise of arbitrary ecclesiastical power, subversive of the inalienable right of every member of the Church of Christ, contrary to the spirit of the Gospel, and inflicted a blot on the reputation of the Methodist Church that time can never efface.

15. *Resolved,* That the passage of the colored testimony resolution, at our late General conference, demands the interference of every member of the Church, and that it is the imperative duty of all who do not wish to be held responsible for its continuance to protest against it in a decided and earnest memorial to the next General conference, and we hereby call on all the members of our Church to record their disapprobation of the above resolution, and require, in terms that can not be misunderstood, its immediate repeal. . . .

Whereas, the Discipline of the Methodist Episcopal Church, p. 176, provides, in substance, that no slaveholder shall be eligible to any official station in the Church, where the laws of the state in which he lives will admit of emancipation, and permit the liberated slave to enjoy freedom therein; and whereas, it appears that one of the bishops of said Church did, in the month of May, 1840, set apart and ordain to the holy office of elder in said Church, a man who was a slaveholder, and lived *at the time* in a state where the laws did allow of emancipation, and did permit the emancipated person to enjoy freedom therein; therefore,

17. *Resolved,* That this convention respectfully request the New England conference of the said Church, at its next session, to address the next General conference on this subject, and to instruct their delegates to that body to take such means as shall bring the matter fully before said General conference, for full examination and adjudication.

18. *Resolved,* That, whereas, in the sight of the most high God, it is not the color of the skin, but the state of the heart which is regarded, it is inconsistent with our Christian profession and character to despise or slight, or make any difference among men on account of their color, but especially in the house of God, and at the communion; and that all legislative enactments, based on this fact, are founded in injustice, contrary to every principle of humanity, and the government of God, who unequivocally declares that he is not a respecter of persons.

SOURCE: Charles Elliot, *History of the Great Secession from the Methodist Episcopal Church in the Year 1845* . . . (Cincinnati, 1855), 970–1.

128. A Biblical Defense of Slavery

Of all the arguments for slavery, the biblical argument was the one most frequently and most universally employed. Since the Scriptures were recognized as the highest court of moral appeal, they were fully capitalized in the defense of human bondage.

A representative biblical argument was presented by John England (1786–1842), bishop of the Charleston Diocese of the Roman Catholic Church. His defense was occasioned by an address given in Georgia by the U.S. Secretary of State, John Forsyth, who had strongly implied that the Apostolic Letter of Pope Gregory XVI, issued in December of 1839, had aligned the Roman Catholic Church on the side of abolitionism. England vigorously refuted the inference, contending that the pope had only condemned the slave trade, not the institution of domestic slavery. The bishop's reply consisted largely of an historical survey of the Catholic tradition in which he conclusively proved that the Roman Church had always sanctioned the institution of slavery. On the other hand, he made clear that the Catholic Church had always striven to protect the rights of the bondmen.

Bishop England's answer to Forsyth was given in a series of *Letters,* eighteen in number, published during 1840–41 in the *United States Catholic Miscellany.* The series was interrupted by more pressing affairs, but was never resumed because of the author's death in 1842. Letters three and four, published on October 13 and 21, 1840, presented a detailed biblical apologetic for slavery. Letter four, which is reproduced below in substance, concentrated upon texts from the New Testament.

When Bishop England published the last letter, he divulged his own views. He explicitly acknowledged a personal antipathy toward slavery, but added, "I also see the impossibility of now abolishing it here. When it can and ought to be abolished is a question for the legislature and not for me." [74]

The author of the *Letters,* a native of Ireland, was sent to America as the first bishop of the newly established Diocese of Charleston, which embraced the two Carolinas and Georgia. Arriving on December 30, 1820, England found a very small diocesan flock of some 3,600 people, scattered over three states.[75] The few existing parishes were not only poverty stricken, but almost priestless. Besides, the See of Charleston itself was torn by what Father Guilday called "trusteemania." [76] Nevertheless, Bishop England entered upon his labors with hope and great vigor, traveling continuously and holding services wherever possible. His industry was truly amazing.

Besides being an eloquent preacher, England was a colorful and provoca-

---

[74] Quoted in Joseph L. O'Brien, *John England, Bishop of Charleston: the Apostle to Democracy* (N.Y., 1934), 152.

[75] Peter Guilday, *The Life and Times of John England* (2 vols., N.Y., 1927), I, 7.

[76] *Ibid.,* 164–282.

tive journalist. In 1822 he founded America's first strictly Catholic periodical, the *United States Catholic Miscellany*. In the same year he founded the
Philosophical and Classical Seminary, in which to train native priests. For
a time the Seminary was attended by many non-Catholics. He also started
a school in Charleston for free Negroes, but public disapproval soon forced
him to close it. The bishop preached widely in the United States, and always
strongly defended the American principle of religious freedom.

In the New Testament we find instances of pious and good men having
slaves, and in no case do we find the Saviour imputing it to them as a
crime, or requiring their servants' emancipation.—In chap. viii, of St. Matthew, we read of a centurion, who addressing the Lord Jesus, said, v. 9,
"For I also am a man under authority, having soldiers under me, and I say
to this man, go, and he goeth: and to another, come, and he cometh: and
to my servant, do this and he doth it." v. 10. "And Jesus hearing this wondered, and said to those that followed him: Amen, I say to you, I have not
found so great faith in Israel." ** v. 13. ["]And Jesus said to the centurion,
go, and as thou hast believed, so be it done to thee. And the servant was
healed at the same hour." St. Luke, in ch. vii, relates also the testimony
which the ancients of Israel gave of this stranger's virtue, and how he loved
their nation, and built a synagogue for them.

In many of his parables, the Saviour describes the master and his servants
in a variety of ways, without any condemnation or censure of slavery. In
Luke xvii, he describes the usual mode of acting towards slaves as the very
basis upon which he teaches one of the most useful lessons of Christian virtue, v. 7. "But which of you having a servant ploughing or feeding cattle,
will say to him, when he is come from the field, immediately, go sit down."
8. "And will not rather say to him, make ready my supper, and gird thyself, and serve me while I eat and drink, and afterwards, thou shalt eat and
drink?" 9. "Doth he thank that servant because he did the things that were
commanded him?" 10. "I think not. So you also, when you shall have
done all the things that are commanded you, say: we are unprofitable servants, we have done that which we ought to do."

After the promulgation of the Christian religion by the apostles, the
slave was not told by them that he was in a state of unchristian durance.
1. Cor. vii, 20. "Let every man abide in the same calling in which he was
called." 21. "Art thou called being a bond-man? Care not for it; but if thou
mayest be made free, use it rather." 22. "For he that is called in the Lord,
being a bond-man, is the free-man of the Lord. Likewise he that is called
being free, is the bond-man of Christ." 23. "You are bought with a price,
be not made the bond-slaves of men." 24. "Brethren, let every man, wherein
he was called, therein abide with God." Thus a man by becoming a Christian was not either made free nor told that he was free, but he was ad-

vised, if he could lawfully procure his freedom, to prefer it to slavery. The 23d verse has exactly that meaning which we find expressed also in chap. vi, v. 20. "For you are bought with a great price, glorify and bear God in your body,["] which is addressed to the free as well as to the slave: all are the servants of God, and should not be drawn from his service by the devices of men, but should "walk worthy of the vocation in which they are called." Eph. iv, i. and the price by which their souls, (not their bodies) were redeemed, is also described by St. Peter I, c. i, 10. "Knowing that you were not redeemed with corruptible gold or silver from your vain conversation of the tradition of your fathers." 19. "But with the precious blood of Christ, as of a lamb unspotted and undefiled."—That it was a spiritual redemption and a spiritual service, St. Paul again shows, Heb. ix, 14. "How much more shall the blood of Christ, who through the Holy Ghost, offered himself without spot to God, cleanse our conscience from dead works to serve the living God?" It is then a spiritual equality as was before remarked, in the words of St. Paul, 1 Cor. xii, 13. "For in one spirit we are baptized into one body, whether Jews or Gentiles, whether bond or free." And in the same chapter he expatiates to show that though all members of the one mystical body, their places, their duties, their gifts are various and different. And in his epistle to the Galatians, chap. iv. he exhibits the great truth which he desires to inculcate by an illustration taken from the institutions of slavery, and without a single expression of their censure.

Nor did the apostles consider the Christian master obliged to liberate his Christian servant. St. Paul in his epistle to Philemon acknowledges the right of the master to the services of his slave for whom however he asks, as a special favor, pardon for having deserted his owner. 10. "I beseech thee for my son Onesimus whom I have begotten in my chains." 11. "Who was heretofore unprofitable to thee, but now profitable both to thee and to thee [sic]." 12. "Whom I have sent back to thee. And do thou receive him as my own bowels." Thus a runaway slave still belonged to his master, and though having become a Christian, so far from being thereby liberated from service, he was bound to return thereto and submit himself to his owner. . . .

Again it is manifest from the Epistle of St. Paul to Timothy that the title of the master continued good to his slave though both should be Christians, c. vii. "Whosoever are servants under the yoke, let them count their masters worthy of all honor, lest the name and doctrine of the Lord be blasphemed." 2. "But they who have believing masters, let them not despise them because they are brethren, but serve them the rather, because they are faithful and beloved, who are partakers of the benefit. These things exhort and teach." And in the subsequent part he declares the contrary teaching to be against the sound words of Jesus Christ, and to spring from ignorant pride. . . .

It will now fully establish what will be necessary to perfect the view which I desire to give, if I can show that masters who were Christians were not required to emancipate their slaves, but had pointed out the duties which they were bound as masters to perform, because this will show under the Christian dispensation the legal, moral and religious existence of slave and master.

The apostle, as we have previously seen, 1 *Tim.* vi, 2, wrote of slaves who had believing or Christian masters. The inspired penman did not address his instructions and exhortations to masters who were not of the household of the Faith. 1 *Cor.* v, 12. "For what have I to do, to judge them that are without?" 13. "For them that are without, God will judge; take away the evil one from amongst yourselves." Thus when he addresses masters; they are Christian masters. Ephes. vi, 9. "And you, masters, do the same things to them (servants) forbearing threatenings, knowing that the Lord both of them and you is in heaven: and there is no respect of persons with him,"—and again, Colos. iv, i, "Masters do to your servants that which is just and equal: knowing that you also have a master in heaven."

We have then in the teaching of the apostles nothing which contradicts the law of Moses, but we have much which corrects the cruelty of the Pagan practice. The exhibition which is presented to us is one of a cheering and of an elevated character. It is true that the state of slavery is continued under the legal sanction, but the slave is taught from the most powerful motives to be faithful, patient, obedient and contented, and the master is taught that though despotism may pass unpunished on earth it will be examined into at the bar of heaven: and though the slave owes him bodily service, yet that the soul of this drudge, having been purchased at the same price as his own, and sanctified by the same law of regeneration, he who is his slave according to the flesh, is his brother according to the spirit.— His humanity, his charity, his affection are enlisted and interested, and he feels that his own father is also, the father of his slave, hence though the servant must readily and cheerfully pay him homage and perform his behests on earth, yet, they may be on an equality in heaven. . . .

To the Christian slave was exhibited the humiliation of an incarnate God, the suffering of an unoffending victim, the invitation of this model of perfection to that meekness, that humility, that peaceful spirit, that charity and forgiveness of injuries which constitute the glorious beatitudes. He was shown the advantage of suffering, the reward of patience, and the narrow road along whose rugged ascents he was to bear the cross, walking in the footsteps of his Saviour. The curtains which divide both worlds were raised as he advanced, and he beheld Lazarus in the bosom of Abraham, whilst the rich man vainly cried to have this once miserable beggar allowed to dip the tip of his finger in water and touch it to his tongue, for he was tormented in that flame.

Thus, sir, did the legislator of Christianity, whilst he admitted the legality of slavery, render the master merciful, and the slave faithful, obedient and religious, looking for his freedom in that region, where alone true and lasting enjoyment can be found.

> SOURCE: *Letters of the Late Bishop England to the Hon. John Forsyth, on the Subject of Domestic Slavery* (Baltimore, 1844), 34–9.

129. A Southern Address to Christendom

On May 16, 1861, the Assembly of the Old School Presbyterians met in Philadelphia under the strained conditions of a raging civil war. Only thirteen of the forty-six southern presbyteries were represented. From the outset sectional feelings were irrepressible. The question of political loyalty inevitably emerged. After various evasive or compromising proposals were rejected, the minister of Brick Presbyterian Church in New York City, Gardiner Spring, finally offered resolutions calling for a declaration of loyalty to the Federal Government.[77] The southern commissioners at once accused their northern brethren of injecting an extraneous political question into the court of Jesus Christ.[78]

On December 4, 1861, commissioners from forty-seven presbyteries, embracing all or parts of eleven southern states, convened in Augusta, Georgia, where they organized the General Assembly of the Presbyterian Church in the Confederate States of America. The highly esteemed minister of the First Presbyterian Church in New Orleans, Benjamin Morgan Palmer, who preached the opening sermon, was unanimously chosen as moderator of the Assembly.[79]

The Assembly adopted a highly significant Address (composed by James Henley Thornwell), which was directed "to all the Churches of Jesus Christ Throughout the Earth." The primary purpose of the document was to justify the action of the southern churchmen in seceding from the parent Assembly and forming a new denomination. The Assembly's defense was essentially twofold. First, the Old School Assembly had violated the church court when it acted upon a purely political question. Second, the cultural and religious interests of the new Confederacy could best be served by a church confined to its national boundaries.

[77] *Minutes of the General Assembly of the Presbyterian Church in the United States of America* [*Old School*], *A.D. 1861* (Phila., 1861), 308. For general background, see William Russell Hoyt, III, "The Religious Thought of Gardiner Spring with Particular Reference to His Doctrine of Sin and Salvation" (typed Ph.D. dissertation, Duke University, 1962), 80–110.

[78] Interestingly, the Synod of South Carolina on the following November unanimously adopted resolutions pledging loyalty to the Confederacy (Benjamin M. Palmer, *The Life and Letters of James Henley Thornwell, D.D., LL.D.* [Richmond, Va., 1875], 509–10). This action, we are told, was taken, not as a synod, but by a convention of Christians acting "in their private capacity." Nonetheless, this action was taken at a regular meeting of the synod and by the same gentlemen who officially constituted the synod.

[79] For a recent illuminating portrait, see Doralyn J. Hickey, "Benjamin Morgan Palmer: Churchman of the Old South" (typed Ph.D. dissertation, Duke University, 1962).

Believing that the antagonism over slavery lay at the root of the events which had dismembered the Federal Union, the Address devoted extended attention to the moral aspect of that peculiar institution. Nowhere in southern literature may one find the proslavery argument developed with greater force or lucidity. It was Thornwell at his forensic best.

The document here presented reproduces that part of the Address which explored the slavery question.

The antagonism of Northern and Southern sentiment on the subject of slavery lies at the root of all the difficulties which have resulted in the dismemberment of the Federal Union, and involved us in the horrors of an unnatural war. . . .

And here we may venture to lay before the Christian world our views as a Church, upon the subject of slavery. We beg a candid hearing.

In the first place, we would have it distinctly understood that, in our ecclesiastical capacity, we are neither the friends nor the foes of slavery, that is to say, we have no commission either to propagate or abolish it. The policy of its existence or non-existence is a question which exclusively belongs to the State. We have no right, as a Church, to enjoin it as a duty, or to condemn it as a sin. Our business is with the duties which spring from the relation; the duties of the masters on the one hand, and of their slaves on the other. These duties we are to proclaim and to enforce with spiritual sanctions. The social, civil, political problems connected with this great subject transcend our sphere, as God has not entrusted to His Church the organization of society, the construction of Governments, nor the allotment of individuals to their various stations. The Church has as much right to preach to the monarchies of Europe, and the despotism of Asia, the doctrines of republican equality, as to preach to the Governments of the South the extirpation of slavery. This position is impregnable, unless it can be shown that slavery is a sin. Upon every other hypothesis, it is so clearly a question for the State, that the proposition would never for a moment have been doubted, had there not been a foregone conclusion in relation to its moral character. Is slavery, then, a sin?

In answering this question, as a Church, let it be distinctly borne in mind that the only rule of judgment is the written word of God. The Church knows nothing of the intuitions of reason or the deductions of philosophy, except those reproduced in the Sacred Canon. She has a positive constitution in the Holy Scriptures, and has no right to utter a single syllable upon any subject, except as the Lord puts words in her mouth. She is founded, in other words, upon express *revelation*. Her creed is an authoritative testimony of God, and not a speculation, and what she proclaims, she must proclaim with the infallible certitude of faith, and not with the hesitating assent of an opinion. The question, then, is brought within a narrow compass: Do the Scriptures directly or indirectly condemn slavery as a sin? If they do not, the dispute is ended, for the Church, without forfeiting her character, dares not go beyond them.

Now, we venture to assert that if men had drawn their conclusions upon this subject only from the Bible, it would no more have entered into any human head to denounce slavery as a sin, than to denounce monarchy, aristocracy or poverty. The truth is, men have listened to what they falsely considered as primitive intuitions, or as necessary deductions from primitive cognitions, and then have gone to the Bible to confirm the crotchets of their vain philosophy. They have gone there determined to find a particular result, and the consequence is, that they leave with having made, instead of having interpreted, Scripture. Slavery is no new thing. It has not only existed for ages in the world, but it has existed, under every dispensation of the covenant of grace, in the Church of God. Indeed, the first organization of the Church as a visible society, separate and distinct from the unbelieving world, was inaugurated in the family of a slaveholder. Among the very first persons to whom the seal of circumcision was affixed, were the slaves of the father of the faithful, some born in his house, and others bought with his money. Slavery again re-appears under the Law. God sanctions it in the first table of the Decalogue, and Moses treats it as an institution to be regulated, not abolished; legitimated and not condemned. We come down to the age of the New Testament, and we find it again in the Churches founded by the Apostles under the plenary inspiration of the Holy Ghost. These facts are utterly amazing, if slavery is the enormous sin which its enemies represent it to be. It will not do to say that the Scriptures have treated it only in a general, incidental way, without any clear implication as to its moral character. Moses surely made it the subject of express and positive legislation, and the Apostles are equally explicit in inculcating the duties which spring from both sides of the relation. They treat slaves as bound to obey and inculcate obedience as an office of religion—a thing wholly self-contradictory, if the authority exercised over them were unlawful and iniquitous.

But what puts this subject in a still clearer light, is the manner in which it is sought to extort from the Scriptures a contrary testimony. The notion of direct and explicit condemnation is given up. The attempt is to show that the genius and spirit of Christianity are opposed to it—that its great cardinal principles of virtue are utterly against it. Much stress is laid upon the Golden Rule and upon the general denunciations of tyranny and oppression. To all this we reply, that no principle is clearer than that a case positively excepted cannot be included under a general rule. Let us concede, for a moment, that the law of love, and the condemnation of tyranny and oppression, seem logically to involve, as a result, the condemnation of slavery; yet, if slavery is afterwards expressly mentioned and treated as a lawful relation, it obviously follows, unless Scripture is to be interpreted as inconsistent with itself, that slavery is, by necessary implication, excepted. The Jewish law forbade, as a general rule, the marriage of a man with his brother's wife. The same law expressly enjoined the same marriage in a given case. The given case was, therefore, an exception, and not to be treated as a violation of the general rule. The law of love has always been the law of God. It was enunciated by Moses almost as clearly as it was enunciated by Jesus Christ. Yet, notwithstanding this law, Moses and the Apostles alike sanctioned the relation of slavery. The conclusion is inevitable, either that the law is not opposed to it, or that slavery is an excepted case. To say that the prohibition of tyranny and oppression include slavery, is to beg the whole question. Tyranny and oppression involve either the unjust usurpation or the unlawful exercise of power. It is the unlawfulness, either in its principle or measure, which constitutes the core of the sin. Slavery must, therefore, be proved to be unlawful, before it can be referred to any such category. The master may, indeed, abuse his power, but he oppresses not simply as a master, but as a wicked master.

But, apart from all this, the law of love is simply the inculcation of universal equity. It implies nothing as to the existence of various ranks and gradations in society. The interpretation which makes it repudiate slavery would make it equally repudiate all social, civil and political inequalities. Its meaning is, not that we should conform ourselves to the arbitrary expectations of others, but that we should render unto them precisely the same measure which, if we were in their circumstance, it would be reasonable and just in us to demand at their hands. It condemns slavery, therefore, only upon the supposition that slavery is a sinful relation—that is, he who extracts the prohibition of slavery from the Golden Rule, begs the very point in dispute.

We cannot prosecute the argument in detail, but we have said enough, we think, to vindicate the position of the Southern Church. We have assumed no new attitude. We stand exactly where the Church of God has always stood—from Abraham to Moses, from Moses to Christ, from Christ to the Reformers, and from the Reformers to ourselves. We stand upon the foundation of the Prophets and Apostles, Jesus Christ Himself being the Chief corner stone. Shall we be excluded from the fellowship of our brethren in other lands, because we dare not depart from the charter of our faith? Shall we be branded with the stigma of reproach, because we cannot consent to corrupt the word of God to suit the intuitions of an infidel philosophy? Shall our names be cast out as evil, and the finger of scorn pointed at us, because we utterly refuse to break our communion with Abraham, Isaac and Jacob, with Moses, David and Isaiah, with Apostles, Prophets and Martyrs, with all the noble army of confessors who have gone to glory from slave-holding countries and from a slave-holding Church, without ever having dreamed that they were living in mortal sin, by conniving at slavery in the midst of them? If so, we shall take consolation in the cheering consciousness that the Master has accepted us. We may be denounced, despised and cast out of the Synagogues of our brethren. But while they are wrangling about the distinctions of men according to the flesh, we shall go forward in our Divine work, and confidently anticipate that, in the great day, as the consequence of our humble labors, we shall meet millions of glorified spirits, who have come up from the bondage of earth to a nobler freedom than human philosophy ever dreamed of. Others, if they please, may spend their time in declaiming on the tyranny of earthly masters; it will be our aim to resist the real tyrants which oppress the soul—Sin and Satan. These are the foes against whom we shall find it employment enough to wage a successful war. And to this holy war it is the purpose of our Church to devote itself with redoubled energy. We feel that the souls of our slaves are a solemn trust, and we shall strive to present them faultless and complete before the presence of God.

Indeed, as we contemplate their condition in the Southern States, and contrast it with that of their fathers before them, and that of their brethren in the present day in their native land, we cannot but accept it as a gracious Providence that they have been brought in such numbers to our shores, and redeemed from the bondage of barbarism and sin. Slavery to them has certainly been overruled for the greatest good. It has been a link in the wondrous chain of Providence, through which many sons and daughters have been made heirs of the heavenly inheritance. The Providential result is, of course, no justification, if the thing is intrinsically wrong; but it is certainly a matter of devout thanksgiving, and no obscure intimation of the will and purpose of God, and of the consequent duty of the Church. We cannot forbear to say, however, that the general operation of the system is kindly and benevolent; it is a real and effective discipline, and without it, we are profoundly persuaded that the African race in the midst of us can never be elevated in the scale of being. As long as that race, in its comparative degradation, co-exists, side by side, with the white, bondage is its normal condition.

As to the endless declamation about human rights, we have only to say that human rights are not a fixed, but a fluctuating quantity. Their sum is not the same in any two nations on the globe. The rights of Englishmen are one thing, the rights of Frenchmen another. There is a minimum without which a man cannot be responsible; there is a maximum which expresses the highest degree of civilization and of Christian culture. The education of the species consists in its ascent along this line. As you go up, the number of rights increases, but the number of individuals who possess them diminishes. As you come down the line, rights are diminished, but the individuals are multiplied. It is just the opposite of the predicamental scale of the logicians. There comprehension diminishes as you ascend and extension increases, and comprehension increases as you descend and extension diminishes. Now, when it is said that slavery is inconsistent with human rights, we crave to understand what point in this line is the slave conceived to occupy. There are, no doubt, many rights which belong to other men—to Englishmen[,] to Frenchmen, to his master, for example—which are denied to him. But is he fit to possess them? Has God qualified him to meet the responsibilities which their possession necessarily implies? His place in the scale is determined by his competency to fulfil its duties. There are other rights which he certainly possesses, without which he could neither be human nor accountable. Before slavery can be charged with doing him injustice, it must be shown that the minimum which falls to his lot at the bottom of the line is out of proportion to his capacity and culture—a thing which can never be done by abstract speculation. The truth is, the education of the human race for liberty and virtue, is a vast Providential scheme, and God assigns to every man, by a wise and holy decree, the precise place he is to occupy in the great moral school of humanity. The scholars are distributed into classes, according to their competency and progress. For God is in history.

To avoid the suspicion of a conscious weakness of our cause, when contemplated from the side of pure speculation, we may advert for a moment to those pretended intuitions which stamp the reprobation of humanity upon this ancient and hoary institution. We admit that there are primitive principles in morals which lie at the root of human consciousness. But the question is, how are we to distinguish them? The subjective feeling of certainty is no adequate criterion, as that is equally felt in reference to crotchets and hereditary prejudices. The very point is to know when this certainty indicates a primitive cognition, and when it does not. There must, therefore, be some eternal test, and whatever cannot abide that test has no authority as a primary truth. That test is an inward necessity of thought, which, in all minds at the proper stage of maturity, is absolutely universal. Whatever is universal is natural. We are willing that slavery should be tried by this standard. We are willing to abide by the testimony of the race, and if man, as man, has every where condemned it—if all human laws have prohibited it as crime—if it stands in the same category with malice, murder and theft, then we are willing, in the name of humanity, to renounce it, and to renounce it forever. But what if the overwhelming majority of mankind have approved it? what if philosophers and statesmen have justified it, and the laws of all nations acknowledged it; what then becomes of these luminous intuitions? They are an *ignis fatuus*, mistaken for a star.

> SOURCE: *Minutes of the General Assembly of the Presbyterian Church in the Confederate States of America, Vol. I, A.D. 1861* (Augusta, Ga., 1861), 55–9.

LITERATURE

For social and cultural background of the period, see Avery O. Craven, *The Coming of the Civil War* (N.Y., 1942; rev. ed., 1957) and Arthur C. Cole,

The Irrepressible Conflict (N.Y., 1934). Craven's main thesis is developed succinctly in *Civil War in the Making, 1815–1860* (Baton Rouge, La., 1959). Two necessary works on southern aspects are Charles S. Sydnor's *The Development of Southern Sectionalism, 1819–1848* (Baton Rouge, La., 1948), and Clement Eaton's *Freedom of Thought in the Old South* (Durham, N.C., 1940).

Slavery as a social and economic institution is carefully explored in Ralph B. Flanders' *Plantation Slavery in Georgia* (Chapel Hill, N.C., 1933), and Charles S. Sydnor's *Slavery in Mississippi* (N.Y., 1933). The latter gives an excellent account of the state Colonization Society. A scholarly study from a conservative standpoint is Ulrich B. Phillips' *American Negro Slavery* (N.Y., 1918). A more realistic interpretation is Kenneth M. Stampp's *The Peculiar Institution: Slavery in the Ante-bellum South* (N.Y., 1956).

The most complete study of the southern antislavery episode is Gordon E. Finnie's "The Antislavery Movement in the South, 1787–1836: Its Rise and Decline and Its Contribution to Abolitionism in the West" (typed Ph.D. dissertation, Duke University, 1962). For briefer investigations, see Alice Dana Adams, *The Neglected Period of Anti-Slavery in America, 1808–1831* (N.Y., 1908), Chaps. 1–5, 11; Stephen B. Weeks, "Anti-Slavery Sentiment in the South," in Southern History Association *Publications,* II (Washington, 1898), 87–130; Weeks, *Southern Quakers and Slavery* (Baltimore, 1896), Chap. 9; William Birney, *James G. Birney and His Times* (N.Y., 1890), Chap. 12; Asa Earl Martin, *The Anti-Slavery Movement in Kentucky Prior to 1850* (Louisville, Ky., 1918); William Warren Sweet, *Religion on the American Frontier: The Baptists, 1783–1830* (N.Y., 1931), Chaps. 5, 14; Kenneth M. Stampp, "The Southern Refutation of the Proslavery Argument," *North Carolina Historical Review,* XXI (1944), 35–45; Walter B. Posey, "The Slavery Question in the Presbyterian Church in the Old Southwest," *Journal of Southern History,* XV (1949), 311–24.

The *African Repository* is a necessary source of light on the work of the American Colonization Society. The Society's *Annual Reports* are also important. A standard book is Early Lee Fox's *The American Colonization Society, 1817–1840* (Baltimore, 1919), although it does not cover the whole history of the organization. For a suggestive essay, see Charles I. Foster, "The Colonization of Free Negroes, in Liberia, 1816–1835," *Journal of Negro History,* XXXVIII (1953), 41–66.

For a systematic approach to the various arguments for slavery, see William S. Jenkins, *Pro-Slavery Thought in the Old South* (Chapel Hill, N.C., 1935). The "moral argument" is given extensive attention. Of the southern churchmen who strongly fortified the proslavery doctrine, the following deserve special attention: Paul Leslie Garber, "The Religious Thought of James Henley Thornwell" (typed Ph.D. dissertation, Duke University, 1939); B. M. Palmer, *The Life and Letters of James Henley Thornwell, D.D., LL.D.* (Richmond, Va., 1875); W. M. Polk, *Leonidas Polk, Bishop and General* (2 vols., N.Y., 1915); Frank Bell Lewis, "Robert Lewis Dabney: Southern Presbyterian Apologist" (typed Ph.D. dissertation, Duke University, 1946); Robert G. Gardner, "John Leadley Dagg; Pioneer American Baptist Theologian" (typed Ph.D. dissertation, Duke University, 1957) and "A Tenth-Hour Apology for Slavery," *Journal of Southern History,* XXVI (1960), 352–67; William A.

Smith, *Lectures on the Philosophy and Practice of Slavery* (Nashville, 1856); Joseph L. O'Brien, *John England: The Apostle to Democracy* (N.Y., 1934); Doralyn J. Hickey, "Benjamin Morgan Palmer: Churchman of the Old South" (typed Ph.D. dissertation, Duke University, 1962).

In studying the antislavery movement, one will find indispensable Dwight L. Dumond's *A Bibliography of Antislavery in America* (Ann Arbor, Mich., 1961). His *Antislavery: The Crusade for Freedom in America* (Ann Arbor, Mich., 1961) is highly illuminating. For a somewhat more objective work, see Gilbert H. Barnes, *The Antislavery Impulse, 1830–1844* (N.Y., 1933). Barnes gives insufficient attention to Garrison and the Quakers. A more comprehensive account is Louis Filler's *The Crusade Against Slavery, 1830–1860* (N.Y., 1960). For a fascinating story of Weld's antislavery labors, see Gilbert H. Barnes and Dwight L. Dumond, eds., *Letters of Theodore Dwight Weld and Angelina Grimké and Sarah Grimké, 1822–1844* (2 vols., N.Y., 1934). Benjamin Thomas' *Theodore Weld: Crusader for Freedom* (New Brunswick, N.J., 1950) is a good supplement to the *Letters*. Another important abolitionist is treated in Dwight L. Dumond's *Letters of James Gillespie Birney, 1831–1857* (2 vols., N.Y., 1938), and in Betty Fladeland's *James Gillespie Birney: Slaveholder to Abolitionist* (N.Y., 1955). An old-line work on the editor of the *Liberator* is Wendell P. and Francis J. Garrison's *William Lloyd Garrison, 1805–1879* (4 vols., Boston, 1885). For other biographies of important antislavery leaders, see Lewis Tappan, *The Life of Arthur Tappan* (N.Y., 1870); Ralph V. Harlow, *Gerrit Smith: Philanthropist and Reformer* (N.Y., 1939); Lucius C. Matlack, *The Life of Orange Scott* (N.Y., 1848); Henry S. Commager, *Theodore Parker* (Boston, 1936; rev. ed., 1947).

On the relation of the churches to the slavery controversy, see: W. W. Sweet, *Methodism in American History* (N.Y., 1933; rev. ed., 1953), Chaps. 12, 14; Lucius C. Matlack, *The Antislavery Struggle and Triumph in the Methodist Episcopal Church* (N.Y., 1881); Donald G. Mathews, "Antislavery, Piety, and Institutionalism: The Slavery Controversies in the Methodist Episcopal Church, 1780 to 1844" (typed Ph.D. dissertation, Duke University, 1962); Robert G. Torbet, *A History of the Baptists* (Phila., 1950), 299–313; Mary B. Putnam, *The Baptists and Slavery: 1840–1845* (Ann Arbor, Mich., 1913); W. W. Barnes, *The Southern Baptist Convention, 1845–1953* (Nashville, 1954), Chaps. 2, 4; L. G. Vander Velde, *The Presbyterian Churches and the Federal Union, 1861–1869* (Cambridge, Mass., 1932); Joseph B. Cheshire, *The [Protestant Episcopal] Church in the Confederate States* (N.Y., 1911); Thomas R. Drake, *Quakers and Slavery in America* (New Haven, 1950); Madeline Hooke Rice, *American Catholic Opinion in the Slavery Controversy* (N.Y., 1944); Charles W. Heathcote, *The Lutheran Church and the Civil War* (N.Y., 1919); Robert Fortenbaugh, "American Lutheran Synods and Slavery," *Journal of Religion,* XIII (1933), 72–92.

PERIOD V
CONFLICTING RESPONSES TO NEW FORCES

1865–1930

INTRODUCTION

THE years from 1865 to 1930 saw remarkable and unexpected transformations in the life of the nation and of its churches. Into these decades were crowded vast changes in the thoughts, practices, and life-styles of the people. The churches actively participated in these changes by stimulating individuals, by advocating higher ideals, and by maintaining significant institutions of learning. But clearly science and technology, with their many by-products, provided the greatest sources of change in these years of transition and conflict.

The churches, committed to the Christianization of a nation, were therefore confronted with many perplexing problems of thought and action. How could the faith be made acceptable to a people whose intellectual life was being transformed by the new scientific views? How could the churches be made a part of a rapidly expanding, diverse and mobile population? With each passing decade, a larger portion of this population lived in the burgeoning cities. Familiar rural patterns of Christian life were proving more and more irrelevant to the dynamically new urban civilization. The churches were thrown into turmoil as many kinds of reactions to the new and continually changing situation developed. What seemed to some to be reasonable ways of meeting new challenges appeared to others to be either an abject surrender to the enemies of faith or a merely superficial adjustment in no way adequate to the realities.

Externally, the churches continued to grow, claiming as members a rising percentage of the American people. This is especially noteworthy in view of the fact that the population, augmented by mighty tides of immigration, more than tripled in this period, reaching some one hundred and twenty million by 1930. The vastness of church expansion is indicated by the fact that though approximately twenty per cent of the population were church members in 1865, by 1930 the total number of adults listed on the rolls of the churches was about fifty-five per cent of the country's adult population.[1] Home missions, church extension, and revivalist movements largely succeeded in planting churches in every corner of the land, and in drawing a majority of the population into some relationship with them. Most Americans continued to think of their country as a Christian nation in spirit, though of course not officially. Protestantism continued to be reckoned as the dominant religious tradition of the nation, though Roman Catholicism, Judaism, and Orthodoxy, largely through the benefits of immigration, were far stronger in 1930 than they had been in 1865. Yet

[1] C. Luther Fry, *The U.S. Looks at Its Churches* (N.Y., 1930), 2.

215

André Siegfried, a perceptive French observer, could say as late as 1927 that "the civilization of the United States is essentially Protestant," adding that "Protestantism is the only national religion, and to ignore that fact is to view the country from a false angle." He was fully aware of the denominational divisions of Protestantism, yet nevertheless could hold firmly to his point: "In order to appreciate the influence of Protestantism in this confusion of sects, we must not look at it as a group of organized churches, for its strength lies in the fact that its spirit is national." [2] Though all churches felt strongly the impact of the intellectual and technological revolutions of these years of transformation, the closer entanglement of Protestant churches with the culture made this an especially critical time of strain and redirection for them.

In the years before the Civil War, a time when the denominational college largely dominated the intellectual scene, the churches had managed to relate Christian faith to the currents of romanticism and idealism in various but generally satisfying ways. The authority of the Bible, so dear to most Protestants, had not been widely challenged. The prestige of science had been rising, to be sure, but not until the dramatic impact of Darwinism shook the world of American thought did the scientific spirit begin seriously to disturb the traditional view of God, man, and nature as held by many Christians.

The epoch-making work of Charles Darwin (1809–82), *The Origin of Species,* was published in England in 1859, but not until the excitement of the Civil War had passed were American scientists and scholars free to turn their attention to his work. Then the theory of evolution, given clarity and feasibility by his extensive researches, became a topic of heated discussion. Darwin's later work, *The Descent of Man* (1871), challenging traditional orthodox theories of man's origin, was even more incisive than his earlier one. Despite opposition, Darwinism rather rapidly made its way in America. The impact of evolutionary thinking fomented intellectual revolution in many quarters. Popularized by a number of able men,[3] evolutionary and scientific thought penetrated everywhere. The methods and attitudes of science were extended to various branches of scholarship, such as the study of history, often with radical results. The rise of humanistic alternatives to religion and the spread of such nontheistic philosophies as materialism and secularism were greatly stimulated among small but influential groups. The democratization of learning through the multiplication of the number of high schools and the increase in the number of uni-

---

[2] *America Comes of Age,* trans. H. H. and Doris Hemming (N.Y., 1927), 33, 38–9.

[3] Central in this group were two Englishmen: the philosopher, Herbert Spencer (1820–1903), and the biologist, Thomas Henry Huxley (1825–95); and two Americans: the historian, John Fiske (1842–1901), and the publicist, Edward Livingston Youmans (1821–87). See Richard Hofstadter, *Social Darwinism in American Thought, 1860–1915* (Phila., 1945), and Bert J. Loewenberg, "Darwinism Comes to America," *Mississippi Valley Historical Review,* XXVIII (1941), 339–68.

versities, many state-supported, helped to spread the new positions and attitudes.

In the churches, the battle over the theory of evolution produced sharp cleavages between those who accepted and those who repudiated it. Then, as evolutionary patterns of thought influenced historical and literary study, the critical approach to the Bible became a second hotly contested issue. Again, many Christians found that the historical understanding of the Bible seemed true and convincing, while others reacted with great hostility, feeling that the sacred citadel of divine authority was being invaded by impious hands.

Science not only contributed directly to the intellectual revolutions of the period, it also played a central role in reshaping the daily lives of most Americans. Applied science made possible the amazing growth of an industrial economy and the expansion of cities into vast concentrations of men and machines. Technology dramatically increased the tempo of communication and transportation; the land was soon bound together by thousands of miles of telephone wire and railroad tracks. Toward the end of the period, the appearance of radio antennae and airports testified to further revolutions in these fields. Churches that had found a secure place in the more leisurely world of rural and small-town America were now confronted with a new industrial order, with all its accompanying problems of laboring masses, city slums, rural depressions, and the general fragmentation of life as the myriad attractions of life in modern urban civilization competed for the time and attention of American citizens. Urbanization meant not only a startling growth in the number and size of cities, it also meant the spread of new patterns of life over the countryside as well as in the metropolises. "It has remained for urbanization, both in its rural and in its city phase, to give the church the greatest inner revolution it has ever known," declared H. Paul Douglass (1871–1953), a pioneer in the sociological study of religion in America.[4] Churchmen found that time-tested ways of evangelism and church extension had to fight a hard and sometimes losing battle against new trends. New methods were developed, but often they too were soon outdated by the swift turn of events.

Furthermore, familiar social and economic views began to seem to some as less than adequate to the new conditions of life and labor in the vast cities. Protestantism, still strong among the middle classes, found it increasingly difficult to attract and to hold working men. Many Christians clung resolutely to the philosophy of individualism which had been so widely dominant in the early part of the century. Indeed, as individualism was threatened by the emerging realities of the industrial order, some adhered to it all the more tightly. Strong men found that the old philosophy allowed them a free hand in a rapidly enriching economy, and those who lost out

---

[4] "Religion—The Protestant Faiths," in Harold E. Stearns, ed., *America Now: An Inquiry into Civilization in the United States* (N.Y., 1938), 514.

in the struggle were often viewed as lazy or incompetent, if not immoral. Though few moved as far up the scale of wealth and power as did that Scottish immigrant, Andrew Carnegie (1835–1919), probably the majority of Americans in the late nineteenth century agreed with the philosophy of his famous essay, "Wealth." [5] The gospel of wealth as formulated by Carnegie rested on the doctrines of the free individual, unfettered competition, the acquisition of wealth by industry and thrift, and the stewardship of the strong. But some of the strong who lived by the individualistic, laissez-faire creed did not trouble themselves much over the matter of stewardship. Dubbed "the robber barons," they exploited the rich and unfenced fields of the rapidly expanding industrial order. With few exceptions, most Americans, including most church members, largely accepted the dominant philosophy of individualism, thinking that by effort and industry they would find their proper place in the scale.

The world in which unqualified individualism as a way of life may have had some relevance was rapidly passing with the growth of giant corporations, big government, and vast cities. In the swift transitions which accompanied industrialization and urbanization, particular groups of Americans were caught in some very unpleasant squeezes. Negroes in southern fields, immigrants in northern slums, farmers in western homesteads, children in eastern factories—and laborers in every quarter—were often caught without protection between the harsh realities of the new order and the no longer adequate social theories of the old. Henry George was but one of the more eloquent voices calling attention to a perplexing dilemma of the time. His *Progress and Poverty* (1879) protested the fact that many Americans were growing poorer even as the levels of wealth were mounting fantastically. Not all the protests were as restrained as his; labor strikes of great intensity erupted. Reform movements were launched to bring about social changes passionately believed by their proponents to be necessary. The agrarian revolt and the Populist movement presented highly controversial reform measures, many of which were later adopted in modified form by the major parties. Of greater significance was the Progressive movement, articulating a gospel of social responsibility as against an individualistic gospel of wealth. Influenced both by the social realities before them and by the messages of the reformers, many American Christians grew deeply concerned over the social question. They addressed themselves to the new problems in various ways, holding positions ranging all the way from a simple and familiar adherence to personal charity through the moderately progressive social gospel to the more radical reconstructionism of Christian socialism.

What made this period such a time of transition and tension for the churches was that the changes in thought and the changes in practice were

[5] Originally published in the *North American Review*, CXLVIII (1889), 653–64; reprinted in Gail Kennedy, ed., *Democracy and the Gospel of Wealth* (Boston, 1949), 1–8.

going on concurrently. The churches had continually to deal with developments that affected their system of thought and their social program at the same time.[6] Within the churches, there were various overall reactions to the challenges. There were some Christians who came to believe that traditional patterns of faith were no longer relevant to the age of science and technology. More sizable groups sought to mediate between their inherited faiths and the patterns of thought and life of the new world. But others resisted the currents of the new age, with varying degrees of intensity. These essentially theological alignments did not correlate exactly (though often closely) with the patterns of response to the social crisis.

Though the cleavages between the various theological positions sometimes became very wide, the fundamental denominational organization of American Christian life was not seriously affected. Indeed, as Sidney E. Mead has observed, in view of the transformation of thought and life in America, "the wonder is not that there was a great deal of confusion, inanity, and hysteria but that as much sanity and order prevailed in them as actually did." [7] From a mid-century perspective, Herbert W. Schneider could look back and note that "the large denominations which embrace over half our population have proved to be amazingly stable and have survived, despite many predictions to the contrary, a series of storms which have tested their intellectual and moral strength as severely as any 'sifting time' in religious history." [8]

The Roman Catholic Church continued to grow in strength throughout this period, largely because of the influx of numbers through immigration. In the National Catholic War Council, which soon after the war became the National Catholic Welfare Conference, the church found a dynamic center of unity and strength. For their part, many of the major (with some of the smaller) Protestant bodies found increased strength and stability as they learned to work together officially in such co-operative agencies as the Foreign Missions Conference of North America (1893), the Home Missions Council (1908), the Federal Council of Churches in the United States of America (1908), and the International Council of Religious Education (1922). These councils were the formal expression of the larger though somewhat vague sense of Protestant unity that encompassed most of the denominations and the parties within them. Both liberals and conservatives found some relief from inner theological tensions by joining together with moderates in crusades to Christianize America. Crusading techniques seemed to offer ways of dealing with the alien and hostile elements of twentieth-century life. In the crusades, men of good will, left, right, and center, all claiming to be true to evangelical Protestantism, could

[6] Arthur M. Schlesinger, "A Critical Period in American Religion, 1875–1900," Massachusetts Historical Society *Proceedings*, LXIV (1930–32), 523–48.

[7] "American Protestantism Since the Civil War. II. From Americanism to Christianity," *Journal of Religion*, XXXVI (1956), 68.

[8] *Religion in 20th Century America* (Cambridge, Mass., 1952), 206.

march side by side in an alliance that was real if often somewhat uneasy. Gaius Glenn Atkins has written:

> The first fifteen years of the twentieth century may sometimes be remembered in America as the Age of Crusades. There were a super-abundance of zeal, a sufficiency of good causes, unusual moral ideal-ism, excessive confidence in mass movements and leaders with rare gifts of popular appeal. The people were ready to cry "God wills it" and set out for world peace, prohibition, the Progressive Party, the "New Freedom" or "the World for Christ in this Generation." The air was full of banners, and the trumpets called from every camp.
>
> The churches shared the general crusading zeal and inaugurated enterprises of their own.[9]

Harrison S. Elliott later reminisced, as he looked back on the years follow-ing his graduation from seminary in 1911: "Those were the days when it seemed as if the kingdom was coming speedily. It is fair to designate the first decade after we graduated from the seminary as a period of great opti-mism and of high idealism. Even the Great War increased rather than dampened our ardor."[10] When America entered World War I, the churches rather too simply devoted their crusading spirit and methods to it.

The great enthusiasm of the crusading spirit and the observable results that accompanied it obscured for most Protestants the strain that had been undergone in adjusting to the rapid transformation of American life. The crusading mood also partly blinded churchmen to the fact that fundamental intellectual issues were being avoided rather than solved. Henry Steele Commager's observation states the matter sharply:

> The church itself confessed to a steady secularization: as it invaded the social and economic fields, it retreated from the intellectual. Philosophy, which for over two centuries had been almost the exclu-sive property of the clergy, slipped quietly from their hands.[11]

Little wonder that in the 1920's, that decade of disillusionment when the idealistic dreams of the century's dawn seemed naïve indeed, it appeared that religion was losing its hold over many Americans. Protestantism es-pecially, as the dominant religious heritage, was regarded with indifference if not with hostility on the part of many articulate individuals, among whom H. L. Mencken and Sinclair Lewis were only the best known. The tensions which the period had set deep within Protestantism erupted into the bitter fundalmentalist-modernist controversy immediately after World War I, providing much exploitable material for the critics of religion, also dampening the enthusiasm of many of the faithful. So this period of transi-

---

[9] *Religion in Our Times* (N.Y., 1932), 156.

[10] "Left—Right—Which Way in Religion?" *The Drew Gateway*, VII (July, 1936), 1.

[11] *The American Mind: An Interpretation of American Thought and Character Since the 1880's* (New Haven, 1950), 167.

tion and turmoil which had seen such peaks of optimism within the culture and the church ended in a slump, revealing something of the toll of the years. Missionary enthusiasm, which had been so high during most of this period, declined markedly in the early 1920's. Falling church attendance and lowered stewardship figures emphasized that church life was in some kind of decline. Winthrop S. Hudson has put this in a vivid way:

> Nothing is more striking than the astonishing reversal in the position occupied by the churches and the role played by religion in American life which took place before the new century was well under way. By the nineteen twenties, the contagious enthusiasm which had been poured into the Student Volunteer Movement, the Sunday School Movement, the Men and Religion Forward Movement, the Interchurch World Movement, and other organized activities of the churches had largely evaporated. . . . Religion, which had been one of the principal subjects of serious and intelligent discussion in the literary monthlies and quarterlies, now became conspicuous by its absence, and was usually resurrected only to serve as a target for the satirical shafts of a Mencken.[12]

To its very end, this was a difficult period for religion, and the aftermath of theological battles, unfulfilled crusades and outworn conventions seemed to be religious retreat. It would have been difficult to predict in 1930 that church advance and theological renewal was to develop in the following decades.

[12] *The Great Tradition of the American Churches* (N.Y., 1953), 196. Cf. Robert T. Handy, "The American Religious Depression, 1925–1935," *Church History*, XXIX (1960), 3–16.

CHAPTER XVI

Radical Tendencies in Religion

THE intellectual and technological revolutions which so deeply influenced American thought and action in the last half of the nineteenth century led to various efforts to reconstruct religion in thoroughgoing fashion. For some, the light of new knowledge shone so brightly as to make the old ways seem dim and remote indeed. Radical attempts to state the essence of religion were often influenced by the religious heritage from the past, but fundamentally they were determined by modern modes of thought. Familiar terms might be employed, but quite new meanings were poured into them. In some cases, those who aimed at thorough reconstruction in religion deliberately cast aside the idioms and practices of the past and sought to begin afresh in the new age of science and technology.

The exponents of "radical religion" by no means formed a homogeneous group. They often contributed to one another's thought, to be sure. They frequently drew on a common body of scientific, historical, and popular material, though with varying degrees of perception. But in their efforts at the reconstruction of religion for modern times, they moved in varying directions. There were those who had no intention of breaking with inherited faith and who often never thought that they had; yet an analysis of their positions shows that what had become decisive or authoritative for them in religion was no longer related directly to classical Christian concepts of faith. It was related instead to modern ideas shaped by new scientific, historical, and philosophical currents of thought. Often such people clung to familiar religious words and customs, but invested them with quite new meaning. But others among the radicals did self-consciously and sometimes even bumptiously break with the Christian heritage and the Christian churches. Between these extremes, the radicals occupied a wide range of viewpoints, some closer to the former and some to the latter, but all in some sense thorough reconstructionists in religion.

Some of those whose religious views came to be essentially reoriented in this period did not break openly with the traditions which had nourished them, but sought to reinterpret them basically in a way which seemed consistent with the new learning. Most of this company remained theistic in orientation, but adopted an approach to religion that was empirical and scientific. Conspicuous among this group were a number of Unitarian leaders. With respect to the Unitarianism of the late nineteenth century, one interpreter declared that "as it was once the liberal side of the old Congregational body, so now it must know itself as the Christian side of the broader scientific movement of our time." [1] One of the most persuasive voices to urge such a reorientation, not only for Unitarianism but for all churches, was Charles William Eliot (1834–1926), for forty years president of Harvard. In his famous address of 1909, "The Religion of the Future," Eliot outlined what the impact of the intellectual revolutions of the time signified for the future of religion.

In the more evangelical denominations were some whose approach to religion may properly be styled radical. For example, in Chicago were Edward Scribner Ames (1870–1958), for thirty-five years professor of philosophy at the University of Chicago and for forty years pastor of the University Church of the Disciples of Christ, and Shailer Mathews (1863–1941), Baptist layman and dean of the Divinity School of the same University. In 1924 the latter summarized in *The Faith of Modernism* the position of those in the evangelical churches who had been decisively influenced by the new currents of scientific and philosophical thinking. In a later work, he declared that "the God of the scientifically minded will assume the patterns of science." [2]

During the first quarter of the twentieth century there was a loss of interest in systematic theology in many theological seminaries, while increasing attention was given to the philosophy of religion, often expressed in a way more generally naturalistic than specifically Christian. Henry Nelson Wieman (1884—) of the Divinity School of the University of Chicago sought to ground all knowledge of God on observation and reason. The "acids of modernity" were felt to some degree within most denominations.

Occasionally a radical was forced out of the churches. Probably most of the heresy trials of the period grew out of the struggle between the staunch conservatives and the moderate liberals, but in at least one famous case, the convicted person was professedly standing for a radically new religious position. In 1906, the Episcopal rector, Algernon Sidney Crapsey (1847–1927), was suspended from the ministry for heresy. He had challenged the church "to become scientific, democratic and socialistic," [3] but as one who professed to have been always a humanist, he was not finally retained by his communion. But where one was suspended, others of similar views remained somewhat uncomfortably within the churches, or quietly drifted away.

At the other extreme were those who did not remain within the regular denominations but who struck out on their own to form new religious movements for the modern age. An early leader in such efforts was Octavius Brooks Frothingham (1822–95). After graduation from the Harvard Di-

---

[1] Joseph Henry Allen, *Our Liberal Movement in Theology, Chiefly as Shown in Recollections of the History of Unitarianism in New England* (Boston, 1892).

[2] *The Growth of the Idea of God* (N.Y., 1931), 184.

[3] *The Last of the Heretics* (N.Y., 1924), 251.

vinity School, Frothingham for a time served as a Unitarian pastor, but his church in New York soon reorganized itself as the "Independent Liberal Church." Frothingham was convinced that there was a wide gulf between all traditional forms of Christianity and the "new church" needed for the new age. He once said:

> For while the old church stood on the dogma of human *depravity*, the new church stands on faith in human *ability*. The old church planted itself on the idea that men must be miraculously saved from hell; the new church plants itself on the idea that men must distance hell by reason. The old church bowed the soul to an institution; the new church makes institutions the creatures of the soul. And between these two groups of principles a gulf is fixed, so deep and wide that they who stand on one side cannot see those who stand on the other.[4]

While some religious radicals sought to bring the "new church" within the bounds of the old, others, like Frothingham, were sure that the gulf was unbridgeable and tried to fashion suitable new institutional expressions for a new religion.

An early, highly publicized organizational manifestation of radical religion was the Free Religious Association, which was formed in 1867. By and large the Association was made up of young thinkers of Unitarian background, men who had been steeped in the thought of Theodore Parker and were committed to the newest developments in the world of science. Frothingham served as first president of the F.R.A. The Association sought to promote the "interests of pure religion" and to encourage the "scientific study of theology." Numbering in its ranks certain strong-minded individuals who believed wholeheartedly in complete freedom of thought without any restrictions, the F.R.A. was troubled by internal dissension from the beginning. During its quarter century of active existence, it contributed significantly to the radical religious ferment of the time, and provided a religious basis for a revolt against Christianity in the name of science. Another important figure in the Free Religious Association was the philosopher, Francis Ellingwood Abbot (1836–1903). In 1870 he commenced the publication of the *Index*, which served as an organ of the Association. Abbot's "Fifty Affirmations" crystalized the main positions of the developing "religion of humanity." The Affirmations began with the declaration that "Religion is the effort of man to perfect himself," and stressed that the universal element in all historical religions is the same. The F.R.A. arose out of transcendentalism but during its rather short life the trend of thought toward empirical and scientific naturalism was clear.

A more permanent expression of the "new church" was the Ethical Culture movement. The ethical movement was close kin to the Free Religious Association—Felix Adler, founder of Ethical Culture, followed

[4] *The Religion of Humanity* (N.Y., 1873), 121–2.

Frothingham as president of the F.R.A. after the latter had served for some ten years. Adler (1851–1933), son of a German Jewish rabbi, came to this country with his family at the age of six. After completing his undergraduate work at Columbia, he studied at Berlin and Heidelberg in order to prepare for the rabbinate. But disturbed by the results of linguistic and philosophical studies, he revolted against his religious heritage. For three years he served as professor of Semitic languages and literature at Cornell. Then in 1876 he resigned to become the principal founder and first leader of the New York Society for Ethical Culture. "The impulse that led originally to the formation of Ethical Societies," he later declared, "sprang from the profound feeling that the life of man needs to be consecrated; furthermore, that the consecration cannot be derived from doctrines which, however vital they may have been in the past, however true they may still be for some, have ceased to be so for oneself." [5]

The members of the Society desired "to separate the grain from the chaff, but also to preserve the grain." Hence they initiated regular Sunday worship and undertook a program of educational and social services. They placed special emphasis on the ethical factor in all of life's relations. A number of the original group of about one hundred had been of Jewish background, but more of Christian upbringing soon entered the movement. The growth of Ethical Culture was very slow, however; by the time of the fiftieth anniversary of the movement in 1926 there were only about six Ethical Societies in existence in the United States, with a total membership of between two and three thousand. There were a few societies abroad. The movement minimized theological interest to devote its full attention to "humanity." Adler, a gifted platform speaker, continued to be the central figure in the movement throughout his life.

The supporters of the Free Religious Association and Ethical Culture devoted themselves to the religion of humanity and considered metaphysical questions marginal, but many of them remained theists of one kind or another. In the early twentieth century, however, a movement developed which stressed a wholly humanistic religious position. It drew considerable support from the pragmatic school of philosophy, particularly as that was stated by Professor John Dewey (1859–1952) of Columbia. From the studies of comparative religion and the psychology of religion came much material which seemed to some to be quite inimical to theistic claims. In university circles especially, there was a noticeable drift toward an agnostic humanism. In the 1920's, a small but articulate minority went even beyond that toward a militant nontheistic humanism. Supporters for this form of radical religion came from the ranks of Unitarian ministers and laymen especially. John H. Dietrich (1878–1958), pastor of the First Unitarian Church of Minneapolis, became unofficial "dean" of the humanists. The new humanists believed that the scientific advance of the time made theirs

---

[5] "Some Characteristics of the American Ethical Movement," *The Fiftieth Anniversary of the Ethical Movement, 1876–1926* (N.Y., 1926), 4.

the only fully tenable position. Several independent humanist societies were formed, and men from various denominational and religious backgrounds were drawn into the movement.

What proved to be the most definitive statement of the humanist trend came after the range of years considered in this chapter, but as the climax of the tendencies of these earlier years. In 1933, humanist leaders published "A Humanist Manifesto," which set forth their position clearly and compactly. The movement was given its theoretical basis by the work of a number of teachers of philosophy and religion at university centers. The most influential signer of the Manifesto, John Dewey, said categorically, "The method we term 'scientific' forms for the modern man (and a man is not modern merely because he lives in 1931) the sole dependable means of disclosing the realities of existence. It is the sole authentic mode of revelation." [6] Men of such conviction believed that the only suitable religion for a modern culture in which science is dominant would be a naturalistic humanism.

Between the extremes of those who broke with the Judeo-Christian heritage to form new religious movements and those who stayed within their denominational homes and sought to reinterpret the faith in terms of a scientific culture was a wide range of attitude and opinion. Some of those whose positions lay between the extremes likewise remained within their churches, but their main interest was drawn to one or another of the new movements. Sometimes they were carried out of their original religious homes by the new currents, or remained only nominally therein. Only a few of the many alternatives that appeared in this time of challenge, ferment, and doubt can be mentioned here.

In the middle of the nineteenth century an interest in "mental healing" arose, pioneered in America by Phineas P. Quimby (1802–66). The movement broadened out in the last quarter of the nineteenth century into a religious current usually called "New Thought," which took its place as part of the general liberalizing tendencies of the time. In his Gifford lectures of 1901–02, William James noted that the Mind-cure or New Thought movement "has taken up into itself a number of contributory elements, and it must now be reckoned with as a genuine religious power." James analyzed the sources of the position in these words:

> One of the doctrinal sources of Mind-cure is the four Gospels; another is Emersonianism or New England transcendentalism; another is Berkeleyan idealism; another is spiritism, with its messages of "law" and "progress" and "development"; another the optimistic popular science evolutionism of which I have recently spoken; and, finally, Hinduism has contributed a strain. But the most characteristic feature of the mind-cure movement is an inspiration much more

[6] Quoted in Albert Einstein, John Dewey, et al., Living Philosophies (N.Y., 1931), 24.

direct. The leaders in this faith have had an intuitive belief in the all-saving power of healthy-minded attitudes as such, in the conquering efficacy of courage, hope, and trust, and a correlative contempt for doubt, fear, worry, and all nervously precautionary states of mind.[7]

New Thought had a considerable influence within many Protestant churches; it also led to the formation of a number of new religious bodies. One of the most prolific of the New Thought writers was Ralph Waldo Trine (1866–1958). His books were widely read and served to popularize New Thought ideas far beyond the inner circles of the movement itself. *In Tune with the Infinite, or Fullness of Peace, Power, and Plenty* was his best-known work, published first in 1897. It continued as a popular seller for over half a century. His works articulated a popular idealistic religious philosophy, and his stress on the "great immutable laws" of the universe helped to make the book attractive to those who wanted to be in tune with recent scientific discovery. The spread of mind-cure ideas in the culture and in the churches was further advanced by the formation of New Thought religious bodies. In 1889, for example, what came to be known as the "Unity School of Christianity" was founded by Charles and Myrtle Fillmore. Unity printed and circulated vast quantities of literature which received a wide reading in many traditional churches; it also organized groups and built churches of its own in many localities. Christian Science, given a precise formulation and a distinctive organizational pattern by Mary Baker Eddy, also strongly reflected the general mood and atmosphere out of which New Thought had arisen.

The growth of the community-church movement in the twentieth century was a complex phenomenon. Some of its supporters were quite orthodox in theology, and were seeking only to minimize the disrupting effects of denominationalism on community life. Some of the community churches retained a formal connection with one or more denominations. But others were formed to provide for the institutional expression of radical religion. One authority, speaking of community churches of this kind, could say in 1928 that the two fundamental features of community churches were "that they substitute the community for the sect as their primary basis of organization, and purpose for dogma as their principle of cohesion." [8] Perhaps the best-known representative of the radical side of the community church development was the forceful John Haynes Holmes (1879—). He turned his Unitarian church in New York City into an independent Community Church, which was to be completely undenominational, entirely public, creedally free, and intensely social. Over one thousand of the some thirteen hundred community churches reported in 1926 were in rural areas, however.

[7] *The Varieties of Religious Experience: A Study in Human Nature* (N.Y., 1902), 93.

[8] David R. Piper, *Community Churches: The Community Church Movement* (Chicago, 1928), 28.

This was explained as "the penetration into rural America of a new idea of the church and its mission, a new idea of what organized religion is for, perhaps even a new conception of Christianity." [9] This was the reason why some people favored community churches: to provide for the institutional embodiment of "a new conception of Christianity," a conception believed to be fully at home in a scientific age. Many of this group were probably closer kin to the radical religionists who broke from organized Christianity to form new associations than to even the more liberal in the churches who were seeking to mediate between Christian faith and the modern world.

In summary, it may be said that those who represented radical tendencies in religion went in quite different directions. Only the more conspicuous developments have been mentioned here. But taken all together, the radicals who separated from the churches and founded new institutions, those who remained within their traditional religious homes, and those who were somewhere between provided an important ferment in the religious life of the time.

130. Christian Science

Mary Baker Eddy (1821–1910) published in 1875 the first edition of *Science and Health*. It was destined to go through many revisions and to become, along with the Bible, the central authority among Christian Scientists as *Science and Health with Key to the Scriptures*. The first chapter of this first edition was entitled "Natural Science," and opened with these words:

> A few years since we clipped the following from the reports on Science:
>
> "At the University of Oxford, a prize of one hundred pounds was offered for the best essay on Natural Science, to refute the materialism of the present age, on the tendency to attribute physical effects to physical causes, rather than to a final spiritual cause." This demand for metaphysics coming from the very fount of erudition meets the wants of the age, and is the one question towering above all others, insomuch as it relates more intimately to the happiness and perfection of man. The control mind holds over matter becomes no longer a question when with mathematical certainty we gain its proof, and can demonstrate the facts assumed. This proof we claim to have gained, and reduced to its statement in science that furnishes a key to the harmony of man, and reveals what destroys sickness, sin, and death.[10]

[9] *Ibid.*, 11.

[10] Mary Baker Glover, *Science and Health* (Boston, 1875), 9. Mary Baker Eddy was born Mary Ann Morse Baker. In 1843 she married George Washington Glover, who died of yellow fever the next year. In 1853 she married Dr. Daniel Patterson; this marriage was dissolved by divorce twenty years later. In 1877 she married Asa Gilbert Eddy, who died in 1882.

This linking of scientific terminology and "mathematical certainty" with a unique metaphysics promising health and wholeness proved in time to speak to one of the felt "wants of the age," and the movement she founded has continued to flourish.

The main facts of Mrs. Eddy's life and the sources of her ideas have been a matter of long and bitter dispute, and much of the literature on the founder and her movement has been decidedly controversial. In 1866, following a fall on the ice, she claimed to have been remarkably healed, and was thus led to the discovery of how to be well and how to cure others. The contention of Mrs. Eddy and her followers has always been that she had been guided through her experiences to a revelation of the divine law of life, to an original discovery of the real meaning of the Bible.[11] On the other hand, there is a considerable body of evidence to show that a good many of her ideas were gained from Phineas P. Quimby, a mental healer of Portland, Maine, who had helped Mrs. Eddy in 1862.[12] The general influence of the intellectual climate of the New England of the time in which transcendentalist thought was strong can also be traced in her writings. Whatever the source of her ideas, Mrs. Eddy soon gave them her own distinctive statement, quite different from the contributions of Quimby or any other. In time a few students were attracted; in 1875, in Lynn, Massachusetts, the first organization of a society was undertaken. Chartered four years later as "The Church of Christ (Scientist)," with headquarters in Boston, the movement slowly spread to other cities. In 1892 the church was reorganized under a self-perpetuating Board of Directors, with Mrs. Eddy, as "pastor emeritus," in firm control as long as she lived. The "Mother Church" in Boston remains the strong center of the movement; other churches of Christian Science are "branches." The religious census of 1906 indicated a membership of about eighty-five thousand, which by 1926 had increased to over two hundred thousand.[13]

Inasmuch as copies of *Science and Health* are readily available, it has seemed most helpful to provide here a selection from the first edition of Mrs. Eddy's spiritual autobiography, *Retrospection and Introspection*. In the passages that follow are reflected such basic Christian Science beliefs as that God is All, that whatever is not God is unreal, that matter is substance in error and hence, with all evil, sin, and sickness, is not real. Mrs. Eddy mentions Plato only to refute him, yet her declaration that "evil is the absence of Good" reminds one of the continuing influence of the Greek philosopher. Sickness, she declared, is a false belief, suffering exists in the mortal mind only, and if they be ruled out there, then they cannot be found anywhere.

[11] E.g., see Sibyl Wilbur, *The Life of Mary Baker Eddy* (N.Y., 1907), 127–35.

[12] Phineas P. Quimby, *The Quimby Manuscripts, Showing the Discovery of Spiritual Healing and the Origin of Christian Science*, ed. Horatio W. Dresser (N.Y., 1921).

[13] C. Luther Fry, *The U.S. Looks at Its Churches* (N.Y., 1930), 140–1.

Foundation-Stones

The following ideas of Deity, antagonized by finite theories, doctrines, and hypotheses, I found to be demonstrable rules in Christian Science, and that we must abide by them.

Whatever diverges from the one divine Mind, or God,—or divides Mind into minds, Spirit into spirits, Soul into souls, and Being into beings, —is a misstatement of the unerring divine Principle of Science, which interrupts the meaning of the omnipotence, omniscience, and omnipresence of Spirit, and is of human, instead of divine origin.

War is waged between the evidences of Spirit and the evidences of the five physical senses; and this contest must go on until peace be declared by the final triumph of Spirit in immutable harmony. Divine Science disclaims sin, sickness, and death, on the basis of the omnipotence and omnipresence of God, or divine good.

All consciousness is Mind, and Mind is God. Hence there is but one Mind; and that one is the infinite good, supplying all Mind by the reflection, not the subdivision, of God. Whatever else claims to be mind, or consciousness, is untrue. The sun sends forth light, but not suns; so God reflects Himself, or Mind, but does not subdivide Mind, or good, into minds, good and evil. Divine Science demands mighty wrestlings with mortal beliefs, as we sail into the eternal haven over the unfathomable sea of possibilities.

Neither ancient nor modern philosophy furnishes a scientific basis for the Science of Mind-healing. Plato believed he had a soul, which must be doctored in order to heal his body. This would be like correcting the principle of music for the purpose of destroying discord. Principle is right; it is practice that is wrong. Soul is right; it is the flesh that is evil. Soul is the synonym of Spirit, God; hence there is but one Soul, and that one is infinite. If the pagan philosopher had known that physical sense, not Soul, causes all bodily ailments, his philosophy would have yielded to Science.

Man shines by borrowed light. He reflects God as his Mind, and this reflection is substance,—the substance of good. Matter is substance in error, Spirit is substance in Truth.

Evil, or error, is not Mind; but infinite Mind is sufficient to supply all manifestations of Intelligence. The notion of more than one Mind, or Life, is as unsatisfying as it is unscientific. All must be of God, and not our own, separated from Him.

Human systems of philosophy and religion are departures from Christian Science. Mistaking divine Principle for corporeal personality, ingrafting upon one First Cause such opposite effects as good and evil, health and sickness, life and death; making mortality the status and rule of divinity,—

such methods can never reach the perfection and demonstration of meta-physical, or Christian Science.

Stating the divine Principle, omnipotence (*omnis potens*), and then departing from this statement, and taking the rule of finite matter, with which to work out the problem of infinity, or Spirit—all this is like trying to compensate for the absence of omnipotence by a physical, false, and finite substitute.

With our Master, life was not merely a sense of existence, but an accompanying sense of power that subdued matter and brought to light immortality, insomuch that the people "were astonished at his doctrine: for he taught them as one having authority, and not as the scribes." Life, as defined by Jesus, had no beginning; it was not the result of organization, or infused into matter; it was Spirit.

The Great Revelation

CHRISTIAN SCIENCE reveals the grand verity, that to believe man has a finite and erring mind, and consequently a mortal mind and soul and life, is error. Scientific terms have no contradictory significations.

In Science, Life is not temporal, but eternal, without beginning or ending. The word *Life* never means that which is the source of death, and of good and evil. Such an inference is unscientific. It is like saying that addition means subtraction in one instance and addition in another, and then applying this rule to a demonstration of the science of numbers; even as mortals apply finite terms to God, in demonstration of infinity. *Life* is a term used to indicate Deity; and every other name for the Supreme Being, if properly employed, has the signification of Life. Whatever errs is mortal, and is the antipodes of Life, or God, and of health and holiness, both in idea and demonstration.

Christian Science reveals Mind, the only living and true God, and all that is made by Him, Mind, as harmonious, immortal, and spiritual: the five material senses define Mind and matter as distinct, but mutually dependent, each on the other, for intelligence and existence. Science defines man as immortal, as coexistent and coeternal with God, as made in His own image and likeness; material sense defines life as something apart from God, beginning and ending, and man as very far from the divine likeness. Science reveals Life as a complete sphere, as eternal self-existent Mind; material sense defines life as a broken sphere, as organized matter, and mind as something separate from God. Science reveals Spirit as All, averring [sic] that there is nothing beside God; material sense says that matter, His antipode, is something besides God. Material sense adds that the divine Spirit created matter, and that matter and evil are as real as Spirit and good.

Christian Science reveals God and His idea as the All and Only. It declares that evil is the absence of good; whereas, Good is God ever-present, and therefore evil is unreal and good is all that is real. Christian Science saith to the wave and storm, "Be still," and there is a great calm. Material sense asks, in its ignorance of Science, "When will the raging of the material elements cease?" Science saith to all manner of disease, "Know that God is all-power and all-presence, and there is nothing beside Him;" and the sick are healed. Material sense saith, "Oh, when will my sufferings cease? Where is God? Sickness is something besides Him, which He cannot, or does not, heal."

Christian Science is the only sure basis of harmony. Material sense contradicts Science, for matter, and its so-called organizations take no cognizance of the spiritual facts of the universe, or of the real man and God. Christian Science declares that there is but one Truth, Life, Love, but one Spirit, Mind, Soul. Any attempt to divide these arises from the fallibility of sense, from mortal man's ignorance, from enmity to God and Divine Science.

Christian Science declares that sickness is a belief, a latent fear, made manifest on the body in different forms of fear, or disease. This fear is formed unconsciously in the silent thought, as when you awaken from sleep and feel ill, experiencing the effect of a fear whose existence you do not realize; but if you fall asleep, actually conscious of the truth of Christian Science,—namely, that man's harmony is no more to be invaded than the rhythm of the universe,—you cannot awake in fear or suffering of any sort.

Science saith to fear, "You are the cause of all sickness; but you are a self-constituted falsity,—you are darkness, nothingness. You are without 'hope and without God in the world.' You do not exist, and have no right to exist, for 'perfect Love casteth out fear.'"

God is everywhere. "There is no speech nor language, where their voice is not heard"; and this voice is Truth that destroys error and Love that casts out fear.

Christian Science reveals the fact, that if suffering exists, it is in the mortal mind only, for matter has no sensation and cannot suffer.

If you rule out every sense of disease and suffering from mortal mind, it cannot be found in the body.

Posterity will have the right to demand that Christian Science be stated and demonstrated in its godliness and grandeur,—that however little be taught or learned, that little shall be right. Let there be milk for babes, but let not the milk be adulterated. Unless this method be pursued, the Science of Christian Healing will again be lost, and human suffering will increase.

Test Christian Science by its effect on society, and you will find that the views here set forth—as to the illusion of sin, sickness, and death—bring forth better fruits of health, righteousness, and Life, than a *belief in their reality has ever done*. A demonstration of the *unreality* of evil destroys evil.

SOURCE: Mary Baker Eddy, *Retrospection and Introspection* (Boston, 1891, 1892), 76–84.

131. The New Religion

One of the most influential prophecies of what religion would be like in a scientific age was supplied by the distinguished Unitarian president of Harvard University in 1909. Called upon to give the closing address to the Summer School of Theology, Charles William Eliot (1834–1926) took the occasion to make a statement that was immediately published in Boston and in London and was soon translated into French and German. It attracted wide and varying comment in the press, and has been reprinted many times.

Eliot had himself been educated at Harvard and had labored in the fields of mathematics and chemistry. As president of Harvard from 1869 to 1909, he had guided the transformation of that institution from college to university, and had encouraged the extensive development of the elective system. During his administration, the Divinity School became the pioneer nondenominational theological seminary in the country.[14]

In his 1909 address, Eliot began with a concise summary of the major intellectual and social forces playing upon religion. He then stated what the religion of the future would probably *not* be; after that he went on to state what the future religion might reasonably be expected to be. Portions of both of the major sections are given here, the negative part in abbreviated form.

DOCUMENT

I shall attempt to state without reserve and in simplest terms free from technicalities, first, what the religion of the future seems likely not to be, and secondly, what it may reasonably be expected to be. My point of view is that of an American layman, whose observing and thinking life has covered the extraordinary period since the *Voyage of the Beagle* was published, anaesthesia and the telegraph came into use, Herbert Spencer issued his first series of papers on evolution, Kuenen, Robertson Smith, and Wellhausen developed and vindicated Biblical criticism, J. S. Mill's *Principles of Political Economy* appeared, and the United States by going to war with Mexico set in operation the forces which abolished slavery on the American continent—the period within which mechanical power came to be widely distributed through the explosive engine and the applications of electricity, and all the great fundamental industries of civilized mankind were reconstructed.

(1) The religion of the future will not be based on authority, either spiritual or temporal. The decline of reliance upon absolute authority is one of the most significant phenomena of the modern world. . . .

[14] See George H. Williams, ed., *The Harvard Divinity School: Its Place in Harvard University and in American Culture* (Boston, 1954), 172–3, 185–6.

(2) It is hardly necessary to say that in the religion of the future there will be no personifications of the primitive forces of nature, such as light, fire, frost, wind, storm, and earthquake. . . .

(3) There will be in the religion of the future no worship, express or implied, of dead ancestors, teachers, or rulers; no more tribal, racial, or tutelary gods; no identification of any human being, however majestic in character, with the Eternal Deity. . . .

(4) In the religious life of the future the primary object will not be the personal welfare or safety of the individual in this world or any other. That safety, that welfare or salvation, may be incidentally secured, but it will not be the prime object in view. The religious person will not think of his own welfare or security, but of service to others, and of contributions to the common good. . . .

(5) The religion of the future will not be propitiatory, sacrificial, or expiatory. . . .

(6) The religion of the future will not perpetuate the Hebrew anthropomorphic representations of God, conceptions which were carried in large measure into institutional Christianity. It will not think of God as an enlarged and glorified man. . . .

(7) The religion of the future will not be gloomy, ascetic, or maledictory. It will not deal chiefly with sorrow and death, but with joy and life. It will not care so much to account for the evil and the ugly in the world as to interpret the good and the beautiful. . . .

Having thus considered what the religion of the future will not be, let us now consider what its positive elements will be.

The new thought of God will be its most characteristic element. This ideal will comprehend the Jewish Jehovah, the Christian Universal Father, the modern physicist's omnipresent and exhaustless Energy, and the biological conception of a Vital Force. The Infinite Spirit pervades the universe, just as the spirit of a man pervades his body, and acts, consciously or unconsciously, in every atom of it. The twentieth century will accept literally and implicitly St. Paul's statement, "In Him we live, and move, and have our being," and God is that vital atmosphere, or incessant inspiration. The new religion is therefore thoroughly monotheistic, its God being the one infinite force; but this one God is not withdrawn or removed, but indwelling, and especially dwelling in every living creature. God is so absolutely immanent in all things, animate and inanimate, that no mediation is needed between him and the least particle of his creation. In his moral attributes, he is for every man the multiplication to infinity of all the noblest, tenderest, and most potent qualities which that man has ever seen or imagined in a human being. In this sense every man makes his own picture of God. Every age, barbarous or civilized, happy or unhappy, improving or degenerating, frames its own conception of God within the limits of its own experiences and imaginings. In this sense, too, a humane religion has to wait for a humane generation. The central thought of the new religion will therefore be a humane and worthy idea of God, thoroughly consistent with the nineteenth-century revelations concerning man and nature, and with all the tenderest and loveliest teachings which have come down to us from the past.

The scientific doctrine of one omnipresent, eternal Energy, informing and inspiring the whole creation at every instant of time and throughout the infinite spaces, is fundamentally and completely inconsistent with the dualistic conception which sets spirit over against matter, good over against evil, man's wickedness against God's righteousness, and Satan against Christ. The doctrine of God's immanence is also inconsistent with the conception that he once set the universe a-going, and then withdrew, leaving the universe to be operated under physical laws, which were his viceregents or substitutes. If God is thoroughly immanent in the entire creation, there can be no "secondary causes," in either the material or the spiritual universe. The new religion rejects absolutely the conception that man is an alien in the world, or that God is alienated from the world. It rejects also the entire conception of man as a fallen being, hopelessly wicked, and tending downward by nature; and it makes this emphatic rejection of long accepted beliefs because it finds them all inconsistent with a humane, civilized, or worthy idea of God. . . .

In all its theory and all its practice it [the religion of the future] will be completely natural. It will place no reliance on any sort of magic, or miracle, or other violation of, or exception to, the laws of nature. It will perform no magical rites, use no occult processes, count on no abnormal interventions of supernal powers, and admit no possession of supernatural gifts, whether transmitted or conferred, by any tribe, class, or family of men. Its sacraments will be, not invasions of law by miracle, but the visible signs of a natural spiritual grace, or of a natural hallowed custom. It may preserve historical rites and ceremonies, which, in times past, have represented the expectation of magical or miraculous effects; but it will be content with natural interpretations of such rites and ceremonies. Its priests will be men especially interested in religious thought, possessing unusual gifts of speech on devotional subjects, and trained in the best methods of improving the social and industrial conditions of human life. . . .

It is obvious, therefore, that the completely natural quality of the future religion excludes from it many of the religious compensations and consolations of the past. . . . The new religion will not attempt to reconcile men and women to present ills by promises of future blessedness, either for themselves or for others. Such promises have done infinite mischief in the world, by inducing men to be patient under sufferings or deprivations against which they should have incessantly struggled. The advent of a just freedom for the mass of mankind has been delayed for centuries by just this effect of compensatory promises issued by churches.

The religion of the future will approach the whole subject of evil from another side, that of resistance and prevention. The Breton sailor, who had had his arm poisoned by a dirty fish-hook which had entered his finger, made a votive offering at the shrine of the Virgin Mary, and prayed for a cure. The workman today, who gets cut or bruised by a rough or dirty instrument, goes to a surgeon, who applies an antiseptic dressing to the wound, and prevents the poisoning. That surgeon is one of the ministers of the new religion. When dwellers in a slum suffer the familiar evils caused by over-crowding, impure food, and cheerless labor, the modern true believers contend against the sources of such misery by providing public baths, play-grounds, wider and cleaner streets, better dwellings, and more effective schools,—that is they attack the sources of physical and moral evil. The new religion cannot supply the old sort of consolation; but it can diminish the need of consolation, or reduce the number of occasions for consolation. . . .

The future religion will have the attribute of universality and of adaptability to the rapidly increasing stores of knowledge and power over nature acquired by the human race. As the religion of the child is inevitably very different from that of an adult, and must grow up with the child, so the religion of a race whose capacities are rapidly enlarging must be capable of a corresponding development. The religion of any single individual ought to grow up with him all the way from infancy to age; and the same is true of the religion of a race. It is bad for any people to stand still in their governmental conceptions and practices, or in the organization of their industries, or in any of their arts or trades, even the oldest; but it is much worse for a people to stand still in their religious conceptions and practices. Now, the new religion affords an indefinite scope, or range, for progress and development. It rejects all the limitations of family, tribal, or national religion. It is not bound to any dogma, creed, book, or institution. It has the whole world for the field of the loving labors of its disciples; and its fundamental precept of serviceableness admits an infinite variety and range in both time and space. It is very simple, and therefore possesses an important element of durability. It is the complicated things that get out of order. Its symbols will not relate to sacrifice or dogma; but it will doubtless have symbols, which will represent its love of liberty, truth and beauty. It will also have social rites and reverent observances; for it will wish to commemorate the good thoughts and deeds which have come down from former generations. It will have its saints; but its canonizations will be based on grounds somewhat new. It will have its heroes; but they must have shown a loving, disinterested, or protective courage. It will have its communions, with the Great Spirit, with the spirits of the departed, and with living fellow-men of like minds. Working together will be one of its fundamental ideas,—of men with God, of men with prophets, leaders, and teachers, of men with one another, of men's intelligence with the forces of nature. It will teach only such uses of authority as are necessary to secure the coöperation of several or many people to one end; and the discipline it will advocate will be training in the development of coöperative good-will.

Will such a religion as this make progress in the twentieth-century world? You have heard in this Summer School of Theology much about the conflict between materialism and religious idealism, the revolt against long-acccepted dogmas, the frequent occurrence of waves of reform, sweeping through and sometimes over the churches, the effect of modern philosophy, ethical theories, social hopes, and democratic principles on the established churches, and the abandonment of churches altogether by a large proportion of the population in countries mainly Protestant. You know, too, how other social organizations have, in some considerable measure, taken the place of churches. . . . Nevertheless, the great mass of the people remain attached to the traditional churches, and are likely to remain so,—partly because of their tender associations with churches in the grave crises of life, and partly because their actual mental condition still permits them to accept the beliefs they have inherited or been taught while young. The new religion will therefore make but slow progress, so far as outward organization goes. It will, however, progressively modify the creeds and religious practices of all the existing churches, and change their symbolism and their teachings concerning the conduct of life. Since its chief doctrine is the doctrine of a sublime unity of substance, force, and spirit, and its chief precept is, Be serviceable, it will exert a strong uniting influence among men.

Christian unity has always been longed for by devout believers, but has been sought in impossible ways. Authoritative churches have tried to force everybody within their range to hold the same opinions and unite in the same observances, but they have won only temporary and local successes. As freedom has increased in the world, it has become more and more difficult to enforce even outward conformity; and in countries where church and state have been separated, a great diversity of religious opinions and practices has been expressed in different religious organizations, each of which commands the effective devotion of a fraction of the population. Since it is certain that men are steadily gaining more and more freedom in thought, speech, and action, civilized society might as well assume that it will be quite impossible to unite all religiously-minded people through any dogma, creed, ceremony, observance, or ritual. All these are divisive, not uniting, wherever a reasonable freedom exists. The new religion proposes as a basis of unity, first, its doctrine of an immanent and loving God, and secondly, its precept, Be serviceable to fellow-men. Already there are many signs in the free countries of the world that different religious denominations can unite in good work to promote human welfare. . . .

Finally, this twentieth-century religion is not only to be in harmony with the great secular movements of modern society—democracy, individualism, social idealism, the zeal for education, the spirit of research, the modern tendency to welcome the new, the fresh powers of preventive medicine, and the recent advances in business and industrial ethics—but also in essential agreement with the direct, personal teachings of Jesus, as they are reported in the Gospels. The revelation he gave to mankind thus becomes more wonderful than ever.

> SOURCE: Charles W. Eliot, *The Religion of the Future,* American
> Unitarian Association, *Tract* 246 (Boston, 1909), 3–10,
> 13–5, 21–6. Used by permission of Beacon Press.

132. *The Faith of a Modernist*

The way in which a scientific approach to religion could decisively influence those who remained within the evangelical denominations is clearly illustrated in the career of Shailer Mathews (1863–1941), dean of the Divinity School of the University of Chicago from 1908 to 1933. Mathews was educated at Colby College and at the Newton Theological Institution. During a summer pastorate while a seminary student, he decided that he would not enter the ministry. He was never ordained. He taught rhetoric and elocution at Colby, then studied in Germany in the fields of history and political economy, and taught in those areas on his return, later adding sociology. In 1894 he began his career at the new University of Chicago as Associate Professor of New Testament History. He later taught in the fields of systematic and historical theology. He became an outstanding Protestant leader, serving as president of the Federal Council of Churches of Christ in America from 1912 to 1916, and of the Northern Baptist Convention in 1915.

Mathews' approach to religion was basically socio-historical. Though he was striving to mediate between inherited faith and the new science, at important points he was moving beyond mediating liberalism. He rejected any appeal to religious authority in favor of a fully scientific, inductive method. His classic definition of modernism, that *"it is the use of the methods of modern science to find, state and use the permanent and central values of inherited orthodoxy"* left "science" as the real authority in matters of faith. A strong distaste for theology was expressed in Mathews' writings; he felt that the center of interest was passing "from theology to life." The tendency of his socio-historical approach was to view all doctrinal statements chiefly as reflections of cultural patterns. In 1930 he published *The Atonement and the Social Process,* in which he made unforgettably clear how theological positions have been influenced by the cultural, political, and intellectual atmosphere of the times in which they were articulated. The next year his *The Growth of the Idea of God* appeared. "The starting point for religion," he insisted, "as for any other form of behavior, is a relationship with the universe described by the scientist." He traced the changes in the understanding of this relationship through history, concluding with the famous definition, "God is our conception, born of social experience, of the personality-evolving and personally responsive elements of our cosmic environment with which we are organically related." [15]

Though radical in methodology, Mathews remained within the orbit of denominational life, confessing his loyalty to Jesus Christ in a nondogmatic way. "The modernist will cherish faith in Jesus Christ as the revealer of the saving God," he wrote, characteristically adding, "but until he is convinced of the historicity of the infancy sections of Matthew and Luke, and holds different conceptions of generation from those given at present by biology, he will not base that faith upon the virgin birth as the one and only means by which God can enter into human experience." [16]

There is one important terminological observation that must be made. In the passage from *The Faith of Modernism* that follows, Mathews referred to liberalism as being further to the theological left than modernism. He was here referring to the liberalism of the nineteenth century of the kind evident in Unitarianism. Actually his use of the term liberalism was thus historically correct, but in the late nineteenth and early twentieth centuries the term liberalism came to be applied to the effort of evangelicals to come to terms with new scientific and historical knowledge. The term "modernist" or "scientific modernist" has been usually applied to those further to the theological left. Mathews never clearly joined this company, but represented certain of its methods and perspectives within the evangelical denominations.

DOCUMENT

Modernism is a projection of the Christian movement into modern conditions. It proceeds within the religious limits set by an ongoing Christian group; it distinguishes permanent Christian convictions from their doctrinal expression; it uses these convictions in meeting the actual needs of our modern world.

The term Modernism itself is somewhat unfortunate. Despite all protestation to the contrary it gives the impression of self-satisfaction, as if only those who hold certain views are intellectually abreast of the times. Yet the terms "Modernism" and "Modernists" have come into such common use that they cannot be avoided. This much, at least, can be said in their favor: they indicate a real tendency in our religious life. This tendency is to be seen when one compares the intellectual habits of Christians as they ex-

---

[15] *The Growth of the Idea of God* (N.Y., 1931), 213, 226.

[16] *The Faith of Modernism* (N.Y., 1924), 176. See also his *New Faith for Old: An Autobiography* (N.Y., 1936), especially Chap. 17, and Kenneth L. Smith, "Shailer Mathews: Theologian of Social Process" (typed Ph.D. dissertation, Duke University, 1959).

pound Christianity. Some rely on scientific method; others, on church authority. The former may be said in general to be those indicated when Modernists are mentioned. But strictly speaking, "Modernism" and "Modernist" imply no new theology or organized denominational movement. The habits of mind and tendencies of thought which the terms have come loosely to represent are to be found in all Christian groups in all parts of the world. Until Modernism is distinguished from fundamentally theological interests, it will be misunderstood. Modernists are not members of a group which prescribes doctrinal views, but Christians who use certain methods of thought are described as Modernists. These methods, with their points of view, must be considered in detail.

I.

There are two social minds at work in our world. The one seeks to reassert the past; the other seeks by new methods to gain efficiency. Such attitudes are the result of our human nature. In all life there are inheritance and variations. All human affairs have their "youth movement" and their "stand patters." Between the two there is always more or less of a struggle. We see it to-day in literature, art, business, and international politics. It is, therefore, only natural that they should appear in the field of Christianity.

Christianity is not a hard and fast system of philosophy or orthodoxy accepted by all those who call themselves Christians. It is that religion which Christians believe and practice. There have always been differences within the church and these differences have been of many sorts. But at bottom Christianity has been the attempt of men to rely upon Christian principles in meeting the needs of their actual life-situations. In making such attempts two types of Christians have always been found. There have been those who, without serious recognition and moral imperatives, have wished to enforce inherited beliefs and institutions; and those who have sought to examine their inheritance, reject whatever has been outgrown and restate its permanent elements from the point of view of and for the satisfaction of new needs. Social and cultural changes, due to forces of many sorts, have lain back of such theological readjustments. . . .

III.

What then is Modernism? A heresy? An infidelity? A denial of truth? A new religion? So its ecclesiastical opponents have called it. But it is none of these. To describe it is like describing that science which has made our modern intellectual world so creative. It is not a denomination or a theology. *It is the use of the methods of modern science to find, state and use the permanent and central values of inherited orthodoxy in meeting the needs of a modern world.* The needs themselves point the way to formulas. Modernists endeavor to reach beliefs and their application in the same way that chemists or historians reach and apply their conclusions. They do not vote in conventions and do not enforce beliefs by discipline. Modernism has no Confession. Its theological affirmations are the formulations of results of investigation both of human needs and the Christian religion. The Dogmatist starts with doctrines, the Modernist with the religion that gave rise to doctrines. The Dogmatist relies on conformity through group authority; the Modernist upon inductive method and action in accord with group loyalty.

An examination of the Modernist movement will disclose distinct aspects of these charcteristics.

1. The Modernist movement is a phase of the scientific struggle for freedom in thought and belief.

The dogmatic mind found its natural and most effective expression in the Roman Catholic Church and in the Protestantism of the sixteenth and seventeenth centuries. Because it developed under the influences of Roman law, its possessors were trained in the methods of the lawyer and the schoolman, and dominated by deductive logic. It regarded doctrine as of the nature of law and church-membership as an obedience to theological statutes passed by church authorities. Its range of interest in philosophy was practically limited to Aristotle, and its theological method was to organize texts of the Bible and bring about the adoption of the resulting formulas or dogmas as authoritative statements comparble with a legal code. Protestantism preserved most of these dogmas while setting up new authority for accepting them. It was not interested in the church as an historical movement, but in the literature of the first stages of that movement. It detached the Bible from history and declared it to be the sole and divinely given basis of revealed truth. Yet the Bible it accepted was determined by authority, and biblical truth was authoritatively said to be expressed in creeds and catechisms and Confessions adopted and enforced by authority. The dogmatic mind has always sought to express its beliefs sharply and clearly and with condemnatory clauses. Its century-long anathematizing of heretics shows that it is quite as truly interested in keeping non-conformists out of the church as in expressing truth held by the church. Naturally it has never been primarily interested in science, international peace, or social justice. It has often attacked scientists; it has never thought of abolishing war; and it has preferred charity and heaven to economic readjustment. One of its most bitter controversies has been over the relation of "works" to faith. . . .

2. Modernists are Christians who accept the results of scientific research as data with which to think religiously.

It would, of course, be unsafe to accept every scientific theory as material for theological thinking. But the Modernist starts with the assumption that scientists know more about nature and man than did the theologians who drew up the Creeds and Confessions. He is open-minded in regard to scientific discovery. Believing that all facts, whether they be those of religious experience or those of the laboratory, can fit into the general scheme of things, he welcomes new facts as rapidly as they can be discovered.

When, therefore, he finds experts in all fields of scientific investigation accepting the general principle of evolution, he makes it a part of his intellectual apparatus. He does this not because he has a theology to be supported, but because he accepts modern science. He has no illusions as to the finality of this or that theory, which, like Darwinism, attempts, though imperfectly, to describe an evolutionary process, but he is convinced that scientists have discovered that there is continuity of development in the physical world, and that, therefore, such continuity must be recognized by religious thinkers. He is cautious about appropriating philosophies, but he is frankly and hopefully an evolutionist because of facts furnished by experts. In this attitude he is reproducing that of earlier religious thinkers when they abandoned the Ptolemaic system of the universe and adopted the Copernican. When he wants to estimate the worth of dogmatic hostility to such attitudes he recalls the attack upon the views of Copernicus by those who had identified Ptolemaic science with religion, and waits for good people to show good sense.

Furthermore, in the light of sociological and historical facts, the Modernist uses the methods of science in his quest for religious assurance. He knows that the Christian religion develops as a group-possession when men's experience and knowledge grow. He is not content simply to accept a doctrine. He seeks to understand its real purpose and service. He therefore seeks to discover why it arose. He searches for its origins and estimates its efficiency in the light of its conformity with social forces and its capacity to nerve men and women for more courageous living. The beliefs of Christians are less extensive than the loyalties of Christians. A religion is a way of living and the Modernist refuses to think of it as an accumulation of decrees. Attitudes and convictions, he discovers from a study of the Christian movement, are not identical with the language and concepts in which they are expressed.

3. Modernists are Christians who adopt the methods of historical and literary science in the study of the Bible and religion.

From some points of view, this, although not the most fundamental, is their most obvious characteristic. It was the critical study of the Scriptures with which the movement started in the Roman Catholic Church and it has laid the foundation for theological discussion in Protestantism. The Modernist is a critic and an historian before he is a theologian. His interest in method precedes his interest in results. The details of his attitude as to the Bible will appear in a later chapter, but in general the Modernist may be said to be first of all a Christian who implicitly trusts the historical method of an approach to Christian truth.

Modernists believe themselves true to the spirit and purpose of Jesus

Christ when they emphasize his teachings and the inner faith of a century-long movement rather than the formulas in which aspects of this faith were authoritatively expressed. In this Modernists are doing for Christianity what Americans did for Americanism when they changed their Constitution in order to give truer application to the principles the Constitution itself expressed. Men who abolished slavery and gave the suffrage to women were more consistently expressing the principle of liberty than the framers of the Constitution themselves, for they limited suffrage to men and permitted the existence of slavery.

4. The Modernist Christian believes the Christian religion will help men meet social as well as individual needs.

Any acquaintance with social facts makes plain how responsive the individual is to social influences. Any intelligent religious program must take such facts into account. But programs differ. Some emphasize rescue and others emphasize salvation. The dogmatic mind has always preferred rescue. In practice it has varied from the asceticism of the monk to the rejection of social idealism. In theology it has limited salvation to elect individuals. On the other hand, students of society know that the relation of the individual to the social order involves him in responsibility for social actions as well as liability to social influences. Therefore, they undertake to transform social forces for the benefit of the individual. Such a policy is furthest possible from a belief that humanity needs only better physical conditions. It is a solemn affirmation that the Christian cannot hold himself guiltless if he permits the existence of economic, political and recreational evils, and that he will be the victim of such evils if he does not undertake to correct or destroy them.

Modernists believe that the Gospel is as significant for social forces as for individuals. They find little hope in rescue of brands from burning; they want to put out the fire. They believe that the same God who so loved the world as to give his only begotten Son that those individuals who believe in him might not perish, also sent his Son into the world that the world might be saved.

But when the Modernist speaks of saving society he does not believe that society will save itself. He believes that the constant need of God's gracious help is to be understood as clearly through the laws given him by the sociologist as by the psychologist. He, therefore, hopefully undertakes to apply the Golden Rule to group-action as truly as to individuals. He would carry Christian attitudes and convictions into our entire life. He urges the duty of sacrifice on the part of nations and of classes, whether they be employers or employees, as truly as on that of individuals. For Jesus Christ to him is more than the savior of isolated individuals. He is the savior of men in society.

This is one reason why the Modernist is an object of suspicion. The dogmatic mind is almost always to be found among social reactionaries. To no small degree Modernism in theology is opposed because Modernists urge reform in economic matters. In the struggle over economic privilege the Modernist is properly feared as one who takes Jesus seriously and believes implicitly that his Gospel applies to wages and war as truly as to oaths, charity and respectability.

5. The Modernist is a Christian who believes that the spiritual and moral needs of the world can be met because they are intellectually convinced that Christian attitudes and faiths are consistent with other realities.

In so far as by trustworthy methods he reaches intellectual conclusions not in accord with those reached by deduction or by major premises given by authority, the Modernist knows himself an emancipator. Christianity is under suspicion in so far as it refuses to submit any tenet to impartial scrutiny. Each intellectual epoch has made that scrutiny. Modernism as a scientific method is for to-day what scholasticism and legal methods were to the past. It is no more negative than is chemistry. If all its conclusions are not the same as those previously held, it is because some things are established beyond question and the perspective of the importance of beliefs has been determined. A scientific method cannot start with authority because it cannot assume conclusions at the beginning of its investigation.

6. Modernists as a class are evangelical Christians. That is, they accept Jesus Christ as the revelation of a Savior God.

The Modernist movement is, therefore, not identical with Liberalism. With all due respect for the influence of Liberalism in clarifying religious thought, its origin and interest tend toward the emphasis of intellectual belief and the criticism and repudiation of doctrines *per se*. The Modernist like any other investigator has a presumption in favor of the reality of that which he is studying. Both historically and by preference his religious starting point is the inherited orthodoxy of a continuing community of Christians. To this group he belongs. The place of evangelical Christianity in social and ethical life, the aid it gives to millions of human hearts, the moral impetus it has given social reforms, forbid treating Christianity as an unborn child of human thought. But if it is to carry conviction as a way of organizing life it must be studied and applied according to methods judged effective by those to whom it is recommended. As the early church fathers were Christians who utilized their Hellenistic training to expound the Christianity brought them by Jews; so the Schoolmen were Christians who followed Aristotle; so the Modernists are Christians who use scientific method to estimate and apply the values of that evangelical inheritance in which they share. One might as well expect a student of politics to deny the existence of the State as to expect a Modernist to be disloyal to the Christian church; to expect a student of medicine to be indifferent to human ills and skeptical as to the use of medicine, as to expect that investigators within the Christian church should be indifferent or skeptical as to faith.

In brief, then, *the use of scientific, historical, social method in under-*

standing and applying evangelical Christianity to the needs of living persons, is Modernism. Its interests are not those of theological controversy or appeal to authority. They do not involve the rejection of the supernatural when rightly defined. Modernists believe that they can discover the ideals and directions needed for Christian living by the application of critical and historical methods to the study of the Bible; that they can discover by similar methods the permanent attitudes and convictions of Christians constituting a continuous and developing group; and that these permanent elements will help and inspire the intelligent and sympathetic organization of life under modern conditions. Modernists are thus evangelical Christians who use modern methods to meet modern needs. Confessionalism is the evangelicalism of the dogmatic mind. Modernism is the evangelicalism of the scientific mind.

> SOURCE: Shailer Mathews, *The Faith of Modernism* (N.Y., 1924), 15-7, 22-4, 29-36. Used by permission of Robert E. Mathews.

133. A Religious Naturalist Defines God

Throughout his major writings in the field of religious thought, Henry Nelson Wieman (1884—) has been supremely concerned with one basic question: How may one know and define God? In answer to the first part of that question, he has consistently maintained that God must be known as any other object in experience, namely, by means of the scientific method or of observation and reason. In answer to the second part, he has defined God in a variety of ways. Before 1930 he commonly defined God as "the most protecting and sustaining behavior of the universe." [17] Shortly thereafter he more often said, "God is that interaction between individuals, groups and ages which generates and promotes the greatest mutuality of good." [18] In the later 1930's, he usually characterized God as a delicate system of complex growth; i.e., growth of creative synthesis, or of meaning and value in the world.[19] In all of these definitions, Wieman studiously avoided all terms which would imply personality or mind in God. According to him, God is superhuman but is neither a person nor a mind.

In the year 1932 Wieman published a lucid essay on "Theocentric Religion," delineating his charcteristic conception of God. The two constructive sections (IV–V) of that essay are contained in the document which follows.

The son of a Presbyterian minister, Wieman was born in Missouri and completed his undergraduate education at Park College. In preparing himself to teach philosophy of religion, he spent a year in Germany attending

---

[17] See, e.g., *The Wrestle of Religion With Truth* (N.Y., 1927), 135; cf. 128.
[18] Wieman, *et al., Is There a God?* (Chicago, 1932), 13.
[19] Henry N. and Regina W. Wieman, *Normative Psychology of Religion* (N.Y., 1935), 50-9; Wieman and Walter M. Horton, *The Growth of Religion* (Chicago, 1938), 348-53.

the lectures of Rudolf Eucken at Jena, and of Wilhelm Windelband and Ernst Troeltsch at Heidelberg. Later he studied at Harvard, majoring with William E. Hocking and Ralph Barton Perry.

Wieman did his first teaching at Occidental College, after which he taught for many years at the University of Chicago. In addition to the books already cited, he is the author of *Religious Experience and Scientific Method* (1926), *Methods of Private Religious Living* (1929), and *The Source of Human Good* (1946).

DOCUMENT

IV

What I am chiefly trying to do in the field of religion is to promote a theocentric religion as over against the prevalent anthropocentric. The first requirement of a theocentric religion is that we make the actuality of God himself, and not our ideas about God, the object of our love and devotion. The second requirement is another side of the same thing. It is that we do not allow our wishes and needs to shape our idea of God, but shall shape it solely in the light of objective evidence. If we cherish our particular idea of God, rather than the mysterious and unexplored actuality of God, we are loving and worshipping ourselves, not God. If we allow our idea of God to be shaped by our desires and needs, we are cuddling ourselves, not serving God.

There is only one method known to man by which he can subordinate his own wishes and needs to objective reality and shape his ideas in the light of authentic evidence rather than hug his own subjectivity. That method is sometimes called scientific method. But it is not limited merely to the techniques of physics and chemistry. If those techniques are the only ones to which the term can be applied, then we do not here mean scientific method. We mean that method which is made up of a combination of observation and reason. By checking the constructs of reason by observation, and directing our observation by the constructs of reason, we gradually acquire an idea of objective reality, and circumvent the thronging urgency of our desires which so persistently hide from us the real nature of objective existence. Only as I hold my ideas in loving and devoted tentativeness, subject to criticism and discarding as corrective evidence is brought to light, can I make God, and not my pet ideas about God, the object of all my living. Only thus is a theocentric religion possible.

I have been widely accused of trying to "reconcile science and religion" and introduce "scientific method" into religion *in order to make religion respectable and acceptable to the intelligentsia*. Nothing has been wider from my thought than that. This accusation is what the psychologists call "projection" on the part of professional religionists. Their business is to make other people religious. Therefore they must try constantly to make religion appealing to others, make it dramatic, preachable or otherwise transmittable [sic]. Hence when they see anyone trying to reformulate our religious thinking, they very naturally jump to the conclusion that he is trying to make religion more acceptable to somebody or other. But that is not my intent. My sole concern is to find some way of escaping from the miasma of subjectivism and making contact with sacred reality.

The only reason I insist on scientific method in religion, is because I want to deal with the objective, existential God, and not merely ideas. We must use ideas, of course; but by means of this method of observation and reason we make our ideas tools, not ends, torches lighting the way, not suns and stars to love and adore. It is because I fight for a theocentric religion, that I insist on holding all beliefs subject to the tests of observation and reason.

Preaching has rendered a great service to religion. But it has imposed one great curse. To be preachable, religion must be dramatic. Therefore professional religionists have insisted that God, and all reality which concerns religion, shall have dramatic form. But the truth is not necessarily dramatic. At any rate, we must first of all have the truth, and then see if it can or cannot be put in dramatic form. But the way institutional religion has functioned, has just reversed this order. We have first insisted on dramatic form, and then tried to see if we could make the results correspond to the truth.

The interpretation of religion offered by Karl Barth has made a very wide appeal because it is so preachable. It is dramatic, traditional and, therefore, appeals to the deep rooted sentiments of church people. Also it claims to deal with objective reality, excluding all merely human desires and ideas with greater rigor and thoroughness than any other. But is this last claim true? It is not. Unquestionably Barth and his followers are sincere. Certainly they have made a desperate effort to escape from the entangling mesh of projected human desires. But they have failed completely in their efforts because they have rejected the only method by which this can be done or even approximated. They have rejected the method of observation combined with reason. Yet this is the only method by which we can even so much as approach objective reality. It is the only way in which we can pierce the interposing screen of our own fanciful constructions.

The idea of God which Barth and his followers finally achieve is simply what tradition hands down to them, but which they claim is the direct revelation of God. How do they know what is revelation and what is not? How do they know that what they accept as revelation is revelation? They do not know and cannot know except by way of observation and reason. What they accept as revelation is mere prejudice, unless its truth is sustained by observation and reason. The only possible way to achieve a theocentric religion is to relinquish all claim to knowledge of God save that which can be obtained by way of observation and reason.

V

Another great obstruction to theocentric religion is the insistence that God is a personality. If observation and reason made it unmistakbly evident that God is a personality, it would be another matter. But observation and reason do not so testify. Also, the grounds on which it is claimed that God must be a personality, are plainly the stronghold of anthropocentric religion as over against theocentric. Some of these grounds are as follows. (1) God must be personality because personality is the highest form of existence that we know. If God is not like man in this respect, he must be lower than man. Here we have anthropocentric religion with a vengeance. (2) God must be a personality because otherwise man can find no satisfaction of his needs. He cannot commune with God, if God is not a personality. If the basic desires and demands of human nature are to be satisfied, God must be a personality. In other words, the needs of man are set up as the standard by which to determine what God must be. This is the most extreme opposite of a theocentric religion, for it tries to determine the nature of God as you would ascertain some utility. Man and his needs are supreme. God is shaped to suit man.

As matter of fact, I believe it can be shown that God is not a personality. A personality can only exist in a society. Personality is generated by interaction between individuals. We do not mean that we first had this interaction, and out of it personalities arose. We mean, rather, that this kind of interaction develops concomitantly with personality. This kind of interaction is communication. It is the sharing of experience. Personalities are developed just in so far as individuals develop a common body of experience which each can share with the others.

Now if personality is thus absolutely dependent upon such social interaction, if it is generated, sustained, enriched, ennobled by social interaction, and is degraded, impoverished and perverted when social interaction goes wrong, it is plain that God cannot be a personality. It is plain that there cannot be a primordial personality, sustaining and promoting the supreme goods of life.

Not only is personality sustained and developed by this social interaction, but no personality can be perfect in an imperfect society. A personality inevitably, by reason of its very nature and the way it is sustained and made, must partake of the evils of the society to which it belongs. If God is a personality he cannot derive his personality from human society, because he would then be no better or stronger than we.

Since personality cannot exist apart from a society, and since the society which generates and sustains God cannot be human society, he must belong to some society of angels. But we have no evidence there is a society of angels. In order to defend personality in God one must resort to the construction of further hypothetical entities for which there is no evidence.

But suppose God is a personality not because of a society of angels, but because of a society in the Godhead itself. Suppose God is a society of two or three. Suppose the old doctrine of the Trinity is correct. We claim, in fact, that is the only ground on which personality in God can be defended. But even that fails to make God a personality. God would then be that interaction between the three members (or two or more) which sustains, generates and renders perfect the personalities *in* God. God would then not be a personality, but a kind of interaction between individuals, which interaction sustains and promotes all the values of personality. As a matter of fact, this is what the old Trinitarian doctrine implied.

Thus we see that under no circumstances can God be thought to be a personality. The idea is self-contradictory. Therefore we conclude that, whatever else God is, he is not a personality. So much for the negative side. Positively, we would say that God is that kind of interaction between things which generates and magnifies personality and all its highest values. God, thus, is more than personality. Personality simply could not function in the way that actuality must function which carries highest possibilities of value and which is, therefore, the rightful object of supreme and passionate devotion for all human kind.

But this interaction which sustains and magnifies personality and all its highest values, cannot be limited merely to the interaction between human individuals. Rather it must be identified with the process of progressive integration. Progressive integration means that interaction between things by which they come to share in common an increasing measure of structure. At the level of human personality this structure shared in common takes on the form of shared experience. Progressive integration at this level is the interaction which develops a richer body of shared experience, accessible to all men who will meet the requirements of participating in it. Such shared experience assumes the form of beauty, truth and love. Art, and that rationality called truth, constitute the form which all experience must assume if it is to be shared in common by all interacting individuals. When it is thus shared it constitutes these individuals into a community wherein the good of each is the good of all and the good of all the good of each. This is love in the religious sense. Maximum mutuality is the highest expression of God in the lives of men.

> SOURCE: Henry Nelson Wieman, "Theocentric Religion," in Vergilius Ferm, ed., *Contemporary American Theology: Theological Autobiographies,* I (N.Y., 1932), 346–51. Used by permission of Vergilius Ferm.

134. Theses of Religious Humanism

The most dramtic expression of humanist views, "A Humanist Manifesto," came after 1930, but as a climax of trends that had long been developing. "When eleven eminent professors of philosophy, theology, economics, medicine, and sociology, and twenty-three other leaders in editorial, literary, educational, and religious fields come out publicly over their own signatures and confess to belief in a new religion called Humanism, and state fifteen theses upon which they all agree," wrote Charles Francis Potter (1885–1962) in 1933, "then something of more than ordinary importance in religious circles has occurred. The fact that these men come from various denominational and religious backgrounds, including Unitarianism, Universalism, Judaism, and Ethical Culture, increases the significance of the new movement." [20]

Among the signers of the fifteen theses of "A Humanist Manifesto" were men prominent in education and journalism: J. A. C. Fagginer Auer of Harvard; Harry Elmer Barnes, then of the Scripps-Howard Newspapers; Edwin A. Burtt of Cornell; John Dewey of Columbia; John H. Dietrich, minister of the First Unitarian Society of Minneapolis; A. Eustace Haydon of the University of Chicago; Robert Morss Lovett of the *New Republic* and of the University of Chicago; Charles Francis Potter, founder and leader of the First Humanist Society of New York; John Herman Randall, Jr., of Columbia; Curtis W. Reese, dean of the Abraham Lincoln Center of Chicago; Roy Wood Sellars of the University of Michigan; and Edwin H. Wilson, editor of the *New Humanist*. The signers felt themselves to be in the vanguard of a mighty movement, for as Potter expressed their mood, "The trend toward Humanism is so marked among the representatives of all the more liberal groups of Christianity and Judaism that it will probably be only a matter of time, and a brief time at that, before Humanism will be generally recognized as the logical faith of those whose modern point of view forces them to abandon the inevitable supernaturalism of the theistic position." [21] Potter, who gave his professional life to the new movement, was himself an example of the trend he expected to become general. Educated at Bucknell University and Newton Theological Institution, he was ordained in 1908 as a Baptist, but later ministered in Unitarian and Universalist churches. Finally he moved to a nontheistic humanist position and organized the First Humanist Society in New York in 1929. He was convinced that the humanization of religion would require the substitution of discovery for revelation, the replacement of salvation by education, the substitution of democracy for monarchy in religion, the replacement of the churches by free religious societies, and the supplanting of the supernatural by the natural. But the mood of the 1930's was not to prove responsive to this culmination of trends from an earlier period.

DOCUMENT

The time has come for widespread recognition of the radical changes in religious beliefs throughout the modern world. The time is past for mere

[20] *Humanizing Religion* (N.Y., 1933), 1.　　　　　　　　　[21] *Ibid.*, 3–4.

revision of traditional attitudes. Science and economic change have disrupted the old beliefs. Religions the world over are under the necessity of coming to terms with new conditions created by a vastly increased knowledge and experience. In every field of human activity, the vital movement is now in the direction of a candid and explicit humanism. In order that religious humanism may be better understood we, the undersigned, desire to make certain affirmations which we believe the facts of our contemporary life demonstrate.

There is great danger of a final, and we believe fatal, identification of the word *religion* with doctrines and methods which have lost their significance and which are powerless to solve the problem of human living in the Twentieth Century. Religions have always been means for realizing the highest values of life. Their end has been accomplished through the interpretation of the total environing situation (theology or world view), the sense of values resulting therefrom (goal or ideal), and the technique (cult), established for realizing the satisfactory life. A change in any of these factors results in alteration of the outward forms of religion. This fact explains the changefulness of religions through the centuries. But through all changes religion itself remains constant in its quest for abiding values, an inseparable feature of human life.

Today man's larger understanding of the universe, his scientific achievements, and his deeper appreciation of brotherhood, have created a situation which requires a new statement of the means and purposes of religion. Such a vital, fearless, and frank religion capable of furnishing adequate social goals and personal satisfactions may appear to many people as a complete break with the past. While this age does owe a vast debt to the traditional religions, it is none the less obvious that any religion that can hope to be a synthesizing and dynamic force for today must be shaped for the needs of this age. To establish such a religion is a major necessity of the present. It is a responsibility which rests upon this generation. We therefore affirm the following:

First: Religious humanists regard the universe as self-existing and not created.

Second: Humanism believes that man is a part of nature and that he has emerged as the result of a continuous process.

Third: Holding an organic view of life, humanists find that the traditional dualism of mind and body must be rejected.

Fourth: Humanism recognizes that man's religious culture and civilization, as clearly depicted by anthropology and history, are the product of a gradual development due to his interaction with his natural environment and with his social heritage. The individual born into a particular culture is largely molded by that culture.

Fifth: Humanism asserts that the nature of the universe depicted by modern science makes unacceptable any supernatural or cosmic guarantees of human values. Obviously humanism does not deny the possibility of realities as yet undiscovered, but it does insist that the way to determine the existence and value of any and all realities is by means of intelligent inquiry and by the assessment of their relation to human needs. Religion must formulate its hopes and plans in the light of the scientific spirit and method.

Sixth: We are convinced that the time has passed for theism, deism, modernism, and the several varieties of "new thought."

Seventh: Religion consists of those actions, purposes and experiences which are humanly significant. Nothing human is alien to the religious. It includes labour, art, science, philosophy, love, friendship, recreation—all that is in its degree expressive of intelligently satisfying human living. The distinction between the sacred and the secular can no longer be maintained.

Eighth: Religious humanism considers the complete realization of human personality to be the end of man's life and seeks its development and fulfillment in the here and now. This is the explanation of the humanist's social passion.

Ninth: In place of the old attitudes involved in worship and prayer the humanist finds his religious emotions expressed in a heightened sense of personal life and in a co-operative effort to promote social well-being.

Tenth: It follows that there will be no uniquely religious emotions and attitudes of the kind hitherto associated with belief in the supernatural.

Eleventh: Man will learn to face the crises of life in terms of his knowledge of their naturalness and probability. Reasonable and manly attitudes will be fostered by education and supported by custom. We assume that humanism will take the path of social and mental hygiene and discourage sentimental and unreal hopes and wishful thinking.

Twelfth: Believing that religion must work increasingly for joy in living, religious humanists aim to foster the creative in man and to encourage achievements that add to the satisfactions of life.

Thirteenth: Religious humanism maintains that all associations and institutions exist for the fulfillment of human life. The intelligent evaluation, transformation, control, and direction of such associations and institutions with a view to the enhancement of human life is the purpose and program of humanism. Certainly religious institutions, their ritualistic forms, ecclesiastical methods, and communal activities must be reconstituted as rapidly as experience allows, in order to function effectively in the modern world.

Fourteenth: The humanists are firmly convinced that the existing acquisitive and profit-motivated society has shown itself to be inadequate and that a radical change in methods, controls, and motives must be instituted. A socialized and co-operative economic order must be established to the end that the equitable distribution of the means of life be possible. The goal of humanism is a free and universal society in which people voluntarily and intelligently co-operate for the common good. Humanists demand a shared life in the shared world.

Fifteenth and last: We assert that humanism will: (*a*) affirm life rather than deny it; (*b*) seek to elicit the possibilities of life, not flee from it, and (*c*) endeavor to establish the conditions of a satisfactory life for all, not merely for the few. By this positive *morale* and intention humanism will be guided, and from this perspective and alignment the techniques and efforts of humanism will flow.

So stand the theses of religious humanism. Though we consider the religious forms and ideas of our fathers no longer adequate, the quest for the good life is still the central task for mankind. Man is at last becoming aware that he alone is responsible for the realization of the world of his dreams, that he has within himself the power for its achievement. He must set intelligence and will to the task.

> SOURCE: "A Humanifest Manifesto," *The New Humanist,* VI (May–June, 1933), 1–4. Used by permission of the American Humanist Association, Yellow Springs, Ohio.

LITERATURE

The general background for the spread of radical religious thought is discussed in the following books: Stow Persons, *American Minds: A History of Ideas* (N.Y., 1958); Merle Curti, *The Growth of American Thought* (N.Y., 1943), Chap. 21; and John H. Randall, Jr., *The Making of the Modern Mind* (rev. ed., Boston, 1940), Chap. 20. The stimulation given to freethought tendencies in American life by the new scientific impulses is treated by Sidney Warren, *American Freethought, 1890–1914* (N.Y., 1943). He deals with the Free Religious Association, socialism and freethought, agnosticism, secularism, and atheism. A fine summary treatment of the various manifestations of "The Religion of Humanity" in the last half of the nineteenth century can be found in Ralph H. Gabriel, *The Course of American Democratic Thought* (N.Y., 1940), Chap. 15. The works of Felix Adler are especially significant for understanding the Ethical Culture movement, especially his *Creed and Deed* (N.Y., 1877) and *An Ethical Philosophy of Life* (N.Y., 1918). David S. Muzzey's essay, "The Founding of the Ethical Movement," in his *Ethics as a Religion* (N.Y., 1951), is illuminating. On the religious humanism that emerged aggressively toward the end of the 1865–1930 period, consult such books as: Stow Persons, *Free Religion: An American Faith* (New Haven, 1947); A. Eustace Haydon, *The Quest of the Ages* (N.Y., 1929); Max C. Otto, *Things and Ideals: Essays in Functional Philosophy* (N.Y., 1924); Charles Francis Potter, *Humanism, A New Religion* (N.Y., 1930), and *Humanizing Religion* (N.Y., 1933); and Roy W. Sellars, *Religion Coming of Age* (N.Y., 1928). John Dewey, *A Common Faith* (N.Y., 1934), succinctly summed up this point of view. The response of the churches to religious humanism can be sampled in a symposium edited by William P. King, *Humanism, Another Battle Line* (Nashville, 1931).

A symposium edited by Gerald Birney Smith, *Religious Thought in the Last Quarter-Century* (Chicago, 1927), reflects the impact of contemporary thought on the Christian churches in the first quarter of the twentieth century. The essay by Smith himself, "Theological Thinking in America" (95–115), is particularly useful, pointing to the areas in which scientific methodology had become decisive. The work has rich bibliographical suggestions. Edwin E. Aubrey's *Present Theological Tendencies* (N.Y., 1936) contains much material relevant to a study of modernist and naturalist theology. Frank Hugh Foster, *The Modern Movement in American Theology: Sketches in the History of American Protestant Thought from the Civil War to the World War* (N.Y., 1939), deals both with liberalism and modernism; the chapter on "The Radical School" is especially pertinent to this section. Henry Nelson Wieman and Bernard E. Meland, *American Philosophies of Religion* (N.Y., 1936), document the tendency of radical philosophy of religion to displace systematic theology in the early decades of the twentieth century. George H. Betts, *The Beliefs of 700 Ministers* (N.Y., 1929), gives an indication of how theological thought moved to the left among many ministers and theological students by the 1920's. Typical works that illustrate the spread of modernist thought in the churches are by Edward Scribner Ames, *Religion* (N.Y., 1929), and Shailer Mathews, *The Faith of Modernism* (N.Y., 1924), *The Atonement and the Social Process* (N.Y., 1930), *The Growth of the Idea of God* (N.Y., 1931), and *New Faith for Old: An Autobiography* (N.Y., 1936).

Important for an understanding of the impact of the psychology of religion on religious thought is William James, *The Varieties of Religious Experience: A Study in Human Nature* (N.Y., 1902). There is a good brief introduction to the way James dealt with religious themes in Lewis White Beck's *Six Secular Philosophers* (N.Y., 1960), 92–105. On the psychology of religion see also the pioneer works by James H. Leuba, *A Psychological Study of Religion: Its Origin, Function and Future* (N.Y., 1912), and by Edwin D. Starbuck, *The Psychology of Religion: An Empirical Study of the Growth of Religious Consciousness* (London & N.Y., new edition, 1915).

For the community church movement as an aspect of the religion of culture, see John Haynes Holmes, *New Churches for Old: A Plea for Community Religion* (N.Y., 1922); Elizabeth R. Hooker, *United Churches* (N.Y., 1926); Henry E. Jackson, *A Community Church* (Boston, 1919); and David R. Piper, *Community Churches: The Community Church Movement* (Chicago, 1928).

There is a vast literature on New Thought and the rise of the religious healing movements. The standard work from the New Thought viewpoint is by Horatio W. Dresser, *A History of the New Thought Movement* (N.Y., 1919). In his useful work, *These Also Believe: A Study of Modern American Cults and Minority Religious Movements* (N.Y., 1949), Charles S. Braden has provided three excellent chapters on New Thought, the Unity School of Christianity, and Christian Science (128–220), together with helpful, selected bibliographical references. See also his *Christian Science Today; Power, Policy, Practice* (Dallas, Tex., 1958), a readable and concise introduction from a liberal Protestant viewpoint.

CHAPTER XVII

The Christocentric Liberal Tradition

THE earliest movement of religious liberalism in America emerged from within New England Calvinism. As already indicated in Volume I of the present work, that movement in its philosophical and ethical features stemmed basically from the Enlightenment.[1] Jonathan Mayhew and Charles Chauncy did much to initiate this pattern of thinking, but to William Ellery Channing belongs the credit for giving it classical expression in his historic Baltimore sermon of 1819. From this movement emerged a new Protestant denomination known as American Unitarianism.

Scarcely, however, had the Channing type of liberalism come to full flower, when it was in turn challenged from within by such men as Ralph Waldo Emerson and Theodore Parker. Thus arose a more radical movement known as transcendentalism.[2] Eventually transcendentalism became the prevailing form of Unitarian theology. This involved, among other things, the triumph of Parker's purely humanitarian conception of Jesus, the final result of which was a break with the classical Christological tradition.

Meanwhile, a distinctly evangelical type of liberalism was emerging within Protestantism. The type began with Horace Bushnell and came to full theological maturity by the opening of World War I. The exponents of this pattern of thinking frequently characterized it during the nineteenth century as "the new theology," or "progressive orthodoxy." After the opening of the present century, however, they generally identified it as "liberal Christianity."

These particular liberals were especially aware of a basic Christological difference between their type of thought and that of those left-wing liberals who took a strictly humanitarian view of Jesus. Thus it is highly significant that the leading theologians with whom we are here concerned deliberately endeavored to construct their system of thought in terms of the person and work of Jesus Christ. "A theology which is not Christocentric," said Egbert C. Smyth of Andover Theological Seminary, "is like a Ptolemaic astronomy,—it is out of true relation to the earth and heavens, to God and the universe." [3] This same conviction led William Adams Brown to develop his influential book, *Christian Theology in Outline*, from the Christological standpoint. He revealed his perspective in these words:

[1] *American Christianity*, I (N.Y., 1960), Chaps. 7, 9.   [2] See *supra*, Chap. 14.
[3] Egbert C. Smyth, *et al.*, *Progressive Orthodoxy* (Boston, 1886), 36.

By the Christological principle, then, we mean the effort to trace in the ever-expanding revelation of God in humanity the vitalizing and transforming influence of the historic Jesus, that from our study we may gain new insight into the character and purpose of God from whom he came, and so be able better to understand the meaning of the world in which we live and the end to which we are called. It is the method which arrives at God through Jesus, and uses the knowledge so gained as the final principle for the interpretation of life.[4]

Loyalty to Christ as "the final principle for the interpretation of life" was not, according to Brown and his fellow liberals, incompatible with the constant search for new truth. Indeed, they insisted that theology must come to terms with all aspects of modern knowledge. They therefore (1) accepted the principle of organic evolution; (2) employed the historical-critical method in their study of the Bible; (3) utilized the findings of psychology and sociology; (4) appropriated the insights of modern philosophy, and especially those of philosophical idealism; and (5) recognized vital moral values in a fully socialized democracy.

In the development of their theological thought, American Christocentric liberals were greatly stimulated by such great German scholars as Schleiermacher and Ritschl, and their successors. During this period numerous younger Americans went to Germany for advanced theological study, including Henry B. Smith, Lewis French Stearns, Egbert C. Smyth, Borden Parker Bowne, Arthur C. McGiffert, Henry Churchill King, Walter Rauschenbusch, and William Adams Brown. Inevitably their minds were deeply affected by this stimulating experience. Through them, Ritschlianism became very influential in this country. Yet it would be a mistake to assume that Christocentric liberalism in America was purely Ritschlian. Brown, for example, bore the distinct stamp of the Ritschlian school of thought;[5] still, he was by no means a straight Ritschlian. He was, for example, explicitly critical of Ritschl's one-sided emphasis upon the historical Jesus.[6] Thus while Brown and other American liberals absorbed important elements of Ritschlianism, they combined those elements with many ingredients drawn from their native Christian heritage. The final result, therefore, was a distinctly American type of Christocentric liberalism.

This chapter will seek to clarify the nature of Christocentric or Christian[7] liberalism by outlining its major doctrines. These doctrines center in four areas: (1) the nature or character of God; (2) the origin, nature, and worth

[4] *Christian Theology in Outline* (N.Y., 1906), 77. William Newton Clarke, the other able systematizer of Christian liberalism, was no less Christological than Brown in his theological method. Cf. *An Outline of Christian Theology* (N.Y., 1898), 5–7.

[5] Cf. Brown, *The Essence of Christianity* (N.Y., 1902), Chaps. 7–8.

[6] Brown, *Christ the Vitalizing Principle of Modern Theology* (N.Y., 1898).

[7] The terms "Christocentric" and "Christian" are used interchangeably in the present discussion. Wherever the term "liberal" is used without any qualifying adjective, it should be understood to refer to the Christocentric type of liberalism.

of man; (3) the mission and person of Jesus Christ; and (4) the kingdom of God.

Interestingly, the Christocentric liberals as a group gave relatively little attention to the question of God's existence. This fact becomes evident if one consults the two greatest American works produced in systematic liberal theology: William Newton Clarke's *An Outline of Christian Theology* (1898), and William Adams Brown's *Christian Theology in Outline* (1906). Neither volume, for example, gave much consideration to the old-line "proofs" of the existence of God. The liberal's main accent lay elsewhere. He took God's existence more or less for granted and concerned himself mainly with the question of God's moral attributes. Clarke made this quite clear when he said, "Not that God is, but what God is, is the first point in the Christian doctrine." [8]

Christian liberalism undertook to re-think the character of God in the light of Christ. In the words of Lewis French Stearns, liberalism tried "to Christologize" the nature of the Divine Being.[9] Underlying this approach was the belief that in Jesus Christ, God had fully and finally unveiled himself in his true nature. Acting upon this belief, the Christian liberal characteristically described God as Christlike.[10]

But what precisely did Christian liberals have in mind when they characterized God as being like Christ? Universally they intended to suggest that, above all else, the God of Jesus is paternal in character. "The name which most concisely sums up the Christian conception of God is Father," said Brown. "In the divine Fatherhood Christian faith finds included the power and authority for which absoluteness stands, the kinship which is involved in personality, and the holy and loving character which Christ has revealed." [11]

By attaching decisive importance to the fatherly attribute of God, the Christian liberal was in effect actually qualifying the divine attribute of sovereignty. Principal A. M. Fairbairn, the great British liberal who exercised considerable influence in America during the late nineteenth century, explicitly recognized this fact. Said he, "The primary and determinative conception is the Fatherhood, and so through it the Sovereignty must be read and interpreted." [12] This shift in emphasis becomes especially revealing when one recalls the fact that most of the early Christocentric liberals were Calvinistic in their theological heritage. Central in Calvinism was the doctrine of absolute divine sovereignty. Therefore former Calvinists like

---

[8] *The Christian Doctrine of God* (N.Y., 1909), 56. Clarke postponed the question of God's existence to the very last section of his treatise.

[9] "The Present Direction of Theological Thought in the Congregational Churches of the United States," in Stearns, *Present Day Theology* (N.Y., 1893), 540–1.

[10] Cf. Francis J. McConnell, *The Christlike God* (N.Y., 1927).

[11] *Christian Theology in Outline*, 100. Cf. Henry Churchill King, *Reconstruction in Theology* (N.Y., 1901), 188–90.

[12] *The Place of Christ in Modern Theology* (N.Y., 1893), 444.

Washington Gladden and George A. Gordon became caustic critics of the doctrine of arbitrary election. Gordon, for example, denounced Calvinism as "the ultimate blasphemy of thought." [13] He not only affirmed the primacy of the principle of the divine Fatherhood, but he relentlessly contended that unless the gospel was available to everybody, it was available to nobody. Gordon's fellow liberals solidly agreed with him.

Thus for the Christocentric liberal, faith in the Divine Fatherhood was no minor matter; on the contrary, it was the root of his passionate concern to preach the gospel to the whole world, and to bring all men into fellowship with God.

The God of the Christian liberal was not only paternal in nature, but he was the indwelling spirit of the universe. As Brown observed, God "is not a transcendent being living in a distant heaven whence from time to time he intervenes in the affairs of earth. He is an ever-present spirit guiding all that happens to a wise and holy end." [14]

This belief in the immanence of God was encouraged by many factors. One of the most important was the theory of organic evolution, according to which change was the result of the operation of resident forces. Those liberal theologians who fell deeply under the spell of evolution tended to think of God almost altogether in terms of an inwardly energizing force or spark.[15] A second potent factor was the Romantic movement. The influence of Romanticism was by no means confined to New England transcendentalism. Particularly through Coleridge, it penetrated the theology of Horace Bushnell and that of many other Christian liberals. A third factor was philosophical idealism, and especially that version of it known as personalistic idealism. Under the teaching of Borden Parker Bowne, for example, personalism spread widely in liberal theological circles. It nourished not only belief in God as cosmic person, but also belief in him as the immanent spirit of the world organism.[16]

Some Christian liberals sensed the danger of an extreme form of divine immanence. One of these was William Newton Clarke, who explicitly criticized an immanentism which bordered on pantheism. His theological thought reveals a judicious balance between God as immanent and as transcendent. "Each conception needs the other," said he. "Transcendence without immanence would give us Deism, cold and barren; immanence without transcendence would give us Pantheism, fatalistic and paralyzing. But neither is without the other; the two coexist in God." [17] A similar position

---

[13] The Christ of Today (Boston, 1895), 184. See also The New Epoch for Faith (Boston, 1901), 261-2.

[14] "The Old Theology and the New," Harvard Theological Review, IV (1911), 16.

[15] Cf. Lyman Abbott, The Theology of an Evolutionist (Boston, 1897), 13.

[16] Borden Parker Bowne, The Immanence of God (Boston, 1905); Francis J. McConnell, The Diviner Immanence (N.Y., 1906); Edgar S. Brightman, ed., Personalism in Theology: A Symposium in Honor of Albert Cornelius Knudson (Boston, 1943).

[17] An Outline of Christian Theology, 130. See also The Christian Doctrine of God, 311-43.

was taken by several other distinguished liberal theologians.[18] Yet, despite the influence of such men, the idea of divine immanence became so strong that many liberals were inclined to lose sight of a truly sovereign God.

Let us now consider a second area of special interest to Christian liberalism: the origin, nature, and worth of human personality. In his idea of the origin of man, the Christocentric liberal clashed with both rigid orthodoxy on the right and naturalistic humanism on the left. Contrary to orthodoxy, he accepted the principle of organic evolution as explaining the divine method of creation. He was not concerned to identify the first man, nor was he especially curious as to the exact manner in which man had risen above his strictly animal existence. All such questions he willingly left to the scientific specialist. On the other hand, the Christian liberal absolutely rejected the humanist's contention that man was the product of purely naturalistic forces. Unwaveringly he insisted that man came into being as a result of God's creative action.

Nothing was more characteristic of Christocentric liberal theology than its accent upon the dignity and worth of human personality. Henry Churchill King at the opening of the twentieth century rightly observed that this particular emphasis "might well be called the most notable moral characteristic of our time." [19] The phrase, "reverence for personality," became something of a slogan in liberal Protestant circles. All forms of society were judged finally by their effect upon personality. For example, an industrial system which subordinated personal values to profitmaking was denounced as sub-Christian. Or a political structure which denied equal rights to any person or group was charged with being not only undemocratic but anti-Christian.

The principle of the worth of persons had at least a twofold religious root. One was the belief that man bore in his being the stamp of the eternal, the *imago Dei*. Being thus endowed, man was sacred to God and should therefore be respected by all human beings. The other root stemmed from the life and teaching of Jesus. Jesus, said the Christian liberal, always regarded personality as superior to all other values. Thus all Christians should follow his example.

A third aspect of the Christian liberal's doctrine of man concerned the human situation. Postulating the fact of organic evolution, he abandoned or basically modified the traditional view that sin entered the world through the fall of Adam. "The notion of the fall," said George A. Gordon, "can no longer serve as an account of the source of moral disorder." [20] His fellow liberals were of the same opinion.[21] Nonetheless, they all recognized the

---

[18] See, for example, Stearns, *Present Day Theology,* 206; Brown, *Christian Theology in Outline,* 200, 229.

[19] *Theology and the Social Consciousness* (N.Y., 1902), 16.

[20] *The New Epoch for Faith* (Boston, 1901), 35.

[21] H. Shelton Smith, *Changing Conceptions of Original Sin: A Study in American Theology Since 1750* (N.Y., 1955), Chap. 8.

reality and universality of sin, regardless of how or when it first entered the human race. Generally speaking, they traced its roots not merely to "the first man," but into the remotest depths of organic life from which man emerged.

The Christian liberal was really more concerned with the effects of sin than with its origin in the race. He strongly opposed the traditional view that sin as such could be transferred from one person to another, and consequently he repudiated the orthodox notion of imputed sin and guilt. On the other hand, the most representative Christian liberals firmly believed that the corrupting effects of sin have been carried down the stream of life through biological reproduction.[22] Rauschenbusch, for example, stressed the vast importance of original sin in this revised form. "Depravity of will and corruption of nature," he argued, "are transmitted wherever life itself is transmitted." [23] With equal seriousness Clarke declared, "When sin has once taken hold of the race, the natural reproduction of life becomes reproduction of life morally injured and faulty. With evil once begun, the race is a succession of tainted individuals,—an organism that works toward continuance of evil." [24]

Some of the greatest Christian liberals pointed to the fact that sin has been transmitted by social tradition as well as through biological channels. They were remarkably realistic in showing how sin produced noxious social structures which became almost irresistible by the individual. Thus Bushnell observed "that evil, once beginning to exist, inevitably becomes organic, and constructs a kind of principate or kingdom opposite to God. . . . Pride organizes caste, and dominates in the sphere of fashion. Corrupt opinions, false judgments, bad manners, and a general body of conventionalisms that represent the motherhood of sin, come into vogue and reign. And so, doubtless, everywhere and in all worlds, sin has it in its nature to organize, mount into the ascendant above God and truth, and reign in a kingdom opposite God." [25] Perhaps no one perceived more clearly the corrupting power of "super-personal forces" than did Walter Rauschenbusch. "The permanent vices and crimes of adults," he wrote, "are not transmitted by heredity, but by being socialized. . . . Just as syphilitic corruption is forced on the helpless foetus in its mother's womb, so these hereditary social evils are forced on the individual embedded in the womb of society and drawing his ideas, moral standards, and spiritual ideals from the general life of the social body." [26]

It is evident, therefore, that Christian liberals like Bushnell and Rauschenbusch saw permanent truth in a modified doctrine of original sin.

<hr>

[22] Bushnell, *Nature and the Supernatural* (N.Y., 1858), Chap. 6; Washington Gladden, *How Much Is Left of the Old Doctrines* (Boston, 1900), 121–4; Clarke, *An Outline of Christian Theology*, 239–45; Brown, *Christian Theology in Outline*, 277–81; Walter Rauschenbusch, *A Theology for the Social Gospel* (N.Y., 1917), 57–9.

[23] *A Theology for the Social Gospel*, 58.   [24] *An Outline of Christian Theology*, 242.

[25] *Nature and the Supernatural*, 135.   [26] *A Theology for the Social Gospel*, 60.

In fact, their view of the radical nature of the human predicament derived in part from the conviction that evil inevitably ran down the racial stream through biological reproduction. In addition, they drew special attention to the fact that socialized evil has incalculable power to corrupt the life of mankind.

Yet one reservation must be made here in order to avoid any misunderstanding. With all his accent upon the reality of sin, the Christocentric liberal did not believe in total or absolute depravity. It is well known that Bushnell, for example, resisted Calvinist orthodoxy at this point. Though he firmly denied that children were naturally good at birth, he nevertheless held that those born of truly Christian parents should be expected "to grow up as Christians, or spiritually renewed persons." [27] This doctrine was based on the premise that the child is not so "unnatured" by original sin that he can at first make only bad choices. Bushnell explicitly contended that the child's very first choice could be for the right as well as for the wrong. Moreover, he taught that the good impulses in the child could, in time and under the proper nurture, win "a qualified sovereignty" over the evil impulses.[28] William Newton Clarke took essentially the same position. According to him, there is a "double flow of good and evil in the common stream of life," and every person at birth must struggle with moral crosscurrents in his nature. Even so, the child may, under adequate spiritual nurture, respond to God at the very outset of his existence.[29]

But although the Christian liberal qualified the theory of absolute native depravity, he still recognized man's basic need to be restored to fellowship with God. Furthermore, he saw no hope that such restoration would result from either self-reformation or mere natural development.[30] Instead, there was needed "a power out of nature" to do what man himself was helpless to accomplish. As Bushnell said, "God is what we want, not a man; God revealed through man, that we may see His Heart, and hide our guilty nature in the bosom of His love." [31]

Bushnell's statement introduces us to the third area of basic concern to the Christian liberal: Christology, or the mission and person of Jesus Christ. The liberal's approach to the work of God in Christ will here be summarized in terms of three basic principles. First, Christian liberals as a group denied that Christ came to "placate" or "satisfy" God. Clarke expressed the prevailing view when he declared: "Since God was working in Christ, there was nothing in God for Christ to overcome. It was no part of Christ's work to make God willing." [32] Second, the whole career of Jesus was lived vicariously; therefore, it is artificial to isolate his death as though it had

[27] Smith, *Changing Conceptions of Original Sin*, 142.
[28] *Discourses on Christian Nurture* (N.Y., 1847), 14.
[29] Clarke, *An Outline of Christian Theology*, 242–5.
[30] Bushnell, *Nature and the Supernatural*, Chap. 8.
[31] *God in Christ* (Century ed., N.Y., 1910), 127.
[32] *An Outline of Christian Theology*, 335.

within itself special saving merit. The cross, in reality, is only the culminating event in a series of events, all of which are saving in character. In fact, Jesus did not in the first place come to die; he died as the consequence of living a life wholly committed to doing God's will.[33] Third, Jesus acted directly in his saving work. In other words, he actually recovered men to God rather than established certain conditions under which God later recovered them. "The work of Christ," contended George B. Stevens, "is not a mere provision for man's salvation, or a condition precedent, but an *actual work of salvation,* a real moral recovery of men from sin to goodness." [34]

The implementation of these principles resulted in what was often characterized as the "moral" theory of the atonement. That theory was not entirely subjectivistic in character, and yet it fell short of the objectivism of the Anselmic doctrine of the atonement.[35] In the closing phase of his theological thought, Bushnell endeavored to supplement his earlier doctrine of the atonement so as to give it a more objective character, but other liberals were not impressed with his achievement.

Even if in the final analysis one should find the so-called moral theory of the atonement inadequate, still it must be remembered that the normative Christocentric liberals insisted that Jesus Christ was the indispensable medium of man's restoration to the Father. How, then, did they think of the person of Christ? In his great address on "The Divinity of Christ," given at Yale in 1848, Bushnell contended that Christ "differs from us, not in degree, but in kind." [36] All the leading Christocentric liberals for at least the next half century took substantially the same position.[37] Since, therefore, they postulated the unique divinity of Christ, they naturally took seriously the trinity and the incarnation. Their interpretations varied on certain points, and yet they were much alike.

Bushnell urged his brethren not to speculate about the interior being of God; nonetheless, he violated his own counsel by affirming "the strict personal unity of God." [38] In this way he tried to counteract a tritheistic tendency which had been encouraged by the influential Hopkinsian, Nathanael Emmons (1745–1840). At first Bushnell himself held an "instru-

---

[33] Bushnell, *The Vicarious Sacrifice, Grounded in Principles of Universal Obligation* (N.Y., 1866), 130.

[34] *The Christian Doctrine of Salvation* (N.Y., 1905), 535. Italics in original.

[35] Hastings Rashdall, *The Idea of the Atonement in Christian Theology* (London, 1925), 350–7.

[36] *God in Christ,* 123.

[37] See, for example, Egbert C. Smyth, *et al., Progressive Orthodoxy,* Chap. 2; Smyth, *et al., The Divinity of Jesus Christ* (Boston, 1893); Gordon, *Ultimate Conceptions of Faith* (Boston, 1903), Chap. 7; Stearns, *Present Day Theology,* Chaps. 8–9; Clarke, *An Outline of Christian Theology,* 285–304; George B. Stevens, *The Christian Doctrine of Salvation* (N.Y., 1905), Part III, Chap. 2; and Brown, *Christian Theology in Outline,* Chap. 19.

[38] *God in Christ,* 136.

mental" theory of the trinity, but in his later thinking he apparently came to believe in something approaching an eternal threeness in the very being of God.[39]

The liberal theologians at Andover Seminary also affirmed the real unity of God; still, they suggested that within the Godhead there was an eternal co-working of Father, Son, and Spirit.[40] George A. Gordon took a more daring trinitarian stand than did his Andover contemporaries; indeed, he insisted that God actually constituted "an ineffable society." [41] Clarke held substantially the same view. According to him, God eternally existed "in three modes," each mode being "a centre of conscious life and activity." [42] Stearns tried to stop short of a social trinity; but even so, he too believed that within God there was some kind of "reciprocal communion." [43]

Some Christocentric liberals, however, deplored all such tritheistic theories. Henry Churchill King, for example, sharply condemned this type of trinitarianism.[44] He considered the interior nature of God to be "necessarily hidden from us." [45] William Adams Brown apparently agreed with King. Though appreciating the intent of men like Gordon, he doubted the value of such *a priori* speculation. He, like Bushnell, preferred to approach the trinity in terms of the Christian revelation. The trinity, he explained, "is not a doctrine about God as he is in himself, but concerning God as revealed. It is the summary of the different ways in which one may know God in experience." [46]

One thing is clear from the foregoing analysis: the Christocentric liberals not only believed in the unique divinity of Jesus Christ, but they seriously endeavored to ground that divinity in the ontological being of God.[47]

When the Christian liberal declared that the Word became flesh, he was called upon to consider not merely the nature of the trinity, but also the nature of the incarnation. The latter was as puzzling to him as the former, and the proposed solutions doubtless satisfied very few liberals, to say nothing of the orthodox theologians.

Once again, Bushnell advised against all attempts to fathom the interior

---

[39] *Christ in Theology* (Hartford, Conn., 1851), 145; "The Christian Trinity a Practical Truth," *Building Eras in Religion* (Centenary ed., N.Y., 1910), 133, 147–8; "Our Relations to Christ in the Future Life," *Sermons on Living Subjects* (Centenary ed., N.Y., 1910), 443–52.

[40] Smyth, *et al., The Divinity of Christ*, 190–7.

[41] *The Christ of Today*, 115; *Ultimate Conceptions of Faith*, 382; "Some Things Worth While in Theology," *Harvard Theological Review*, III (1910), 391.

[42] *An Outline of Christian Theology*, 174, 177.   [43] *Present Day Theology*, 200–1.

[44] *Reconstruction in Theology*, 192; *Theology and the Social Consciousness*, 222–3.

[45] *Theology and the Social Consciousness*, 201–4, 223.

[46] *Christian Theology in Outline*, 156.

[47] According to Frank H. Foster (*The Modern Movement in American Theology* [N.Y., 1939], 103), "the liberal theology became largely unitarian" by 1892. However, such evidence as he cited does not really support his claim.

being of the God-man. Nevertheless, he at once undertook to show wherein the traditional two-nature formulation was entirely indefensible.[48] Accordingly he insisted that one must hold relentlessly to the the strict unity of Christ's person. Precisely how the divine and the human were actually united in Jesus remained an impenetrable mystery to Bushnell.[49]

Later Christian liberals also asserted the strict unity of Christ's person, but they concerned themselves more with his humanity than did Bushnell, who admitted that he was not even sure that Christ had a human soul. At first the Andover liberals largely agreed with Bushnell in respect to Christ's humanity. In their view, the human nature into which the Word entered was merely some sort of abstraction, which could become personal "only with, in, and through the Logos." Hence, as they admitted, the personality of Jesus is not at all human, but "falls into the central point of Absolute Personality." [50] Within the next decade, however, the Andover progressives ceased to draw so rigid a line between the divine and the human in Jesus Christ. Instead, they undertook to restate the divinity of Christ in terms of the widely accepted doctrine of divine immanence.[51]

William Newton Clarke developed his theory of the incarnation on the premise that Jesus "was a genuine person," with one consciousness and one will.[52] On the other hand, he held that Jesus' consciousness "was neither that of God nor that of man exclusively, but was that of the unique God-man who was constituted by the Incarnation." [53] That consciousness, however, was at first "certainly human," and even entailed the limitations of a child; only later in life, after much maturing, did Jesus become conscious that "he was related to God as others were not." [54] Here Clarke was clearly reflecting the Kenotic interpretation of the incarnation.

William Adams Brown did not care for Clarke's idea that Jesus began as human and ended as divine. He dismissed the notion of two distinct natures in Jesus, and considered him in terms of a single person, who, though fully human, enjoyed perfect fellowship with the Father.[55]

These efforts to rationalize the incarnation were, as already indicated, far from satisfying. Underlying them, however, was a fundamental conviction that Jesus was the truly unique Son of God, not simply the man of Nazareth.

The fourth and final area of major interest to Christocentric liberals was that of the kingdom of God. Their concern with the concept of the kingdom derived from a twofold faith. The first was the belief that the idea of the kingdom of God, as revealed in the life and teaching of Jesus, was the best category through which to express the Christian pattern of a truly redeemed community of persons. The second was the belief that

---

[48] *God in Christ*, 148–55.   [49] *Ibid.*, 161–4.
[50] Smyth, *et al., Progressive Orthodoxy*, 29–30.
[51] Smyth, *et al., The Divinity of Christ*, Chap. 7.
[52] *An Outline of Christian Theoloy*, 297.   [53] *Ibid.*, 298.   [54] *Ibid.*, 298–9.
[55] *Christian Theology in Outline*, 343–52.

Jesus' idea of the kingdom of God was the only adequate category through which to interpret the Christian goal of history. This twofold conception of the kingdom was succinctly articulated by Brown at the opening of the present century. "By the kingdom of God," said he, "we mean that society of redeemed personalities, of which Christ is at once the ideal and the mediator, the union of whose members, one with another and with God in the community of holy love, progressively realized in history, constitutes the end for which the world exists." [56]

The content of Brown's lucid statement requires no detailed elaboration here, but three of the more basic elements deserve summary accent. First of all, the kingdom of God was a present social reality, not something lying wholly in the future, and Jesus Christ was both its abiding norm and its living mediator. Second, the kingdom of God epitomized the all-embracing goal of history. Third, the kingdom of God was to be progressively actualized in the world. Christocentric liberals as a group wholeheartedly endorsed this threefold emphasis. This meant, among other things, that they necessarily interpreted the gospel in terms of its social thrust. Brown therefore spoke representatively when he said, "An unsocial Christianity is a contradiction in terms." [57]

This completes our brief survey. It clearly indicates that the Christological principle was absolutely indispensable to the shaping of the most characteristic patterns of Christocentric liberal theology. The impact of this movement of thought was by no means insignificant. By the advent of the twentieth century, Christian liberalism had in fact become the prevailing mode of thought in many of the greatest Protestant theological seminaries in America.

135. God's Design in History

One of the first American Christocentric liberals to incorporate the principle of evolution in a Christian philosophy of history was Newman Smyth (1843–1925). In his *Old Faiths in New Light* (1879) Smyth accepted the idea of evolution, but argued that the direction of evolution was determined by the incarnation. Making extensive use of the findings of modern biblical criticism, he described the historical process by which God had crowned the morally progressive series of biblical events with his own absolute self-revelation in Jesus Christ, the Word made flesh. The Christ who came preaching the gospel of the kingdom was more than human; he "ushered in a still higher reign than the age of man." In reality he embodied the New Humanity, the ideal of all true humanity.

Although Smyth's doctrine was generally optimistic, that optimism was not based upon naturalistic principles but upon God's sovereign direction

---

[56] *Christian Theology in Outline*, 182–3.   [57] *Ibid.*, 193.

of history. Furthermore, the kingdom of God was not to be completed in the present world order but only in a new creation after the resurrection. "We [always] live broken lives in an unfinished world," said Smyth.[58]

After taking his A.B. at Bowdoin College in 1863, Smyth enlisted in the Union army and served until the end of the Civil War. On being mustered out at Appomattox Court House, he entered Andover Theological Seminary, where Edwards A. Park was the dominant theological mind. Park's "orthodox rationalism" repelled him, for he was already veering away from New England Calvinism. Later study with Isaac A. Dorner at the University of Berlin completed his theological emancipation.[59]

When Andover Seminary entered upon its liberal era, Smyth was invited by the trustees to take the chair vacated by Park, but forces sympathetic to Park's type of orthodoxy frustrated the move.[60] Consequently the promising young theologian continued in the parish ministry, his greatest pastorate being First (Center) Congregational Church in New Haven, where he served from 1882 to 1907. Despite the demands of a large flock, he carried on scholarly research and wrote many influential books, among them *Through Science to Faith* (1902), and *Constructive Natural Theology* (1913).

The following document is reproduced from *Old Faiths in New Light*, and constitutes the author's final summation.

DOCUMENT

It remains for us now to gather up in one general conclusion the separate lines of our reasoning. We began by accepting loyally the results of scientific research into the present constitution of things. We trust our senses, and the logic of the senses, just so far as the human understanding can work out a positive science. We admit that the course of visible nature can be best summed up in some general law of evolution. We do not question, and have no moral interest in questioning, a physical evolution, and a mechanism coextensive with the bounds of nature, so far as by such conceptions the sum total of our scientific knowledge can be at present expressed to the best advantage. But ours is by birthright the duty, also, of subjecting visible nature to the interpretation of the spirit, and of reading the formulas of things in the light of our own moral ideas. The science whose source is within us, can never yield to any sciences whose sources are in the world without us. Perfect knowledge must be the harmony of both. Our objection to evolution is not that it may not be true; but that, if proved true, it is only a half-truth. We dare not put a part for the whole; we refuse to measure the possibilities of the universe by the diameter of the

---

[58] *Old Faiths in New Light* (N.Y., 1879), 290.
[59] Smyth, *Recollections and Reflections* (N.Y., 1926), 87.
[60] William J. Tucker, *My Generation* (Boston, 1919), 105-20.

little circle of our knowledge. Besides the curve of the earth which we can measure, there is the immeasurable sweep of the sky above us. A philosophy worthy of the name must admit both sciences—the science of the natural, and the science of the spiritual which transcends nature,—or its conclusions will be only half-truths. Physical evolution finds its complement only in a higher truth. The one thought of the Creator is expressed in two parts of speech, a noun and a verb; matter and mind, body and soul, nature and the supernatural, are the two parts, the noun and the verb, of the one creative word. But the prevalent evolutionary philosophy is a grammar simply of the noun to the neglect of the verb. It is a science only of one part of the creative speech; it goes off exultingly with the substantive, and leaves metaphysics to learn, if it can, what is really affirmed of it. It takes nature as the only part of the divine speech worth knowing, and separates it from all the affirmations of our consciousness. But we cannot so easily and so arbitrarily construe the Creator's thought. It may be difficult to see how in some points the noun and the verb agree; how together they make one intelligible meaning; but no difficulty in our earthly grammar can warrant us in giving up one iota of the sentence set before us for our study; and if we should, it would be easier to sacrifice matter to spirit, than spirit to matter. But we hold fast to both noun and verb; to the great generic substantive without us—the world that is made, and which stands for something; and also to that which is affirmed within us—thought, will, love.

Wherever mechanism can be found, even within the domain of life, we are ready to receive the proofs of it.[61] But mechanism explains nothing, not even its own motion. We have given in the preceding chapters evidences of the presence and working of something which is without the mechanism of things, and whose energy cannot be reduced to any physical equivalents. We noticed the historical growth of a revelation, which it is difficult to account for as a spontaneous generation of nature. We traced the processes of the manifestation of a divine life with man. We have seen in the development of a progressive revelation the evolution of a power greater than natural forces, and working out its benign results according to a higher law. The natural evolution of the Semitic stock does not contain the whole development of the history of Israel. We then beheld standing among men, one whose generation no natural science can declare, whose Person is a wonder, and whose life is a miracle, if this world and the powers of this world are all of the universe; but whose advent is hardly a surprise, and whose work is a unity, if we view it in relation to a divine order, and as the culmination of a supernatural evolution of nature. We beheld in that consummation of the creation the beginning of a new reign higher than the

---

[61] The burden of proof is really on the side of materialism. Consciousness holds everything to be like itself, until it is proved to be different. Everything is spiritual until shown to be material. [Smyth]

dynasty of man, the ushering in of a new kingdom of a constitution beyond the earthly which it shall supersede, even the kingdom of heaven. We have listened to the prophecies of the final glory of that kingdom, and find in them the worthy end and consummation of the whole divine process, or supernatural evolution, of the creation—of nature, life, and human history. So far as we can read from the face of this present world the story of its own past, and the probabilities of its future, we learn that it has not always been, and that it cannot last forever. We discover in the present visible nature the signs that it is but a part and moment of a diviner whole. The seen cannot be, as we have repeatedly said, the demonstration of the Unseen; but the more we learn of nature, the more confidence we may have in the spirit's affirmations of faith. We have seen that this world is unfinished, and this apparent or visible nature incomplete—its evolution a contradiction and destruction of itself—unless we believe that it is continuous with a supernatural realm, and a preparation for that which is perfect, which is to come.

This conclusion will at once be subjected by many to the reproach of dualism, and it will be said that evolution excludes the supposition of a twofold development of the creation. But, as matter of fact, we find a twofoldness in experience which we may hide from ourselves for the moment under some mask of words, but which we cannot obliterate so long as we are thinking men. We do not make, we simply recognize, the dualism which exists in the constitution of nature. There are two kinds of force, two lines of law, two orders of development, two processes of evolution,—body and mind, nature and spirit, earth and heaven. We secure only a fictitious unity when we ignore either kind of being, or seek to reduce either to the terms of the other. The desire to reduce the universe to a unit, is the *ignis fatuus* of much positive science. It lures rash scientific speculation into extremes of folly. Haeckel's boastful monism, for example, or claim that he has reduced all things in heaven and earth to one kind of protoplasmic matter, involves the double absurdity of asking the human mind to commit suicide, and also of attempting to bring nature into subjection by beating the very breath of life out of it. Science, then, would have to perform the office of undertaker to a dead world. Nature, however, is not a mere collection of specimens preserved for our dissection; and philosophy still has a higher task to fulfil than to keep the doors of a museum-world. There is an "inner life of things," and a unity of the spirit in the creation. We have followed, in our discussion, the course of a twofold development, and found in nature and history repeated and manifold signs of a double evolution—a supernatural as well as natural law, and order, and growth;—but the two are one in their origin, their aim, and their end. The supernatural evolution, whose signs and evidences we cannot deny, is not a work of spiritual power against nature; rather we have conceived of it throughout as a *connatural* evolution—a development with nature, and through nature, of something which is more than nature; the result or goal of which is a new nature, the second nature, the glorified creation, the new heaven, and new earth of the Scriptures. The unity is real, the dualism which we observe apparent. The dualism exists in time, and to our finite intelligence; the unity is in eternity, and to the mind of the Omniscient. A monistic theory is conceivable only when we bring in the idea of the living God as the everywhere present Spirit, and eternal unity of the creation. The oneness of all things amid infinite diversity is a truth of the Spirit. All the sciences seek for this unity, but religion alone finds it. When Comte proposed as the end of positive science the reduction of all phenomena to one law, he really brought back again the banished age of theology. The one comprehensive formula for all existing things is—God. By Him all things consist. The unity of the creation is a truth of the Godhead. The science of the senses may knock in vain for this truth to be opened to it, but the poet finds it revealed wherever he looks. It is not a lesson of biology, but a truth of life disclosed to the living soul. He who possesses what Wordsworth called "the first great gift, a vital soul," who has "the feeling intellect, reason in her most exalted mood," becomes the true seer, the interpreter of the thought of God hidden in nature's heart. The divine secret of existence which the logic of Mr. Mill could not break open, which the science of the Royal Academy cannot torture to confess itself in its laboratory, is the truth pervading all things, which the feeling intellect of Wordsworth discerned, and the sense and the mystery of it made him the great poet of nature's spiritual aspects and prophetic moods. To the poet's vital soul nature wore an expression of divinity on her very face.

> "The unfettered clouds and region of the heavens;
> Tumult and peace, the darkness and the light;
> Were all the workings of one mind, the features
> Of the same face, blossoms upon one tree;
> Characters of the great Apocalypse
> The types and symbols of Eternity,
> Of first, and last, and midst, and without end."

We need never hesitate, therefore, to bring old faiths into new light. Our spiritual life can suffer and grow pale only if we shut it out from the increasing light, and leave it to grow in the darkness. The clear shining of knowledge may dissipate a thousand fancies which we have mistaken for realities; but it shall bring to faith health, and vigor, and renewed life. While many run to and fro, and knowledge is increased, Christianity cannot be preserved as a cloistered virtue, or a scholastic art; but out in the breezy world, under the open sky, rejoicing in the light, its strength shall not be abated, nor its eye grow dim. Reverently and humbly, but nothing doubting, the Christian apologist of today may follow wherever new paths of knowledge seem opening to our approach; and though he goes down into the depths, or wanders through realms of strange shadows, and endless confusions, nevertheless, after he has traversed all the spheres into which thought can find entrance, if he remains true to the spirit sent for his guidance, his better self,—like Dante following Beatrice from world to world—he shall find himself at last by the gates of Paradise, walking in a cloud of light, full of all melodious voices.

SOURCE: Newman Smyth, Old Faiths in New Light (2nd ed., N.Y., 1879), 383-91.

136. Christ, the Moral Power of God

Christocentric liberals reacted sharply against traditional ideas of the work of Christ, and the American theologian who formulated the view which was to win increasing favor was Horace Bushnell (1802-76). In the year 1848 he advocated what he then called a subjective-objective view of the atonement.[62] The principal end of Christ's work, he maintained, was to renovate man's character and restore him to fellowship with God. The renovating event, Bushnell admitted, was entirely subjective, but he contended that by using the biblical "altar forms" that event could be outwardly dramatized and thus be enhanced in its personal effect. This was the import, he said, of the Jewish ritualistic sacrifices. Bushnell was careful to warn that nothing in his theory assumed that God had to be appeased or placated.

The new doctrine raised an uproar among Bushnell's Congregational brethren, and for many years he was the center of heated controversy.[63] Undaunted, he vigorously reasserted his views in *The Vicarious Sacrifice* (1866), although he let the term subjective-objective fall into the background of the discussion.

Shortly before his death, "the unexpected arrival of fresh light" led the author to publish *Forgiveness and Law* (1874) as a substitute for Parts III and IV of *The Vicarious Sacrifice*. Though still immovably insisting that Christ's main role was to renovate character, he now conceded that propitiation was a necessary factor in releasing the forgiving nature of the Father. Even so, all punitive elements were still renounced. This phase of Bushnell's thought has been largely ignored. It was the doctrine as set forth in *The Vicarious Sacrifice* which prevailed in later Christian liberalism, and therefore the document is reproduced from that work.

Following his graduation from Yale Divinity School, where he revolted against Nathaniel Taylor's speculative orthodoxy, Bushnell in 1833 was called to the North Church (Congregational) in Hartford, Connecticut. Declining health led him to retire from that church in 1859. Though an unusually able preacher, he was most distinguished for his writing. His

---

[62] *God in Christ* (Centenary ed., N.Y., 1910), 185-275.
[63] Bushnell, *Christ in Theology* (Hartford, Conn., 1851), 212-348.

published works included, in addition to those already mentioned, *Christian Nurture* (1847–61), *Nature and the Supernatural* (1858), *Sermons on Christ and His Salvation* (1864), and *Sermons on Living Subjects* (1872).

DOCUMENT

The healings of Christ in bodies, we have just seen, are in fact an outward type of the more radical and sublime cure he undertakes, by his sacrifice, to work in fallen character. In this cure, we have the principal aim and object of his mission. We may sum up thus all that he taught, and did, and suffered, in the industry of his life and the pangs of his cross, and say that the one, comprehensive, all-inclusive aim, that draws him on, is the change he will operate in the spiritual habit and future well-being of souls. In this fact it is, and only in this, that he becomes a Redeemer. He is here in vicarious sacrifice, not for something else, but for this. . . .

It is very commonly assumed that Christ is here for another and different main object; viz., to suffer before God's justice, and prepare, in the satisfying of that, a way of possible forgiveness for men. From this I must dissent, though without proposing here any controversy, farther than may be implied in the maintenance and due illustration of my proposition above stated. What was necessary to be done for the preparation of forgiveness will be considered, at a more advanced stage of the discussion. I only say, for the present, that this is no principal matter in his work, the principal matter being to inaugurate a grand, restorative, new-creating movement on character—the reconciliation, that is, of men to God. The other, the preparation of forgiveness, take what view of it we may, unless we make forgiveness the same thing as reconciliation, can be only a secondary and subordinate matter, the principal work and wonder of all being what Christ undertakes and is able to do, in the bad mind's healing and recovery to God.

That some very great and wonderful change, or recasting of soul is, in some way, necessary—as well as to provide the forgiveness of sins—is generally admitted and asserted with abundant emphasis; but it is not as generally perceived that Christ has any particular agency in it. It is not denied that his teachings have great value, or that what is called his expiatory suffering for sin is effective in a degree, on men's feeling, as well as efficacious in the satisfaction of justice; and it is continually put to his credit, in this same suffering and satisfaction, that he has purchased the Holy Spirit, and sends him forth to work the needed change in souls. In this way, some compensation is made for the loss that accrues by a failure to conceive the immediate and really immense agency of Christ in such changes; still there is a loss. No conception of Christ really meets the true significance of his mission, that does not find him working centrally in the great Soul-Healing himself; related presently to it, in all the matter of his suffering and sacrifice. It is not his simply to forgive, or obtain the forgiveness of sin, in the lowest and most nearly negative sense of remission; his great and vastly more significant endeavor is, to make the sin itself let go of the sinner, and so deliver him inwardly that he shall be clear of it. And to accomplish this requires an almost recomposition of the man; the removal of all his breakage, and disorder, and derangement, and the crystalization over again, if I may so speak, of all his shattered affinities, in God's own harmony and law. And, in order to this result, whatever agencies beside concur in it, three things, included in the sacrifice and suffering of Jesus, appear to be specially needed.

1. There is a want of something done, or shown, to preëngage the feeling, or raise a favoring prejudice in it; so that, when advance is made, on God's part, in a call to repentance, the subject may not be repelled, but drawn rather. Otherwise it is like to be as it was in the garden, when the culprit hearing God calling after him, fled and hid himself. No bad soul likes to meet the Holy one, but recoils painfully, shivers with dread, and turns away. But the foremost thing we see in Christ is not the infinite holiness, or sovereign purity; he takes us, first, on the side of our natural feeling; showing his compassions there, passing before us visaged in sorrow, groaning in distressful concern for us, dying even the bitterest conceivable death, because the love he bears to us can not let go of us. In a word we see him entered so deeply into our lot, that we are softened and drawn by him, and even begin to want him entered more deeply, that we may feel him more constrainingly. In this way a great point is turned in our recovery. Our heart is engaged before it is broken. We like the Friend before we love the Saviour.

2. It is another point of consequence, in the matter of our recovery, that we have some better, more tender, and so more piercing, conviction of sin, than we get from our natural remorse, or even from the rugged and blunt sentence of law. It is well, indeed, to be shot through with fiery bolts from Sinai, but these hard, dry wounds, these lacerations of truth, want searching and wounding over again, by the gentle surgery of love, before we are in a way to be healed. In this more subduing, and more nearly irresistible convincing, we have, in part, the peculiar efficacy of the cross. We look on him whom we have pierced, and are pierced ourselves. Through the mighty bosom struggle of the agony and death, we look down, softened, into the bosom wars and woes Christ pities and dies for in us. And when we hear him say—"Of sin because ye believe not on me"—we are not chilled, or repelled, as by the icy baptism of fear and remorse, but we welcome the pain. As Simeon himself declared, "he is set for the fall," as well as "for the rising again"; and we even bless the fall that so tenderly prepares the rising.

In this manner it was, that the conversion of Paul began at the point of that piercing word—"I am Jesus of Nazareth, whom thou persecutest."

Penetrated and felled by that arrow of the divine love, his "exceedingly mad" feeling dies, and his resistance, from that moment, is gone.

3. There greatly needs to be, and therefore, in Christ, is given, a type of the new feeling and life to be restored. Abstract descriptions given of holiness or holy virtue, do not signify much to those who never knew them inwardly by their effects. To conceive a really divine character by specification, or receive it by inventory is, in fact, impossible. No language can give the specification, and no mind could take the meaning of it accurately, if it were given. Hence the necessity that we have some exposition that is practical and personal. We want no theologic definition of God's perfections; but we want a friend, whom we can feel as a man, and whom it will be sufficiently accurate for us to accept and love. Let him come so nigh, if possible, let him be so deeply inserted into our lot and our feeling, that we can bury ourselves in him and the fortunes of his burdened life, and then it will be wonderful, if having God's own type in his life, we do not catch the true impress from it in ourselves.

In these three points, we perceive, that the suffering life and death of Jesus are the appropriate and even necessary equipment of his doing force, in what he undertakes for character. . . .

A great power then is wanted, which can pierce, and press, and draw, and sway, and, as it were, new crystalize the soul, which still is not any kind of force. And considering what the change is which the Scripture itself proposes, we even look to see some different, higher kind of power brought into the field, and magnified as the hope of our salvation. In Christ, accordingly, we find this higher power so magnified—a power that we may call the Moral Power of God. . . .

Is it then that Christ is to be such a kind of power as we mean when we speak of example? Certainly not, if we take the word example, in its most proper and common signification. An example, we conceive, is a model that we copy, and set ourselves, by our own will, to reproduce in ourselves. Many teachers have been rising up, in all the past ages, and propounding it as the true theory of the gospel, that Christ came forth to be a Redeemer, in the way of being an example. But no theory of the kind has ever been able, under the very meager and restricted word example, to get any show of general acceptance. For the truth is that we consciously want something better than a model to be copied; some vehicle of God to the soul, that is able to copy God into it. Something is wanted that shall go before and beget, in us, the disposition to copy an example.

Sometimes the example theory has been stated broadly enough to include the demonstration of the divine love in Christ's life. Sometimes, also, this demonstration of the divine love, apart from any thing said of example, has been put forward as the object of his mission; love being regarded as the sufficient reconciling power of God on human character. But no such view has ever gained a wide acceptance; not for the reason, I must think, that God's love is not a great power on the feeling of mankind, or that, when it is revealed in Christ, it does not go far to make up the requisite power; but that consciously we need other and sturdier elements to produce impressions, equal to the change proposed in our spiritual transformation. Mere love, as we commonly conceive the word, suffers disrespect. We need somehow to feel that the love is a principled love, grounded in immovable convictions of right. There is no so very intense power in love, when descending even to the greatest possible sacrifice, if we are allowed to think of it as being only a mood of natural softness, or merely instinctive sympathy. Many animals will rush after one of their kind in distress, and pitch themselves into the toils of their captors, by mere sympathy of kind. To magnify love therefore, even the love of the cross, as being itself the new-creating power of God, would be a very great mistake, if the righteous rule of God is not somehow included. When Jesus in his sacrifice takes our lot upon his feeling, and goes even to the cross for us, we need also to conceive that he does this for the right, and because the everlasting word of righteousness commands him. Not all that belongs to this matter can be said as effectively here as it may be, when we come, in the Third Part, to consider the relations of the sacrifice to law. So much is added here only to fasten, or sufficiently affirm, the conviction, that no purely favoring, sympathetic kind of intervention, however self-sacrificing, can be any sufficient power on character to be a salvation.

By the moral power of God, or of Christ as the manifested reality of God, we understand, comprehensively the power of all God's moral perfections, in one word, of his greatness. And by greatness we mean greatness of character; for there is no greatness in force, no greatness in quantity, or height, or antiquity of being, no greatness any where but in character. In this it is that so great moral power is conceived to be developed, in the self-devoting sacrifice of Christ's life and death. . . .

I have only to add, as a considerable argument for the moral view of Christ and his sacrifice, in distinction from all others, that the time of his coming coincides with this only. Had he come, having it for his principal object to satisfy God's justice and be substituted, in that manner, for the release of transgression, there appears to be no reason why he should have delayed his coming for so many ages. If the effect was to be on God, God was just as capable, at the very first, of feeling the worth of his sacrifice, as at any time afterward; and, if this was to be the salvation, why should the salvation be delayed? But if he came to be the moral power of God on men, nothing is so difficult as the due development of any such moral power; because the capacity, or necessary receptivity for it, has itself to be prepared. Thus, if Christ had come to the monster age before the flood, when raw force was every thing, and moral greatness nothing, his death and passion, all the significance of his suffering and sacrifice, would have been lost, and probably would not even have been preserved in the remembrance of history. The world was too coarse, and too deep in the force-principle of violence, to apprehend a visitation so thoughtful and deep in the merit of character. There was no room or receptivity, as yet, for Christ in the world. A long drawn scheme of economy is previously needed, to prepare that receptivity; a drill of outward sacrifice and ceremony, a providential milling of captivities, deliverances, wars, plagues, and other public judgments; commemorated in hymns, interpreted and set home by the preaching of a prophet ministry; till finally there is a culture of mind, or of moral perception produced, that is sufficiently advanced, to receive the meaning of Christ in his sacrifice, and allow him to get an accepted place in the moral impressions of mankind. Conceiving, in this manner, that he came to be the moral power of God on character, there is good and sufficient reason for his delay. He came as soon as he could, or, as the Scripture says, "in the fullness of time"; came in fact, at the very earliest moment, when it was possible to get hold of history.

Indeed, so very slow is the world in getting ready for the due impression of what lies in moral power, that only a very partial opening to it is prepared even now. The world is still too coarse, too deep in sense and the force-principle, to feel, in any but a very small degree, the moral power of God in the Christian history. Slowly and sluggishly this higher sense is unfolding, but there is a perceptible advance, and we may anticipate the day, when there will be a sense opened wide enough for Christ, in his true power, to enter; thus to fill, and new-create in good, all souls that live. Then, and not till then, will it be known how grand a fact the moral power of God in the person of his Son may be.

> SOURCE: Horace Bushnell, *The Vicarious Sacrifice, Grounded in Principles of Universal Obligation* (N.Y., 1866), 151–6, 169–72, 182–4.

137. Barriers to the Scriptures

The liberal scholar employed the historical-critical method in biblical study, but the traditionalist denounced that method as an enemy of Christian faith. These conflicting views led to numerous controversies during the latter half of the nineteenth century. One of the most exciting was generated by the inaugural address of Charles A. Briggs (1841–1913), given when he was inducted into the newly created Edward Robinson Professorship of Biblical Theology in Union Theological Seminary (New York). Briggs defended modern biblical scholarship and vigorously condemned the "inerrancy dogma" of Protestant orthodoxy. The heart of his address is reproduced in the document here presented.

As a result of the uproar, Briggs was suspended from the Presbyterian ministry, and Union withdrew from the jurisdiction of the Presbyterian

Church.[64] Briggs of course continued his services at Union, where he had been a member of the faculty since 1876. Prior to his appointment to the Robinson Chair, he taught Hebrew and cognate languages.

That Briggs should have raised a controversial storm is surprising, since his own theological views were, on the whole, remarkably conservative. In his Christology, for example, he was completely loyal to the Chalcedonian tradition.[65] Perhaps it was Briggs's caustic style more than the actual substance of his views which provoked the reaction.

DOCUMENT

The Bible is the book of God, the greatest treasure of the Church. Its ministry are messengers to preach the Word of God, and to invite men to His presence and government. It is pharisaic to obstruct their way by any fences or stumbling-blocks whatever. It is a sin against the divine majesty to prop up divine authority by human authority, however great or extensive. . . . And yet this is the way men have been dealing with the Bible, shutting out the light of God, obstructing the life of God, and fencing in the authority of God.

(1.) *Superstition.*—The first barrier that obstructs the way to the Bible is *superstition*. We are accustomed to attach superstition to the Roman Catholic Mariolatry, Hagiolatry, and the use of images and pictures and other external things in worship. But superstition is no less superstition if it take the form of *Bibliolatry*. It may be all the worse if it concentrate itself on this one thing. But the Bible has no magical virtue in it, and there is no halo enclosing it. It will not stop a bullet any better than a mass-book. It will not keep off evil spirits any better than a cross. It will not guard a home from fire half so well as holy water. If you desire to know when and how you should take a journey, you will find a safer guide in an almanac or a daily newspaper. The Bible is no better than hydromancy or witchcraft, if we seek for divine guidance by the chance opening of the Book. The Bible, as a book, is paper, print, and binding,—nothing more. It is entitled to reverent handling for the sake of its holy contents, because it contains the divine word of redemption for man, and not for any other reason whatever.

(2.) *Verbal Inspiration.*—The second barrier, keeping men from the Bible, is the dogma of *verbal inspiration*. The Bible in use in our churches and homes is an English Bible. Upon the English Bible our religious life is founded. But the English Bible is a translation from Hebrew, Aramaic, and Greek originals. It is claimed for these originals by modern dogmaticians that they are verbally inspired. No such claim is found in the Bible itself, or in any of the creeds of Christendom. And yet it has been urged by the

[64] Lefferts A. Loetscher, "C. A. Briggs in the Retrospect of Half a Century," *Theology Today*, XII (1955), 27–42. See also Loetscher, *The Broadening Church: A Study of Theological Issues in the Presbyterian Church Since 1869* (Phila., 1954), 48–62.

[65] Charles A. Briggs, "The Christ of the Church," *American Journal of Theology*, XVI (1912), 196–217.

common opinion of modern evangelicalism that there can be no inspiration without *verbal inspiration*. But a study of the original languages of the Bible finds that they are languages admirably fitted by divine Providence for their purpose, but still, languages developing in the same way essentially as other human languages. The text of the Bible, in which these languages have been handed down, has shared the fortunes of other texts of other literature. . . .

(3.) *Authenticity.*—The third barrier is the *authenticity of the Scriptures*. The only authenticity we are concerned about in seeking for the divine authority of the Scriptures is *divine authenticity,* and yet many theologians have insisted that we must prove that the Scriptures were written by or under the superintendence of prophets and apostles. Refusing to build on the authority of the living Church, they have sought an authority in the dead Church; abandoning the authority of institutional Christianity, they have sought a prop in floating traditions. These traditions assign authors to all the books of the Bible, and on the authority of these human authors, it is claimed that the Bible is divine. . . . It is just here that the Higher Criticism has proved such a terror in our times. Traditionalists are crying out that it is destroying the Bible, because it is exposing their fallacies and follies. It may be regarded as the certain result of the science of the Higher Criticism that Moses did not write the Pentateuch or Job; Ezra did not write the Chronicles, Ezra, or Nehemiah; Jeremiah did not write the Kings or Lamentations; David did not write the Psalter, but only a few of the Psalms; Solomon did not write the Song of Songs or Ecclesiastes, and only a portion of the Proverbs; Isaiah did not write half of the book that bears his name. The great mass of the Old Testament was written by authors whose names or connection with their writings are lost in oblivion. If this is destroying the Bible, the Bible is destroyed already. But who tells us that these traditional names were the authors of the Bible? The Bible itself? The creeds of the Church? Any reliable historical testimony? None of these! Pure, conjectural tradition! . . . It will ere long become clear to the Christian people that the Higher Criticism has rendered an inestimable service to this generation and to the generations to come. What has been destroyed has been the fallacies and conceits of theologians; the obstructions that have barred the way of literary men from the Bible. Higher Criticism has forced its way into the Bible itself and brought us face to face with the holy contents, so that we may see and know whether they are divine or not. . . .

(4.) *Inerrancy.*—The fourth barrier set up by theologians to keep men away from the Bible is the dogma of the inerrancy of Scripture. This barrier confronts Historical Criticism. It is not a pleasant task to point out errors in the sacred Scriptures. Nevertheless Historical Criticism finds them, and we must meet the issue whether they destroy the authority of the Bible or not. It has been taught in recent years, and is still taught by some theologians, that one proved error destroys the authority of Scripture. I shall venture to affirm that, so far as I can see, there are errors in the Scriptures that no one has been able to explain away; and the theory that they were not in the original text is sheer assumption, upon which no mind can rest with certainty. If such errors destroy the authority of the Bible, it is already destroyed for historians. Men cannot shut their eyes to truth and fact. But on what authority do these theologians drive men from the Bible by this theory of inerrancy? The Bible itself nowhere makes this claim. The creeds of the Church nowhere sanction it. It is a ghost of modern evangelicalism to frighten children. The Bible has maintained its authority with the best scholars of our time, who with open minds have been willing to recognize any error that might be pointed out by Historical Criticism. . . .

(5.) *Violation of the Laws of Nature.*—The fifth obstruction to the Bible has been thrown up in front of modern science. It is the claim that the *miracles* disturb, or violate, the laws of nature and the harmony of the universe; and so the miracles of the Bible have become to men of science sufficient evidence that the Bible is no more than other sacred books of other religions. But the theories of miracles that have been taught in the Christian Church are human inventions for which the Scriptures and the Church have no responsibility whatever. . . .

The miracles of the Bible were the work of God either by direct divine energy or mediately through holy men, energized to perform them; but there is no reason why we should claim that they in any way violate the laws of nature or disturb its harmonies. We ought not to be disturbed by the efforts of scholars to explain them under the forms of divine law, in accordance with the order of nature. . . .

(6.) *Minute Prediction.*—Another barrier to the Bible has been the interpretation put upon *Predictive Prophecy,* making it a sort of history before the time, and looking anxiously for the fulfilment of the details of Biblical prediction. Kuenen has shown that if we insist upon the fulfilment of the details of the predictive prophecy of the Old Testament, many of these predictions have been reversed by history; and the great body of the Messianic prediction has not only never been fulfilled, but cannot now be fulfilled, for the reason that its own time has passed forever. . . .

We have passed through these barriers that men have thrown up in front of the Word of God, the breastworks against Philosophy, History, and Science. It is not surprising that multitudes of the best men of our age have rejected a Bible thus guarded and defended, as if it could not sustain the light of day. Doubtless there are many who are thinking that the critics are destroying the Bible. They have so identified these outworks with the Bible itself that *their* Bible vanishes with these barriers. I feel deeply for them. . . . But I feel more deeply for those many men, honest and true, whom they have been keeping away from the Bible. I would say to all such: We have undermined the breastworks of traditionalism; let us blow them to atoms. We have forced our way through the obstructions; let us remove them from the face of the earth, that no man hereafter may be kept from the Bible, but that all may freely enter in, search it through and through, and find God enthroned in its very centre.

> SOURCE: Charles A. Briggs, *The Authority of Holy Scripture: An Inaugural Address* (N.Y., 1891), 29–41.

138. Jesus Christ, Religious Ultimate

No Christocentric liberal was ever more deeply concerned over the general drift toward a merely human view of Jesus than George A. Gordon (1853–1929) of Boston. In one of his most widely read books, *The Christ of To-day* (1895), he wrote: "If there is complete identity between Christ and humanity in respect of being and range of powers, men are ready to believe on him; but if it is said that there is any otherness, any eternal difference between him and his brethren, it is felt that that must be a metaphysical fiction." [66]

In the year 1902 Gordon delivered the Lyman Beecher Lectures at Yale and later published them in a volume entitled *Ultimate Conceptions of Faith* (1903). One of the most important ultimates therein discussed was Jesus Christ. The following document is reproduced from that volume, and contains the substance of Gordon's Christology.

After finishing his theological study at Bangor Theological Seminary, Gordon entered Harvard University, where he majored in philosophy. His performance was brilliant, and he graduated with high honors. So partial was he to the Greek theological tradition that he has been called "the Origen of our age." [67]

A preacher of great power, Gordon was for more than forty years minister of Old South Church in Boston. Meanwhile he lectured in all the leading American universities and wrote numerous highly esteemed books, including, in addition to those already mentioned, *The New Epoch for Faith* (1901), *Immortality and the New Theodicy* (1897), *Through Man to God* (1906), *Religion and Miracle* (1909), and *Humanism in New England Theology* (1920).

DOCUMENT

To me the Christological tradition of the church is unspeakably precious. The church is not founded upon theism, but upon Christian theism. The testimony of the creeds is impressive when one recalls the fact that the creeds are witnesses to what was vital in the life of the church. Nothing

---

[66] *The Christ of To-day* (6th ed., Boston, 1897), 96.

[67] John W. Buckham, *Progressive Religious Thought in America* (Boston, 1919), 133. This work contains an excellent analysis of Gordon's theological thought.

can be so surely fatal to the pulpit as a meagre Christology. For the preacher of Christianity the person of its founder is central and sovereign. He kindles love where every other inspiration fails; he sustains enthusiasm where without him human nature would break down; he commands the homage of his people through their gratitude and their hope. Wherever the church has been living and mighty Jesus Christ has been felt to be absolutely indispensable to its faith, its love, and its power. He has thus identified himself with his message. His religion lives in his life among men. He stands in the historic experience of his disciples in a unique and in an inseparable association with God.

To me, thinking in profound sympathy with the highest Christological tradition of the church, Jesus seems to be the perfect man. His manhood, his perfect manhood, is the obvious truth of his existence. This obvious truth becomes the premise from which is elicited the divine meaning of his career. Jesus as the perfect man is fitted for unique moral union with that in God which the Fourth Gospel calls ὁ λόγος, which Paul designates ὁ χριστός, which the Epistle to the Hebrews names ὁ υἱος, which the Nicene creed covers by the same word. It will be seen that a social conception of the nature of God is the logical precedent for the true appreciation of the person of Jesus. Indeed a social conception of the being of God is the logical precedent to the just appreciation of mankind. . . . The point now calling for definite statement is the unique association of the life of Jesus with God inside that general association with God, in which a living humanity must stand. The Filial in God, Eternal in his being, wrought into our entire humanity, in consequence of which men are men, is in perfect union with Jesus. The Incarnation has its meaning in this unique identification of the soul of Jesus with the Eternal filial in God; and this unique identification is through the perfect manhood of Jesus. The conception of God's being for which the Trinity stands, as we shall see later, is the ground of humanity, and the ground of the unique meaning of the life of Jesus. He is the supreme historic utterance of the Eternal Son; he is in perfect moral union with that in God so named. Before his advent Jesus was not; but the Son of God whose perfect human expression he is, is eternal in the heavens. The preëxistence of Jesus I do not find in the teaching of the great theologians, with the exception of Origen, and he teaches the preëxistence of all soul. It is not Jesus who preëxists before his advent; it is the Logos, the Christ, the eternal Son who preëxists. Preëxistence concerns primarily the doctrine of God, and only in a secondary sense the person of Jesus. The position here maintained is that Jesus the perfect man is the sovereign historic expression of the eternal Son in the bosom of the Father, and that Jesus as perfect man is in an association with God ideal, unique, and unsearchable.

With the exception of the idea of preëxistence, this is essentially the position of Origen on the Incarnation. In the teaching of Origen the doctrine of God is first, logically first. In himself God is eternally the Father, and the Son, and the Holy Ghost. Before all worlds God was thus an ineffable society in himself. Souls were then in existence in that pre-temporal world. According to the high use or the abuse of freedom they drew near to God, or fell away from him into time. Among the uncounted multitude of souls in that eternal world there was one preëminent and perfect soul. Between all souls and the Eternal Son there is kinship; between this preëminent and perfect soul there is ineffable union. This preëminent and perfect soul became, in the flesh, Jesus the ideal man, and as such Jesus became the sovereign organ in time of the Eternal Son in the Godhead.

If we ignore the idea of preëxistence in this scheme, it seems to me to cover with remarkable adequacy the thought of this generation concerning Jesus. The kinship between God and man is a fundamental position of faith to-day. It is a living and fruitful truth. In virtue of it we are able to discover in God an eternal humanity, and in human existence an infinite significance. It cannot be said too often or with too great emphasis that there is between God and every man an inseparable association; that there is in every man a genuine incarnation of God. But the obliteration of the possibility of distinction in the association between God and man is against the facts of religious history, and it is against the facts in the record of the life of Jesus. His soul is easily seen to be the sovereign soul, the soul of unique and unapproachable distinction. And this soul of unique distinction has assigned to it a unique vocation. That vocation is that Jesus serve as the supreme organ of the Eternal Son in God. The need of this vocation on the divine side, and on the human, the reality of this vocation in the life of Jesus, and the sovereign distinction of Jesus in the fulfillment of his vocation, are positions that belong together and that support one another. The ancient insights into the monumental meaning of the life of Jesus must not be allowed to fade from our faith; they must be kept and adjusted to the modern insights into the divine worth of man as man; insights for which we are indebted to a new appreciation of Christianity in the light of the general progress of society. And having ventured to connect with my own sense of the meaning of the Incarnation the great name of Origen, I will add to this exposition his concluding words: "The above, meanwhile, are the thoughts which have occurred to us, when treating of subjects of such difficulty as the incarnation and deity of Christ. If there be any one, indeed, who can discover something better, and who can establish his assertions by clearer proofs from holy Scriptures, let his opinion be received in preference to mine." [68]

The point of chief moment is the moral aspect of the subject. We have in Jesus the highest expression of the wisdom and love of God, the final single utterance of that in the Infinite which chiefly concerns our race,—his goodness, his pity, his perfect moral being, and our complete involvement with that being. Jesus is thus the world's sovereign symbol for God, the world's sovereign assurance of God. As prophet, as priest, and as king, God is with him; for God he speaks, for God he suffers, for God he rules. And

[68] Origen, *De Principiis*, Book II, chap. vi. [Gordon]

if humanity is ever to be filled with the eternal harmonies, it will be because the song of good-will that brightened the heavens over the manger in Bethlehem is played by the power of Jesus Christ into all its thoughts and sympathies, into all its achievements and hopes.

> SOURCE: George A. Gordon, *Ultimate Conceptions of Faith* (Boston, 1903), 290–6.

139. The Divine Fatherhood

In 1895 Washington Gladden (1836–1918) rightly observed that the concept of the Fatherhood of God was at that time a "ruling idea." [69] Four years later he published an unusually illuminating essay in *The Homiletic Review,* in which he told how the idea of the Divine Fatherhood had brought about a significant revision in American Protestant thought. The gist of that essay constitutes the document presented below.

Gladden's life spanned the dynamic period in which the United States moved from a rural society into one of the world's most powerful industrial civilizations, and his social and religious thought kept pace with the rapidly changing situation. Gladden started his life in a country village in Pennsylvania and ended it in Columbus, Ohio, a city of industrial power. Although he never attended a theological seminary, he had the good fortune to study at Williams College while the great Mark Hopkins presided over that institution. After completing two short pastorates in New York and Massachusetts, respectively, he was for four years religious editor of the *Independent* (1871–75). Then followed another brief pastorate in Massachusetts. His greatest ministry, however, was at First Congregational Church in Columbus, Ohio, where he preached from 1882 until his death in 1918.

Gladden was a distinguished leader in two closely related liberal movements: the new theology and the social gospel. On behalf of both he wrote almost constantly, his better known books being *Applied Christianity* (1886), *Who Wrote the Bible? A Book For the People* (1891), *Social Facts and Forces* (1897), *Christianity and Socialism* (1905), *How Much Is Left of the Old Doctrines* (1900), and *Present Day Theology* (1913). [70] For the most part, Gladden's books were popular tracts for the times, but his great hymn, "O Master, Let Me Walk With Thee," which now finds a place in practically all Protestant hymnbooks, is of enduring value.

DOCUMENT

That the doctrine of the Fatherhood of God is the substance of the truth to which Jesus bore witness, is plain to any candid reader of the New Testament. . . . The truth that God is a Father has, indeed, always had some sort of recognition. It would have been hardly possible for men who

---

[49] *Ruling Ideas of the Present Age* (Boston, 1895), Chap. 2.

[70] For an account of Gladden's ministry, see his own lucid autobiography, *Recollections* (Boston, 1909).

had the Sermon on the Mount in their hands and who daily repeated the
Lord's Prayer utterly to ignore it; but it has not been the organizing idea of
Christian theology. The Greek theologians of the early centuries put much
emphasis upon it; but in the Western church, since Augustine's day, a
different conception has prevailed. Especially is this true of the theology of
the Reformation. The central idea of that is the sovereignty of God, rather
than His Fatherhood. Upon this theology most of us who are more than
fifty years of age were brought up. We were taught to call God Father, but
there was a persistent doubt in our minds as to our right to address Him by
that name, and all our customary thought made Him Monarch or Im-
perator. The one thing that was kept before our minds was that He had
a government, and that we sustained certain relations to it which were
of the utmost consequence to us. The paternal character was wholly submerged in the kingly character. Fatherhood was a vague and distant possibility; the immediate, awful, overwhelming fact was sovereignty. . . .

The change will give theology a new center of motion; in fact, it will
transform theology from an unmoral to a moral science. Theology of which
sovereignty is the center is not a moral science. The essence of sovereignty
is force; the justice of God, according to the old conception, was His determination to have His own will. . . . The constructive idea is no longer
force; it is righteousness and love. No more radical change is conceivable. . . .

It must not be inferred that the substitution of Fatherhood for sovereignty
weakens the divine government, for there is no rule so watchful or so absolute as that of the father over the child. When the politicians wish to
stigmatize a government as exercising too much control over its subjects,
they call it a paternal government. The power is there, but it is not the
"fundamental and primary fact"; it is a subordinate and secondary fact.
Power is the instrument of love; love is not the vassal of power. . . .

The character in which power is supreme and love is subaltern is not
a moral character. The theology in which force is "fundamental and primary" and Fatherhood is exceptional and contingent is not a moral theology.
And the change from an unmoral to a moral theology is, I repeat, as radical
a change as it is possible to conceive.

That it must have consequences, should be evident enough. It began
to show itself in the unconscious revolt against the doctrine of the damnation of non-elect infants. This doctrine could never have been believed if
the fact of the divine Fatherhood had not been kept out of sight. In the
colloquy of Wigglesworth's famous poem [71] between the infants in hell
and the stern Power who rejects their plea, there is not a hint of any paternal
relation: He is "great Creator" and "Judge most dread"; they are "Adam's
brood"; the poet does not permit them to mention the fact that they are
children of the Father in heaven. . . .

Precisely the same effect followed with respect to the unconditional

[71] *The Day of Doom* (1662).

decree by which the numbers of the elect and of the non-elect were from all eternity unchangeably determined. It was logical; it seemed to follow inevitably from the doctrine of an absolute Will; but it was quite impossible to conceive of a Father treating His children after this manner, and the doctrine had to go. There are those who affect to believe that it is still part of the faith of the Church; let them venture to preach it, just as it is formulated in the third chapter of the Westminster Confession!

The ghastly belief that the whole heathen world—all who have not heard of Christ—are doomed to everlasting misery, was the prevailing belief of the first half of this century. . . . The doctrine of the Fatherhood, as Jesus taught it, when once accepted, makes the maintenance of such a theory of the fate of the heathen nations simply impossible. At the same time it multiplies and strengthens all the higher and stronger missionary motives. If these people in darkness and misery are the children of our Father, our own brethren and sisters, how can we sit still in our ceiled houses and leave them weltering in such degradation? . . .

The doctrine of retribution in all its phases has felt the plastic power of the doctrine of the divine Fatherhood. It is not true, as we have seen, that the fact of retribution is any less certain now than once it was; the new conception of the moral law as containing within itself a self-enforcing energy, has given to this truth a positiveness and solemnity which it never knew before. But the reactions against evil which are incorporated in the natural order, and which thus express the will of God against disobedience, are primarily intended as dissuasions from sin. . . . Of no truth are we more sure than this, that nothing will be left undone that infinite love can do to restrain the transgressor, to reclaim the fallen, and to bring the wanderer home. We know this, because we know that we, being evil, would do as much as this, and we are sure that our heavenly Father will do much more.

But will the Father's love ultimately overcome all resistance and restore all His prodigal children? . . . I can not be sure. The power of the perverse human will to resist light and love is a terrible fact. The prerogative of freedom is all that makes a man, but it seems to involve his unmaking also. Many an earthly father finds his largest wisdom and his deepest love and his completest self-sacrifice powerless to save his son. It is possible to resist the Holy Ghost. . . .

The notion that the mercy of God is limited in time—that up to a certain date He is pitiful and kind to His children, and beyond that date inexorable—will not live in the same world with the doctrine of the divine Fatherhood. There is no real fatherhood, in earth or in heaven, of which this is true. . . .

It would be easy to show how the acceptance of Christ's doctrine of the divine Fatherhood has rendered incredible those theories of the atonement which teach expiation of God's wrath by suffering, and the substitution of the pain of an innocent being for the penalty due to a guilty one. All legal or forensic theories are of course out of the question; the work is purely ethical. . . .

It may also be evident that the doctrine of the Fatherhood throws light upon the interpretation of the Bible. If God is the Being whom Jesus represented Him to be, some of the Old Testament writers must have had imperfect conceptions of Him. But because He is a Father, He was very patient with the ignorance and darkness of the childhood of the world, giving His people from generation to generation as much truth as they could receive; sometimes adapting the revelation to their childish apprehension, and turning their faces always toward the fuller light which was yet to come. . . .

Of only one other doctrine can we speak, the doctrine of man. This doctrine, more than any other, ought to feel the vivifying power of Christ's revelation of Fatherhood. If what Jesus tells us is true, that we are, every one of us, children of the Father in heaven; if this is the fact which we are to believe concerning ourselves; if it is not merely a figure of speech to enkindle our imagination, but the literal truth; if it is not a remote possibility to which saints attain, but the actual condition into which every man is born, and from which no man can any more escape than he can escape from the fact that he is the son of his earthly parents—if all this is true, what a tremendous truth it is! . . .

For this truth stops not short on the frontiers of theology, if theology has frontiers; it follows man wherever he goes, and gives law to all his life. If God is the Father of all men, all men are brethren; and there can be but one law for home and school and shop and factory and market and court and legislative hall. One child of the common Father can not enslave another nor exploit another; the strong and the fortunate and the wise can not take advantage of the weak and the crippled and the ignorant, and enrich themselves by spoiling their neighbors; each must care for the welfare of all, and all must minister to the good of each. This is the law of brotherhood which directly follows from Christ's doctrine of Fatherhood, and which is beginning to be seriously considered, all over the world, as the only solution of the problems of society.

SOURCE: Washington Gladden, "The Fatherhood of God as a Theological Factor," *The Homiletic Review,* XXXVII (January–June, 1899), 201–8.

140. The Kingdom of God on Earth

The first decade of the twentieth century saw American liberal Protestants on tiptoe to "bring in" the kingdom of God. The spirit of that optimistic era is forcefully reflected in an address on "The Kingdom of God," delivered several times during 1909 by Arthur Cushman McGiffert (1861–

1933). When Arthur Cushman McGiffert, Jr., brought out a volume of his father's writings, entitled *Christianity as History and Faith* (1934), he placed that address last because it presented "a thesis and a phraseology dear to the author's heart." The following document contains the constructive section of that address.

McGiffert's graduate education included advanced study with the great historian, Adolf Harnack. That masterly German scholar engraved his ideas so firmly upon the mind of the young American that he maintained a Ritschlian perspective throughout the rest of his life. After a brief stay at Lane Theological Seminary, McGiffert was called, in 1893, to the chair of church history in Union Seminary (New York), where he wielded great influence both as teacher and as scholar. In 1917 he became president of Union, and guided that institution until failing health forced his retirement in 1926. His *History of Christianity in the Apostolic Age* (1897) constituted a landmark in American scholarship, while his final publication, *The History of Christian Thought* (2 vols., 1932–33), continues to be used as a standard work in the leading theological seminaries.

DOCUMENT

What then is this new age? What are its characteristic features and its peculiar needs?

The modern age is marked by a vast confidence in the powers of man. For many centuries it was the custom to think of man as a weak and puny thing. Humility and self-distrust were the cardinal virtues, pride and self-reliance and independence the root of all vice. The change is not the fruit of speculation, a mere philosophical theory as to man's relation to the universe, but the result of the actual and growing conquest of the world in which we live. . . . What this man most needs . . . from Christianity is not condemnation for the pride of accomplishment, exhortations to humility and the offer of healing from above, but the chance to use his strength in ways that are most worth while—higher ideals, larger opportunities, vaster realms of service.

Another marked characteristic of the modern age is its widespread and controlling interest in the present world. . . . Characteristic of a former time was its conviction that all had been learned and accomplished that man was capable of, that the golden age lay in the past and that nothing better was to be looked for. Characteristic of the present time is its faith in the future, based upon its solid experience of the past.

And again, what the age needs from Christianity is not a demonstration that this earth is a poor and unsatisfying place, and an exhortation to set one's heart upon another life beyond the grave but the vision of a work worth doing now and here, a work worth doing for this world, in which the thought and interest of the modern age so largely centre.

Another characteristic of our age is its growing social concern. . . . Our generation is burning with zeal for social, economic, and civic reform, and is controlled by the idea of human brotherhood and marked by its practice as no generation ever was before.

And again, what such an age needs from Christianity is not to be told the supreme importance of personal salvation but to be given a social ideal grand enough to fire its imagination, to arouse its enthusiasm and to enlist its devotion.

Has Christianity then a message for the modern world? Let us see. The greatest fact in modern Christian history is the rediscovery of Jesus. He is better known and understood today than he has ever been before. The development of historical study and criticism, which has revolutionized traditional opinion upon all sorts of matters, has given us a new insight into the origin and growth of Christianity. The Jesus of the Gospels has been finally set free from the integuments in which the devotion and the misunderstanding of the Christian church early enswathed him, and has been allowed for the first time to speak for himself. And the striking feature of the situation is that he speaks a language which the modern age, with its genial confidence in man, its vivid interest in the present world and its profound concern for social betterment, is peculiarly fitted to understand. His message is just the message that the modern world is looking for. The kingdom of God was the burden of his preaching, not a kingdom lying in another world beyond the skies but established here and now—"Thy kingdom come, Thy will be done in earth"; not a kingdom made up of isolated human lives moving along their several and separate paths toward heaven, but of the society of all humankind banded together in common labour under the control of a common purpose. And not by some supernatural and miraculous means was the kingdom to come while men sat by and gazed in awe upon the power of the Almighty, but by the work of Jesus himself and of those that came after him, by the devotion and energy of human lives working at one with the Divine Will. When Jesus said "Follow me" he meant nothing else than labouring with him at the same task in the same spirit.

The kingdom of God on earth, what does it mean? We answer perhaps glibly enough: the control of the lives of men and of all their relationships one with another and of all the institutions in which those relationships find expression by the spirit of Jesus Christ who has shown us what God is and what he would have this world be. The answer is tremendous in its sweep but it needs to be given a more definite content. What is actually involved in the kingdom of God on earth? Is it only a vague form of words, a beautiful but intangible mirage, or is it really something concrete and practical? Does it affect only ethics and religion, or social, economic, and civic matters as well? Does it mean only the improvement of individual character, or also the transformation of society and the state? The modification of details in our existing systems, or their radical reconstruction? The grafting of new principles on the old, or the repudiation of all we have and the birth of a new world? Can our present civilization really be Christianized, or must it give way to an altogether different order? Is it a dangerous thing, this kingdom of God? Does it cut too deep to be welcome, or is it simply the fulfillment of our faith and hope? And how is the kingdom to be established? What methods are to be adopted, what principles followed and along what lines must the work proceed? It is not to answer them that I have propounded such momentous questions as these. Who indeed can answer them today? It is only to emphasize the vastness and complexity of the problem. In it the church of the twentieth century, to which has been committed the responsibility of leadership, has the most difficult problem it has to face. We Protestants have hardly more than played with it hitherto. In the Middle Ages the Catholics grappled with it, and actually evolved an international state which they called the kingdom of God and which dominated western Europe for centuries. It was a grand conception, magnificently carried out, but it was not the kind of kingdom Jesus was thinking of, nor the kind of kingdom the world needs today. We live in the modern age and the modern age has turned its back forever on mediævalism, whether in state or church. We do not want the spirit of otherworldliness to distract men from their duty to this world but to inspire them to it; we do not want the future to overshadow the present but to transfigure it; we do not want the supernatural to crowd out the natural but to fill it with living meaning; we do not want a recrudescence of priestly or ecclesiastical authority but the birth of the spirit of Christian service. Freedom, spontaneity, individuality, opportunity, confidence, and self-reliance—all these precious gains of the modern age we must preserve. But we must have also love, sympathy, fellowship, co-operation and an ideal worthy of our common devotion, our common effort and our common sacrifice.

The kingdom for which mediæval Christians toiled so faithfully was for still another reason quite a different thing from the kingdom of God which Jesus had in mind. He did not mean another institution set up in the midst of the existing institutions of the world into which a man could enter from without. The kingdom of God which he preached is not in any sense identical with the Christian church. It is the reign of God, of his purposes, of his ideals, of his spirit in the relationships and in the institutions of the world. It is the world itself brought into harmony with God's will. Not a dualism of two kingdoms but one kingdom only, God's world and ours controlled by the spirit of Christ. For this the Christian church is called to labour, not to enlarge and glorify itself and to seek to dominate but to make itself the most efficient instrument for the transformation of the world into the kingdom of God. . . .

It is a divine thing, this kingdom of God. In it God's supreme purpose finds expression, his purpose to promote the reign of the spirit of love among men. It is for this that God is; and this is what God's love for the world means. In human brotherhood the Divine Fatherhood finds fulfillment. Through human brotherhood alone the Father's purpose for his children comes to accomplishment, and through human brotherhood alone his children discover him. God himself is back of the kingdom. We did not invent it. Its ideals are not of our making. They have been given us. They are higher than we could have dreamed of. They lift us above ourselves. We rise to meet them and find expressed in them the best that we can know. In this kingdom the divine and the human are inextricably interwoven. In it there is communion with God, as his desires fill our souls and his purposes are made our own, and in it there is the power of God, as the inspirations of his presence lay hold upon us. And yet it realizes itself only in the experience of men. We do not find it by turning our backs upon the world and ceasing to be human, we find it only here in human life itself. It is rooted in the inner man, in his affections, his will, his character, but it comes to visible expression in all sorts of ways, as the external relationships of life are brought one after another under the control of the inner disposition.

It is both material and spiritual, this kingdom of God. It ministers to the body and to the soul. Not as in earlier days when the church thought only of the spirit and looked upon the body with contempt; not as today so many social reformers—even Christian ones—seem to think only of the body and disregard altogether the higher things of the spirit. Unlike both, Jesus ministered at once to the outer and the inner man. The kingdom of God which he proclaimed means the weal of the one as of the other. It means a social order in which there shall be food and drink and clothing and shelter, a just share of the physical goods of life for all God's children, and in which there shall be also for all of them the consolation of divine communion, the inspirations of human fellowship, the glow of sympathy, the joy of service, the trinity of faith and hope and love.

It is a Christian thing, this kingdom of God. The greatest gift of God to the world is Jesus Christ. It is just this which differentiates the kingdom of God we preach from all man-made Utopias. His life, his character, his teaching, his work, his spirit of service dominating the world—this is what the kingdom means. It is not merely our self-taught love and devotion but the love and devotion of the Christ kindled in our hearts as we have looked upon him and caught the inspiration of his vision of God. The prophets too preached the kingdom of God, but they had not seen Jesus; and it is not the kingdom of the prophets we proclaim to the world but the kingdom of the Christ. In him God has given the full revelation of his purpose for the world, and his aims, his motives, his estimate of values, his hopes it is that we would have the world share.

It is a uniting, not a dividing force, this kingdom of God. Not setting the present over against the past, the church over against the world, the conservative over against the radical, one community, one nation, one sect over against another. It gathers them all up into one. . . . Not by jealousy and envy, not by sectarian zeal and religious fanaticism, not by national bigotry and class prejudice, not by the forcing of opinions and customs upon others but by the union of all men of good-will of every race and religion and condition, by the sharing of their visions and by the linking of their faiths and hopes and efforts shall the kingdom of God come.

The great task of the Christian church of the twentieth century is ready to its hand. Upon the church devolves the chief responsibility for the bringing of the kingdom, for to it has been vouchsafed the supreme vision, in Jesus' revelation of his Father's will. . . .

We are on the eve of great happenings. No one familiar with history and able to read the signs of the times can for a moment doubt it. Unfortunately the church, as too often in the past, has in many places lost its leadership. It continues to minister beautifully and efficiently to its own members and to bless the lives of multitudes of them, but it is not in the van of progress, and much of the best life of the world has turned its back upon it and is pushing on alone.

We Christians are apt to be much too easily satisfied. . . . We are content with too little, and the great modern world, with its teeming masses, its eager enthusiasms, its burning problems and its untold possibilities, is in danger of slipping away from us. Yet what a message we have for it! The kingdom of God on earth—the control of all the relationships of life and of all the institutions of society by the spirit of Jesus Christ.

> SOURCE: Arthur Cushman McGiffert, "The Kingdom of God," *Christianity as History and Faith,* ed. Arthur Cushman McGiffert, Jr. (N.Y., 1934), 300–10. Copyright 1934 Charles Scribner's Sons; renewal copyright © 1962 Charles Scribner's Sons and A. C. McGiffert, Jr. Used by permission.

141. The Problem of the Parousia

Shortly before the opening of the twentieth century New Testament scholarship was beginning to admit, contrary to earlier critical opinion, that Jesus' teaching contained eschatological and apocalyptical elements. This newer point of view was thus inhospitable to the liberal theological claim that Jesus had viewed the coming of the kingdom of God in terms of gradual growth. In 1905, when William Newton Clarke (1840–1912) published *The Use of the Scriptures in Theology,* he was well aware of the recent trend in biblical thought, but still he tried to justify the older interpretation. He tacitly conceded that the advent-expectation might be an element in the teaching of Jesus, and yet he insisted that it did not constitute a really "Christian element" of the Bible and should therefore be discarded by theologians. The document which follows reproduces the gist of his argument.

Clarke began his professional career as a pastor, but from 1890 until 1908 he taught theology at Colgate University. One of his most brilliant students later said of him, "He . . . was one of the most inspiring teachers I ever sat under." [72] Clarke's greatest book, *An Outline of Christian Theology* (1898), was forged in his classroom. That *Outline,* said a well-informed theologian, "has been perhaps the most influential book of its kind in American religious thinking." [73]

DOCUMENT

When the Messiah should come, what was he expected to do? Hopes in Israel varied, but not widely. He was to establish a kingdom in Israel, and reign over the chosen people, and make Israel rule over the nations. The ancient kingdom of David, sacred and glorious in national memory, was the type which he would fulfil and glorify. Israelites of past ages would be raised from the dead to share in the glory of his kingdom. The living Israel would be purified from sin that it might reign with him, and would enter the kingdom through the ordeal of a judgment. Thus the chosen people would be glorified with the Messiah in his kingdom at Jerusalem, while the nations would either be blessed in his reign or be punished for their hatred of Israel. This, with variations, was the hope.

Jesus appeared, and was rejected by the nation in general, but by a minority was welcomed as the Messiah. When he had gone, the Messiah, as these believed, had been among them. And what had he done? He founded no kingdom in his lifetime, nor took any step in that direction, beyond the claim that was implied in his final entrance to Jerusalem. At the hands of Israel the Messiah died. But death was followed by resurrection, and soon he was gone from the earth and was exerting spiritual power upon men from the heavenly world. A church sprang up in his name, which started within the Jewish circle but soon went abroad among the nations, where alone, and not among the people of the Messiah, it was permanently established. He was as far as possible from fulfilling the sacred expectations about the Christ, and yet, in the sure conviction of his early followers, he was the Christ. Surely, then, the expectations would yet be realized: fulfilment was only delayed. He had gone from the world in which he was to reign, but the heavens could not retain him: he would quickly return, the dead would be raised, the judgment would be held, the kingdom would be established, and the Messiah would reign in majesty on the earth. This Christian rendering of the Jewish expectation took power-

[72] Harry Emerson Fosdick, *The Living of These Days: An Autobiography* (N.Y., 1956), 65.

[73] Gerald Birney Smith, *Current Christian Thinking* (Chicago, 1928), 83. For a good analysis of Clarke's theology, see Bernard C. Cochran, "William Newton Clarke: Exponent of the 'New Theology'" (Typed Ph.D. dissertation, Duke University, 1961).

ful hold upon the Jewish Christians, and was passed on by them to the Gentiles who believed, and formed a mighty inspiration in the life of the early church.

But the expectation was not realized. The Messiah did not return in glory. A wholly different course of events unfolded. A spiritual work was done, and it was a work that formed a true continuation of what Jesus had done in life and death, a genuine development from his actual mission. There came new holiness and fellowship with God, new love and fellowship with men, new hope of immortality. There came a living and growing church on earth. This was what Jesus had introduced. The Christ who lived brought in a future like himself. Though the advent-hope continued, there came no realization whatever of that hope or any of its elements. The movement of history followed according to the influence of the Christ who came, not according to the hopes of those who pictured him beforehand.

How could it be otherwise? From what should a movement of history come forth? from what was expected to occur, or from what had occurred? Expectations do not determine what history shall be: facts and working influences do that. The Jesus who lived and died was the one from whom the Christian development took its character, not the Davidic king long hoped for but never born. The history that followed Christ has been Christian, imperfectly of course but really: it would have been Jewish, not Christian, if the ancient hope had been realized. In other words, the fulfilment of the preChristian advent-hope ought not to have come, and could not come. Now that we are far enough away to look at it, we can see that the advent-hope was part and parcel of Judaism, and no part of the gift of Christ at all. It came most naturally into the early Christian life, seeing that the first disciples did not understand the Master very well, and it was natural that for a time it should remain a living hope. But it was never anything else than a Jewish remainder, a survival, an intrusion of something incongruous into the Christian field.

The advent-hope had its usefulness for the early Christians, for after Jesus the real Christ had lived and been loved, and died and been glorified, the hope of seeing him again had a quality that no Jewish expectation could ever possess. Christian faith, hope, and love all entered glowingly into the looking for his return. So the hope kept the image of the unseen Saviour vividly present to the church, and brightened dark days with a heavenly light. Nevertheless, Christ himself had doomed it to disappointment by being what he was. The real Messiah had started history in another direction, and the visible return to Messianic glory on earth was no item in the development that came forth from him.

Consequently the advent-hope ought to have been dropped out of Christianity, when time had refuted it and experience had shown the kingdom coming in another way. It was discredited long before the New Testament was complete, for it was never anything but hope of an event close at hand. The Scriptures know absolutely nothing of a return of Christ after two thousand years. But it has had a different fate, full of pathetic interest. It was taken to be a part of Christianity itself. Was it not a part of early Christian life? Did not the apostles cherish it?—and they could not be mistaken. Does it not glow on the pages of the Bible? Still therefore the expected event was thought to be only delayed, and so the millennial conception of the kingdom, and the vivid advent-hope, have survived until this day, side by side with that spiritual experience which has borne agelong testimony that the real Christ is working on another plan.

This discredited hope of a soon-returning Christ and a visible kingdom has long been kept alive in perpetual disappointment by the accepted doctrine of the Scriptures. But the sound historical interpretation which is now possible assigns to it no place at all in the gift and revelation of Christ, and therefore our principle requires us to drop it and all that belongs to it out of our Christian theology. Visible advent, simultaneous resurrection, assemblage of all men for judgment, millennial reign of Christ on earth,— all is Jewish survival, historically discredited by the work of Christ himself: it is a remainder from pre-Christian life and hope, demonstrated to be non-Christian by the different course of Christian history; wherefore it forms no part of Christian theology. Under the wholesome influence of our principle this whole group of topics will disappear, and the Christianity that proceeded from the actual work of Christ will stand delivered from the contradictory conception that has been bound in with it through all these ages.

I am not overlooking the important question that has already been suggested to every listener. Everyone remembers that the advent-expectation can be quoted from the lips of Jesus Christ himself. There stands the great apocalyptic passage in the twenty-fourth chapter of Matthew's Gospel, with other sayings of similar effect, picturing the coming kingdom in the common manner of Jewish hope, and announcing the visible advent of the Messiah as close at hand. How can one say the advent-hope is not Christian when it has this endorsement? Is there then a non-Christian element in the words of Christ himself? Had he too his ideas inherited from an expiring age, existing side by side with his vision of eternal truth? Did he conceive the coming kingdom in the mistaken manner of the time? or are the words of expectation that never came true attributed to him by others, and not his own?

As to the interpretation of these sayings, we must judge between two ways. One is that while his conception of the spiritual character of the coming kingdom rose immeasurably above the thought of the time, and was a Saviour's own conception, he still conceived the time and form of the kingdom in the manner which the past had consecrated. The other is that the collectors of the synoptic record, preserving the tradition of the church, gathered in with his words some that were not his, and so attributed to him the accepted view of the kingdom, which they had no doubt that he entertained. Probably there is no third interpretation. The time has not yet come for general agreement here, but the question has arisen in the course of candid study, and is destined to remain long in discussion. Therefore let the discussion be open and without reproach. Many persons feel it necessary to hold that Jesus spoke the words, in order to preserve the credit of the evangelists and the accuracy of the record, lest we should lose our sense of certainty as to what he said and did. This is the popular feeling. Others feel it necessary to hold that he did not speak the words, in order to preserve the spiritual sanity and consistency of our Lord himself, and avoid the conclusion that he misconceived the nature of his own work and kingdom,—an object quite as important, one would think, as the maintaining of the credit of the evangelists. Others again, disclaiming any object except to read his life as they find it, think the evidence shows that he spoke the words, or at least some of them, and further, that he conceived the kingdom in the manner of the Old Testament, though with vast heightening of its spiritual character. Some of these, with deepest reverence toward him, regard the retention of the old idea as an unimportant element in the life of him who was bearing to the world the everlasting message. These are not surprised if the messenger of God in the limitations of humanity thought in the manner of his time. They ask how he could have addressed his own generation if he had not. What he lived for, they would say, was not to show at once, or even to see at once, all truth that was involved in his mission, but to reveal that central truth and eternal life in which the true kingdom in its own time would consist. They see so clearly the revealing and redeeming glory of Jesus Christ as not to be troubled by this limitation upon his foresight. So these interpreters, though they find the advent-hope expressed in genuine words of Jesus, would agree with me in judging it to be no part of his gift to the world.

> SOURCE: William Newton Clarke, *The Use of the Scriptures in Theology* (N.Y., 1905), 102–11.

142. The Intolerance of Fundamentalism

The decade following World War I witnessed a militant campaign of the fundamentalists to purge the American Protestant churches of all persons who refused to subscribe to their type of rigid orthodoxy, an orthodoxy which centered in the celebrated "five points," such as biblical inerrancy, the virgin birth, and the second coming of Christ. The outcome was a rancorous ten-year conflict commonly known as the fundamentalist-modernist controversy.

In June of 1922, in an effort to allay the strife, Harry Emerson Fosdick (1878—), a Baptist and the pre-eminent voice of the American Protestant pulpit, delivered a sermon in New York's First Presbyterian Church, where he was then guest minister, entitled "Shall the Fundamentalists Win?" Far from cooling tempers, it set off the hottest controversy that ever raged about any sermon in American history. For at least two years, it was headlined in the leading newspapers across the nation. The author, a representative Christocentric liberal, was assailed as fiercely by the radicals on his left as by the fundamentalists on his right.[74] Both parties wanted him to cut loose from his historic Christian moorings, but for different reasons: the fundamentalists, because he was too liberal; the radicals, because he was too conservative.

Determined to oust him from the pulpit at First Church, Presbyterian fundamentalists in 1923 carried their grievance to the General Assembly, where, led by the eloquent William Jennings Bryan of anti-evolution fame, they succeeded in having the Assembly condemn the doctrines then being preached to that congregation. The Assembly also directed the Presbytery of New York to take steps to maintain loyalty to the Westminster Confession of Faith. When this action failed to achieve the desired result, the next Assembly (1924) invited Fosdick to become a regular Presbyterian minister and subscribe to Presbyterian doctrinal standards. Seeing the intent of that maneuver, he tendered his resignation as guest minister. After much persuasion, Fosdick accepted the pastorate of the Park Avenue Baptist Church, which he soon developed into the great Riverside Church (dedicated in 1930), and where he carried on a notable ministry until his retirement in 1946. After a short rest, he threw himself into a movement to restore the decaying community near Riverside Church, and meanwhile resumed a heavy program of writing. His more than thirty books have been read by millions. Phenomenally popular have been *The Manhood of the Master* (1913), *The Meaning of Prayer* (1915), and *On Being A Real Person* (1943).

The following document is reproduced from the sermon, "Shall the Fundamentalists Win?"

DOCUMENT

This morning we are to think of the Fundamentalist controversy which threatens to divide the American churches, as though already they were not sufficiently split and riven. A scene, suggestive for our thought, is depicted in the fifth chapter of the Book of the Acts, where the Jewish leaders hale before them Peter and other of the apostles because they had been preaching Jesus as the Messiah. Moreover, the Jewish leaders propose to slay them, when in opposition Gamaliel speaks: "Refrain from these men, and let them alone; for if this counsel or this work be of men, it will be overthrown; but if it is of God ye will not be able to overthrow them; lest haply ye be found even to be fighting against God." . . .

Already all of us must have heard about the people who call themselves the Fundamentalists. Their apparent intention is to drive out of the evan-

[74] Harry Emerson Fosdick, *The Living of These Days*, 152–68.

gelical churches men and women of liberal opinions. I speak of them the more freely because there are no two denominations more affected by them than the Baptist and the Presbyterian. We should not identify the Fundamentalists with the conservatives. All Fundamentalists are conservatives, but not all conservatives are Fundamentalists. The best conservatives can often give lessons to the liberals in true liberality of spirit, but the Fundamentalist program is essentially illiberal and intolerant. The Fundamentalists see, and they see truly, that in this last generation there have been strange new movements in Christian thought. A great mass of new knowledge has come into man's possession: new knowledge about the physical universe, its origin, its forces, its laws; new knowledge about human history and in particular about the ways in which the ancient peoples used to think in matters of religion and the methods by which they phrased and explained their spiritual experiences; and new knowledge, also, about other religions and the strangely similar ways in which men's faiths and religious practices have developed everywhere. . . . The new knowledge and the old faith cannot be left antagonistic or even disparate, as though a man on Saturday could use one set of regulative ideas for his life and on Sunday could change gear to another altogether. We must be able to think our modern life clear through in Christian terms, and to do that we also must be able to think our Christian faith clear through in modern terms.

There is nothing new about the situation. It has happened again and again in history, as, for example, when the stationary earth suddenly began to move and the universe that had been centered in this planet was centered in the sun around which the planets whirled. Whenever such a situation has arisen, there has been only one way out: the new knowledge and the old faith had to be blended in a new combination. Now, the people in this generation who are trying to do this are the liberals, and the Fundamentalists are out on a campaign to shut against them the doors of the Christian fellowship. Shall they be allowed to succeed?

It is interesting to note where the Fundamentalists are driving in their stakes to mark out the deadline of doctrine around the Church, across which no one is to pass except on terms of agreement. They insist that we must all believe in the historicity of certain special miracles, pre-eminently the virgin birth of our Lord; that we must believe in a special theory of inspiration— that the original documents of the Scripture, which of course we no longer possess, were inerrantly dictated to men a good deal as a man might dictate to a stenographer; that we must believe in a special theory of the atonement —that the blood of our Lord, shed in a substitutionary death, placates an alienated Deity and makes possible welcome for the returning sinner; and that we must believe in the second coming of our Lord upon the clouds of heaven to set up a millennium here, as the only way in which God can bring history to a worthy denouement. Such are some of the stakes which are being driven to mark a deadline of doctrine around the Church.

If a man is a genuine liberal, his primary protest is not against holding these opinions, although he may well protest against their being considered the fundamentals of Christianity. This is a free country and anybody has a right to hold these opinions or any others, if he is sincerely convinced of them. The question is, Has anybody a right to deny the Christian name to those who differ with him on such points and to shut against them the doors of the Christian fellowship? The Fundamentalists say that this must be done. In this country and on the foreign field they are trying to do it. They have actually endeavored to put on the statute books of a whole State binding laws against teaching modern biology. If they had their way, within the Church, they would set up in Protestantism a doctrinal tribunal more rigid than the Pope's. In such an hour, delicate and dangerous, when feelings are bound to run high, I plead this morning the cause of magnanimity and liberality and tolerance of spirit. I would, if I could reach their ears, say to the Fundamentalists about the liberals what Gamaliel said to the Jews, "Refrain from these men, and let them alone: for if this counsel or this work be of men, it will be overthrown; but if it is of God ye will not be able to overthrow them; lest haply ye be found even to be fighting against God."

That we may be entirely candid and concrete and may not lose ourselves in any fog of generalities, let us this morning take two or three of these Fundamentalist items and see with reference to them what the situation is in the Christian churches. Too often we preachers have failed to talk frankly enough about the differences of opinion which exist among evangelical Christians, although everybody knows that they are there. Let us face this morning some of the differences of opinion with which somehow we must deal.

We may well begin with the vexed and mooted question of the virgin birth of our Lord. I know people in the Christian churches, ministers, missionaries, laymen, devoted lovers of the Lord and servants of the Gospel, who, alike as they are in their personal devotion to the Master, hold quite different points of view about a matter like the virgin birth. Here, for example, is one point of view: that the virgin birth is to be accepted as historical fact; it actually happened; there was no other way for a personality like the Master to come into this world except by a special biological miracle. That is one point of view, and many are the gracious and beautiful souls who hold it. But, side by side with them in the evangelical churches is a group of equally loyal and reverent people who would say that the virgin birth is not to be accepted as an historic fact. . . . So far from thinking that they have given up anything vital in the New Testament's attitude toward Jesus, these Christians remember that the two men who contributed most to the Church's thought of the divine meaning of the Christ were Paul and John, who never even distantly allude to the virgin birth.

Here in the Christian churches are these two groups of people and the question which the Fundamentalists raise is this, Shall one of them throw the other out? Has intolerance any contribution to make to this situation? Will it persuade anybody of anything? Is not the Christian Church large enough to hold within her hospitable fellowship people who differ on points like this and agree to differ until the fuller truth be manifested? The Fundamentalists say not. They say that the liberals must go. Well, if the Fundamentalists should succeed, then out of the Christian Church would go some of the best Christian life and consecration of his [sic] generation— multitudes of men and women, devout and reverent Christians, who need the Church and whom the Church needs.

Consider another matter on which there is a sincere difference of opinion between evangelical Christians: the inspiration of the Bible. One point of view is that the original documents of the Scripture were inerrantly dictated by God to men. Whether we deal with the story of creation or the list of the dukes of Edom or the narratives of Solomon's reign or the Sermon on the Mount or the thirteenth chapter of First Corinthians, they all came in the same way, and they all came as no other book ever came. They were inerrantly dictated; everything there—scientific opinions, medical theories, historical judgments, as well as spiritual insight—is infallible. That is one idea of the Bible's inspiration. But side by side with those who hold it, lovers of the Book as much as they, are multitudes of people who never think about the Bible so. Indeed, that static and mechanical theory of inspiration seems to them a positive peril to the spiritual life. . . .

Here in the Christian Church to-day are these two groups, and the question which the Fundamentalists have raised is this, Shall one of them drive the other out? Do we think the cause of Jesus Christ will be furthered by that? If He should walk through the ranks of this congregation this morning, can we imagine Him claiming as His own those who hold one idea of inspiration and sending from Him into outer darkness those who hold another? You cannot fit the Lord Christ into that Fundamentalist mold. . . .

Consider another matter upon which there is a serious and sincere difference of opinion between evangelical Christians: the second coming of our Lord. The second coming was the early Christian phrasing of hope. No one in the ancient world had ever thought, as we do, of development, progress, gradual change, as God's way of working out His will in human life and institutions. They thought of human history as a series of ages succeeding one another with abrupt suddenness. The Graeco-Roman world gave the names of metals to the ages—gold, silver, bronze, iron. The Hebrews had their ages, too—the original Paradise in which man began, the cursed world in which man now lives, the blessed Messianic Kingdom some day suddenly to appear on the clouds of heaven. It was the Hebrew way of expressing hope for the victory of God and righteousness. When the Christians came they took over that phrasing of expectancy and the New Testament is aglow with it. The preaching of the apostles thrills with the glad announcement, "Christ is coming!"

In the evangelical churches to-day there are differing views of this matter. One view is that Christ is literally coming, externally, on the clouds of heaven, to set up His Kingdom here. I never heard that teaching in my youth at all. It has always had a new resurrection when desperate circumstances came and man's only hope seemed to lie in divine intervention. It is not strange, then, that during these chaotic, catastrophic years there has been a fresh rebirth of this old phrasing of expectancy. "Christ is coming!" seems to many Christians the central message of the Gospel. In the strength of it some of them are doing great service for the world. But, unhappily, many so overemphasize it that they outdo anything the ancient Hebrews or the ancient Christians ever did. They sit still and do nothing and expect the world to grow worse and worse until He comes.

Side by side with these to whom the second coming is a literal expectation, another group exists in the evangelical churches. They, too, say, "Christ is coming!" They say it with all their hearts; but they are not thinking of an external arrival on the clouds. They have assimilated as part of the divine revelation the exhilarating insight which these recent generations have given to us, that development is God's way of working out His will. . . . And these Christians, when they say that Christ is coming, mean that, slowly it may be, but surely, His will and principles will be worked out by God's grace in human life and institutions, until "He shall see of the travail of His soul and shall be satisfied."

These two groups exist in the Christian churches and the question raised by the Fundamentalists is, Shall one of them drive the other out? Will that get us anywhere? Multitudes of young men and women at this season of the year are graduating from our schools of learning, thousands of them Christians who may make us older ones ashamed by the sincerity of their devotion to God's will on earth. They are not thinking in ancient terms that leave ideas of progress out. They cannot think in those terms. There could be no greater tragedy than that the Fundamentalists should shut the door of the Christian fellowship against such.

I do not believe for one moment that the Fundamentalists are going to succeed. Nobody's intolerance can contribute anything to the solution of the situation which we have described. If, then, the Fundamentalists have no solution of the problem, where may we expect to find it? In two concluding comments let us consider our reply to that inquiry.

The first element that is necessary is a spirit of tolerance and Christian liberty. When will the world learn that intolerance solves no problems? This is not a lesson which the Fundamentalists alone need to learn; the liberals also need to learn it. Speaking, as I do, from the viewpoint of liberal opinions, let me say that if some young, fresh mind here this morning is holding new ideas, has fought his way through, it may be by intellectual and spiritual struggle, to novel positions, and is tempted to be intolerant about old opinions, offensively to condescend to those who hold them and to be harsh in judgment on them, he may well remember that people who held those old opinions have given the world some of the noblest character and the most rememberable service that it ever has been blessed with, and that we of the younger generation will prove our case best, not by controversial intolerance, but by producing, with our new opinions, something of the depth and strength, nobility and beauty of character that in other times were associated with other thoughts. It was a wise liberal, the most adventurous man of his day—Paul the Apostle— who said, "Knowledge puffeth up, but love buildeth up."

Nevertheless, it is true that just now the Fundamentalists are giving us one of the worst exhibitions of bitter intolerance that the churches of this country have ever seen. As one watches them and listens to them he remembers the remark of General Armstrong of Hampton Institute, "Cantankerousness is worse than heterodoxy." There are many opinions in the field of modern controversy concerning which I am not sure whether they are right or wrong, but there is one thing I am sure of: courtesy and kindliness and tolerance and humility and fairness are right. Opinions may be mistaken; love never is. . . .

The second element which is needed, if we are to reach a happy solution of this problem, is a clear insight into the main issues of modern Christianity and a sense of penitent shame that the Christian Church should be quarreling over little matters when the world is dying of great needs. If, during the war, when the nations were wrestling upon the very brink of hell and at times all seemed lost, you chanced to hear two men in an altercation about some minor matter of sectarian denominationalism, could you restrain your indignation? You said, "What can you do with folks like this who, in the face of colossal issues, play with the tiddledywinks and peccadillos of religion?" So, now, when from the terrific questions of this generation one is called away by the noise of this Fundamentalist controversy, he thinks it almost unforgivable that men should tithe mint and anise and cummin, and quarrel over them, when the world is perishing for the lack of the weightier matters of the law, justice, and mercy, and faith. . . .

The present world situation smells to heaven! And now, in the presence of colossal problems, which must be solved in Christ's name and for Christ's sake, the Fundamentalists propose to drive out from the Christian churches all the consecrated souls who do not agree with their theory of inspiration. What immeasurable folly!

Well, they are not going to do it; certainly not in this vicinity. I do not even know in this congregation whether anybody has been tempted to be a Fundamentalist. Never in this church have I caught one accent of intolerance. God keep us always so and ever increasing areas of the Christian fellowship; intellectually hospitable, open-minded, liberty-loving, fair, tolerant, not with the tolerance of indifference, as though we did not care about the faith, but because always our major emphasis is upon the weightier matters of the law.

> SOURCE: Harry Emerson Fosdick, "Shall the Fundamentalists Win?" *The Christian Work,* CII (June 10, 1922), 716–9, 722. Used by permission of the author.

143. Christianity and Other Faiths

The study of comparative religion led Christian liberals to develop a missionary apologetic which conflicted with that of orthodox Protestants. The latter generally held that the non-Christian religions were entirely false and should be rejected in toto. The liberals, on the other hand, recognized certain positive values in other religions, but nevertheless regarded Christianity as a higher faith in which the nobler elements of those religions are fulfilled. In a sense, the non-Christian religions were to Christianity what the Old Testament was to the New. In other words, they served as a preparatory revelation to be completed in the Christian revelation.

In the year 1909 John W. Buckham (1864–1945) presented the viewpoint of Christocentric liberalism more or less typically in his article, "Christianity Among the Religions," published in *The Hibbert Journal.* The core of that essay is reprinted in the document below. Section I is omitted, since it is introductory to the central thesis of the author.

A graduate of the University of Vermont and of Andover Theological Seminary, Buckham held two New England pastorates between 1888 and 1903. In the latter year he joined the faculty of Pacific Theological Seminary (now Pacific School of Religion), where he taught theology until his retirement in 1937. His more important books included *Christ and the Eternal Order* (1906), *Personality and the Christian Ideal* (1909), *Progressive Religious Thought in America* (1919), *Personality and Psychology* (1924), and *The Humanity of God* (1928). He delivered the Taylor Lectures at Yale in 1914. Educated at Andover Seminary when Christocentric liberalism dominated the faculty, Buckham retained that stamp of thinking for the remainder of his life, although after World War I he became considerably less optimistic. Referring to his Andover days, he said: "It seemed to many of us who were studying theology and beginning our ministry in the eighties and nineties as if humanity were on the eve of the golden age. . . . The kingdom of God appeared to be at hand." [75]

[75] *Progressive Religious Thought in America* (Boston, 1919), 316–7.

II.

The study of Comparative Religion is revealing Christianity in a wholly new light, from the vantage-ground of a fresh view-point. For the first time we are getting perspective. In two ways the gain is inestimable. Comparison is disclosing the inherent strength and superiority of Christianity as it could appear in no other way. All values are clarified by comparison. . . . Other religions do not lose when placed beside Christianity except relatively, but Christianity gains. There is at once a clearer understanding, both of them and of itself. The presence of the best reveals in the same instant the goodness of the good and the supremacy of the best. It was the folly of unfaith to hesitate so long to place Christianity upon a common base level with other religions, fully, freely, and without prejudice. For only as it stands on the same level can its true height be seen. . . .

The supremacy of Christianity appears by comparison, both in what it includes and in what it excludes. All that is worthiest and highest in other religions proves by comparison to be in Christianity. Is it the reverence of Hebraism, the freedom of Hellenism, the moral earnestness of Zoroastrianism, the mysticism of Brahmanism, the sacrificial spirit of Buddhism? All are here in Christianity, and here, not in excess of emphasis, but in full and balanced harmony. And in much, too, that is in other religions and not in Christianity, its supremacy may be seen quite as clearly. Angles of distortion, ignoble and limiting ideas of God, asceticisms that wrong humanity, conceptions of nature and spirit that fetter and retard the spirit,—how free on the whole from these defects of other religions Christianity is. Not that such excrescences have not become attached to Christianity and worked serious ill, but they do not belong to its spirit and essence.

We must not, however, suffer this broader outlook upon religion as a whole to blind our eyes to the true character of Christianity, lest we rob it of its own individuality. The fact that Christianity conjoined Hebraism and Hellenism by no means reduces it to a mere syncretism. Nor does the fact that it has incorporated elements from other religions make it an eclecticism. No one who understands Christianity would hesitate to say that it is far more than a union of Hebrew and Greek elements. Whatever Christianity has taken up it has assimilated. This is its secret—a marvellous *power of assimilation*. With that astonishing alchemy which indicates originality of organism, Christianity has made its own, transformed, renewed whatever it has laid hold upon. Syncretisms combine, eclecticisms choose and construct, but only life assimilates. . . .

When we come to ask for the secret of this assimilative power, we find ourselves approaching that problem which has proved so fascinating of late: What is the essence of Christianity, where is the hiding of its power?

It is not difficult, by analysing Christianity, as Harnack has done, to discover certain potent fundamental truths—the fatherhood of God, the worth of the soul, the kingdom of God—which, at least in the emphasis and fervour it gives to them, are distinctively and characteristically Christian. But after all, close as these truths lie to the heart of Christianity, they are not its inner essence. Our New Theology is in great part characterised by its showing that Christianity won its way by uniting two great truths concerning God which no other religious philosophy has harmonised—Transcendence and Immanence; but no one would think of finding even in that synthesis, important as it is, the essence of the Christian religion. The ethics of Christianity, too, and even its cult, reflect a simplicity and sincerity which help to account for the strong hold which Christianity secured and kept over the human mind; but none of these things solve the problem of its essence. To reach that, one must go deeper into that profound and subtle realm that holds the hidden springs of all that moves us most—*personality*. At the very source and centre of Christianity there glows a Person who—say what we may of the incompleteness of his life-story and the later misconceptions which have obscured his true character—is the most compelling, transforming Fact in human history. . . . Making the largest possible allowance for idealisation in the portrait of Jesus in the gospels, there remains, as a necessary basis for it, a personality so strong, so pure, so noble, as to leave an indelible impress upon the human mind, which "far from fading, rather grows," and gives promise of growing till it shall remould humanity into its likeness. . . .

But is not Jesus himself also a product of evolution? Yes, in a sense Jesus certainly was a racial religious product. Generations of spiritual culture entered into his individuality. He was the consummate flower blooming on the most vigorous branch that has put forth from the religious trunk of humanity. And yet that does not explain him wholly; it does not touch the deepest secret of his being. That transcendent Self within him which rose above the physical, the temporal, the racial, which met and mastered limitation and circumstance, and all the slings and arrows of outrageous fortune, and turned all into splendid victory—how shall we account for that? It cannot be accounted for, save as one sees in him another self beside the merely racial man—the Second Man from heaven. Not that this twofold selfhood is peculiar to Jesus Christ—it belongs to man as man,—but that the eternal Self, which in us is but inconstant and indistinct, in him was so full-orbed and supreme that of him, as of no other, the author of the Fourth Gospel could write: "And the Word became flesh." . . .

III.

The conviction is gaining ground that the hour has struck for a universal human religion, that the advance of humanity, as a whole, requires that mankind move henceforth under one spiritual leadership toward a common goal. Whether this is so, is too large a question to be dealt with in this or in any single paper. Suffice to say that the present writer shares the conviction, together with its appropriate supplement, that Christianity is the only religion that can possibly fulfil this office. In the light of the study of Comparative Religion, it seems an extreme, almost a fanatical aim, to advance Christianity as entitled to supersede all other faiths; and yet it is only in the light of such a study that this aim gets its highest encouragement.

A sufficient reason—whether there be others or not—for pressing Christianity as the only religion fit to become the world's religion is that the others—to put it squarely, and I think fairly—have failed. Buddhism, Confucianism, Mohammedanism, with the minor religions, have all failed. Not that they have failed in the sense of not holding their own outwardly, and even making gains, nor in the sense of not containing a great deal of truth, and of accomplishing great good—but in the sense of not having done for their adherents and for humanity what religion ought to do. Not that Christianity itself has been absolutely successful; far enough from that. But Christianity has, at least, not failed. In spite of serious deficiencies and limitations on the part of Christians, Christianity has, by comparison, accomplished vastly more for human progress than any other of the world's faiths. And not only by its works does Christianity make itself known, but also, and supremely, by that inherent, essential superiority which manifests itself to the eye of unprejudiced and pure rational judgment, discerning the things that are excellent.

In nothing is the true supremacy of the Christian Faith better attested than in the inner regeneration which takes place in other faiths when Christianity comes into close contact with them. This is the most remarkable religious fact, perhaps, in the life of the Orient to-day. Buddhism in India, in China, and in Japan is undergoing a marked purification in the direction of Christian ideals. Mohammedanism itself is becoming leavened with Christian principles to an extent but little understood. . . .

Why not, then, be content with this result? Why not let Christianity do its work indirectly, and depend upon these rooted religions to develop into a purity and power sufficient for the needs of their own races? The answer is that these religions, in spite of temporary resuscitation, are effete, and have not the power of development and adaptation; they lack the moral and spiritual vigour and resources to meet the multiplying demands of advancing humanity. It is the old parable of the new wine and the old wineskins.

But, granted the need of a universal religion, and that none of the Oriental religions is able to meet the need, why should it be any individual religion, and not rather a new and greater religion made up of the best in all the religions, a religion of religions, a splendid hybrid obtained by what has been termed the "cross-fertilisation of religions"? At first blush there is a certain fascination in this idea. It has an air of breadth and cosmopolitanism that gives it glitter, but it soon fades. It is seen that a religion which is coldly compounded of various religions, which is everything in general and nothing in particular, is no religion at all. . . . The dream of a polyglot religion is evaporating. What humanity needs and will demand is a religion with a character of its own and a history of its own, a religion whose roots have gone down deep into the soil of many generations, which has grown up in its own strength and with a sense of its own mission, against which storms have beaten and suns have burned in vain, and which has stood the test of time and transplanting, and changing civilizations. A religion which has thus sufficient might of its own, and yet sufficient real breadth and inclusiveness to absorb and conserve the truth of other religions, is far better fitted to become the religion of mankind than any syncretism or eclecticism.

IV.

If Christianity is to be set forward, not simply as a missionary religion, a world-evangel, to summon responsive souls out of other religions unto itself, but rather as a world-religion, a faith for universal humanity, its adherents must strike away all the shackles that bind it, all the cumbersome, adventitious non-essentials that have become attached to it, and restore to it the freedom of its qualities, the strength and simplicity of its original unobscured vision and unencumbered power. Too many intelligent men of our own time, who have never looked for the essence of Christianity, have identified it with dogmas and forms which really have no more to do with real Christianity than clothing has to do with the man. Whatever any school of Christians may protest as to the infidelity of refusing to identify Christianity with a miraculous revelation, or an infallible Bible, of [or] predestination, or substitutionary atonement, or eternal punishment, it is inexcusable for an educated person to be blind to the fact that these doctrines never were, nor can be, a part of essential Christianity. The Christian faith has won its way sometimes with the aid of these doctrines, sometimes in spite of them, but never because of them. Christianity is a religion of rational freedom, and if it has too often been forced to assume the form of religion of external authority, the result can only be a transient travesty of its true character, certain in time to be cast aside.

And not only must Christianity be divested of its *impedimenta* if it is to make conquest of the world, there must be restored to it also that genius of adaptation to varied human need and environment which enabled it to break the bonds of Judaism and respond to the unconscious call of the Gentile world. This inexhaustible adaptability, this power of lending itself to the deeper needs of varied races without losing its own character and individuality, is, I repeat, characteristic of Christianity. . . .

It is a natural blunder to imagine that we of the West have made Christianity exclusively our own, explored it, exhausted it, stamped upon it its final form. We carry it back to the Orient as if it were our gift to the peoples that gave it birth. In a sense it is, in another sense it is their gift to us. Already Christianity is escaping our hands to do its own great work in its own way. The day of the missionary, noble as it has been and is, already draws toward its close. Vitalised and vitalising Christian churches and civilisations are rising with firm but not ungrateful insistence to claim the right to develop in their own way. Again the herald of the Coming One is forced to proclaim with mingled sadness and joy, "He must increase, but I must decrease."

V.

The result of placing Christianity among the religions, of subjecting it to a free and impartial comparison with other faiths, is thus twofold. In the first place, its kinship with other religions is proved. The religious development of the race is one, culminating in Christianity. The Christian faith has drawn up into itself and assimilated the highest ideas and aspirations of mankind. The life-blood of the religion of humanity flows in its veins; its victories are the fruitage, in part, of all the spiritual struggles of the race from its infancy. In the second place, such a comparison reveals the inherent supremacy of Christianity, its historical uniqueness, the vitalising personality of its Christ, its unparalleled power of adaptation and development, thus laying upon it, with increasing urgency, the divine obligation of universality.

> SOURCE: John W. Buckham, "Christianity Among the Religions,"
> *The Hibbert Journal,* VII (October, 1908—July, 1909),
> 513–21. Used by permission of *The Hibbert Journal.*

LITERATURE

Of first importance as a source reference is Nelson R. Burr's *A Critical Bibliography in Religion,* in J. Ward Smith and A. Leland Jamison, eds., *Religion in American Life* (4 vols., Princeton, 1961), Vol. IV, Part 5, Sec. 3, A–E. For superior short essays on Christocentric liberalism, see Theodore T. Munger, "The New Theology," *The Freedom of Faith* (N.Y., 1883), 3–69; George A. Gordon, "The Contrast and Agreement Between the New Orthodoxy and the Old," *Andover Review,* XIX (1893), 1–18; "Some Things Worth While in Theology," *Harvard Theological Review,* III (1910), 375–402; Lewis French Stearns, "The Present Direction of Theological Thought in the Congregational Churches of the United States [1891]," *Present Day Theology* (N.Y., 1893), 533–45; W. A. Brown, "The Old Theology and the New," *Harvard Theological Review,* IV (1911), 1–24; Arthur C. McGiffert, Jr., "Protestant Liberalism," in David E. Roberts and Henry Pitney Van Dusen, eds., *Liberal Theology: An Appraisal* (N.Y., 1942), 106–20; Henry P. Van Dusen, "The Liberal Movement in Theology," in Samuel M. Cavert and Henry P. Van Dusen, eds., *The Church*

Through Half a Century (N.Y., 1936), 67–88. Two longer surveys are John W. Buckham's *Progressive Religious Thought in America* (Boston, 1919), and Frank H. Foster's *The Modern Movement in American Theology* (N.Y., 1939). Egbert C. Smyth and his seminary associates are explored critically in Daniel Day Williams' *The Andover Liberals* (N.Y., 1941). For twentieth-century trends in liberal theology, see Gerald B. Smith, *Current Christian Thinking* (Chicago, 1928), Chaps. 3, 6–7, 9.

For treatments of special aspects of liberal theology, see A. C. McGiffert, "Divine Immanence," in *The Rise of Modern Religious Ideas* (N.Y., 1915), Chap. 10; John W. Buckham, *The Humanity of God* (N.Y., 1928), emphasizing the Divine Fatherhood; Borden Parker Bowne, *The Immanence of God* (Boston, 1905); Francis J. McConnell, *The Christlike God* (N.Y., 1927); John Dillenberger, *Protestant Thought and Natural Science* (N.Y., 1960), Chap. 8; Munger, "Evolution and the Faith," in *The Appeal to Life* (N.Y., 1887), 209–43; Walter Horton, "Science and Theology," in Cavert and Van Dusen, eds., *op. cit.,* Chap. 4; E. Clinton Gardner, "Horace Bushnell's Doctrine of Depravity," *Theology Today,* XII (1955), 10–26; H. Shelton Smith, *Changing Conceptions of Original Sin: A Study in American Theology Since 1750* (N.Y., 1955), Chaps. 7 and 8; William Adams Brown, "The Place of Christ in Modern Theology," *American Journal of Theology,* XVI (1912), 31–50; Gerald B. Smith, "The Christ of Faith and the Jesus of History," *American Journal of Theology,* XVIII (1914), 521–44; Eugene W. Lyman, "The Place of Christ in Modern Theology," *Journal of Religion,* IX (1929), 184–203; Henry Sloane Coffin, *The Meaning of the Cross* (N.Y., 1931); Harry Emerson Fosdick, *Christianity and Progress* (N.Y., 1922).

There is no comprehensive study of Christocentric liberalism, and therefore the critical student should devote his primary attention to the basic writings of the major liberal thinkers. Bushnell, the brilliant fountainhead of the movement, must be given sustained study, especially his *Nature and the Supernatural* (N.Y., 1858), and *The Vicarious Sacrifice* (N.Y., 1866). Mary B. Cheney's *Life and Letters of Horace Bushnell* (N.Y., 1880) contains some important letters. Barbara M. Cross has cast some interesting new light on Bushnell's pastoral ministry in her *Horace Bushnell: Minister to a Changing America* (Chicago, 1958). An older work still of some value is Theodore T. Munger's *Horace Bushnell, Preacher and Theologian* (Boston, 1899). Lewis French Stearns' *The Evidence of Christian Experience* (N.Y., 1891) is indispensable for an understanding of the evangelical basis of liberalism. Newman Smyth's *The Religious Feeling* (N.Y., 1877) and *Old Faiths in New Light* (N.Y., 1879) deserve more attention than they have received. His *Recollections and Reflections* (N.Y., 1926) contains many sidelights on liberal theology. One of the greatest Christocentric thinkers of his time was George A. Gordon, whose *The Christ of Today* (Boston, 1895) sounded the alarm against the decline of classical Christology. His most enduring work is *Ultimate Conceptions of Faith* (Boston, 1903), but others of value include *Immortality and the New Theodicy* (Boston, 1897), *Humanism in New England Theology* (Boston, 1920), *The New Epoch for Faith* (Boston, 1901), and *Religion and Miracle* (Boston, 1909). His autobiography, *My Education and Religion* (Boston, 1925), is important supplementary reading. Arthur Cushman McGiffert's theological views are best disclosed in *Christianity as History and Faith,* ed. A. C. McGiffert, Jr. (N.Y., 1934). In addition to Borden Parker Bowne's

The Immanence of God (Boston, 1905), and *Personalism* (Boston, 1908), one should consult his *Studies in Christianity* (Boston, 1909). A valuable guide to the understanding of this great personalist is Francis J. McConnell's *Borden Parker Bowne* (N.Y., 1929). Henry Churchill King's best book in religious thought is *Reconstruction in Theology* (N.Y., 1901). An excellent essay showing that Eugene W. Lyman belonged essentially to the Christocentric liberal tradition is Walter M. Horton's "Eugene W. Lyman: Liberal Christian Thinker," in David E. Roberts and Henry Pitney Van Dusen, eds., *Liberal Theology: An Appraisal* (N.Y., 1942), 3–44. This volume contains a full list of Lyman's publications.

One of the two greatest systematizers of Christocentric liberalism was William Newton Clarke, whose *An Outline of Christian Theology* (N.Y., 1898) was enormously influential. His *The Christian Doctrine of God* (N.Y., 1909) and *The Use of the Scriptures in Theology* (N.Y., 1905) are valuable supplements to the *Outline*. For a highly illuminating essay on Clarke's contribution to modern theology, see W. A. Brown, "The Theology of William Newton Clarke," *Harvard Theological Review*, III (1910), 167–80. W. A. Brown's *Christian Theology in Outline* (N.Y., 1906) is more scholarly than Clarke's *Outline*, and also gives a better historical background in its treatment of the various doctrines. Brown's theological views are further elaborated in *The Essence of Christianity* (N.Y., 1902), Chap. 8; *The Christian Hope* (N.Y., 1912); *God at Work: A Study of the Supernatural* (N.Y., 1933); *Finding God in a New World* (N.Y., 1935); and *How to Think of Christ* (N.Y., 1945). Much light is thrown upon Brown's life and thought in his autobiography, *A Teacher and His Times* (N.Y., 1940).

CHAPTER XVIII

Variant Orthodoxies

AMERICAN life, including church life, had from early days been intensely dynamic—mobile, adaptive, activistic. But almost to the end of the nineteenth century this dynamism had failed to find deep and conscious expression in the theology of the orthodox churches. The churches were reproducing, or at least attempting to reproduce, the theology of earlier generations with the least possible variation; in other words, they were not theologizing analytically and seriously about the realities of their own existence. It is true, revivalism had developed a streamlined, simplified theology for those who came under its influence, but it was mostly a negative, stripping-off process, and it had seldom been done deliberately or systematically. American theology in 1865 had much furniture in the storeroom which it never used in the living room. The social and cultural changes of the late nineteenth and early twentieth centuries constituted a time of testing of American theology. Amid the heart-searching in the cultural crisis, what had been latent factors pointing toward some restatement of the faith now became patent and self-conscious. On the other hand, those who deliberately chose to retain the faith unchanged now had to define it anew against both challengers and innovators. In the process of defining it in terms of the new issues and against new opponents the resisters, too, inevitably made alterations in it. Previous chapters have dealt with those who undertook radical theological revision [1] and with those who mediated between the new views and historic orthodoxy.[2] The present chapter will concern itself with those who resisted theological change.

Christians who resisted the new theological forces usually did so in one or more of the following ways: (1) by re-emphasis on the authority of the church; (2) by means of a "scholastic" theology; or (3) by preoccupation with pietism or apocalypticism. The immediate objectives of resistance were to preserve the principle of authority, whether it was the authority of pope, of apostolic succession, of an inerrant Bible, or of a theological system. These authorities were not, of course, regarded as ultimate ends in themselves but were jealously guarded because they were considered indispensable avenues of approach to God, or because they were regarded as having a special and direct divine sanction. To sacrifice them, it was felt, would be to lose hold of the absolute and to fall into the morass of contemporary relativism. Thus, many of the men considered in the present chapter were

---

[1] See *supra*, Chap. 16.   [2] See *supra*, Chap. 17.

fighting a crusade, defending the Ark of the Covenant, with a desperation and a finality which it was almost impossible for their more urbane opponents—champions of bright, new ideas—fully to appreciate.

The outstanding example of resistance to change by re-emphasis on the authority of the church was of course the Roman Catholic Church. Because this type of authority is centered in a living institution, the church, it allows adjustment, continually renewed compromise between tradition and the new realities, with the church defining what is the essential meaning of tradition in relation to the emerging situation. While this procedure makes some room for modification of definitions, methods, and processes, it can permit, in the case of Roman Catholicism at least, no thoroughgoing reconstruction. The dominating role of the past is seen in the condemnation of the theological bogey, "Americanism," and in the far more determined repudiation of "Modernism."

Among American Episcopalians, too, the authority of church tradition —as transmitted through bishops in apostolic succession—acted as a brake on theological and social change, but to a much lesser degree than among Roman Catholics. Before the end of the nineteenth century High Church Anglicans in both England and the United States were assimilating many of the theological innovations of the time and were interested in social reform, within, of course, the existing social structure. Far more conservative theologically was the numerically small Reformed Episcopal Church which separated from the Protestant Episcopal Church in 1873, not over contemporary theological issues but over churchmanship, as a protest against exclusion of non-Episcopalians from Episcopal communion. The conservatism of the seceders was not based on the authority of the church, but, like the conservatism of many other Protestant evangelical bodies, was based on scholasticism and pietism.

A second, and, among American Protestants, a far more important way of resisting change was by resort to theological scholasticism. Lutheranism and the Reformed faith in the seventeenth century each developed a type of scholastic theology. The Protestant Reformation of the sixteenth century had claimed to rediscover faith as a vital principle, as personal trust in the living God known in Jesus Christ. Ensuing theological controversy more and more diverted emphasis to propositional correctness, to the elaboration of definitions, and to the statement of the faith in terms which would be convincing to the reason. Amid this orthodox rationalism, the Reformation's central dynamic concept of faith as vital trust in God was obscured. Furthermore, this "digging in" process that went on during the seventeenth and eighteenth centuries rendered theology less mobile and less adaptable to new cultural situations. The faith congealed and resisted further change.

Among American Lutherans the influence of theological scholasticism was evident in the vigorous reaction against Samuel S. Schmucker's "American Lutheranism." [3] Following this crisis, Lutheranism in the United States became increasingly strict in its confessionalism, subscribing not only the irenic and ecumenically-minded Augsburg Confession, but in many cases also the polemic and somewhat scholastic Formula of Concord, first published in 1580. Increasingly committed to its elaborate confessionalism, American Lutheranism was able successfully to resist theological change throughout the nineteenth century. This was particularly true of the Missouri Synod of Lutherans and of the related Synodical Conference. Many branches of American Lutheranism, during part of the time, found a further protective insulation in language barriers. [4] But Lutheranism retained, in an even more central position than did other Protestant bodies, the great substantive principle of the Reformation, salvation by grace received through faith alone. This principle retained latent dynamism and remained as a potential corrective to any scholasticism. The second quarter of the twentieth century found American Lutheranism, having surmounted its language barrier, in process of uniting its own household, entering prominently into the ecumenical movement, and dealing more directly with contemporary American theological issues. By 1930, American Lutheranism was beginning to assume its full role as one of the largest and weightiest of the American churches and was bringing to the national community a distinctive historic type of Protestantism, which had been preserved more nearly in its original classical type than had almost any other form of American Protestantism.

A very influential type of scholasticism was found among the American Reformed and Presbyterian Churches in the nineteenth century. It perhaps received its most elaborate and consistent American expression in Princeton Theological Seminary. Using as its philosophical foundation Scottish common-sense realism, [5] this theology patterned its method after the method of the natural sciences. The Bible was said to be to the theologian what nature is to the natural scientist; and from these biblical data, by an "inductive" method, the theologian should quarry and arrange his systematic theology. [6] To be sure, belief in the inspiration of Scripture was not declared necessary for salvation. All that was necessary for salvation was confidence in the Bible as a reasonably trustworthy historical record. In the biblical writings one reads of Jesus of Nazareth, and one becomes a Christian by saving faith in him as the unique Son of God. But having come to saving faith in Christ, so the argument ran, one discovers that Christ accepted the Old Testament Scriptures as the inspired Word of God and promised the Holy Spirit to the writers of the New Testament. Therefore, on the

---

[3] See *supra*, 101.

[4] Cf. Heinrich H. Maurer, "Studies in the Sociology of Religion," *American Journal of Sociology*, XXX (1924–25), 257–86, 408–38, 534–50, 665–82; XXXI (1925–26), 39–57, 485–506; XXXIV (1928–29), 282–95.

[5] Cf. Sydney E. Ahlstrom, "The Scottish Philosophy and American Theology," *Church History*, XXIV (1955), 257–72.

[6] Charles Hodge, *Systematic Theology*, I (N.Y., 1871), 1–18.

authority of Christ, the Christian should accept the entire Scriptures as the inspired Word of God, from which, inductively, he can then draw a systematic theology. Many in the late nineteenth and twentieth centuries found this "objective" theological method a welcome antidote to the subjectivism and uncertainty which was implicit in much of the liberalism of the times. But this type of scholasticism, with its "objectivity" and its method patterned on the highly external and impersonal method of the natural sciences, found it impossible to do full justice to the historic Reformed emphasis on the witness of the Holy Spirit to the heart of the Christian. Furthermore, the method was peculiarly vulnerable to attack from the new biblical criticism. But in spite of its weaknesses, the method continued to enjoy wide vogue in fundamentalist and in neo-fundamentalist circles even after 1930.

A third way of resisting change, which was widely employed among American Protestants, was by absorption in pietism, sometimes combined with apocalypticism. In the late nineteenth century, the heritage of revivalism bifurcated. Part of it, abandoning the old revivalistic technique, combined its emphasis on inner spiritual experience with the new romantic-idealistic emphasis on feelings to form a basic ingredient in the new liberal theology. The rebellion against rigidity in theology and in methods which was seen in a man like Charles G. Finney, together with his subjective and pragmatic standard of spiritual values, inclined toward the new liberal theology. On the other hand, after the Civil War much of American revivalism became fixed in method and content and professionalized in personnel. Its early spontaneity and unpredictableness largely disappeared. Originally dynamic and revolutionary, it now became stereotyped and a chief bulwark of religious conservatism. But in circles where its theological presuppositions remained unchallenged, it still retained considerable power.

Pietism and scholasticism constituted the two chief foundations of Protestant conservatism after 1865. But the two were uneasy yokefellows. Scholasticism was learned, sometimes pedantic, but inclined toward a cold and objective temper, with little skill or daring in soul surgery. Pietism, on the other hand, still traveled light theologically, but retained much of its early fervor and practical skill in spiritual midwifery. Pietism and scholasticism could unite forces against such a common foe as theological liberalism, but left to themselves, they were happier apart. In the 1920's, scholasticism supplied to the fundamentalist movement whatever intellectual weight it possessed, while pietism supplied to it its outreach and zeal and a degree of creative imagination.

In the period, 1865–1930, the pietistic tradition produced such revivalists as Dwight L. Moody (1837–99), Samuel P. Jones (1847–1906), R. A. Torrey (1856–1928), J. Wilbur Chapman (1859–1918), and Billy Sunday (1863–1935). Their procedures had become highly stylized. Great city "campaigns" enlisted the support of the Protestant churches *en masse*, covered the city with publicity and promotional organization, and won hundreds, sometimes thousands, of converts. What had once been an effort to achieve complete spontaneity now utilized the high-pressure methods of big business. The pietistic tradition in this period also expressed itself in important institutions. In 1886 the Moody Bible Institute of Chicago was founded, followed by the Bible Institute of Los Angeles (1907) and many similar institutions, imbuing thousands of laymen and some ministers with positive conceptions of Christian experience and with a rather rigid system of Christian beliefs. Bible conferences and faith missions further carried these views across the country and around the world.

Pietism was interested not only in conversion but in Christian holiness after conversion. Ever since the time of John Wesley, revivalism in the English-speaking world had been periodically accompanied by perfectionist teaching, the view that it is possible for a Christian to live free from all known sin.[7] In 1859 William E. Boardman, an American Presbyterian who had come under Methodist influence, published *The Higher Christian Life,* which taught the possibility of a life of perfect holiness. Giving his whole time after 1870 to propagating the doctrine, he went, in 1873, to London, where Moody and Sankey were conducting their highly successful revival in England and Scotland (1873–75). In the wake of this, Boardman and the like-minded Robert Pearsall Smith, in the interests of their particular brand of perfectionism, conducted a series of remarkable conventions, culminating in great meetings at Oxford in 1874 and at Brighton in 1875. Out of these meetings grew the English Keswick Movement. Both before and after Boardman's trip to England, the "Higher Life" doctrines were exerting influence in America. In 1910, Charles G. Trumbull (1872–1941), editor of the *Sunday School Times,* which enjoyed considerable circulation among American conservatives, was converted to the Keswick type of perfectionism and propagated it ardently through the *Times* and at conferences held in Princeton, New Jersey, and later in Keswick, New Jersey. Keswick perfectionism, though rooted in Wesleyanism, was definitely quietistic, teaching that the Christian can attain full holiness only when he abandons all efforts and allows the Holy Spirit to live within him the life of Christ.[8]

Far more numerous than the advocates of Keswickism were the adherents of various "holiness" movements in America. Many of these were offshoots of Methodism, aspiring to recover Methodism's "original" emphasis on holiness. Their striving after an absolute ethic was often intense and their spirit, in early stages at least, highly separatistic. There was a strong spirit of protest against the "worldliness" which was thought to prevail within

---

[7] Cf. *supra,* 42.

[8] For a hostile but informing brief treatment, cf. Benjamin B. Warfield, *Perfectionism* (2 vols., N.Y., 1931), I, 312–21; II, 463–611. Steven Barabas, *So Great Salvation: The History and Message of the Keswick Convention* (London, 1952), is sympathetic. *Victory in Christ: A Report of Princeton Conference, 1916* (Phila., 1916), contains addresses by Charles G. Trumbull.

the more conventional churches, and there was little tendency to co-operate with other Christians, even with other holiness groups. As time passed, however, these groups tended gradually toward the more conventional type of American denominationalism. Among the fastest growing and most important of the holiness bodies were those known as Pentecostals, of which the largest was the Assemblies of God.[9]

Apocalypticism has sometimes accompanied revivalism in America. There have been two principal interpretations of the predicted return of Christ to earth—the postmillennial and the premillennial. The postmillennial view held that Christ's return would be after his predicted millennial reign. The millennial kingdom, thus placed before Christ's return, was made continuous with the present life of the church and was regarded as the climax of the church's history in the present world, when the power of the Holy Spirit would show itself more fully in the holiness of individual Christians and even in the transformation of social institutions. Jonathan Edwards taught this doctrine in the eighteenth century, as did his disciple, Samuel Hopkins. It was one of the inspirations underlying the founding of American foreign missions and the development of the "benevolent empire" in the early nineteenth century. In the latter part of the nineteenth century this concept of the climactic reign of Christ on earth through his church was interpreted in still more secular and sociological terms by the new social gospel.

Simultaneously with the secularization of the postmillennial interpretation of Christ's return, there was among many in the American evangelical churches a revival of the premillennial view of Christ's return—that is, the more radically supernatural conception that he would return to earth before the millennium, and then set up on earth a kingdom under his personal, visible rule. This view received great impetus from a nondenominational Prophetic Conference which was held in Holy Trinity Episcopal Church, New York, in 1878. By repudiating the idea that the history of the Christian church would climax in a millennium of blessing and righteousness, premillennialism created a gulf between the "church" and the "world," which would be effectively bridged only by the physical return of Christ. Logically, and usually also actually, premillennialism disparaged all social meliorative activities of the church as hopeless. The church should concentrate on saving souls, plucking "brands from the burning," in the short time remaining before Christ's return. Though highly critical of the social gospel, the revived premillennialism showed notable zeal in evangelism and in foreign missions. While it did not completely capture revivalism, it was often found in conjunction with it. Both pietism and apocalypticism,

---

[9] Literature from within the movement remains uncritical and patriotic. Cf. Stanley H. Frodsham, *With Signs Following: The Story of the Pentecostal Revival in the Twentieth Century* (rev. ed., Springfield, Mo., 1946). On the "holiness" group, cf. Elmer T. Clark, *The Small Sects in America* (rev. ed., N.Y., 1949).

whether separately or together, refused to come to terms with the theological and social changes of the day—pietism by ignoring them and preoccupying itself with the inner spiritual life, and apocalypticism by escaping into an age of future blessedness. But scholastic theology, with its strong emphasis on reason, shied away from the excessive supernaturalism of premillennialism, although on occasion it allied itself uncomfortably with premillennialism against the common enemy, liberalism.[10]

The premillennialism which was revived by the Prophetic Conference of 1878 and by a series of subsequent similar conferences was led by clergymen of such churches as the Presbyterian, Reformed, Episcopal, and Congregational, and found its chief following within the conventional denominations. But a more extreme type of apocalypticism was to be found outside of the conventional churches. The failure of William Miller's prediction that Christ would return physically to earth in 1844 was followed by a continuing Adventist movement, the most important branch of which was the Seventh-day Adventists, which, in addition to observing Saturday as the Sabbath, developed a very elaborate and somewhat unique interpretation of biblical prophecy.

Much farther removed from the conventional churches were the Jehovah's Witnesses, who were founded by "Pastor" Charles Taze Russell (1852–1916) in 1872 and in 1931 adopted the name "Jehovah's Witnesses." They combined apocalypticism with outspoken criticism of existing social institutions. Contemporary class struggle and speculative concern about the meaning of history are both echoed in this movement which has found most of its following among the less privileged social groups.

The theological issues of the period, 1865–1930, were closely related to practical problems of church work. The activism of the times and increasing emphasis on efficiency caused the churches to take a pragmatic view of theology. Theology must not divert energy from more "practical" matters. Above all, it must not, by producing bitter controversy, divide the church and weaken its missionary and educational enterprises. Rather, when efficiency required larger unions, many were ready to sacrifice theological distinctions for the sake of the larger practical objectives.

The so-called fundamentalist movement, which reached its height in the later 1920's, was in part precipitated by the impetus given to church unity by World War I. Many in the churches suddenly became fearful that essential Christian truth was being lightly discarded. But the immediate roots of the fundamentalist controversy reached back many decades into American history, a fact which has too commonly been ignored in discussions of fundamentalism. Its roots went directly into the 1880's and 1890's when the issues created by biblical criticism and theological change were

[10] Shirley J. Case, *The Millennial Hope* (Chicago, 1918); D. H. Kromminga, *The Millennium in the Church* (Grand Rapids, Mich., 1945); C. Norman Kraus, *Dispensationalism in America* (Richmond, Va., 1958).

being discussed among the evangelical denominations. From then on, debate continued intermittently.[11] World War I, by accelerating the pressure for change, caused many long-standing grievances to come to a head. The war also fomented a spirit of aggressiveness and combat which was conspicuous on both sides in the fundamentalist-modernist controversy. Perhaps the war, with its avowed purpose of complete victory, contributed something further to the theological battle. According to slogans of the day, the war was fought "to make the world safe for democracy"; it was "a war to end war." That is, the war fostered an idea that by an immediate all-out struggle issues could be settled "once and for all." Long aggravated by the steady gains of the new theology, resisters of change sought a "show-down" fight which would permanently end the peril. The attempt has been made to establish the rural character of fundamentalism, but this is dubious.[12] Cities such as Philadelphia, Minneapolis, Fort Worth, Denver, and Los Angeles were chief centers of fundamentalist strength.

At its peak, the fundamentalist-modernist controversy seriously disturbed many of the leading denominations of the country.[13] A few minor schisms resulted, but the desire to retain united strength for church work prevented large disruptions. The fundamentalists failed to impose their sharply defined theological requirements on a single major denomination where the struggle was waged, and by the end of the 1920's the controversy had largely subsided.

Fundamentalism challenged naturalism in the name of historic Christianity. It was important and necessary that a challenge be made, but fundamentalism's definition of the "enemy" and its definition of the issue were not acceptable. Like the papal encyclical of 1907 against modernism, fundamentalists inclined to attribute to evangelical liberals radical implications of their positions which these theologians themselves vigorously repudiated. In defining the issues, fundamentalism did not point in the direction which the most representative evangelical thought was soon to take. The doctrine of the incarnation is central for historic Christianity. But this was not properly formulated or adequately defended by fundamentalism's emphasis on the virgin birth of Christ. The conception of revelation from God is basic to Christianity, but insistence on the inerrancy of the Bible in no sense takes the measure of the problem. The question of the relation of God to the physical universe has been a central problem in western thought since the rise of natural science three centuries ago, but it is not properly dealt with by insisting on the historicity of physical miracles like the raising of Lazarus. Fundamentalism drew a necessary line between historic Christianity

[11] For an example of the early beginnings of this controversy in a leading denomination, see Lefferts A. Loetscher, *The Broadening Church: A Study of Theological Issues in the Presbyterian Church Since 1869* (Phila., 1954).

[12] Norman F. Furniss, *The Fundamentalist Controversy, 1918–1931* (New Haven, 1954), 26–9.

[13] *Ibid.*, 103–76; Stewart G. Cole, *The History of Fundamentalism* (N.Y., 1931), 65–225.

and naturalism, but it drew the line at the wrong place. With the gradual decline of the fundamentalist controversy, the way was open for a more profound and more creative discussion of basic Christian truth.

144. Papal Infallibility Defended

In an era of doubt and uncertainty the claims of the Roman Catholic Church to authority appealed to many. This authoritarianism reached its climax in the dogma of papal infallibility as promulgated by the Vatican Council in 1870. The dogma declares:

When the Roman pontiff speaks *ex cathedra,* that is, when discharging the office of the Shepherd and Doctor of all Christians, in virtue of his supreme apostolic authority [he] defines a doctrine to be held by the Universal Church concerning faith or morals, he enjoys (by divine assistance promised to him in the blessed Peter) that infallibility by which the Divine Redeemer wished his Church to be instructed in the definition of doctrine concerning faith or morals; and therefore such definitions of the Roman Pontiff are irreformable of themselves, and not by virtue of the consent of the Church.[14]

This in effect made church councils superfluous, or at least reduced them to an advisory role. The Vatican Council also asserted the pope's universal episcopate, that is, his direct authority in every diocese. Roman Catholic church government was thus made even more vigorous and effective, though at the price of becoming an absolute monarchy. Loss of the papacy's temporal power later in this same year, 1870, proved ultimately to be a blessing in disguise by relieving the papal court of the burden of purely political administration. The decisions of the Vatican Council had the effect of further widening the distance between Roman Catholicism and Protestantism.

The council attracted much non-Catholic attention in the United States. American newspapers covered it in stories and editorials, which were prevailingly hostile and sometimes factually incorrect. But as the months of deliberation wore on, from the opening session on December 8, 1869, to the climactic vote on infallibility on July 18, 1870, newspaper interest declined noticeably.[15]

American prelates attended the council—six archbishops, thirty-nine bishops, and one abbot. Among them was Bernard John McQuaid, American-born son of an Irish factory worker, since 1868 bishop of Rochester, New York. Twenty letters of Bishop McQuaid, which he wrote while

[14] J. B. Bury, *History of the Papacy in the Nineteenth Century (1864–1878),* ed. R. H. Murray (London, 1930), 134.
[15] J. R. Beiser, *The Vatican Council and the American Secular Newspapers, 1869–70* (Washington, 1941).

in Rome attending the council, are extant. Concerning the mooted infallibility doctrine, McQuaid reported that "the feeling is very strong, *pro* and *con*," [16] and that the American, German, French, British, and Eastern bishops were being outvoted by the Italians, Spaniards, and South Americans.[17] Anticipating the adoption of the infallibility doctrine, he feared that "the damage to the Church will be immense. In some countries there will be large schisms. . . . If some decrees are passed as they have been presented to us, we can look for hard times in all countries in which Catholics and protestants are expected to live together." [18] The day before the final vote he wrote despondently, "They have ended by making the definition [of infallibility] as absolute and strict as it was possible to make it. As a consequence a large *non placet* vote will be recorded against it. What will be the consequence in some of these European countries God only knows." [19] But the results for the Catholic Church were not so calamitous as the good bishop feared. Though a vigorous and able minority had opposed the definition of infallibility, in the end not a single bishop refused to accept it. It is true, the Old Catholic Church, with its center of strength in Germany, separated as a result of this council, but it did not draw out any large proportion of the parent body. Bishop McQuaid himself, though he had been among those at the council who courageously resisted the definition of infallibility, accepted it when once adopted and in his cathedral on August 28, 1870, sought by the address here presented to ensure acceptance of it in his own diocese.

DOCUMENT

The question is simple enough. The definition is clear enough. The Pope is declared to be infallible. This is the ordinary language used, and men are horrified that a man like this should be made infallible, raised above man, made somet[h]ing like God in heaven, one that cannot err, one that cannot be deceived. When we use the term: "The Pope is Infallible," in that sense, it is not correct—it is not true. The Pope is infallible in certain things. He is not a man that is made infallible in all things. The doctrine declares that the head of the Church, the Sovereign Pontiff, exercising the office of supreme head of the Church, IN MATTERS OF FAITH AND MORALS as contained in the Scriptures, as revealed by Christ and contained in the apostolic traditions, cannot err, not because his nature has been changed, but he cannot err, when thus acting in such matters, by the divine assistance that is thus given him—that is, when he has fulfilled the office of Peter, Prince of the Apostles, in teaching the Universal Church the things of morals and of faith revealed by Christ, the assistance of God will be with him to keep [him] from error. But in politics, in busi-

[16] H. J. Browne, "The Letters of Bishop McQuaid from the Vatican Council," *Catholic Historical Review*, XLI (1955–56), 412.

[17] *Ibid.*, 416. [18] *Ibid.*, 430, 431. [19] *Ibid.*, 440–1.

ness matters, and the government of his own State, in temporal affairs, in scientific subjects or literary subjects, he stands where all other men stand, and his knowledge is worth the capacity of his mind, and the education it has received. God has never promised to be with him under such circumstances nor in such cases.

And now many minds are much troubled outside of the Catholic Church. Why were they not troubled when the Church was declared to be infallible? They were more willing to admit the infallibility of the Pope and 500 Bishops than the infallibility of the Pope alone. The question is not about the power of infallibility, because the God that can make 500 Bishops united together infallible, is just as able to make one infallible, and when you bring 500 together, and they discuss a point as Catholics understand it, the result of their discussion and the result only has divine assistance. But men seem to think that in this gathering of 500 men there was a certain amount of security. There was just the amount of security that you would find in our Halls of Congress. A body of men assembled, having no promise of divine assistance, they might study, they might examine, they might discuss matters and come to a decision, but this decision might be as fallible as the decision of a single one; and so 500 Bishops coming together, unless the divine power, that was promised by Christ, was with them, they are just as liable to err as any other 500 men. And when we speak of the Council and its decision being infallible, it is not because there was a gathering of 500 learned, and wise, and able men, but because we looked for the Spirit of God to come down and rest upon the counsels of those men, so that the decision that went forth was not the act of a simple gathering, of the united wisdom of those men, but it was something that had within it power, light, and knowledge from the Spirit of God. The decision given out was an infallible decision, because it was in accordance with the Spirit of God.

And now, when the Holy Father, acting in the capacity spoken of, not writing letters, not discussing the matter as a theologian, but, when addressing the Universal Church, not an instruction to this Bishop or to that one, but giving a solemn definition to the whole Church in matters of faith and morals as contained in the Scriptures and the Apostolic traditions— therefore, there can be no revelation, no inspiration, no new religion, nothing else than the deposit of faith which Christ left on earth—and when speaking thus and of these things, his definitions are infallible, they cannot err, they are the true doctrines. The doctrine then and thus given by the Holy Father is the true doctrine—the very doctrine which Christ our Lord gave.

Now, you will say, there was a variety of opinions and much disputing among the Bishops with regard to this matter. Well, there was; and what was the point of the dispute, and upon what did they differ? It was whether, in making these definitions, the Holy Father should consult the Bishops just as in the Council he has consulted them. And whilst in the text of the definition, in the first part of it you will notice, when it is properly placed before you, we are told, in the past this the Holy Father has always done and, no doubt, to the end of time he always will do. But the definition does not admit that this consulting of the Bishops is at all necessary to his rendering of an infallible definition. Some said it was. The smaller number said it was. The much greater number said it was not, and the result of the discussion and the definition that comes to us explicitly and clearly is that it is by no means necessary on the part of the Sovereign Pontiff to consult the Bishops before rendering an infallible definition on faith and morals. Some might say: "But since his present condition differs but little from his former one, why pass this definition and bring up the question, and so excite the minds of men?" The minds of men will be excited by something or other to the end of the world, and many judged it expedient that this definition should be passed to prevent trouble in the future, such as has arisen in the past. Now, for example, this is the first Council in 300 years, but during that time heresies arose—in Europe more than in this country. Men's minds are taken up with religious questions; sharp, acute minds work upon philosophical subjects, and in bringing out these philosophical subjects they trench upon the ground of faith. It is the peculiar office of the head of the Church to be ever ready to note when the faith is being assailed and to warn the Church of it and guard her from danger. This is the office of the Holy Father. This office he has always been exercising within the last 300 years. He has performed this work steadily, and as decision after decision has been given out, his definition has been received by the Church.

> SOURCE: F. J. Zwierlein, *The Life and Letters of Bishop McQuaid,*
> II (Rochester, N.Y., 1926), 60–2. Used by permission of
> Lewis J. Zwierlein.

145. Dwight L. Moody Proclaims God's Love

Revivalism, with its emphasis on spiritual experience and spontaneity, had often been associated in American history with mildly progressive theological tendencies. The Edwardean theologians, who were closely associated with revivalism, had successively modified their inherited Calvinism, and Charles G. Finney spoke impatiently of his church's creed as a "paper pope." By the end of the nineteenth century, the most direct heirs of Edwards and Finney were sponsoring the new liberal theology. Thus the American revivalistic heritage bifurcated. While a part of it contributed indirectly to the rise of liberalism and ceased to be revivalistic, the other branch became theologically stereotyped. This had long been true of frontier revivalism, and was true also of city evangelism in the post-Civil War period.

The city evangelists faced the tensions that were growing out of rapid industrialization and ideological change. They sometimes made passing references to social problems, and their theology was so simplified that men of differing beliefs and varying ecclesiologies were willing to support them in the hope that they could aid the churches in meeting the new urban crisis. But for all its simplicity and occasional ambiguity, the message quite consistently proclaimed by the city evangelists was a bulwark of the emerging fundamentalism.

Dwight Lyman Moody (1837–99) was perhaps the greatest of the city evangelists. Born on a Massachusetts farm, losing his father at the age of four, he had little formal education. At twenty-three he was well started toward prosperity in Chicago, but gave it up for the precarious income of a free-lance Christian lay worker. He was busy with Sunday school, Y.M.C.A., and work for Civil War soldiers in the United States Commission. An amazingly successful evangelistic tour of Great Britain (1873–75) with the singer, Ira D. Sankey, first gave him national fame. Great revival campaigns in Brooklyn, Philadelphia, New York, Chicago, Boston, Baltimore, St. Louis, and San Francisco which followed (1875–81) were the peak of his career. Thereafter much of his attention was directed to the founding of Northfield Seminary for girls, Mount Hermon School for boys, Moody Bible Institute, and to conferences and student work.

Moody combined transparent sincerity with the application to soul saving of the techniques of big business. Publicity, ministerial endorsement, financial support, lay workers—all were organized to the last detail. Moody remained a layman without theological education and spoke with great simplicity and directness. He translated the gospel into the literary style of the contemporary popular magazines which were deeply tinged with Victorian sentimentality.

Moody's central theme was God's yearning love for all men. The thunders of hell had receded. Though he welcomed the support of men like Henry Drummond and Lyman Abbott, who represented the newer theological tendencies, his own preaching was based on biblical literalism and a few fundamentals of faith. Social questions, he assumed, are to be solved by the conversion of individuals.[20]

The selection is from Moody's sermon on "God's Love for the Sinner," his most characteristic theme. Characteristic, too, are his references to the inquiry room, his easy, chatty style, and his warm, sentimental illustration from home life.

[20] For suggestive evaluations of Moody in the context of his times, cf. William G. McLoughlin, Jr., *Modern Revivalism: Charles Grandison Finney to Billy Graham* (New York, 1959), 166–281; Bernard A. Weisberger, *They Gathered at the River: The Story of the Great Revivalists and their Impact upon Religion in America* (Boston, 1958), 175–219.

We find a good many people in the inquiry-room night after night that tell us they cannot pray. They would like to pray, they say. Their sins are troubling them; they are weary and heavy laden, many of them cast down under their sins. They want to get rid of the burden, but they keep running after this man and that man, asking them to pray for them. Now, if a man can't pray, it must be because he has a false impression about God. It is a false idea which hinders you from praying to God now in your hearts—praying to Him here, not in your closet at home, but here in the silence of your hearts. The great truth we want to remember is that God loves the sinner. He hates sin, yea, with a perfect hatred; but he loves the sinner. God is love. Oh, that all in this assembly might feel this and be drawn towards Him! If you really want to be saved, just come to God, and He will save you. A man came to me in the inquiry-room the other night and said: "I cannot pray, I have not strength to pray, I am too vile." Now, God has given us just the words to meet this case. In the 5th chapter of Romans, at the 6th verse, we read: "For when we were without strength, in due time Christ died for the ungodly." It is a good thing to know that we have no strength, and to bear in mind that Christ died for the ungodly. Then this text has a lesson for another class. There was once a woman at an inquiry-meeting who thought she was not very bad, and, of course, she could find neither peace nor light while she believed in herself. Soon after, she heard a minister preach from this same text: "Christ died for the ungodly." She thought over this for a moment and said: "Oh, if I was only ungodly, I might get salvation!" But before the sermon was over the woman found that she was a great sinner; and, at the close, she took her place with the ungodly and got salvation then and there. . . .

I can imagine some mother saying: "If God loves me, why does He chasten me?" Not twenty-four hours ago a woman came into the inquiry-room and said: "If God loves me, why has He bereaved and afflicted me?" Well now, there was an answer for that woman in the twelfth chapter of Hebrews, at the fifth verse: "And ye have forgotten the exhortation which speaketh unto you as unto children: My son, despise not the chastening of the Lord, nor faint when thou art rebuked of Him."

I remember a few years ago, that my little girl used to be in the habit of getting up cross some mornings. You know how it is when any member of your family does not get up in a sweet temper; it disturbs all the rest of the family. Well, one morning she got up cross, and spoke in a cross way, and, finally, I said to her, "Emma, if you speak in that way again, I shall have to punish you." Now it was not because I didn't love her; it was because I did love her, and if I had to correct it was for the good of the little child. Well, that went off all right. One morning she got up cross again. I said nothing, but when she was getting ready to go to school she came up to me and said, "Papa, kiss me." I said, "Emma, I cannot kiss you this morning." She said, "Why, father?" "Because you have been cross again this morning; I cannot kiss you." She said, "Why, papa, you never refused to kiss me before." "Well, you have been naughty this morning." "Why don't you kiss me?" she said again. "Because you have been naughty. You will have to go to school without your kiss." She went into the other room where her mother was and said, "Mamma, papa don't love me. He won't kiss me. I wish you would go and get him to kiss me." But her mother said, "You know, Emma, that your father loves you, but you have been naughty." So she couldn't be kissed, and she went down stairs crying as if her heart would break, and I loved her so well that the tears came into my eyes. I could not help crying, and when I heard her going down stairs I could not keep down my tears. I think I loved her then better than I ever did, and when I heard the door close I went to the window and saw her going down the street weeping. I didn't feel good all that day. I believe I felt a good deal worse than the child did, and I was anxious for her to come home. How long that day seemed to me! And when she came home at night and came to me and asked me to forgive her, and told me how sorry she felt, how gladly I took her up and kissed her, and how happy she went up stairs to her bed. It is just so with God. He loves you, and when He chastises you, it is for your own good. . . .

In the Song of Solomon we read of the Lord: "His left hand is under my head, and His right arm doth embrace me. His banner is love!" God wants us all to come under that banner to-day. There was a man who came to this country from England and was naturalized; and after a year or two he went to Cuba. War broke out in 1867 there; and this man, though perfectly innocent, was arrested as a spy by the Spanish authorities, court-martialled, tried and condemned to be shot. He appealed to the English and American consuls, and they examined him and found that he was innocent, and went to the Spanish authorities and said, "He is not guilty of this charge; he must not be shot." But the Spanish officials said he had been tried by their laws and found guilty, and must die. There was no telegraph to Cuba then, and no time to hear from their Governments about the matter. The law must take its course. The morning of the day of execution came. The man was carried, with his coffin, to the spot where his open grave had just been dug. As he is sitting on the coffin, and just while the soldiers are awaiting the order "Fire," suddenly the noise of a carriage rapidly driven is heard. The American and English consuls step to the place of the condemned man. One wraps around him the Star Spangled Banner, the other the Union Jack. They say to the soldiers, "Fire on these flags if you dare!" And they dared not fire, and the man was released. It was not the flags which they feared, but the two powerful Governments which were behind the flags. To-day, God calls you to come under His banner of love. Legions of angels will help you, and God Himself will protect you and keep you. But if you do not accept His love, if you reject His salvation, do not think that God will receive harlots and drunkards, and sinners, unredeemed, into His kingdom. If you die in your sins, there is not in the Bible one ray of hope to show that there will be opportunity to repent hereafter. Now is the accepted time of salvation. Come under the banner of love. May the God of grace help you to come under the banner now and recognize Him as your Lord and Saviour. May you come to-night and be saved.

> SOURCE: D. L. Moody, *"To All People." Comprising Sermons, Bible Readings, Temperance Addresses, and Prayer-meeting Talks* (N.Y., 1877), 322–3, 331–4.

146. Biblical Inerrancy

The Presbyterian Church in the U.S.A. divided into Old School and New School branches in 1837 over questions of theology, church government, and slavery. The Civil War powerfully stimulated integrating forces in American life, and in 1869 the two branches reunited. Expressing the "honeymoon" spirit of the reunion, a theological journal, the *Presbyterian Review,* began to appear in 1880, under the joint editorship of a representative of the more liberal New School tradition, Charles A. Briggs of Union Theological Seminary, New York, and a representative of the more conservative Old School tradition, A. A. Hodge of Princeton Theological Seminary. Things went fairly smoothly until the editors, taking cognizance of the controversy over biblical criticism raised in Scotland by the case of William Robertson Smith, professor at Aberdeen, ran a series of eight articles (1881–83) on the critical study of the Bible, alternating between conservative and liberal spokesmen.[21] The series was extremely significant in calling wider popular attention to biblical criticism than had previously been done in America, and in starting a chain of events that led to Briggs's inaugural address of 1891 and to his final suspension from the Presbyterian ministry in 1893, events which disseminated the new views across the country far more widely still.

The first in the series of eight *Presbyterian Review* articles on issues raised by biblical criticism appeared in April, 1881, under the joint authorship of A. A. Hodge (1823–86), professor of theology at Princeton Theological Seminary, and Benjamin B. Warfield (1851–1921), professor of New Testament at Western Theological Seminary, Allegheny (later Pittsburgh). This article, from which the present document is taken, was one of the clearest and most balanced statements of the inerrancy of the Bible that the biblical controversy in America produced, either at that time or later. The precise and sharply chiseled definition of terms was the ripe fruit of generations of scholastic development of the doctrine, with some distinctive features of

---

[21] Cf. Lefferts A. Loetscher, *The Broadening Church,* 28–37.

its own, most notably the clear-cut limitation of inerrancy to the original (and now lost) biblical manuscripts. By this device, the claim to inerrancy could be renewed and even heightened, and at the same time be removed from the possibility of empirical refutation. On the other hand, if inerrancy was confined to the lost biblical autographs, it could have no practical value for Christian living today.

Contrary to some exponents of inerrancy, the article distinguished between revelation and inspiration, in order that inspiration might be defined more narrowly as God's superintendence over the process of writing the Bible, whether at a particular moment the biblical writers were recording revelation or other matters. Drawing on their Calvinistic view that God can overrule and control men even while men are acting spontaneously, the authors insisted that their doctrine of superintendence was not one of "dictation," but that the biblical writers, often with conscious creativity, wrote their own ideas in their own respective literary styles. The doctrine of biblical inerrancy here set forth became for a time the official position of the Presbyterian Church and was the basis on which Briggs was suspended from the ministry, but the doctrine was abandoned by the church during the fundamentalist-modernist controversy of the 1920's.[22]

The article is a classic statement of a doctrine which fundamentalists continued to hold in the middle of the twentieth century. At that later date, among more scholarly fundamentalists the name of Warfield was almost uniquely revered by reason of his wide learning and conservative views, and his writings were being reprinted and circulated.

DOCUMENT

The word Inspiration, as applied to the Holy Scriptures, has gradually acquired a specific technical meaning, independent of its etymology. At first this word, in the sense of God-breathed, was used to express the entire agency of God in producing that divine element which distinguishes Scripture from all other writings. It was used in a sense comprehensive of supernatural revelation, while the immense range of providential and gracious divine activities concerned in the genesis of the Word of God in human language was practically overlooked. But Christian scholars have come to see that this divine element, which penetrates and glorifies Scripture at every point, has entered and become incorporated with it in very various ways, natural, supernatural, and gracious, through long courses of providential leading, as well as by direct suggestion, through the spontaneous action of the souls of the sacred writers, as well as by controlling influence from without. It is important that distinguishable ideas should be connoted by distinct terms, and that the terms themselves should be fixed in a definite sense. Thus we have come to distinguish sharply between Revelation, which is the frequent, and Inspiration, which is the constant attribute

[22] *Ibid.*, 56-7, 61, 133-4.

of all the thoughts and statements of Scripture, and between the problem
of the genesis of Scripture on the one hand, which includes historic processes
and the concurrence of natural and supernatural forces, and must account
for all the phenomena of Scripture; and the mere fact of Inspiration on the
other hand, or the superintendence by God of the writers in the entire
process of their writing, which accounts for nothing whatever but the
absolute infallibility of the record in which the revelation, once generated,
appears in the original autograph. It will be observed that we intentionally
avoid applying to this inspiration the predicate "influence." It summoned,
on occasion, a great variety of influences, but its essence was superintendence.
This superintendence attended the entire process of the genesis of Scripture,
and particularly the process of the final composition of the record. It inter-
fered with no spontaneous natural agencies, which were, in themselves,
producing results conformable to the mind of the Holy Spirit. On occasion
it summoned all needed divine influences and suggestions, and it sealed the
entire record, and all its elements, however generated with the imprimatur
of God, sending it to us as His Word.

The importance of limiting the word "Inspiration" to a definite and
never varying sense, and one which is shown, by the facts of the case, to
be applicable equally to every part of Scripture, is self-evident, and is
emphasized by the embarrassment which is continually recurring in the
discussions of this subject, arising sometimes from the wide, and sometimes
from the various, senses in which this term is used by different parties. The
history of theology is full of parallel instances, in which terms of the
highest import have come to be accepted in a more fixed and narrow sense
than they bore at first, either in Scriptural or early ecclesiastical usage, and
with only a remote relation to their etymology; as, for instance, Regeneration, Sacrament, etc.

Presuppositions

From this definition of the term it is evident that, instead of being in
the order of thought, the first religious truth which we embrace, upon
which, subsequently, the entire fabric of true religion rests, it is the last and
crowning attribute of those sacred books from which we derive our religious
knowledge. Very many religious and historical truths must be established
before we come to the question of Inspiration; as, for instance, the being
and moral government of God, the fallen condition of man, the fact of a
redemptive scheme, the general historical truth of the Scriptures, and the
validity and authority of the revelation of God's will, which they contain—
i.e., the general truth of Christianity and its doctrines. Hence it follows
that, while the Inspiration of the Scriptures is true, and being true is a
principle fundamental to the adequate interpretation of Scripture, it nevertheless is not in the first instance a principle fundamental to the truth of the
Christian religion. In dealing with sceptics it is not proper to begin with

the evidence which immediately establishes Inspiration, but we should first establish Theism, then the historical credibility of the Scriptures, and then the divine origin of Christianity. Nor should we ever allow it to be believed that the truth of Christianity depends upon any doctrine of Inspiration whatever. Revelation came in large part before the record of it, and the Christian Church before the New Testament Scriptures. Inspiration can have no meaning if Christianity is not true, but Christianity would be true and divine, and being so, would stand, even if God had not been pleased to give us, in addition to His revelation of saving truth, an infallible record of that revelation absolutely errorless, by means of Inspiration.

In the second place it is also evident that our conception of revelation and its methods must be conditioned upon our general views of God's relation to the world, and His methods of influencing the souls of men. The only really dangerous opposition to the Church doctrine of Inspiration comes either directly or indirectly, but always ultimately, from some false view of God's relation to the world, of His methods of working, and of the possibility of a supernatural agency penetrating and altering the course of a natural process. But the whole genius of Christianity, all of its essential and most characteristic doctrines, presuppose the immanence of God in all His creatures, and His concurrence with them in all of their spontaneous activities. In Him, as an active, intelligent Spirit, we all live and move and have our being. He governs all His creatures and all their actions, working in men even to will, and spontaneously to do His good pleasure. The currents, thus, of the divine activities do not only flow around us conditioning or controlling our action from without, but they none the less flow within the inner current of our personal lives confluent with our spontaneous self-movements, and contributing to the effects whatever properties God may see fit that they shall have.

There is also a real logical and ideal, if not a physical, continuity between all the various provinces and methods of God's working; providence and grace, the natural and the supernatural, all constitute one system in the execution of one plan. All these agents and all these methods are so perfectly adjusted in the plan of God that not one interferes with any other, and all are so adjusted and controlled as that each works perfectly, according to the law of its own nature, and yet all together infallibly bring about the result God designs. In this case that design is a record without error of the facts and doctrines He had commissioned His servants to teach. . . .

Several points remain to be more particularly considered, concerning which, some difference of opinion at present prevails.

1st. Is it proper to call this Inspiration "plenary"? This word, which has often been made the occasion of strife, is in itself indefinite, and its use contributes nothing, either to the precision or the emphasis of the definition. The word means simply "full," "complete," perfectly adequate for the attainment of the end designed, whatever that might have been. There ought not to be on any side any hesitancy to affirm this of the books of the Bible.

2d. Can this Inspiration be properly said to be "verbal"? The objection to the application of this predicate to Inspiration is urged upon three distinct grounds:

(1). We believe that the great majority of those who object to the affirmation that Inspiration is verbal, are impelled thereto by a feeling, more or less definite, that the phrase implies that Inspiration is, in its essence, a process of verbal dictation, or that, at least in some way, the revelation of the thought, or the inspiration of the writer, was by means of the control which God exercised over his words. And there is the more excuse for this misapprehension because of the extremely mechanical conceptions of Inspiration maintained by many former advocates of the use of this term "verbal." This view, however, we repudiate as earnestly as any of those who object to the language in question. At the present time the advocates of the strictest doctrine of Inspiration, in insisting that it is verbal, do not mean that, in any way, the thoughts were inspired by means of the words, but simply that the divine superintendence, which we call Inspiration, extended to the verbal expression of the thoughts of the sacred writers, as well as to the thoughts themselves, and that, hence, the Bible considered as a record, an utterance in words of a divine revelation, is the Word of God to us. Hence, in all the affirmations of Scripture of every kind, there is no more error in the words of the original autographs than in the thoughts they were chosen to express. The thoughts and words are both alike human, and, therefore, subject to human limitations, but the divine superintendence and guarantee extends to the one as much as the other.

(2). There are others, who, while insisting as strongly as any upon the presence of the divine element in Scripture, developed through special providences and gracious dealings, religious experiences and mental processes, in the very manner we have just set forth under the head of the "Genesis of Scripture," yet substantially deny what we have here called "Inspiration." They retain the word "Inspiration," but signify by it the divine element in the revelation, or providential, or gracious dealing aforesaid, and they believe that the sacred writers, having been divinely helped to certain knowledge, were left to the natural limitations and fallibility incidental to their human and personal characters, alike in their thinking out their several narrations and expositions of divine truth, and in their reduction of them to writing. This view gives up the whole matter of the immediate divine authorship of the Bible as the Word of God, and its infallibility and authority as a rule of faith and practice. We have only the several versions of God's revelations, as rendered mentally and verbally, more or less adequately, yet always imperfectly, by the different sacred writers. This class of objectors are, of course, self-consistent in rejecting verbal inspiration in any sense. But this view is not consistent either with the claims of

Scripture, the consciousness of Christians, or the historic doctrine of the Church.

(3). There are others who maintain that the Scriptures have been certainly inspired so far forth as to constitute them in all their parts, and, as a whole, an infallible and divinely authoritative rule of faith and practice, and yet hold that, while the thoughts of the sacred writers concerning doctrine and duty were inspired and errorless, their language was of purely human suggestion, and more or less accurate. The question as to whether the elements of Scripture relating to the course of nature and to the events of history are without error, will be considered below; it is sufficient to say under the present head, that it is self-evident that, just as far as the thoughts of Scripture, relating to any element or topic whatsoever, are inspired, the words in which those thoughts are expressed must be inspired also. Every element of Scripture, whether doctrine or history, of which God has guaranteed the infallibility, must be infallible in its verbal expression. No matter how in other respects generated, the Scriptures are a product of human thought, and every process of human thought involves language. "The slightest consideration will show that words are as essential to intellectual processes as they are to mutual intercourse. . . . Thoughts are wedded to words as necessarily as soul to body. Without it the mysteries unveiled before the eyes of the seer would be confused shadows; with it they are made clear lessons for human life."

Besides this the Scriptures are a *record* of divine revelations, and, as such, consist of words, and as far as the record is inspired at all, and as far as it is in any element infallible, its inspiration must reach to its words. Infallible thought must be definite thought, and definite thought implies words. But if God could have rendered the thoughts of the apostles regarding doctrine and duty infallibly correct without words, and then left them to convey it to us in their own language, we should be left to precisely that amount of certainty for the foundation of our faith as is guaranteed by the natural competency of the human authors, and neither more nor less. There would be no divine guarantee whatever. The human medium would everywhere interpose its fallibility between God and us. Besides, most believers admit that some of the prophetical parts of Scripture were verbally dictated. It was, moreover, promised that the Apostles should speak as the Spirit gave them utterance. "The Word of God came unto the prophet." The Church has always held, as expressed by the Helvetic Confession, II., "that the canonical Scriptures *are the Word of God.*" Paul claims that the Holy Spirit superintended and guaranteed his words as well as his thoughts (I Cor. ii. 13). The things of the Spirit we teach "not in the words which man's wisdom teacheth, but which the Holy Ghost teacheth," (συγκρίνοντες), combining spiritual things with spiritual, *i.e.,* spiritual thoughts with spiritual words.

It is evident, therefore, that it is not clearness of thought which inclines any of the advocates of a real inspiration of the Holy Scriptures to deny that it extends to the words. Whatever discrepancies or other human limitations may attach to the sacred record, *the line* (of inspired or not inspired, of infallible or fallible) *can never rationally be drawn between the thoughts and the words of Scripture.*

3d. It is asked again: In what way, and to what extent, is the doctrine of Inspiration dependent upon the supposed results of modern criticism, as to the dates, authors, sources, and modes of composition of the several books? To us the following answer appears to be well founded, and to set the limits within which the Church doctrine of inspiration is in equilibrium with the results of modern criticism fairly and certainly:

The doctrine of Inspiration, in its essence and, consequently, in all its forms, presupposes a supernatural revelation and a supernatural providential guidance, entering into and determining the genesis of Scripture from the beginning. Every naturalistic theory, therefore, of the evolution of Scripture, however disguised, is necessarily opposed to any true version of the Catholic doctrine of Inspiration. It is, also, a well-known matter of fact that Christ himself is the ultimate witness on whose testimony the Scriptures, as well as their doctrinal contents, rest. We receive the Old Testament just as Christ handed it to us, and on His authority. And we receive as belonging to the New Testament all, and only those books which an apostically instructed age testifies to have been produced by the Apostles or their companions, *i.e.,* by the men whom Christ commissioned, and to whom He promised infallibility in teaching. It is evident, therefore, that every supposed conclusion of critical investigation which denies the apostolical origin of a New Testament book, or the truth of any part of Christ's testimony in relation to the Old Testament and its contents, or which is inconsistent with the absolute truthfulness of any affirmation of any book so authenticated, must be inconsistent with the true doctrine of Inspiration. On the other hand, the defenders of the strictest doctrine of Inspiration should cheerfully acknowledge that theories as to the authors, dates, sources, and modes of composition of the several books, which are not plainly inconsistent with the testimony of Christ or His Apostles as to the Old Testament, or with the apostolic origin of the books of the New Testament, or with the absolute truthfulness of any of the affirmations of these books so authenticated, cannot in the least invalidate the evidence or pervert the meaning of the historical doctrine of Inspiration.

4th. The real point at issue between the more strict and the more lax views of Inspiration maintained by believing scholars remains to be stated. It is claimed and admitted equally on both sides that the great design and effect of Inspiration is to render the sacred Scriptures in all their parts a divinely infallible and authoritative rule of faith and practice; and hence that in all their elements of thought and expression concerned in the great purpose of conveying to men a revelation of spiritual doctrine or duty, the

Scriptures are absolutely infallible. But if this be so, it is argued by the more liberal school of Christian scholars, that this admitted fact is not inconsistent with other facts which they claim are matters of their personal observation; to wit, that in certain elements of Scripture which are purely incidental to their great end of teaching spiritual truth, such as history, natural history, ethnology, archæology, geography, natural science, and philosophy, they, like all the best human writings of their age, are, while for the most part reliable, yet limited by inaccuracies and discrepancies. While this is maintained, it is generally at the same time affirmed, that when compared with other books of the same antiquity, these inaccuracies and discrepancies of the Bible are inconsiderable in number, and always of secondary importance, in no degree invalidating the great attribute of Scripture, its absolute infallibility and its divine authority as a rule of faith and practice.

The writers of this article are sincerely convinced of the perfect soundness of the great Catholic doctrine of Biblical Inspiration, *i.e.,* that the Scriptures not only contain, but ARE THE WORD OF GOD, and hence that all their elements and all their affirmations are absolutely errorless, and binding the faith and obedience of men. Nevertheless we admit that the question between ourselves and the advocates of the view just stated, is one of fact, to be decided only by an exhaustive and impartial examination of all the sources of evidence, *i.e.,* the claims and the phenomena of the Scriptures themselves. There will undoubtedly be found upon the surface many apparent affirmations presumably inconsistent with the present teachings of science, with facts of history, or with other statements of the sacred books themselves. Such apparent inconsistencies and collisions with other sources of information are to be expected in imperfect copies of ancient writings; from the fact that the original reading may have been lost, or that we may fail to realize the point of view of the author, or that we are destitute of the circumstantial knowledge which would fill up and harmonize the record. Besides, the human forms of knowledge by which the critics test the accuracy of Scripture are themselves subject to error. In view of all the facts known to us, we affirm that a candid inspection of all the ascertained phenomena of the original text of Scripture will leave unmodified the ancient faith of the Church. In all their real affirmations these books are without error.

It must be remembered that it is not claimed that the Scriptures any more than their authors are omniscient. The information they convey is in the forms of human thought, and limited on all sides. They were not designed to teach philosophy, science, or human history as such. They were not designed to furnish an infallible system of speculative theology. They are written in human languages, whose words, inflections, constructions, and idioms bear everywhere indelible traces of human error. The record itself furnishes evidence that the writers were in large measure dependent for their knowledge upon sources and methods in themselves fallible; and that their personal knowledge and judgments were in many matters hesitating and defective, or even wrong. Nevertheless the historical faith of the Church has always been, that all the affirmations of Scripture of all kinds, whether of spiritual doctrine or duty, or of physical or historical fact, or of psychological or philosophical principle, are without any error, when the *ipsissima verba* of the original autographs are ascertained and interpreted in their natural and intended sense.

> SOURCE: Archibald A. Hodge and Benjamin B. Warfield, "Inspiration," *Presbyterian Review,* II (1881), 225-8, 232-8.

147. Jehovah's Witnesses

The century of change and upheaval following the Civil War quite understandably witnessed renewed interest in millennialism. This interest appeared among a minority within the conventional churches as premillennialism, which at times assumed the more radical form of dispensationalism.

One of the most interesting and zealous of the millennial movements was the Jehovah's Witnesses. Charles Taze ("Pastor") Russell (1852–1916), its founder, was reared in a Congregational family, but revolted against the traditional doctrine of eternal punishment which was being widely challenged at the time. The Seventh-day Adventists turned his attention toward millennial views. Presently he was teaching that Christ actually did return to earth—invisibly—in 1874, would be set upon his throne in 1914, and would enter God's temple in 1918. He would soon return visibly, but the date cannot be foreknown. When he comes, he will judge the living and the dead and set up his millennial kingdom. At the end of the millennium the wicked will not suffer eternal punishment, but will be annihilated.

As the document here presented indicates, Russell taught an extreme type of separatism. The Christian must withdraw from involvement in all political and—so far as possible—even social institutions in order to preserve Christian truth and purity. Individuals are bad, but institutions are far worse, because they compound human sin. The historical process corrupts even well-meaning human endeavors. This is particularly true, he said, of the religious institutions, the churches. Related to his pessimistic view of society, Russell predicted a class struggle, but, unlike Karl Marx, he insisted that his followers remain aloof from it, for he considered neither side morally pure. Social righteousness will be established only by Christ's physical coming. Jehovah's Witnesses emphasize a biblical literalism but, paradoxically, are heterodox in their views of the person of Christ.

The withdrawal of Jehovah's Witnesses from political, military, and social involvement has been interpreted by their enemies as misanthropy, and has been the chief cause of the outrageous persecution which has often been inflicted upon them. The group is notable for its zeal. Though there are no membership statistics, it is evident that the movement is expanding, especially among the less privileged in the cities.[23]

DOCUMENT

Though the powers that be, the governments of this world, were ordained or arranged for by God, that mankind might gain a needed experience under them, yet the Church, the consecrated ones who aspire to office in the coming Kingdom of God, should neither covet the honors and the emoluments of office in the kingdoms of this world, nor should they oppose these powers. They are fellow citizens and heirs of the heavenly kingdom (Eph. 2:19), and as such should claim only such rights and privileges under the kingdoms of this world as are accorded to *aliens*. Their mission is not to help the world to improve its present condition, nor to have anything to do with its affairs at present. To attempt to do so would be but a waste of effort; for the world's course and its termination are both clearly defined in the Scriptures and are fully under the control of him who in his own time will *give us* the kingdom. The influence of the *true* Church is now and always has been small—so small as to count practically nothing politically; but however great it might appear, we should follow the example and teaching of our Lord and the apostles. Knowing that the purpose of God is to let the world fully test its own ability to govern itself, the true Church should not, while in it, be *of* the world. The saints may influence the world only by their separateness from it, by letting *their light* shine; and thus through their lives the spirit of truth REPROVES the world. Thus—as peaceable, orderly obeyers and commenders of every righteous law, reprovers of lawlessness and sin, and pointers forward to the promised Kingdom of God and the blessings to be expected under it, and not by the method commonly adopted of mingling in politics and scheming with the world for power, and thus being drawn into wars and sins and the general degradation—in glorious chastity should the prospective Bride of the Prince of Peace be a power for good, as her Lord's representative in the world.

The Church of God should give its *entire attention* and effort to preaching the Kingdom of God, and to the advancement of the interests of that Kingdom according to the plan laid down in the Scriptures. If this is faithfully done, there will be no time nor disposition to dabble in the politics of present governments. The Lord had no time for it; the apostles had no time for it; nor have any of the saints who are following their example.

The early Church, shortly after the death of the apostles, fell a prey to this very temptation. The preaching of the coming Kingdom of God, which

[23] The leading study is Herbert W. Stroup, *The Jehovah's Witnesses* (N.Y., 1945). Cf. also Charles T. Russell, *Studies in the Scriptures: A Helping Hand for Bible Students* (7 vols., Allegheny, Pa., 1897–1902), and the numerous writings of the late "Judge" Joseph F. Rutherford, Russell's successor as leader of the movement.

would displace all earthly kingdoms, and of the crucified Christ as the heir of that Kingdom, was unpopular, and brought with it persecution, scorn and contempt. But some thought to improve on God's plan, and, instead of suffering, to get the Church into a position of favor with the world. By a combination with earthly powers they succeeded. As a result Papacy was developed, and in time became the mistress and queen of nations.—Rev. 17: 3-5; 18:7.

By this policy everything was changed: instead of suffering, came honor; instead of humility, came pride; instead of truth, came error; and instead of being persecuted, she became the persecutor of all who condemned her new and illegal honors. Soon she began to invent new theories and sophistries to justify her course, first deceiving herself, and then the nations, into the belief that the promised millennial reign of Christ HAD COME, and that Christ the King was represented by her popes, who reigned over the kings of the earth as his vicegerents. Her claims were successful in deceiving the whole world. "She made all nations *drunk*" with her erroneous doctrines (Rev. 17:2), intimidating them by teaching that eternal torment awaited all who resisted her claims. Soon the kings of Europe were crowned or deposed by her edict, and under her supposed authority.

Thus it comes that the kingdoms of Europe to-day claim to be Christian kingdoms, and announce that their sovereigns reign "by the grace of God," *i.e.*, through appointment of either Papacy or some of the Protestant sects. For though the Reformers abandoned many of Papacy's claims to ecclesiastical jurisdiction, etc., they held to this honor which the kings of earth had come to attach to Christianity. And thus the Reformers fell into the same error, and exercised the authority of monarchs in appointing and sanctioning governments and kings, and denominating such "Christian kingdoms," or kingdoms of Christ. So we hear much to-day of that strange enigma, *"The Christian World"*—an enigma indeed, when viewed in the light of the true principles of the Gospel. Our Lord said of his disciples, "They are not of the world, even as I am not of the world." And Paul exhorts us, saying, "Be not conformed to this world."—John 17:16; Rom. 12:2.

God never approved of calling these kingdoms by the name of Christ. Deceived by the Church nominal, these nations are sailing under false colors, claiming to be what they are not. Their only title, aside from the vote of the people, is in God's *limited* grant, spoken to Nebuchadnezzar— until he come whose right the dominion is.

The claim that these imperfect kingdoms, with their imperfect laws and often selfish and vicious rulers, are the "kingdoms of our Lord and his Anointed" is a gross libel upon the true Kingdom of Christ, before which they must shortly fall, and upon its "Prince of Peace" and righteous rulers. —Isa. 32:1.

Another serious injury resulting from that error is that the attention of the children of God has thereby been attracted away from the promised heavenly kingdom; and they have been led to an improper recognition of and intimacy with earthly kingdoms, and to almost fruitless attempts to engraft upon these wild, worldly stocks the graces and morals of Christianity, to the neglect of the gospel concerning the true Kingdom and the hopes centering in it. Under this deception, some are at present very solicitous that the name of God should be incorporated into the Constitution of the United States, that *thereby* this may become a Christian nation. The Reformed Presbyterians have for years refused to vote or hold office under this government, *because* it is not Christ's Kingdom. Thus they recognize the impropriety of Christians sharing in any other. We have great sympathy with this sentiment, but not with the conclusion, that if God's *name* were mentioned in the Constitution, that fact would transform this government from a kingdom of this world to a kingdom of Christ, and give them liberty to vote and to hold office under it. O, how foolish! How great the deception by which the "Mother of harlots" has made all nations drunk (Rev. 17:2); for in a similar manner it is claimed that the kingdoms of Europe were transferred from Satan to Christ, and became "Christian nations."

Let it be seen that the best and the worst of earth's nations are but "kingdoms of this world," whose lease of power from God is now about expired, that they may give place to their ordained successor, the Kingdom of Messiah, the Fifth Universal Empire of earth (Dan. 2:44; 7:14, 17, 27) —and it will do much to establish truth and to overthrow error.

But as it is, the actions of Papacy in this regard, sanctioned by the Protestant Reformers, go unquestioned among Christian people. And since they should uphold the Kingdom of Christ, they feel themselves bound to champion the present falling kingdoms of so-called Christendom, whose time is fast expiring; and thus their sympathies are often forced to the side of oppression, rather than to the side of right and freedom—to the side of the kingdoms of this world, and the prince of this world, rather than to the side of the coming true Kingdom of Christ.—Rev. 17:14; 19:11–19.

The world is fast coming to realize that the "kingdoms of this world" are not Christlike, and that their claim to be of Christ's appointment is not unquestionable. Men are beginning to use their reasoning powers on this and similar questions; and they will act out their convictions so much more violently, as they come to realize that a deception has been practiced upon them in the name of the God of Justice and the Prince of Peace. In fact, the tendency with many is to conclude that Christianity itself is an imposition without foundation, and that, leagued with civil rulers, its aim is merely to hold in check the liberties of the masses.

O that men were wise, that they would apply their hearts to understand the work and plan of the Lord! Then would the present kingdoms melt down gradually—reform would swiftly follow reform, and liberty follow liberty, and justice and truth would prevail until righteousness would be established in the earth. But they will not do this, nor can they in their present fallen state; and so, armed with selfishness, each will strive for mastery, and the kingdoms of this world will pass away with a great time of trouble, such as was not since there was a nation. Of those who will be vainly trying to hold to a dominion which has passed away, when the dominion is given to him whose right it is, the Lord speaks, urging that they are fighting against him—a conflict in which they are sure to fail.

SOURCE: Charles T. Russell, *Millennial Dawn*, Vol. I: *The Plan of the Ages* (Allegheny, Pa., 1886), 266–71.

148. The Pope's Encyclical on Americanism

From the early years of the republic some American Roman Catholics desired to maintain a degree of autonomy, partly in reaction to anti-Catholic taunts of domination by a "foreign potentate." Thus, just after the American Revolution, Bishop John Carroll asked the Congregation of Propaganda that the office of prefect-apostolic be transformed into a diocesan episcopate as soon as possible. Early in the nineteenth century, Bishop John England stressed development of a truly American Church with an American clergy; and later in the century Archbishops Gibbons and Ireland desired the Church to recognize and to take full account of American ways and ideals. These considerations were continually being presented to Rome by leading American Catholics. But the heresy of so-called "Americanism" went beyond this.

French liberal Catholics, harassed by anticlerical laws, held up the example of American Catholicism which was growing rapidly in the midst of a free, liberal society. Their exaggeration of American Catholic divergences was heightened by an inaccurate translation into French in 1897 of *The Life of Father Hecker* which had been published in the United States six years before. Isaac Thomas Hecker (1819–88) was reared a Methodist, experimented with transcendentalism, and became a Roman Catholic in 1844, being ordained to the priesthood five years later. He founded the Paulist Fathers who were notably successful in their object of converting Protestants to the Roman Catholic faith. It was charged that Hecker's strategy was to stress beliefs which Catholics and Protestants held in common rather than the distinctive beliefs of Catholics. This was an important item in the concept of "Americanism" and an additional object of heated debate among Catholics.

Pope Leo XIII felt it necessary to condemn "Americanism" by the encyclical *Testem benevolentiae* on January 22, 1899. He named such errors as the adaptation of the faith to non-Catholics and to modern civilization; the muting of aspects of Catholicism; and distorted emphasis on the operation of the Holy Spirit on individuals as an accommodation to the American revivalistic atmosphere. The pope was very careful not to accuse American Catholics of actually holding the condemned views, but merely said that these views had been ascribed to some American Catholics by a foreign source. The pope was careful also to avoid condemning America, or American society. The encyclical succeeded in pleasing both sides. Conservatives rejoiced to see the principles officially repudiated, while Cardinal Gibbons took the occasion to deny that American Catholics held any such views.[24] The encyclical showed the kind of perils the American Catholic Church was thought by some in high quarters to be facing and the ecclesiastical power which stood ready to hold American Catholicism in the faith.

DOCUMENT

We send you this letter as a testimony of that devoted affection in your regard, which during the long course of Our Pontificate, We have never ceased to profess for you, for your colleagues in the Episcopate, and for the whole American people, willingly availing Ourselves of every occasion to do so, whether it was the happy increase of your church, or the works which you have done so wisely and well in furthering and protecting the interests of Catholicity. The opportunity also often presented itself of regarding with admiration that exceptional disposition of your nation, so eager for what is great, and so ready to pursue whatever might be conducive to social progress and the splendor of the State. But although the object of this letter is not to repeat the praise so often accorded, but rather to point out certain things which are to be avoided and corrected, yet because it is written with that same apostolic charity which We have always shown you, and in which We have often addressed you, We trust that you will regard it likewise as a proof of Our love; and all the more so as it is conceived and intended to put an end to certain contentions which have arisen lately among you, and which disturb the minds, if not of all, at least of many, to the no slight detriment of peace.

You are aware, beloved Son, that the book entitled "The Life of Isaac Thomas Hecker," chiefly through the action of those who have undertaken to publish and interpret it in a foreign language, has excited no small controversy on account of certain opinions which are introduced concerning the manner of leading a Christian life. We, therefore, on account of Our apostolic office, in order to provide for the integrity of the faith, and to guard the security of the faithful, desire to write to you more at length upon the whole matter.

The principles on which the new opinions We have mentioned are based may be reduced to this: that, in order the more easily to bring over to Catholic doctrine those who dissent from it, the Church ought to adapt herself somewhat to our advanced civilization, and, relaxing her ancient

[24] John T. Ellis, *American Catholicism* (Chicago, 1956), 117–9; Joseph McSorley, *Father Hecker and His Friends* (St. Louis, 1953); Thomas T. McAvoy, *The Great Crisis in American Catholic History, 1895–1900* (Chicago, 1957).

rigor, show some indulgence to modern popular theories and methods. Many think that this is to be understood not only with regard to the rule of life, but also to the doctrines in which the *deposit of faith* is contained. For they contend that it is opportune, in order to work in a more attractive way upon the wills of those who are not in accord with us, to pass over certain heads of doctrines, as if of lesser moment, or to so soften them that they may not have the same meaning which the Church has invariably held. Now, Beloved Son, few words are needed to show how reprehensible is the plan that is thus conceived, if we but consider the character and origin of the doctrine which the Church hands down to us. . . .

The rule of life which is laid down for Catholics is not of such a nature as not to admit modifications, according to the diversity of time and place. The Church, indeed, possesses what her Author has bestowed on her, a kind and merciful disposition; for which reason from the very beginning she willingly showed herself to be what Paul proclaimed in his own regard: *I became all things to all men, that I might save all.* The history of all past ages is witness that the Apostolic See, to which not only the office of teaching but also the supreme government of the whole Church was committed, has constantly adhered *to the same doctrine, in the same sense and in the same mind:* but it has always been accustomed to so modify the rule of life that, while keeping the divine right inviolate, it has never disregarded the manners and customs of the various nations which it embraces. If required for the salvation of souls, who will doubt that it is ready to do so at the present time? But this is not to be determined by the will of private individuals, who are mostly deceived by the appearance of right, but ought to be left to the judgment of the Church. In this all must acquiesce who wish to avoid the censure of Our predecessor Pius VI., who proclaimed the 18th proposition of the Synod of Pistoia "to be injurious to the Church and to the Spirit of God which governs her, inasmuch as it subjects to scrutiny the discipline established and approved by the Church, as if the Church could establish a useless discipline or one which would be too onerous for Christian liberty to bear."

But in the matter of which we are now speaking, Beloved Son, the project involves a greater danger and is more hostile to Catholic doctrine and discipline, inasmuch as the followers of these novelties judge that a certain liberty ought to be introduced into the Church, so that, limiting the exercise and vigilance of its powers, each one of the faithful may act more freely in pursuance of his own natural bent and capacity. They affirm, namely, that this is called for in order to imitate that liberty which, though quite recently introduced, is now the law and the foundation of almost every civil community. On that point We have spoken very much at length in the Letter written to all the bishops about the constitution of States; where We have also shown the difference between the Church, which is of divine right, and all other associations which subsist by the free will of men. It is of importance, therefore, to note particularly an opinion which is adduced as a sort of argument to urge the granting of such liberty to Catholics. For they say, in speaking of the infallible teaching of the Roman Pontiff, that after the solemn decision formulated in the Vatican Council, there is no more need of solicitude in that regard, and, because of its being now out of dispute, a wider field of thought and action is thrown open to individuals. A preposterous method of arguing, surely. For if anything is suggested by the infallible teaching of the Church, it is certainly that no one should wish to withdraw from it; nay, that all should strive to be thoroughly imbued with and be guided by its spirit, so as to be the more easily preserved from any private error whatsoever. To this we may add that those who argue in that wise quite set aside the wisdom and providence of God; who when He desired in that very solemn decision to affirm the authority and teaching office of the Apostolic See, desired it especially in order the more efficaciously to guard the minds of Catholics from the dangers of the present times. The license which is commonly confounded with liberty; the passion for saying and reviling everything; the habit of thinking and of expressing everything in print, have cast such deep shadows on men's minds, that there is now greater utility and necessity for this office of teaching then ever before, lest men should be drawn away from conscience and duty. It is far, indeed, from Our intention to repudiate all that the genius of the time begets; nay, rather, whatever the search for truth attains, or the effort after good achieves, will always be welcome by Us, for it increases the patrimony of doctrine and enlarges the limits of public prosperity. But all this, to possess real utility, should thrive without setting aside the authority and wisdom of the Church. . . .

Lastly, not to delay too long, it is also maintained that the way and the method which Catholics have followed thus far for recalling those who differ from us is to be abandoned and another resorted to. In that matter, it suffices to advert that it is not prudent, Beloved Son, to neglect what antiquity, with its long experience, guided as it is by apostolic teaching, has stamped with its approval. From the word of God we have it that it is the office of all to labor in helping the salvation of our neighbor in the order and degree in which each one is. The faithful indeed will most usefully fulfil their duty by integrity of life, by the works of Christian charity, by instant and assiduous prayer to God. But the clergy should do so by a wise preaching of the Gospel, by the decorum and splendor of the sacred ceremonies, but especially by expressing in themselves the form of doctrine which the apostles delivered to Titus and Timothy. So that if among the different methods of preaching the word of God, that sometimes seems preferable by which those who dissent from us are spoken to, not in the church but in any private and proper place, not in disputation but in amicable conference, such method is indeed not to be reprehended; provided, however, that those who are devoted to that work by the authority of the bishop be men who have first given proof of science and virtue. For We think that there are very many among you who differ from Catholics rather through ignorance than because of any disposition of the will, who, perchance, if the truth is put before them in a familiar and friendly manner, may more easily be led to the one sheepfold of Christ.

Hence, from all that We have hitherto said, it is clear, Beloved Son, that We cannot approve the opinions which some comprise under the head of Americanism. If, indeed, by that name be designated the characteristic qualities which reflect honor on the people of America, just as other nations have what is special to them; or if it implies the condition of your commonwealths, or the laws and customs which prevail in them, there is surely no reason why We should deem that it ought to be discarded. But if it is to be used not only to signify, but even to commend the above doctrines, there can be no doubt but that our Venerable Brethren the bishops of America would be the first to repudiate and condemn it, as being especially unjust to them and to the entire nation as well. For it raises the suspicion that there are some among you who conceive of and desire a church in America different from that which is in the rest of the world. One in the unity of doctrine as in the unity of government, such is the Catholic Church, and, since God has established its centre and foundation in the Chair of Peter, one which is rightly called Roman, for where Peter is there is the Church. Wherefore he who wishes to be called by the name of Catholic ought to employ in truth the words of Jerome to Pope Damasus, "I following none as the first except Christ am associated in communion with your Beatitude, that is, with the Chair of Peter; upon that Rock I know is built the Church; whoever gathereth not with thee scattereth."

What We write, Beloved Son, to you in particular, by reason of Our office, we shall take care to have communicated to the rest of the bishops of the United States, expressing again that love in which we include your whole nation, which as in times past has done much for religion and bids fair with God's good grace to do still more in the future.

To you and all the faithful of America We give most lovingly as an augury of divine assistance Our Apostolical Benediction.

> SOURCE: John J. Wynne, S.J., ed., *The Great Encyclical Letters of Pope Leo XIII* (N.Y., 1903), 441–5, 451–3.

149. The Pope Condemns "Modernism"

The early part of the pontificate of Leo XIII (1878–1903) brought to the Roman Catholic Church a great advance in theological scholarship. Somewhat belatedly, as was the case also with American Protestants during the same years, Catholic theologians in Europe and America were suddenly confronted with the radical biblical and historical views which had been developing among German Protestant scholars. But the pope later began to draw back from some of the dangerous results to which his encouragement of theological scholarship was unintentionally leading. In 1893 his encyclical *Providentissimus Deus* set forth a rigid view of biblical inspiration, and in 1899 in a letter to the French prelates he opposed liberal theology. In 1902, the year before his death, he created a Biblical Commission. His successor, Pius X (1903–14), proceeded more resolutely against the new tendencies, his most notable measure being the encyclical against modernism in 1907, *Pascendi Dominici Gregis*,[25] portions of which are here presented.

Pascendi treated modernism as a conspiracy and as an integrated system, essentially the same wherever found, whereas those more sympathetic to it regarded it rather as a method and a spirit, having many common presuppositions, to be sure, but differing widely in specific doctrinal positions. Throughout the encyclical, too, there is evident the method of attributing to opponents the most radical implications of their views whether they accepted such implications or not. Many did not. With rigid systematization, the encyclical attributed to the modernist seven different roles and attacked him in each—philosopher, believer, theologian, historian, critic, apologist, and reformer. The remedy which the encyclical proposed against modernism was vigorous ecclesiastical prosecution. George Tyrrell (1861–1909) in England and Alfred Loisy (1857–1940) in France were excommunicated. Within a few years modernism was driven out of the church or forced underground. The policy has of course profoundly influenced the theological atmosphere of the Catholic Church in the United States.

DOCUMENT

[THE MODERNIST AS BELIEVER [26]]

Thus far, Venerable Brethren, We have considered the Modernist as a Philosopher. Now if we proceed to consider him as a believer, and seek to know how the believer, according to Modernism, is marked off from the Philosopher, it must be observed that, although the Philosopher recognizes the *reality of the divine* as the object of faith, still this *reality* is not to be found by him but in the heart of the believer, as an object of feeling and affirmation, and therefore confined within the sphere of phenomena; but the question as to whether in itself it exists outside that feeling and affirmation is one which the Philosopher passes over and neglects. For the Modernist believer, on the contrary, it is an established and certain fact that the *reality* of the divine does really exist in itself and quite independently of the person who believes in it. If you ask on what foundation this assertion of the believer rests, he answers: In the personal *experience* of the individual. On this head the Modernists differ from the Rationalists only to fall into the views

[25] James H. Nichols, *History of Christianity, 1650–1950, Secularization of the West* (N.Y., 1956), 294–305.

[26] The bracketed headings are supplied editorially, and are not a part of the original text.

of the Protestants and pseudo-Mystics. The following is their manner of stating the question: In *the religious sense* one must recognize a kind of intuition of the heart which puts man in immediate contact with the *reality* of God, and infuses such a persuasion of God's existence and His action both within and without man as far to exceed any scientific conviction. They assert, therefore, the existence of a real experience, and one of a kind that surpasses all rational experience. If this experience is denied by some, like the Rationalists, they say that this arises from the fact that such persons are unwilling to put themselves in the moral state necessary to produce it. It is this *experience* which makes the person who acquires it to be properly and truly a believer.

How far this position is removed from that of Catholic teaching! . . .

There is yet another element in this part of their teaching which is absolutely contrary to Catholic truth. For what is laid down as to *experience* is also applied with destructive effect to *tradition*, which has always been maintained by the Catholic Church. Tradition, as understood by the Modernists, is a communication with others of an *original experience*, through preaching by means of the intellectual formula. To this formula, in addition to its *representative* value, they attribute a species of *suggestive* efficacy which acts firstly in the believer by stimulating the *religious sense*, should it happen to have grown sluggish, and by renewing the *experience* once acquired, and secondly, in those who do not yet believe by awakening in them for the first time the *religious sense* and producing the *experience*. . . .

We have proceeded sufficiently far, Venerable Brethren, to have before us enough, and more than enough, to enable us to see what are the relations which Modernists establish between faith and science—including, as they are wont to do under that name, history. And in the first place it is to be held that the object-matter of the one is quite extraneous to and separate from the object-matter of the other. For faith occupies itself solely with something which science declares to be for it *unknowable*. Hence each has a separate scope assigned to it: science is entirely concerned with phenomena, into which faith does not at all enter; faith, on the contrary, concerns itself with the divine, which is entirely unknown to science. Thus it is contended that there can never be any dissension between faith and science, for if each keeps on its own ground they can never meet and therefore never can be in contradiction. And if it be objected that in the visible world there are some things which appertain to faith, such as the human life of Christ, the Modernists reply by denying this. For though such things come within the category of phenomena, still in as far as they are *lived* by faith and in the way already described have been by faith *transfigured* and *disfigured*, they have been removed from the world of sense and transferred into material for the divine. Hence should it be further asked whether Christ has wrought real miracles, and made real prophecies, whether He rose truly from the dead and ascended into Heaven, the answer of agnostic science will be in the negative and the answer of faith in the affirmative—yet there will not be, on that account, any conflict between them. For it will be denied by the philosopher as a philosopher speaking to philosophers and considering Christ only in His *historical reality;* and it will be affirmed by the believer as a believer speaking to believers and considering the life of Christ as *lived again* by the faith and in the faith.

It would be a great mistake, nevertheless, to suppose that, according to these theories, one is allowed to believe that faith and science are entirely independent of each other. On the side of science that is indeed quite true and correct, but it is quite otherwise with regard to faith, which is subject to science, not on one but on three grounds. For in the first place it must be observed that in every religious fact, when one takes away the *divine reality* and the *experience* of it which the believer possesses, everything else, and especially the *religious formulas,* belongs to the sphere of phenomena and therefore falls under the control of science. Let the believer go out of the world if he will, but so long as he remains in it, whether he like it or not, he cannot escape from the laws, the observation, the judgments of science and of history. Further, although it is contended that God is the object of faith alone, the statement refers only to the *divine reality,* not to the *idea* of God. The latter also is subject to science which, while it philosophises in what is called the logical order, soars also to the absolute and the ideal. It is therefore the right of philosophy and of science to form its knowledge concerning the idea of God, to direct it in its evolution and to purify it of any extraneous elements which may have entered into it. Hence we have the Modernist axiom that the religious evolution ought to be brought into accord with the moral and intellectual, or as one whom they regard as their leader has expressed it, ought to be subject to it. Finally, man does not suffer a dualism to exist in himself, and the believer therefore feels within him an impelling need so to harmonise faith with science that it may never oppose the general conception which science sets forth concerning the universe.

Thus it is evident that science is to be entirely independent of faith, while on the other hand, and notwithstanding that they are supposed to be strangers to each other, faith is made subject to science. . . .

[THE MODERNIST AS CRITIC]

As history takes its conclusions from philosophy, so too criticism takes its conclusions from history. The critic, on the data furnished him by the historian, makes two parts of all his documents. Those that remain after the triple elimination above described go to form the *real* history; the rest is attributed to the history of the faith or, as it is styled, to *internal* history. For the Modernists distinguish very carefully between these two kinds of history, and it is to be noted that they oppose the history of the faith to *real* history precisely as real. Thus, as we have already said, we have a twofold Christ: a real Christ, and a Christ, the one of faith, who never really existed;

a Christ who has lived at a given time and in a given place, and a Christ who has never lived outside the pious meditations of the believer—the Christ, for instance, whom we find in the Gospel of S. John, which, according to them, is mere meditation from beginning to end. . . .

[THE MODERNIST AS APOLOGIST]

The Modernist apologist depends in two ways on the philosopher. First, *indirectly,* inasmuch as his subject-matter is history—history dictated, as we have seen, by the philosopher; and, secondly, *directly,* inasmuch as he takes both his doctrines and his conclusions from the philosopher. Hence that common axiom of the Modernist school that in the new apologetics controversies in religion must be determined by psychological and historical research. The Modernist apologists, then, enter the arena, proclaiming to the rationalists that, though they are defending religion, they have no intention of employing the data of the Sacred Books or the histories in current use in the Church, and written upon the old lines, but *real* history composed on modern principles and according to the modern method. In all this they assert that they are not using an *argumentum ad hominem,* because they are really of the opinion that the truth is to be found only in this kind of history. They feel that it is not necessary for them to make profession of their own sincerity in their writings. They are already known to and praised by the rationalist as fighting under the same banner. . . .

[THE MODERNIST AS REFORMER]

It remains for Us now to say a few words about the Modernist as reformer. From all that has preceded, it is abundantly clear how great and how eager is the passion of such men for innovation. In all Catholicism there is absolutely nothing on which it does not fasten. They wish philosophy to be reformed, especially in the ecclesiastical seminaries. They wish the scholastic philosophy to be relegated to the history of philosophy and to be classed among obsolete systems, and the young men to be taught modern philosophy which alone is true and suited to the times in which we live. They desire the reform of theology: rational theology is to have modern philosophy for its foundation, and positive theology is to be founded on the history of dogma. As for history, it must be written and taught only according to their methods and modern principles. Dogmas and their evolution, they affirm, are to be harmonised with science and history. In the Catechism no dogmas are to be inserted except those that have been reformed and are within the capacity of the people. Regarding worship, they say, the number of external devotions is to be reduced, and steps must be taken to prevent their further increase, though, indeed, some of the admirers of symbolism are disposed to be more indulgent on this head. They cry out that ecclesiastical government requires to be reformed in all its branches, but especially in its disciplinary and dogmatic departments.

They insist that both outwardly and inwardly it must be brought into harmony with the modern conscience, which now wholly tends towards democracy; a share in ecclesiastical government should therefore be given to the lower ranks of the clergy, and even to the laity, and authority which is too much concentrated, should be decentralised. The Roman Congregations, and especially the *Index* and the *Holy Office,* must be likewise modified. The ecclesiastical authority must alter its line of conduct in the social and political world; while keeping outside political organisations, it must adapt itself to them, in order to penetrate them with its spirit. With regard to morals, they adopt the principle of the Americanists, that the active virtues are more important than the passive, and are to be more encouraged in practice. They ask that the clergy should return to their primitive humility and poverty, and that in their ideas and action they should admit the principles of Modernism; and there are some who, gladly listening to the teaching of their Protestant masters, would desire the suppression of the celibacy of the clergy. What is there left in the Church which is not to be reformed by them and according to their principles?

> SOURCE: *The Programme of Modernism* (N.Y., 1908), 167–8, 170–4, 199–200, 205–6, 212–4. Used by permission of John Day Company.

150. A Theological Battle Line

During the fundamentalist-modernist controversy after World War I, J. Gresham Machen (1881–1937) emerged as perhaps the ablest theological exponent of the fundamentalist position, though he preferred to call himself simply a Calvinist. Born in Baltimore, he cherished throughout his life the traditions of the Old South, including a Jeffersonian opposition to machine-age centralization. After graduating from Johns Hopkins University and Princeton Seminary, he spent a year abroad at the universities of Marburg and Göttingen. At Marburg he felt the strong magnetism of the popular Ritschlian theologian, Wilhelm Herrmann, but reacted vigorously against the theological reconstruction which he proposed, regarding it as a threat to the very life of Christianity. Inner misgivings concerning his call to the ministry caused him to wait eight years before seeking ordination. After he had ministered to soldiers under the auspices of the Young Men's Christian Association (1918–19), his teaching and preaching acquired new popular appeal. In his teaching and writings he insisted that Christianity was based on the actions of God in history and therefore could not ignore critical questions raised by history and science. He repudiated irrationalism and anti-intellectualism.

His book, *Christianity and Liberalism* (1923), from which the document is taken, grew out of a lecture to laymen. Like the encyclical of Pope Pius X against modernism, Machen identified all forms of liberalism with radical naturalism and unhesitatingly attributed to liberal writers what he considered to be the ultimate implications of their views. Quite consistently, he followed his premises to their conclusion and desired a division of the church which would separate "liberalism" from "Christianity." [27]

DOCUMENT

In the sphere of religion, in particular, the present time is a time of conflict; the great redemptive religion which has always been known as Christianity is battling against a totally diverse type of religious belief, which is only the more destructive of the Christian faith because it makes use of traditional Christian terminology. This modern non-redemptive religion is called "modernism" or "liberalism." Both names are unsatisfactory; the latter, in particular, is question-begging. The movement designated as "liberalism" is regarded as "liberal" only by its friends; to its opponents it seems to involve a narrow ignoring of many relevant facts. And indeed the movement is so various in its manifestations that one may almost despair of finding any common name which will apply to all its forms. But manifold as are the forms in which the movement appears, the root of the movement is one; the many varieties of modern liberal religion are rooted in naturalism —that is, in the denial of any entrance of the creative power of God (as distinguished from the ordinary course of nature) in connection with the origin of Christianity. The word "naturalism" is here used in a sense somewhat different from its philosophical meaning. In this non-philosophical sense it describes with fair accuracy the real root of what is called, by what may turn out to be a degradation of an originally noble word, "liberal" religion. . . .

Modern liberalism may be criticized (1) on the ground that it is unChristian and (2) on the ground that it is unscientific. We shall concern ourselves here chiefly with the former line of criticism; we shall be interested in showing that despite the liberal use of traditional phraseology modern liberalism not only is a different religion from Christianity but belongs in a totally different class of religions. But in showing that the liberal attempt at rescuing Christianity is false we are not showing that there is no way of rescuing Christianity at all; on the contrary, it may appear incidentally, even in the present little book, that it is not the Christianity of the New Testament which is in conflict with science, but the supposed Christianity of the modern liberal Church, and that the real city of God, and that city alone, has defences which are capable of warding off the assaults of modern unbelief. However, our immediate concern is with the other side of the problem; our principal concern just now is to show that the liberal attempt at reconciling Christianity with modern science has really relinquished everything distinctive of Christianity, so that what remains is in essentials

[27] Ned B. Stonehouse, *J. Gresham Machen: A Biographical Memoir* (Grand Rapids, Mich., 1954); Lefferts A. Loetscher, "John Gresham Machen," *Dictionary of American Biography*, XXII, *Supplement Two* (N.Y., 1958), 411–2.

only that same indefinite type of religious aspiration which was in the world before Christianity came upon the scene. In trying to remove from Christianity everything that could possibly be objected to in the name of science, in trying to bribe off the enemy by those concessions which the enemy most desires, the apologist has really abandoned what he started out to defend. . . .

It must be admitted that there are many Christians who do not accept the doctrine of plenary inspiration. That doctrine is denied not only by liberal opponents of Christianity, but also by many true Christian men. There are many Christian men in the modern Church who find in the origin of Christianity no mere product of evolution but a real entrance of the creative power of God, who depend for their salvation, not at all upon their own efforts to lead the Christ life, but upon the atoning blood of Christ—there are many men in the modern Church who thus accept the central message of the Bible and yet believe that the message has come to us merely on the authority of trustworthy witnesses unaided in their literary work by any supernatural guidance of the Spirit of God. There are many who believe that the Bible is right at the central point, in its account of the redeeming work of Christ, and yet believe that it contains many errors. Such men are not really liberals, but Christians; because they have accepted as true the message upon which Christianity depends. A great gulf separates them from those who reject the supernatural act of God with which Christianity stands or falls.

It is another question, however, whether the mediating view of the Bible which is thus maintained is logically tenable, the trouble being that our Lord Himself seems to have held the high view of the Bible which is here being rejected. Certainly it is another question—and a question which the present writer would answer with an emphatic negative—whether the panic about the Bible, which gives rise to such concessions, is at all justified by the facts. If the Christian make full use of his Christian privileges, he finds the seat of authority in the whole Bible, which he regards as no mere word of man but as the very Word of God. . . .

Miracles are rejected by the modern liberal Church, and with the miracles the entirety of the supernatural Person of our Lord. . . .

The question . . . does not concern the historicity of this miracle or that; it concerns the historicity of all miracles. That fact is often obscured, and the obscuration of it often introduces an element of something like disingenuousness into the advocacy of the liberal cause. The liberal preacher singles out some one miracle and discusses that as though it were the only point at issue. The miracle which is usually singled out is the Virgin Birth. The liberal preacher insists on the possibility of believing in Christ no matter which view be adopted as to the manner of His entrance into the world. Is not the Person the same no matter how He was born? The impression is thus produced upon the plain man that the preacher is accepting the main outlines of the New Testament account of Jesus, but merely has difficulties with this particular element in the account. But such an impression is radically false. It is true that some men have denied the Virgin Birth and yet have accepted the New Testament account of Jesus as a supernatural Person. But such men are exceedingly few and far between. It might be difficult to find a single one of any prominence living to-day, so profoundly and so obviously congruous is the Virgin Birth with the whole New Testament presentation of Christ. The overwhelming majority of those who reject the Virgin Birth reject also the whole supernatural content of the New Testament, and make of the "resurrection" just what the word "resurrection" most emphatically did not mean—a permanence of the influence of Jesus or a mere spiritual existence of Jesus beyond the grave. Old words may here be used, but the thing that they designate is gone. . . .

Christianity differs from liberalism in the way in which the transformation of society is conceived. But according to Christian belief, as well as according to liberalism, there is really to be a transformation of society; it is not true that the Christian evangelist is interested in the salvation of individuals without being interested in the salvation of the race. And even before the salvation of all society has been achieved, there is already a society of those who have been saved. That society is the Church. The Church is the highest Christian answer to the social needs of man.

And the Church invisible, the true company of the redeemed, finds expression in the companies of Christians who constitute the visible Church to-day. But what is the trouble with the visible Church? What is the reason for its obvious weakness? There are perhaps many causes of weakness. But one cause is perfectly plain—the Church of to-day has been unfaithful to her Lord by admitting great companies of non-Christian persons, not only into her membership, but into her teaching agencies. It is indeed inevitable that some persons who are not truly Christian shall find their way into the visible Church; fallible men cannot discern the heart, and many a profession of faith which seems to be genuine may really be false. But it is not this kind of error to which we now refer. What is now meant is not the admission of individuals whose confessions of faith may not be sincere, but the admission of great companies of persons who have never made any really credible confession of faith at all and whose entire attitude toward the gospel is the very reverse of the Christian attitude. Such persons, moreover, have been admitted not merely to the membership, but to the ministry of the Church, and to an increasing extent have been allowed to dominate its councils and determine its teaching. The greatest menace to the Christian Church to-day comes not from the enemies outside, but from the enemies within; it comes from the presence within the Church of a type of faith and practice that is anti-Christian to the core.

We are not dealing here with delicate personal questions; we are not presuming to say whether such and such an individual man is a Christian or not. God only can decide such questions; no man can say with assurance whether the attitude of certain individual "liberals" toward Christ is saving faith or not. But one thing is perfectly plain—whether or no liberals are Christians, it is at any rate perfectly clear that liberalism is not Christianity. And that being the case, it is highly undesirable that liberalism and Christianity should continue to be propagated within the bounds of the same organization. A separation between the two parties in the Church is the crying need of the hour. . . .

The plain fact is that liberalism, whether it be true or false, is no mere "heresy"—no mere divergence at isolated points from Christian teaching. On the contrary it proceeds from a totally different root, and it constitutes, in essentials, a unitary system of its own. That does not mean that all liberals hold all parts of the system, or that Christians who have been affected by liberal teaching at one point have been affected at all points. There is sometimes a salutary lack of logic which prevents the whole of a man's faith being destroyed when he has given up a part. But the true way in which to examine a spiritual movement is in its logical relations; logic is the great dynamic, and the logical implications of any way of thinking are sooner or later certain to be worked out. And taken as a whole, even as it actually exists to-day, naturalistic liberalism is a fairly unitary phenomenon; it is tending more and more to eliminate from itself illogical remnants of Christian belief. It differs from Christianity in its view of God, of man, of the seat of authority and of the way of salvation. And it differs from Christianity not only in theology but in the whole of life. It is indeed sometimes said that there can be communion in feeling where communion in thinking is gone, a communion of the heart as distinguished from a communion of the head. But with respect to the present controversy, such a distinction certainly does not apply. On the contrary, in reading the books and listening to the sermons of recent liberal teachers—so untroubled by the problem of sin, so devoid of all sympathy for guilty humanity, so prone to abuse and ridicule the things dearest to the heart of every Christian man—one can only confess that if liberalism is to return into the Christian communion there must be a change of heart fully as much as a change of mind. God grant that such a change of heart may come! But meanwhile the present situation must not be ignored but faced. Christianity is being attacked from within by a movement which is anti-Christian to the core.

SOURCE: J. Gresham Machen, *Christianity and Liberalism* (N.Y., 1923), 2, 7–8, 75–6, 107–8, 158–60, 172–3. Used by permission of Trustees for Westminster Theological Seminary.

151. Calvinism Flayed as Incipient Liberalism

The Lutheran Churches in the United States largely escaped the modernist-fundamentalist controversy of the 1920's. This was partly because, previous to World War I, they had been somewhat isolated from the rest of American religious life; partly because their religious authority was not only the Bible but also the doctrine of salvation by faith as a norm of orthodoxy and of Christian experience; and partly because their confessionalism and theological conservatism since the middle of the nineteenth century delayed and reduced the theological crisis for them.

The Missouri Synod, with most of its membership in the Midwest, was the stronghold of Lutheran conservatism in the United States. In spite of its insistence on simon-pure Lutheranism, the Missouri Synod was committed to some positions that were really quite un-Lutheran, such as biblical literalism; a congregational form of church government; and (in spite of the body's strongly avowed opposition to everything that was distinctive of the Calvinistic churches) an almost Calvinistic emphasis on predestination.

Early in 1839 a band of German emigrants, dissatisfied with the "rationalism" which they found in their native Saxony, settled in St. Louis and in Perry County, Missouri, a hundred miles farther down the Mississippi River. Soon disillusioned by the immorality of their autocratic bishop, Martin Stephan, they banished him and recognized as their new leader the able and earnest Carl Ferdinand Wilhelm Walther (1811–87). Under the guidance of Walther they adopted a democratic church polity which gave the laity equal voice with the clergy and which recognized the autonomy of each local congregation. Before the end of 1839 the settlers built in Perry County a college for the education of ministers, which ten years later moved to St. Louis and took the name Concordia Seminary. This gave the Missouri Lutherans unified control over their supply of ministers and was of crucial importance in perpetuating the denomination's orthodoxy. Parochial elementary schools were started in the earliest days, the pastor himself assuming this added responsibility where a teacher could not be secured. Missouri Lutherans soon acquired and still have the largest parochial school system in the United States, next to the Roman Catholics, though with the abandonment of the German language in the twentieth century, Lutheran parochial school enrollment declined.[28] These schools provided systematic indoctrination and contributed further to the intensification and perpetuation of the denominational pattern. In 1844 Walther began publishing *Der Lutheraner,* a periodical which helped to rally like-minded Lutherans in various parts of the country. Three years later, at a meeting in Chicago, there was organized with Walther as president "The Synod of Missouri, Ohio, and Other States" which at its centennial in 1947 took the name "The Lutheran Church–Missouri Synod." From the beginning the Saxon settlers in Missouri constituted the nucleus of the Synod and supplied its characteristic spirit. The

[28] Carl Mauelshagen, *American Lutheranism Surrenders to Forces of Conservatism* (Athens, Ga., 1936), 207.

influence of "Missouri" was further extended by the organization in 1872, under its predominance, of a federation of Lutheran synods with the name "The Evangelical Lutheran Synodical Conference of North America."

Interestingly, the settlers from Luther's own state of Saxony proved to be his most vocal champions in America. Like the Southern Baptists, the Missouri Lutherans maintained an amazing degree of strict doctrinal uniformity even while disavowing centralized ecclesiastical machinery. Many Lutheran bodies subscribed only the broad and irenic Augsburg Confession (1530), whereas the Missouri Lutherans subscribed all six Luthern creeds, including the much more controversial and scholastic Formula of Concord (1577). "Missouri" has been resolutely opposed to exchange of pulpits or intercommunion with non-Lutherans, and has been highly critical of other Lutheran bodies for alleged laxity of doctrine and unionistic tendencies. The result has been that, even among Lutherans, "Missouri" and its related Synodical Conference have traveled alone. Politically, too, the Missouri Lutherans have represented the Lutheran tradition in its most conservative form. They accepted quite literally Luther's doctrine of the authority of existing civil government, the duty of obeying such government in everything not contrary to conscience, and the duty, even when government makes demands contrary to conscience, of offering only passive resistance. They also held that the church should confine its activity strictly to spiritual matters, and should not attempt to deal with economic or political problems. The social gospel was rejected as an error of "Calvinistic sectarianism."

There was a growing constituency in America to which the finality and assurance of Missouri Synod's doctrinal emphasis appealed. In 1872, at its twenty-fifth anniversary, the Synod had 72,120 members, and before 1930 its membership passed a million, the largest of the Lutheran bodies in the United States. This Synod exerts great influence, especially in the Midwest, in favor of an extremely conservative type of Protestantism.

John H. C. Fritz (1874–1953), author of the article here presented in part, was a representative Missouri Lutheran. Educated at Concordia College, Fort Wayne, and at Concordia Seminary, St. Louis, he held three pastorates before becoming professor (1920–53) and dean (1920–40) at Concordia Seminary. In 1919–20 he was president of the Western District of his church. His article, while implying some sympathy with fundamentalism, refuses to make common cause with it, and seeks to emphasize Lutheran distinctiveness in a quite characteristic way.

DOCUMENT

The Fundamentalists are that party in the non-Lutheran Protestant churches of our day which is making a fight for the fundamentals of the Christian religion over against the Modern Liberalists, who deny these fundamental truths of the Bible and of historic Christianity. The Fundamentalists are sincere; this cannot be said of all the Modern Liberalists. The Fundamentalists are fighting for a good cause; the Modern Liberalists are not.

Will the Fundamentalists win out in their fight against the Modern Liberalists? Our conviction is that they will not, and cannot, unless they submit to a radical revision of their position by adopting an entirely different attitude toward the truth as it is revealed in the Scriptures and toward those who deny this truth. . . .

The spirit of indifferentism and compromise has been characteristic of the Reformed theology since its very earliest history. *It is, in fact, an essential part of its system.* If it were to eliminate it from its system, it would cease to be what it is. Reformed theologians to this very day cannot understand why Luther accused Zwingli and his followers at Marburg in the year 1529 of having a different spirit (*"Ihr habt einen andern Geist"*). They will even now not forgive Luther for having refused to Zwingli the hand of fellowship. They cannot understand why our Lutheran church-body stands for doctrinal purity and therefore refuses to have pulpit- and altar-fellowship with such as disagree with it in doctrine. Such a position, they tell us, is narrow,—if they are at all willing to dismiss the case with such a mild reprimand. Such plain words in Scripture as "Hold fast the form of sound words," 2 Tim. 1, 13; "Mark them which cause divisions and offenses contrary to the doctrine which ye have learned, and avoid them," Rom. 16, 17; "Though we or an angel from heaven preach any other gospel unto you than that which we have preached unto you, let him be accursed," Gal. 1, 8; "Beware of false prophets," Matt. 7, 15; and many others, similar plain words and commands of Scripture, are by them not at all understood.

That very spirit of Zwingli of which Luther spoke was a compromising spirit, a spirit which would not make a clean-cut and clear-cut issue of the truth, a spirit which would let truth and error stand side by side in the Church. What the result of that position has been is clearly seen in the deplorable condition of the non-Lutheran denominations of our day. The course which the admission of error into the Church takes can work out only in one way. In his *Conservative Reformation* Dr. Krauth says: "When error is admitted into the Church, it will be found that the stages of its progress are always three. It begins by asking *toleration*. Its friends say to the majority: You need not be afraid of us; we are few and weak; only let us alone; we shall not disturb the faith of others. The Church has her standards of doctrine; of course, we shall never interfere with them; we only ask for ourselves to be spared interference with our private opinions. Indulged in this for a time, error goes on to assert *equal rights*. Truth and error are two balancing forces. The Church shall do nothing which looks like deciding between them; that would be partiality. It is bigotry to assert any superior right for the truth. We are to agree to differ, and any favoring of the truth because it is truth is partisanship. What the friends of truth and error hold in common is fundamental. Anything on which they differ is *ipso facto* non-essential. Anybody who makes account of such a thing is a disturber of the peace of the Church. Truth and error are two coordinate powers, and the great secret of church-statesmanship is to preserve the balance between them. From this point error soon goes on to its natural end, which is to assert *supremacy*. Truth started with *tolerating;* it comes to be merely tolerated, and that only for a time. Error claims a preference for its judgments on all disputed points. It puts men into positions, not as at first in spite of their departure from the Church's faith, but in consequence of it. Their recommendation is that they repudiate that faith, and position is given them to teach others to repudiate it, and to make them skilful in combating it."

How shall we account for the peculiar position held toward the truth by the theologians of the Reformed Church, to which also the Fundamentalists of our day belong? Their peculiar position toward the truth, and consequently also toward those who deny the truth, is due to their peculiar position held toward the Scriptures. In the first place, they are not agreed that the Bible is the *verbally* inspired Word of God; in the second place, none of them accepts the divine principle of Bible interpretation: *Scriptura Scripturam interpretatur,* nor that other hermeneutical principle, which is closely related to it: *Sensus literalis unus est;* on the contrary, *they let man assume the right to interpret the Scripture as he understands it.* This wrong principle of Scripture interpretation has opened the floodgates to the various and manifold differing opinions in the Church and to the spirit of sectarianism. This wrong attitude toward the Scriptures is the weakness of non-Lutheran Protestantism and the very thing which in the course of time, in the very measure in which the wrong principle is being *consistently* applied, is bringing about its ruin.

The fact is that in their attitude toward the Scriptures the Fundamentalists and the Modern Liberalists do not essentially differ; *they differ only in degree.* Both the Fundamentalists and the Modern Liberalists accord to human reason the right to interpret what God says in the Bible; the only difference is that the Modern Liberalists have consistently carried out the principle and have therefore also applied it to such doctrines as the deity of Christ and the atonement, while the Fundamentalists have not yet gone to the same extent, in other words, are yet more or less inconsistent.

To the Fundamentalists this criticism, we know, will seem harsh. But we ask, Is it not true? The fact of the existence of the denominations, differing as they do in doctrine, can be explained only on the basis of a wrong principle of Scripture interpretation. If all men in the Church would admit that the Bible must be taken as it reads, taken at its face value, then there could be no differences of opinion as to doctrine; and without differences as to doctrine there could be no denominationalism in the Christian Church. The grievance which Zwingli had against Luther was that Luther clung too closely to the letter of the Scriptures, and it is this same grievance which the churches of the Reformed theology have against our Lutheran Church today. It is our intolerant spirit over against any departure from the *one* true meaning which the words of the Scripture convey that they detest. If we would grant to every man, as they do, the right of his own private opinion in interpreting the Scriptures, then they would not accuse us of narrowness and bigotry. If we, however, would take their position, we would be just as unable and as ineffectual as they are to combat error and, in the same way as they are doing, expose ourselves to the same dangers and put ourselves under the same condemnation.

> SOURCE: John H. C. Fritz, "Will the Fundamentalists Win Out in Their Fight Against the Modern Liberalists?" *Theological Monthly*, IV (1924), 234, 237–40. Used by permission of Concordia Publishing House.

152. Science and Religion

The Southern Baptist Convention was organized as a separate body in May, 1845, when the existing Baptist Foreign Mission Board declared itself unwilling on principle to appoint slaveholding missionaries. The new denomination proved to be particularly adapted to the South, gaining special strength among the large rural population. With its deep rural roots, it was a bulwark of social and theological conservatism.

The spokesmen for liberal theology were few in number among Southern Baptists in the 1920's,[29] and did not constitute a serious challenge to the dominant views. But, stimulated by the fundamentalist-modernist controversy which was being nationally publicized at the time, and desiring to overawe its own liberal minority, the Southern Baptist Convention in 1925 adopted the most complete statement of faith in its history. For this action it gave the following reason: "The present occasion for a reaffirmation of Christian fundamentals is the prevalence of naturalism in the modern teaching and preaching of religion."

The statement which the Convention adopted in 1925 was a slight modification of the New Hampshire Confession (drafted in 1833 and revised in 1853), which is the most widely accepted confession among Baptists in the United States.[30] The 1925 revision left the article on "The Scriptures" unchanged, but, reflecting contemporary discussions, inserted affirmations of the virgin birth, bodily resurrection, and physical return of Christ, and, in the section on "The Fall of Man," declared: "Man was created by the special act of God as recorded in Genesis." Not incorporated

[29] Cf. Norman F. Furniss, *The Fundamentalist Controversy*, 119–26; Edwin Mims, *The Advancing South: Stories of Progress and Reaction* (Garden City, N.Y., 1926), 279–311; Virginius Dabney, *Liberalism in the South* (Chapel Hill, N.C., 1932), 287–308.

[30] For the text of the New Hampshire Confession, cf. William J. McGlothlin, *Baptist Confessions of Faith* (Phila., 1911), 301–7.

in the revised Confession but immediately subjoined to it was the statement here reproduced condemning evolution under the title "Science and Religion." In spite of Baptist principles of local autonomy, section three of this statement assumed authority to enforce strict theological criteria for teaching in Baptist institutions.

The Convention in 1926 again condemned evolution and was partially successful in persuading its educational institutions and boards to concur in the condemnation. But the effort provoked considerable resistance. As the 1920's came to a close, the controversy in the nation was dying down. Pragmatic considerations were discouraging theological controversy in other activistic American denominations, and the Southern Baptists, who were entering a new era of denominational promotion and organizational efficiency, did not wish the church's work to be impaired by controversy. Thus the Baptists, too, were ready to turn their attention to other things.[31]

DOCUMENT

1. We recognize the greatness and value of the service which modern science is rendering to the cause of truth in uncovering the facts of the natural world. We believe that loyalty to fact is a common ground of genuine science and the Christian religion. We have no interest or desire in covering up any fact in any realm of research. But we do protest against certain unwarranted procedures on the part of some so-called scientists. First, in making discoveries, or alleged discoveries, in physical nature, a convenient weapon of attack upon the facts of religion; second, using the particular sciences, such as psychology, biology, geology and various others, as if they necessarily contained knowledge pertaining to the realm of the Christian religion, setting aside the supernatural; third, teaching as facts what are merely hypotheses. The evolution doctrine has long been a working hypothesis of science, and will probably continue to be, because of its apparent simplicity in explaining the universe. But its best exponents freely admit that the causes of the origin of species have not been traced, nor has any proof been forthcoming that man is not the direct creation of God as recorded in Genesis. We protest against the imposition of this theory upon the minds of our children in denominational, or public schools, as if it were a definite and established truth of science. We insist that this and all other theories be dealt with in a truly scientific way, that is, in careful conformity to established facts.

2. We record again our unwavering adherence to the supernatural elements in the Christian religion. The Bible is God's revelation of himself through men moved by the Holy Spirit, and is our sufficient, certain and authoritative guide in religion. Jesus Christ was born of the Virgin Mary, through the power of the Holy Spirit. He was the divine and eternal Son

[31] Furniss, *Fundamentalist Controversy*, 125. For Southern Baptist history in general, cf. William W. Barnes, *The Southern Baptist Convention, 1854-1953* (Nashville, 1954).

of God. He wrought miracles, healing the sick, casting out demons, raising the dead. He died as the vicarious, atoning Saviour of the world, and was buried. He arose again from the dead. The tomb was emptied of its contents. In his risen body he appeared many times to his disciples. He ascended to the right hand of the Father. He will come again in person, the same Jesus who ascended from the Mount of Olives.

3. We believe that adherence to the above truths and facts is a necessary condition of service for teachers in our Baptist schools. These facts of Christianity in no way conflict with any fact in science. We do not sit in judgment upon the scientific views of teachers of science. We grant them the same freedom of research in their realm that we claim for ourselves in the religious realm. But we do insist upon a positive content of faith in accordance with the preceding statement as a qualification for acceptable service in Baptist schools. The supreme issue today is between naturalism and super-naturalism. We stand unalterably for the supernatural in Christianity. Teachers in our schools should be careful to free themselves from any suspicion of disloyalty on this point. In the present period of agitation and unrest they are obligated to make their positions clear. We pledge our support to all schools and teachers who are thus loyal to the facts of Christianity as revealed in the Scriptures.

> SOURCE: *Annual of the Southern Baptist Convention*, 1925, 75–6. Used by permission.

LITERATURE

For the Roman Catholic Church in the United States in this period, John T. Ellis' annotated bibliography, *A Guide to American Catholic History* (Milwaukee, 1959) is a helpful introduction. *The Life of James Cardinal Gibbons, Archbishop of Baltimore, 1834–1921* (2 vols., Milwaukee, 1952), by John T. Ellis, is almost a history of American Catholicism for the period. The leading Catholic historical periodical, the *Catholic Historical Review* (1915—), publishes both articles and source materials. The Vatican Council of 1869–70 is informingly treated in Cuthbert Butler, *The Vatican Council: The Story Told from Inside in Bishop Ullathorne's Letters* (2 vols., London, 1930), while reactions in America are surveyed by J. Ryan Beiser in *The Vatican Council and the American Secular Newspapers, 1869–1870* (Washington, 1941). The best treatment of the "Americanism" issue is Thomas T. McAvoy's *The Great Crisis in American Catholic History, 1895–1900* (Chicago, 1957), and valuable information on Catholic "Modernism" will be found in Alexander R. Vidler's *The Modernist Movement in the Roman Church: Its Origins and Outcome* (Cambridge, England, 1934). Robert D. Cross's *The Emergence of Liberal Catholicism in America* (Cambridge, Mass., 1958) is particularly helpful for the last two decades of the nineteenth century.

Fundamentalism has been treated in a number of studies. Stewart G. Cole in *The History of Fundamentalism* (N.Y., 1931) summarizes the controversy among Northern Baptists, Presbyterians, Disciples, Methodists, and Episcopalians, respectively, and also deals with nondenominational fundamentalist organizations.

Norman F. Furniss' *The Fundamentalist Controversy, 1918–1931* (New Haven, 1954), with a fresh working of the sources, devotes more attention to the evolution issue and adds sections on the Southern Baptists and Southern Presbyterians. Lefferts A. Loetscher's *The Broadening Church: A Study of Theological Issues in the Presbyterian Church Since 1869* (Phila., 1954) analyzes the theological history of fundamentalism since the Civil War, as seen in a major denomination. Gabriel A. Hebert's *Fundamentalism and the Church of God* (London, 1957) is by an Australian Anglican. It is not, as the title might suggest, a treatment of the American fundamentalist movement, but deals in a suggestive way with theological problems related to the fundamentalist discussions. Robert T. Handy's "Fundamentalism and Modernism in Perspective," *Religion in Life,* XXIV (Summer, 1955), 381–94, offers a theological analysis.

Fundamentalism received its name from a series of little volumes which were widely distributed, *The Fundamentals: A Testimony to the Truth* (12 vols., Chicago, 1909–12). J. Gresham Machen's *Christianity and Liberalism* (N.Y., 1923) was about the clearest statement of the antithesis between fundamentalism and liberalism which the controversy produced. More irenic presentations of conservative theology were Edgar Y. Mullins, *Christianity at the Crossroads* (N.Y., 1924), and Francis L. Patton, *Fundamental Christianity* (N.Y., 1926).

Holiness and similar movements, many of which contributed to the total volume of theological conservatism in the United States, are presented in Elmer T. Clark's *The Small Sects in America* (rev. ed., N.Y., 1949). Dispensationalism, an extreme form of premillennialism, has been conspicuous in portions of the fundamentalist movement. C. Norman Kraus' *Dispensationalism in America: Its Rise and Development* (Richmond, Va., 1958) relates dispensationalism to the American setting, whereas Clarence Bass's *Backgrounds to Dispensationalism* (Grand Rapids, Mich., 1960) is concerned principally with its English roots in J. N. Darby.

Evolution was a subject of concern for many decades. Stow Persons, ed., *Evolutionary Thought in America* (New Haven, 1950) treats various aspects of the subject, including its theological implications. Bert J. Loewenberg's "Darwinism Comes to America, 1858–1900," *Mississippi Valley Historical Review,* XXVIII (1941), 339–68, admirably relates the debates about evolution to the larger social and intellectual backgrounds. For a leading theologian's resistance to Darwin's views, cf. Charles Hodge, *What Is Darwinism?* (N.Y., 1874). Sympathetic to Bryan's fundamentalism is Wayne C. Williams, *William Jennings Bryan* (N.Y., 1936), while Bryan is answered by a leading scientist in Henry Fairfield Osborn's *The Earth Speaks to Bryan* (N.Y., 1925).

Revivalism has been an important tributary to fundamentalism in the period since the Civil War. William G. McLoughlin's *Modern Revivalism: Charles Grandison Finney to Billy Graham* (N.Y., 1959) ably shows how, through its ministerial and lay supporters, revivalism was related to the theological and economic pressures of the times. Suggestive and highly readable is Bernard A. Weisberger's *They Gathered at the River: The Story of the Great Revivalists and Their Impact Upon Religion in America* (Boston, 1958). The revivalism of the immediately preceding period is ably treated by Timothy L. Smith in his *Revivalism and Social Reform in Mid-Nineteenth-Century America* (N.Y., 1957). Lefferts A. Loetscher's "Presbyterianism and Revivals in Philadelphia Since 1875,"

Pennsylvania Magazine of History and Biography, LXVIII (1944), 54–92, summarizes the revivalism of this period in relation to a representative metropolitan body. For D. L. Moody, cf. Wilbur M. Smith, *An Annotated Bibliography of Dwight L. Moody* (Chicago, 1948), and William R. Moody, *D. L. Moody* (N.Y., 1930). Billy Sunday is critically evaluated in his total context by William G. McLoughlin, Jr., *Billy Sunday Was His Real Name* (Chicago, 1955).

Jehovah's Witnesses are the subject of scholarly analysis in Herbert H. Stroup's *The Jehovah's Witnesses* (N.Y., 1945), with bibliography, 171–3.

On the Missouri Lutherans, some material will be found in the general bibliography by Herbert H. Schmidt, "The Literature of the Lutherans in America," *Religion in Life,* XXVII (1958), 583–603. The theological periodical of the Missouri Lutherans, under its three successive names, is invaluable for authentic character: *Theological Quarterly* (St. Louis, 1897–1920); *Theological Monthly* (St. Louis, 1921–29); and *Concordia Theological Monthly* (St. Louis, 1931–59). Three published doctoral dissertations and one on microfilm are well documented: Carl Mauelshagen, *American Lutheranism Surrenders to Forces of Conservatism* (Athens, Ga., 1936); Carl S. Mundinger, *Government in the Missouri Synod* (St. Louis, 1947); Walter O. Forster, *Zion on the Mississippi: The Settlement of the Saxon Lutherans in Missouri, 1839–1841* (St. Louis, 1953); and Ernest T. Bachman, "The Rise of 'Missouri Lutheranism' " (typed Ph.D. dissertation, University of Chicago, 1946; microfilm). A series of six articles by Heinrich H. Maurer, under the general title of "Studies in the Sociology of Religion," offers valuable sociological analysis of American religion, mostly Missouri Lutheranism, in *American Journal of Sociology,* XXX (1924–25), 257–86, 408–38, 534–50, 665–82; XXXI (1925–26), 39–57, 485–506.

For the Southern Baptists, the bibliography by Leo T. Crisman is useful: "The Literature of the Baptists," *Religion in Life,* XXV (1955–56), 117–31. William W. Barnes treats the denominational history as a whole, *The Southern Baptist Convention: A Study in the Development of Ecclesiology* (Seminary Hill, Tex., 1934), while Robert A. Baker's *Relations between Northern and Southern Baptists* (Fort Worth, Tex., 1948) deals with a special aspect. The *Encyclopedia of Southern Baptists* (2 vols., Nashville, Tenn., 1958) contains much information, particularly concerning organizational matters.

CHAPTER XIX

The Quickening of Social Conscience

THE rapid growth of American industry after the Civil War brought to a head social problems which posed serious moral issues for the churches. As industry expanded it consolidated into ever larger units. While corporations were merging, wealth was being concentrated in the hands of fewer persons, so that by 1890 one per cent of the families owned more than half of the wealth of the country.[1] This concentrated wealth, by overshadowing the individual and even by corrupting government officials, was threatening to destroy the political equality which had been won earlier in the century. What was still more serious, the vast industrial machine was making men and classes and even industries so dependent on each other that the ordinary individual was becoming insignificant and powerless. Labor tried unsuccessfully to create an effective counterbalance to concentrated capital. Bloody strikes and riots in 1877, 1886, 1892, and 1894 alerted the churches as nothing else had done to the underlying moral aspects of the industrial problem.

The churches were deterred from giving moral leadership in the industrial crisis by laissez-faire economics, which they inclined to accept almost as theological orthodoxy. Laissez-faire economics was the ghost of the Christian doctrine of God's personal providence dressed in the ill-fitting clothes of eighteenth-century scientific law. It taught that there is a good Creator who undergirded human relations with beneficent principles, and that if only man would avoid interfering with these principles everything would work out for the best. Thus if an individual served his own enlightened self-interest it was supposed that he was serving the good of the whole. On its face this seemed convincingly Christian, but in the true spirit of the Enlightenment it eliminated the crucial doctrines of the Fall and of human sin, doctrines which point to the necessity for regulation and restraint. Laissez faire thus encouraged an unrealistic optimism and lack of moral discipline which would have horrified classical Protestantism or medieval Catholicism. Laissez faire, as held by Americans after 1865, had been given some Christian accents by Scottish realism, but had also been intensified by social Darwinism's doctrine of the survival of the fittest.[2]

The American churches, both Protestant and Catholic, were at first singularly unprepared to cope with the moral problems of the new industrial

[1] Harold U. Faulkner, *The Decline of Laissez Faire, 1897–1917* (N.Y., 1951), 21.
[2] Cf. Joseph Dorfman, *The Economic Mind in American Civilization*, III, *1865–1918* (N.Y., 1949), 49–82; Henry F. May, *Protestant Churches and Industrial America* (N.Y., 1949), 3–25; Richard Hofstadter, *Social Darwinism in American Thought* (Phila., 1945).

era. Protestantism had largely accepted the compartmentalizing and secularizing of life which had been initiated by the Renaissance and which had been given special character in America by the separation of church and state. The heritage from later Puritanism, from the frontier, and from revivalism had made Protestants of the late nineteenth century individualistic to an unusual degree at the very moment when a corporate approach to the emerging industrial problems was needed. The doctrine of the church and the conception of the solidarity of society, both of which would have had great value in the social crisis, had suffered serious erosion in the American environment. In some quarters, Protestantism had lost its dynamism and ethical vitality and, in scholastic fashion, thought of Christian truth as consisting of propositional statements. In the more numerous areas where a dynamic spirit did prevail, emphasis, in pietistic fashion, was usually concentrated on inner spiritual experience and on individual conduct.

American Catholics, like Protestants, were quite unprepared to give strong moral leadership to the emerging industrial society. It is true that the Catholics were heirs of the medieval ideal of a Christian society under the influence of the church. They still viewed the church as a divine organism and retained somewhat more of a solidaristic conception of society than did their Protestant neighbors. But Catholics belonged to a church which in other parts of the world had large vested interests, and they insisted on regarding property rights as almost sacrosanct, in spite of the fact that their American adherents were mostly working people. Socialism was abhorrent. Inconsistently with their own tradition, for a time they accepted laissez faire and repudiated as "socialistic" government regulation of economic life.[3]

The rising social sciences offered valuable social resources to both Protestants and Catholics. The term "sociology" had been coined by Auguste Comte in 1837. By 1880 sociology was being accepted as an academic discipline in a number of leading American educational institutions. In the same year, a Lutheran clergyman, J. H. W. Stuckenberg, published his notable volume, *Christian Sociology*. Sociology's central concern with relations between persons and between groups contributed to the idea of social solidarity and proved invaluable to an understanding of the new industrial society. Before 1900 many Protestant seminaries, and after the turn of the century many Catholic seminaries, were adding courses in sociology to their curricula.[4] Social psychology also made available new social understanding and techniques for social action.

[3] Cf. Henry J. Browne, "Catholicism in the United States," in James Ward Smith and A. Leland Jamison, eds., *Religion in American Life*, Vol. I: *The Shaping of American Religion* (Princeton, 1961), 95-6, 101; Aaron I. Abell, *American Catholicism and Social Action: A Search for Social Justice, 1865-1950* (Garden City, N.Y., 1960), 27; Robert D. Cross, *The Emergence of Liberal Catholicism in America* (Cambridge, Mass., 1958), 106, 114.

[4] C. Howard Hopkins, *The Rise of the Social Gospel in American Protestantism, 1865-1915* (New Haven, 1940), 167; Aaron I. Abell, *The Urban Impact on American Protestantism, 1865-*

Socialism, too, as far as its limited influence extended, called attention to the interrelatedness of the new economic life. In 1877 the Socialist Labor Party of North America was organized and in 1898, the Social Democratic Party, which three years later became the Socialist Party of America. During most of the 1880's, the American clergy unanimously opposed socialism. After 1890, however, many leaders of Protestant social thought adopted ideas from socialism, while a small minority of them became avowed socialists. In 1889 the Society of Christian Socialists was organized by a group of Boston clergymen under the leadership of W. D. P. Bliss. The Society accepted many of the ideas and objectives of socialism, although repudiating its antireligious bias. George D. Herron (1862–1925), professor at Iowa College, was one of the most influential representatives of this type of thought. Christian socialism, although important in stimulating the churches to think socially, did not achieve large ends in its own right.[5] Roman Catholics, on their part, maintained a continuous attack on socialism, but in spite of that it stimulated them to increased social awareness.

Protestants expressed their new social attitudes in theological terms which were closely related to the theological changes currently taking place.[6] Over against the individualism which was becoming more and more ineffective in the new industrial civilization, exponents of social Christianity offered a social doctrine of the kingdom of God. They did not expect isolated individuals to change society, but thought of the transforming power as itself a society, a community of the ethically earnest. This kingdom of God was no longer regarded as other-worldly, but as this-worldly and ethical. The idea of the kingdom seems to have been preferred to the idea of the church as a corrective of an exaggerated individualism principally for two reasons. For one thing, in many areas of American Christianity individualism had so weakened the idea of the church that there was little substance left in it. But, more important, the kingdom seemed to provide for Christians and non-Christians a common base for ethical action in a way which the church could not do. This was so because the kingdom was now redefined broadly as the community which included all who were ethically interested, whereas the church had long been more exclusively defined as the community of the redeemed. Walter Rauschenbusch (1861–1918), leading theologian of social Christianity, gave classic formulation to this new conception of the kingdom of God.

Other aspects of the new theology also contributed to its social involvement. Accentuation of God's immanence, like the new definition of the kingdom, helped to break down the barrier between secular and sacred and to prepare the way for the direct application of Christian principles to

---

1900 (Cambridge, Mass., 1943), 224–45; John A. Ryan, *Social Doctrine in Action: A Personal History* (N.Y., 1941), 78–9, 107.

[5] May, *Protestant Churches and Industrial America*, 261–2; James Dombrowski, *The Early Days of Christian Socialism in America* (N.Y., 1936).

[6] For a discussion of theological changes in this period see *supra,* Chaps. 16 and 17.

society as a whole. Philosophic idealism encouraged this emphasis on the divine immanence. God is not outside of the social process but within it. This combined with the doctrine of evolution to create an optimistic attitude toward social problems and toward history as a whole. God is now in the act of working out his purposes in society. Many of the leaders of the new social Christianity sought to make ethics central in religion, thus giving further urgency to the demand for immediate social renewal. Current critical studies of the Bible also contributed to this tendency by setting forth the Old Testament prophets as great ethical leaders and the "historic Jesus" as exemplar and reformer. "Jesus stepped down from his pedestal and became a real character," said Shailer Mathews (1863–1941).[7] Christian leaders like Washington Gladden (1836–1918) challenged the idea that economic life—the law of supply and demand, for example—was beyond the range of Christian ethics. Gladden advocated rational self-love, based on the Golden Rule and combining egoism and altruism, as a workable social principle.[8]

The term "social gospel" was applied to this type of thinking just before the turn of the century and became more general by 1910. From 1865 to 1880 was a time of preliminary budding, with the real flowering in the 1890's. Soon after the turn of the century, denominational and interdenominational bodies set up social agencies and programs.[9] Men like Gladden and Josiah Strong (1847–1916) and an increasing number of others urged that the rights of labor be recognized and that industrial peace be sought on this basis. They warned that there must be social changes and improvement in the condition of the lower classes if revolution was to be avoided. They urged just wages, and a few of them advocated profit sharing by labor. They denounced concentration of wealth, unrestrained competition, and laissez faire. "When the kingdom of God is fully come in the world," wrote Josiah Strong in 1902, "I imagine that the Manchester school of political economy will have just about as much influence on earth as it now has in heaven."[10]

The social gospel was not a revolutionary attack on capitalistic society from the outside, but a reforming effort from within. Its ideal of the kingdom of God had striking resemblance to bourgeois America of its day. Leaders of the theological revival of the 1930's later charged that this particular form of social Christianity, with its confidence in the rationality and disinterestedness of man's conduct, was less realistic than either proletarian

[7] *New Faith for Old: An Autobiography* (N.Y., 1936), 123.

[8] Washington Gladden, *Recollections* (Boston, 1909), 251; Hopkins, *Rise of the Social Gospel*, 88–9.

[9] Hopkins, *Rise of the Social Gospel*, 122, 196–7, 280.

[10] *The Next Great Awakening* (N.Y., 1902), 172; cf. also Strong, *Our Country* (N.Y., 1885), 123–5, 211; Strong, *The New Era* (N.Y., 1893), 10, 36, 134; Gladden, *Recollections*, 300–4. The Manchester School, led by Richard Cobden (1804–65) and John Bright (1811–89), worked for free trade in Britain. It held to laissez-faire economic theory.

radicalism or biblical prophetic religion.[11] But the social gospel showed timely awareness that society is more than the aggregate of individuals composing it; it realized that Christianity had deep ethical obligations to this society; and it sought to state these obligations in terms of the theology of its day. Before the end of the nineteenth century it was gaining entrance into many seminaries. Soon after the turn of the century this form of social Christianity was receiving official recognition by leading denominations and was noticeably influencing political progressivism. The social gospel was a primary factor in creating the Federal Council of Churches in 1908, and continued to be a powerful force in Protestantism throughout the period here under review.

Roman Catholic leaders began to deal with the problems of the new American industrial society in a constructive way in the 1880's. Before the Civil War, Catholics, as an oppressed minority who did not share the prevailing optimism concerning progress and man's perfectibility, remained largely aloof from the humanitarian crusades. Instead, they created their own benevolent agencies—schools, orphanages, homes, hospitals. By the 1880's some Catholic leaders, including James Cardinal Gibbons (1834–1921), Archbishop of Baltimore, and Archbishop John Ireland (1838–1918) of St. Paul, were convinced that the church should involve itself more directly in American life. Related to this objective was concern for American workingmen, many of whom were Catholics.[12] Catholic conservatives, led by Archbishop Michael A. Corrigan of New York, and by Germans of the Midwest, opposed both Americanization and social reform.

Henry George (1839–97), advocating a single tax on land, stimulated the social thinking of some Catholics in the 1880's, although very few followed his economic views all the way.[13] Father Edward McGlynn (1837–1900), moved by extensive unemployment in his St. Stephen's parish in New York City, in 1886 supported Henry George's candidacy for mayor of New York. As a result he was suspended, later excommunicated, but finally, in 1892, restored to the priesthood. Father McGlynn was a powerful orator and his widely publicized case stimulated interest among Catholics in social questions. Rome, however, condemned (1889) Henry George's book, *Progress and Poverty,* but as a concession to Cardinal Gibbons declared that the condemnation need not be published.[14] A notable example of the growing concern for workingmen on the part of American Catholics was Cardinal Gibbons' memorial to the Roman Congregation of Propa-

[11] Dombrowski, *The Early Days of Christian Socialism in America,* 18–30.

[12] Thomas T. McAvoy, *The Great Crisis in American Catholic History, 1895–1900* (Chicago, 1957), 44; Aaron I. Abell, in *The Image of Man,* ed. M. A. Fitzsimmons, Thomas T. McAvoy, and Frank O'Malley (Notre Dame, Ind., 1959), 385–91. On the "Americanism" issue, cf. *supra,* 336–40.

[13] Ryan, *Social Doctrine in Action,* 9; Abell, *American Catholicism and Social Action,* 61–2.

[14] John Tracy Ellis, *The Life of James Cardinal Gibbons, Archbishop of Baltimore, 1834–1921* (2 vols., Milwaukee, 1952), I, 547–94.

ganda in 1887. This succeeded in averting a condemnation of the Knights of Labor in the United States.[15]

Leo XIII's encyclical *Rerum novarum* (1891) brought into the church a new attitude toward labor questions. Private property remained inviolable, socialism was condemned, and great emphasis was laid on private charity. But labor associations (defined to include employers as well as employees) were sanctioned and government regulation of industry was endorsed, which marked an important change. The influence of these new teachings on American Catholics was not, however, immediately apparent. Until the turn of the century, fear of socialism restrained Catholic social thinking.[16] At the opening of the twentieth century many Catholics favored industrial legislation, particularly in the interest of minimum wages, and were becoming increasingly concerned with problems of social justice. Catholics were also establishing social settlements in various cities.

Monsignor John A. Ryan (1869–1945) was a creative force in Catholic social thinking. He had been influenced by the liberal Archbishop John Ireland and by such non-Catholics as Henry George and Richard T. Ely. In the presidential campaign of 1896 he actively supported William Jennings Bryan. From 1915 to 1939 he taught political economy and moral theology in the Catholic University of America. A diligent student of economics, Ryan held that the ethical value of commodities or of labor must be determined independently of their purely economic value. He favored minimum-wage legislation, compulsory arbitration, and urged that economic life become less competitive and more co-operative. At St. Paul Seminary, Minnesota, whose faculty he joined in 1902, he taught the first course in economics and sociology given in any Catholic seminary in the United States. Fellow churchmen followed the trail which he blazed. He was the author of the social declaration adopted by the Catholic bishops in 1919 and known as the Bishops' Program of Social Reconstruction. The church, with its venerable corpus of social doctrine and with its increased size and influence in American society, was now launched upon a program of carefully planned and well-organized social action. In the social area more than anywhere else there developed a degree of co-operation between Catholics and other religious bodies. The Bishops' Program of 1919 and subsequent actions of the National Catholic Welfare Conference became an important influence on American society.

Social issues less directly related to industrialization also challenged the churches, both Protestant and Catholic, during the period 1865–1930. The political reconstruction of the South, which sought to ensure the "loyalty" of the South and the new freedom of the Negro, found a close parallel in

---

[15] Henry J. Browne, *The Catholic Church and the Knights of Labor* (Washington, 1949).

[16] John F. Cronin, *Catholic Social Principles: The Social Teaching of the Catholic Church Applied to American Economic Life* (Milwaukee, 1950), 42; Ryan, *Social Doctrine in Action*, 44; Abell, in *The Image of Man*, 389–90; Ellis, *The Life of James Cardinal Gibbons*, I, 535–8.

the churches. Northern teachers, many of them with religious motivation and abolitionist background, seeking to re-educate the South, soon antagonized southern traditions and devoted themselves largely to schooling the recently emancipated slaves.[17] Northern denominations which had coreligionists in the South—most conspicuously the Methodists, Baptists, and Old School Presbyterians—demanded that Southerners repent of the "sins" of slavery and "treason" as a condition of ending the divisions which had been caused by slavery and secession. This provocation, added to lingering bitterness on both sides, prolonged the sectional divisions into the twentieth century.[18] By the 1880's, however, a few southern churchmen, like Atticus G. Haygood, president of Emory College, were championing the rise of a "new" reconstructed South. The structure of religion in the South was greatly altered by the decision of the freedmen, especially Baptists and Methodists, to organize separate Negro religious bodies.

Closely related to industrialization was the rise of cities. The immigration of great numbers of Roman Catholics and Jews caused many Protestant churches to flee to the more congenial suburbs. Roman Catholic churches, surrounded by immigrants of their own faith, were often more successful in the inner city. Protestants developed new techniques in the effort to reach city dwellers. The Salvation Army, coming to the United States in 1879, combined revivalistic preaching with physical relief. In the 1880's Methodists and Lutherans developed the work of deaconesses to care for the needy. Following earlier pioneering by William A. Muhlenberg and Thomas K. Beecher, St. George's Church, New York City, in 1882 conducted the full program of an "institutional church." Churches of this type rendered social, educational, and recreational services to their communities throughout the week. Social settlements, a minority of which, like Andover House (opened in 1892) and the Union Settlement (1895) of Union Theological Seminary, were religiously motivated, did much to throw a bridge of understanding across the gulf of social separation.[19] Cities were perhaps the worst-governed political units in the country. From time to time, clergymen, like Washington Gladden in Columbus, Ohio, and Charles H. Parkhurst in New York City, led effective—but usually very temporary—outbursts of reform.[20]

Immigrants coming to the United States in unprecedented numbers compounded the social problems already created by industrialization and urbanization. Starting in the 1880's, immigrants from northern and western

[17] Hugh L. Swint, *The Northern Teacher in the South, 1865-1870* (Nashville, 1941).

[18] Cf. Ralph E. Morrow, *Northern Methodism and Reconstruction* (East Lansing, Mich., 1956).

[19] Abell, *The Urban Impact on American Protestantism,* casts much light on the relation of Protestants to the urban problem.

[20] Charles H. Parkhurst, *Our Fight with Tammany* (N.Y., 1895); cf. the interdenominational efforts in Lefferts A. Loetscher, "Presbyterians and Political Reform in Philadelphia," *Journal of the Presbyterian Historical Society,* XXIII (1945), 2-18, 119-36.

Europe were outnumbered by those from southern and eastern Europe, whose appearance, culture, and folkways were in sharp contrast with those of older Americans, and whose religion was usually either Roman Catholic or Jewish. American nativism revived in the 1880's and 1890's, declined in the early twentieth century, then became more widespread than ever during American participation in World War I. In general, the Protestant churches shared the prevailing apprehensions concerning the flood of immigration. Protestants became active in home missions for Catholic immigrants, but with very limited success.[21] The psychological and sociological barriers which separated the older Protestants from the newer arrivals are revealed in the solemn warnings against an alleged immigrant "peril" which were voiced by some of the very denominations and missionary leaders most active in trying to win the newcomers.[22] Roman Catholics gained greatly from the newer immigration, being largely successful in retaining for their church those who came from Catholic countries.[23]

The rural problem was the counterpart of the industrial and urban problem. Discontented farmers, especially in the West and South, organized Farmers' Alliances in the 1880's. The People's, or Populist, Party arose in 1891, and in 1896 unsuccessfully supported the Democratic candidate for president, William Jennings Bryan. The churches sometimes offered devout exhortations and supplied biblical metaphors, as in Bryan's famous "Cross of Gold" speech, but there is no evidence that church leaders attempted to redefine Christian principles in relation to the new rural conditions in any way parallel to what the formulators of the social gospel were attempting to do in relation to industrial life. In the early twentieth century, however, as cities drained off much of the best rural leadership, the churches made sociological analyses of rural society, and with denominational or interdenominational subsidies sought, with very partial success, to meet the new rural needs.[24]

Two crusades which antedated the Civil War were the subject of more attention by Protestants than any other social concerns during the period 1865–1930—temperance and Sabbath observance.

The temperance movement had brought about state prohibition in Maine in 1851, but this failed to start a prevailing trend. The National Prohibition Party, organized in 1869, and even more the Woman's Christian Temperance Union, organized in 1874, propagandized zealously. More effective, however, was the Anti-Saloon League, organized in 1895, which vigorously supported candidates for political office, regardless of party affiliation or voting record on other issues, so long as they voted "dry." The

[21] Theodore Abel, *Protestant Home Missions to Catholic Immigrants* (N.Y., 1933), 103–7.
[22] Charles L. Thompson, *The Soul of America* (N.Y., 1919), 136.
[23] Gerald Shaughnessy, *Has the Immigrant Kept the Faith?* (N.Y., 1925).
[24] Charles O. Gill and Gifford Pinchot, *The Country Church: The Decline of Its Influence and the Remedy* (N.Y., 1913); Edwin L. Earp, *The Rural Church Movement* (N.Y., 1914); Edmund de S. Brunner, *The Church and the Agricultural Crisis* (Boston, 1928).

League was so closely related to the Protestant churches as to be almost their unofficial arm. The ultimate end of these efforts was achieved in national constitutional prohibition by the adoption of the Eighteenth Amendment, operative in 1920. Evangelical denominations—most notably the Methodists, Baptists, and Presbyterians—gave powerful support to the temperance drive. Quarterly lessons in the Sunday schools, frequent pulpit references, and resolutions by ecclesiastical bodies implemented their stand.[25]

"Sabbath" observance received much attention from the churches. There was continued bemoaning of the laxity of the "Continental Sunday" which was charged against immigrants from the European Continent, especially Germans. Disproportionately great efforts were made to prevent the national expositions of the period from remaining open on Sunday, to keep streetcars from running on Sunday, and to discourage the reading of Sunday newspapers. But in spite of sermons, repeated editorials in church newspapers, and resolutions by ecclesiastical bodies, the mores of an industrial and urban society changed. Later still, after two world wars, clergymen with entirely good conscience were observing Sunday in ways which their grandfathers had castigated.

American national destiny was the subject of renewed attention after the Civil War, and the churches were deeply interested in it. Since the early nineteenth century the foreign-missionary movement had been giving American Christians an interest in the outside world which offered at least some counterpoise to the national concerns which preoccupied the country throughout most of the nineteenth century. The earliest appeal for foreign missionary support was almost exclusively evangelical, to secure conversions. But as the social gospel emerged at home in the closing decades of the nineteenth century, it was echoed in appeals to alleviate social needs in the non-Christian world.[26] The promotion of foreign missions, whether evangelistic or social, by emphasizing the need of non-Christian peoples and the obligations of American Christians to them, sometimes tended unintentionally to increase America's self-esteem.

The hypothesis, which was entering American intellectual circles in the 1880's, that the "Anglo-Saxons" were a superior breed,[27] supplied a rationale for American dreams of imperialism. A leading exponent of the social gospel, Josiah Strong, espoused Anglo-Saxonism in his widely circulated book, Our Country (1885). Combining this idea with social Darwinism's

[25] E. H. Cherrington, The Evolution of Prohibition in the U.S.A.: A Chronological History of the Liquor Problem (Westerville, O., 1920), is written from the viewpoint of the Anti-Saloon League; while D. Leigh Colvin, Prohibition in the United States: A History of the Prohibition Party and of the Prohibition Movement (N.Y., 1926), is written by a former vice-presidential candidate of the Prohibition Party. Cf. also Peter Odegard, Pressure Politics: The Story of the Anti-Saloon League (N.Y., 1928).

[26] Cf. James S. Dennis, Christian Missions and Social Progress: A Sociological Study of Foreign Missions (3 vols., N.Y., 1897-1906).

[27] Edward N. Saveth, in Saveth, ed., Understanding the American Past: American History and Its Interpretation (Boston, 1954), 11-5.

principle of the "survival of the fittest" and with the Christian doctrine of God's providence, Strong declared that the "Anglo-Saxons" were destined by God to carry the benefits of their superior civilization to less vigorous races and to master them. When the United States openly adopted imperialistic policies in the closing years of the nineteenth century, churchmen prevailingly supported the new expansionism. Almost until the outbreak of hostilities with Spain, most of the Protestant clergy opposed war, but once the struggle was entered and the new possessions secured, they favored retaining the acquisitions for the greater opportunity which this would provide for missionary work.[28] Spain was a stanchly Catholic nation and American Catholics saw the war in somewhat different perspective from American Protestants. Before the final rupture with Spain, Archbishop Ireland, at the request of Pope Leo XIII, went to Washington to use what influence he could to avert war. Later, Cardinal Gibbons, when interrogated by President McKinley, advised against retaining the Philippine Islands.[29]

The peace movement, which derived part of its strength from the churches, revived after the Civil War, and became more vigorous at the turn of the century, strongly supporting the first and second Hague Conferences in 1899 and 1907. At the outbreak of World War I, the churches overwhelmingly favored Woodrow Wilson's policy of neutrality and peace, but after the United States entered the war, the great majority of churches and clergymen supported the war effort enthusiastically.[30] There were some, however, like Robert E. Speer, who balanced their support with a degree of restraint and self-criticism.[31] A very few, like the Quaker Rufus M. Jones, held to a pacifist position. In general it can be said that Christian social thinking was more advanced in relating Christian principles to industrial society at home than in relating these principles to international affairs.

153. The Social Responsibility of the State

The overthrow of chattel slavery did not lead to legislation to alleviate "wage slavery." Instead, the laissez-faire economics, which had been quietly taken for granted and widely practiced earlier in the century, became more articulate and aggressive after 1865.

American churchmen were slow to urge legislation in behalf of the workingman. But as workers became defenseless against concentrated capital, some clergymen began to see that property rights as currently inter-

---

[28] Attitudes of clergymen toward American destiny and imperialism are analyzed, in relation to social and ideological forces of the time, by John E. Smylie in "Protestant Clergymen and America's World Role, 1865–1900: A Study of Christianity, Nationality, and International Relations" (typed Th.D. dissertation, Princeton Theological Seminary, 1959).

[29] McAvoy, *The Great Crisis in American Catholic History, 1895–1900,* 205; Ellis, *The Life of James Cardinal Gibbons,* II, 98.

[30] Ray H. Abrams, *Preachers Present Arms* (N.Y., 1933).

[31] Robert E. Speer, *The Christian Man, the Church and the War* (N.Y., 1918).

preted conflicted with personal rights. In the interest of the latter they called for legislative action.

One of the first clergymen to raise the issue after the Civil War was George Nye Boardman (1825–1915). A graduate of Middlebury College and of Andover Seminary and later a student under Nathaniel W. Taylor at Yale Divinity School, he was pastor of the First Presbyterian Church of Binghamton, New York, in 1866 when he wrote the article here presented. In 1871 he became professor of systematic theology at Chicago Theological Seminary, and in 1899 published *A History of New England Theology*. While agreeing that private enterprise was the chief source of wealth, Boardman refused to admit that unrestrained selfishness could serve the highest ends of society. The unmodified law of supply and demand threatened the laborer with a bare subsistence wage. He did not suggest labor unions as a remedy, but demanded that the state be concerned with the welfare of society and not merely with police functions. The principle which he endorsed was a broad one and could readily be extended far beyond the poor laws and free schools advocated.[32]

DOCUMENT

Another question on which the clergy have a right to speak, and in the solution of which they occupy a vantage-ground, relates to the aim of governments. Is the world governed too much? Are the intents of government essentially negative, having in view the protection of the people against evils, or do they propose also to promote interests by positive legislation? Is government to leave the poor to take care of themselves, leave feeble interests to take care of themselves, or is its office that of protection and support to the needy? There can be no doubt that the main source of human wealth and comfort is in private enterprise and individual industry. Any philosophy that teaches the young that the government is not the chief almoner of blessings; that it has very little to do with the really positive enjoyments and attainments of mankind; that it plays but an insignificant part in human life, is to be hailed as a friend, and commissioned to its important work. Still we must not hold that governments are ordained simply to prevent wrongs; they have interests also to promote. Could legislation prevent every possible wrong, that might answer its end; but the only practical means of effecting this is by making sure certain necessary interests of the people. Recent legislation in favor of homesteads, in favor of widows, in distribution of bounty-lands, indicates a recognition of the duty here referred to. Without an attempt to decide the question, Whose servant governments are, there is to us something repulsive in the thought that it should disregard the social relations which God has established, and should consider itself as simply the minister of cold justice. It may without

[32] For other early Protestant critics of laissez faire, cf. Hopkins, *The Rise of the Social Gospel*, 24–35.

injury rise to a higher level at once, and stand as the protector of interests without which society cannot exist. We lose much in defining the province of governments by losing sight of the fact that there is a self-seeking which is also benevolence, that there are social interests which are identical with personal interests. But political economy is attempting now to establish itself on the principle that self-seeking will secure the best result through checks upon itself, not by being identical with seeking the good of others. It holds that commercial war is the natural state of man, i.e. competition is the natural state of business. Political economy teaches, or is attempting to teach, that the world will be best provided for, when every man provides for himself as best he can; that justice is best promoted by each man's making sure of his own rights. But the question is: Are men able to fight each other in this way, and all with success—is there a victory for every man? Is it not true that there must be some superintending power, protecting the weak, repressing violence? Is infinite war the same as peace,—every man's holding every other in place the same as every one's leaving every one untouched? Does infinite selfishness amount to the same thing as infinite benevolence? Morality and virtue are confessedly the highest or cheapest good if they can universally prevail; but inasmuch as they can only be imperfect in their influence, are we to enforce them by law, or are we to adopt infinite vice as the same thing as perfect virtue, and so set each man's injustice to act as a guard against any injustice towards himself? Is all legislation a mere carrying out of this principle, so that the murderer is hung, not because righteousness requires it, but because self-protection requires it? And, to carry the matter out perfectly, is a man to contend for the gratifications of self at the present moment in opposition to the self of any other time? Is he to say, of all times, *now* is the most important, only the pleasures of the present hour must not vitiate the pleasures of the present hour by giving occasion to fear for the future?

Perhaps the clergyman is in a better position to view this question than any other man, and the word of God aids him to a reply to the question, though it be one of social economy. It is supposable, indeed, that the poor and needy should contend with the strong, and appeal from physical to moral means to carry on a contest; and the poor man might declare that he and his family would starve rather than degrade themselves and degrade labor by working for inadequate wages; and so the man in power, the possessor of wealth, might have his choice between starving his neighbors or paying them fairly for their work. But this is only a supposition. The world is not peopled by heroes; men do work for such wages as they can get, and live uncomfortably if they cannot live comfortably. There is thus always a large class of the population who depend for the comforts of life on the virtue, benevolence, or justice of their employers; and the clergyman will demand a somewhat higher grade of these qualities than the mere man of the world. He will remember that the family is the atom of society;

that whatever crushes that pulverizes it, reduces it to individuality and to selfishness—is sin against God. He will remember that the church cannot exist without the family, that national existence even depends upon it, and therefore that its rights must be sacredly guarded. While therefore he will, with Chalmers, teach the parents providence, and throw around all the restraints of duty, he will also claim that there is a morality for the rich, for the employer, that they may not wantonly crush the instincts of the poorer classes, and doom to single life, aimless, dreary, ending in suicide perhaps, those who are dependent upon the daily wages they receive. Nor will the clergyman be satisfied when those to whom he preaches are barely sustained in life; there are some moral qualities indispensable to the family which extreme poverty destroys. Not to speak of the wanton laceration of the family and the profaning of its sanctity which is seen in connection with slavery, there are families to be found in every land in which fathers and mothers are obliged to labor till their muscles are knotted and their bones misshapen, till weariness is ingrained in the very tissues, till the feeling of fatigue is general and continuous, till patience is gone, till complaint, sighing, fault-finding have settled down upon the family circle like a blight; and these are in reality families no longer. When the children who are so unfortunate as to survive infancy are driven out by taskmasters, while they should still be at play or at school—when they are obliged to *earn* the bread they *eat*—the house is a slave-pen, the household has no ties that can characterize it as a family. When children show in their countenances an unnatural maturity, are wrinkled with age, and especially are prematurely old in sin, are unnaturally vicious, because they can find no diversions but in crimes against nature, then they are not really members of a family, and, practically, there is not any way open for them into the kingdom of heaven, the family of God.

The minister of Christ looking upon men in such condition as this, asks himself: Is there no protection for this class of the human race; are they to be left to themselves, and to the "tender mercies" of their employers? He will see that often there are men who with the utmost kindness furnish the poor with labor, who most benevolently care for them; but he will certainly sometimes see that the employer, driven by competition to afford his products at the lowest price, and yet resolved to make his own profits the highest possible, heartlessly sets the poor man's wages at the smallest amount. Such a view will disclose a meaning which the inspiring Spirit intended, if the apostle did not, in the text: "The wages of sin is death." A bare look at humanity shows that death is its doom if not reward. The race dies constantly, not from old age, but dies out from the distemper of poverty and consequent crime. The less favored ones are living briefly in wretchedness, and dying hopelessly; those extruded from the inner circle of privileges—the extremities of humanity, as it were—are falling constantly the victims of a wasting consumption that seems to be devouring the outskirts of the race; children are thrown into the arms of death at birth; man, hardened and debased, dies blaspheming his God; woman, wronged, crushed, in despair hurls herself unbidden to the bar of her Judge, and so death is the awful wages we receive for our work. The human race hardly increases in numbers; does not at all improve in morals, except where the Saviour of the world rescues a people for himself. He who preaches the gospel to the poor will have no doubt, in view of such facts, that governments, and all social institutions, are to be based on positive virtue, on morality, not on selfishness, not on each man's ability to take care of himself. He will have no hesitation in deciding that legislation in favor of the poor, in the form of poor-laws, or as the compulsory support of free schools, is only the legitimate increase of the wages paid by the employer; it is the wages due to the family over and above that due to the individual.

> SOURCE: George N. Boardman, "Political Economy and the Christian Ministry," *Bibliotheca Sacra*, XXIII (1866), 100–4.

154. The New South

The agonies of Reconstruction in the South were experienced within the churches, in none more so than in the Methodist Church. During the Civil War, Northern Methodists had been particularly fervent in their support of the Federal Government. A War Department directive of November 30, 1863, placed at the disposal of Bishop Edward R. Ames for the use of the Methodist Episcopal Church "all houses of worship belonging to the Methodist Episcopal Church South in which a loyal minister, appointed by a loyal bishop of said church, does not now officiate." [33] Seizures under this and similar orders to other denominations were of course bitterly resented in the South. The General Conference of the Methodist Episcopal Church in 1864 endorsed the program of ecclesiastical Reconstruction already begun, so that by the end of the war machinery for absorbing the Methodist Episcopal Church, South, was already in operation.

The ending of the war produced a brief time of uncertainty as to policy among Methodists in both North and South. But ecclesiastical and political Reconstruction were so closely intertwined that soon many Northern Methodists were declaring ecclesiastical absorption necessary to cement the Federal Union. By the autumn of 1865 they were thoroughly committed to a long-range program of permeating the South. [34]

For a short time Southern Methodists, too, were uncertain as to what course to pursue. Their church had lost a third of its membership, they had been unable to hold their quadrennial General Conference in 1862, and

---

[33] *The War of the Rebellion: A Compilation of the Official Records of the Union and Confederate Armies*, Series I, Vol. XXXIV, Part II (Washington, 1891), 311.

[34] Hunter D. Farish, *The Circuit Rider Dismounts: A Social History of Southern Methodism, 1865–1900* (Richmond, Va., 1938), and Ralph E. Morrow, *Northern Methodism and Reconstruction* (East Lansing, Mich., 1956).

their organization was demoralized. Some, like Braxton Craven, were ready for absorption by the Northern Methodists. Craven, a Southern Methodist minister soon to resume the presidency of Trinity College, North Carolina, had been a slaveholder and a Confederate Army officer. On July 24, 1864, he wrote to Bishop Edward R. Ames, approving the reunion of Methodism, essentially along northern lines.[35] But other counsels were to prevail. War-time animosities continued strong on both sides. A convention of Southern Methodists at Louisville in 1864 had protested against the ecclesiastical interference of the North, but it was a declaration issued by twenty-four ministers and a dozen laymen at Palmyra, Missouri, on June 22, 1865, which proved decisive in crystallizing opinion at the crucial moment.[36] In August, 1865, the three bishops of the church took up the plea for continued existence,[37] and by the time the General Conference met in May, 1866, the church was raising high its bulwarks against Reconstruction.

In spite of this continuing heritage of bitterness on both sides, some southern churchmen by the end of the Reconstruction period were willing to welcome the advent of a new South. A distinguished example of this type was the Methodist, Atticus G. Haygood (1839–96). Born in Georgia of southern parentage, he served as chaplain in the Confederate Army. His mother was driven from her home in Atlanta by General Sherman's soldiers. After the war he served as pastor and presiding elder, then as Sunday-school secretary of his denomination. From 1875 to 1884 he was president of Emory College of which he was an alumnus. During part of his presidency he edited the *Wesleyan Christian Advocate,* a weekly paper for Methodists in Georgia and Florida. His desire for the advancement of the Negro is seen in his book, *Our Brother in Black, His Freedom and His Future* (1881), and in his resigning of his college presidency to work for the John F. Slater Fund for promoting Negro education. In 1890 he became a bishop.[38] The Thanksgiving sermon here given reflects Haygood's hearty acceptance of emancipation and of the new South.

DOCUMENT

There is one great historic fact which should, in my sober judgment, above all things, excite every-where in the South profound gratitude to Almighty God: *I mean the abolition of African slavery.*

If I speak only for myself, (and I am persuaded that I do not,) then be it so. But I, for one, thank God that there is no longer slavery in these

[35] Text in Nora C. Chaffin, "A Southern Advocate of Methodist Unification in 1865," *North Carolina Historical Review,* XVIII (1941), 42–7.

[36] Farish, *The Circuit Rider Dismounts,* 52–4; W. M. Leftwich, *Martyrdom in Missouri,* II (St. Louis, 1870), 303–20; W. H. Lewis, *The History of Methodism in Missouri,* III (Nashville, 1890), 171–9.

[37] Text in "Pastoral Address of the Southern Methodist Bishops," *Southern Christian Advocate,* August 31, 1865.

[38] Edgar H. Johnson, "Atticus Green Haygood," *Dictionary of American Biography,* VIII (N.Y., 1932), 452–3.

United States! I am persuaded that I only say what the vast majority of our people feel and believe. I do not forget the better characteristics of African slavery as it existed among us for so long a time under the sanction of national law and under the protection of the Constitution of the United States; I do not forget that its worse features were often cruelly exaggerated, and that its best were unfairly minified; more than all, I do not forget that, in the providence of God, a work that is without a parallel in history was done on the Southern plantations—a work that was begun by such men as Bishop Capers, of South Carolina, Lovick Pierce and Bishop Andrew, of Georgia, and by men like-minded with them—a work whose expenses were met by the slave-holders themselves—a work that resulted in the Christianizing of a full half million of the African people, who became communicants of our Churches, and of nearly the whole four or five millions who were brought largely under the all-pervasive and redeeming influence of our holy religion.

I have nothing to say at this time of the particular "war measure" that brought about their immediate and unconditioned enfranchisement, only that it is history, and that it is done for once and for all. I am not called on, in order to justify my position, to approve the political unwisdom of suddenly placing the ballot in the hands of nearly a million of unqualified men —only that, since it is done, this also is history that we of the South should accept, and that our fellow-citizens of the North should never disturb. But all these things, bad as they may have been and unfortunate as they may yet be, are only incidental to the one great historic fact, that *slavery exists no more*. For this fact I devoutly thank God this day! And on many accounts:

1. For the negroes themselves. While they have suffered and will suffer many things in their struggle for existence, I do nevertheless believe that in the long run it is best for them. How soon they shall realize the possibilities of their new relations depends largely, perhaps most, on themselves. Much depends on those who, under God, set them free. By every token this whole nation should undertake the problem of their education. That problem will have to be worked out on the basis of co-operation; that is, they must be helped to help themselves. To make their education an absolute gratuity will perpetuate many of the misconceptions and weaknesses of character which now embarrass and hinder their progress. Much also depends upon the Southern white people, their sympathy, their justice, their wise and helpful co-operation. This we should give them, not reluctantly, but gladly, for their good and for the safety of all, for their elevation and for the glory of God. How we may do this may be matter for discussion hereafter.

2. I am grateful that slavery no longer exists, because it is better for the white people of the South. It is better for our industries and our business,

as proved by the crops that free labor makes. But by eminence it is better for our social and ethical development. We will now begin to take our right place among both the conservative and aggressive forces of the civilized and Christian world.

3. I am grateful because it is unspeakably better for our children and children's children. It is better for them in a thousand ways. I have not time for discussion in detail now. But this, if nothing else, proves the truth of my position: there are more white children at work in the South to-day than ever before. And this goes far to account for the six million bales of cotton. Our children are growing up to believe that idleness is vagabondage. One other thing I wish to say before leaving this point. We hear much about the disadvantages to our children of leaving them among several millions of freedmen. I recognize them, and feel them; but I would rather leave my children among several millions of free negroes than among several millions of negroes in slavery.

But leaving out of view at this time all discussion of the various benefits that may come through the enfranchisement of the negroes, I am thankful on the broad and unqualified ground, that there *is now no slavery in all our land*.

Does any one say to me this day: "You have got new light; you have changed 'the opinions you entertained twenty years ago.'" I answer humbly, but gratefully, and without qualification: I have got new light. I do now believe many things that I did not believe twenty years ago. Moreover, if it please God to spare me in this world twenty years longer, I hope to have, on many difficult problems, more new light. I expect, if I see the dawn of the year 1900, to believe some things that I now reject and to reject some things that I now believe. And I will not be alone.

In conclusion, I ask you to indulge me in a few reflections that are, I believe, appropriate to this occasion.

And first of all, *as a people, let us of the South frankly recognize some of our faults and lacks, and try to reform and improve*. I know this is a hard task. And it is all the harder because we are the subjects of so much denunciation and misrepresentation by our critics of the Northern States, and of other countries. Much of this comes through sincere ignorance; much of it through the necessities of party politics; some of it, I fear, through sinful hatred; and much of it through habit. Many have so long thrown stones at us that it has become a habit to do so. The rather Pharisaic attitude that many public men at the North have assumed toward us has greatly embarrassed and arrested our efforts to discover our faults and to amend them. But all this only furnishes a reason for beginning the sooner and trying the harder. What is really good—and there is much that is good— let us stand by, and make it better if we can.

There are some unpleasant things that ought to be said. They are on my conscience. Will you bear with me while I point out some of the weaker points in our social make-up—some of the more serious lacks in our development?

First, then, let us endeavor to overcome our intense provincialism. We are too well satisfied with ourselves. We think better of ourselves than the facts of our history and our present state of progress justify. Some of us are nearly of the opinion that the words "the South" is a synonym for universe. As a people we have not enough felt the heartbeat of the world outside of us. We have been largely shut off from that world. Slavery did this, and this suggests another reason for gratitude that it exists no more. On this point I will add only one word more. Had we been less provincial, less shut in by and with our own ideas, had we known the world better, we would have known ourselves better, and there would have been no war in 1861.

Secondly, there is a vast mass of illiteracy among us. There is white as well as black illiteracy. There are multiplied thousands who can neither read nor write. They must be taught.

Thirdly, let us recognize our want of a literature. We have not done much in this line of things. It is too obvious to dispute about, it is too painful to dwell upon.

Fourthly, let us wake up to our want of educational facilities. Our public-school system is painfully inadequate. Our colleges and universities are unendowed, and they struggle against fearful odds in their effort to do their work. We are one hundred years behind the Eastern and Middle States. We are also behind many of the new States of the West.

Fifthly, consider how behindhand we are with our manufacturing interests. And remember that nature never did more to furnish a people with the conditions necessary to successful manufactures. Does any one say, we lack capital? I answer, No, my friend, it was always so. It was so when we had capital. I have thought of these things a great deal. I have been placed where I was obliged to think of them, and I have reached this conclusion with perfect confidence of its correctness: Our provincialism, our want of literature, our lack of educational facilities, and our manufactures, like our lack of population, is all explained by one fact and one word—slavery. But for slavery, Georgia would be as densely peopled as Rhode Island. Wherefore, among many other reasons, I say again, I thank God that it is no more among us!

I mention, lastly, *some traits of character we should cultivate.*

First, the humble but all-prevailing virtues of industry and economy in business. There should be no non-producing classes among us—no wasting classes. The Northern people have more money than the Southern people, chiefly for the reason that they work more and save more.

Secondly, let us cultivate the sentiments and habits of political and social toleration. This is sorely needed among us. We need to feel that a man may vote against us and be our friend; we need to feel that we can be his friend although we vote against him.

Thirdly, let us cultivate respect for all law and authority as God's appointment. This is not a characteristic quality of our people. The educating influences of many generations have been unfavorable to the development of this sentiment as a mental habit, or, rather, as a mental characteristic. We must plant ourselves and bring up our children on the platform of St. Paul and St. Peter, as read and considered in the beginning of this discourse. Law, authority, we must reverence and obey as the ordinance of God.

Finally, let us cease from politics as a trust and a trade. Our duty of citizenship we must perform, but we should look no longer to political struggles as the means of deliverance from all our difficulties. If we succeed we would be disappointed. Political success may enrich a few place-hunters, who ride into office upon the tide of popular enthusiasm; but it will bring little reward to the masses of the people. There is no help for it; if we prosper, we must work for it. Our deliverance will come through millions of hard licks, and millions of acts of self-denial, through industry, economy, civil order, and the blessing of God upon obedience. . . .

There is no reason why the South should be despondent. Let us cultivate industry and economy, observe law and order, practice virtue and justice, walk in truth and righteousness, and press on with strong hearts and good hopes. The true golden day of the South is yet to dawn. But the light is breaking, and presently the shadows will flee away. Its fullness of splendor I may never see; but my children will see it, and I wish them to get ready for it while they may.

> SOURCE: Atticus G. Haygood, *The New South: Gratitude, Amendment, Hope. A Thanksgiving Sermon for November 25, 1880* (Oxford, Ga., 1880), 11–6.

155. Cardinal Gibbons Defends the Knights of Labor

The Knights of Labor was the most important labor organization of its day. Formed in 1869, it had more than half a million members by 1886, mostly unskilled workers. Its leader, Terence V. Powderly, was a Roman Catholic, as were two-thirds of the members. The organization, particularly by some of its provisions for oath-bound secrecy, aroused Roman Catholic hostility, and in 1884 the Holy See condemned the Knights in the Canadian Province of Quebec.

The great majority of the American hierarchy were opposed to a similar condemnation for the United States as it would alienate labor from the church, would be an injustice to workers, and would drive them to greater radicalism. The memorial sent to Cardinal Simeoni of the Sacred Congregation by James Cardinal Gibbons (1834–1921) has been called "a shrewd mixture of moral principle and expediency." [39] Acknowledging shortcomings of the Knights, the memorial noted also injustices to labor which needed righting. The principle of labor association was defended, and specific criticisms of the Knights were answered. The memorial emphasized the growing power of the masses and the loss which would result to the church if they were alienated. Besides, the Knights were already declining.

The memorial won its point, and the Holy Office refrained from condemning the organization in the United States. The document was probably drafted chiefly by Archbishop John Ireland and Bishop John J. Keane, but Cardinal Gibbons alone signed it.[40] The memorial, which is here reproduced, was an important milestone in the development of American Catholic social concern.

DOCUMENT

To His Eminence Cardinal Simeoni, Prefect of the Sacred Congregation of the Propaganda: [41]

YOUR EMINENCE:

In submitting to the Holy See the conclusions which after several months of attentive observation and reflection, seem to me to sum up the truth concerning the association of the Knights of Labor, I feel profoundly convinced of the vast importance of the consequences attaching to this question, which forms but a link in the great chain of the social problems of our day, and especially of our country. . . .

1. In the first place, in the constitution, laws and official declarations of the Knights of Labor, there can clearly be found assertions and rules [though there may be found . . . things—peuvent bien se trouver des assertions ou des règles] which we would not approve; but we have not found in them those elements so clearly pointed out by the Holy See, which places them among condemned associations. . . .

2. That there exists among us, as in the other countries of the world, grave and threatening social evils, public injustices, which call for strong resistance and legal remedy, is a fact which no one dares to deny, and the truth of which has been already acknowledged by the Congress and the President of the United States. Without entering into the sad details of these wrongs,—which does not seem necessary here,—it may suffice to mention only that monopolies on the part of both individuals and of corporations, have already called forth not only the complaints of our working classes but also the opposition of our public men and legislators; that

---

[39] Robert D. Cross, *The Emergence of Liberal Catholicism in America*, 116.

[40] Henry J. Browne, "Catholicism in the United States," in J. W. Smith and A. L. Jamison, eds., *Religion in American Life*, Vol. I: *The Shaping of American Religion* (Princeton, 1961), 97.

[41] The lesser differences in the readings, which usually show the toning down of the original French for American readers, will be indicated in brackets within the text. The other variations will be cited in the notes. [H. J. Browne]

the efforts of these monopolists, not always without success, to control legislation to their own profit, cause serious apprehension among the disinterested friends of liberty; that the heartless avarice which, through greed of gain, pitilessly grinds not only the men, but particularly the women and children in various enployments, make it clear to all who love humanity and justice that it is not only the right of the laboring classes to protect themselves, but the duty of the whole people to aid them in finding a remedy against the dangers with which both civilization and the social order are menaced by avarice, oppression and corruption.

It would be vain to deny either the existence of the evils, the right of legitimate resistance, or the necessity of a remedy. At most doubt might be raised about the legitimacy of the form of resistance and the remedy employed by the Knights of Labor. This then ought to be the next point of our examination.

3. It can hardly be doubted that for the attainment of any public end, association—the organization of all interested persons—is the most efficacious means, a means altogether natural and just. This is so evident, and besides so conformable to the genius of our country, of our essentially popular social conditions, that it is unnecessary to insist upon it. It is almost the only means to invite public attention, to give force to the most legitimate resistance, to add weight to the most just demands. . . .

4. Let us now consider the objections made against this sort of organization.

(a) It is objected that in these organizations Catholics are mixed with Protestants, to the peril of their faith. Naturally, yes, they are mixed with Protestants in the workers' associations,[42] precisely as they are at their work; for in a mixed people like ours, the separation of religions in social affairs is not possible. But to suppose that the faith of our Catholics suffers thereby is not to know the Catholic workers of America who are not like the workingmen of so many European countries—misguided and perverted children, looking on their Mother the Church as a hostile stepmother—but they are intelligent, well instructed and devoted children ready to give their blood, as they continually give their means (although small and hard-earned) [hard-earned—chétifs et péniblement gagnés] for her support and protection. And in fact it is not in the present case that Catholics are mixed with Protestants, but rather that Protestants are admitted to the advantages of an association, two-thirds of whose members and the principal officers [many of whose members and officers—des deux tiers des membres et les officiers principaux] are Catholics; and in a country like ours their exclusion would be simply impossible.

(b) But it is said, could there not be substituted for such an organization confraternities which would unite the workingmen under the direction

---

[42] The first part of the parallel was omitted in the English "avec les Protestants dans les associations des travailleurs, précisément comme ils sont dans les travaux mêmes." [H. J. Browne]

of the priests and the direct influence of religion? I answer frankly that I do not believe that either possible or necessary in our country. I sincerely admire the efforts of this sort which are made in countries where the workers are led astray by the enemies of religion; but thanks be to God, that is not our condition. We find that in our country the presence and explicit influence of the clergy would not be advisable where our citizens, without distinction of religious belief, come together in regard to their industrial interests alone. Without going so far, we have abundant means for making our working people faithful Catholics, and simple good sense advises us not to go to extremes.

(c) Again, it is objected that the liberty of such an organization exposes Catholics to the evil influences of the most dangerous associates, even of atheists, communists and anarchists. That is true; but it is one of the trials of faith which our brave American Catholics are accustomed to meet almost daily, and which they know how to disregard with good sense and firmness. The press of our country tells us and the president of the Knights of Labor has related to us, how these violent and aggressive elements have endeavored to seize authority in their councils, or to inject their poison into the principles of the association; but they also verify with what determination these evil spirits [machinators—mauvais esprits] have been repulsed and defeated. The presence among our citizens of this destructive element, which has come for the most part from certain nations of Europe, is assuredly for us an occasion of lively regrets and careful precautions; it is an inevitable fact, however, but one which the union between the Church and her children in our country renders comparatively free from danger. In truth, the only grave danger would come from an alienation between the Church and her children, which nothing would more certainly occasion than imprudent condemnations.

(d) An especially weighty charge is drawn from the outbursts of violence, even to bloodshed, which have characterized [accompanied—charactérizé] several of the strikes inaugurated by labor organizations. Concerning this, three things are to be remarked: first, strikes are not an invention of the Knights of Labor, but a means almost everywhere and always resorted to by employees in our land and elsewhere to protest against what they consider unjust and to demand their right; secondly in such a struggle of the poor and indignant multitudes against hard and obstinate monopoly, anger and violence [outbursts of anger—colère et le violence] are often as inevitable as they are regrettable; thirdly, the laws and chief authorities of the Knights of Labor, far from encouraging violence or the occasions of it, exercise a powerful influence to hinder it, and to keep strikes within the limits of good order and legitimate action. A careful examination of the acts of violence which have marked the struggle between capital and labor during the past year, leaves us convinced that it would be unjust to attribute them to the association of the Knights of Labor. This was but one of several associations of workers that took part in the strikes, and their chief officers, according to disinterested witnesses, used every possible effort to appease the anger of the crowds and to prevent the excesses which, in my judgment, could not justly be attributed to them. Doubtless among the Knights of Labor as among thousands of other workingmen, there are violent, or even wicked and criminal men, who have committed inexcusable deeds of violence, and have urged their associates to do the same; but to attribute this to the organization, it seems to me, would be as unreasonable as to attribute to the Church the follies and crimes of her children against which she protests.[43] I repeat that in such a struggle of the great masses of the people against the mail-clad power, which, as it is acknowledged, often refuses them the simple rights of humanity and justice, it is vain to expect that every error and every act of violence can be avoided; and to dream that this struggle can be prevented, or that we can deter the multitudes from organizing, which is their only practical means [hope—moyen pratique] of success, would be to ignore the nature and forces of human society in times like ours. The part of Christian prudence evidently is to try to hold the hearts of the multitude by the bonds of love, in order to control their actions by the principles of faith, justice and charity, to acknowledge frankly the truth and justice in their cause, in order to deter them from what would be false and criminal, and thus to turn into a legitimate, peaceable and beneficent contest what could easily become for the masses of our people a volcanic abyss, like that which society fears and the Church deplores in Europe.

Upon this point I insist strongly, because, from an intimate acquaintance with the social conditions of our country I am profoundly convinced that here we are touching upon a subject which not only concerns the rights of the working classes, who ought to be especially dear to the Church which our Divine Lord sent to evangelize the poor, but with which are bound up the fundamental interests of the Church and of human society for the future. This is a point which I desire, in a few additional words to develop more clearly.

5. Whoever meditates upon the ways in which divine Providence is guiding contemporary history cannot fail to remark how important is the part which the power of the people takes therein at present and must take in the future. We behold, with profound sadness, the efforts of the prince of darkness to make this power dangerous to the social weal by withdrawing the masses of the people from the influence of religion, and impelling them towards the ruinous paths of license and anarchy. Until now our country presents a picture of altogether different [most consolingly different —tout différent] character—that of a popular power regulated by love of good order, by respect for religion, by obedience to the authority of the laws, not a democracy of license and violence, but that true democracy

---

[43] "Proteste," was translated "strives and protests." [H. J. Browne]

which aims at the general prosperity through the means of sound principles and good social order.

In order to preserve so desirable a state of things it is absolutely necessary that religion should continue to hold the affections, and thus rule the conduct of the multitudes. As Cardinal Manning has so well written,[44] "In the future era the Church has no longer to deal with princes and parliaments, but with the masses, with the people. Whether we will or no this is our work; we need a new spirit, a new direction of our life and activity." To lose influence over the people would be to lose the future altogether; and it is by the heart, far more than by the understanding, that we must hold and guide this immense power, so mighty either for good or for evil. Among all the glorious titles of the Church which her history has merited for her, there is not one which at present gives her so great influence as that of *Friend of the People.* Assuredly, in our democratic country, it is this title which wins for the Catholic Church not only the enthusiastic devotedness of the millions of her children, but also the respect and admiration of all our citizens, whatever be their religious belief. It is the power of precisely this title which renders persecution almost an impossibility, and which draws toward our holy Church the great heart of the American people.

And since it is acknowledged by all that the great questions of the future are not those of war, of commerce or finance, but the social questions, the questions which concern the improvement of the condition of the great masses of the people, and especially of the working people, it is evidently of supreme importance that the Church should always be found on the side of humanity, of justice toward the multitudes who compose the body of the human family. . . .

6. Now let us consider for a moment the consequences which would inevitably follow from a contrary course, from a lack of sympathy for the working class, from a suspicion of their aims, from a hasty condemnation of their methods.

(a) First, there is the evident danger of the Church's losing in popular estimation her right to be considered the friend of the people. The logic of men's hearts goes swiftly to its conclusions, and this conclusion would be a pernicious one for the people and for the Church. To lose the heart of the people would be a misfortune for which the friendship of the few rich and powerful would be no compensation.

(b) There is a great danger of rendering hostile to the Church the political power of our country, which openly takes sides with the millions who are demanding justice and the improvement of their condition. The accusation of being, *"un-American,"* that is to say, alien to our national spirit, is the most powerful weapon which the enemies of the Church know how to employ against her. It was this cry which aroused the Know-Nothing

[44] In the English version this quotation is introduced with the words, "A new task is before us." [H. J. Browne]

persecution thirty years ago, and the same would be quickly used again if the opportunity offered itself. . . .

(c) A third danger, and the one which touches our hearts the most, is the risk of losing the love of the children of the Church, and of pushing them into an attitude of resistance against their Mother. The whole world presents no more beautiful spectacle than that of their filial devotion and obedience. . . .

7. But besides the danger which would result from such a condemnation and the impossibility of having it respected and observed [putting it into effect—de la faire respecter et observer] one should note that the form of this organization is so little permanent, as the press indicates nearly every day, that in the estimation of practical men in our country, it cannot last very many years. . . .[45]

8. In all this discussion I have not at all spoken of Canada, nor of the condemnation concerning the Knights of Labor in Canada. For we would consider it an impertinence to involve ourselves in the ecclesiastical affairs of another country which has a hierarchy of its own, and with whose needs and social conditions we do not pretend to be acquainted.[46] We believe, however, that the circumstances of a people almost entirely Catholic, as in lower Canada, must be very different from those of a mixed population like ours. . . .

With complete confidence, I leave the case [47] to the wisdom and prudence of your Eminence and the Holy See.

Rome, February 20, 1887.

J. CARDINAL GIBBONS,
Archbishop of Baltimore.

SOURCE: Henry J. Browne, *The Catholic Church and the Knights of Labor* (Washington, 1949), 365–78. Used by permission of The Catholic University of America Press.

156. Leo XIII's "Rerum Novarum"

When Leo XIII's encyclical, *Rerum novarum,* appeared in 1891, the Holy See was seeking foreign aid against the kingdom of Italy, which twenty-one years before had seized the Papal States. The papacy was therefore increasingly inclined to look for support to western lands where new and more liberal currents were flowing. What influence, if any, Cardinal

[45] The English read: "It is also very important that we should carefully consider another reason against condemnation, arising from the unstable and transient character of the organization in question. It is frequently remarked by the press and by attentive observers that this special form of association has in it so little permanence that, in its present shape, it is not likely to last many years." [H. J. Browne]

[46] "Les besoins" was not translated. [H. J. Browne]

[47] The English inserted, "the decision of the case." [H. J. Browne]

Gibbons and American interests had on the encyclical has been a matter of debate.[48]

The basic social concepts of *Rerum novarum* were conservative. Private property and social stratification were fully accepted by the encyclical, while socialism was strenuously repudiated. The Marxian dialectic of inevitable class war was rejected, and much hope was attached to voluntary Christian charity—that is, Christian love—of the powerful for the weak and vice versa. The role of the church was emphasized, as giving spiritual motivation and social direction. Particularly significant was the assertion of the right of the state to legislate for the protection of the workingman, and the right of workingmen to form associations. These associations were to be under the influence of the church, and in close association with employers. There was much about them that resembled medieval guilds.

Many in Europe and America were surprised at the advanced stand which the encyclical took. For a time conservative Catholics in America remained silent about it, but by the end of the century it was being received and used. Its principles have become the foundation of labor policy among American Catholics. Expanding Catholic interest in American social problems and the co-operation of Catholics at times with non-Catholics in efforts to solve these problems did much to reduce anti-Catholic prejudice.[49] Portions of *Rerum novarum* are here presented.

DOCUMENT

THAT the spirit of revolutionary change, which has long been disturbing the nations of the world, should have passed beyond the sphere of politics and made its influence felt in the cognate sphere of practical economics is not surprising. The elements of the conflict now raging are unmistakable: in the vast expansion of industrial pursuits and the marvellous discoveries of science; in the changed relations between masters and workmen; in the enormous fortunes of some few individuals, and the utter poverty of the masses; in the increased self-reliance and closer mutual combination of the working classes; as also, finally, in the prevailing moral degeneracy. The momentous gravity of the state of things now obtaining fills every mind with painful apprehension; wise men are discussing it; practical men are proposing schemes; popular meetings, legislatures, and rulers of nations are all busied with it—and actually there is no question which has taken a deeper hold on the public mind. . . .

Socialists and Private Property

To remedy these wrongs the Socialists, working on the poor man's envy of the rich, are striving to do away with private property, and contend that

[48] Ellis, *The Life of James Cardinal Gibbons*, I, 530–1, 578.

[49] Aaron I. Abell, *American Catholicism and Social Action*, 11–89; Abell, "The Reception of Leo XIII's Labor Encyclical in America, 1891–1919," *Review of Politics*, VII (1945), 464–7.

individual possessions should become the common property of all, to be administered by the State or by municipal bodies. They hold that by thus transferring property from private individuals to the community, the present mischievous state of things will be set to rights, inasmuch as each citizen will then get his fair share of whatever there is to enjoy. But their contentions are so clearly powerless to end the controversy that were they carried into effect the workingman himself would be among the first to suffer. They are, moreover, emphatically unjust, because they would rob the lawful possessor, bring State action into a sphere not within its competence, and create utter confusion in the community.

It is surely undeniable that, when a man engages in remunerative labor, the impelling reason and motive of his work is to obtain property, and thereafter to hold it as his very own. If one man hires out to another his strength or skill, he does so for the purpose of receiving in return what is necessary for sustenance and education; he therefore expressly intends to acquire a right full and real, not only to the remuneration, but also to the disposal of such remuneration, just as he pleases. Thus, if he lives sparingly, saves money, and, for greater security, invests his savings in land, the land, in such case, is only his wages under another form; and, consequently, a workingman's little estate thus purchased should be as completely at his full disposal as are the wages he receives for his labor. But it is precisely in such power of disposal that ownership consists, whether the property consist of land or chattels. Socialists, therefore, by endeavoring to transfer the possessions of individuals to the community, strike at the interests of every wage earner, for they deprive him of the liberty of disposing of his wages, and thus of all hope and possibility of increasing his stock and of bettering his condition in life. . . .

Man's Natural Right and His Social and Domestic Duties

The rights here spoken of, belonging to each individual man, are seen in a much stronger light if they are considered in relation to man's social and domestic obligations.

In choosing a state of life, it is indisputable that all are at full liberty either to follow the counsel of Jesus Christ as to virginity, or to enter into the bonds of marriage. No human law can abolish the natural and primitive right of marriage, or in any way limit the chief and principal purpose of marriage, ordained by God's authority from the beginning. *Increase and multiply.* Thus we have the Family; the "society" of a man's own household; a society limited indeed in numbers, but a true "society," anterior to every kind of State or nation, with rights and duties of its own, totally independent of the commonwealth.

That right of property, therefore, which has been proved to belong naturally to individual persons, must also belong to a man in his capacity of head of a family; nay, such a person must possess this right so much the more clearly in proportion as his position multiplies his duties. For it is a most sacred law of nature that a father must provide food and all necessaries for those whom he has begotten; and, similarly, nature dictates that a man's children, who carry on, as it were, and continue his own personality, should be provided by him with all that is needful to enable them honorably to keep themselves from want and misery in the uncertainties of this mortal life. Now, in no other way can a father effect this except by the ownership of profitable property, which he can transmit to his children by inheritance. A family, no less than a State, is, as we have said, a true society, governed by a power within itself, that is to say, by the father. Wherefore, provided the limits be not transgressed which are prescribed by the very purposes for which it exists, the Family has, at least, equal rights with the State in the choice and pursuit of those things which are needful to its preservation and its just liberty. . . .

Our first and most fundamental principle, therefore, when we undertake to alleviate the condition of the masses, must be the inviolability of private property. This laid down, We go on to show where we must find the remedy that we seek.

The Church Alone Can Solve the Social Problem

We approach the subject with confidence, and in the exercise of the rights which belong to Us. For no practical solution of this question will ever be found without the assistance of Religion and of the Church. It is We who are the chief guardian of Religion, and the chief dispenser of what belongs to the Church, and we must not by silence neglect the duty which lies upon Us. Doubtless this most serious question demands the attention and the efforts of others besides Ourselves—of the rulers of States, of employers of labor, of the wealthy, and of the working population themselves for whom We plead. But We affirm without hesitation that all the striving of men will be vain if they leave out the Church. . . .

The Christian Interdependence of Capital and Labor

The great mistake that is made in the matter now under consideration, is to possess oneself of the idea that class is naturally hostile to class; that rich and poor are intended by nature to live at war with one another. So irrational and so false is this view, that the exact contrary is the truth. Just as the symmetry of the human body is the result of the disposition of the members of the body, so in a State it is ordained by nature that these two classes should exist in harmony and agreement, and should, as it were, fit into one another, so as to maintain the equilibrium of the body politic. Each requires the other; capital cannot do without labor, nor labor without capital. Mutual agreement results in pleasantness and good order; perpetual conflict necessarily produces confusion and outrage. Now, in preventing such strife as this, and in making it impossible, the efficacy of Christianity is marvelous and manifold. First of all, there is nothing more powerful than Religion (of which the Church is the interpreter and guardian) in drawing rich and poor together, by reminding each class of its duties to the other, and especially of the duties of justice. Thus Religion teaches the laboring man and the workman to carry out honestly and well all equitable agreements freely made, never to injure capital, nor to outrage the person of an employer; never to employ violence in representing his own cause, nor to engage in riot and disorder; and to have nothing to do with men of evil principles, who work upon the people with artful promises, and raise foolish hopes which usually end in disaster and in repentance when too late. Religion teaches the rich man and the employer that their work-people are not their slaves; that they must respect in every man his dignity as a man and as a Christian; that labor is nothing to be ashamed of, if we listen to right reason and to Christian philosophy, but is an honorable employment, enabling a man to sustain his life in an upright and creditable way; and that it is shameful and inhuman to treat men like chattels to make money by, or to look upon them merely as so much muscle or physical power. Thus, again, Religion teaches that, as among the workmen's concerns are Religion herself, and things spiritual and mental, the employer is bound to see that he has time for the duties of piety; that he be not exposed to corrupting influences and dangerous occasions; and that he be not led away to neglect his home and family or to squander his wages. Then, again, the employer must never tax his work-people beyond their strength, nor employ them in work unsuited to their sex or age. His great and principal obligation is to give to every one that which is just. . . .

The State's Share in the Relief of Poverty

It cannot, however, be doubted that to attain the purpose of which We treat, not only the Church, but all human means must conspire. All who are concerned in the matter must be of one mind and must act together. It is in this, as in the Providence which governs the world; results do not happen save where all the causes co-operate.

Let us now, therefore, inquire what part the State should play in the work of remedy and relief.

By the State We here understand, not the particular form of government which prevails in this or that nation, but the State as rightly understood; that is to say, any government conformable in its institutions to right reason and natural law, and to those dictates of the Divine wisdom which We have expounded in the Encyclical on the Christian Constitution of the State. The first duty, therefore, of the rulers of the State should be to make sure that the laws and institutions, the general character and administration of the commonwealth, shall be such as to produce of themselves public well-being and private prosperity. This is the proper office of wise statesmanship and the work of the heads of the State. Now a State chiefly prospers and flourishes by morality, by well-regulated family life, by respect for religion and justice, by the moderation and equal distribution of public burdens, by the progress of the arts and of trade, by the abundant yield of the land—by everything which makes the citizens better and happier. Here, then, it is in the power of a ruler to benefit every order of the State, and amongst the rest to promote in the highest degree the interests of the poor; and this by virtue of his office, and without being exposed to any suspicion of undue interference—for it is the province of the commonwealth to consult for the common good. And the more that is done for the working population by the general laws of the country, the less need will there be to seek for particular means to relieve them. . . .

Whenever the general interest or any particular class suffers, or is threatened with, evils which can in no other way be met, the public authority must step in to meet them. Now, among the interests of the public, as of private individuals, are these: that peace and good order should be maintained; that family life should be carried on in accordance with God's laws and those of nature; that Religion should be reverenced and obeyed; that a high standard of morality should prevail in public and private life; that the sanctity of justice should be respected, and that no one should injure another with impunity; that the members of the commonwealth should grow up to man's estate strong and robust, and capable, if need be, of guarding and defending their country. If by a strike, or other combination of workmen, there should be imminent danger of disturbance to the public peace; or if circumstances were such that among the laboring population the ties of family life were relaxed; if Religion were found to suffer through the workmen not having time and opportunity to practice it; if in workshops and factories there were danger to morals through the mixing of the sexes or from any occasion of evil; or if employers laid burdens upon the workmen which were unjust, or degraded them with conditions that were repugnant to their dignity as human beings; finally, if health were endangered by excessive labor, or by work unsuited to sex or age—in these cases there can be no question that, within certain limits, it would be right to call in the help and authority of the law. The limits must be determined by the nature of the occasion which calls for the law's interference—the principle being this, that the law must not undertake more, nor go further, than is required for the remedy of the evil or the removal of the danger. . . .

Save the Laborers from the Cruelty of Speculators in Labor

If we turn now to things exterior and corporeal, the first concern of all is to save the poor workers from the cruelty of grasping speculators, who use human beings as mere instruments for making money. It is neither justice nor humanity so to grind men down with excessive labor as to stupefy their minds and wear out their bodies. Man's powers like his general nature, are limited, and beyond these limits he cannot go. His strength is devoted and increased by use and exercise, but only on condition of due intermission and proper rest. Daily labor, therefore, must be so regulated that it may not be protracted during longer hours than strength admits. How many and how long the intervals of rest should be, will depend upon the nature of the work, on circumstances of time and place, and on the health and strength of the workman. Those who labor in mines and quarries, and in work within the bowels of the earth, should have shorter hours in proportion, as their labor is more severe and more trying to health. Then, again, the season of the year must be taken into account; for not unfrequently a kind of labor is easy at one time which at another is intolerable or very difficult. Finally, work which is suitable for a strong man cannot reasonably be required from a woman or a child. . . .

Multiply Workingmen's Associations

In the last place—employers and workmen may themselves effect much in the matter of which We treat, by means of those institutions and organizations which afford opportune assistance to those in need, and which draw the two orders more closely together. Among these may be enumerated: Societies for mutual help; various foundations established by private persons for providing for the workman, and for his widow or his orphans, in sudden calamity, in sickness, and in the event of death; and what are called "patronages," or institutions for the care of boys and girls, for young people, and also for those of more mature age.

The most important of all are Workmen's Associations; for these virtually include all the rest. History attests what excellent results were effected by the Artificers' Guilds of a former day. They were the means not only of many advantages to the workmen, but in no small degree of the advancement of art, as numerous monuments remain to prove. Such associations should be adapted to the requirements of the age in which we live—an age of greater instruction, of different customs, and of more numerous requirements in daily life. It is gratifying to know that there are actually in existence not a few Societies of this nature, consisting either of workmen alone, or of workmen and employers together; but it were greatly to be desired that they should multiply and become more effective. . . .

The Advantages of Lawful Combination

And here we are reminded of the Confraternities, Societies, and Religious Orders which have arisen by the Church's authority and the piety of the Christian people. The annals of every nation down to our own times testify to what they have done for the human race. It is indisputable on grounds of reason alone, that such associations, being perfectly blameless in their objects, have the sanction of the law of nature. On their religious side, they rightly claim to be responsible to the Church alone. The administrators of the State, therefore, have no rights over them, nor can they claim any share in their management; on the contrary, it is the State's duty to respect and cherish them, and, if necessary, to defend them from attack. It is notorious that a very different course has been followed, more especially in our own times. In many places the State has laid violent hands on these communities, and committed manifold injustice against them; it has placed them under the civil law, taken away their rights as corporate bodies, and robbed them of their property. In such property the Church had her rights, each member of the body had his or her rights, and there were also the rights of those who had founded or endowed them for a definite purpose, and of those for whose benefit and assistance they existed. Wherefore, We cannot refrain from complaining of such spoliation as unjust and fraught with evil results; and with the more reason because, at the very time when the law proclaims that association is free to all, We see that Catholic societies, however peaceable and useful, are hindered in every way, whilst the utmost freedom is given to men whose objects are at once hurtful to Religion and dangerous to the State.

Associations of every kind, and especially those of working men, are now far more common than formerly. In regard to many of these there is no need at present to inquire whence they spring, what are their objects or what means they use. But there is a good deal of evidence which goes to prove that many of these societies are in the hands of invisible leaders, and are managed on principles far from compatible with Christianity and the public well-being; and that they do their best to get into their hands the whole field of labor and to force workmen either to join them or to starve. Under these circumstances the Christian workmen must do one of two things: either join associations in which their religion will be exposed to peril, or form associations among themselves—unite their forces and courageously shake off the yoke of unjust and intolerable oppression. No one who does not wish to expose man's chief good to extreme danger will hesitate to say that the second alternative must by all means be adopted. . . .

As far as regards the Church, its assistance will never be wanting, be the time or the occasion what it may; and it will intervene with greater effect in proportion as its liberty of action is the more unfettered; let this be carefully noted by those whose office it is to provide for the public welfare. Every minister of holy Religion must throw into the conflict all the energy of his mind, and all the strength of his endurance; with your authority, Venerable Brethren, and by your example, they must never cease to urge upon all men of every class, upon the high as well as the lowly, the Gospel doctrines of Christian life; by every means in their power they must strive for the good of the people; and above all they must earnestly cherish in themselves, and try to arouse in others, Charity, the mistress and queen of virtues. For the happy results we all long for must be chiefly brought about by the plenteous outpouring of Charity; of that true Christian Charity which is the fulfilling of the whole Gospel law, which is always ready to sacrifice itself for others' sake, and which is man's surest antidote against worldly pride and immoderate love of self; that Charity whose office is described and whose God-like features are drawn by the Apostle St. Paul in these words: *Charity is patient, is kind, . . . seeketh not her own, . . . suffereth all things, . . . endureth all things.*

On each of you, Venerable Brethren, and on your Clergy and people, as an earnest of God's mercy and a mark of our affection, We lovingly in the Lord bestow the Apostolic Benediction.

Given at St. Peter's in Rome, the fifteenth day of May, 1891, the fourteenth year of our Pontificate.

LEO XIII., Pope.

SOURCE: John A. Ryan and Joseph Husslein, eds., *The Church and Labor* (N.Y., 1920), 57–9, 62–3, 65–7, 74–5, 77–8, 81, 85, 87–88, 93–94. Used by permission of Msgr. Lawrence F. Ryan.

157. A Radical View of Property Rights

George D. Herron (1862–1925) represented a radical type of Protestant social Christianity. Born in Indiana of devout parents, he early had a sense of personal mission. He had little formal education, but read widely and became a Congregational minister. An address before the Minnesota Congregational Club in 1890 on "The Message of Jesus to Men of Wealth" brought him national fame. After ministering in Burlington, Iowa (1891–93), he became professor of applied Christianity at Iowa (later Grinnell) College (1893–99). Herron's overflowing classrooms, popular lecture tours, and numerous publications extended his influence. He and the president of the college, George A. Gates, made their campus a center of the Kingdom movement, which reached its climax in 1894 and 1895 in earnest groups discussing how society might be transformed into the kingdom of God. By 1896 the churches were rejecting Herron's social radicalism.[50] In 1901 he was divorced, remarried, and deposed from the ministry. He spent the remainder of his life in Europe.

Herron was more rhetorician than systematic thinker or organizer. Along with his social emphasis he retained much individualism. He became convinced that the institution of private property was un-Christian, but until his later years expected Christian individuals to introduce a better social order on a voluntary basis. He saw the cross of Christ as the necessary principle of self-sacrifice, and stressed a stewardship which would consider all property consecrated to the general welfare.[51] After the turn of the

[50] Robert T. Handy, "George D. Herron and the Kingdom Movement," *Church History*, XIX (1950), 97–115; also Handy, "George D. Herron and the Social Gospel in American Protestantism, 1890–1901" (typed Ph.D. dissertation, University of Chicago, 1949).

[51] Cf. George D. Herron, *The New Redemption: A Call to the Church to Reconstruct Society According to the Gospel of Christ* (N.Y., 1893).

century, however, Herron became less hopeful of Christian motivation and moved further toward the Marxian conception of class struggle and coercion. In his heyday, Herron's ideas were widely discussed and he was an important stimulus even to many who vigorously disagreed with him. The passage here selected from Herron's *Between Caesar and Jesus* (1899) finds him not yet having fully abandoned individualistic voluntaryism, and quite characteristically vague as to the means of implementing his ideals.

DOCUMENT

The undeviating hostility of Christ and his witnesses to individual wealth cannot be evaded by following John Wesley's immoral advice to make all one can and then give all one can. The philanthropy of economic extortion is the greatest immediate menace to religion and social progress. The gifts that come not from wilful extortion, but from as clean hands as the system of things will suffer any man to have, are apt to be even more misleading than the benevolence of avarice, because they seem to justify and make Christian what is really anti-Christ. Let us honor such contributions as they deserve to be honored, or concede the economic and historical necessity of individual wealth in the social evolution; but let us not deceive ourselves, and become false teachers to the people, by speaking of such wealth as Christian. Wealth is a power in the world, and often a power for good, while a rich man may be very useful and generous, and his motives noble; but, however religious and philanthropic he be, the rich man stands in the antithesis of the Christian attitude towards the world. We cannot honestly imagine one in Christ's state of mind, one feeling as Christ felt, one coming at the world from his point of view, giving himself to acquiring individual wealth. Strictly speaking, a rich Christian is a contradiction of terms. This is a hard saying, and it places every one of us in positions of dreadful inconsistency and difficulty; but it is the bald, naked reality of Jesus' teaching. Let us confess that we are all alike guilty; that none of us are really Christian, if it comes to this; but let us be men enough to look the truth straight in the face. As Charles Kingsley makes one of his characters say, the worm that dieth not and the fire that is not quenched are a great blessing, if one may only know the truth by them at last. The shame and sorrow that the truth brings, I must face with you; for none are guiltier for the existing order of things than those of us who teach in colleges endowed by individual wealth.

Of course, one should not throw away, nor destroy, nor desecrate any property that is in his hands. He ought not and cannot individually extricate himself from the system that now exists. But the very least that a Christian can do, in the existing order, is to administer what he possesses for the common good, in the most literal sense of the term. A man cannot be Christian without being practically communistic; as a possessor of property, he is simply a steward having in trust what belongs to others. With this, he must exhaust his possibilities in changing the system from one of private ownership and competition into the common ownership and co-operative service of the kingdom of heaven. Sometimes, I think that a single man of great economic power, accepting such a stewardship, with the heart of Christ in him, could change the world.

The question as to whether economic brotherhood is practicable is a question of whether Christianity is practicable. If Jesus dwelt at the heart of God, and knew the law and secret of the universe, it is not worth while trying to establish society on any other basis than that of the universal communism of the Father who maketh his sun to rise on the evil and the good, and sendeth rain on the just and unjust; the Father who, when his children had wasted the abundant resources of life which he had already given them, redeemed them by giving them more resources. Before we dismiss such a social basis as a dream, let us well consider our free schools, the free street railways in the Australian city, the free highways unto the ends of the earth, and many other initiatives in the common life of to-day, which indicate that we are in the beginnings of a tremendous change upward into communism which Jesus disclosed as universal life and order.

In the fulness of its times, we shall have a new Christian synthesis upon which to base the religious movement which the social spirit seeks, and it will guide society through storm and change. The details of that synthesis do not yet appear; but in the outline emerging from the confusion of our faith, we may behold an economic of the kingdom of heaven. It will so state the facts and forces which are the sum of Jesus' idea, in such clear terms of present social need, as to afford a definite, tangible, working programme of social faith. It comes, after the long winter of apostolic faith, as a new religion springing up from the seed of Christ in the human soil. It promises a faith for which men will once more be ready to live or die with equal joy. It will be, as was prophesied by the last words of a beloved teacher, Dr. Edwin Hatch, "a Christianity which is not new but old, which is not old but new, a Christianity in which the moral and spiritual elements will again hold their place, in which men will be bound together by the bond of mutual service, which is the bond of the sons of God, a Christianity which will actually realize the brotherhood of men, the ideal of its first Christian communities."

The original idea of Jesus, once out in the social open, as a mode and economy of life, to be seen as it humanly is, will sweep the world. His early standard, once lifted amidst the perplexity and strife, and millions will rally to it as if on wings, not one of whom can be changed by our system of religion. His kingdom of heaven once more at hand, and the Christian conscience that overran the Roman empire, that wrought the spiritual chivalry of Francis Xavier and Loyola, that went crusading at the call of Hermit Peter and Abbot Bernard, that endured Spanish rack and fire and English gallows and dungeons, that crossed winter seas to found Pilgrim homes and build Puritan states, will arise in a messianic passion vaster than any summoned to change the world by crises past, and our economic problem will dissolve away in its fervent heat, to disclose the friendly stars of the new heaven lighting the new earth with the everlasting truth that love is law.

SOURCE: George D. Herron, Between Caesar and Jesus (N.Y., 1899), 136–40.

158. The Church and Industry

The rise of the social gospel was a major factor in bringing about the organization of the Federal Council of Churches of Christ in America, which was officially launched by thirty-three Protestant denominations at Philadelphia in 1908. Pioneers of Christian unity, such as Frank Mason North, Elias B. Sanford, and Josiah Strong, were keenly aware that the churches, working independently of one another, could not cope successfully with the problems of the new industrial order. At its organizing meeting in Philadelphia, the Council adopted a document which had been prepared by the Committee on the Church and Modern Industry. This paper proved to be an historic milepost in the growth of the social consciousness of co-operative Protestantism.

Section nine, extracted from the other sections, later became known as "the social creed of the churches," and eventually was adopted by most of the major denominations. It was considerably broadened in scope by the Federal Council in 1912, and retained this form until revised in 1932. Section nine reveals its deeper religious significance only when read in the setting of the entire report. The preceding sections state the Christian basis of section nine, and should therefore be included as an integral part of the creed. What is here presented includes the other sections also.

DOCUMENT

1. This Federal Council places upon record its profound belief that the complex problems of modern industry can be interpreted and solved only by the teachings of the New Testament, and that Jesus Christ is final authority in the social as in the individual life. . . . The interest of the Church in men is neither recent nor artificial. No challenge of newly posted sentries can exclude it from the ground where are struggle and privation and need. It has its credentials and knows the watchword.

2. Christian practice has not always harmonized with Christian principle. . . . In the mighty task of putting conscience and justice and love into a "Christian" civilization, the Church, with all its splendid achievements, has sometimes faltered. But it has gone farther and suffered more, a thousand fold, to accomplish this end than any other organized force the world has ever known.

3. The Church now confronts the most significant crisis and the greatest opportunity in its long career. In part its ideals and principles have become the working basis of organizations for social and industrial betterment which do not accept its spiritual leadership and which have been estranged from its fellowship. We believe, not for its own sake but in the interest of the kingdom of God, the Church must not merely acquiesce in the movements outside of it which make for human welfare, but must demonstrate not by proclamation but by deeds its primacy among all the forces which seek to lift the plane and better the conditions of human life.

This Council, therefore, welcomes this first opportunity on behalf of the Churches of Christ in the United States officially represented, to emphasize convictions which have been in fragmentary ways already expressed.

[4.] We recognize the complex nature of industrial obligations, affecting employer and employee, society and government, rich and poor, and most earnestly counsel tolerance, patience and mutual confidence; we do not defend or excuse wrong doing in high places or in low, nor purpose to adapt the ethical standards of the Gospel to the exigencies of commerce or the codes of a confused industrial system.

5. While we assert the natural right of men—capitalists and working-men alike—to organize for common ends, we hold that the organization of capital or the organization of labor cannot make wrong right, or right wrong; that essential righteousness is not determined by numbers either of dollars or of men; that the Church must meet social bewilderment by ethical lucidity, and by gentle and resolute testimony to the truth must assert for the whole Gospel, its prerogative as the test of the rightness of both individual and collective conduct everywhere.

6. We regard with the greatest satisfaction the effort of those employers, individual and corporate, who have shown in the conduct of their business, a fraternal spirit and a disposition to deal justly and humanely with their employes as to wages, profit-sharing, welfare work, protection against accidents, sanitary conditions of toil, and readiness to submit differences to arbitration. We record our admiration for such labor organizations as have under wise leadership throughout many years, by patient cultivation of just feelings and temperate views among their members, raised the efficiency of service, set the example of calmness and self-restraint in conference with employers, and promoted the welfare not only of the men of their own craft but of the entire body of workingmen.

7. In such organizations is the proof that the fundamental purposes of the labor movement are ethical. In them great numbers of men of all nationalities and origins are being compacted in fellowship, trained in mutual respect, and disciplined in virtues which belong to right character and are at the basis of good citizenship. By them society at large is benefited in the securing of better conditions of work, in the Americanization of our immigrant population, and in the educational influence of the multitudes who in

the labor unions find their chief, sometimes their only, intellectual stimulus.

8. We note as omens of industrial peace and goodwill, the growth of a spirit of conciliation, and of the practice of conference and arbitration in settling trade disputes. We trust profoundly that these methods may supplant those of the strike and the lockout, the boycott and the black-list. Lawlessness and violence on either side of labor controversies, are an invasion of the rights of the people and must be condemned and resisted. We believe no better opportunity could be afforded to Christian men, employers and wage-earners alike, to rebuke the superciliousness of power and the obstinacy of opinion, than by asserting and illustrating before their fellows in labor contests, the Gospel which deals with men as men and has for its basis of fraternity the Golden Rule.

We commend most heartily the societies and leagues in which employers and workingmen come together upon a common platform to consider the problems of each in the interest of both, and we urge Christian men more freely to participate in such movements of conciliation. We express our gratitude for the evidences that in ever widening circles the influence of the agencies established by some of the churches is distinctly modifying the attitude of the workingmen and the Church toward each other.

9. We deem it the duty of all Christian people to concern themselves directly with certain practical industrial problems. To us it seems that the churches must stand—

For equal rights and complete justice for all men in all stations of life.

For the right of all men to the opportunity for self-maintenance, a right ever to be wisely and strongly safeguarded against encroachments of every kind. For the right of workers to some protection against the hardships often resulting from the swift crises of industrial change.

For the principle of conciliation and arbitration in industrial dissensions.

For the protection of the worker from dangerous machinery, occupational disease, injuries and mortality.

For the abolition of child labor.

For such regulation of the conditions of toil for women as shall safeguard the physical and moral health of the community.

For the suppression of the "sweating system."

For the gradual and reasonable reduction of the hours of labor to the lowest practicable point, and for that degree of leisure for all which is a condition of the highest human life.

For a release from employment one day in seven.

For a living wage as a minimum in every industry, and for the highest wage that each industry can afford.

For the most equitable division of the products of industry that can ultimately be devised.

Right: Dwight L. Moody, peerless
American Evangelist

Below: Jehovah's Witnesses
administering Baptism

John G. Machen, militant foe of
Liberal Christianity

James Cardinal Gibbons, Archbishop of
Baltimore for forty-three years

Rufus M. Jones, Quaker Educator and Theologian

For suitable provision for the old age of the workers and for those incapacitated by injury.

For the abatement of poverty.

10. To the toilers of America and to those who by organized effort are seeking to lift the crushing burdens of the poor, and to reduce the hardships and uphold the dignity of labor, this Council sends the greeting of human brotherhood and the pledge of sympathy and of help in a cause which belongs to all who follow Christ.

> SOURCE: Elias B. Sanford, *Origin and History of the Federal Council of the Churches of Christ in America* (Hartford, Conn., 1916), 494–8.

159. A Pacifist Speaks Out

Many American clergymen entered and continued through the years of World War I with nineteenth-century optimism undimmed. Only the Kaiser seemed to stand between them and the bright new world of their dreams. Religion still retained a predominantly ethical character: the Christian in private and in public life must and can fulfill God's will; society and even international relations are perfectible. The tradition of God's purpose in American history remained strong. Emphasis on God's immanence and slighting of his transcendent judgment of life made it easy to identify religion and patriotism, God's will and American national policy. Not until the disillusionment of post-war years was this type of thinking to be seriously challenged.

There were a minority, however, who dared to view national purpose with more self-criticism. Some members of the Society of Friends maintained their historic pacifism even while acknowledging that it was far easier for conscientious individuals to hold such a position than for a responsible government to do so.

Rufus M. Jones (1863–1948), in the document here offered, set forth "The Quaker Peace Position" before the United States entered the war. During portions of both world wars he was chairman of the American Friends Service Committee for European Relief (1917–27, 1934–44). From 1893, Jones taught at Haverford College, his alma mater, in which he became professor of philosophy in 1904. His wide lecturing and extensive writing were devoted to a variety of subjects, including philosophy, social questions, spiritual experience, and Quaker history.

DOCUMENT

The world at large has had for the most part a very vague conception of the central religious ideas of Quakerism, but everybody who knows the name "Quaker," knows and always has known, that it is the popular name of a people who stand unconditionally for peace. Their peace-testimony has in the mind of the great public always been their most characteristic mark and badge. This Quaker position has been treated sometimes with ridicule and sometimes with respect, but in either case their fundamental attitude has seldom been understood. It will perhaps not be out of place in the midst of this din and clash of arms to interpret briefly the Quaker idea.

We have grown familiar during the last score of years with the accumulation of economic reasons against war, and we have followed with interest the congresses and conferences that have piled up and driven home these impressive economic arguments. They, however, generally, if not always, end with a caveat, or hedging clause to the effect that "peace at any price" is no part of the intention and is not implied in the argument.

The Quaker idea is fundamentally different from this economic idea. The Quaker is not primarily concerned with the question whether war pays or does not pay for the people engaged in it; whether it succeeds in its aim or does not succeed. The Quaker flatly insists that it is absolutely and eternally wrong morally, that Christianity and war are utterly incompatible. He does not blame or judge others—and they are vastly the majority—who think differently; but for himself the light of his truth is clear, and he cannot see otherwise.

This position goes back to and is grounded in the Quaker's idea of the nature of human personality, for this is the tap-root of all Quaker idealisms. There is something divine, something of God, in every person. The eternal passion of God, the whole redemptive story of the gospels, gets its significance in the tremendous fact that man and God belong together, are meant for each other and that beings like us are potential sons of God. To become a person, in the real sense of the word, is to awake to the consciousness of the divine relationship, to feel the inherent possibilities of sonship with God, to draw upon the inexhaustible supplies of grace, to enter into the actual inheritance of this divine-human privilege, and to live in it and practice it.

But this process of realizing the possibilities of life, this mighty business of becoming persons, can go on only in an atmosphere of human love and fellowship, and in an environment of co-operation. Great as is the influence of the divine operation in the realization of this higher life of man, it is forever conjoined with human assistance and with human elements. Men cannot come to their spiritual stature, they cannot realize their potential nature, in a social atmosphere of hate and anger, when they are occupied with killing men like themselves. In that inward climate, the higher impulses and the diviner contacts are weakened or missed altogether and the truer ideal of manhood is frustrated and defeated. Even if war paid in territory and in commerce, it would still be an impossible hazard for a people, because it checks and blocks the whole business of the higher life of man, it interferes with all the essential processes that go to the making of spiritual personality.

For one who has found his way through Christ to the full meaning of life, to the real worth of man, to the inestimable ministry of love and brotherhood, war is simply impossible. It is no longer a question of expediency; with the Quaker view of life one cannot engage in killing men, whatever may be involved in the refusal.

Through pain and struggle the world has slowly discovered the immense possibilities of democracy. We are just at the dawn of a real human emancipation. Vast processes of liberation are at work. Human rights, quite undreamed of when the Declaration of Independence was written, are gradually being won and enjoyed by common men and women. Social transformations are well under way which some day will bring new heavens and a new earth.

But war interferes with all these social undertakings; it postpones the realization of all ideals and human hopes. Pledged as he is, to the advancement of human emancipation and to the achievement of a society which furnishes and guarantees richer and fuller and freer opportunities of life, the Quaker opposes all war and war methods because he believes they defeat this supreme business in which the best men and women are engaged.

Holding such views of man and of life, partaking of a kingdom in which war is flatly an impossible course, what is the Quaker's business and mission in a world organized as ours is today? One of the first things that is laid upon him is the business of making his idea of life, his grasp of Christianity, clear and luminous to men. He should simplify it, strip it of outgrown phraseology and make it march with quick, vital, human interpretation. He should, then, be ready to take unflinchingly whatever amount of suffering is involved in his truth, and he should verify it in its length and depth by going all the way through with his faith, even at the uttermost cost; for no prophet-visions of life can ever be wrought into the fabric of the everyday world except through the patient suffering of those who are privileged to see.

It becomes, further, a very essential part of his business, as George Fox, the Quaker founder, saw, to live in the virtue of that life and power which does away with the occasion of war. That is, if Quakerism is to be anything more than an empty abstraction and the name for an ideal in a vacuum, the Quaker is bound to practice a kind of life that abolishes the spirit that leads to war—the spirit of avarice and covetousness, tendencies of suspicion and hate, actions of injustice and selfishness. He must exhibit, hard as is the call, a life that puts his ideas of God and man, of divine and human interfellowship, of love and self-giving, full into play. He must weave his idea into the visible stuff of daily life.

Then he must be gentle and tenderly respectful toward all Christians who feel the stern necessity of continuing the world-old way of settling differences and of working out national issues. It is never safe to assume the rôle of special favorite or sole guardian of truth, or remnant of the elect. Other Christians are also serious and honest, sincere and conscientious, and possessed of their profound convictions; and the Quaker, in holding on the way which seems sun-clear to him, must avoid all reflection upon the motives or the Christian loyalty of other faiths.

And whether in times of war or times of peace, the Quaker is under peculiar obligation to assist and to forward movements and forces which make for peace in the world and which bind men together in ties of unity and fellowship. In times of war, every avenue of loving service, of heroic devotion, or of self-forgetful ministry should be entered, that the Quaker may vie with the soldier in his blood-red loyalty and devotion to his cause.

The moment war is over, and in times of peace, those who hold this high and costly faith in God and man must not be content to conduct mild and lukewarm peace meetings and to issue commonplace resolutions—"helpless as spilled beans on a dresser," as Hosea Bigelow puts it. They must take a thoroughly virile and robust part in the work of creating higher national ideals and in forming a truer public sentiment, and a healthier social atmosphere. There must be no withdrawal from the complicated life of the world into any of the subtle forms of cloistered piety. Religious ideals must be interpreted and reinterpreted in terms of present day thought; the ties of human sympathy must be linked up and woven in between all classes of men; every opportunity must be seized for directing and perfecting methods of public education, and for raising the moral tone and quality of the press; and a full share of responsibility for the character of local and national government must be taken up and born with the same fidelity that the Quaker has always shown to the inner voice in matters of intimate, personal duty.

A peace-testimony is, thus, a heavy undertaking, and calls for all the courage and all the sacrifice of a battlefield, though the "weapons" are of a vastly different sort from Krupp guns and Mauser rifles.

It is obviously far easier to work out and consistently to maintain such a peace position as this for the individual and for a small group of religious idealists than to put it into effective operation for a great nation living in complicated relations with the peoples of the world. The Quaker is forced to admit that so far in the history of the races no great nation has yet risked its honor and its very existence in an unconditional experiment of peace at all costs and hazards. It is a plain, clear fact that men everywhere are, even at this late stage of evolution, powerfully supplied with fighting instincts. This present war proves conclusively that the fighting instinct is far from being smothered or eradicated. Never has the flower of a nation gone more willingly to danger and death than in this latest crowning year of man's civilization; and it is probably true that more persons during human history have gone to danger and death under the spur and thrust of this instinct than for any other single cause, perhaps, indeed, for all causes put together.

Then, again, we cannot miss the fact that nations have been and still are carried forward into wars almost unconsciously by the emotional force of deep-seated ideas, or theories or doctrines in reference to their supposed destiny—often enough doctrines essentially ungrounded or false. Certain economic theories or abstract ideas of peril to be feared from expanding and developing races, frequently obsess nations, produce fears, suspicions, and hates, and finally eventuate in war.

Nations are composed of many types of persons; they are striking instances of "multiple personality." There will for generations to come be higher and lower selves in the nations of the world, and we must not expect a millennium nation to come by express train or by aeroplane. Statesmen will still form entangling alliances when we are not watching, and they will get their nation into such a "fix" that citizens will be swept with the war-spirit and will bring the ancient instincts into play.

What we must do, then, is to form in as large groups as possible higher convictions, more idealistic faiths, and greater compulsions, which in the long run—in these matters the run is often very long!—will penetrate and permeate ever wider groups, and so make new nations, or at least a new national spirit. . . .

The preparation, however, for putting the Quaker ideal full into play among the nations of the world is no doubt still a long future process. It calls for a far greater perfection of international courts, perhaps even the formation of an international parliament. It involves, further, a sounder education; the cultivation of clearer, truer insight; a keener and more searching analysis of facts; a greater elimination of prejudices in the formation of historic and economic theories and a stronger control of will under the impact of such obstract [sic] theories. Just such moral, intellectual and volitional advance, however, is the true glory of a nation and the promotion of it is the real business of the best patriots.

> SOURCE: Rufus M. Jones, "The Quaker Peace Position," *The Survey*, XXXIV (1915), 22–3. Used by permission.

160. The Social Gospel and the Kingdom of God

In Walter Rauschenbusch (1861–1918) the American social gospel found its major prophet and its greatest theologian. His German-born father was a member of the faculty of Rochester Theological Seminary, having special responsibility for the training of pastors for German Americans.

Following in the footsteps of his father, Walter entered the Baptist ministry. After completing his theological education at Rochester Seminary in 1886, he volunteered to enter foreign missionary service, but this door was closed because of his reputed liberal views of the Old Testament.[52] He then sought a pastorate, but suffered a second rejection by a strong mid-western church. After these two failures, he accepted a call at a salary of $900 to the small Second German Church of New York City, located on the edge of "Hell's Kitchen." Laboring there in a squalid tenement section for eleven years (1886–97), he came to see that the acute social problems with which he was surrounded demanded a rethinking of the gospel as he had previously understood it. The New York mayoralty campaign of Henry George in 1886 also contributed to his social awakening, but he needed a comprehensive Christian concept with which to deal with social issues. It was then that the phrase, so familiar in the teachings of Jesus, "kingdom of God," dawned upon him "as a new revelation." This furnished him with a concept large enough to embrace the social as well as the personal prob-lems of life. Thus it was no accident that, with two close friends, Leighton Williams and Nathaniel Schmidt, he organized in 1892 a voluntary society called "The Brotherhood of the Kingdom."

In 1897 he joined the faculty of Rochester Seminary, becoming professor of church history in 1902, and remaining at the seminary until his death. His arresting book, *Christianity and the Social Crisis* (1907), made him leader of the social-gospel movement. Among his other widely read books in this same field were *Christianizing the Social Order* (1912), and *A Theology for the Social Gospel* (1917).

In his earlier treatises Rauschenbusch reflected the optimistic temper of the other evangelical liberals of the time, but the stunning experience of World War I gave to his *A Theology for the Social Gospel* a somewhat more realistic note. The heart of that book is chapter thirteen, the core of which constitutes the accompanying document.

DOCUMENT

If theology is to offer an adequate doctrinal basis for the social gospel, it must not only make room for the doctrine of the Kingdom of God, but give it a central place and revise all other doctrines so that they will articulate organically with it. . . .

To those whose minds live in the social gospel, the Kingdom of God is a dear truth, the marrow of the gospel, just as the incarnation was to Atha-nasius, justification by faith alone to Luther, and the sovereignty of God to Jonathan Edwards. It was just as dear to Jesus. He too lived in it, and from it looked out on the world and the work he had to do.

Jesus always spoke of the Kingdom of God. Only two of his reported sayings contain the word "Church," and both passages are of questionable authenticity. It is safe to say that he never thought of founding the kind of institution which afterward claimed to be acting for him.

Yet immediately after his death, groups of disciples joined and con-

[52] Dores R. Sharpe, *Walter Rauschenbusch* (N.Y., 1942), 58.

solidated by inward necessity. Each local group knew that it was part of a divinely founded fellowship mysteriously spreading through humanity, and awaiting the return of the Lord and the establishing of his Kingdom. This universal Church was loved with the same religious faith and reverence with which Jesus had loved the Kingdom of God. It was the partial and earthly realization of the divine Society, and at the Parousia the Church and the Kingdom would merge.

But the Kingdom was merely a hope, the Church a present reality. The chief interest and affection flowed toward the Church. Soon, through a combination of causes, the name and idea of "the Kingdom" began to be displaced by the name and idea of "the Church" in the preaching, literature, and theological thought of the Church. Augustine completed this process in his *De Civitate Dei*. The Kingdom of God which has, throughout human history, opposed the Kingdom of Sin, is today embodied in the Church. The millennium began when the Church was founded. This practically substituted the actual, not the ideal Church for the Kingdom of God. The beloved ideal of Jesus became a vague phrase which kept intruding from the New Testament. Like Cinderella in the kitchen, it saw the other great dogmas furbished up for the ball, but no prince of theology restored it to its rightful place. The Reformation, too, brought no renascence of the doctrine of the Kingdom; it had only eschatological value, or was defined in blurred phrases borrowed from the Church. The present revival of the Kingdom idea is due to the combined influence of the historical study of the Bible and of the social gospel.

When the doctrine of the Kingdom of God shriveled to an undeveloped and pathetic remnant in Christian thought, this loss was bound to have far-reaching consequences. We are told that the loss of a single tooth from the arch of the mouth in childhood may spoil the symmetrical development of the skull and produce malformations affecting the mind and character. The atrophy of that idea which had occupied the chief place in the mind of Jesus, necessarily affected the conception of Christianity, the life of the Church, the progress of humanity, and the structure of theology. I shall briefly enumerate some of the consequences affecting theology. This list, however, is by no means complete.

1. Theology lost its contact with the synoptic thought of Jesus. Its problems were not at all the same which had occupied his mind. It lost his point of view and became to some extent incapable of understanding him. His ideas had to be rediscovered in our time. Traditional theology and the mind of Jesus Christ became incommensurable quantities. It claimed to regard his revelation and the substance of his thought as divine, and yet did not learn to think like him. The loss of the Kingdom idea is one key to this situation.

2. The distinctive ethical principles of Jesus were the direct outgrowth of his conception of the Kingdom of God. When the latter disappeared

from theology, the former disappeared from ethics. Only persons having the substance of the Kingdom ideal in their minds, seem to be able to get relish out of the ethics of Jesus. Only those church bodies which have been in opposition to organized society and have looked for a better city with its foundations in heaven, have taken the Sermon on the Mount seriously.

3. The Church is primarily a fellowship for worship; the Kingdom is a fellowship of righteousness. When the latter was neglected in theology, the ethical force of Christianity was weakened; when the former was emphasized in theology, the importance of worship was exaggerated. The prophets and Jesus had cried down sacrifices and ceremonial performances, and cried up righteousness, mercy, solidarity. . . .

4. When the Kingdom ceased to be the dominating religious reality, the Church moved up into the position of the supreme good. To promote the power of the Church and its control over all rival political forces was equivalent to promoting the supreme ends of Christianity. This increased the arrogance of churchmen and took the moral check off their policies. . . .

5. The Kingdom ideal is the test and corrective of the influence of the Church. When the Kingdom ideal disappeared, the conscience of the Church was muffled. It became possible for the missionary expansion of Christianity to halt for centuries without creating any sense of shortcoming. It became possible for the most unjust social conditions to fasten themselves on Christian nations without awakening any consciousness that the purpose of Christ was being defied and beaten back. . . .

6. The Kingdom ideal contains the revolutionary force of Christianity. When this ideal faded out of the systematic thought of the Church, it became a conservative social influence and increased the weight of the other stationary forces in society. If the Kingdom of God had remained part of the theological and Christian consciousness, the Church could not, down to our times, have been salaried by autocratic class governments to keep the democratic and economic impulses of the people under check.

7. Reversely, the movements for democracy and social justice were left without a religious backing for lack of the Kingdom idea. . . .

8. Secular life is belittled as compared with church life. Services rendered to the Church get a higher religious rating than services rendered to the community. Thus the religious value is taken out of the activities of the common man and the prophetic services to society. Wherever the Kingdom of God is a living reality in Christian thought, any advance of social righteousness is seen as a part of redemption and arouses inward joy and the triumphant sense of salvation. When the Church absorbs interest, a subtle asceticism creeps back into our theology and the world looks different.

9. When the doctrine of the Kingdom of God is lacking in theology, the salvation of the individual is seen in its relation to the Church and to the future life, but not in its relation to the task of saving the social order. Theology has left this important point in a condition so hazy and muddled

that it has taken us almost a generation to see that the salvation of the individual and the redemption of the social order are closely related, and how.

10. Finally, theology has been deprived of the inspiration of great ideas contained in the idea of the Kingdom and in labor for it. The Kingdom of God breeds prophets; the Church breeds priests and theologians. The Church runs to tradition and dogma; the Kingdom of God rejoices in forecasts and boundless horizons. . . .

These are some of the historical effects which the loss of the doctrine of the Kingdom of God has inflicted on systematic theology. The chief contribution which the social gospel has made and will make to theology is to give new vitality and importance to that doctrine. . . .

In the following brief propositions I should like to offer a few suggestions, on behalf of the social gospel, for the theological formulation of the doctrine of the Kingdom. Something like this is needed to give us "a theology for the social gospel."

1. The Kingdom of God is divine in its origin, progress and consummation. It was initiated by Jesus Christ, in whom the prophetic spirit came to its consummation, it is sustained by the Holy Spirit, and it will be brought to its fulfilment by the power of God in his own time. The passive and active resistance of the Kingdom of Evil at every stage of its advance is so great, and the human resources of the Kingdom of God so slender, that no explanation can satisfy a religious mind which does not see the power of God in its movements. The Kingdom of God, therefore, is miraculous all the way, and is the continuous revelation of the power, the righteousness, and the love of God. . . .

2. The Kingdom of God contains the teleology of the Christian religion. It translates theology from the static to the dynamic. It sees, not doctrines or rites to be conserved and perpetuated, but resistance to be overcome and great ends to be achieved. Since the Kingdom of God is the supreme purpose of God, we shall understand the Kingdom so far as we understand God, and we shall understand God so far as we understand his Kingdom. As long as organized sin is in the world, the Kingdom of God is characterized by conflict with evil. But if there were no evil, or after evil has been overcome, the Kingdom of God will still be the end to which God is lifting the race. It is realized not only by redemption, but also by the education of mankind and the revelation of his life within it.

3. Since God is in it, the Kingdom of God is always both present and future. Like God it is in all tenses, eternal in the midst of time. It is the energy of God realizing itself in human life. Its future lies among the mysteries of God. It invites and justifies prophecy, but all prophecy is fallible; it is valuable in so far as it grows out of action for the Kingdom and impels action. No theories about the future of the Kingdom of God are likely to be valuable or true which paralyze or postpone redemptive action on our part. To those who postpone, it is a theory and not a reality. It is

for us to see the Kingdom of God as always coming, always pressing in on the present, always big with possibility, and always inviting immediate action. We walk by faith. Every human life is so placed that it can share with God in the creation of the Kingdom, or can resist and retard its progress. The Kingdom is for each of us the supreme task and the supreme gift of God. By accepting it as a task, we experience it as a gift. By labouring for it we enter into the joy and peace of the Kingdom as our divine father-land and habitation.

4. Even before Christ, men of God saw the Kingdom of God as the great end to which all divine leadings were pointing. Every idealistic inter-pretation of the world, religious or philosophical, needs some such concep-tion. Within the Christian religion the idea of the Kingdom gets its dis-tinctive interpretation from Christ. (a) Jesus emancipated the idea of the Kingdom from previous nationalistic limitations and from the debasement of lower religious tendencies, and made it world-wide and spiritual. (b) He made the purpose of salvation essential in it. (c) He imposed his own mind, his personality, his love and holy will on the idea of the Kingdom. (d) He not only foretold it but initiated it by his life and work. . . .

5. The Kingdom of God is humanity organized according to the will of God. Interpreting it through the consciousness of Jesus we may affirm these convictions about the ethical relations within the Kingdom: (a) Since Christ revealed the divine worth of life and personality, and since his salvation seeks the restoration and fulfilment of even the least, it follows that the Kingdom of God, at every stage of human development, tends toward a social order which will best guarantee to all personalities their freest and highest development. This involves the redemption of social life from the cramping influence of religious bigotry, from the repression of self-assertion in the relation of upper and lower classes, and from all forms of slavery in which human beings are treated as mere means to serve the ends of others. (b) Since love is the supreme law of Christ, the Kingdom of God implies a progressive reign of love in human affairs. We can see its advance wherever the free will of love supersedes the use of force and legal coercion as a regulative of the social order. This involves the redemption of society from political autocracies and economic oligarchies; the substitution of redemptive for vindictive penology; the abolition of constraint through hunger as part of the industrial system; and the abolition of war as the supreme expression of hate and the completest cessation of freedom. (c) The highest expression of love is the free surrender of what is truly our own, life, property, and rights. A much lower but perhaps more decisive expres-sion of love is the surrender of any opportunity to exploit men. No social group or organization can claim to be clearly within the Kingdom of God which drains others for its own ease, and resists the effort to abate this fundamental evil. This involves the redemption of society from private property in the natural resources of the earth, and from any condition in industry which makes monopoly profits possible. (d) The reign of love

tends toward the progressive unity of mankind, but with the maintenance of individual liberty and the opportunity of nations to work out their own national peculiarities and ideals.

6. Since the Kingdom is the supreme end of God, it must be the purpose for which the Church exists. The measure in which it fulfils this purpose is also the measure of its spiritual authority and honour. The institutions of the Church, its activities, its worship, and its theology must in the long run be tested by its effectiveness in creating the Kingdom of God. . . .

7. Since the Kingdom is the supreme end, all problems of personal salvation must be reconsidered from the point of view of the Kingdom. It is not sufficient to set the two aims of Christianity side by side. There must be a synthesis, and theology must explain how the two react on each other. The entire redemptive work of Christ must also be reconsidered under this orientation. Early Greek theology saw salvation chiefly as the redemption from ignorance by the revelation of God and from earthliness by the impartation of immortality. It interpreted the work of Christ accordingly, and laid stress on his incarnation and resurrection. Western theology saw salvation mainly as forgiveness of guilt and freedom from punishment. It interpreted the work of Christ accordingly, and laid stress on the death and atonement. If the Kingdom of God was the guiding idea and chief end of Jesus—as we now know it was—we may be sure that every step in His life, including His death, was related to that aim and its realization, and when the idea of the Kingdom of God takes its due place in theology, the work of Christ will have to be interpreted afresh.

8. The Kingdom of God is not confined within the limits of the Church and its activities. It embraces the whole of human life. It is the Christian transfiguration of the social order. The Church is one social institution alongside of the family, the industrial organization of society, and the State. The Kingdom of God is in all these, and realizes itself through them all. During the Middle Ages all society was ruled and guided by the Church. Few of us would want modern life to return to such a condition. Functions which the Church used to perform, have now far outgrown its capacities. The Church is indispensable to the religious education of humanity and to the conservation of religion, but the greatest future awaits religion in the public life of humanity.

SOURCE: Walter Rauschenbusch, *A Theology for the Social Gospel* (N.Y., 1917), 131-45. Reprinted with permission of the publisher. Copyright 1917 by The Macmillan Company. Copyright 1945 by Pauline Rauschenbusch.

161. The Bishops' Social Program

Roman Catholics in 1917 organized the National Catholic War Council in order to meet special needs of World War I. A papal decree in 1922 made the organization permanent under a new name, National Catholic Welfare

Conference. With its Administrative Committee of ten prelates, the Conference has come to wield great influence within and beyond the Catholic Church. Of the Conference's eight departments, the Social Action Department, organized in 1920, soon became the most widely known.

In 1919 Msgr. John A. Ryan (1869–1945),[53] professor of moral theology and industrial ethics at the Catholic University of America in Washington, D.C., drafted a document, here presented, which was adopted by the Administrative Committee of the Conference and came to be known as "The Bishops' Program of Social Reconstruction." It was advanced for its day, but nearly all of its proposals have since become a part of American industrial society.

DOCUMENT

FOREWORD

The ending of the Great War has brought peace. But the only safeguard of peace is social justice and a contented people. The deep unrest so emphatically and so widely voiced throughout the world is the most serious menace to the future peace of every nation and of the entire world. Great problems face us. They cannot be put aside; they must be met and solved with justice to all.

In the hope of stating the lines that will best guide us in our right solution the following pronouncement is issued by the Administrative Committee of the National Catholic War Council. Its practical applications are, of course, subject to discussion, but all its essential declarations are based upon the principles of charity and justice that have always been held and taught by the Catholic Church, while its practical proposals are merely an adaptation of those principles and that traditional teaching to the social and industrial conditions and needs of our own time.

† Peter J. Muldoon, *Chairman,*
    Bishop of Rockford

† Patrick J. Hayes,
    Bishop of Tagaste

† Joseph Schrembs,
    Bishop of Toledo

† William T. Russell,
    Bishop of Charleston

Washington, D.C.
February 12, 1919

Social Reconstruction

"Reconstruction" has of late been so tiresomely reiterated, not to say violently abused, that it has become to many of us a word of aversion. Politicians, social students, labor leaders, businessmen, charity workers, clergymen, and various other social groups have contributed their quota of

---

[53] Cf. Patrick W. Gearty, *The Economic Thought of Monsignor John A. Ryan* (Washington, 1953).

spoken words and printed pages to the discussion of the subject; yet the majority of us still find ourselves rather bewildered and helpless. We are unable to say what parts of our social system imperatively need reconstruction; how much of that which is imperatively necessary is likely to be seriously undertaken; or what specific methods and measures are best suited to realize that amount of reconstruction which is at once imperatively necessary and immediately feasible. . . .

No Profound Changes in the United States

It is not to be expected that as many or as great social changes will take place in the United States as in Europe. Neither our habits of thinking nor our ordinary ways of life have undergone a profound disturbance. The hackneyed phrase: "Things will never again be the same after the war," has a much more concrete and deeply felt meaning among the European peoples. Their minds are fully adjusted to the conviction and expectation that these words will come true. In the second place, the devastation, the loss of capital and of men, the changes in individual relations, and the increase in the activities of government have been much greater in Europe than in the United States. Moreover, our superior natural advantages and resources, the better industrial and social condition of our working classes still constitute an obstacle to anything like revolutionary changes. It is significant that no social group in America, not even among the wage earners, has produced such a fundamental and radical program of reconstruction as the Labor Party of Great Britain. . . .

Present Wage Rates Should Be Sustained

The general level of wages attained during the war should not be lowered. In a few industries, especially some directly and peculiarly connected with the carrying on of war, wages have reached a plane upon which they cannot possibly continue for this grade of occupations. But the number of workers in this situation is an extremely small proportion of the entire wage-earning population. The overwhelming majority should not be compelled or suffered to undergo any reduction in their rates of remuneration, for two reasons: first, because the average rate of pay has not increased faster than the cost of living; second, because a considerable majority of the wage earners of the United States, both men and women, were not receiving living wages when prices began to rise in 1915. In that year, according to Lauck and Sydenstricker, whose work is the most comprehensive on the subject, four fifths of the heads of families obtained less than $800, while two thirds of the female wage earners were paid less than $400. Even if the prices of goods should fall to the level on which they were in 1915—something that cannot be hoped for within five years—the average present rates of wages would not exceed the equivalent of a decent livelihood in the case of the vast majority. The exceptional instances to the contrary are practically all among the skilled workers. Therefore, wages on the whole should not be reduced even when the cost of living recedes from its present high level.

Even if the great majority of workers were now in receipt of more than living wages, there are no good reasons why rates of pay should be lowered. After all, a living wage is not necessarily the full measure of justice. All the Catholic authorities on the subject explicitly declare that this is only the minimum of justice. In a country as rich as ours, there are very few cases in which it is possible to prove that the worker would be getting more than that to which he has a right if he were paid something in excess of this ethical minimum. Why, then, should we assume that this is the normal share of almost the whole laboring population? Since our industrial resources and instrumentalities are sufficient to provide more than a living wage for a very large proportion of the workers, why should we acquiesce in a theory which denies them this measure of the comforts of life? Such a policy is not only of very questionable morality, but is unsound economically. The large demand for goods which is created and maintained by high rates of wages and high purchasing power by the masses is the surest guarantee of a continuous and general operation of industrial establishments. It is the most effective instrument of prosperity for labor and capital alike. The principal beneficiaries of a general reduction of wages would be the less efficient among the capitalists, and the more comfortable sections of the consumers. The wage-earners would lose more in remuneration than they would gain from whatever fall in prices occurred as a direct result of the fall in wages. On grounds both of justice and sound economics, we should give our hearty support to all legitimate efforts made by labor to resist general wage reductions.

Housing for Working Classes

Housing projects for war workers which have been completed, or almost completed by the government of the United States, have cost some forty million dollars, and are found in eleven cities. While the federal government cannot continue this work in time of peace, the example and precedent that it has set, and the experience and knowledge that it has developed, should not be forthwith neglected and lost. The great cities in which congestion and other forms of bad housing are disgracefully apparent ought to take up and continue the work, at least to such an extent as will remove the worst features of a social condition that is a menace at once to industrial efficiency, civic health, good morals, and religion.

Reduction of the Cost of Living

During the war the cost of living has risen at least 75 per cent above the level of 1913. Some check has been placed upon the upward trend by government fixing of prices in the case of bread and coal and a few other commodities. Even if we believe it desirable, we cannot ask that the government continue this action after the articles of peace have been signed; for neither public opinion nor Congress is ready for such a revolutionary policy. If the extortionate practices of monopoly were prevented by adequate laws and adequate law enforcement, prices would automatically be kept at as low a level as that to which they might be brought by direct government determination. Just what laws, in addition to those already on the statute books, are necessary to abolish monopolistic extortion is a question of detail that need not be considered here. In passing, it may be noted that government competition with monopolies that cannot be effectively restrained by the ordinary antitrust laws deserves more serious consideration than it has yet received.

More important and more effective than any government regulation of prices would be the establishment of co-operative stores. . . .

The Legal Minimum Wage

Turning now from those agencies and laws that have been put in operation during the war to the general subject of labor legislation and problems, we are glad to note that there is no longer any serious objection urged by impartial persons against the legal minimum wage. The several states should enact laws providing for the establishment of wage rates that will be at least sufficient for the decent maintenance of a family, in the case of all male adults, and adequate to the decent individual support of female workers. In the beginning the minimum wages for male workers should suffice only for the present needs of the family, but they should be gradually raised until they are adequate to meet future needs as well. That is, they should be ultimately high enough to make possible that amount of saving which is necessary to protect the worker and his family against sickness, accidents, invalidity, and old age.

Social Insurance

Until this level of legal minimum wages is reached the worker stands in need of the device of insurance. The State should make comprehensive provision for insurance against illness, invalidity, unemployment, and old age. So far as possible the insurance fund should be raised by a levy on industry, as is now done in the case of accident compensation. The industry in which a man is employed should provide with all that is necessary to meet all the needs of his entire life. Therefore, any contribution to the insurance fund from the general revenues of the State should be only slight and temporary. . . .

Labor Participation in Industrial Management

The right of labor to organize and to deal with employers through representatives has been asserted above in connection with the discussion of the War Labor Board. It is to be hoped that this right will never again be called in question by any considerable number of employers. In addition to this, labor ought gradually to receive greater representation in what the English group of Quaker employers have called the "industrial" part of business management—"the control of processes and machinery; nature of product; engagement and dismissal of employees; hours of work, rates of pay, bonuses, etc.; welfare work; shop discipline; relations with trade unions." The establishment of shop committees, working wherever possible with the trade union, is the method suggested by this group of employers for giving the employees the proper share of industrial management. There can be no doubt that a frank adoption of these means and ends by employers would not only promote the welfare of the workers, but vastly improve the relations between them and their employers, and increase the efficiency and productiveness of each establishment.

There is no need here to emphasize the importance of safety and sanitation in work places, as this is pretty generally recognized by legislation. What is required is an extension and strengthening of many of the existing statutes, and a better administration and enforcement of such laws everywhere.

Vocational Training

The need of industrial, or as it has come to be more generally called, vocational training, is now universally acknowledged. In the interest of the nation, as well as in that of the workers themselves, this training should be made substantially universal. While we cannot now discuss the subject in any detail, we do wish to set down two general observations. First, the vocational training should be offered in such forms and conditions as not to deprive the children of the working classes of at least the elements of a cultural education. A healthy democracy cannot tolerate a purely industrial or trade education for any class of its citizens. We do not want to have the children of the wage earners put into a special class in which they are marked as outside the sphere of opportunities for culture. The second observation is that the system of vocational training should not operate so as to weaken in any degree our parochial schools or any other class of private schools. Indeed, the opportunities of the system should be extended to all qualified private schools on exactly the same basis as to public schools. We want neither class divisions in education nor a State monopoly of education.

Child Labor

The question of education naturally suggests the subject of child labor. Public opinion in the majority of the states of our country has set its face inflexibly against the continuous employment of children in industry before the age of sixteen years. Within a reasonably short time all of our states, except some of the stagnant ones, will have laws providing for this reasonable standard. The education of public opinion must continue, but inasmuch as the process is slow, the abolition of child labor in certain sections seems unlikely to be brought about by the legislatures of those states, and since the Keating-Owen Act has been declared unconstitutional, there seems to be no device by which this reproach to our country can be removed except that of taxing child labor out of existence. This method is embodied in an amendment to the Federal Revenue Bill which would impose a tax of 10 per cent on all goods made by children. . . .

Ultimate and Fundamental Reforms

Despite the practical and immediate character of the present statement, we cannot entirely neglect the question of ultimate aims and a systematic program; for other groups are busy issuing such systematic pronouncements, and we all need something of the kind as a philosophical foundation and as a satisfaction to our natural desire for comprehensive statements.

It seems clear that the present industrial system is destined to last for a long time in its main outlines. That is to say, private ownership of capital is not likely to be supplanted by a collectivist organization of industry at a date sufficiently near to justify any present action based on the hypothesis of its arrival. This forecast we recognize as not only extremely probable, but as highly desirable; for, other objections apart, Socialism would mean bureaucracy, political tyranny, the helplessness of the individual as a factor in the ordering of his own life, and in general social inefficiency and decadence.

Main Defects of Present System

Nevertheless, the present system stands in grievous need of considerable modifications and improvement. Its main defects are three: Enormous inefficiency and waste in the production and distribution of commodities; insufficient incomes for the great majority of wage earners, and unnecessarily large incomes for a small minority of privileged capitalists. . . .

A New Spirit a Vital Need

"Society," said Pope Leo XIII, "can be healed in no other way than by a return to Christian life and Christian institutions." The truth of these words is more widely perceived today than when they were written, more than twenty-seven years ago. Changes in our economic and political systems will have only partial and feeble efficiency if they be not reinforced by the Christian view of work and wealth. Neither the moderate reforms advocated in this paper nor any other program of betterment or reconstruction will prove reasonably effective without a reform in the spirit of both labor and capital. The laborer must come to realize that he owes his employer and society an honest day's work in return for a fair wage, and that conditions cannot be substantially improved until he roots out the desire to get a maximum of return for a minimum of service. The capitalist must likewise get a new viewpoint. He needs to learn the long-forgotten truth that wealth is stewardship, that profit-making is not the basic justification of business enterprise, and that there are such things as fair profits, fair interest, and fair prices. Above and before all, he must cultivate and strengthen within his mind the truth which many of his class have begun to grasp for the first time during the present war; namely, that the laborer is a human being, not merely an instrument of production; and that the laborer's right to a decent livelihood is the first moral charge upon industry. The employer has a right to get a reasonable living out of his business, but he has no right to interest on his investment until his employees have obtained at least living wages. This is the human and Christian, in contrast to the purely commercial and pagan, ethics of industry.

> SOURCE: *Our Bishops Speak . . . 1919–1951* (Milwaukee, 1952), 243–4, 248, 251–7, 259–60. Used by permission of National Catholic Welfare Conference, Washington, D.C.

LITERATURE

On Reconstruction, C. Vann Woodward's *Reunion and Reaction: The Compromise of 1877 and the End of Reconstruction* (Boston, 1951) is a stimulating study offering economic explanations, while Paul H. Buck's *The Road to Reunion, 1865–1900* (Boston, 1937) emphasizes cultural factors. Clerical background is provided in Chester F. Dunham, *The Attitude of the Northern Clergy toward the South, 1860–1865* (Toledo, O., 1942). Sectional tensions were exposed and intensified by teachers, as shown in Hugh L. Swint's *The Northern Teacher in the South, 1862–1870* (Nashville, 1941). W. M. Leftwich's *Martyrdom in Missouri* (2 vols., St. Louis, 1870) is a loosely-written but colorful contemporary Border-State Methodist's complaint. The important role of Methodists in Reconstruction is treated by Hunter D. Farish in *The Circuit Rider Dismounts: A Social History of Southern Methodism, 1865–1900* (Richmond, Va., 1938), and by Ralph E. Morrow in *Northern Methodism and Reconstruction* (East Lansing, Mich., 1956). The New York *Christian Advocate* and the *Methodist Quarterly Review* voice the contemporary northern viewpoint of the Methodist Episcopal Church. Presbyterians are dealt with in Lewis G. Vander Velde's *The Presbyterian Churches and the Federal Union, 1861–1869* (Cambridge, Mass., 1932).

As background for the social gospel, the standard economic history of Harold U. Faulkner, *American Economic History* (7th ed., N.Y., 1954), is useful. Joseph Dorfman's *The Economic Mind in American Civilization, III, 1865–1918* (N.Y., 1949) is broad-gauge and informing. The basic social-gospel histories are Henry F. May, *Protestant Churches and Industrial America* (N.Y., 1949); C. Howard Hopkins, *The Rise of the Social Gospel in American Protestantism, 1865–1915* (New Haven, 1940); Aaron I. Abell, *The Urban Impact on American Protestantism, 1865–1900* (Cambridge, Mass., 1943); and James Dombrowski, *The Early Days of Christian Socialism in America* (N.Y., 1936). *The Protestant Search for Political Realism, 1919–1941* (Berkeley, Calif., 1960), by Donald B. Meyer, deals primarily with a later period but offers a penetrating critique of this period.

Autobiographies of those who led in theology and social concern supply color and inner understanding of the forces of change involved, as for example, Washington Gladden's *Recollections* (Boston, 1909); Lyman Abbott's *Reminiscences* (Boston, 1914); William Jewett Tucker's *My Generation* (Boston, 1919); and Shailer Mathews' *New Faith for Old* (N.Y., 1936). To these should be added Robert T. Handy's "George D. Herron and the Kingdom Movement," in *Church History*, XIX (1950), 97–115, and Dores R. Sharpe's *Walter Rauschenbusch* (N.Y., 1942). All six of these, except Tucker, were authors of numerous writings applying Christianity to the society of their day. These writings are particularly representative, as well as those of Josiah Strong.

Charles M. Sheldon's *In His Steps: What Would Jesus Do?* (Chicago, 1897) is a simple novel that reflects many of the implications of the social gospel. Its circulation is estimated to have been in excess of 20,000,000 copies. Henry George's *Progress and Poverty* (written 1879, contained in Vols. I and II of *The Writings of Henry George*, 10 vols., N.Y., 1898–1900), and Edward Bellamy's *Looking Backward, 2000–1887* (Boston, 1888) were "secular" writings which greatly stimulated Christian social thinking. Thorstein Veblen, *Theory of the Leisure Class* (N.Y., 1899), especially Chap. 13, "Devout Observances," is highly critical of religion. The influence of social interest on the origin and life of the Federal Council of Churches is indicated in John A. Hutchison's *We Are Not Divided: A Critical and Historical Study of the Federal Council of the Churches of Christ in America* (N.Y., 1941).

Roman Catholic social concern is informingly treated with ample documentation and with a helpful bibliographical essay in *American Catholicism and Social Action: A Search for Social Justice, 1865–1950* (Garden City, N.Y., 1960), by Aaron I. Abell. Much of the best of American Catholic history is found in the biographies of prelates, and this is true of social history also, as, e.g., in John Tracy Ellis, *The Life of James Cardinal Gibbons, Archbishop of Baltimore* (2 vols., Milwaukee, 1952); Frederick J. Zwierlein, *Life and Letters of Bishop McQuaid* (3 vols., Rochester, N.Y., 1925–27); James H. Moynihan, *The Life of Archbishop John Ireland* (N.Y., 1953); and Patrick H. Ahern, *The Life of John J. Keane, Educator and Archbishop* (Milwaukee, 1955). The thought of Monsignor John A. Ryan, leader in American Catholic social thinking, is treated in his autobiography, *Social Doctrine in Action: A Personal History* (N.Y., 1941), and in Patrick W. Gearty's *The Economic Thought of Monsignor John A. Ryan* (Washington, 1953). An important discussion of the church's relation to labor is Henry J. Browne's *The Catholic Church and the Knights of Labor* (Washington, 1949). Cf. also John A. Ryan, ed., *The Church and Labor* (N.Y., 1920). Henry George, in *The Condition of Labor: An Open Letter to Pope Leo XIII* (N.Y., 1891), criticized Leo's encyclical *Rerum novarum*.

Tensions growing out of immigration are ably analyzed in their relation to social and intellectual forces of the time by John Higham, *Strangers in the Land: Patterns of American Nativism, 1860–1925* (New Brunswick, N.J., 1955). Prejudices of historians of immigration are laid bare in Edward N. Saveth, *American Historians and European Immigrants, 1875–1925* (N.Y., 1948). Relation of Protestants and of Catholics to immigrants of Catholic background are the subjects, respectively, of Theodore Abel, *Protestant Home Missions to Catholic Immigrants* (N.Y., 1933) and of Gerald Shaughnessy, *Has the Immigrant Kept the*

Faith: A Study of Immigration and Catholic Growth in the United States, 1790–1920 (N.Y., 1925).

The attitude of the clergy toward World War I requires more theological analysis than has yet been given to it. John M. Mecklin's "The War and the Dilemma of the Christian Ethic," *American Journal of Theology*, XXIII (1919), 14–40, attempted this at close range. Granville Hicks discussed "The Parsons and the War" in the *American Mercury*, X (Feb., 1927), 129–42. A suggestive state sampling of general public opinion has been made by Cedric C. Cummin's *Indiana Public Opinion and the World War, 1914–1917* (Indianapolis, 1945). Ray H. Abrams' *Preachers Present Arms* (N.Y., 1933) is a sociological analysis in which the author's presuppositions stand out very clearly. The wartime sermons of such preachers as Henry van Dyke, Harry Emerson Fosdick, and Newell Dwight Hillis are important social landmarks of the day.

PERIOD VI
REVALUING THE HERITAGE
1930–1960

INTRODUCTION

THE continuing world-wide social upheaval of the period after 1930 affected the American churches profoundly. The stock market crash of October, 1929, which ended the precarious post-war "normalcy" of the Harding-Coolidge era, shook American society more deeply than had World War I. The era of an expanding economy and unlimited opportunity seemed ended. Ahead lay the threat of permanent class cleavages like those of the more static Old World. Though most Protestants were above the economic level of greatest destitution, the churches were confronted on all sides with suffering and social anxiety. Various Holiness churches effectively ministered to the victims of unemployment and poverty, and achieved phenomenal growth. But for the more conventional older denominations there was no religious revival such as had often accompanied previous economic deflations.

Franklin D. Roosevelt, delivering his inaugural address amid closed banks and a paralyzed economy, in March, 1933, announced that "the only thing we have to fear is fear itself." The New Deal, launched in a Hundred Days of breath-taking legislation, proceeded to regulate industrial life, agriculture, labor relations, the security exchanges, social security. A social revolution, sounding a note of equalitarianism and professing many of the ideals of the social gospel, was under way. Many evangelical churchmen who were critical of Roosevelt's leadership in the repeal of the Eighteenth Amendment, were deeply impressed with the announced purposes of the New Deal even while reserving criticism for the centralizing effect of such agencies as "NRA" and "AAA." [1]

The attack on Pearl Harbor, December 7, 1941, precipitated a more positive attitude toward military action on the part of the American churches. At the end of World War I, the cartoon of the American doughboy leaving France with the words "Lafayette, we quit," fairly represented American withdrawal into isolationism. For a time the churches supported the idea of a League of Nations, even in the face of increasing Senate opposition to it. Great numbers of churchmen in the interwar period "repented" of their endorsement of World War I and expressed high expectations for the romantic multilateral Kellogg-Briand Pact of 1928 "outlawing" war. The churches supported World War II, not this time as a crusade or an absolute good, but as a grim necessity and the lesser of two evils. Though pacifism in nearly all of the churches had declined sharply, most of the churches gave moral support to conscientious objectors among their members. Roman

[1] Paul A. Carter, *The Decline and Revival of the Social Gospel: Social and Political Liberalism in American Protestant Churches, 1920–1940* (Ithaca, N.Y., 1954), 163–79.

Catholics, while loyally committed to the war effort, were somewhat more apprehensive than others about the consequences of strengthening atheistic Russia.[2] The atomic bomb, which ended the war and ushered in a new era, created moral problems in which churchmen at once began to show concern.[3] Roman Catholic discussion during the post-war period inclined toward the medieval ideal of the limited "just war," whereas many Protestants tended to doubt whether in an atomic era war could be limited in purpose or method.[4] When communists invaded South Korea in 1950, the Federal Council of Churches endorsed military action by the United States, in what proved to be a limited war.[5] Amid the international upheaval following World War II, the United States, without major alteration in its policy of immigration restriction, enacted special legislation to receive a limited number of displaced persons. Local churches, both Protestant and Catholic, helped settlers individually to secure homes, jobs, and friends.

Communism created many problems for democracy and for the American churches. In the 1930's, Russia, fearful of being isolated, temporarily muted its ideal of international revolution. Her new "democratic" constitution of 1936 and her aid to the Loyalists in the Spanish Civil War won the admiration of many. The Soviet Union exploited to the full this more friendly atmosphere by organizing numerous communist "front" organizations which enlisted many of the unsuspecting, including some clergymen. On the other hand, the Russian blood purges of 1937–38 and the Hitler-Stalin nonaggression pact that ushered in World War II disillusioned many friends of Russia. When, by the end of 1941, the United States found itself at war on the side of Russia against Germany, friendliness to the Soviet Union reached a new high, only to be dashed again by the "cold war" that followed. Communism, avowedly atheistic, never made infiltration of the churches a major objective. The effort to secure access to Negroes through their ministers achieved only very limited and temporary success. The clergy who participated in communist "front" organizations in the 1930's and 1940's were disproportionately few, and nearly all of them later withdrew.

Technological development in the United States continued at an ac-

[2] F. Ernest Johnson, "The Impact of the War on Religion in America," *American Journal of Sociology*, XLVIII (1942), 353–60; Ray H. Abrams, "The Churches and the Clergy in World War II," *Annals of the American Academy of Political and Social Science*, CCLVI (March, 1948), 110–9.

[3] Cf. Federal Council of the Churches of Christ in America, *Atomic Warfare and the Christian Faith: Report* (N.Y., 1946); and Federal Council, *The Christian Conscience and Weapons of Mass Destruction* (N.Y., 1950).

[4] Suggestively discussed in Paul Ramsey, *War and the Christian Conscience: How Shall Modern War Be Conducted Justly?* (Durham, N.C., 1961).

[5] Arthur H. Darken, "The National Council of Churches and Our Foreign Policy," *Religion in Life*, XXIV (1955), 113–26. In 1950, the Federal Council merged with seven other interdenominational bodies to form the National Council of the Churches of Christ in the United States of America. Cf. *infra*. 585–9.

celerating pace after 1930. The machine tightened its hold on industry by means of automation, invaded the office, and mechanized farming to such an extent that a declining number of farmers was able to feed a rapidly expanding population. In the 1950's, industrial labor began to constitute a smaller proportion of the population, and labor unions faced the possible loss of some of the great power which they had acquired during the New Deal and war years. With continued mechanization it was difficult for the churches to keep alive the ideal that one's "vocation" in the world was a significant Christian service. It was the day of the technical expert. As corporations became larger and their ownership more widely spread, they came increasingly under the control of nonowning managers.

While rural labor declined absolutely and industrial labor declined proportionately in numbers, technical experts, white-collar workers, and personal service callings of all sorts expanded so greatly as to alter the character and proportionate size of the middle class. The result of these sudden social changes was insecurity of social position and almost frantic status seeking. Meanwhile, industrial society was producing culture standardization and a loss of individuality. "The man in the grey flannel suit," the "organization man" who was "other-directed," was becoming a stereotype. The rebellion of an occasional "beatnik" seemed purposeless and futile. The greater laxness of sex life, which followed World War I, increased, as documented by the sensational reports of Alfred C. Kinsey.[6]

There was high population mobility during World War II, and the churches rapidly extended their ministrations to the new centers of defense industries, while chaplains and visiting ministers served the great army training camps. After the war the United States, like much of the rest of the world, experienced a "population explosion," while population mobility remained very high. Movement was toward the metropolises, especially toward their suburbs. In the suburbs arose homogeneous middle- and upper-class communities which contrasted sharply with the heterogeneous, atomistic center city. It was in suburbia, comfortably withdrawn from the racial and economic conflicts of the inner city and factory, that the Protestant churches of this period experienced most of their growth. This gave them a seemingly strong position with the upper and expanding middle classes, but it removed them farther from the laboring class, and often gave an artificial, hothouse character to their busy church life. This tended more than ever to leave the inner city to the Roman Catholics, to Holiness sects, and to segregated Negro churches.[7] The 1950 United States census showed that fifty-seven per cent of the population lived in metropolitan areas.

[6] Max Lerner, *America as a Civilization: Life and Thought in the United States Today* (N.Y., 1957), gives an informing summary of social change, with bibliographies.

[7] Gibson Winter, *The Suburban Captivity of the Churches: An Analysis of Protestant Responsibility in the Expanding Metropolis* (Garden City, N.Y., 1961); Kenneth D. Miller, "Our Growing Suburbs and Their Churches," *Religion in Life*, XXIV (1955), 516–23.

According to a study by the National Council of Churches, these areas contained forty-six per cent of the nation's Protestants, seventy-five per cent of the Roman Catholics, and almost all of the Jews.[8]

In the area of theology, new creativity appeared in American Protestantism in the 1930's. Neo-orthodoxy gave a fresh impetus to nearly every one of the theological disciplines. In biblical studies, there was new interest in biblical theology. Church history experienced vigorous reaction against positivistic methodology, and stress was laid on theological interpretation. Ethics, too, was viewed more theologically. The strategy of the new orthodoxy was not to make grudging retreats before modern culture; but, after rethinking and where necessary restating basic Christian truth, to assume the offensive and to challenge modern thought and life all along the line. Amid the important social and theological changes of the period there was a revaluing of the heritage of the churches which resulted in changed attitudes toward theological liberalism, toward the social gospel, and toward the problem of denominational isolation.

There were some who rejected both neo-orthodoxy and neo-liberalism, and held to a neo-fundamentalism. Nearly all of the major Protestant denominations had by this time adopted more progressive views, and neo-fundamentalists within them were a dissenting minority. The revivalistic, Adventist, and Holiness churches constituted one of the most vigorous and fastest growing areas of neo-fundamentalism. These Adventist and Holiness bodies were much divided among themselves and only to a limited degree regarded themselves as included within a neo-fundamentalist "movement." These groups were outstandingly successful in overseas missions, especially in Latin America, where they often greatly outnumbered the conventional Protestant bodies. It has even been suggested that the Adventist and Holiness churches should be regarded as a major "third force" in Christianity alongside Roman and Orthodox Catholicism and Protestantism.[9]

Roman Catholic theology in America achieved new vigor in this period. With greater confidence and a true sense of belonging, Catholics sought to relate their theology more directly to American life and thought. There was fresh desire, too, to utilize the resources of medieval scholasticism, as Pope Leo XIII had urged. The founding in 1939 of *The Thomist: A Speculative Quarterly* reflected this interest. The promulgation of the dogma of the Assumption of the Virgin Mary by Pope Pius XII on November 1, 1950,[10] was an event of major significance in the Catholic world.

A striking phenomenon of the times was a great increase in religious

---

[8] Benson Y. Landis, "Trends in Church Membership in the United States," *Annals of the American Academy of Political and Social Science*, CCCXXXII (Nov., 1960), 7.

[9] Cf. two articles by Henry P. Van Dusen: "Caribbean Holiday," *Christian Century*, LXXII (Aug. 17, 1955), 946–8; "The Challenge of the Sects," *Christianity and Crisis*, XVIII (July 21, 1958), 103–6.

[10] In the bull *Munificentissimus Deus*. The translated text is in the *Thomist*, XIV (1951), 3–21.

interest following World War II and climaxing in the late 1950's. There had previously been signs of religious decline. Before the entry of the United States into World War I, a new critical sophistication was becoming apparent in American culture which continued into the post-war period.[11] By 1914, immigration of non-Protestants, Catholic urban strength, Protestant complacency and theological erosion had weakened the pre-eminence of Protestant influence in American life.[12] In the middle 1920's, and continuing for a decade, there was a falling off in church attendance, in social concern, and in the support of home and foreign missions.[13] But tendencies more favorable to religion also appeared. By the 1930's, American literature, especially fiction, was showing renewed interest in moral problems and even in underlying religious values, though not in conventional orthodoxy. Books with religious themes appeared on the best-seller lists,[14] but, interestingly, the sale of books technically classified as "religious" did not increase in this period in relation to total book sales.[15]

After World War II, church and Sunday school attendance and *per capita* giving increased greatly.[16] The amount spent on new religious buildings expanded from $251,000,000 in 1948 to $935,000,000 in 1959.[17] The proportion of members of religious bodies in the total population rose strikingly in the 1940's.[18] Catholic growth in the eight years 1950–58 was more rapid than Protestant, representing a forty-two per cent gain compared with Protestantism's twenty-three per cent.[19] A statistical analysis suggested that in the fifty-year period, 1906–56, denominations that were conservative in theology, worship, and polity experienced the most growth. In that fifty-year period, however, Catholicism's rate of growth was only seventh among the eleven largest denominations.[20]

[11] Henry F. May, *The End of American Innocence: A Study of the First Years of Our Time, 1912–1917* (N.Y., 1959); May, "Shifting Perspectives on the 1920's," *Mississippi Valley Historical Review*, XLIII (1956–57), 405–27.

[12] Winthrop S. Hudson, *American Protestantism* (Chicago, 1961), 128–34.

[13] Robert T. Handy, "The American Religious Depression, 1925–1935," *Church History*, XXIX (1960), 3–16.

[14] Nelson R. Burr, *A Critical Bibliography of Religion in America*, in Smith and Jamison, eds., *Religion in American Life*, Vol. IV, 850–1, 884–5, 897–902.

[15] In 1920 books on "religion" constituted 8.14% of book sales; in 1930 they constituted 8.31%; in 1940, 7.44%; in 1950, 6.59%; in 1959, 7.56% and in 1961, 7.14%. These figures are derived from statistics in *American Library and Book Trade Annual, 1961* (N.Y., 1960), 74; *Publishers' Weekly: The Book Industry Journal*, CLXXXI (Jan. 15, 1962), 46.

[16] Will Herberg, *Protestant-Catholic-Jew: An Essay in American Religious Sociology* (Garden City, N.Y., 1955), 62–3.

[17] Benson Y. Landis, "Trends in Church Membership," *Annals of the American Academy of Political and Social Science*, CCCXXXII (Nov., 1960), 3.

[18] In 1900, 36% were members; in 1910, 41.2%; in 1920, 45.6%; in 1930, 47.8%; in 1940, 48.9%; in 1950, 57.6%; and in 1958, 63%, *ibid.*, 4; Richard D. Lambert, "Current Trends in Religion—A Summary," *ibid.*, 147.

[19] Landis, "Trends in Church Membership," *Annals of the American Academy of Political and Social Science*, CCCXXXII, 5.

[20] Richard C. Wolf, "1900–1950 Survey: Religious Trends in the United States," *Christianity Today*, III (April 27, 1959), 3–6.

Conspicuous in this revival of religious interest, and reflecting the outer and inner upheaval of the times, was the quest for peace of spirit. Protestant, Catholic, and Jewish clergymen treated the theme in best sellers [21] and on radio and television.

By the late 1950's there were signs that the quickening of religious interest was passing its peak. The widely publicized and highly organized evangelistic "crusades" of Billy Graham still drew the attendance of hundreds of thousands in leading cities.[22] But some were suggesting that the revival as a whole had been too much merely "a maturing national religion," a creedless faith in faith, "religion-in-general . . . the result of the conjunction of one side of the American creed with one side of the Christian revelation." [23] It was notable that the "revival" scarcely challenged the secularism of the times. Some, noting the diminished influence of Protestantism on American culture, even spoke hyperbolically of a "post-Protestant" era.

The altered position of Protestantism in American life was an important phenomenon of the times. In the half-century ending in 1956, the Eastern Orthodox bodies increased by 1,754.7 per cent to a membership of 2,396,906. By 1958 Catholics constituted 22.8 per cent of the population and Protestants 35.5 per cent. Jews in the same year reported 5,500,000.[24] It is not surprising, therefore, that spokesmen of both Catholicism and Judaism declared that American culture was no longer Protestant but pluralistic,[25] a fact which Protestants could not deny. As Catholics grew stronger, non-Catholics became concerned about their influence on government. These fears increased when President Roosevelt in 1939 appointed Myron C. Taylor as his "personal representative with the rank of ambassador" to the pope. In 1947, the concern of non-Catholics led to the organization of Protestants and Other Americans United for Separation of Church and State. On November 20, 1948, the American Catholic hierarchy, opposing the theory of absolute separation of church and state, set as a goal "free cooperation between government and religious bodies—cooperation involving no special privilege to any group and no restriction on the religious liberty of any citizen." The question of tax assistance for Catholic parochial schools was a particularly controversial issue during this period. On the more positive side, the creation of the National Conference of Christians

[21] Joshua L. Liebman, *Peace of Mind* (N.Y., 1946); Fulton J. Sheen, *Peace of Soul* (N.Y., 1949); Norman Vincent Peale, *The Power of Positive Thinking* (N.Y., 1952).

[22] William G. McLoughlin, Jr., *Billy Graham: Revivalist in a Secular Age* (N.Y., 1960).

[23] Martin E. Marty, *The New Shape of American Religion* (N.Y., 1959), 10, 40; cf. also A. Roy Eckardt, *The Surge of Piety in America* (N.Y., 1958).

[24] Landis, "Trends in Church Membership," *Annals of the American Academy of Political and Social Science*, CCCXXXII, 5; Wolf, "1900–1950 Survey: Religious Trends in the United States," *Christianity Today*, III, 4.

[25] E.g., Herberg, *Protestant-Catholic-Jew;* John Courtney Murray designated a fourth category, secularism, in his "America's Four Conspiracies," in John Cogley, ed., *Religion in America: Original Essays on Religion in a Free Society* (N.Y., 1958).

and Jews in 1928 contributed toward constructive relations between Protestants, Catholics, and Jews.

Specialized functions of the ministry developed under the impact of social change, interest of the ecumenical movement in ministerial orders, and emphasis on lay ministry. For the pastor, more time came to be devoted to administration, less to pulpit preparation.[26] Pastoral theology emerged as an important discipline based on developments in psychology.[27] The greater diversification of the pastor's responsibility and the desire to develop a fuller lay ministry was reflected in the idea of "pastor-director," emphasized by H. Richard Niebuhr in the survey of theological education which he directed for the American Association of Theological Schools.[28]

As theological orientation and world conditions changed, some challenged the foreign missionary movement, while others took the occasion to reassert the absolute claims of Christianity.[29] Following World War II, the communist victory in China closed that land against missions, and the world-wide revolt against colonialism hastened the development of self-support, self-government, and self-propagation among all of the younger churches. The role of missionaries from the United States became more and more an auxiliary and advisory one.

The ecumenical movement, in which American churchmen were conspicuous, achieved new significance with the organization of the World Council of Churches in 1948. Contemporaneous with growing international awareness of "one world" and with the increase of secularism and of other forces hostile to the church, this quest for Christian unity among most of the leading non-Roman churches of the world was chiefly the outgrowth of forces within the churches themselves. By bringing into conversation widely diverse Christian traditions, the movement stimulated theological understanding and brought to the Christian world greater unity and power.

[26] Samuel W. Blizzard, "The Minister's Dilemma," *Christian Century*, LXXIII (April 25, 1956), 508–10.

[27] Seward Hiltner, "Pastoral Theology and Psychology," in Arnold S. Nash, ed., *Protestant Thought in the Twentieth Century: Whence and Whither?* (N.Y., 1951), 179–99.

[28] H. Richard Niebuhr, *et al., Survey of Theological Education in the United States and Canada* (3 vols., N.Y., 1956–57).

[29] *Re-thinking Missions: A Laymen's Inquiry after One Hundred Years* (N.Y., 1932); Hendrik Kraemer, *The Christian Message in a Non-Christian World* (London, 1938).

CHAPTER XX

The Post-Liberal Theological Mind

THE Christocentric liberal movement, which began with Horace Bushnell, reached the end of its creative period with the appearance of Walter Rauschenbusch's *A Theology for the Social Gospel* (1917). Although less comprehensive than the systematic treatises of William Newton Clarke and William Adams Brown, it belonged essentially to the same theological tradition. The chief distinction of *A Theology* lay in the fact that it organized every basic theological concept around the key category of the Kingdom of God, a category which, according to the author, embraced "the marrow of the gospel." [1] This book was the classic expression of the American social-gospel movement, and yet for two reasons it failed to achieve its full potentiality. In the first place, it was immediately submerged by the events of World War I. In the second place, the post-war social and theological climate became increasingly inhospitable to its basic assumptions.

Rauschenbusch himself foresaw that the post-war world would require drastic changes in the life and thought of the church, and yet he ventured to predict that the social-gospel movement would be revived "with pent-up energy" in the new era. [2] That prediction, however, never came true. Lively social action followed the war, but the liberal theology upon which it was based soon became so entangled in controversy that it eventually foundered.

Liberalism's first controversy grew out of a militant fundamentalist effort to purge the churches of all "modernists." The conflict flared up soon after the war and lasted some ten years. In the end, the ultra-conservatives failed in their primary objective, but at least they forced their opponents into a self-defensive posture. In the middle twenties, while the fundamentalist pressure was still strong, the liberals were drawn into dialogue with a small but vociferous party known as religious humanists. [3] These insurgents openly challenged the liberals to forsake their theistic tradition and espouse a religious faith based entirely upon the authority of modern scientific method. Although a few liberals went far in that direction, most of them rejected the new religion of science. But once again, involvement in contro-

[1] *A Theology for the Social Gospel* (N.Y., 1917), 131.
[2] *Ibid.*, 4.
[3] Gerald B. Smith, *Current Christian Thinking* (Chicago, 1928), Chap. 5; Walter M. Horton, *Theism and the Modern Mood* (N.Y., 1930), Chap. 2; William P. King, ed., *Humanism, Another Battle Line* (Nashville, 1931), especially D. C. Macintosh's essay, "Contemporary Humanism," 41–72. See also *supra*, 249–53.

versy prevented them from utilizing their full energies in creative theological effort.

While the humanist pressure was still increasing, the liberal movement was subjected to the impact of the "dialectical" or "crisis" theology of Karl Barth and his followers.[4] An American translation of Barth's *Das Wort Gottes und die Theologie* came out in 1928,[5] and at once excited vigorous discussion. Then followed Emil Brunner's *The Theology of Crisis* (1929), which sharply assailed the whole liberal movement. In 1931 Wilhelm Pauck published his *Karl Barth: Prophet of a New Christianity?* While not uncritical of dialectical theology, Pauck acknowledged that Barth's indictment of theological liberalism should be taken seriously. In 1932 H. Richard Niebuhr published a translation of Paul Tillich's *Die religiöse Lage der Gegenwart.*[6] Although not a Barthian, Tillich explicitly condemned European Protestant liberalism for its subserviency to capitalist culture. Then came the most devastating American polemic of its time, Reinhold Niebuhr's *Moral Man and Immoral Society* (1932), which analyzed the whole structure of liberal culture and found it much too unrealistic to solve the problems of a technological and industrial society. In particular it castigated the romantic moralists in education, sociology, and religion.

By this time Protestant liberalism was in great ferment, with many of its adherents beginning to question the future of their movement. Only a year after Niebuhr had published his *Moral Man,* a close colleague at Union said, "The most important fact about contemporary American theology is the disintegration of liberalism."[7] A young Oberlin theologian sweepingly announced in 1934 that the entire system of liberalism had "collapsed and must be replaced."[8]

Walter Horton's announcement now appears to have been somewhat premature. By the end of the 1930's, however, many influential Protestant liberals had publicly acknowledged that their theological views had been either deeply chastened or substantially revised.[9] By then they generally

---

[4] Other influences which were soon felt in the American scene included the Lund type of Lutheran thought (Aulén and Nygren), Eastern Orthodoxy (Berdyaev), and Neo-Thomism (Maritain), but these were minor as compared with the Barthian impact. For a good short survey of the various European streams that flowed into America, see Sydney E. Ahlstrom, "Continental Influence on American Christian Thought Since World War I," *Church History,* XXXVII (1958), 256–73.

[5] *The Word of God and the Word of Man,* tr. Douglas Horton (Boston, 1928).

[6] *The Religious Situation,* tr. H. Richard Niebuhr (N.Y., 1932). The force of Tillich's ideas was greatly increased by the translator's able preface.

[7] John C. Bennett, "After Liberalism—What?" *Christian Century,* L (1933), 1403.

[8] Walter M. Horton, *Realistic Theology* (N.Y., 1934), ix. America's most influential liberal minister, Harry Emerson Fosdick, declared in a notable sermon that "we must go beyond modernism." "Beyond Modernism," *Christian Century,* LII (1935), 1549–52.

[9] See the twenty-four autobiographical essays on "How My Mind Has Changed in This Decade," *Christian Century,* LVI (Jan. 18–Sept. 20, 1939). Barth, the only non-American, closed the series.

agreed that American Protestant thought was entering upon a new era. The new tendencies were variously labeled "neo-orthodoxy," "realistic theology," or "neo-supernaturalism." As viewed from a later perspective, those characterizations failed to indicate the great diversity of ideas and tendencies which were emerging.[10] Hence, the present essay will not attempt to apply any single category to this highly multiform movement, but instead will endeavor to analyze it in terms of its distinctive marks or characteristic traits.

Since the reader will occasionally encounter the term "post-liberal" in the remainder of this chapter, perhaps a word of explanation at the outset will avoid a possible misunderstanding. As here used, the term does not signify the exclusion of all elements of historic liberalism from the newer tendencies of thought, but only that the older liberalism as a coherent system is no longer intact.

First of all, the post-liberal mind reasserted the sovereignty of God. Negatively, this included a protest against the prevailing tendency to glorify man and all his works. Several features of liberal thinking had served to cultivate man's consciousness of his moral and spiritual autonomy. One of these was the idea of divine immanence. Walter M. Horton was only articulating a widely held notion when, in 1930, he began his provisional definition of God by saying, "God is my own better self." [11] Horton's complete view of deity of course involved much more than that statement implied, but to begin a definition in that anthropocentric fashion inevitably tended to obscure the transcendence of God and to nourish within man a feeling of his own goodness and self-sufficiency. This is no merely academic issue, for indeed well-known liberals in the early part of this century explicitly encouraged this very spirit. "A religion that is to promote and sustain democracy," said Arthur C. McGiffert of Union Seminary in 1919, "must first of all be a religion of faith in man." [12] "Religious education in a democracy," he specified, "should not be such as to encourage the delusive belief in supernatural agencies and dependence upon them, but it should be such as to convince everybody that things can be controlled and moulded by the power of man." [13] That is an amazing statement, yet it was by no means exceptional in its time.

The humanist movement was a second factor which reinforced a religion of faith in man. In the decade of the 1920's religious humanism was supremely self-confident, and its main concern was to undermine belief in the existence of God, the assumption being that only a religion without God would encourage man to devote himself single-mindedly to the promotion of human values. Max C. Otto of the University of Wisconsin, for

[10] Cf. Sydney E. Ahlstrom, "Neo-Orthodoxy Demythologized," *Christian Century*, LXXIV (1957), 649–51.
[11] *Theism and the Modern Mood*, 107.
[12] "Democracy and Religion," *Religious Education*, XIV (1919), 158.
[13] *Ibid.*, 157.

Reinhold Niebuhr, Prophet of
Christian Realism

Father Virgil Michel, Pioneer of the
Liturgical Movement

Martin Luther King, Jr. *(second from right)* bidding farewell to a group of Chicago
Antisegregationists released from jail in Albany, Georgia

Three American Methodisms in their Uniting Conference at
Kansas City, Missouri, in 1939

Participants in the Oberlin Faith and Order Conference (1957):
left, Dr. Graham Cotter (Canada); *center,* Bishop Johannes Lilje (Germany);
right, the Rev. Edward James Odom (U. S.)

example, earnestly admonished his fellowmen to acknowledge their absolute cosmic isolation so that they might then "with new zest . . . build on earth the fair city we have looked for in a compensatory world beyond." [14]

A third factor which nourished anthropocentrism was the psychology of religion, a subject which became so captivating during the first quarter of the twentieth century that it almost eclipsed theology as an academic discipline in some divinity schools.[15] The new movement of religious education, which was enormously popular during this same period, derived its basic theory almost entirely from data provided by psychology and sociology, and practically ignored theology. In 1931 Walter Horton expressed a widely held conviction when he said, "Theology must . . . agree without reservation to alter, amend, or cancel altogether whatsoever there may be in the dogmas of the past that is flatly and decisively contradicted by any new facts that psychology may reveal." [16] To give psychology any such veto power over theology is in effect to subjugate the latter to the former. Edward Scribner Ames drew the final conclusion from Horton's thesis when he said, "The psychology of religious experience becomes the conditioning science for the various branches of theology, or rather, it is the science which in its developed forms becomes theology or the philosophy of religion." [17] This tendency of thought becomes all the more alarming when it is remembered that the psychology of religion focused its primary attention upon the reactions or mental functions of the human subject, not upon ultimate Reality. Humanists, such as Ames and James H. Leuba, were not at all disturbed by this emphasis, because they denied the existence of a Divine Being. But even a personalistic theist like George A. Coe also largely confined his study to aspects of human consciousness and gave little serious attention to the reign of God.

This whole emphasis upon the religious consciousness was anathema to most post-liberals, and they recoiled from "psychologism" as a mortal enemy of theocentric religion. Reporting in 1936 on the new theological perspective of an influential group of some twenty-four younger Protestant churchmen, Samuel M. Cavert wrote:

> At the center of attention the realists place, not the religious subject, with his experiences and judgments, but the religious object. . . . What they are concerned about is the objective structure of things —a structure to which man must conform, whether or not it satisfies

[14] *Things and Ideals* (N.Y., 1924), 290. Cf. his *The Human Enterprise* (N.Y., 1940), 338.
[15] The leading treatises included Edwin D. Starbuck, *Psychology of Religion* (N.Y., 1899); William James, *Varieties of Religious Experience* (N.Y., 1902); E. S. Ames, *The Psychology of Religious Experience* (N.Y., 1910); James H. Leuba, *A Psychological Study of Religion* (N.Y., 1912); George A. Coe, *The Psychology of Religion* (Chicago, 1916); Harrison S. Elliott, *The Bearing of Psychology upon Religion* (N.Y., 1916); James B. Pratt, *The Religious Consciousness* (N.Y., 1920).
[16] *A Psychological Approach to Theology* (N.Y., 1931), 23.
[17] *The Psychology of Religious Experience.* 26.

his own desires and interests and values. God is not to be equated with the highest reaches of human aspiration and imagination. He is no projection of man's ideals or of his social consciousness. He is objective Reality.[18]

This was more or less typical of the general drift of the new theological realism. Even the distinguished religious naturalist, Henry Nelson Wieman, also stressed the necessity of a theocentric religion, although his idea of God diverged radically from the classical theistic tradition.[19]

But while the American post-liberals reasserted the principle of a transcendent God, they did not, as did the earlier Barth, accept the notion of a "wholly other" God. Divine transcendence did not mean for them a type of supernaturalism which set God entirely apart from natural and historical events. Theocentrism, in other words, did not denote an other-worldly type of religion. Indeed, it has been the post-liberal realists who have done most to preserve the enduring values of the older social-gospel movement.

A second distinctive mark of post-liberal thinking has been a renewed appreciation of biblical revelation. The assumption underlying this interest is that God can be known only if he reveals himself, and that the place where he has decisively disclosed himself is in the Bible. Consequently, "biblical religion" has been receiving far more attention than it perhaps ever got in the heyday of liberalism.

The new accent upon biblical revelation has given a strong impetus to biblical studies. Nor is this movement confined to Protestant circles. In recent decades Catholic biblical exegesis has indeed made notable progress, especially since the issuance of the encyclical *Divino Afflante Spiritu* (1943).[20] Catholic scholarship in the area of the Dead Sea Scrolls, for example, is highly distinguished. Significant advances are being made in America under the leadership of such men as Father John L. McKenzie of Loyola University (Chicago). The *Catholic Biblical Quarterly,* launched in 1939, is publishing many scholarly articles which are being read by a growing number of non-Catholic students. A hopeful omen for the ecumenical movement lies in the fact that American Catholic and Protestant biblical scholars are beginning to discuss their critical findings and common exegetical problems in inter-faith conferences. In 1959 the Catholic Biblical Association made the far-reaching proposal that Catholic and Protestant biblical scholars collaborate in the preparation of a modern English version of the Scriptures which could be used in public education.[21] If this effort

---

[18] "The Younger Theologians," *Religion in Life,* V (1936), 524–5.

[19] Wieman, "Theocentric Religion," in Vergilius Ferm, ed., *Contemporary American Theology: Theological Biographies,* I (N.Y., 1932), 339–52; "Neo-Orthodoxy and Contemporary Religious Reaction," in Wieman, *et al., Religious Liberals Reply* (Boston, 1947), 3–15. See also *supra,* 245–9.

[20] Gustave Weigel, S.J., *Catholic Theology in Dialogue* (N.Y., 1961), 29–48.

[21] *Ibid.,* 37.

were successful, it could go far toward opening the way for a larger use of the Bible in the public schools.

Of great significance is the revival of interest in biblical theology. During the late nineteenth century this subject received much attention, but around the opening of our century it was outmoded by the history-of-religion movement.[22] Biblical scholars then distinguished their function sharply from that of the theologian, and they became absorbed in problems connected with the origin and evolution of Israelite religion and of early Christianity. Much attention was given to the diversity of religious ideas contained in the Old and New Testaments, and anything resembling a unified biblical theology was considered impossible. Robert H. Pfeiffer's *Introduction to the Old Testament* (1941) is a late example of this type of historico-critical scholarship.

A strikingly different viewpoint soon manifested itself. The revival of biblical theology, which rose to tidal force on the European Continent in the 1930's, reached America in the 1940's. Despite rumblings of discontent among some old-line historicists,[23] interest in biblical thought has steadily mounted, as is evidenced by a swelling stream of books, including Paul Minear's *Eyes of Faith* (1946), Frederick C. Grant's *An Introduction to New Testament Thought* (1950), Bernhard W. Anderson's *Rediscovering the Bible* (1951), G. Ernest Wright's *God Who Acts* (1952), and John Bright's *The Kingdom of God* (1953).

Among the many effects of this current development of biblical theology, two will be mentioned here. First, the Old Testament is assuming a new significance in the life of the church. It is no longer a book primarily for the scientific antiquarian; instead, it is being seen as the beginning of a revelational and covenantal movement which finds its ultimate fulfilment in the New Testament. As W. Eichrodt, the author of a three-volume treatise on Old Testament theology, has said, "Old Testament religion with all its undeniable uniqueness of character is understood in its real essence only when considered in the light of the fulfilment which it received in Christ."[24] Second, systematic (dogmatic) theology is being deeply influenced by the new type of biblical scholarship; indeed, it is tending in some circles to become almost an appendage to biblical theology. This is especially true where theology is viewed as solely kerygmatic in character.

A third distinctive mark of the post-liberal mind has been a decisive reaction against an optimistic interpretation of the human situation. Probably the most vulnerable aspect of every version of American Protestant

[22] Clarence Tucker Craig, "Biblical Theology and the Rise of Historicism," *Journal of Biblical Literature*, LXII (1943), 281–94; James D. Smart, "The Death and Rebirth of Old Testament Theology," *Journal of Religion*, XXIII (1943), 1–11, 125–36.

[23] Cf. William A. Erwin, "The Reviving Theology of the Old Testament," *Journal of Religion*, XV (1945), 235–46.

[24] Quoted by James D. Smart, "The Death and Rebirth of Old Testament Theology," *Journal of Religion*, XXIII (1943), 135.

liberalism was its failure to perceive the fundamental nature of man's moral predicament. Even Christocentric liberalism had lost much of its earlier anthropological realism by the time of World War I.[25] Here and there a lonely prophet lifted his voice against the mood of moral complacency. In 1913, just before the war began, Dean W. W. Fenn of Harvard Divinity School wrote:

> To a serious thinker, Modern Liberalism often seems too jocund for life as it actually is. . . . A religious doctrine which cannot bear the weight of the heartbreaking disasters of life will prove a broken reed piercing the hand of him who leans upon it. Every fall is a fall upward—tell that to a man who by his sin has fallen from a position of honor and power into deep and damaging disgrace. If all's right with the world, something is wrong with man's moral sense.[26]

Another prominent dissenter was Harry Emerson Fosdick, who in his Cole Lectures at Vanderbilt University in 1922 penetratingly exposed the manner in which faith in human progress had "blanketed the sense of sin." "In spite of the debacle of the Great War," he declared, "this is one of the most unrepentant generations that ever walked the earth, dreaming still of automatic progress toward an earthly paradise." [27]

But the Fenns and the Fosdicks of those days were exceedingly scarce, and their somber warning made little impression upon their fellow clergymen, to say nothing of the rank and file in the pew. Not until the Great Depression had paralyzed the American economy was the time ripe for an Amos of the stature of Reinhold Niebuhr. But even then his *Moral Man and Immoral Society* (1932) was anathema to most secular and religious liberals, who still generally clung to the optimistic notion that mankind on the whole was gradually taming human egoism and progressively achieving mutuality among men and nations. Niebuhr admitted that rational and religious resources could do much to mitigate the imperialistic impulses of men and of groups, but he denied that those impulses would ever be completely subdued. He emphasized the fact that group imperialism is always more difficult to bring under moral control than that of the individual self.

Niebuhr did more than any other moralist or theologian to awaken both secularists and religionists to the reality and gravity of sin. His initial concern (as in *Moral Man*) was with social evil, but in his Gifford Lectures he unfolded a profound conception of sin. Of particular interest is the fact that Niebuhr argued seriously for a revival of the idea—not, of course, the old doctrine—of original sin. "The utopian illusions and sentimental aberrations of modern liberal culture," he observed, "are really all derived from

[25] Mary Francis Thelen, *Man as Sinner in Contemporary American Realistic Theology* (N.Y., 1946), 13–32, 54–9; H. Shelton Smith, *Changing Conceptions of Original Sin: A Study in American Theology Since 1750* (N.Y., 1955), Chap. 8.

[26] "Modern Liberalism," *American Journal of Theology*, XVII (1913), 516–7.

[27] *Christianity and Progress* (N.Y., 1922), 171.

the basic error of negating the fact of original sin." [28] As a result of the efforts of Niebuhr and of many other Christian realists, the older romantic view of man now has little standing in informed circles. Even where theologians still hold to much of the older type of liberalism, they have disavowed optimistic interpretations of human nature and of human history.[29]

A fourth primary feature of the post-liberal mind has been a revival of interest in Christology. Throughout the latter half of the last century, American Christocentric liberals prevailingly defended a substantially high doctrine of the person of Jesus in the face of a growing reductionist tendency of thought. This was particularly true of Bushnell and his immediate successors. Early in the present century, however, evangelical liberals became increasingly engrossed in the Jesus of history. Whereas their theological predecessors had found the term "person" of Christ a fitting category, they themselves preferred to speak of the "personality" of Jesus. The latter term involved no necessary metaphysical presuppositions, and it also denoted traits of character which were more or less observable in any historical figure.

In the year 1909 a famed American historian of Christian doctrine declared: "The greatest fact in modern Christian history is the rediscovery of Jesus. He is better known and understood today than he has ever been before." [30] McGiffert here expressed what was then a common belief among Protestant liberals in this country. That belief rested upon the assumption that modern historico-critical research had successfully isolated a primitive layer of Synoptic Gospel teaching (Q) in which the real Jesus—Jesus as he actually lived and taught apart from all theological coloring by his followers—had come to light. The image of "the man of Nazareth" was remarkably clear; he was a prophet-teacher of a new righteousness the substance of which was the infinite worth and brotherhood of man under the Divine Fatherhood. Harnack shaped that image classically in his *What Is Christianity?*

This conception of the Jesus of history captivated American liberals, especially those who labored to advance the social-gospel movement. Some leaders in this movement did not seriously concern themselves with the Christological question. They feared that any such concern might divert attention from the social task of the churches. Thus the greatest theologian of the social gospel wrote: "The speculative problem of christological dogma was how the divine and human natures united in the person of Christ; the problem of the social gospel is how the divine life of Christ can get control of human society." [31]

[28] *The Nature and Destiny of Man* (2 vols., N.Y., 1941–43), I, 373–n. 4.

[29] This is true, for example, of L. Harold DeWolf; cf. his *A Theology of the Living Church* (rev. ed., N.Y., 1960), Chaps. 23–24.

[30] Arthur C. McGiffert, *Christianity as History and Faith*, ed. A. C. McGiffert, Jr. (N.Y., 1934), 302.

[31] Rauschenbusch, *A Theology for the Social Gospel*, 148.

Despite the shattering blow delivered by Schweitzer's *Quest of the Historical Jesus,* some prominent liberals persisted in their claim that the real Jesus had rejected an eschatological-apocalyptical view of the kingdom of God in favor of a conception of the kingdom that was to come gradually within the evolving processes of history.[32]

Throughout the first third of the twentieth century, Christology was widely neglected by American scholarship. Since around 1940, however, the one-sided emphasis upon the Jesus of history has been in process of theological correction. Many scholars would now agree with John Knox, that "Christology is the most important area of Christian theology." [33] Toward the new Christological thinking Knox himself has contributed three unusually fertile volumes: *The Man Christ Jesus* (1941), *Christ the Lord* (1945), and *On the Meaning of Christ* (1947).[34] W. Norman Pittenger published *Christ and Christian Faith* in 1941, and followed it with *The Incarnate Word* in 1959. The latter is especially illuminating. In his *Realistic Theology* (1934) Walter Horton began a re-exploration of Christological thought which he culminated in *Our Eternal Contemporary* (1942). In volume two of *The Nature and Destiny of Man* and in *Faith and History* (1949) Reinhold Niebuhr has dealt freshly with important aspects of the person and work of Christ.[35] Highly suggestive is Paul Tillich's *Existence and the Christ* (1957). Other important works could be cited, but these are sufficient to indicate that the Christological problem is now in the forefront of American Protestant thinking.

Although these current treatments of Christology reflect divergent views at many points, they also reveal some significant common emphases. First, they all reject the older liberal tendency to draw a sharp distinction between the Jesus of history and the Christ of faith. Second, they insist upon the full humanity of Christ. Third, they prevailingly recognize the indispensability of the teachings of Jesus.

A fifth characteristic of much post-liberal thinking has been a serious endeavor to understand the Christian nature of the church. This is something relatively new in the history of American Protestantism. It is true that some early Puritan thought, the Mercersburg theology, and High-Church Anglicanism did show a measure of interest in ecclesiology, but Protestant orthodoxy as a whole has been largely indifferent toward ecclesiology. The same must be said also of Protestant liberalism. Investigation indicates that not a single Christocentric liberal from the time of Bushnell until World War I published a major treatise on the nature of the church. Furthermore, the subject was almost entirely ignored in the two most in-

---

[32] See, for example, Charles Foster Kent, *The Social Teachings of Jesus and the Prophets* (N.Y., 1917), 275–8; Rauschenbusch, *A Theology for the Social Gospel,* 218–20.

[33] *On the Meaning of Christ* (N.Y., 1947), 2.

[34] All three are now available in one volume, *Jesus: Lord and Christ* (N.Y., 1958).

[35] Paul Lehmann, "The Christology of Reinhold Niebuhr," in Charles W. Kegley and Robert W. Bretall, eds., *Reinhold Niebuhr: His Religious, Social, and Political Thought* (N.Y., 1956), 252–80.

fluential works in liberal systematic theology.[36] Leaders in the social-gospel phase of liberalism definitely feared that an emphasis upon the church would deflect attention from the kingdom of God. Rauschenbusch, for example, argued that the early Christian movement lost its prophetic character when the church replaced the kingdom of God as the object of primary interest.[37]

Nor does the history of Roman Catholic thought reveal as much concern with ecclesiology as many Protestants have assumed.[38] Prior to the Reformation, systematic treatises in this area were indeed a rarity. Even the authoritative *Summa* of Thomas Aquinas treated the subject as a subordinate aspect of Christology. The Reformation era produced Catholic tractates in numbers, but they reflected the defects of their polemical birth and did not notably advance the understanding of ecclesiology. The later centuries, for one reason or another, also failed to produce an understanding of the church as a total reality.[39]

It is within the present century, therefore, that both Catholics and Protestants have become most profoundly moved to renew their search for a doctrine of the church in all its Christian depth and fulness. On the Catholic side, a vital new trend began in 1924 with the publication of Karl Adam's *Das Wesen des Katholizismus,* in which the Pauline symbol of the church as the Body of Christ was made central rather than the traditional idea of the church as the kingdom of God.[40] Obviously the Pauline concept is much more dynamic and organic in import than the old kingdom idea, and it also provides a foundation upon which to develop a liturgy of unlimited richness. On its face, it would also seem to offer a much better concept around which to discuss ecumenical issues between Catholics and Protestants.

At first the innovation met with general disfavor among academic theologians, but when, in 1943, Pius XII threw his support to the new symbol in his great encyclical, *Mystici Corporis Christi,*[41] opposition speedily subsided. In accordance with the pope's instruction, the Pauline phrase, *sōma tou Christou,* is rendered as the Mystical Body of Christ, in order to "distinguish the Body of the Church, which is a society whose Head and Ruler is Christ, from His physical Body, which born of the Virgin Mother of God now sits at the right hand of the Father and rests hidden under the Eucharistic veil." [42] This idea of the church as the Mystical Body has the hearty support of American Catholicism's brilliant ecclesiologist, the Rev. Gustave Weigel, S.J., of Woodstock College.

---

[36] William Newton Clarke, *An Outline of Christian Theology* (N.Y., 1898); William Adams Brown, *Christian Theology in Outline* (N.Y., 1906). In later years, however, Brown made amends; cf. his *The Church: Catholic and Protestant* (N.Y., 1935).

[37] *A Theology for the Social Gospel,* Chap. 13.

[38] Gustave Weigel, S.J., *Catholic Theology in Dialogue,* 9–12.   [39] *Ibid.,* 102.

[40] *The Spirit of Catholicism,* tr. Justin McCann, O.S.B. (rev ed., N.Y., 1937), Chap. 3.

[41] For English text, see "Mystici Corporis Christi," *The Catholic Mind,* XLI (1943), 1–44

[42] *Ibid.,* par. 73.

Protestant interest in ecclesiology has grown steadily over the past quarter-century. Since Charles Clayton Morrison published his pioneering book on the church, *What is Christianity?* (1940), numerous other works on the same theme have made their appearance, such as Nels Ferré's *The Christian Fellowship* (1940), Theodore Wedel's *The Coming Great Church* (1945), Clarence Tucker Craig's *The One Church* (1951), and J. Robert Nelson's *The Realm of Redemption* (1951). The awakening is also reflected in the fact that the books in recent systematic theology [43] are generally giving extensive consideration to ecclesiology.

It is well known that differences vary enormously among non-Roman conceptions of the church, ranging all the way from the Quaker idea on the left to that of the Anglo-Catholic on the right. Hence, anything like substantial agreement probably lies far in the future. Nonetheless, the leading minds are beginning to meet at some promising points. This fact was revealed in an important study of the nature of the church conducted under the auspices of the American Theological Committee of the World Conference on Faith and Order.[44] Though differing in many respects, members of the committee apparently agreed to the following statement:

> What is the Church? It is the sphere of God's salvation in the present, and it is prophetic of his ultimate triumph in the Kingdom of God. It is constituted by the revelation of his grace in Jesus Christ. . . . It is marked by the presence of his Holy Spirit with all of its evidence of divine power.[45]

That statement obviously obscures basic differences on such questions as the nature of the ministry and the sacraments; nevertheless, it contains the seeds out of which further agreement will undoubtedly grow.[46]

Within the more churchly communions, the revival of ecclesiological thought has been closely linked with a remarkable liturgical awakening. The movement within the Roman Church began in Europe more than a century ago, but only in the last forty years has it taken vital root in American Catholicism. American developments received their major impetus from St. John's Abbey (Collegeville, Minn.), where one of the leading spirits was the Rev. Virgil Michel (1890–1938).[47] A vigorous press for the advancement of the liturgical awakening was set up there, and in 1926 a monthly, *Orate Fratres* (now *Worship*), was launched under the editorship of Dom Michel.

[43] For example, L. Harold DeWolf's *A Theology of the Living Church.*
[44] "Report on the Study of the Church," *Christendom,* IX (1944), 270–87.
[45] *Ibid.,* 286–7.
[46] For a summary of ecclesiological agreements and disagreements within Christendom in general, see Walter M. Horton, *Christian Theology: An Ecumenical Approach* (rev. ed., N.Y., 1958), Chap. 7.
[47] Paul Marx, O.S.B., *The Life and Work of Virgil Michel* (Washington, 1957). For Dom Michel's own story of the origin of the liturgical movement in the U.S., see John Tracy Ellis, ed., *Documents of American Catholic History* (Milwaukee, 1955), 644–7.

The concept of the church as the Mystical Body of Christ is central in the present Catholic liturgical movement, and around this concept are being developed resources for corporate worship which may well become one of the most revitalizing forces in Roman Catholic piety.[48] From a Protestant standpoint, one of the most significant aspects of this liturgical revival is the new accent upon "the priesthood of the laity."

Lutherans and Episcopalians also are experiencing a fresh advance in liturgical thinking, a development which is drawing much inspiration from *Worship* and other Catholic publications.[49] Other non-Roman communions are beginning to show an interest in the liturgical movement, as is indicated by an increasing output of new service books designed to enrich congregational worship.

These, then, are five major characteristics of the post-liberal mind: (1) the revival of a theocentric emphasis; (2) a renewed interest in biblical revelation; (3) the recovery of a realistic view of human nature; (4) a return to the question of Christology; and (5) the search for a more vital doctrine of the church. Considered in their total impact, these new tendencies indicate that current theological thinking has advanced substantially beyond the liberalism of 1930.

Significantly, almost every one of these recent developments has involved an effort to recover some aspect of Christian thought which was neglected during the twentieth-century period of liberalism. Have these correctives, then, gone far enough; and is there now an increasing need to reactivate some of the neglected elements of Christian liberalism? For a growing number, the answer appears to be "yes."

Indeed, some of the very theologians who did most to advance the post-liberal movement have been giving an affirmative answer to that question. John Bennett, for example, has contended that "it's time to go beyond neo-orthodoxy." [50] At least two factors seem to underlie this new attitude. One of these is a growing concern over the general drift toward ultra-conservatism in religious thought. The drift is evident in the waxing strength of a type of rigid evangelicalism which bears basic continuity with the old fundamentalism of the 1920's.[51] The dogma of biblical inerrancy, for example, is

[48] For a well-documented study by a Lutheran historian, see Ernest B. Koenker, *The Liturgical Renaissance in the Roman Catholic Church* (Chicago, 1954). Also valuable is Charles Davis, *Liturgy and Doctrine* (N.Y., 1960).

[49] See Herman A. Preus, "Liturgical Revival in American Lutheranism," *Worship*, XXXIII (1959), 523–30; Arthur C. Piepkorn, "The Protestant Worship Revival and the Lutheran Liturgical Movement," in Massey H. Shepherd, Jr., ed., *The Liturgical Renewal of the Church* (N.Y., 1960), 55–97; Shepherd, ed., *The Eucharist and Liturgical Renewal* (N.Y., 1960).

[50] John C. Bennett, "It's Time to Go Beyond Neo-Orthodoxy," *Advance*, CL (May 9, 1958), 4–5, 23–4. See also Paul Tillich, "Beyond the Usual Alternatives," *Christian Century*, LXXV (1958), 553–5; Reinhold Niebuhr, "The Quality of Our Lives," *Christian Century*, LXXVII (1960), 568–72.

[51] Cf. Arnold W. Hearn, "Fundamentalist Renascence," *Christian Century*, LXXV (1958), 528–30.

as stoutly maintained by the new evangelicals as it was by their fundamentalist predecessors.[52] The most sophisticated periodical voice of this theological movement is *Christianity Today,* a fortnightly with a wide circulation. It is critical of so-called neo-orthodoxy, theological liberalism, and the ecumenical movement as represented in the National and World Councils of Churches.

The second factor is a realization that many former liberals were too iconoclastic in their wholesale condemnation of the liberal tradition. True enough, the more perceptive critics occasionally specified certain liberal emphases which were worth preserving.[53] As a rule, however, these incidental reservations had little effect upon the general flight from liberalism. Furthermore, the term liberal was often used without any effort to distinguish between the various types of liberalism, and therefore the impression was left that Christian liberalism was as unsound as humanistic liberalism.

Doubtless still other factors have been operative in creating the new temper; but whatever they may be, there is an emerging conviction among some of the more perceptive theologians that the time has come to revive elements of the liberal tradition. H. Richard Niebuhr expressed the mood of a growing number when he said: "I believe that the Barthian correction of the line of march begun in Schleiermacher's day was absolutely essential, but that it has become an overcorrection and that Protestant theology can minister to the church's life more effectively if it resumes the general line of march represented by the evangelical, empirical and critical movement."[54] Karl Barth himself, indeed, now seems to favor renewing contact with the masters of classical liberalism. Thus in an address of 1957 he declared that thinkers like Holtzmann, Harnack, and Troeltsch "will not cease to speak to us. And we cannot cease to listen to them."[55] If that declaration really means what it says, then the famed theologian may go still further in modifying his earlier orthodoxy.

It is not the role of the historian to undertake to predict what lies ahead in religious thought. Nonetheless, history warrants his believing that the emerging tendency to look with a critical eye upon theological achievements of the past generation is a good sign that the theological mind is in a state of vitality. In theology, as in all other disciplines, complacency is the first step toward intellectual sterility.

162. The Modernist Apostasy

Few men in the 1930's renounced their liberal faith more uncompromisingly than Edwin Lewis (1881–1959) of Drew University. He wrote his

[52] See, for example, Edward John Carnell, *The Case for Orthodox Theology* (Phila., 1959), 33–50.
[53] See, for example, Reinhold Niebuhr, "Ten Years That Shook My World," *Christian Century,* LVI (1939), 544.
[54] "Reformation: Continuing Imperative," *Christian Century,* LXXVII (1960), 250.
[55] *The Humanity of God* (Richmond, Va., 1960), 33.

first book, *Jesus Christ and the Human Quest* (1924), on the premises of theological liberalism, but within a few years he became convinced that he had mistakenly tried to ground Christianity in philosophy rather than in revelation. The result was a radical shift to the position that "Christianity . . . contains its own philosophy," and therefore has no need to be adjusted to any other.[56]

Lewis first revealed his new faith in an emotion-laden essay, "The Fatal Apostasy of the Modern Church," which he published in *Religion in Life* in the fall of 1933. The essay instantly drew fire from many of his Methodist brethren, some charging that he had gone Barthian and others that he had lapsed into fundamentalism. Stung by his critics, Lewis replied in *A Christian Manifesto* (1934) that was even more uncompromising. To the end of his life the convert kept the faith, although he later admitted that the *Manifesto* had put some matters too strongly.

At the age of nineteen, Lewis left his native England for Canada, where he served as a Methodist missionary. Later he came to the United States and held pastorates in the East and the West. In 1916 he joined the faculty of his alma mater, Drew Theological Seminary, where he taught systematic theology until his retirement in 1951. Among his more solid post-liberal books are *A Philosophy of the Christian Revelation* (1940) and *The Creator and the Adversary* (1948).[57]

The following document is reproduced from "The Fatal Apostasy."

DOCUMENT

Modern theological liberalism undoubtedly rendered the church an important service. It helped to break the strangle-hold of terms and phrases which had become in all too many cases merely empty shibboleths. It re-established, after the fashion of the thirteenth century, the rights of the intellect in the evaluation of the things of the spirit. It garnered for the use of the church the rich harvest of scholarship in many fields—biblical, historical, sociological, psychological. It served notice to a world too often skeptical that a man could believe in Jesus and at the same time be fully aware of all the amazing kaleidoscopic changes occurring in contemporary life. For such a service we cannot but be grateful. Nevertheless, all is not well with us. Liberalism has not brought us to the Promised Land. We may have gained a battle, but the campaign is still on, and there is more than a suspicion that the gain made at one point involved a serious loss elsewhere. We yielded positions whose strategic significance is becoming more and more manifest. We so stressed the Bible as coming to us in "the words of men" that the sense in which it is also "the word of God" has become increasingly vague. We so freely allowed the influence of contemporary forces in the development of doctrine as to have endangered the continuity

---

[56] "From Philosophy to Revelation," *Christian Century*, LVI (June 14, 1939), 762–4.

[57] For a brief analysis of Lewis' theological views, see David W. Soper, *Major Voices in American Theology* (Phila., 1953), 17–36.

of that living core of truth and reality for which contemporary forces were but the *milieu*. We exposed all the delicate nuances of spiritual experience to the cold dispassionate gaze of psychology, until it has become a question whether psychology of religion is not in danger of destroying the very thing it lives by. And in particular we were so determined to recover for the church "the human Jesus" that we lost sight of the fact that the church is the creation of "the divine Christ," or at least of faith in Christ as divine. Have we sown the wind, and is the whirlwind now upon us?

The Gospels and The Church

The *Hibbert Journal* symposium [58] of a generation ago, "Jesus, or Christ?" was a sign of the times. It showed very clearly the results of the "Jesus-study" of the latter part of the nineteenth century. It prophesied an increasing emphasis on "the religion of Jesus," a prophecy which has been abundantly fulfilled. In many quarters of the modern church it is now taken for granted that "the Jesus of the Gospels" is the primary datum for Christianity. . . .

But perhaps the case is not so simple as it seems. Say what we will, the stubborn fact remains that the Gospels are themselves the product of a community which already had "seated Christ at the right hand of God," and that, failing that audacious act of their mind and heart, we had had no Gospels at all. If the dangerous expression may be permitted, it was "Christ" who saved "Jesus" to us. That is to say, although Jesus was saved to posterity by "the Christian community," that community organized itself not around the fact that a man named Jesus had lived and taught and wrought and died, but around the belief that in that same Jesus had "dwelt all the fullness of the Godhead bodily." . . .

The Original Christian Message

The Christian "facts" are not to be limited to what fell between Bethlehem and Calvary. What was then said and done was but part of a larger whole—of a movement taking place within the very being of God. Men believed that this was implied in the indubitable historical and experiential facts. They therefore wrought out the idea of "pre-existence" as applied to their Lord, identified him as the permanently active occasion of that life of fellowship in which the church as they knew it was constituted, and from this were led on step by step to formulate finally the doctrine of the Trinity. It is easy enough to complain that this was to transform "the simple Gospel" into a *Weltanschauung,* yet we have no evidence that the so-called simple Gospel was ever preached, even at the beginning, apart from at least some of the elements of this philosophy. . . .

What then is the object of Christian faith? Not a man who once lived and died, but a Contemporary Reality, a God whose awful holiness is

[58] "Jesus or Christ?" *Hibbert Journal Supplement for 1909* (London, 1909).

"covered" by one who is both our representative and his, so that it is "our flesh that we see in the Godhead," that "flesh" which was historically Jesus of Nazareth but is eternally the divine Christ whose disclosure and apprehension Jesus lived and died to make possible. . . . It was that thought that created and sustained the church, and the church languishes to-day because it has substituted that thought with one of lesser power as it is of lesser truth. . . .

The Repudiation of Christianity

We do not like Christianity, not because it is intrinsically incredible but because it is so vastly humiliating. We do not *want* it to be true that "the Son of Man came to give himself a ransom for many," and so we find "critical" reasons for doubting that the words were ever spoken—as though by proving that Jesus did not say them we should prove that they were not true! We do not *want* it to be true that "the Word became flesh and dwelt among us": therefore we get rid of one of the most profound, heart-searching, and revolutionary truths ever uttered—the truth which must always be the touch-stone of any proposed Christology—by the simple device of labeling it "Platonism." We do not *want* it to be true that "through one act of righteousness the free gift came unto all men to justification of life": this being so, we ask by what right Paul "distorted" the simple Gospel of brotherhood and service and good will by introducing into it misleading analogies from temple and law-court.

No; we do not like Christianity. We do not like its cosmic audacity. We do not like its moral pessimism. We do not like the way it smashes the beautiful orderliness of our metaphysical systems. We do not like its uncompromising insistence on the possibility of our being damned souls, whose only hope is in the sovereign grace of God—a God who voluntarily endured self-immolation as the cost of his own graciousness. We be *men*— men whose prerogative it is to stand before God, face him without a tremor, and *demand;* not slaves whose duty it is to kneel before him with covered face, humbly and reverently and gratefully to *accept.* Away with this doctrine of grace! Away with this whole mythology of Incarnation! Away with this outworn notion of Atonement! Make way for emancipated man!

The Plight of The Church

But in this pride lies our shame, our weakness, and our defeat. What has it done for us? What has it done for the church—at least, for evangelical Protestantism? How far have we gotten with our various substitutes? Look over our churches: they are full of people who, brought up on these substitutes, are strangers to those deeper experiences without which there had been no New Testament and no Church of Christ. . . .

And to a large extent, this plight of the church is traceable to a weakening of its dogmatic basis. Whether the phrase, "humanitarian Christology," is defensible or not is a question. Unless Christ is conceived as one who "stands on the divine side of causality in effecting redemption," it is difficult to see why we need a doctrine of him at all. If Jesus is not specifically related to God's eternal purpose to enter sacrificially the stream of our humanity, to the end that he might thereby change its direction and set it flowing toward himself, then we no more need a doctrine of Jesus than we need a doctrine of Jeremiah or a doctrine of Paul. There is no permanent resting-place between *some form* of the Logos Christology and a "humanitarian Christology" (allowing the phrase) which in effect surrenders the whole idea of direct divine sacrificial saving activity. And what we mean theologically by a Logos Christology we mean practically by a Christ-centered religion rather than a "religion of Jesus." If the emulation of "the religion of Jesus" were presented as the possible end of a Christ-centered faith, that would be different. What we are actually doing, however, is supposing that unregenerate men can be "like Jesus"! Even a casual acquaintance with great sections of modern Protestantism makes it evident that it has departed very widely from the Christocentric emphasis. We must recover that emphasis, or perish. The divine Christ saved the human Jesus from disappearing, and if the human Jesus is to continue to mean for men all that he should, it must still be through the divine Christ. Christ must continue to save Jesus!

It is not that men cannot live "the good life" without faith in the divine Christ. It is not that there cannot be a profound appreciation of the character of Jesus without it. But Christianity does not consist simply in the good life and in moral appreciation and endeavor. It *is* this, of course. . . .

But what *does* the modern church believe? The church is becoming creedless as rapidly as the innovators can have their way. The "Confession of Faith"—what is happening to it? Or what about the "new" confessions that one sees and hears—suitable enough, one imagines, for, say, a fraternal order. And as for the Apostles' Creed—"our people will not say it any more": which means, apparently, that "our people," having some difficulties over the Virgin Birth and the resurrection of the body, have elected the easy way of believing in nothing at all—certainly not in "the Holy Catholic Church." So we are going to allow them to be satisfied with "The Social Creed of the Churches," quite forgetful of the fact that unless the church has a "religious" creed besides a "social" creed the church as such will cease to exist long before it has had time to make its "social" creed effective in the life of the world. "But the social creed *is* religious." Yes; but has its religion proved dynamic enough, impelling enough, to maintain itself at the high point—the Himalayanly high point—necessary to make its creed effective? The church has set itself to do more at the very time that it is lessening its power to do anything.

"What Must We Do To Be Saved?"

The church, especially the American evangelical churches, must re-enthrone Christ, the divine Christ, in the life and thought of the people, or cease to exist. Not that the church merely as an institution is the necessary desideratum. But the church in the high New Testament sense of "the body of Christ"—this *must* be saved for the sake of the world. Here is the world's one redeeming force because here is the world's one redeeming message—if the message be *complete*. It is that completeness whose lack is the secret of our impotence. Can we recover it? Nay rather, do we here highly resolve that we *will* recover it? Let us be done with compromise, and let us affirm—affirm magnificently, affirm audaciously. Let us affirm God—his unchanging love for man, his unchanging hatred of sin, his sacrificial presence in all the life and work of Jesus. Let us affirm Christ—Christ as the meaning of God, Christ as what God *is* in virtue of that mysterious "kenosis" by which he made himself one with a human life, and at the same time that he was doing the utmost he could do for men endured the worst—a Cross—that men could do against him. Let us affirm the Spirit— the divine concern to bring to bear upon the hearts and consciences of men the impact of what God in Christ has done and is forever doing on their behalf, to the end that they may be moved to repentance, to that faith which ensures forgiveness, to that love which brings moral empowerment, and to that surrender of the will which makes God's purposes their purposes. Let us affirm the church—the community of the redeemed, those who in all their life seek the regnancy of the spirit of Jesus, carrying on and extending the mystery of the Incarnation against that day when God, the Christ-God, shall be all and in all. Let us affirm the Kingdom—the Christianizing of life everywhere.

> SOURCE: Edwin Lewis, "The Fatal Apostasy of the Modern Church," *Religion in Life,* II (Autumn, 1933), 483-4, 486-92. Copyright 1933 by Pierce and Smith; copyright renewed 1961 by Abingdon Press. Used by permission.

163. The Captivity of the Church

The leaders in post-liberal Protestant thought were acutely aware of the church's failure to maintain its spiritual independence from "the world." No one spoke more directly to this situation in the 1930's than did H. Richard Niebuhr (1894-1962). The church had fallen prey to a corrupt civilization, he urged, because it had not been true to its Divine Head. In 1935 Niebuhr elaborated this thesis penetratingly in a little book entitled *The Church Against the World,* which he wrote in collaboration with Wilhelm Pauck and Francis P. Miller. A section of that essay, entitled "The Captive Church," is largely reproduced in the document that follows. It is the author's conviction that the "captivity of the church is the first fact with which we need to deal in our time."

A native of Missouri, Niebuhr was educated at Elmhurst College, Eden Theological Seminary, and Yale University, receiving his Ph.D. from the latter. He taught at Eden from 1919–22 and again from 1927–31. He served as President of Elmhurst from 1924–27. From 1931 until his death in 1962 he taught Christian ethics at Yale. For many years he stood in the forefront of American theologians.[59] His more influential books include *The Social Sources of Denominationalism* (1929), *The Kingdom of God in America* (1937), *The Meaning of Revelation* (1941), *Christ and Culture* (1951), and *Radical Monotheism and Western Culture* (1960).

DOCUMENT

The church is in bondage to capitalism. Capitalism in its contemporary form is more than a system of ownership and distribution of economic goods. It is a faith and a way of life. It is faith in wealth as the source of all life's blessings and as the savior of man from his deepest misery. It is the doctrine that man's most important activity is the production of economic goods and that all other things are dependent upon this. On the basis of this initial idolatry it develops a morality in which economic worth becomes the standard by which to measure all other values and the economic virtues take precedence over courage, temperance, wisdom and justice, over charity, humility and fidelity. Hence nature, love, life, truth, beauty and justice are exploited or made the servants of the high economic good. Everything, including the lives of workers, is made a utility, is desecrated and ultimately destroyed. Capitalism develops a discipline of its own but in the long run makes for the overthrow of all discipline since the service of its god demands the encouragement of unlimited desire for that which promises—but must fail—to satisfy the lust of the flesh and the pride of life.

The capitalist faith is not a disembodied spirit. It expresses itself in laws and social habits and transforms the whole of civilization. It fashions society into an economic organization in which production for profit becomes the central enterprise, in which the economic relations of men are regarded as their fundamental relations, in which economic privileges are most highly prized, and in which the resultant classes of men are set to struggle with one another for the economic goods. Education and government are brought under the sway of the faith. The family itself is modified by it. The structure of cities and their very architecture is influenced by the religion. So intimate is the relation between the civilization and the faith, that it is difficult to participate in the former without consenting to the latter and becoming entangled in its destructive morality. . . .

No antithesis could be greater than that which obtains between the

[59] For an analysis of his unique contribution, see Paul Ramsey, ed., *Faith and Ethics: The Theology of H. Richard Niebuhr* (N.Y., 1957).

gospel and capitalist faith. The church has known from the beginning that the love of money is the root of evil, that it is impossible to serve God and Mammon, that they that have riches shall hardly enter into life, that life does not consist in the abundance of things possessed, that the earth is the Lord's and that love, not self-interest, is the first law of life. Yet the church has become entangled with capitalist civilization to such an extent that it has compromised with capitalist faith and morality and become a servant of the world. . . . The entanglement with capitalism appears in the great economic interests of the church, in its debt structure, in its dependence through endowments upon the continued dividends of capitalism, and especially in its dependence upon the continued gifts of the privileged classes in the economic society. This entanglement has become the greater the more the church has attempted to keep pace with the development of capitalistic civilization, not without compromising with capitalist ideas of success and efficiency. At the same time evidence of religious syncretism, of the combination of Christianity with capitalist religion, has appeared. The "building of the kingdom of God" has been confused in many a churchly pronouncement with the increase of church possessions or with the economic advancement of mankind. The church has often behaved as though the saving of civilization and particularly of capitalist civilization were its mission. It has failed to apply to the morality of that civilization the rigid standards which it did not fail to use where less powerful realities were concerned. The development may have been inevitable, nevertheless it was a fall.

The bondage of the church to nationalism has been more apparent than its bondage to capitalism, partly because nationalism is so evidently a religion, partly because it issues in the dramatic sacrifices of war—sacrifices more obvious if not more actual than those which capitalism demands and offers to its god. Nationalism is no more to be confused with the principle of nationality than capitalism is to be confused with the principle of private property. Just as we can accept, without complaint against the past, the fact that a private property system replaced feudalism, so we can accept, without blaming our ancestors for moral delinquency, the rise of national organization in place of universal empire. But as the private property system became the soil in which the lust for possessions and the worship of wealth grew up, so the possibility of national independence provided opportunity for the growth of religious nationalism, the worship of the nation, and the lust for national power and glory. And as religious capitalism perverted the private property system, so religious nationalism corrupted the nationalities. Nationalism regards the nation as the supreme value, the source of all life's meaning, as an end-in-itself and a law to itself. It seeks to persuade individuals and organizations to make national might and glory their main aim in life. It even achieves a certain deliverance of men by freeing them from their bondage to self. In our modern polytheism it enters into close relationship with capitalism, though not without friction and occasional conflict, and sometimes it appears to offer an alternative faith to those who have become disillusioned with wealth-worship. Since the adequacy of its god is continually called into question by the existence of other national deities, it requires the demonstration of the omnipotence of nation and breeds an unlimited lust for national power and expansion. But since the god is limited the result is conflict, war and destruction. Despite the fact that the nationalist faith becomes obviously dominant only in times of sudden or continued political crisis, it has had constant and growing influence in the West, affecting particularly government and education.

The antithesis between the faith of the church and the nationalist idolatry has always been self-evident. The prophetic revolution out of which Christianity eventually came was a revolution against nationalist religion. The messianic career of Jesus developed in defiance of the nationalisms of Judaism and of Rome. In one sense Christianity emerged out of man's disillusionment with the doctrine that the road to life and joy and justice lies through the exercise of political force and the growth of national power. The story of its rise is the history of long struggle with self-righteous political power. Yet in the modern world Christianity has fallen into dependence upon the political agencies which have become the instruments of nationalism and has compromised with the religion they promote. The division of Christendom into national units would have been a less serious matter had it not resulted so frequently in a division into nationalistic units. The close relation of church and state in some instances, the participation of the church in the political life in other cases, has been accompanied by a syncretism of nationalism and Christianity. . . .

Capitalism and nationalism are variant forms of a faith which is more widespread in modern civilization than either. It is difficult to label this religion. . . . The rather too technical term "anthropocentrism" seems to be the best designation of the faith.[60] It is marked on its negative side by the rejection not only of the symbols of the creation, the fall and the salvation of men, but also of the belief in human dependence and limitation, in human wickedness and frailty, in divine forgiveness through the suffering of the innocent. Positively it affirms the sufficiency of man. Human desire is the source of all values. The mind and the will of man are sufficient instruments of his salvation. Evil is nothing but lack of development. Revolutionary second-birth is unnecessary. Although some elements of the anthropocentric faith are always present in human society, and although it was represented at the beginning of the modern development, it is not the source but rather the product of modern civilization. Growing out of the success of science and technology in understanding and modifying some

[60] For a fuller analysis of the factors which have nourished the anthropocentric and anthropocratic spirit, see H. Richard Niebuhr, "Religious Realism and the Twentieth Century," in D. C. Macintosh, ed., *Religious Realism* (N.Y., 1931), 413–28.

of the conditions of life, it has substituted veneration of science for scientific knowledge, and glorification of human activity for its exercise. Following upon the long education in which Protestant and Catholic evangelism had brought Western men to a deep sense of their duty, this anthropocentrism glorified the moral sense of man as his natural possession and taught him that he needed no other law than the one within. Yet, as in the case of capitalism and nationalism, the faith which grew out of modern culture has modified that culture. During the last generations the anthropocentric faith has entered deeply into the structure of society and has contributed not a little to the megapolitanism and megalomania of contemporary civilization.

The compromise of the church with anthropocentrism has come almost imperceptibly in the course of its collaboration in the work of culture. It was hastened by the tenacity of Christian traditionalism, which appeared to leave churchmen with no alternative than one between worship of the letter and worship of the men who wrote the letters. Nevertheless, the compromise is a perversion of the Christian position. The more obvious expressions of the compromise have been frequent but perhaps less dangerous than the prevailing one by means of which Christianity appeared to remain true to itself while accepting the anthropocentric position. That compromise was the substitution of religion for the God of faith. Man's aspiration after God, his prayer, his worship was exalted in this syncretism into a saving power, worthy of a place alongside science and art. Religion was endowed with all the attributes of Godhead, the while its basis was found in human nature itself. The adaptation of Christianity to the anthropocentric faith appeared in other ways: in the attenuation of the conviction of sin and of the necessity of rebirth, in the substitution of the human claim to immortality for the Christian hope and fear of an afterlife, in the glorification of religious heroes, and in the efforts of religious men and societies to become saviors.

The captive church is the church which has become entangled with this system or these systems of worldliness. It is a church which seeks to prove its usefulness to civilization, in terms of civilization's own demands. It is a church which has lost the distinctive note and the earnestness of a Christian discipline of life and has become what every religious institution tends to become—the teacher of the prevailing code of morals and the pantheon of the social gods. It is a church, moreover, which has become entangled with the world in its desire for the increase of its power and prestige and which shares the worldly fear of insecurity.

SOURCE: H. Richard Niebuhr, "Toward the Independence of the Church," in H. R. Niebuhr, Wilhelm Pauck, and Francis P. Miller, *The Church Against the World* (Chicago, 1935), 128–39. Copyright 1935. Harper & Row, Publishers, Incorporated.

164. Two Views of Man

Naturalistic versions of religion attracted considerable attention in America during the first third of this century, but interest in religious naturalism has declined in recent decades. This declension may be due in part to the critical analysis to which religious naturalism has been subjected. A notable example is the historic Calhoun-Wieman dialogue of 1936–37.[61]

Unlike some theologians, Robert L. Calhoun (1896–) has always recognized a certain value in Henry Nelson Wieman's version of naturalistic theism and in the various types of religious humanism, but he has never found those modes of thought ultimately adequate. Nowhere has Calhoun more acutely exposed the weakness of nontheistic humanism than in an essay which he wrote for the Oxford World Conference (1937), entitled "The Dilemma of Humanitarian Modernism." Profoundly perceptive is the last section of the essay, in which the Christian view of man is contrasted with that of humanitarian modernism. The subjoined document contains the heart of that section.

In reading the document, one should bear in mind the sense in which Calhoun uses the two important terms, "modernism" and "humanitarianism." By the former he means not primarily any particular school of thought, but rather a certain temper which is preoccupied with the immediate context of events and which commonly disregards the supratemporal ground of existence. By humanitarianism he refers to a social disposition which is concerned to relieve human suffering and promote the welfare of the less fortunate.

Like most other younger theologians in the 1930's, Calhoun was severely buffeted in his encounter with neo-orthodoxy, but he never surrendered the hard core of theological liberalism.[62] Meanwhile, however, he has shifted his primary interest from philosophy to theology, and has also come to recognize that the Christian revelation must be the starting point of theology. But although he begins with revelation, he insists that revelation cannot dispense with reason. His guiding principle could be summed up as *fides quaerens intellectum.*

Since 1923 Calhoun has taught at Yale, giving major attention to historical theology. In recent years he has been especially interested in the ecumenical movement and has done much to undergird it with a vital theology. He has published numerous articles, essays, and books, but his

---

[61] Robert L. Calhoun, "God as More Than Mind," *Christendom*, I (1936), 333–49; Henry Nelson Wieman, "God Is More Than We Can Think," *ibid.*, 428–42; Calhoun, "How Shall We Think of God?" *ibid.*, 593–611; Wieman, "Faith and Knowledge," *ibid.*, 762–78; Calhoun, "The Power of God and the Wisdom of God," *ibid.*, II (1937), 36–49; Wieman, "The Absolute Commitment of Faith," *ibid.*, 202–14; Calhoun, "A Final Statement," *ibid.*, 215–8.

[62] Cf. "A Liberal Bandaged but Unbowed," *Christian Century*, LVI (May 3, 1939), 701–4.

God and the Common Life (1935) is his most distinguished contribution to theological scholarship.

DOCUMENT

To pass from such high-minded naturalism to the Christian understanding of man is to move into additional dimensions of belief. Much in what is affirmed by pragmatism, and by the unreflective modernism to which it gives one sort of voice, can be affirmed also by a contemporary Christian, sometimes in frank divergence from views often maintained hitherto in the name of Christianity. But such affirmations, when set in the frame of Christian faith, take on meanings beyond any for which naturalism has room. Moreover, at certain points the affirmations of Christian faith contradict both assertions and denials of naturalistic and humanistic modernism. Christian faith rejects the view that nature is ultimate; that man is self-sufficient; that culture is the supreme object of loyalty, and the ground of human salvation. It rejects with equal stubbornness the humanism which makes a god of human personality, and the inhumane primitivism which holds human personality in contempt.

The base line upon which all these agreements and differences converge is the boundary between ways of life and thought which lay primary stress upon things that are seen, and those which lay primary stress upon things that are not seen. Modernism of all varieties belongs to the first class, Christianity to the second. For modernism, the center of gravity for human life and thought is wholly within the range of human experience; for Christianity it is outside that range, though crucially related to it.

This basic distinction has many particular aspects. Thus, in its theory of knowledge modernism tends to positivism and gnosticism, Christianity to faith-realism. The one contents itself with the panorama of current events, and speaks or acts as though in knowing these, one can know all that is of importance for human life. The other affirms that even if all phenomena were known by man, and nothing beyond these, what is most important of all would remain unknown; and further, that this most important Reality can never be fully known by man, as one knows a color or a pain, but partially at best, by faith, or by reason continuously grounded in an act of faith. Modernism tends to narrow men's attention to the immediate present and proximate future. Christianity tries to keep men aware of all history as a living movement in time, which at every moment points beyond itself to what is eternal, and has its significance fundamentally in that relationship. Modernism regards nature as ultimate and self-explanatory; human culture and personality as given natural facts. Christianity declares that nature, culture and personality are problems, not solutions; and that all of them must find theoretic and practical solution, if at all, through faith in a sovereign God.

The essential difference between Christian faith and modernism, whether inside or outside the nominally Christian churches and sects, is a difference of actual perspective or orientation. This difference is decisive, and irreconcilable except through essential change in one or the other. But it should not require anathemas nor bloodless wars of extermination from either side. In detailed content and aims, they have much ground for common understanding, and much to learn from each other. . . .

This means, in the first place, ungrudging acknowledgment of the positive gains for human life which modernism has fostered. It must be said by Christian thinkers in the most forthright manner that the explicit turning of men's attention from ultimate to proximate aspects of reality, in the manner of the special sciences, is one indispensable factor in man's laborious quest after truth and enlightened living. When concern with first and final causes crowds out due attention to particular details, our whole outlook is falsified. Faith in God cannot take the place of patient search for understanding of nature and man, nor of painstaking technical procedures through which detailed knowledge is put to work. Science and technology are certainly not enough, but they are indispensable: and hitherto modernism, not traditional Christianity, has most candidly welcomed them. . . .

At the same time, while giving full credit for sound emphasis in modernism, it must be said no less plainly that its purview is too narrow and its perspective false. This is true both of frankly non-Christian thought, and of these [those] forms of liberalism and of "the social gospel" within the churches which identify the Kingdom of God with a cultural ideal or an improved social order. In trying to be realistic about religious tradition, modernism becomes unrealistic about man. It sees him predominantly if not exclusively as a "cultured" being, able to live his life fully within the more decorous precincts of current civilization, which collectively are often romanticized into a genial sort of *Magna Mater*. . . . Man cannot live by culture alone. His fierce, deep-seated drives require at once more ample scope and more powerful discipline than culture by itself can provide. This Christian faith sees far more clearly than modernism, and by so much is more realistic about man. It sees him as at once less admirable in his present actuality, and more profound in his ultimate significance, than modernism takes him to be.

First of all, man the animal is, for Christian faith, a creature responsible to his Creator. . . .

In response to God's creative word he has emerged from the stream of organic evolution, with ears partly though imperfectly attuned to God's continuing summons, which will not let him rest. That summons is partly conveyed, though by no means automatically interpreted, through the processes that go on within man, and in nature around him; which have their ultimate meaning not simply as being themselves, but as being vehicles for the divine word to which man is not merely subjected but *responsible,* having therein his distinctive status as man.

A corresponding difference of perspective sets off the Christian belief about man as social being. Modernism tends to deal with culture and with history in the same manner as with physical nature, regarding it as self-explanatory, and a sufficient frame of reference for the behavior of human persons. . . .

For modernism, human society is ultimate and human ills are curable by it. For Christian faith, man is not simply the more or less inept child of a culture. He is that, no doubt. But far more ominously he is, individually and collectively, a sinner against the eternal word of God. The frame of reference for his conduct is not merely the behavior patterns of an existing culture, but the fabric of a world order in which all cultures are grounded, and which is itself continuously molded by God's will. Against this fabric not only individuals and groups, but whole cultures stand under judgment, and in so far as they fail grossly to meet its demands, whether by overt rebellion or merely through inertia, they die.

The requirement which thus lies upon men is not simply the constraint of stubborn facts, but the obligation implicit in worth and in the liability of persons to its claims. Such obligation differs from factual compulsion (from which it is, of course, never entirely separate) in that the response for which it calls is not a forced surrender but a voluntary devotion, in which the responding self is not constricted but fulfilled, or realized. The summons is, in principle, a demand for willingness to lose one's life for the Kingdom of God, and thus to find it. It is a call to the highest good of which man is capable; to the fulfilment, not the destruction, of his root nature, and the satisfaction of his most distinctive hungers. For Christian faith, the call to such devotion comes centrally through Jesus Christ, and the voice that speaks most clearly in his life and death is trusted, in Christian living, as the voice of God. To the more superficial, so-called "natural" inclinations of men (including Christians) toward self-indulgence and self-glorification, such a call is either unintelligible or a positive affront, and the usual response is apathy or refusal. This is sin. It is not merely to reject some demand or habit pattern of society. This, though entitled to its own proper meed of love and devotion, is always partly and in some respects radically of another mind than the mind of Jesus Christ. To sin is not then simply to disobey society but to contradict the will of God, which is the deepest law of man's own being.

The conflicts which arise thence are among the most profound and most destructive with which we have to cope in ourselves. Not merely pain, nor frustration of particular desires, nor collision of individual wills, nor even social conflicts between competing groups. These can be endured, inside fairly wide limits, without essential disintegration of human selves;

and within somewhat narrower limits, they can even be regarded as conducive to growth toward maturity. Of the really disruptive processes which break down human selfhood, some are disasters which men suffer but do not cause—deterioration of brain cells, starvation of bodies and minds, overloading of the weak in the natural struggle for existence; but some spring directly from the self-contradiction which is sin—man's vain attempt to deny his own humanity by denying his responsibility to God. Thence arise the destructive tensions within individual selves, whose symptoms are indecision, vacillation, cowardice, anxiety and moral anguish; or, still worse, acquired cruelty and brutal callousness. Thence arise also, in large part, the insidious treacheries, prides and fears which take shape in the oppression of weaker groups by stronger; and as the stress of group conflict increases, issue in the ghastly inhumanities of despotism and war. It is this profound self-contradiction in man, this denial of the responsibility which makes him human, that breaks down selves and societies from within. . . .

Such denial is at once an act and a disposition, individual and communal. It is the disposition of every infant, every adult, every social group (including the organized churches and sects), and every culture to affirm its own wants and will as ultimate. It is also each particular decision which expresses and confirms this tendency. Mankind and every human self is "fallen" not from some original perfection (which no creature has ever had), but simply into the plight of selfhood responsible yet not truly responsive to God. This "fall" is at once a rise from and a lapse below animal innocence. Other animals cannot be "demonic." Men and their cultures not only can, but continually become so in fact. In failing or refusing to acknowledge the sovereignty of God, they deny their own nature as human, and condemn themselves thereby to inner conflict, incurable by anything they themselves can do, which tends continually to their own destruction.

This demonic tendency in human life modernism can neither understand nor cope with. By its own secularistic optimism, indeed, it helps, quite unintentionally, to foster both the self-assertiveness and the delusive self-confidence which lead again and again to the savage inhumanities which modernists, like all decent folk, deplore. This indictment rests also, of course, against organized Christendom. Professed Christians of modernistic temper share the tendency to overvalue human culture, and are all too easily sucked in to the defense of their own segment of it against other segments, subordinating the supracultural claims of the gospel to the demands of nation, folk or class. Traditionalistic Christians, in essentially similar fashion, have always been prone to confuse their acknowledged responsibility to God with the right to identify the demands of the actual church, or some part of it, with the divine will. Entrenchment of vested interests, repression of dissent, and persecutions are the not unnatural outcome; and the peculiar ruthlessness of religious wars bears witness to the liability of churches of all sorts to demonic self-exaltation. But in Christian faith, fallible men are continually being confronted anew with the majesty of God which condemns, and the love of God which can destroy, all demonries. In modernism, there is sincere abhorrence of these, but neither clear insight into their nature nor power to nullify their spells. Intelligence and good will are indispensable, but not enough. The enlistment of emotion and the other powerful drives mobilized in a transcendental religious faith is needed also.

In its understanding of man's origin, duty and present plight, therefore, Christian faith differs crucially from modernism, for all that they have much in common. They diverge, finally, in their understanding of human destiny. For modernism, as we have seen, man's destiny is in his own hands, and his salvation depends finally upon himself. This salvation is conceived in terms of earthly progress, effected through individual learnings and growth, and social amelioration. The ideal is by no means a vulgar or a trivial one, though it can easily be cheapened—more easily, perhaps, than the harsh judgments of prophetic religion (though these also are often turned into cloaks for all-too-human arrogance and cruelty). In the modernist ideal of the good life, all that is choice in human culture in the regions of intellect, aesthetic appreciation, moral sensitiveness and vigor, humane love and loyalty has its place. For progressive realization of this ideal, modernism looks to man, to his natural capacities, and the natural and social stimuli which can be made to play upon them. Education, in the broadest and most literal sense, is the way of salvation; the drawing out, in a fluid series of controlled situations, of a more and more effectively selected sum of human responses. Such progress, limited only by the duration of human life on the earth, is the modernist's ruling hope.

Once more Christian faith dissents, not because at particular points this view is bad, but because with all its good it leaves out what is basic to the whole, and thereby falsifies the total perspective. Christian faith denies, first of all, that salvation of any kind is to be had except from God. That men can learn and grow, and that they may well come better to understand and control their natural and cultural environment and themselves, it need not question. But even such learning and growth, it declares, can take place only by the grace of God. Not man but God maintains the equilibria of nature, and the compensatory rhythms of history. Cultures grow and decline not mainly because of what men do, but mainly because of what God does, around men and within them. Apart from his providence, not even the wavering steps we call human progress could be made.

But Christian faith says more: that such progress is not in itself to be called salvation. What men most deeply need is not bigger and better things, nor even finer and finer individuals and social orders. These certainly, if they can be had, but these will never be enough. What men most deeply need is blessedness, "the peace of God, which passeth all understanding." Whatever the future may hold, some men and women have found here stability and fullness of life with God. But it comes from beyond the here-and-now, to men and women for whom this present has seemed to open, like a glass become translucent, upon incomprehended depths of being and of good before which human restlessness is stilled. Not that struggle ceases, nor that sin is canceled. Man does not become a superman, immune to these things. The point is that somehow, beyond human knowing and doing, peace dawns in the midst of struggle, without in the least annulling its arduousness and pain.

A part of the truth is that *meaning* comes into the turmoil, which before it did not have, of a sort which man had neither foreseen nor specifically desired. But more than meaning. There comes conviction of the overshadowing presence of God. Not this or that detail of the present landscape need be changed. Only the whole is made new. The presence of a loved one, or devotion to a new-found cause, may similarly make nothing different and everything new within a limited area, for a while. The presence of God to those who believe makes a new heaven and a new earth, for life. It should not relax but quicken the struggle for specific human betterments; only the struggle now is lived and seen in the light of eternity. This dimension of being modernism by itself does not recognize, nor count as a factor for human destiny. To Christian faith, it is the chief thing of all.

Herein is the dilemma of humanitarian modernism: that it condemns its own best impulses to continual thwarting and recurrent disaster. This is, for Christian faith, a simple variant of the central dilemma of mankind. Man is a problem to himself not chiefly because of his more obvious vices, but because the very strength in him, the better part of his effort and aspiration, so continually goes wrong. That greed and lying should get him into trouble need be no matter for surprise. But that truth-seeking and generosity should betray him is a cruel puzzle. No wonder that in bewilderment men turn again and again from the disappointing ways of genteel culture to the primitive devotions of tribalism, war and tyranny. But that way madness lies. Inhumanity is no solution for the dilemmas of human living: for men cannot by volition cease to be men, and their efforts to do so aggravate the death-dealing conflicts among them and within them. The only real cure is for them to be made, by the grace of God, not less but more fully humane. Truth-seeking and generosity need more ample room.

SOURCE: Robert L. Calhoun, "The Dilemma of Humanitarian Modernism," in T. E. Jessop, *et al.*, *The Christian Understanding of Man*, Vol. II: Oxford Conference Books (Chicago, 1938), 68–71, 73, 75–81. Copyright Harper & Row, Publishers, Incorporated.

165. Christian Truth in Myth

In their devotion to modern scientific method, theological liberals were inclined to reject all religious conceptions which could not be rationalized in terms of natural cause-effect relations. Accordingly, such ideas as the Creation and the Fall were often dismissed as useless in theological discourse. In recent times a need has been felt to revive their usage despite their rational absurdity. No American thinker has done more to restore these old terms to theological respectability than Reinhold Niebuhr (1892—). But he has sought to restore them in the form of myth and symbol. In the year 1937 Niebuhr devoted two essays to this problem. In the first essay, "The Truth in Myths," [63] he observed that mythical elements are enshrined in every religious tradition and that the mythical heritage contains both primitive (pre-scientific) myths and permanent (supra-scientific) myths. Only the latter sort of myth, he said, could be retained in a scientific age, but liberal religion had unfortunately sacrificed all mythical elements to the impoverishment of Christian faith.

The second essay, "As Deceivers, Yet True," is printed in full in the accompanying document. As will be observed, it adumbrates most of the key ideas of Niebuhr's Christian philosophy of history, ideas which he elaborated in mature form in his Gifford Lectures, *The Nature and Destiny of Man* (1941–43), and in *Faith and History* (1949).

In his graduate study at Yale, Niebuhr was deeply influenced by two favorite professors, Frank C. Porter and Douglas C. Macintosh, both distinguished theological liberals. Yet his thirteen-year pastorate (1915–28) in the great industrial city of Detroit, Michigan, speedily opened his eyes to the weaknesses of liberalism. His very first book, *Does Civilization Need Religion?* warned that religious liberalism was far too romantic to cope with the facts of nature and of history.[64] In 1939 he sketched his pilgrimage from liberalism to Christian realism in a classic essay.[65]

In the fall of 1928 Niebuhr joined the faculty of Union Theological Seminary as professor of Christian ethics, and remained there until his retirement in 1960. His influence upon contemporary American religious thought has been unsurpassed.

DOCUMENT

Among the paradoxes with which St. Paul describes the character, the vicissitudes and the faith of the Christian ministry, the phrase "as deceivers

---

[63] "The Truth in Myths," in J. S. Bixler *et al.,* eds., *The Nature of Religious Experience* (N.Y., 1937), 117–35.

[64] *Does Civilization Need Religion?* (N.Y., 1927), 9–10. See also his diary, *Leaves from the Notebook of a Tamed Cynic* (Chicago, 1929), 90–1.

[65] "Ten Years That Shook My World," *Christian Century,* LVI (April 26, 1939), 542–6.

yet true" [66] is particularly intriguing. Following immediately after the phrase "by evil report and good report" it probably defines the evil reports which were circulated about him as charges of deception and dishonesty. This charge is refuted with his "yet true." But the question arises why the charge is admitted before it is refuted. Perhaps this is done merely for the sake of preserving an unbroken line of paradoxical statements. If this be the case, a mere canon of rhetorical style has prompted a very profound statement. For what is true in the Christian religion can be expressed only in symbols which contain a certain degree of provisional and superficial deception. Every apologist of the Christian faith might well, therefore, make the Pauline phrase his own. We do teach the truth by deception. We are deceivers, yet true.

The necessity for the deception is given in the primary characteristic of the Christian world view. Christianity does not believe that the natural, temporal and historical world is self-derived or self-explanatory. It believes that the ground and the fulfilment of existence lie outside of existence, in an eternal and divine will. But it does not hold, as do many forms of dualism, that there is an eternal world separate and distinct from the temporal world. The relation between the temporal and the eternal is dialectical. The eternal is revealed and expressed in the temporal but not exhausted in it. God is not the sum total of finite occasions and relationships. He is their ground and they are the creation of His will. But, on the other hand, the finite world is not merely a corrupt emanation from the ideal and eternal. Consequently the relation of time and eternity cannot be expressed in simple rational terms. It can be expressed only in symbolic terms. A rational or logical expression of the relationship invariably leads either to a pantheism in which God and the world are identified, and the temporal in its totality is equated with the eternal; or in which they are separated so that a false supernaturalism emerges, a dualism between an eternal and spiritual world without content and a temporal world without meaning or significance.

I

Before analysing the deceptive symbols which the Christian faith uses to express this dimension of eternity in time, it might be clarifying to recall that artists are forced to use deceptive symbols when they seek to portray two dimensions of space upon the single dimension of a flat canvas. Every picture which suggests depth and perspective draws angles not as they are but as they appear to the eye when it looks into depth. Parallel lines are not drawn as parallel lines but are made to appear as if they converged on the horizon; for so they appear to the eye when it envisages a total perspective. Only the most primitive art and the drawings made by very small children reveal the mistake of portraying things in their true proportions rather than as they are seen. The necessity of picturing things as they seem

[66] II Cor. 6:8.

rather than as they are, in order to record on one dimension what they are in two dimensions, is a striking analogy, in the field of space, of the problem of religion in the sphere of time.

Time is a succession of events. Yet mere succession is not time. Time has reality only through a meaningful relationship of its successions. Therefore time is real only as it gives successive expressions of principles and powers which lie outside of it. Yet every suggestion of the principle of a process must be expressed in terms of the temporal process, and every idea of the God who is the ground of the world must be expressed in some term taken from the world. The temporal process is like the painter's flat canvas. It is one dimension upon which two dimensions must be recorded. This can be done only by symbols which deceive for the sake of truth.

Great art faces the problem of the two dimensions of time as well as the two dimensions of space. The portrait artist, for instance, is confronted with the necessity of picturing a character. Human personality is more than a succession of moods. The moods of a moment are held together in a unity of thought and feeling, which gives them, however seemingly capricious, a considerable degree of consistency. The problem of the artist is to portray the inner consistency of a character which is never fully expressed in any one particular mood or facial expression. This can be done only by falsifying physiognomic details. Portraiture is an art which can never be sharply distinguished from caricature. A moment of time in a personality can be made to express what transcends the moment of time only if the moment is not recorded accurately. It must be made into a symbol of something beyond itself.

This technique of art explains why art is more closely related to religion than science. Art describes the world not in terms of its exact relationships. It constantly falsifies these relationships, as analysed by science, in order to express their total meaning.

II

The Christian religion may be characterised as one which has transmuted primitive religious and artistic myths and symbols without fully rationalising them. Buddhism is much more rational than Christianity. In consequence Buddhism finds the finite and temporal world evil. Spinozism is a more rational version of God and the world than the biblical account; but it finds the world unqualifiedly good and identical with God. In the biblical account the world is good because God created it; but the world is not God. Every Christian myth, in one way or another, expresses both the meaningfulness and the incompleteness of the temporal world, both the majesty of God and his relation to the world.

We are deceivers yet true, when we say that God created the world. Creation is a mythical idea which cannot be fully rationalised. It has therefore been an offense to the philosophers who, with the scientists, have substituted the idea of causality for it. They have sought to explain each subsequent event by a previous cause. Such an explanation of the world leads the more naïve thinkers to a naturalism which regards the world as self-explanatory because every event can be derived from a previous one. The more sophisticated philosophers will at least, with Aristotle, seek for a first cause which gives an original impetus to the whole chain of causation. But such a first cause does not have a living relationship with the events of nature and history. It does not therefore account for the emergence of novelty in each new event. No new fact or event in history is an arbitrary novelty. It is always related to a previous event. But it is a great error to imagine that this relationship completely accounts for the new emergence. In both nature and history each new thing is only one of an infinite number of possibilities which might have emerged at that particular juncture. It is for this reason that, though we can trace a series of causes in retrospect, we can never predict the future with accuracy. There is a profound arbitrariness in every given fact, which rational theories of causation seek to obscure. Thus they regard a given form of animal life as rational because they can trace it historically to another form or relate it in terms of genus and species to other types of life. Yet none of these relationships, whether historical or schematic, can eliminate the profound arbitrariness of the givenness of things.

It is therefore true, to account for the meaningfulness of life in terms of the relation of every thing to a creative centre and source of meaning. But the truth of creation can be expressed only in terms which outrage reason. Involved in the idea of creation is the concept of making something out of nothing. The *Shepherd* of Hermas declares "First of all believe that God is one, who created and set in order all things and caused the universe to exist out of nothing." This was the constant reiteration of Christian belief, until in very modern times it was thought possible to substitute the idea of evolutionary causation for the idea of creation. The idea of creation out of nothing is profoundly ultrarational; for human reason can deal only with the stuff of experience, and in experience the previous event and cause are seen, while the creative source of novelty is beyond experience.

The idea of creation relates the ground of existence to existence and is therefore mythical rather than rational. The fact that it is not a rational idea does not make it untrue or deceptive. But since it is not rational it is a temptation to deceptions. Every mythical idea contains a primitive deception and a more ultimate one. The primitive error is to regard the early form in which the myth is stated as authoritative. Thus the Christian religion is always tempted to insist that belief in creation also involves belief in an actual forming of man out of a lump of clay, or in an actual creative activity of six days. It is to this temptation that biblical literalism succumbs. But there is also a more ultimate source of error in the mythical statement of religious belief. That is to regard the relation of each fact and event in history to a Divine Creator as obviating the possibility of an organic relation to other facts and events according to a natural order. By this error, which Etienne Gilson [67] calls "theologism," Christian theology is constantly tempted to deny the significance of the natural order, and to confuse the scientific analysis of its relationships. At the rise of modern thought Malebranche developed a doctrine of "occasionalism" which expressed this error of Christian theology in its most consistent form. But it has been a persistent error in Christian thought and one which arises naturally out [of] the mythical statement of the idea of creation. The error is analogous to that of certain types of art which completely falsify the natural relations of objects in order to express their ultimate significance.

We are deceivers, yet true, when we say that man fell into evil. The story of the fall of man in the Garden of Eden is a primitive myth which modern theology has been glad to disavow, for fear that modern culture might regard belief in it as a proof of the obscurantism of religion. In place of it we have substituted various accounts of the origin and the nature of evil in human life. Most of these accounts, reduced to their essentials, attribute sin to the inertia of nature, or the hypertrophy of impulses, or to the defect of reason (ignorance), and thereby either explicitly or implicitly place their trust in developed reason as the guarantor of goodness. In all of these accounts the essential point in the nature of human evil is missed, namely, that it arises from the very freedom of reason with which man is endowed. Sin is not so much a consequence of natural impulses, which in animal life do not lead to sin, as of the freedom by which man is able to throw the harmonies of nature out of joint. He disturbs the harmony of nature when he centres his life about one particular impulse (sex or the possessive impulse, for instance) or when he tries to make himself, rather than God, the centre of existence. This egoism is sin in its quintessential form. It is not a defect of creation but a defect which becomes possible because man has been endowed with a freedom not known in the rest of creation.

The idea of the fall is subject to the error of regarding the primitive myth of the garden, the apple and the serpent, as historically true. But even if this error is not committed, Christian thought is still tempted to regard the fall as an historical occurrence. The fall is not historical. It does not take place in any concrete human act. It is the presupposition of such acts. It deals with an area of human freedom which, when once expressed in terms of an act, is always historically related to a previous act or predisposition. External descriptions of human behaviour are therefore always deterministic. That is the deception into which those are betrayed who seek to avoid the errors of introspection by purely external descriptions of human behaviour. What Christianity means by the idea of the fall can only be known in introspection. The consciousness of sin and the consciousness of God are inextricably involved with each other. Only as the full

[67] In his *Unity of Philosophical Experience.* [Niebuhr]

dimension of human existence is measured, which includes not only the dimension of historical breadth but the dimension of trans-historical freedom, does the idea of the fall of man achieve significance and relevance.

It is interesting to note that Christian theology has usually regarded the fall as an historical occurrence, even when it did not accept the primitive myth of the Garden of Eden. It therefore spoke of a perfection before the fall as if that too were an historical era. Even the sophisticated dialectical theology of Barth and his school speaks of the perfection before the fall as historical, and consequently elaborates a doctrine of human sinfulness which approaches, and sometimes surpasses, the extremism of the historic doctrine of total depravity. The perfection before the fall is an ideal possibility which men can comprehend but not realise. The perfection before the fall is, in a sense, the perfection before the act. Thus we are able to conceive of a perfectly disinterested justice; but when we act our own achievements will fall short of this standard. The rationalists always assume that, since men are able to conceive of perfect standards of justice, such standards will be realised as soon as all men become intelligent enough to conceive them. They do not realise that intelligence offers no guarantee of the realisation of a standard, and that the greatest idealists, as well as the most cynical realists or the most ignorant victims of an immediate situation, fall short in their action; nor that such falling short arises not simply from the defect of the mind but from an egoistic corruption of the heart. Self intrudes itself into every ideal, when thought gives place to action. The deceptions to which the idea of the fall give rise are many; and all of them have been the basis of error at some time or other in the history of Christian theology. We are deceivers, yet true in clinging to the idea of the fall as a symbol of the origin and the nature of evil in human life.

III

We are deceivers, yet true, when we affirm that God became man to redeem the world from sin. The idea of eternity entering time is intellectually absurd. This absurdity is proved to the hilt by all the theological dogmas which seek to make it rational. The dogmas which seek to describe the relation of God the Father (the God who does not enter history) and God the son (the God of history) all insist that the Son is equal to the Father and is yet not equal to Him. In the same way all the doctrines of the two natures of Christ assert that he is not less divine for being human and temporal and not less human and temporal for being fully divine. Quite obviously it is impossible to assert that the eternal ground of existence has entered existence and not sacrificed its eternal and unconditioned quality, without outraging every canon of reason. Reason may deal with the conditioned realities of existence in their relationships and it may even point to the fathomless depth of creativity out of which existential forms are born. But it cannot assert that the Divine Creator has come into creation without losing His unconditioned character. The truth that the Word was made flesh outrages all the canons by which truth is usually judged. Yet it is the truth. The whole character of the Christian religion is involved in that affirmation. It asserts that God's word is relevant to human life. It declares that an event in history can be of such a character as to reveal the character of history itself; that without such a revelation the character of history cannot be known. It is not possible to arrive at an understanding of the meaning of life and history without such a revelation. No induction from empirical facts can yield a conclusion about ultimate meaning because every process of induction presupposes some canon and criterion of meaning. That is why metaphysical systems which pretend to arrive at ultimate conclusions about the meaning of life are either covert theologies which unconsciously rationalise some revelation, accepted by faith; or they merely identify rationality with meaning, a procedure which forces them into either pantheism or acosmism. They must either identify the world with God on the supposition that temporal events, fully understood in all their relationships, are transmuted from finiteness and contingency into an unconditioned totality; or they must find the existential world evil in its finiteness because it does not conform in its contingent, existential relationships to a rational idea of unity.

For Christian faith the world is neither perfect nor meaningless. The God who created it also reveals Himself in it. He reveals Himself not only in a general revelation, that is, in the sense that His creation is His revelation; but in a special revelation. A general revelation can only point to the reality of God but not to His particular attributes. A theology which believes only in a general revelation must inevitably culminate in pantheism; because a God who is merely the object of human knowledge and not a subject who communicates with man by His own initiative is something less than God. A knowledge of God which depends only upon a study of the behaviour of the world must inevitably be as flat as the knowledge of any person would be, which depended merely upon the observation of the person's behaviour. The study of human behaviour cannot give a full clue to the meaning of a personality, because there is a depth of freedom in every personality which can only communicate itself in its own "word." That word may be related to an analysis of behaviour and become the principle of interpretation for the analysis. But it is not the consequence of the analysis. Without such a word the picture of any personality would be flat, as the interpretations of the divine which eliminate revelation are flat.

In Christian thought Christ is both the perfect man, "the second Adam" who had restored the perfection of what man was and ought to be; and the Son of God, who transcends all possibilities of human life. It is this idea which theology sought to rationalise in the doctrines of the two natures of Christ. It cannot be rationalised and yet it is a true idea. Human life stands in infinity. Everything it touches turns into infinity. Every moral standard, rigorously analysed, proves to be no permanently valid standard at all short of perfect and infinite love. The only adequate norm of human conduct is love of God and of man, through which all men are perfectly related to each other, because they are all related in terms of perfect obedience and love to the centre and source of their existence. In the same way all evil in human life is derived from an effort to transmute finite values into infinities, to seek infinite power, and infinite wealth and infinite gratification of desire. There is no sharp line between the infinity in man and the infinity beyond man and yet there is a very sharp line. Man always remains a creature and his sin arises from the fact that he is not satisfied to remain so. He seeks to turn creatureliness into infinity; whereas his salvation depends upon subjecting his creaturely weakness to the infinite good of God. Christ, who expresses both the infinite possibilities of love in human life and the infinite possibilities beyond human life, is thus a true revelation of the total situation in which human life stands. There is every possibility of illusion and deception in this statement of the Christian faith. Men may be deceived by the primitive myth of the Virgin Birth and seek to comprehend as a pure historical fact, what is significant precisely because it points beyond history. Or they may seek to explain the dogma of the Incarnation in terms which will make it an article in a philosophical creed. Such efforts will lead to varied deceptions; but the deceptions cannot destroy the truth of the Incarnation.

Yet the revelation of God in the Incarnation is not of itself the redemption. Christianity believes that Christ died to save men from sin. It has a gospel which contains a crucifixion as well as an incarnation, a cross as well as a manger. This doctrine of the atoning death of the Son of God upon the cross has led to many theological errors, among them to theories of substitutionary atonement which outrage the moral sense. There is in fact no theory of the atonement which is quite as satisfying as the simple statements of the vicarious death of Christ in the Gospels. This may mean that faith is able to sense and appropriate an ultimate truth too deep for human reason. This is the foolishness of God which is wiser than the wisdom of men. The modern world has found not only the theories of atonement but the idea of atonement itself absurd. It rebelled not only against theories of a sacrifice which ransomed man from the devil's clutches or of a sacrifice which appeased the anger of a vindictive divine Father; it regarded the very idea of reconciliation between God and man as absurd.

The reason for this simple rejection of the Christian drama of salvation lies in the modern conception of human nature, rather than in any rejection of the theological absurdities attached to the idea of Christ's atoning death. Modern man does not regard life as tragic. He thinks that history is the record of the progressive triumph of good over evil. He does not recognise the simple but profound truth that man's life remains self-contradictory in its sin, no matter how high human culture rises; that the highest expression of human spirituality, therefore, contains also the subtlest form of human sin. The failure to recognise this fact gives modern culture a non-tragic conception of human history. To recognise this fact, and nothing more, is to reduce human history to simple tragedy. But the basic message of Christian faith is a message of hope in tragedy. It declares that when the Christ, by whom the world was made, enters the world, the world will not receive him. "He came unto his own and his own received him not." Human existence denies its own deepest and most essential nature. That is tragic. But when that fact is understood, when men cease to make the standards of a sinful existence the norms of life but accept its true norm, even though they fail to obey it, their very contrition opens the eyes of faith. This is the Godly sorrow that worketh repentance. Out of this despair hope is born. The hope is simply this: that the contradictions of human existence, which man cannot surmount, are swallowed up in the life of God Himself. The God of Christian faith is not only creator but redeemer. He does not allow human existence to end tragically. He snatches victory from defeat. He is Himself defeated in history but He is also victorious in that defeat.

There are theologies which interpret this article in the Christian creed as if life were really pure tragedy, but for the atoning love of Christ. But the fact is that the atoning death of Christ is the revelation of ultimate reality which may become the principle of interpretation for all human experience. It is not a principle yielded by experience, but it is applicable to experience and validated by it. It is an actual fact that human life, which is always threatened and periodically engulfed by the evil which human sin creates, is also marvellously redeemed by the transmutation of evil into good. This transmutation is not a human but a divine possibility. No man can, by taking thought, turn evil into good. Yet in the total operations of providence in history this transmutation occurs. The Christian faith consequently does not defy the tragic facts of human existence by a single victory over tragedy; nor does it flee the tragedy of temporal existence into a heavenly escape. These forms of the Christian faith are deceptions.

Most profoundly the atonement of Christ is a revelation of what life actually is. It is tragic from the standpoint of human striving. Human striving can do no better than the Roman law and the Hebraic religion, both the highest of their kind, through which the Lord was crucified. Yet this crucifixion becomes the revelation of that in human history which transcends human striving. And without this revelation, that which is beyond tragedy in life could not have been apprehended. Without the cross men are beguiled by what is good in human existence into a false optimism and by what is tragic into despair. The message of the Son of God who dies upon the cross, of a God who transcends history and is yet in history, who condemns and judges sin and yet suffers with and for the sinner, this message is the truth about life. It cannot be stated without deceptions; but the truths which seek to avoid the deceptions are immeasurably less profound. Compared to this Christ who died for men's sins upon the cross, Jesus, the good man who tells all men to be good, is more solidly historical. But he is the bearer of no more than a pale truism.

We are deceivers, yet true, when we declare that Christ will come again at the last judgment, that he who was defeated in history will ultimately triumph over it, will become its judge and the author of its new life. No doctrine of Christianity has led to more deceptions and illusions than the hope of the second coming of Christ. This doctrine has been so frequently appropriated and exploited by sectarian fanatics that the church has been a little ashamed of it. We have made even less of the apocalyptic literature into which Hebraic prophecy culminated and in which Christ was nurtured. The imagery of this literature is so extravagant, and at times so fantastic, that Christian thinkers have been content, on the whole, to leave it alone. Yet the doctrine of Christ's second coming involves all the profoundest characteristics of the Christian religion. It is this doctrine which distinguishes Christianity both from naturalistic utopianism and from Hellenistic otherworldiness [sic]. In it the Christian hope of the fulfilment of life is expressed paradoxically and dialectically, holding fast to its essential conception of the relation of time to eternity. History is not regarded as meaningless, as in Greek thought, particularly in later neo-Platonism. For this reason the realm of fulfilment is not above history, in some heaven in which pure form is abstracted from the concrete content of historical existence. The realm of fulfilment is at the end of history. This symbolises that fulfilment both transcends and is relevant to historical forms. The end of history is not a point in history.

The chronological illusion, that it is a point in history, so characteristic of all myths which point to the trans-historical by a symbol of time, is particularly fruitful of error in the doctrine of the second coming. It has led to fantastic sectarian illusions of every type. Yet it is significant that the dispossessed and disinherited have been particularly prone to these illusions, because they were anxious to express the Christian hope of fulfilment in social as well as in individual terms. Sectarian apocalypticism is closely related to modern proletarian radicalism, which is a secularised form of the latter. In both, the individualism of Christian orthodoxy is opposed with conceptions which place the corporate enterprises of mankind, as well as individuals, under an ultimate judgment and under ultimate possibilities of fulfilment. In these secular and apocalyptic illusions the end of time is a point in time beyond which there will be an unconditioned society. But there is truth in the illusions.

The more bourgeois version of this illusory apocalypticism is the idea of progress in which the unconditioned ground of history is explicitly denied, but an unconditioned fulfilment in terms of infinite duration is implicitly affirmed. The Kingdom of God, as the absolute reign of God, is transmuted into a principle of development, immanent in history itself. Against such a conception Christian thought is forced to maintain as rigorous opposition as against dualistic otherworldliness. The ultimate fulfilment of life transcends the possibilities of human history. There is no hope of overcoming the contradictions, in which life stands, in history. But since these contradictions are not the consequence of mere finiteness and temporality, but the fruits of human freedom, they are not overcome merely by translating the temporal into the eternal. Since they persist in all human striving, fulfilment is not a human but a divine possibility. God must overcome this inescapable contradiction.

Therefore it is Christ who is both the judge of the world and the author of its fulfilment; for Christ is the symbol both of what man ought to be and of what God is beyond man. In Christ we have a revelation of both the human possibilities which are to be fulfilled and the divine power which will fulfil them. In Christ, too, we have the revelation of the significance of human history and of the ground of its meaning which transcends history.

We are therefore deceivers, yet true, when we insist that the Christ who died on the cross will come again in power and glory, that he will judge the quick and the dead and will establish his Kingdom. We do not believe that the human enterprise will have a tragic conclusion; but the ground of our hope lies not in human capacity but in divine power and mercy, in the character of the ultimate reality, which carries the human enterprise. This hope does not imply that fulfilment means the negation of what is established and developed in human history. Each moment of history stands under the possibility of an ultimate fulfilment. The fulfilment is neither a negation of its essential character nor yet a further development of its own inherent capacities. It is rather a completion of its essence by an annihilation of the contradictions which sin has introduced into human life.

> SOURCE: Reinhold Niebuhr, "As Deceivers, Yet True," *Beyond Tragedy* (N.Y., 1937), 3-24. Copyright 1937 Charles Scribner's Sons. Reprinted by permission of the publisher.

166. *"The New Being"*

Nothing is more distinctive of post-liberal theology than its quest for a true understanding of the person and work of Jesus Christ. Herein lies one of the most original contributions of Paul J. Tillich (1886—). To know Tillich at all is to associate him with the potent words, "The New Being." In the fall of 1950 he published a little classic in *Religion in Life* on the meaning of those words. The document below presents that magnificent essay in full. It adumbrates all the distinctive ideas of the author's Christological thought, ideas which he later fully elaborated in *Existence and the Christ* (1957). Summarizing the soteriological role of the Christ in the latter volume, Tillich said: "It is the Christ who brings the New Being, who saves men from the old being, that is, from existential estrangement and its self-destructive consequences." [68]

Before coming to America in 1933, Tillich had taught in four German universities: Berlin, Marburg, Dresden, and Frankfurt. From 1933 to 1955 he taught philosophical theology at Union Theological Seminary in New York. Between 1955 and 1962 he was University Professor at Harvard. In the fall of 1962 he accepted the John Nuveen Professorship in the Divinity School of the University of Chicago. In addition to lecturing widely in colleges and universities, Tillich has published numerous works which have attracted widespread scholarly attention, among them *The Interpretation of History* (1936), *The Protestant Era* (1948), *The Courage to Be* (1952), and *Systematic Theology* (2 vols., 1951–57). As Barth is contemporary Protestantism's greatest kerygmatic theologian, so Tillich is its greatest philosophical theologian. [69]

DOCUMENT

If I were asked to sum up the Christian message for our time in two words, I would say with Paul, it is the message of a "New Creation." Let me repeat one of his sentences (II Cor. 5:17) in the words of an exact translation: "If anyone is in union with Christ he is a new being; the old state of things has passed away; there is a new state of things." Christianity is the message of the New Creation, the New Being, the New Reality which has appeared with the appearance of Jesus who for this reason, and just for this reason, is called the Christ. For the Christ, the Messiah, the selected and anointed One, is he who brings the new state of things.

We all live in the old state of things, and the question asked of us is whether we *also* participate in the new state of things. We belong to the old creation, and the demand made upon us by Christianity is that we *also* participate in the new creation. We have known ourselves in our old being, and we have to ask ourselves whether we also have experienced something of a new being.

What is this new being? Paul answers first by saying what it is *not*. It is neither circumcision nor uncircumcision, he says (Gal. 6:5). For Paul and for the readers of his letter this meant something very definite. It meant that neither to be a Jew nor to be a pagan is ultimately important; that only one thing counts, namely, the union with him in whom the new reality is present. Circumcision or uncircumcision, what does that mean for *us?* Again it can mean something very definite, but at the same time something very universal. It means that no religion as such produces the new being. Circumcision is a religious rite, observed by the Jews; sacrifices

[68] *Systematic Theology*, Vol. II: *Existence and the Christ* (Chicago, 1957), 150.

[69] For an appraisal of Tillich's contribution to religious thought, see Charles W. Kegley and Robert W. Bretall, eds., *The Theology of Paul Tillich* (N.Y., 1952).

are religious rites, observed by the pagans; baptism is a religious rite, observed by the Christians. All these rites do not matter, only a new creation. And since these rites stand, in the words of Paul, for the whole religion to which they belong, we can say: no religion matters, only a new state of things. Let us think about this striking assertion of Paul. What it first says is that Christianity is more than a religion; it is the message of a new creation. Christianity as a religion is not important. It is like circumcision or like uncircumcision: no more, no less!

Are we able even to imagine the consequences of the apostolic pronouncement for our situation? Christianity in the present world encounters several forms of circumcision and uncircumcision. Circumcision can stand today for everything called religion, uncircumcision for everything called secular but making half-religious claims. There are the great religions besides Christianity—Hinduism, Buddhism, Islam, and the remnants of classical Judaism; they have their myths and their rites—so to speak, their "circumcision"—which gives each of them their distinction. There are the secular movements: Fascism and Communism, Secular Humanism, and Ethical Idealism. They try to avoid myths and rites; they represent, so to speak, uncircumcision. Nevertheless, they also claim ultimate truth and demand complete devotion. How shall Christianity face them? Shall Christianity tell them: come to us, we are a better religion, our kind of circumcision or uncircumcision is higher than yours? Shall we praise Christianity, our way of life, the religious as well as the secular? Shall we make of the Christian message a success story, and tell them, like advertisers: try it with us, and you will see how important Christianity is for everybody? Some missionaries and some ministers and some Christian laymen use these methods. They show a total misunderstanding of Christianity.

The apostle who was a missionary and a minister and a layman all at once says something different. He says: no religion matters, neither ours nor yours. But I want to tell you that something has happened that matters, something that judges you and me, your religion and my religion. A new creation has occurred, a new being has appeared; and we are all asked to participate in it. And so we should say to the pagans and Jews wherever we meet them: don't compare your religion and our religion, your rites and our rites, your prophets and our prophets, your priests and our priests, the pious amongst you and the pious amongst us. All this is of no avail! And above all don't think that we want to convert you to English or American Christianity, or to the religion of the Western World. We do not want to convert you to us, not even to the best of us. This would be of no avail. We only want to show you something we have seen and to tell you something we have heard: that in the midst of the old creation there is a new creation, and that this new creation is manifest in Jesus who is called the Christ.

And when we meet Fascists and Communists, scientific humanists and ethical idealists, we should say to them: don't boast too much that you have no rites and myths, that you are free from superstitions, that you are perfectly reasonable, uncircumcised in every sense. In the first place, you also have your rites and myths, your bits of circumcision; they are even very important to you. But even if you were completely free from them, you have no reason to point to your *un*circumcision. It is of no avail. Don't think that we want to convert you away from your secular state to a religious state, that we want to make you religious and members of a very high religion—the Christian—and of a very great denomination within it, namely, our own. This would be of no avail. We want only to communicate to you an experience we have had, that here and there in the world and now and then in ourselves is a new creation, usually hidden, but sometimes manifest, and certainly manifest in Jesus who is called the Christ.

This is the way we should speak to all those outside the Christian realm, whether they are religious or secular. And we should not be worried too much about the Christian religion, about the state of the churches, about membership and doctrines, about institutions and ministers, about sermons and sacraments. This is circumcision; and the lack of it, the secularization which today is spreading all over the world, is uncircumcision. Both are nothing, of no importance, if the ultimate question is asked—the question of a new reality. *This* question, however, is of infinite importance. About it we should worry more than anything else between heaven and earth. The new creation, this is our ultimate concern; this should be our infinite passion—the infinite passion of every human being. This matters; this alone matters ultimately. In comparison with it everything else, even religion or nonreligion, even Christianity or non-Christianity, matters very little—and ultimately nothing.

And now let me boast for a moment about the fact that we are Christians and let us become fools by boasting, as Paul called himself when he started boasting. It is the greatness of Christianity that it can see how small it is. The importance of being a Christian is that we can stand the insight that it is of no importance. It is the spiritual power of religion that he who is religious can fearlessly look at the vanity of religion. It is the maturest fruit of Christian understanding to understand that Christianity, as such, is of no avail. This is boasting, not personal boasting, but boasting about Christianity. As boasting it is foolishness. But as boasting about the fact that there is nothing to boast about, it is wisdom and maturity. Having as having not, this is the right attitude toward everything great and wonderful in life—even religion and Christianity. But it is not the right attitude toward the new creation. Toward it the right attitude is, longing for it passionately, infinitely.

And now we ask again: what is this new being? The new being is not something that simply replaces the old. It is a renewal of the old which has been corrupted, distorted, split, almost destroyed—but not wholly destroyed. Salvation does not destroy creation; it transforms the old creation into a new one. Therefore we can speak of the new in terms of a *re*-newal, threefold—*re*-conciliation, *re*-union, *re*-surrection.

I

In II Cor. 5, Paul combines new creation with reconciliation. The message of reconciliation is: *be* reconciled to God. Cease to be hostile to him, for he is never hostile to you. The message of reconciliation is not that God needs to be reconciled. How could he be? Since he is the source and power of reconciliation, who could reconcile him? Pagans and Jews and Christians, all of us have tried and are trying to reconcile him by rites and sacraments, by prayers and services, by moral behavior and works of charity. But if we try this, if we try to give something to him, to show good deeds which may appease him, we fail. It is never enough; we never can satisfy him because there is an infinite demand upon us. And since we cannot appease him, we grow hostile toward him.

Have you ever noticed how much hostility against God dwells in the depth of the good and honest people, in those who excel in works of charity, in piety and religious zeal? This cannot be otherwise; for one is hostile, consciously or unconsciously, toward those by whom one feels rejected. Everybody is in this predicament, whether he calls that which rejects him "God," or "nature," or "destiny," or "social conditions." Everybody carries a hostility toward the existence into which he has been thrown, toward the hidden powers which determine his life and that of the universe, toward that which makes him guilty and threatens him with destruction because he has become guilty. We all feel rejected and hostile toward what has rejected us. We all try to appease it, and, in failing, we become more hostile. This happens often unnoticed by ourselves. But there are two symptoms which we hardly can avoid noticing: the hostility against ourselves and the hostility against others. One speaks so often of pride and arrogance and self-certainty and complacency in people. But this is in most cases the superficial level of their being. Below this, on a deeper level, there is self-rejection, disgust, and even hate of oneself.

Be reconciled to God. That means, at the same time, be reconciled to ourselves. But we are not; we try to appease ourselves. We try to make ourselves more acceptable to our own judgment and, when we fail, we grow more hostile toward ourselves. And he who feels rejected by God and who rejects himself feels also rejected by the others. As he grows hostile toward destiny and hostile toward himself, he also grows hostile toward other men. If we often are horrified by the unconscious or conscious hostility people betray toward us or by our own hostility toward people whom we believe we love, let us not forget: they feel rejected by us; we feel rejected by them. They tried hard to make themselves acceptable to us, and they failed. We tried hard to make ourselves acceptable to them, and we failed. And their and our hostility grew.

Be reconciled to God. That means, at the same time, be reconciled with the others. But it does *not* mean, try to reconcile the others, as it does not mean, try to reconcile yourselves, try to reconcile God. You will fail. This is the message: a new reality has appeared in which you *are* reconciled. To enter the new being we do not need to show anything. We must only be open to be grasped by it, although we have nothing to show.

II

Being reconciled, that is the first mark of the new reality. And being reunited is its second mark. Reconciliation makes reunion possible. The new creation is the reality in which the separated is reunited. The new being is manifest in the Christ because in him the separation never overcame the unity between him and God, between him and mankind, between him and himself. This fact gives his picture in the Gospels the overwhelming and inexhaustible power. In him we look at a human life that maintained the union in spite of everything that drove him into separation. He represents and mediates the power of the new being because he represents and mediates the power of an undisrupted union. Where the new reality appears one feels united with God, the ground and meaning of one's existence. One has what has been called the love of one's destiny, and what, today, we might call the courage to take upon ourselves our own anxiety. Then one has the astonishing experience of feeling reunited with oneself. There is a center, a direction, a meaning for life.

All healing—bodily and mental—creates this reunion of oneself with oneself. Where there is real healing, *there* is the new being, the new creation. But real healing is not where only a part of body or mind is reunited with the whole, but where the whole itself, our whole being, our whole personality is united with itself. The new creation is healing creation because it creates reunion with oneself. And it creates reunion with the others.

Nothing is more distinctive of the old being than the separation of man from man. Nothing is more passionately demanded than social healing, than the new being within history. Religion and Christianity are under strong accusation that they have not brought reunion into human history. Who could deny the truth of this challenge? Nevertheless, mankind still lives; and it could not live any more if the power of separation had not permanently been conquered by the power of reunion, of healing, of the new creation. Where one is grasped by a human face as human, although one has to overcome personal distaste, or racial strangeness, or national conflicts, or the differences of sex, of age, of beauty, of strength, of knowledge, and all the other innumerable causes of separation—*there* the new creation happens! Mankind lives because this happens again and again.

And if the church which is the assembly of God has an ultimate significance, this is its significance: that here the reunion of man to man is pronounced and confessed and realized, even if in fragments and weaknesses and distortions. The church is the place where the reunion of man with man is an actual event, though the Church of God is permanently betrayed by the Christian churches. But, although betrayed and expelled, the new creation saves and preserves that by which it is betrayed and expelled: churches, mankind, and history.

III

The church, like all its members, relapses from the new into the old being. Therefore, the third mark of the new creation is re-surrection. The word "resurrection" has for many people the connotation of dead bodies leaving their graves or other fanciful imagery. But resurrection means the victory of the new state of things, the new being born out of the death of the old. Resurrection is not an event that might happen in some remote future, but it is the power of the new being to create life out of death, here and now, today and tomorrow. Where there is a new being, *there* is resurrection—namely, the creation into eternity out of every moment of time. The old being has the mark of disintegration and death. The new being puts a new mark over the old one. Out of disintegration and death something is born of eternal significance. That which is immersed in dissolution emerges in a new creation. Resurrection happens *now,* or it does not happen at all. It happens in us and around us, in soul and history, in nature and universe.

Reconciliation, reunion, resurrection, this is the new creation, the new being, the new state of things. Do we participate in it? The message of Christianity is not Christianity, but a new reality. A new state of things has appeared, it still appears; it is hidden and visible, it is there and it is here. Accept it, enter into it, let it grasp you.

SOURCE: Paul J. Tillich, "The New Being," *Religion in Life,* XIX (Autumn, 1950), 511-7. Copyright 1950 by Pierce and Smith. Reprinted with minor changes in *The New Being* published by Charles Scribner's Sons and used with their permission.

167. For a New Liberalism

No American scholar of our time has been more sensitive to the changing currents in religious thought than Walter Marshall Horton 1895—). In his first major book, *Theism and the Modern Mood* (1930), he reflected the prevailing faith in empirical theological method, but in his *Realistic Theology* (1934) he radically altered his earlier viewpoint. Yet by mid-century he had become fearful that neo-orthodoxy was veering too far toward old-line orthodoxy and sounded an alarm in the Eugene Lyman Lecture, "Liberalism Old and New," delivered at Sweet Briar College, Virginia, in 1952. That excellent discourse deserves to be better known. The gist of it is reprinted in the following document.

It is only fair to say that all along Walter Horton had insisted that the old liberalism involved certain values of permanent worth; indeed, in his *Realistic Theology* he elaborated those values in some detail.[70] Yet the rest of the book tended to submerge those values. At any rate, Horton has written a good deal in recent years designed to create a countermovement against neo-orthodoxy.

A native of Massachusetts, Horton graduated from Harvard in 1917, after which he pursued advanced studies at Union Theological Seminary and Columbia University. Since 1925 he has taught systematic theology at Oberlin Graduate School of Theology. Publishing his first article when only twenty-four years old, he has always been a prolific writer. Among his better known works, besides those already mentioned, are *A Psychological Approach to Theology* (1931), *Contemporary Continental Theology* (1936), *Contemporary English Theology* (1938), *Our Eternal Contemporary* (1942), and *Christian Theology: An Ecumenical Approach* (1955; rev. ed., 1958).

DOCUMENT

I hold no brief for the continuance, unaltered, of the older type of liberalism that prevailed at the turn of the century. As far back as 1934 I became convinced of its radical defects, and announced its demise (prematurely, some critics have said) without too much regret. What I do believe to be possible and needful in this age of neo-orthodox hegemony is the development of a *new liberalism,* relevant to the new situation, which would continue the old liberalism somewhat as the butterfly continues the caterpillar, sloughing off its old dried-up skin but perpetuating its vital principle.

The *possibility* of such a new liberalism first appeared to me ten years ago, when I made a study of Professor Lyman's whole theological development for the symposium on *Liberal Theology* issued in his honor after his retirement. It became very clear in the course of this study that Lyman was a liberal from start to finish, but never fell into the glaring errors usually denounced by the critics of the older liberalism; and toward the end of his teaching career he analyzed the "Permanent Values in Liberal Christian Theology" [71] in terms that foreshadowed a new formulation of the liberal position.

The *need* of such a reformulated liberalism has become particularly evident to me since the Second World War. A mood of pessimism and futility has descended upon our age, from which neo-orthodoxy—which did so much to rescue us from Utopian optimism and foolish complacency in the critical years before that war—has so far been unable to deliver us.

[70] *Realistic Theology* (N.Y., 1934), 16–34. See also his autobiographical essay, "Between Liberalism and the New Orthodoxy," *Christian Century,* LVI (May 17, 1939), 637–40.

[71] *Union Review,* May, 1940, pp. 5 et seq. [Horton]

Neo-orthodoxy has probably not yet rendered its full potential services to Christian thought, especially in America; but it needs a new strong opposition party to point out its dangers and correct its defects, just as the old liberalism needed opposition and correction, twenty-five years ago. . . .

I suggest that the best way to define the needed new position is first to describe the old liberalism in its popular form, at the turn of the century; then to consider wherein the new orthodoxy justly criticized and corrected the older liberal view, in the period following the First World War; finally to consider how the new liberalism needs to criticize and correct the new orthodoxy in its turn, while taking due account of its lasting contributions to Christian thought. We shall follow this sequence four times, corresponding to the four "permanent values" which Professor Lyman saw in liberal Christian theology, and corresponding also to the four major themes with which all religious thought is necessarily concerned: (1) *Faith and Reason,* or the Pathways to Religious Knowledge; (2) *God,* or the Ground of Trust; (3) *Christ,* or the Way of Salvation; and (4) the *Kingdom of God,* or the Goal of Hope.

1. *Faith and Reason.*

The old liberalism certainly *intended* to maintain what Lyman calls "a close and vital relation between faith and reason." . . .[72]

I fear it must be admitted that in its popular form, the old liberalism did not maintain a proper balance between faith and reason, but tended to dissolve the distinctive affirmations of the Christian faith in some rational scheme, which thus took the place of Biblical revelation as the principal authoritative source of Christian teaching. . . .

We must all be grateful to the neo-orthodox movement for bringing back the Bible to the central place in Christian thought that properly belongs to it, and for doing this without reverting to uncritical or anti-scientific views of Biblical authority. At this point, neo-orthodoxy carries on the liberal tradition while correcting a serious unintentional lapse from the best liberal principles: the tendency to interpret reason and experience as *substitutes* for the Christian revelation, rather than as the faculties by which it is received and understood. Again, we have to thank neo-orthodoxy for calling attention to what Kierkegaard called the "existential" element in religious faith, and the "paradoxical" form in which religious affirmations are typically expressed, *suggesting* and *symbolizing* truths that can never be adequately *conveyed* in rationally lucid propositions. Here too, there is no incompatibility with liberalism. . . .

Real conflict emerges when some neo-orthodox insist that the way of special Biblical revelation, full as it is of paradoxical oppositions and mysterious symbolism, is the *only* way to faith in God, and that natural theol-

---

[72] This and corresponding quotations are from the above cited article in the *Union Review.* [Horton]

ogy, rational philosophy, and general revelation outside the Bible have *no* place in Christian thought. "There is no way from man to God; there is only a way from God to man," says Barth. That is to say, whenever man tries to think or argue his way to God by the use of reason, he commits idolatry and reduces God to the stature of a finite object. God must be allowed to speak for Himself; and when He speaks, all sorts of apparently contradictory assertions are to be expected. There is in all this a solemn and needed warning against trying to measure God's infinity by finite stand-ards; but when *only* paradoxical statements about God are admitted, the concept of God becomes systematic nonsense, an abyss of darkness in which the "numinous" completely drives out the luminous, and no intelligible word comes forth from the thunders and lightnings that enwrap the Holy Mount. . . .

We may venture to predict, then, that the new liberalism will give a central place to Biblical revelation in its theory of religious knowledge, and will not try to confine the mystery and majesty of God's being in a closed rational system, but will continue to maintain a place for reason as a con-firmatory approach to faith, as a principle of harmony among religious ideas, and as a most necessary check upon the fanatical dogmatism of rival religious revelations—whose probable recourse is to violence and oppression, if reason refuses to judge between them.

2. God

In any system of religious thought, the conception of religious knowl-edge and the conception of God are closely interrelated. God is believed to be what the admitted evidence discloses. We must expect to find, then, that the older liberalism lost the balance of its concept of God in proportion as it lost its original balance between faith and reason. It is true, as Pro-fessor Lyman says, that liberalism at its best maintains "the union of the transcendence and immanence of God"; but as the old liberalism so largely slipped over into a one-sided rationalism, by the same process it slipped over into a one-sided immanentism. . . .

When social order is disturbed and social chaos breaks loose, as has re-peatedly occurred in the years since 1914, faith in the immanent God is severely shaken. Some, shocked at the implication that God is responsible for the horrors they face, shift to the idea of a limited God, struggling against the dark forces that are beyond Him as they are beyond us; others give up faith altogether, and become religious humanists; but most typi-cally, and most widely, the adjustment to the new world-situation is made by shifting the emphasis from God's immanence to His transcendence, as is done in neo-orthodoxy. . . .

Recently, however, it has become evident that the exclusive neo-orthodox emphasis on divine transcendence is a case of over-compensation, which needs to be corrected in its turn. A divine Judge can be located aloft in the sky, so to speak, raining down disciplinary thunder-bolts like angry Jupiter; but a God of grace must have healing contact with earth and man. Both Barth and Niebuhr now recognize that our age is in danger of despair, and desperately needs the assurance of God's forgiving, healing, life-giving grace; [73] but though both men recognize that this is part of the Gospel, they are considerably hampered in preaching it by their habitual one-sided stress upon divine transcendence, which makes God seem too distant to be gracious. A new liberalism, unhampered by this stress, and maintaining a better balance than the old liberalism between transcendence and immanence, should be able to preach judgment as well as Barth or Niebuhr, while preaching grace as well as Wesley or Moody. The whole Christian message requires both at once. . . .

3. Christ

The transcendence and immanence of God are closely related to the conception of Christ as the Way of Salvation. An over-emphasis on immanence brings God and man so near that all men are divine and a Savior is not needed; an over-emphasis on transcendence holds God and man so far apart that a divine-human Mediator between them becomes quite inconceivable.

When the old liberalism's one-sided immanentism is consistently applied to the doctrine of Christ, it gives us a Christ barely distinguishable from the rest of the human race, and a human race barely distinguishable from God. Perhaps the boldest and clearest expression of this point of view is to be found in *The New Theology*, published in 1907 by R. J. Campbell, then the liberal minister of the City Temple in London. "Strictly speaking," says Campbell, "the human and the divine are two categories which shade into and imply each other; humanity is Divinity, viewed from below, Divinity is humanity viewed from above." . . .[74]

This type of liberal optimism about human nature, this confidence that man is moving toward his true destiny through the steady unfolding of the God within him, has certainly not been justified by the events of the twentieth century. The moral to be drawn from these events can be tersely expressed in the text of one of Reinhold Niebuhr's sermons: "Cursed be the man that putteth his trust in man!" Man in the twentieth century has been let down and frustrated so often by his fellow-men, that he feels caught in a sort of prison, from which he cannot escape unless released from outside; and his Rescuer has to be endued with something more than human power; he needs power from above, strong enough to break bars of brass. Under these circumstances a respectful hearing must be given to the neo-orthodox

---

[73] Barth is quoted as saying, "Pessimism is *also* a heresy." [Horton]

[74] R. J. Campbell, *The New Theology*, pp. 74, 75. [Horton]

doctrine of Christ, as one who comes from above, from a transcendent world, and whose divine-humanity is not merely a slight heightening of average humanity, but the amazing Miracle and "Absolute Paradox"[75] of heaven come down to earth, and the Creator becoming a creature.

A respectful hearing, but also a critical hearing. *Respectful,* because it is evident that the dimension of transcendent depth needed to be restored to that conception of Christ which we have described; and when this is done, it is bound to become a more difficult and paradoxical idea than it was before. *Critical,* because of the real danger that in restoring the dimension of transcendence, the dimension of immanence may be lost, and so the saviorhood of Christ may be denied again just as it is being reaffirmed. The intention of neo-orthodoxy is of course to reaffirm the doctrine of Christ as the God-man, "who for us men and for our salvation came down from heaven . . . and was made man"; but in its handling of the earthly life of this heavenly visitant, it often shows itself strangely negative. There is nothing specific in the life or the teaching of Jesus that can be pointed to as clearly manifesting the presence of God. His incognito is impenetrable except to the eye of faith; and faith, according to Kierkegaard, declares that "History has nothing whatever to do with Christ. . . . He is the paradox, which history can never digest or convert into a common syllogism."[76] This is the point where Christ's saviorhood threatens to slip away again; for if the Savior gives no clear guidance, no specific help, *here on the plane of history where we live,* he is not the Lord we seek and we must look for another.

There is truth in Kierkegaard's view that must be weighed and accepted by the new liberalism. It is true that no *merely* historical approach to the life and teaching of Jesus can recognize him as Savior; only if faith sees in him the Wisdom and Power of the same eternal God in whose hands our destinies still rest, can it trust him as Savior. But how can faith see God's Wisdom and Power in Jesus, if the story of his life and the history of his influence are as utterly mystifying, as darkly opaque as Kierkegaard says? Why all the excitement in Galilee and Jerusalem, if not because even the secular and unbelieving mind could perceive a strange grandeur in this lowly but extraordinary Man? Why have men called him Lord and God all through the centuries, and bowed to him rather than to Mohammed or Confucius or some other, if they have not found in his recorded words and deeds some credible sign of God's presence? . . . It is one of the duties of the new liberalism to see that the man Jesus, through whose human lips the first apostles were called, is not carelessly by-passed by the new orthodoxy. Only a transcendent *and* immanent Christ can be the Way to the transcendent and immanent God.

[75] Kierkegaard's expression. [Horton]
[76] Bretall, *A Kierkegaard Anthology,* p. 392. [Horton]

4. The Kingdom of God

The last of the four permanent values in liberalism, according to Professor Lyman, is to be found in "the close and vital relation which it sees between the religious and ethical in the Christian way of life," a relation which is particularly clear in its conception "that God wills the redemption of society as well as the individual, and that as individuals experience redemption they become centers of redemptive living in society."

Such an explicit avowal of belief in the social gospel and its hope of a Kingdom of God on earth takes courage to make, nowadays. Every one knows how many illusions were connected with this hope, at the turn of the century, and how tragically these illusions have been dissipated. . . .

What then? Is the prayer, "Thy Kingdom come on earth," no longer to be prayed? Is the hope of a better social order, which human hands can help in some measure to build, no longer part of the Christian hope? Sweepingly negative answers have been given to these questions. In Barth's early writings, there is for example a purely eternalistic or Platonic conception of the Kingdom of God. That means there is nothing to hope for in future history; man's true hope lies in turning his eyes vertically upward, to that eternal Kingdom in the heavens which overarches all times. This Kingdom is as near to us now as it ever will be. Now I think it has been one of the great and lasting contributions of neo-orthodoxy to reassert the eternal meaning of the Kingdom of God after a period of feverish futurism, when Utopian dreams of coming happiness on earth almost crowded the hope of heaven out of men's minds; but excessive concentration on the eternal hope may undermine the sense of social responsibility, and strip future history of all meaning. . . .

How should the new liberalism revise its version of the social gospel, and its conception of the Kingdom of God on earth, in order to play its proper part in this fruitful new collaboration of liberal and orthodox thought? *Negatively,* I would say, by dropping its hope of realizing the Kingdom of God fully within history, and by ceasing to identify the progress of the Kingdom with the success of particular human plans and programs. *Positively,* by working out a new view of God's advancing Providence in history, which would be a moral substitute for the abandoned doctrine of progress. Crucial to such a view would be the ancient conviction that God always saves a remnant, whenever judgment descends upon a nation or a civilization; and on this remnant a new order, fitter to endure, is founded. Evil and good grow together, between judgments; but there is a divisive quality in evil which forever tends towards its destruction, and definitely rules out the possibility of a final victory of evil; while good has inward strength that survives many crucifixions and forever rises to new resurrections. Though God's good Kingdom is thus stronger than evil, its final and eternal victory can come only through great tribulations and be snatched, so to speak, out of the very jaws of the still insurgent Anti-Christ. If liberals recognize this much truth in the orthodox view of history, they have a right to ask the orthodox, in their turn, not to gaze perpetually at the far heavenly horizon, but to lend a hand in that portion of the task of realizing the Kingdom on earth which God assigns to this generation.

> SOURCE: Walter Marshall Horton, *Eugene William Lyman Lec-ture: Liberalism Old and New.* Sweet Briar College, November 14, 1952 (Sweet Briar, Va., 1952), 7–22. Used by permission of the author.

168. The Unity of the Bible

At first most biblical scholars in America resisted the new movement in biblical theology, fearing that it would retard or jeopardize developments in modern historical criticism. Critical scholarship in recent decades had concerned itself primarily with the origin and growth of biblical religion, and therefore it mainly emphasized the great variety of ideas to be found in the Old and New Testaments. Thus many scholars argued that it was a mistake to try to impose upon the Bible any unifying theological principle.

One of the first American biblical scholars to challenge the traditional viewpoint was G. Ernest Wright (1909—). While Wright acknowledged that the Bible embraced a wide variety of ideas, he insisted that there is a basic unity to be found in the Scriptures as a whole. In the year 1952 he set forth the essence of his doctrine in a lucid essay, "Wherein Lies the Unity of the Bible?" The subjoined document reprints most of that important essay.

Before joining the faculty of Harvard Divinity School in 1958, Wright taught Old Testament at McCormick Theological Seminary. A specialist in archaeology, he is editor of *The Biblical Archaeologist.* He is co-author with Floyd V. Filson of *Westminster Historical Atlas to the Bible* (1945; rev. ed., 1956). His other writings include *The Challenge to Israel's Faith* (1944), and *God Who Acts: Biblical Theology as Recital* (1952).

DOCUMENT

I

The problem of the unity of the Bible confronts us in all of our attempts to teach and to preach biblical faith in a modern setting. No sooner do we present one set of generalizations on the basis of one selection of biblical passages or books than we may be confronted with other passages which seem to say the opposite. When we attempt to present in some sys-tematic way the theology of the Bible, which should be the chief agent for the presentation of its unity, we are confronted with the seemingly insuperable obstacle that the Bible was never written with any attention whatever to systematic presentation of theological propositions. For that reason biblical scholars cannot make up their minds as to what biblical theology is or can be. Is it a history of biblical ideas? But how can one make a systematic presentation of ideas undergoing historical change and exhibiting considerable fluidity through a historical process? Is it then a systematic cross-section of those ideas at some one period which we select as normative? If so, how can one call it a *biblical* theology, when it is the theology of only one period? To complicate matters, one may say that it is difficult enough to write a theology of either Testament, but to put both together and insist on a theology of the whole Bible because the latter is the scripture of the church is a still greater embarrassment. Perhaps, then, we should say with Professor Burrows that biblical theology is merely packaging the foods of biblical research for the consumer in the modern Church, that it can be nothing more than the popularization and preaching of the faith to modern man. Yet the study of the Bible is a serious discipline, and as a matter of objective fact there ought to be some way by which we can present it as a whole in as responsible and serious a manner as is done in other disciplines. The fact is that we are so presenting it continually. What troubles us is that we are both unclear and uneasy as to the principles which guide us in doing so.

Personally, I see no solution to the problem confronting us, unless it is possible that our presuppositions can be re-examined and found faulty in some measure so that we can make a fresh start in our thinking. This problem of the Bible's unity has always been an important one for the Church, but because of the historical research of the past century it is more acute for us than for almost any previous generation, unless we except the first centuries of the Christian era. And because of our insistence on proper, careful, historical exegesis certain methods of interpretation previously used are no longer available to us. What, then, are we to do?

Part of our difficulty, it seems to me, lies in our conception of the place where the unity ought to be. It is, for example, illustrated by our understanding of the word, "theology." Theology to us means propositional dogmatics; it means the systematic presentation of the intellectual content of religion in an abstract manner. In the Church it has proceeded along certain customary lines; e.g. the doctrines of God, man, Christ, the Church, etc., elaborated in different ways but fundamentally the same in essential conception. Most of the biblical theologies attempted in the past two hundred years have simply taken over this conception of the nature of theology, and have attempted to impose its categories on the Bible. But in doing so, the Bible is forced to speak in an idiom not germane to it. We are imposing something on the Bible which the latter does not have, with the result that through our theologies the Bible never speaks in its own manner. In the Presbyterian church, for example, every ordained person must say that he believes in the system of doctrine contained in the Holy Scriptures. But to what is one confessing in this instance? Does the Scripture contain a *system of doctrine* in any literal sense of the phrase? The Westminster Confession of Faith contains a very elaborate definition of God, beginning: "There is but one only living and true God, who is infinite in being and perfection, a most pure spirit, invisible, without body, parts, or passions, immutable, immense, eternal, incomprehensible, almighty, most wise, most holy, most free, most absolute . . ." etc. As a matter of fact, this definition when compared with the simple, moving, vivid and arresting nature of the biblical presentations appears dull and pretentious; and somehow it does not lead us into the presence of the God being defined. It simply removes him from us with its abstractions as an object of rational systematization which inevitably introduces rational argumentation.

Is it possible that theology can have another meaning? Is its sole meaning that given it by the systematic theologians? Unless it does have another, and characteristically biblical meaning, then we cannot use it in any attempt to present biblical faith as a unitary whole over against the other faiths of mankind. I personally should like to insist that there is such a thing as Biblical Theology, the chief unitary discipline of the Bible; but I should define it, not as propositional dogmatics, but as *the confessional recital of the Acts of God in a particular history, together with the inferences to be drawn from them.* The unity of the Bible is not to be found *primarily* in an abstract system of ideas, nor in a systemic attempt to rationalize dogmatic propositions by means of the outline drawn from systematic theology (God, man, sin, redemption). It is rather to be found in a certain view of history, as the directed handiwork of God, from which the inferences for faith and life are drawn.

In all of the intensive work of the past century in which this and that is compared to, or said to be derived from, the pagan environment, we have tended to lose sight of one thing particularly which more than any other distinguishes the Bible from all other religious literatures. That is its peculiar and characteristic interest in history. In biblical worship one of the chief elements is the confessional recital of events, for the very telling of the story is an act of confession. Biblical history is obviously no secular affair; it centers in the narrations of those events singled out because they are the great formative and redemptive acts of God which have determined the course of history or because they show man's response in faith or rebellion to the God who has revealed himself by his historical acts. For example, the chief events of the Old Testament were the freeing from Egyptian bondage and the gift of the land for an inheritance. These historical events are interpreted as the handiwork of God, whence inferences are drawn. Since Israel was a tiny, obscure group with nothing whatever to commend it to the world, the Exodus meant to the nation that Yahweh had shown a peculiar, unexplainable, and unmerited grace which drew this people to him in a special relation. Hence the doctrine of the Chosen People, the election. Hence also the characteristic apprehension of the grace and righteousness of God. Since the land of Canaan was God's gift, it was not owned by Israel as a natural right. It was a conditional loan, whence derived the whole Israelite doctrine of property and inheritance. The so-called "attributes" of God cannot be analyzed as abstractions because they are all inferences about God, drawn from the way he has acted; i.e., from the interpretation of historical events. The pagan background of Israel's chief religious festivals is clear, but the most important thing to notice is that the Sabbath, the spring, and the fall festivals were all changed radically, so that they became commemorations of events. Historical memory and participation became central in the worship, and this has been carried over into the church, as is illustrated by the rehearsal of history in the services of worship, in the division of the Christian year, and in the Lord's Supper.

In other words, the nature of the biblical God is known, not primarily through nature, nor through internal religious experience typified in mysticism, but rather through the study of history. There God is seen at work, whereas nature is largely demythologized and made the servant of God's work in history. Personality is an important means of revelation in the Bible, but men are not known as great heroes or martyrs in the pagan sense. Instead, they are known either as those who by faith respond obediently and in love to God's call to a historical vocation, or else they are seen as those who rebel against him. The language of inner religious experience is thus not sufficiently objective to depict the knowledge of God or the life of faith. Neither is the conception of revelation by the words and teachings of men alone. God in truth does reveal himself by the Word, but the latter cannot be characterized as a series of abstract spiritual or moral teachings which can be taken out of their setting and strung together with other similar sayings to form "the Bible of the world." God's Word by prophet, lawgiver, and apostle is always tied in with the history; it is an accompaniment and interpreter of the history. It is not an independent *esse*, which can adequately be comprehended apart from history. . . .

The biblical interest in God, therefore, is not in his *being* as a static object of reflection, but in his active lordship of history. Neither is the biblical interest in man to be found in man's *nature*, but rather in *what man has done* in response to God's lordship. For this reason the biblical doctrine of God and man cannot be depicted in the manner customary in systematic dogmatics. They can only be ascertained by means of a confessional recital of history.

These are some of the reasons by which I should argue that there is such a thing as biblical theology, a theology which both characterizes and unifies the Bible, and one which is itself and not anything else. Hence the word "theology" is not to be defined solely as the systematicians do: namely, as the abstract and propositional discussion of the rational content of faith.

Instead, *biblical theology is the confessional rehearsal of history, together with the inferences to be drawn from it.*

What kind of unity does this conception give to the Bible? It is certainly not a static unity of all parts or of the ideas within the parts. It is a unity which holds within it, and which provides for, a great amount of variety. The primary unity lies in the kerygmatic core of the Bible, whereas the concentration upon history and the problem of life within history is the occasion for great variety in conception, presentation, and particular interest. So many things are true when kept within a particular situation which are not true when universalized in order to make them fit all situations. The formula by which the Deuteronomist interprets the history of Israel may thus be held to be essentially valid for the data with which he deals, but it does not apply entirely to the function of the Servant of Second Isaiah, nor to the lives of Job or of Jesus, etc. Priests, prophets, and the wise men may all have their individual vocations and interests which lead them along separate paths, often in seeming contradiction. But behind them all is the kerygmatic core of the faith, or, if it is lacking, then there inevitably will be controversy, as the presence of Job and Ecclesiastes in the wisdom literature makes clear.

II

What is this kerygmatic core of the Bible, this confessional rehearsal of events interpreted as the redemptive activity of God? It is to be noted that biblical faith does not start with certain abstract ideas or principles which it then seeks to expound and apply. It instead starts with the confessional recital of history and draws out the inferences from that. . . .

Here, then, is what God has done, what he has promised, and what he demands as the condition of the fulfillment of promise. The Deuteronomic and Chronicler's histories of the people in their land are both written by inferential application of these presuppositions to subsequent events. To the old kerygma the problem of government brought a new element, the promise and covenant to and with David and his dynasty, which subsequently became central in Messianic theology. The prophets made clear the implications of the proclamation to succeeding generations, so that its meaning was seen always to be directly relevant to every historical situation. The psalmists preserve the liturgical response of worshippers to it in different situations. The wisdom writers sought to make clear what prudential daily life under "the fear of Yahweh" meant, though their lack of the truly kerygmatic perspective shows their close relation to the international sources of this practical ethics and became the occasion for theological skepticism of much of wisdom's basis (in Job and Eccles.)—a problem not resolved until the Intertestamental Period.

Here, then, is variety in plenty, but central to it is the confessional recital of God's saving and redemptive acts, while those elements in which this recital were not central caused trouble and further reflection. In Acts 13 we have the first record of a sermon attributed to Paul. It begins in vss. 17–23 with a confessional summary of what God has done. The following are the central articles of faith which it contains: (1) The God of Israel chose the fathers (Patriarchs); (2) he delivered their progeny with uplifted arm from Egyptian slavery and bore with them in the wilderness; (3) he directed the Conquest and divided the land to them by lot; (4) after the judges, Samuel and the rejected Saul, he raised up David to be their king, as a man after his own heart; (5) of whose seed, according to promise, he raised up a Saviour, Jesus.

This confession begins with the Patriarchs and ends in the Old Testament with David. Thence it passes immediately to Jesus Christ, thus suggesting that the events from Abraham to David are the most significant history of the former times and that Christ is the continuation, the clarification, and the fulfillment of the redemptive purposes of God within it. The accuracy of this attempt to draw out the central elements of both Testaments has been confirmed by both form and literary criticism; the primary unity of the Bible must lie at this point.

> SOURCE: G. Ernest Wright, "Wherein Lies the Unity of the Bible?"
> *The Journal of Bible and Religion,* XX (1952), 194–8.
> Used by permission.

169. The Revival of Catholic Biblical Studies

Biblical criticism in the Roman Catholic Church suffered a severe blow in the early part of this century as a result of the modernist controversy. Almost a generation was to pass before modern biblical scholarship could be significantly revived. The current revival was given its greatest stimulus in 1943, when Pius XII issued his encyclical letter, *Divino Afflante Spiritu,*[77] urging that a much larger scholarly effort be devoted to the solution of basic problems in biblical exegesis. He stressed the importance of exploring the new data which are accumulating in such fields as archaeology and philology.[78] The pope also urged the parish priests to become more active in disseminating "the heavenly treasures of the Divine Word by sermons, homilies and exhortations." [79]

The papal declaration has greatly spurred scientific biblical research among Catholic scholars in various countries. In 1958 the Rev. John L. McKenzie, S.J. (1910—) published a significant article in the *Journal of Biblical Literature* in which he indicated lines of exegetical progress and specified some of the immediate problems that remain to be solved. A substantial part of that article is reprinted in the document which follows.

---

[77] For English text, see *The Catholic Mind,* XLII (1944), 257–83.
[78] *Ibid.,* pars. 21–4, 31, 49, 51.   [79] *Ibid.,* par. 59.

Father McKenzie, a native of Indiana, received his education at Xavier University (Ohio), Saint Mary's College (Kansas), and Weston College (Mass.). From 1942 to 1960 he taught Old Testament at West Baden College (Indiana), and since the latter year has been Professor of Biblical History at Loyola University in Chicago. He is author of *The Two-Edged Sword* (1956).

DOCUMENT

Any discussion of contemporary Catholic Exegesis must begin from the publication in 1943 of *Divino Afflante Spiritu,* the encyclical letter of Pope Pius XII on the promotion of biblical studies. . . .

The Modernist controversy of the first decade of this century left deep wounds on the body of Catholic theological and biblical scholarship. It would take entirely too long to review the history of this crisis; it is sufficient to note that Catholic theology and exegesis up to the beginning of the second world war exhibited what many have called the mentality of the beleaguered fortress. In the prevailing climate of opinion it was better to adhere to what was thought to be safe doctrine than to make sorties into hostile territory. In such a defensive atmosphere creative scholarship was extremely unlikely, and in fact there is not much creative scholarship to which we can point over a period of some thirty years. . . .

The papal declaration was not received with equal enthusiasm by all theologians, and some seemed to interpret it as in no way modifying their earlier opinions. At the present writing, fifteen years after the publication of the encyclical, opposition to creative biblical scholarship speaks only in whispers, and it no longer inhibits original work which goes beyond commonly accepted theological opinion.

Perhaps the most important statement of the encyclical was the declaration that there exist a great many unsolved exegetical problems to which no certain answer is found either in the traditional teaching of the Church or in commonly accepted theological opinion. Exegetes are urged to take up these unsolved problems, and other members of the Church are warned to abhor that intemperate zeal which regards anything new as to be for that reason opposed or suspected. . . .

The encyclical affirms that the first duty of the interpreter is to discover the literal sense, the genuine meaning of the Bible. And lest any one should misunderstand this to be a restatement of the fundamentalist principle of interpretation, the encyclical goes on to say that the genuine meaning of the text cannot be understood without historical and cultural studies of the world of the ancient Near East, without comparison of the Bible with other ancient literatures, and without determining the precise literary form of the separate books and portions of the Bible. This sweeping encouragement to historical investigation and to the study of *Gattungsgeschichte* is as unreserved as one could desire. It would be wrong, of course, to think that historical and literary criticism began only in 1943 among Catholic exegetes. I have already observed that a consensus on the necessity of these methods existed before the encyclical, which would hardly have been published had not such a consensus existed. Since 1943, however, these studies have been carried on with much more intensity. . . .

The revolt against historicism and the demand for a biblical theology in the Protestant churches has had a parallel in the Catholic Church. Here there was no revolt against historicism, because there never had been any historicism against which to revolt. But there was a stout affirmation of the "historical character" of the Bible without any attention whatever to the study of literary forms. The purely defensive and almost entirely controversial scholarship of the era of the siege mentality had by 1943 proved its sterility beyond all question. As a group the Catholic clergy and laity had lost all interest in anything biblical scholarship had to say. They thought— and I am not questioning the correctness of their judgment—that biblical scholarship contributed nothing to enrich their faith and realize their ideals. No one who accepts the Bible as the word of God can feel comfortable when this book is praised by every one and read and understood by almost no one. And so among Catholics also there was a demand for a theological treatment of the Bible which would make sense. If biblical scholars could not or would not furnish such a treatment, then the field was left wide open for the amateurs. Modern historical and critical scholarship has arrived none too soon to keep popular thinking about the Bible from soaring off into space. There is not yet a large body of literature available to the Catholic clergy and laity on the theological significance of the Bible, especially in English; but the material is being treated in scholarly books and journals, and future popular literature ought to have a basis in sound scholarship. Up to this time it appears that this type of popular literature must be written by the exegete if it is to be written at all.

The felt need for the theological interpretation of the Bible has centered since 1946 on the question of the unity of OT and NT. A mass of literature on the subject has arisen, but the question is still open. In Europe, especially in France immediately after the second world war, this question was answered by a revival of typology. The proposal for a return to the typological exegesis of the Fathers was stated most articulately and fully by Jean Daniélou and Henri de Lubac, who differed from each other in some detail.[80] But they both agreed that the "spiritual meaning" is found everywhere throughout the OT, and that the discovery of the spiritual sense is independent of scientific and literal interpretation. This denial of any religious value in scientific biblical scholarship was a very disturbing element in the theory; it seems ultimately to make any "spiritual" exegesis anti-intellectual,

---

[80] Cf. in particular Henri de Lubac, *Histoire et Esprit* (Paris: Aubier, 1950). In a review of this book I included a rather full summary of De Lubac's thesis and a critique of his principles of exegesis (*Theological Studies*, XII [1950], 365–84). [McKenzie]

and to remove all control from the interpretation of the Bible except the spiritual insight of the interpreter. The controversy about spiritual exegesis really never reached the Catholics of this country, and it has been dormant in Europe for the last half-dozen years. The theory, as one might expect, has been generally rejected by exegetes. But exegetes would not be justified simply in rejecting the theory unless they were willing to supply the need by a spiritual interpretation based on the genuine meaning of the Bible as investigated by the tools of historical and literary criticism. This they are doing.

The question of typology, however, is not thereby finished. Typology is so much a part of the traditional Catholic interpretation of the Bible that it cannot be abandoned by the modern scholar. The encyclical speaks expressly of the necessity of continuing typological interpretation. Most exegetes recognize that the traditional typology of the Fathers of the Church cannot be combined with modern scientific study and that typology must be redefined before it can be employed in our interpretation. This work has not been done.

In recent years the theory of typology has been largely replaced by the theory of the *sensus plenior,* the "fuller sense." [81] Raymond E. Brown has thus defined the fuller sense: "The *sensus plenior* is that additional, deeper meaning intended by God but not clearly intended by the human author, which is seen to exist in the words of a biblical text (or group of texts or even a whole book) when they are studied in the light of further revelation or development in the understanding of revelation." [82] Brown is at some pains to escape the objection often leveled by critics of the theory that the *sensus plenior* escapes definition; he lists definitions given by twenty-one different authors which, he believes, are in substantial agreement. . . .

It is my own personal impression, both from reading and from conversation with Catholic exegetes, that the majority of them lean towards this theory. I should be happy to be proved wrong; some colleagues in Germany told me last year that no German Catholic exegete is interested in the fuller sense. There is an articulate minority which finds the theory unacceptable. I believe the criticisms of G. Courtade and R. P. Bierberg are entirely valid and have not been met by the defenders of the fuller sense.[83] Even if a more substantial agreement has been reached in the definition of the fuller sense, the definition still lacks precision; and when a more detailed exposition is given, the lack of a unified concept which one can grasp becomes apparent. . . .

[81] The theory is fully set forth by Joseph Coppens in *Les harmonies des deux Testaments* (Tournai-Paris: Casterman, 1949) and Raymond E. Brown in *The* Sensus Plenior *of Sacred Scripture* (Baltimore: St. Mary's University, 1955). [McKenzie]

[82] *Op. cit.,* p. 92.

[83] G. Courtade, *Recherches de science religieuse,* XXXVI (1949), 136–41; R. P. Bierberg, *CBQ,* X (1948), 182–95. [McKenzie]

To sum up, then, the problems of hermeneutics as they appear to this observer: as our first task—although it is not strictly a problem of hermeneutics—I put the continued investigation by historical and critical methods of the genuine meaning of the Bible. We have, I believe, not nearly exhausted the wealth of material furnished by the study of ancient Near Eastern literature and culture and by the corresponding studies of the Hellenistic world of NT times. Such works as those produced by the school of Lucien Cerfaux excel in the NT field; but Catholic scholars have produced nothing comparable for the OT. I put this task first because it is a necessary preliminary to the construction of a biblical theology. Any subsequent work which will be done on the theological application of the Bible to Catholic belief and practice will be a waste of time unless it rests on such serious and rigorously critical work. After this will come the theological exploration of biblical themes; and here we must include a better statement of the unity of OT and NT. . . . I am inclined to believe that any statement of the unity of OT and NT before much solid exegetical and theological work is done in each of them is likely to be premature. Simplification is wonderful, but it often comes at too high a price. The articles of D. M. Stanley, principally in *Theological Studies* and the *Catholic Biblical Quarterly* are superb examples of the exploration of NT theological themes.

The work must first be done on the scholarly level; but the Catholic biblical scholar cannot afford to speak to no one except his colleagues in biblical scholarship. It is not merely a question of whether he desires to be heard by the Catholic clergy and laity; it is a question of whether they are willing to support him if they think he has no message for them. Hence, while it is essential that the theological interpretation and application be carried on first by scientific methods, the task cannot be regarded as finished unless the results of scholarly work are made available to a wider public. Popularization at the present moment could easily be premature; but Catholic scholars ought to lose no opportunity to make themselves heard on the theological significance of the Bible. Should they succeed in doing this, they will have done no more than fulfil the mission which is assigned to them in the encyclical *Divino Afflante Spiritu*.

I believe that if they fulfil this mission they will also help to construct a bridge between Catholics and members of other communions. The confessional differences which divide us will not be closed in the foreseeable future; but these differences, if divided Christians can agree at least on the minimum essentials of Christian charity, ought not to become the source of human personal differences.

SOURCE: John L. McKenzie, S.J., "Problems of Hermeneutics in Roman Catholic Exegesis," *Journal of Biblical Literature*, LXXVII (1958), 197–204. Used by permission of the *Journal*.

170. The New Fundamentalism

Among those seeking to repristinate an ultra-conservative version of evangelical theology, the editor of *Christianity Today,* Carl F. H. Henry (1912—), is second to none. In 1956, when that fortnightly was founded, he became its editor. Under his direction, the journal has been used with all vigilance to advance an enlightened fundamentalism.

Especially illuminating is a series of four articles which the editor published in *Christianity Today* in 1957 under the general title, "Dare We Revive the Modernist-Fundamentalist Conflict?" [84] That title was inspired by the appearance of Harry Emerson Fosdick's autobiography, *The Living of These Days* (1955), which, said Henry, "spins a halo of self-justification." Hence, the opening article sharply rebuked the famed champion of modernism for his "unrepentant liberalism." The next article, on the other hand, drubbed old-line fundamentalism, charging it with narrowness of theological and historical perspective, indifference toward ecclesiology, and lack of social concern. The third article expressed approval of the current revival of interest in theology, but found neo-orthodoxy—identified as neo-supernaturalism—wanting. The final article indicated the responsibility which now rests upon true believers in "biblical supernaturalism." The substance of that article is reprinted in the document below.

Carl Henry, a native of New York City, took his undergraduate work at Wheaton College and completed his divinity studies at Northern Baptist Theological Seminary. In 1949 he received the Ph.D. from Boston University. Prior to his present position he taught at Northern Baptist Seminary and Fuller Theological Seminary. Among his best known books are *The Uneasy Conscience of Modern Fundamentalism* (1947), *The Protestant Dilemma* (1949), *Fifty Years of Protestant Theology* (1950), and *Christian Personal Ethics* (1957).

DOCUMENT

A higher spirit to quicken and to fulfill the theological fortunes of this century will require more than the displacement of modernism, more than the revision of neo-orthodoxy, more than the revival of fundamentalism. Recovery of apostolic perspective and dedication of the evangelical movement to biblical realities are foundational to this hope.

Exalt Biblical Theology

Evangelical theology has nothing to fear, and much to gain, from aligning itself earnestly with the current plea for a return to biblical theology. To measure this moving front of creative theology sympathetically, to understand its concern and courage and to name its weaknesses without

[84] *Christianity Today,* I (June 10–July 22, 1957).

depreciating its strength will best preserve relevant theological interaction with the contemporarry debate.

The evangelical movement must make its very own the passionate concern for the reality of special divine revelation, for a theology of the Word of God, for attentive hearing of the witness of the Bible, for a return to biblical theology.

Positive Preaching

Rededication to positive and triumphant preaching is the evangelical pulpit's great need. The note of Christ's lordship over this dark century, of the victory of Christianity, has been obscured. If it be evangelical, preaching must enforce the living communication of the changeless realities of divine redemption. The minister whose pulpit does not become the life-giving center of his community fails in his major mission. Perspective on Christianity's current gains and final triumph will avoid a myopic and melancholy discipleship. The Christian pulpit must present the invisible and exalted Head of the body of Christ; linked to him this earthly colony of heaven moves to inevitable vindication and glory. The perplexing problems of our perverse social orders find their hopeful solution only in this regenerative union. Out of its spiritual power must spring the incentives to creative cultural contributions.

Enlarge Christian Living

The evangelical fellowship needs a fresh and pervading conception of the Christian life. Too long fundamentalists have swiftly referred the question, "What distinguishes Christian living?" to personal abstinence from dubious social externals. The Christian conscience, of course, will always need to justify outward behavior, in home, in vocation and in leisure. But Christian ethics probes deeper. It bares the invisible zone of personality wherein lurk pride, covetousness and hatred.

Unfortunately, fundamentalism minimized the exemplary Jesus in the sphere of personal ethics. The theme of Christ's oneness with God was developed so exclusively in terms of his deity that the import of his dependence upon God for all human nature was lost. The manhood of Jesus is essentially one with ours; its uniqueness is in the zone of sinlessness, not of humanness. His uncompromised devotion and dependence upon God, his sustained relationship of mutual love, embodied the ideal pattern of human life in perfect fellowship with God. In view of his unbroken union with God, his humanity holds a central significance for all humanity.

In this light, a new importance attaches to the Nazarene's learning of the Father's will in the course of obedient dependence. His struggle with temptation to magnificent victory over all the assaults of evil, his exemplary trust, his unwavering reliance on God even in the darkest hours, his interior calm of soul, the wellspring of love that flowed from his being—in all these experiences Christ models for us an ideal spiritual relationship with God. In Jesus of Nazareth, God is fully resident; in God, Jesus is fully at home. He lives out the "rest in God" that actualizes the "abiding" to which we are called.

Another way in which evangelicals need to move beyond the fundamentalist ethic is in comprehending the whole of the moral law in fuller exposition of love for God and neighbor, and in the larger experience of the Holy Spirit in New Testament terms of ethical virtue. Often quite legalistically, and with an absoluteness beyond New Testament authority, fundamentalism's doctrine of surrender, of rededication, has merely proscripted worldly practices, from which the believer was discouraged. Unemphasized, however, are the fruit of the Spirit and those many virtues which differentiate dedicated living in terms of biblical Christianity.

Social Concern

We need a new concern for the individual in the entirety of his Christian experience. He is a member of all life's communities, of faith, of the family, of labor, of the state, of culture. Christianity is by no means the social gospel of modernism, but is nonetheless vibrant with social implications as a religion of redemptive transformation. To express and continue the vitality of the gospel message, marriage and the home, labor and economics, politics and the state, culture and the arts, in fact, every sphere of life, must evidence the lordship of Christ.

Obviously, the social application of Christian theology is no easy task. For one thing, fundamentalism fails to elaborate principles and programs of Christian social action because it fails to recognize the relevance of the gospel to the sociocultural sphere. Modernism defines Christian social imperatives in secular terms and uses the Church to reorganize unregenerate humanity. Its social sensitivity gave modernism no license to neglect the imperative of personal regeneration. Evangelistic and missionary priorities, on the other hand, gave fundamentalism no license to conceal the imperative of Christian social ethics. Despite the perils, no evasion of responsibility for meaningfully relating the gospel to the pressing problems of modern life is tolerable.

The divine life is a "being in love," a social or a family fellowship in which personality expresses the outgoing, creative relationships of redemption. A worker by God's creation, man sees vocation as a divinely entrusted stewardship by which to demonstrate love to God and service to man. As divinely ordained, the state declares God's intention and the dignity of man's responsibility for preserving justice and repressing iniquity in a sinful order. This world challenges man to interpret literature, art, music, and other media in reference to eternal order and values.

Approach to Science

Evangelical confidence in the ontological significance of reason makes possible a positive, courageous approach to science. For more than a century and a half modern philosophy has regrettably minimized the role of reason. Kant disjoined it from the spiritual world. Darwin naturalized and constricted it within the physical world. Dewey allowed it only a pragmatic or an instrumental role. These speculations took a heavy toll in Christian circles. A segment of evangelical Christianity nonetheless maintained its insistence upon the Logos as integral to the Godhead, the universe as a rational-purposive order, and man's finite reason is [as] related to the image of God.

Yet for more than a generation the evangelical attitude in scientific matters has been largely defensive. Evolutionary thought is met only obliquely. American fundamentalism often neglected scrutinizing its own position in the light of recent historical and scientific research. It even failed to buttress its convictions with rigorous theological supports.

Yet modernism, despite its eager pursuit of such revision, achieved no true correlation of Christianity and science. While modernism adjusted Christianity swiftly to the prevailing climate of technical conviction, its scientific respect was gained by a costly neglect of Christianity's import to science.

Today a new mood pervades the scientific sphere. That mood may not fully validate the evangelical view of nature, but it does at least deflate the presuppositions on which the older liberalism built its bias against the miraculous. The evangelical movement is now given a strategic opportunity to transcend its hesitant attitude toward scientific endeavor, and to stress the realities of a rational, purposive universe that coheres in the Logos as the agent in creation, preservation, redemption, sanctification and judgment. . . .

Doctrine of the Church

The evangelical movement needs also the sustained study of the New Testament doctrine of the Church and a greater concern for the unity of regenerate believers. Its program for reflecting the unity of the body of Christ in contemporary history is inadequate in several regards.

Evangelical discussions of the unity of the Church are shaped to protest the ecumenical framework as a compromise to be avoided. Ecumenical Christianity blesses a cooperation broader than the New Testament fellowship; it needs to be reminded that not all union is sacred—that the more inclusive the union, the greater the danger of compromising and secularizing its Christian integrity. By contrast, the evangelical movement easily restricts cooperation more narrowly than does the Bible. It must learn that not all separation is expressive of Christian unity. The principle of separation itself may acquire an objectionable form and content, related more to divisive temper than to theological fidelity. In the face of the inclusive church movement, the evangelical spirit reacts too much toward independency. Through refusal to cooperate with believers whose theological conservatism and dedication to Christ are beyond question, evangelical Christianity is in danger of divisiveness and disruptiveness.

Sound Doctrine and New Life

Evangelical insistence that the unity of the body of Christ requires a basic doctrinal agreement and a regenerate membership is sound. The ecumenical temperament encourages the breakdown of denominational barriers at too great a price whenever it minimizes doctrinal positions. Interdenominationalism in our century has sprung from a peculiar assortment of motives. Fundamentalists stimulated denominational desertion through discontent with theologically inclusive programs ventured by liberal leadership in the established denominations. Such was not in actuality an antithesis to denominationalism, since denominational tenets were not called into question. Indeed, most evangelicals prefer to support New Testament programs within their own denominational lines, allowing interdenominational cooperation to spring from multidenominational dedication to common evangelical priorities. The compromise of priorities in denominational circles, however, led to interdenominationalism at the expense of denominationalism and quickened the sense of an extradenominational unity based on common doctrine and faith.

The liberal interdenominational urge had a different motivation, namely, a virtual depreciation of denominationalism as unworthy sectarianism insofar as any fixed creedal positions are affirmed. This exaltation of the experiential unity of the Church through the disparagement of doctrinal soundness is the great peril of ecumenical ecclesiology today. Its constant danger is the elevation of the concern for unity above the concern for truth.

Precision in Beliefs

Evangelical emphasis on an indispensable doctrinal basis for Church unity needs, however, to be defined with greater precision. Such concern accounts for evangelical uneasiness over the creedal vagrancy of the World Council of Churches whose nebulous emphasis is only on "Jesus Christ as Lord and Savior." [85] Since the evangelical movement includes churches that are both creedal and noncreedal in heritage, a specific creedal unity has not been elaborated, although common theological tenets are listed. This evangelical listing of a doctrinal minimum raises difficulties for creedal churches, inasmuch as they consider no article of faith dispensable. To

---

[85] The actual phrase used by the World Council was, however, "our Lord Jesus Christ as God and Saviour"—cf. "The Constitution of the World Council of Churches," art. 1, in *Findings and Decisions, First Assembly of the World Council of Churches* (N.Y., 1948), 91.

Reformed churchmen, evangelical formulas often appear open to objectionable development. They prefer a strict creedal fellowship, a restriction that excludes progress toward the unity of diverse evangelical elements. The evangelical failure to fully elaborate essential doctrines has resulted in fragmentation by granting priority to secondary emphases (in such matters as eschatology). Evangelical Christianity has been slow to establish study conferences in biblical doctrine, to encourage mutual growth and understanding. Ironically, study sessions on theological issues are now often associated with movements whose doctrinal depth and concern are widely questioned. The significance of Christian doctrine, its dispensability or indispensability, its definition as witness or revelation, the elements identified respectively as core and periphery—these are issues on which evangelical Christianity must be vocal.

Fellowship of Disciples

Evangelical Christianity too frequently limits the term "evangelical" to those identified with a limited number of movements. This needlessly stresses a sense of Christian minority and discourages cooperation and communication with unenlisted evangelicals. But the tensions of American church history in this turbulent century cannot be automatically superimposed upon all world evangelical communities. Ecumenical leadership in the Federal Council of Churches and its successor, the National Council of Churches, failed to reflect the viewpoint of that considerable genuinely evangelical segment of its constituency. In the World Council of Churches, leaders on the Continent also have often found themselves theologically far to the right of American spokesmen, and have found American evangelicals in the World Council disappointingly unvocal. Long before the establishment of organizations like the World Evangelical Fellowship, many European churches have approached the World Council in quest of an enlarging evangelical fellowship. Evangelical world alternatives to inclusive movements arose after most large historic denominations were already enlisted in the World Council. Does evangelical loyalty within these committed denominations necessarily depend upon public repudiation of the World Council, and upon entrance instead into minority movements quite withdrawn from the stream of influential theological discussion? Even the National Association of Evangelicals in the United States must accept the absence of Southern Baptists and Missouri Lutherans, whose antipathy for theological inclusivism keeps these denominations also outside the National Council. The question that obviously remains, of course, is whether an evangelical who prefers identification with the broader movements can justify his participation, if he knows his own spiritual heritage, except in the capacity of a New Testament witness? Must not a silent evangelical in this climate always ask himself whether the silence which once perhaps was golden, now, through a dulling of love for truth and neighbor, has become as sounding brass or tinkling cymbal [?] Indeed, must not the evangelical always and everywhere address this question to himself in whatever association he is placed?

Lack of evangelical communication across the lines of inclusive and exclusive movements is not wholly due to the exclusivists. Ecumenical enthusiasts have encouraged neither fellowship nor conversation with exclusivist evangelicals. This coldness contributed needlessly to the fundamentalist suspicion of all outside their own constituency, and did little to mitigate the incivility that some fundamentalists reserved for such individuals. The unity of the believing Church requires communication between evangelicals on a basis of mutual tolerance and respect.

Concern for Unity

Unfortunately for the evangelical cause, the concern for the unity of the Church is now largely associated in the public mind with the inclusive vision. The failure of evangelicals to hear what the Spirit says in the New Testament to the churches has created the void now being filled by inclusivist conceptions of unity. The evangelical church needs with new earnestness to seek unity in its fragmenting environment, needs to reflect to the disunited world and to the disunited nations the sacred unity of the body of Christ.

Although evangelicals have criticized the broad basis of ecumenical merger and unity, they have achieved in their own ranks few mergers on the theological-spiritual level. Without conceding that denominationalism is evil or that health increases in proportion to the reduction of denominations, may there not be evidence that evangelical Christianity is overdenominationalized? If doctrinal agreement enhances the deepest unity of believers, may we not expect progress in the elimination of unneccessary divisions by emphasizing the spiritual unity of the Church? Evangelical Christianity, if it takes seriously its own emphasis on the unity of the body, must show visible gains in demonstrating unity in church life.

Contemporary Christianity would gain if the discussion of ecclesiastical tolerance were set in a New Testament context. The scriptural respect for individual liberty in matters of religious belief must not obscure definite requirements for identification with the body of Christian believers. The New Testament upholds specific doctrinal affirmations as indispensable to genuine Christian confession. In this biblical setting, divisiveness is depicted primarily as a theological question, not (as is usually the case today) as a matter of ecclesiastical attitude and relationship. The modernist tendency to link Christian love, tolerance and liberty with theological inclusivism is therefore discredited. Modernist pleas for religious tolerance and the caustic indictments of fundamentalist bigotry often were basically a strategic device for evading the question of doctrinal fidelity. This flaunting of tolerance, however, was discredited when inclusivist leaders suppressed or excluded evangelicals not sympathetic to the inclusive policy. The "tolerance plea" swiftly dismissed as divisive what was not clearly so in fact. Divisiveness meant disapproval of the inclusive policy, tolerance meant approval. But the New Testament does not support the view that devotion to Christian liberty and progress and to the peace and unity of Christ's Church is measured by the devaluation of doctrine in deference to an inclusive fellowship. From the biblical point of view, doctrinal belief is a Christian imperative, not a matter of indifference.

Whenever it professes a genuine regard for the scriptural point of view, the inclusive movement is driven to soul-searching in respect to doctrinal latitude and its own propaganda for organic church union. Within the World Council, in contrast with the National Council, exists a forum from which this ambiguity can be challenged. Evangelicals in this movement, if they bear an evangelical witness, must constantly call the Commission on Faith and Order to judge the theological and ecclesiastical question from the standpoint of Scripture.

The fact must not be ignored, however, that different evangelical conceptions of the visible Church are prevalent. Although historically the Christian churches have all insisted upon a minimal theological assent for admission to membership, Reformed churches share Calvin's view that even in the Church wheat and tares—professing and believing Christians—will dwell together until their final separation in the judgment. Baptist churches have traditionally placed greater emphasis on a regenerate membership and on a pure church. Even the disciplinary procedure of the more broadly conceived Reformed churches, however, considers church members flouting or indifferent to creedal standards as guilty as grave sin. Christian churches in the past stressed both a minimal requirement for membership and a maximal indulgence for avoidance of discipline or exclusion. But modernist leaders asserted the inevitability of doctrinal change. Heresy trials became an oddity in contemporary church history, not because of an absence of heresy, but because of the lack of zeal to prosecute heretics.

We dare not own any other authority over life and deed but the living God. We dare not own any other God than the righteous and merciful God revealed in Jesus Christ. We dare not own another Christ but Jesus of Nazareth, the Word become flesh who now by the Spirit is the exalted head of the body of believers. We dare not own any other Spirit than the Spirit who has breathed out Scripture through chosen men, that doubt may vanish about what God is saying to the Church and to the world. We dare not own any other Scripture than this Book. Let other men proclaim another god, another Christ, another spirit, another book or word—that is their privilege and their peril. But if once again the spiritual life of our world is to rise above the rubble of paganism into which it is now decaying, it will be only through the dynamic of revelation, regeneration, and redemption, through the sacred message which once brought hope. We have a task to do, a task of apostolic awesomeness; let us rise to the doing. The hour for rescue is distressingly late.

> SOURCE: Carl F. H. Henry, "Dare We Renew the Controversy? The Evangelical Responsibility," *Christianity Today,* I (July 22, 1957), 23–6, 38. Copyright 1957. Used by permission of *Christianity Today.*

171. Priesthood of the Laity

The current liturgical movement in the Roman Catholic Church is, among other things, notable for its concern to magnify the role of the laity in eucharistic worship. In his encyclical, *Mediator Dei* (1947), Pius XII declared:

> It is, therefore, desirable, Venerable Brethren, that all the faithful should be aware that to participate in the eucharistic sacrifice is their chief duty and supreme dignity, and that not in an inert and negligent fashion, giving way to distractions and day-dreaming, but with such earnestness and concentration that they may be united as closely as possible with the High Priest, according to the Apostle, "Let this mind be in you which was also in Christ Jesus." [Phil. 2:5.] And together with Him and through Him let them make their oblation and in union with Him let them offer up themselves.[86]

Since the issuance of the pope's encyclical, many attempts have been made to delineate more precisely the part which the faithful have in the celebration of the Mass. There seems to be a growing tendency to relate the laity more integrally to the Mass,[87] and yet there is latent fear that this trend could ultimately infringe upon the office of the ordained priest. Indeed, several paragraphs in *Mediator Dei* indicate that Pius XII himself was well aware of this very danger.[88]

The Rev. Charles E. Miller, C.M., has published two instructive articles on this vital question, the first of which appeared in *Worship* in April of 1959.[89] This article dealt solely with the historical background of lay participation in the eucharistic sacrifice. The second, however, which was published in the same journal the following month, elaborated Miller's own position. The subjoined document presents that stimulating article in full, including all of the author's footnotes.

A native of Louisiana (New Orleans), Father Miller received his edu-

---

[86] "Mediator Dei," *The Catholic Mind,* XLVI (June, 1948), sec. 80.

[87] For a good discussion of this aspect, see Ernest B. Koenker, *The Liturgical Renaissance in the Roman Catholic Church,* Chap. 5. See also Josef A. Jungmann, S.J., *Liturgical Worship* (N.Y., 1941).

[88] Cf. *Mediator Dei,* pars. 82, 83, 92, 93, 96.

[89] "Lay Participation in the Mass: Theological Basis," *Worship,* XXXIII (April, 1959), 285–9.

cation at St. Mary's Seminary (Missouri), Immaculate Heart College (California), and St. Louis University. He is now Vice Rector of St. John's Seminary College, Camarillo, California.

DOCUMENT

In our previous article we treated of the priesthood of the laity, and of how it has been interpreted through the centuries, and particularly in modern times. There remains the question of how that priesthood of the laity becomes operative in the sacrifice of the Mass: do the baptized laity "offer the Sacrifice" in the sense that their offering has an intrinsic relation to the essence of the Mass—to the separate consecrations which are effected by the ordained priest alone?

Two Aspects of the Consecration

Before we approach the encyclical *Mediator Dei* we must be aware of a fact which seems to have been presupposed by Pius XII: viz., that the consecration, while being one act, has two aspects; that of immolation and that of oblation.[90] The "immolation" in a sacrifice is the act by which the change or destruction of the victim is effected whereby it is constituted as a sacrifice, a *res sacra*. The "oblation" is the offering of what is immolated to God as a sign of acknowledgment of His supreme dominion and man's subjection.

Moreover, it must be observed, as Merkelbach well points out, that a twofold formal element must be distinguished in sacrifice. Considered precisely as an act of religion, the formal element is the oblation or offering to God; but considered precisely as a sacrifice, the formal element is the immolation.

As St. Thomas states, "every sacrifice is an oblation but not every oblation is a sacrifice." [91] That which makes an oblation to be a sacrifice, and so distinct from other oblations, is the immolation. Hence, the immolation is the formal element of sacrifice as such.[92]

Teaching of "Mediator Dei"

That the priest alone as the instrument of Christ immolates should be patent. Pius XII made the fact explicit: "The unbloody immolation at the consecration . . . is performed by the priest and by him alone. . . ."

But does the Church, and do the faithful, share in the oblation? Pius XII said: "It is because the priest places the divine Victim on the altar that he offers it to God the Father as an oblation. . . . Now the faithful par-

---

[90] De le Taille, *Mysterium Fidei*, pp. 327 ff.; quoted by Paul F. Palmer, S.J., "The Lay Priesthood: Real or Metaphorical?" *Theological Studies*, VIII (Dec., 1947), pp. 606 ff. [Miller]

[91] *Summa Th.*, II-II, q. 85, a. 3, ad. 3. [Miller]

[92] Henricus Merkelbach, O.P., *Summa Theologiae Moralis*, III, *De Sacramentis* (1949 ed.), no. 304, p. 253. [Miller]

ticipate in this oblation understood in this limited sense (*oblatio restricti nominis*) after their own fashion and in a twofold manner. . . ." [93]

Obviously the Pope is here referring to the oblation identified with the consecration. That is to say, the act whereby the priest makes the Victim present on the altar is not only an immolation but an oblation: the entire sacrifice is complete in the one act of consecration. Pius therefore says that the faithful, whom he has already excluded from the immolation, participate in the oblation.

Though theologians have continued to maintain even after the encyclical that the faithful do not share at all in the essence of the Mass, but only in the prayers of offering following it, it seems obvious that Pius teaches that the people share in the oblation effected by the priest in making the Victim present on the altar.

That the Pope is speaking of the oblation identified with the consecration, an oblation distinct from immolation which belongs to the priest alone, is corroborated from these words of the Pontiff: "Let the faithful, therefore, consider to what a high dignity they are raised by the sacrament of baptism. They should not think it enough to participate in the eucharistic Sacrifice with the general intention which befits members of Christ . . . but let them further . . . be most closely united with the High Priest and His earthly minister *at the time the consecration of the divine Victim is effected.* . . ." [94]

If the people had no relation to the consecration, it would surely be idle for the Pope to urge them to be "most closely united" with the priest "at the time the consecration of the divine Victim is effected."

In an earlier paragraph,[95] moreover, he had stated that it is not merely for an extrinsic reason, such as saying the prayers with the priest or even by offering the bread and wine to the priest, that the people are said to offer the sacrifice, but for more profound reasons (the Latin is, *intima ratio*), which he goes on to expound in the manner just described. Then too, one is not inclined to believe that the Pontiff wishes to reduce what he has called "the chief duty and supreme dignity" of the faithful to the position of applauding spectators.

Finally, if the Church did not share in the oblation understood in this sense, the Church would be totally excluded from a Mass stripped of all accidental prayers—an exclusion which can hardly be admitted, for the Pope says: "The whole Church can be said by right (*jure*) to offer the Victim through Christ." [96]

In What Sense the Faithful Share in the Oblation

We must next see in exactly what sense the people share in this oblation, for the Pope qualifies what he states by saying that they share in a limited

[93] *AAS*, Vol. 14 (1947), pp. 555 ff. [Miller]   [94] *Mediator Dei*, no. 104. [Miller]
[95] *Ibid.*, no. 90.   [96] *Ibid.*, no. 93.

sense (*oblatio restricti nominis*), and in a twofold way. They offer the sacrifice, first through the hands of the priest, and secondly, to a certain extent (*quodammodo*) in union with him.

The Pope goes on to explain that the faithful offer the sacrifice through the hands of the priest because the priest represents Christ the Head who offers in the name of all His members,[97] so that the whole Church can be said by right to make the oblation of the Victim through Christ. That is to say, the priest represents Christ, but Christ offers, not as a Head devoid of the rest of His body, but a Head in union with His members as a whole. All the members offer because the Head offers.

This is obviously an objective manner of offering, independent of all intentions or human acts on the part of the members. Awake or asleep, all the members, the whole Church, are sharing in the offering of the sacrifice, for it is the whole Christ that offers.

There is a second manner of offering, depending on and flowing from this first manner: the faithful offer to a certain extent in union with the priest.

The Pope says "to a certain extent" because, as he goes on to explain, the faithful do not offer the Victim in union with the priest in the sense that, being members of the Church no less than the priest, they perform a visible liturgical rite, but because they "unite their hearts in praise, impetration, expiation and thanksgiving with the prayers or intenton of the priest, even of the High Priest Himself, so that in the one and same offering of the Victim according to a visible sacerdotal rite, they may be presented to God the Father."[98]

This second mode of offering is subjective, that is, it is a human act, an act of religion, made possible because of the first or objective mode of offering. In other words, in the second manner of offering the faithful bring their interior sentiments into accord with the external rite, as the Pope says is necessary.[99]

A pagan could have the best internal sentiments in the world, but the Mass would not be his worship—the Mass would not be his sacrifice because he is not one with Christ. A pagan cannot subjectively offer the Mass because he does not do so objectively, that is, as a member of Christ the Priest.

To explain further: a man gives you a gift with his right hand. The right hand objectively gives you the gift—it does what the man does because of its union with the man. If the hand could become rational and join with the man in the act by its intention and desire, it would give the gift subjectively as well.

In the Mass, without Christ and His minister the faithful can do noth-

---

[97] The Latin text is ". . . *altaris minister personam Christi utpote Capitas gerit, membrorum omnium nomine offerentis. . . .*" [Miller]

[98] *Mediator Dei,* no. 93. [Miller]   [99] *Ibid.*

ing; when Christ and His minister offer the Victim, the faithful because of their union do so objectively (that is, through the hands of the priest), and this is the basis for their subjective offering (that is, to a certain extent in union with the priest).

As we have already seen, if sacrifice be considered precisely as sacrifice, the formal element is the immolation and the material element is the oblation. The priest alone obviously performs the liturgical rite, whereby he effects in the one act of consecration the immolation and oblation. The people do not perform the rite; they effect neither the immolation nor the oblation.

Nevertheless, though they do not effect the oblation, they do share in the oblation in the sense already explained. Hence they share in that which is the material element of sacrifice, understood precisely as sacrifice; and since a material element is a part of the essence, they can be said in this sense to share in the essence of the Mass.

Now the oblation is what makes the sacrifice a true act of religion, that is, an act of worship. It seems to be for this reason that the Pope, while excluding the people from the liturgical rite,[100] does definitely refer them to true liturgical worship: "By the waters of baptism, as by common right, Christians are made members of the Mystical Body of Christ the Priest, and by the 'character' which is imprinted on their souls, they are appointed to give worship to God. Thus they participate according to their condition in the priesthood of Christ. . . . It is by reason of this participation that the offering made by the people is also included in liturgical worship." [101]

That the Pope is here speaking of real and active power by means of the sacramental character of baptism (and not merely a metaphorical or passive power) in relation to the sacrifice of the Mass is confirmed by the Instruction of the Sacred Congregation of Rites of September 3, 1958: "The laity also exercise an active liturgical participation by virtue of the baptismal character. Because of the baptismal character it is true that in the holy sacrifice of the Mass they offer in a certain manner with the priest the divine Victim to God the Father." [102]

Here we can see the advance that St. Thomas' doctrine of the character made over St. Augustine's idea of the oneness with Christ the Priest. As St. Paul teaches, in the Body there are many members and their functions are diverse (I Cor. 12:12, 27, 28). There is only one priesthood of Christ, but it is shared in different ways.[103] It is not enough to say that all are one with Christ the Priest, but one must determine to what extent one shares in that priesthood.

---

[100] Cf. Allocution of Pius XII on the Priesthood, *Irish Ecc. Record*, 82, p. 434. [Miller]

[101] *Mediator Dei*, nos. 88 and 92. [Miller]

[102] Instruction of SRC, Sept. 3, 1958, no. 93b. [Miller]

[103] James E. Rea, *The Common Priesthood of the Members of the Mystical Body* (Washington: The Catholic U. of America Press, 1947), pp. 151 ff. [Miller]

St. Thomas showed that the character is the determinant. The character of orders gives one the power to be an active instrumental cause with Christ the principal cause in the consecrating of the divine Victim, which is the immolation and oblation according to a visible, liturgical rite. The priest in orders (instrumentally) alone makes possible the sacrifice and the laity concur in the external rite only mediately,[104] that is, through the hands of the priest and to a certain extent in union with him. Without a priest, the layman is helpless.

This limited priesthood of the laity is different from that of orders not only in degree but in kind,[105] as Pius the XII stated.[106] The layman in no way whatsoever immolates; he concurs in the oblation really but only mediately and can do nothing without a priest. The ordained minister immolates and makes the oblation without any intermediary and in his own person and acts in independence of all save Christ, the Head of the Church.

The baptismal character, then, truly gives the power to offer the Victim of the Mass, but it does not give power to perform the rite, that is, to act immediately; it gives only the power to act with the priest by intention because one is in union with Christ the Priest. It is truly the power whereby the laity exercise an active liturgical participation and offer in a certain manner the divine Victim to God.[107]

A word should be said about the accidental prayers expressing oblation surrounding the essence of the sacrifice. The whole canon should be considered, as many authors point out, as one act of sacrifice; it is extended because our human nature cannot adequately express everything in a single act. These prayers make explicit and articulate what is already contained in the essence of the Mass, and so these prayers express a reality, not merely a velleity or fiction. The prayers are an "attestation that the Church consents in the oblation made by Christ, and *offers it along with Him*." [108]

The Pope, therefore, points out: "The prayers by which the divine Victim is offered to God are generally expressed in the plural number; and in these it is indicated more than once that the people also participate in this august sacrifice inasmuch as they offer the same." [109]

Conclusion

The view of the lay priesthood presented here does not "depreciate or minimize" the lay priesthood (in accord with the wishes expressed by the Pope in his allocution), but preserves its dignity and reality. Furthermore, far from derogating from the exalted nature of the priesthood of orders, this view exalts it all the more, for it shows how completely dependent the faithful are on Christ's chosen minister, without whom there could be no common priesthood of the laity at all.

[104] Palmer, *op. cit.*, pp. 612 ff. [Miller]
[105] Rea, *op. cit.*, p. 191. [Miller]
[106] Allocution, *loc. cit.* [Miller]
[107] Instruction SRC, *loc. cit.* [Miller]
[108] *Mediator Dei*, no. 86, quoting St. Robert Bellarmine; underscoring mine. [Miller]
[109] *Ibid.*, no. 87.

We can well conclude with the summary presented by Father Rea:
The common priesthood is a real participation of the priesthood of Christ, and as such a potency really, though mediately, to offer the eucharistic Sacrifice; it is not simply a metaphor to be emptied of all reality by the prefixing of the adjective "spiritual." It is a real but analogous priesthood participating in the reality of the one priesthood of Christ, which is the sole source and origin of all priesthood.[110]

> SOURCE: Charles E. Miller, C.M., "Lay Participation in the Mass: Theological Basis (II)," *Worship*, XXXIII (May, 1959), 347–53. Used by permission of *Worship*.

LITERATURE

The contemporary literary output on theological themes is so vast that only the barest sampling is here possible. One should not miss the series of thirty-four articles published in the *Christian Century*, LVI (Jan. 18–Sept. 20, 1939) under the general title, "How My Mind Has Changed in This Decade." Of the early articles discussing the pros and cons of religious liberalism, the following are especially luminous: Henry P. Van Dusen, "The Sickness of Liberal Religion," *The World Tomorrow*, XIV (1931), 256–9; Harry E. Fosdick, "Beyond Modernism," *Christian Century*, LII (1935), 1549–52; John C. Bennett, "After Liberalism—What?" *Christian Century*, L (1933), 1403–6; A. C. McGiffert, Jr., "The Future of Liberal Christianity in America," *Journal of Religion*, XV (1935), 161–75; Wilhelm Pauck, "What is Wrong with Liberalism?" *Journal of Religion*, XV (1935), 146–60; Henry Sloane Coffin, "Can Liberalism Survive?" *Religion in Life*, IV (1935), 194–203.

Walter Horton's *Realistic Theology* (N.Y., 1934) is an early reflection of the influence of neo-orthodoxy. The same is true of John C. Bennett's *Christian Realism* (N.Y., 1941). In his "The Younger Theologians," *Religion in Life*, V (1936), 520–31, Samuel M. Cavert shows wherein the younger liberals changed their minds. Daniel Day Williams' *What Present Day Theologians Are Thinking* (rev. ed., N.Y., 1959) is an excellent short survey, with emphases upon the Bible, Christ, church, and Christian ethics. Less comprehensive, though helpful, is Roger Hazelton's *New Accents in Contemporary Theology* (N.Y., 1960). For a series of essays on various aspects of American religious thought, see Arnold Nash, ed., *Protestant Thought in the Twentieth Century* (N.Y., 1951).

For critical expositions of the thought of several leaders of the new theological movement, see George Hammar, *Christian Realism in Contemporary American Theology* (Uppsala, Sweden, 1940), giving attention to Reinhold Niebuhr, Walter M. Horton, and Henry P. Van Dusen; Mary Frances Thelen, *Man As Sinner in Contemporary American Realistic Theology* (N.Y., 1946), stressing the views of the two Niebuhrs, Horton, John C. Bennett, and Robert L. Calhoun; Charles W. Kegley and Robert W. Bretall, eds., *Reinhold Niebuhr: His Religious, Social, and Political Thought* (N.Y., 1956); Kegley and Bretall, eds., *The Theology of Paul Tillich* (N.Y., 1952); Paul Ramsey, ed., *Faith and Ethics:*

---

[110] Rea, *op. cit.*, pp. 233 ff. [Miller]

The Theology of H. Richard Niebuhr (N.Y., 1957). Each of those works contains a good bibliography. For two splendid books dealing with Reinhold Niebuhr's contribution to religious thought, see Gordon Harland, *The Thought of Reinhold Niebuhr* (N.Y., 1960), and Hans Hoffmann, *The Theology of Reinhold Niebuhr* (N.Y., 1956). George H. Tavard's *Paul Tillich and the Christian Message* (N.Y., 1961) is a perceptive analysis and evaluation.

Interest in biblical theology has revived. For a brief historical background see Clarence T. Craig, "Biblical Theology and the Rise of Historicism," *Journal of Biblical Literature,* LXII (1943), 281–94. "The Death and Rebirth of Biblical Theology" is superbly treated in James D. Smart's *The Interpretation of Scripture* (Phila., 1962), Chaps. 8 and 9. An excellent survey of current literature on biblical theology may be found in Floyd V. Filson, "The Unity of the Old and the New Testaments," *Interpretation,* V (1951), 134–52. G. Ernest Wright takes up the pros and cons of biblical theology in his "Neo-Orthodoxy and the Bible," *Journal of Bible and Religion,* XIV (1946), 87–93. For a most illuminating essay see W. D. Davies, "The Scene in New Testament Theology," *Journal of Bible and Religion,* XX (1952), 231–8. Recent developments in Old Testament theology are analyzed in Emil G. Kraeling's *The Old Testament Since the Reformation* (London, 1955), Chap. 17. Good essays by biblical specialists are contained in *The Study of the Bible Today and Tomorrow* (Chicago, 1947), ed. H. R. Willoughby. For an illuminating discussion of the interrelation of the Scriptures and theology, see Gustave Weigel's *Catholic Theology in Dialogue* (N.Y., 1961), 29–48.

Of the many books reflecting renewed interest in the Christological question, the following deserve special attention: Walter M. Horton, *Our Eternal Contemporary* (N.Y., 1942); John Knox, *On the Meaning of Christ* (N.Y., 1947); Floyd V. Filson, *One Lord, One Faith* (Phila., 1943); John W. Bowman, *The Intention of Jesus* (Phila., 1943); and W. Norman Pittenger, *The Word Incarnate* (N.Y., 1959). The closely related doctrine of the trinity is ably treated in Claude Welch's *In His Name* (N.Y., 1952).

Clarence T. Craig's *The One Church* (N.Y., 1945) is a careful study of the biblical basis of the church. In his *The Coming Great Church* (N.Y., 1945) Theodore Wedel has astutely analyzed the problems which must be solved in order to achieve comprehensive ecumenicity. Walter Horton, in his *Christian Theology: An Ecumenical Approach* (rev. ed., N.Y., 1958), 104–43, reveals the extent to which scholarly agreement has already been reached on the doctrine of the church. Highly instructive is J. Robert Nelson's *The Realm of Redemption: Studies in the Doctrine of the Nature of the Church in Contemporary Protestant Theology* (London, 1951). The Roman Catholic doctrine of the church is ably presented in Gustave Weigel's *Catholic Theology in Dialogue,* 9–28.

For a brief history of the liturgical movement in the various communions, see Massey H. Shepherd, Jr., "The History of the Liturgical Renewal," in Shepherd, ed., *The Liturgical Renewal of the Church* (N.Y., 1960), 21–52. Ernest B. Koenker's *The Liturgical Renaissance in the Roman Catholic Church* (Chicago, 1954) is a keen theological analysis by a Lutheran scholar. The great pioneer in the American phase of the Roman Catholic liturgical movement is given thorough treatment in Paul Marx, O.S.B., *The Life and Work of Virgil Michel*

(Washington, D.C., 1957). Charles Davis discusses helpfully the doctrinal basis of the liturgical movement in the Roman Communion in his *Liturgy and Doctrine* (N.Y., 1960). A. H. Reinhold's *The American Parish and the Roman Liturgy* (N.Y., 1958) is instructive. For an admirable short study, see Arthur C. Piepkorn's "The Protestant Worship Revival and the Lutheran Liturgical Movement," in Shepherd, ed., *op. cit.*, 55–97. Also valuable is the little book of addresses edited by Massey H. Shepherd, Jr., under the title, *The Eucharist and Liturgical Renewal* (N.Y., 1960).

CHAPTER XXI

Realism in Social Christianity

THE encounter of the churches with the domestic and world crises which have troubled American life since 1930 contributed to a considerable reshaping of the patterns of Christian social thought and action. Within Protestantism, the heritage of the social gospel remained strong until the outbreak of World War II. Donald B. Meyer has summed up much evidence concerning the situation in the early 1930's by saying:

. . . within the Protestant pastorate the scanty band of prophecy had grown to something of a genuine minority. Perhaps one in four Northern urban Protestant churches was likely to be led by a man for whom social change was an accepted ideal, sometimes vivid, often socialist. In Northern seminaries the proportion was apt to be higher.[1]

But the social-gospel group formed a "dominant minority" within Protestantism, for its leaders were conspicuous in many major denominations in the North, notably in Congregational, Episcopal, Baptist, Methodist, and Presbyterian bodies. Such leaders were frequently heard in church assemblies and read in the religious press. They were active in interdenominational agencies, especially in the Federal Council of Churches. While the Protestant majority held to more traditional social and political views, it was the socially conscious minority which was especially vocal and active as the economic depression of the 1930's forced the social question to the fore.

The Great Depression touched many aspects of the life of the churches. "Outwardly the churches suffered along with the rest of the nation," Robert M. Miller has written. "Memberships dropped, budgets were slashed, benevolent and missionary enterprises set adrift, ministers fired, and chapels closed." [2] Thus confronted with the disastrous effects of economic decline, the churches participated in a discussion of the pressing public questions of the day, providing an opportunity for exponents of Christian social concern to have a wide hearing. For example, a survey of periodical articles in religion for the 1930's revealed the following:

The most striking increase in religious discussion in magazines has been in the field of Christian ethics. *Readers' Guide* entries under this heading and under "Church and Social Problems," "Christian Socialism," and "Christian Sociology" increased from 17 per 100,000 in 1929 to 140 in 1932, and in 1941 they were still more than twice

[1] *The Protestant Search for Political Realism, 1919–1941* (Berkeley, Calif., 1960), 175–6.
[2] *American Protestantism and Social Issues, 1919–1939* (Chapel Hill, N.C., 1958), 63.

their 1929 level. The rise and recession of this curve is notably similar to the rise and decline in the amount of unemployment and to other indices of the economic depression.[3]

In this atmosphere, a number of the denominations for the first time formed official agencies of Christian social action. Some of the most progressive church pronouncements on public issues were made during this period.[4] Many Christians found much to commend in the liberal social legislation of Franklin D. Roosevelt's "New Deal" administration. One enthusiast stated this clearly in a report to an interdenominational home missions council: "I do not know the shades of your political passions before November 3,[5] but I suspect that I shall be right in feeling sure that dedicated as you are to the social gospel of Jesus, you must follow with sympathy the trends in national government to meet and heal human suffering." [6]

Both the theological premises and the working strategies of the social gospel were subjected to sharp attack, however, in this same depression decade. The decline of liberal theology and the emergence of neo-orthodox currents of thought undermined the theoretical foundations on which the social gospel had been built. That gospel had drawn on Marxist analysis in criticizing bourgeois society, but such developments in the Soviet Union as the Stalinist purges, followed by the pact with Hitler, served in practical ways to reveal the theoretical limitations of Marxism. By the late 1930's, only a very few Christians agreed with positive assessments of Russian developments as made by such men as Harry F. Ward (1873—).[7] Liberal social Christianity had not devoted much attention to matters of political strategy, relying largely on the power of the spoken and written word to influence significantly church and public opinion. To a growing band of those who called themselves "realists," many of whom had grown up under the inspiration of the social gospel, this was much too optimistic and impractical. It seriously misunderstood the limitations of voluntary co-operation as a means of dealing with stubborn social evils, they affirmed, and it did not take sufficient account of man's sinfulness. In his widely read books, Reinhold Niebuhr (1892—) led the attack on the views of man and society that had dominated the social gospel.[8] Niebuhr's relentless criticism

[3] Hornell Hart, "Religion," *American Journal of Sociology,* XLVII (1941–42), 894.

[4] Paul A. Carter, *The Decline and Revival of the Social Gospel: Social and Political Liberalism in American Protestant Churches, 1920–1940* (Ithaca, N.Y., 1954), Chap. 11.

[5] November 3, 1936 was election day, on which Roosevelt won his second term as President by an overwhelming landslide.

[6] Home Missions Council and Council of Women for Home Missions, *Annual Report, January, 1936–January, 1937* (N.Y., n.d.), 63.

[7] For a full discussion of Ward's views, see Ralph L. Roy, *Communism and the Churches* (N.Y., 1960); Meyer, *Protestant Search for Political Realism.*

[8] On Niebuhr, see *supra,* 455–65. Cf. also Meyer, *Protestant Search for Political Realism;* J. Neal Hughley, *Trends in Protestant Social Idealism* (N.Y., 1948), Chap. 7; Charles W. Kegley and Robert W. Bretall, eds., *Reinhold Niebuhr: His Religious, Social, and Political Thought* (N.Y., 1956); and Gordon Harland, *The Thought of Reinhold Niebuhr* (N.Y., 1960).

of the theories and strategies of liberal social Christianity contributed to its decline.

The attack on the social gospel came from outside as well as from inside the movement. In the 1930's, Christians of conservative and reactionary social viewpoints became more articulate and aggressive. Up to about 1935, most Protestants who attempted to relate Christian faith to social issues were liberals; those of conservative stamp generally tended to think of their social and their religious views as separate concerns. But in 1935, the Rev. James W. Fifield, Jr. (1899—), pastor of a large Congregational church in Los Angeles, founded Spiritual Mobilization, a movement which opposed "pagan stateism" and stood for very conservative social and economic positions. In the same year, a group of Methodist business men formed the Conference of Methodist Laymen to oppose what they considered to be leftist tendencies in the churches. Since then, many other organizations of conservative orientation have been formed. In 1951, for example, the Circuit Riders, Inc., launched a drive to oppose the propagation of socialistic or any other anti-American teachings in the Methodist Church.[9] As the conservative movement spread, it covered as wide a range of views as did liberal social Christianity, but it was one in opposing the influence of the latter in the churches and in the interdenominational agencies. In general, it saw liberalism as moving away from the American way of life under the influence of socialism and communism. For their part, the liberals stoutly argued that their views arose out of their Christian convictions and were deeply concerned with preserving the American heritage of democracy and freedom for all the people. They detected in certain of the currents of thought and action which sought to resist the threat of communism the danger of a repression of civil liberties. In countering the threats on the left, they affirmed, there was a danger of succumbing to the rigidities of the right. Many conservatives charged that communism had significantly influenced certain leaders within the churches, but only in a very few cases was this charge shown to have any truth.[10]

The conservatives, however, in their debate with the liberals, did implicitly grant an important point for which the social gospel had long argued: that Christians should be genuinely concerned about social realities as part of their faith, and that their attempts to deal with public issues

[9] For critical discussions of these movements, see Ralph L. Roy, *Apostles of Discord: A Study of Organized Bigotry and Disruption on the Fringes of Protestantism* (Boston, 1953), and George D. Younger, "Protestant Piety and the Right Wing," *Social Action*, XVII (May 15, 1951), 5–35. Characteristic expressions of the conservative critique of liberal social Christianity may be found in John T. Flynn, *The Road Ahead: America's Creeping Revolution* (N.Y., 1949), and Edmund A. Optiz, *The Powers That Be: Case Studies of the Church in Politics* (Los Angeles, 1956). A sociological treatment of the conflict in economic ethics in contemporary churches may be found in Chap. 5 of J. Milton Yinger's *Religion in the Struggle for Power: A Study in the Sociology of Religion* (Durham, N.C., 1946).

[10] Roy, *Communism and the Churches*.

should not be divorced from religious conviction. One of the major contributions of the social gospel to Protestant life was thus accepted, though in a way quite different from that envisioned by the liberal prophets.

Both because of changes in the social and economic situation, and as a consequence of the attacks made upon it, the social gospel as a movement declined after 1940. Despite the vigorous efforts of such conspicuous liberals as Bishop G. Bromley Oxnam (1891—) of the Methodist Church, the movement never recovered its previous force. In the general prosperity that marked these decades, the social question was no longer the burning one that it had been in depression days. Many Americans of both major political parties had come to accept the necessity of corporate responsibility for victims of social misfortune, so that the sense of urgency which had undergirded much Christian concern for society had lessened.

Protestant awareness of major public issues did not subside, however; the social gospel had left too lasting a stamp on church life for that. New patterns of social ethical thought and action had to be worked out. The most conspicuous leader in this effort was Reinhold Niebuhr, who had been informed both by the classical Christian views of man as sinner and by the liberal awareness of the social dimensions of life. In his efforts to describe a realistic Christian ethic, Niebuhr has sought to point the way between a too simple hope that an ideal social order can be won by exhorting people to love one another, and a cynicism which sets the principles of power or self-interest above the law of love. The Christian should labor for the closest proximation of justice as is possible amid the moral ambiguities and power struggles of life.[11] John C. Bennett (1902—) has been closely related to Niebuhr in this "neo-Protestant movement in theology and ethics" which "can best be understood as a transitional synthesis of Protestant orthodoxy with Protestant liberalism."[12] Bennett has sharply criticized various widely accepted Christian social strategies, including those of both liberal and conservative Protestantism. He has argued for a strategy that emphasized both the relevance and the transcendence of the Christian ethic, which takes account of the universality and persistence of sin, and which admits the elements of technical autonomy in social policies.[13]

The ethical thought of H. Richard Niebuhr (1894–1962) also became very influential in the post-war period. Fundamental motifs in his ethics include the relativism of life in faith, existentialist personalism, moral action as response, and a sense of flux and process in experience.[14] In part under the influence of Richard Niebuhr, but also drawing on the contributions of Dietrich Bonhoeffer (1906–45), German Protestant martyr, a contextual,

[11] E.g., see his *Christian Realism and Political Problems* (N.Y., 1953).
[12] Waldo Beach, in Arnold S. Nash, ed., *Protestant Thought in the Twentieth Century: Whence and Whither* (N.Y., 1951), 137.
[13] *Christian Ethics and Social Policy* (N.Y., 1946).
[14] Paul Ramsey, ed., *Faith and Ethics: The Theology of H. Richard Niebuhr* (N.Y., 1957); 120–2; H. Richard Niebuhr, *Christ and Culture* (N.Y., 1951), Chap. 7.

relational Christian social ethics, sometimes styled "koinonia" ethics, made its appearance in the 1950's. Distinguishing themselves from those of imperative-centered or metaphysics-centered views, the contextualists focus on the nature of moral decisions and the situations in which moral agents must act.[15]

Protestant concepts of political responsibility underwent an important transition under the impact of realistic thought. The social gospel, on the whole, was not deeply interested in politics. It was concerned with crusading for particular measures which it viewed as especially important, but, somewhat typical of the Protestantism out of which it came, it had no theology of politics. Stimulated both by a growing awareness of the power of politics as demonstrated by the rise of dictatorships and also by involvement in world Christian discussion of political realities, Christian social leaders began increasingly to call attention to the importance of political awareness at local, national, and world levels. The inescapable political dimensions of all human action were emphasized. Protestant social ethicists tended to dwell more on the necessity of the Christian's becoming responsibly concerned with the decision-making processes of politics rather than on the details of political choice.[16]

In this whole body of Christian social thought, the importance of ecumenical discussions concerning Christianity and society, to which Americans contributed much and from which they learned much, is very evident. The Life and Work Movement and its successor, the World Council of Churches, have stimulated much thought and writing in the field of social ethics; the concept of the "responsible society," which was developed in the ecumenical context, has proved to be very fruitful and provocative.[17]

Those who were charged with the responsibility of carrying out the social-action programs of the churches drew on these new currents in ethical thought for guidance in their activities. Throughout the entire period covered by this chapter, Christians were significantly concerned with three major areas of public interest: economic and industrial life, race relations, and international justice and peace. New ways of addressing these questions emerged as the new trends in social realism replaced the social gospel.

Changing patterns in Protestant economic thinking can be studied by comparing two carefully prepared and representative statements, one published in 1932 and the other in 1954. In 1932 the Federal Council of Churches adopted a statement, "Social Ideals of the Churches." The heart of the document was a summary of the ideals for which the churches should

[15] James Gustafson, "Christian Ethics and Social Policy," in Ramsey, ed., *Faith and Ethics,* 119–39; Paul L. Lehmann, "The Foundation and Pattern of Christian Behavior," in John A. Hutchison, ed., *Christian Faith and Social Action* (N.Y., 1953), 93–116.

[16] E.g., see John C. Bennett, *Christians and the State* (N.Y., 1958); William Muehl, *Politics for Christians* (N.Y., 1956).

[17] Edward Duff, *The Social Thought of the World Council of Churches* (N.Y., 1956); Walter G. Muelder, *Foundations of the Responsible Society* (N.Y., 1959).

stand, based upon the earlier "social creed" of the churches.[18] Many of the ideals dealt with economic life. In 1954 the General Board of the National Council of Churches [19] adopted a statement, "Christian Principles and Assumptions for Economic Life." This declaration climaxed in thirteen "norms for guidance" for Christian judgment of economic institutions and practices. There were many similarities between the two statements, but the second paid much more attention to the theological basis of its pronouncements, moving far beyond the simple "Kingdom of God" theology which was so strong in the earlier social-gospel movement. It was also decidedly more interested in the nature of the church as seen from a theological perspective. It emphasized that a prime objective of the churches is their ministry to individuals, and placed on the layman primary responsibility for making Christian influence felt in economic life. In 1932 the prophetic role of the church was given chief attention, but in 1954 it was recognized that the church's task is both prophetic and conserving. Whereas the earlier document called for more socialization, the latter was very much aware of the dangers of collectivism, and recognized clearly how the union of political and economic power can pose a threat to freedom. The 1954 declaration emphasized that there are real conflicts between the positive values of order, freedom, and justice. Therefore there can be no completely Christian economic system, it asserted, and Christians should seek such adjustments of economic institutions and practices as will most fully serve the three values.[20] In 1932, there was almost uncritical sympathy for labor in its struggle against capital. By 1954, the situation had been significantly altered by the effect of New Deal legislation and by the rise of "big labor." Still friendly to labor, the 1954 statement was much more aware of the ambiguities and complexities of industrial conflict. The two statements arise out of significantly changed theological and ethical contexts and clearly illustrate the shift from the confident idealism of the social gospel to the cautious realism of the ethics of responsibility.[21] The social-action study materials and programs of the churches reflected these new understandings of social-economic reality.

The earlier social gospel had focused largely though not exclusively on problems arising from the conflict of capital and labor. Since 1940, some of the issues previously somewhat subordinated emerged as major interests.

[18] For the social creed, see *supra*, 394–7.

[19] The National Council of Churches was formed in 1950 through a merger of the Federal Council with seven other major interdenominational agencies. See *infra*, 585–9.

[20] Robert T. Handy, "From 'Social Ideals' to 'Norms for Guidance,'" *Christianity and Crisis*, XIV (1954–55), 187–91.

[21] For a full elaboration of the general positions reflected in "Christian Principles and Assumptions for Economic Life," see the ten-volume series on "Ethics and Economic Life," prepared by a study committee originally appointed by the Federal Council of Churches. E.g., John C. Bennett, *et al.*, *Christian Values and Economic Life* (N.Y., 1954). An interpretation of the series was prepared by Marquis W. Childs and Douglass Cater, *Ethics in a Business Society* (N.Y., 1954).

Concern with racial injustice became especially conspicuous. In 1960, J. Oscar Lee wrote:

The churches have been especially preoccupied with this problem in the past twenty years. This interest has included: an examination of the pattern of racial segregation in American society; a determination of the religious and ethical implications of racial segregation; and movement to eliminate racial segregation from the life and work of the churches. One result of this process is that an increasing number of Christians agree that racial segregation must be rejected since it is a violation of the spirit and the teaching of the Christian gospel.[22]

The detention in relocation camps of Americans of Japanese ancestry during World War II troubled many Americans, and was one factor in the new concern for minorities.[23] But the treatment of Negroes in American life weighed more and more heavily on the conscience of Christians. Churches became more aware of their own involvement in patterns of segregation, and serious efforts to change those patterns were undertaken. Many denominations took official stands favoring desegregation.[24] The historic Supreme Court decision of May 17, 1954, calling for an end of segregation in the public schools, greatly heightened the attention given to racial matters in the nation and in the churches. New strategies of resistance to discrimination on the part of the Negroes, such as bus boycotts and lunchcounter sit-ins, were applied. The leaders of these movements, outstanding among whom was the Rev. Martin Luther King, Jr. (1929——), often drew heavily from Christian sources in shaping their programs, and appealed to all Christians for support.

Christian thought and action concerning war and peace also underwent some important transitions in this period. The social gospel in the 1920's and 1930's had been strongly influenced by pacifism; indeed, many of the movement's leaders were convinced pacifists.[25] But during the 1930's, the realistic trends in social-ethical thought ran counter to pacifism. The realists insisted that conflict of interest between men and nations was inescapable, and that to hope to preserve the values of freedom, justice and order with-

[22] "Religion Among Ethnic and Racial Minorities," *The Annals of the American Academy of Political and Social Science,* CCCXXXII (November, 1960), 113.

[23] Toru Matsumoto, *Beyond Prejudice: A Story of the Church and Japanese Americans* (N.Y., 1946).

[24] Liston Pope, *The Kingdom Beyond Caste* (N.Y., 1957); Kyle Haselden, *The Racial Problem in Christian Perspective* (N.Y., 1959).

[25] Hughley, *Trends in Protestant Social Idealism,* Chaps. 1–5; Carter, *Decline and Revival of the Social Gospel,* Chap. 14; Meyer, *Protestant Search for Political Realism,* Chap. 18; Miller, *American Protestantism and Social Issues,* Part V. See also Kirby Page, "20,870 Clergymen on War and Economic Justice," *The World Tomorrow,* XVII (1934), 222–56. The article reported on a questionnaire in which nearly 13,000 American clergymen declared their determination not to sanction or participate in any future war.

out possible recourse to the painful necessities of military force was utopian. Reinhold Niebuhr dramatically resigned from the Fellowship of Reconciliation, a pacifist organization.[26] The realists pointed to the grim facts of international life in the 1930's: the Sino-Japanese War, the invasion of Ethiopia by Italy, and especially the rise of Hitler in Germany. Many of them advocated responsible American involvement in World War II before the Japanese bombing of Pearl Harbor forced the issue. Early in 1941, for example, a group of Christian leaders founded *Christianity and Crisis,* a biweekly journal edited by Reinhold Niebuhr, in which pacifist ideas were challenged as perfectionist and utopian, and which called for participation by America in the fight for freedom against tyranny. Leading pacifists, such as Kirby Page (1890–1957) and A. J. Muste (1885—), stood by their earlier positions, as did such historic peace churches as the Quakers and the Brethren, but the pacifist movement lost much of the support it had enjoyed since World War I. The realists, however, were aware of the tragic nature of the decision for war, and had few illusions concerning the nature of modern warfare. In the churches, there was little of the jingoistic, crusading attitude that had characterized them during World War I. Participation in the war was undertaken more in the spirit of painful necessity. Conscientious objectors were for the most part given fair treatment during the war.

Though pacifism in the churches waned, devotion to the cause of peace did not. In many ways the churches expressed their concern for the development of a permanent and lasting peace. While there was some opposition, most responsible Christian bodies favored the development of international co-operation through the United Nations. As atomic weapons were perfected so that it became clear that civilization might not survive a new total war, the Christian social conscience grew more troubled. By the late 1950's there was some resurgence of pacifism—"nuclear pacifism"—cast not so much in an absolutist vein as in the conviction that unrestricted war with weapons of mass destruction must be avoided at almost any cost. Concern for international peace and order was expressed in many ways in the churches: for example, through the work of the Department of International Affairs of the National Council of Churches, through the efforts of denominational agencies, and through the continuing activities of those smaller churches which were historically committed to pacifism.

The patterns of Roman Catholic social thought and action in this period were developed along the lines which had been laid down in *Rerum novarum* (1891) and in the Bishops' Program of 1919.[27] The important new element was the publication in 1931, on the fortieth anniversary of *Rerum novarum,* of an encyclical by Pius XI on reconstructing the social order, *Quadragesimo anno.* Addressing himself to the problems of unemployment and social

---

[26] *Christian Century,* LI (1934), 17–19. [27] See *supra,* 407–14.

justice, the pope approved of social planning, and urged that the direction of economic life be assigned to autonomous vocational groups. While various segments of American Catholic life reacted with differing degrees of enthusiasm, socially-minded Catholics found much to help their cause in the papal statement, which attracted favorable attention also from Protestants and others who were concerned with public issues. In the depression years, the Catholic social movement was a force for social justice. The Social Action Department of the National Catholic Welfare Conference under the leadership of Monsignor John A. Ryan (1869–1945) did much to heighten the social awareness and effectiveness of the Catholic Church. Catholic leaders were pleased to find that most of the immediate measures as set forth in the Bishops' Program became in some form part of national policy under the New Deal.

In this decade of high social interest, variant understandings of the basic Catholic social teachings were advocated. The "radio priest," Father Charles E. Coughlin (1891—) of Royal Oak, Michigan, attracted much attention as he launched a movement of social justice that envisioned the nationalization of "public necessities," including banking and currency. When his movement ventured into political fields and took on anti-Semitic traits, he lost his following.[28] More characteristic of central Catholic social positions was the Catholic League for Social Justice, founded in 1932 by a layman, Michael O'Shaughnessy (1874—). Building on the foundation of papal social teaching, the League won the endorsement of many bishops and exerted a pervasive influence on Catholic life in the 1930's. Another facet of Catholic social concern was expressed through the National Legion of Decency, founded in 1934 to work for higher moral standards, particularly in motion pictures. In 1938, a National Organization for Decent Literature (NODL) was founded.[29]

In the 1940's and 1950's, there was much discussion among Catholics of the Industry Council plan, which called for labor-management co-operation in industry under governmental co-ordination. Many Catholic theorists declared that the Industry Councils would put into practice the ideals of the encyclicals. But the system was opposed by conservatives who were suspicious of collectivist trends in any form and who opposed economic planning. An able spokesman for the conservative view was the Rev. Edward A. Keller, professor of economics at Notre Dame.[30] But the leaders of the Social Action Department found in the Industry Councils a plan

---

[28] Aaron I. Abell, *American Catholicism and Social Action: A Search for Social Justice, 1865–1950* (Garden City, N.Y., 1960), 241–2.

[29] Harold C. Gardiner, *Catholic Viewpoint on Censorship* (Garden City, N.Y., 1958), Part II, Chap. 2.

[30] Abell, *American Catholicism and Social Action*, 267–72. The conservative movement was somewhat analogous to the one in Protestantism. Father Keller also was in favor of the so-called "right to work" laws, to which liberals were generally opposed. See his *The Case for Right-to-Work Laws: A Defense of Voluntary Unionism* (Chicago, 1956).

that gave meaning and direction to their work. An Industry Council Association was formed in 1951 to advance the plan, though it was recognized that there was no realistic hope of its being adopted in the immediate future.

Catholic political thought in this period was marked by the emergence of a "dynamic" view of church-state relations. American Catholic political thinking has tended to be quite static. Earlier tendencies toward a fruitful coming to terms of Catholic tradition with American democracy were checked by Leo XIII's condemnation of "Americanism" in the encyclical *Testem benevolentiae* (1899). American Catholicism's defensive status as a minority group in the culture tended to set as standard static and traditional patterns of political thought which looked back to the middle ages for models. But by the middle of the twentieth century, Roman Catholics in America had become a powerful force—numerous, well-organized, and aggressive. Hence many Catholic theologians were anxious to explore the possibility of fresh applications of Catholic principles to the realities of American life. Was there an inherent conflict between official Catholic teaching on church-state relations and the American heritage of democracy and freedom? Many Catholics and many non-Catholics said yes, but under the leadership of the Rev. John Courtney Murray, S.J. (1904—), an influential group of Catholic thinkers said no, and put forth a dynamic view, arguing from Catholic principles and history for an acceptance by Catholics of political democracy and religious freedom.

The patterns of Catholic social action in the period can be summarized by reference to the three major areas of public interest previously mentioned. In the field of economic and industrial life, Catholic actionists were busy during the 1930's in helping to strengthen the labor unions. This was promoted especially by the Catholic Worker movement, founded in 1933 by Dorothy Day (1898—), with the help of Peter Maurin (1877–1949). The monthly *Catholic Worker* soon attained a circulation of over one hundred thousand. Houses of hospitality provided centers for discussion and reform.[31] In 1937 the Association of Catholic Trade Unionists (ACTU) was formed. It sought to stimulate the healthy growth of the unions, to co-ordinate Catholic efforts within unionism, and to oppose communist and racketeering influences in the labor movement.[32] A particularly successful aspect of ACTU work was the forming of night schools for workers. The labor-school idea was soon adopted by other socially-minded Catholics. Hence there were nearly a hundred of these schools in existence when the communist effort to infiltrate the unions was at its height in the immediate post-war years. Catholics were thus ready to play an important role at a critical point in labor-union history.

---

[31] Dorothy Day, *Houses of Hospitality* (London, 1939). See also her book, *From Union Square to Rome* (Silver Spring, Md., 1938).

[32] Leo R. Ward, ed., *The American Apostolate: American Catholics in the Twentieth Century* (Westminster, Md., 1952), Chaps. 5 and 6.

In the field of race relations, there was marked development in this period. The Catholic mission to the Negroes, undertaken after the Civil War, had been cast in the patterns of segregation. Early in the 1920's a protest movement on the part of Negro Catholics took shape with the formation of the Federated Colored Catholics of America. The Federation was not itself very effective, but it helped to pave the way for a series of clergy conferences on Negro welfare. In the 1930's, Catholic college students became actively involved in opposing segregation. In 1934, the Catholic Interracial Council of New York City was organized under the leadership of the Rev. John La Farge, S.J. In books and in the Council's monthly *Interracial Review,* Father La Farge and others campaigned against segregation in Catholic institutions. The movement gained in strength during and after World War II; in such cities as St. Louis, New Orleans, Raleigh, N.C., and Washington, church leaders opened churches and schools on a desegregated basis in advance of public opinion.[33]

In their devotion to international justice and peace, American Roman Catholics built on the foundations laid by various popes.[34] In 1927, the Catholic Association for International Peace was formed; through its writings and meetings it sought to oppose ultra-pacifism and isolationism and to promote a juridically directed system of world organization. Catholic principles for world peace were set forth by Pius XII in a series of widely quoted Christmas Messages during the early years of World War II; these principles have guided Catholics in their continuing work for international order and peace.[35]

Trends in Catholic social thought were authoritatively expressed by Pope John XXIII in 1961 in the encyclical, *Mater et Magistra.* Issued on the seventieth anniversary of *Rerum novarum* and the thirtieth of *Quadragesimo anno,* the new encyclical built on the former statements, but went beyond them in its concern for "the universal common good." Maintaining that social justice must permeate all economic activity, it insisted that social charity must also pervade social justice under the protection of the state. In time, this encyclical may prove to have opened a new period in Catholic social concern, as *Rerum novarum* did seventy years earlier.

By 1960, the social-action programs of the churches were less conspicuous than they had been in the early 1930's, although they continued to play important roles. Chiefly through the contribution of realistic social ethics, they had in general come to be more directly related to Christian theology and more relevantly aimed at social actualities.

[33] John La Farge, *The Catholic Viewpoint on Race Relations* (Garden City, N.Y., 1956), 61–74; John T. Ellis, *American Catholicism* (Chicago, 1956), 145–6.

[34] Harry C. Koenig, ed., *Principles for Peace: Selections from Papal Documents, Leo XIII to Pius XII* (Washington, 1943).

[35] Guido Gonella, tr. T. Lincoln Bouscaren, *A World to Reconstruct: Pius XII on Peace and Reconstruction* (Milwaukee, 1944).

172. Political Conflict in Ethical Perspective

The name of Reinhold Niebuhr has already appeared many times in the treatment of the present period (1930–60), for he contributed significantly to social and theological thought throughout the period. Between his first book, *Does Civilization Need Religion?* (1927), and *The Structure of Nations and Empires* (1959), he produced sixteen books and hundreds of articles and editorials.[36] The central figure in the Fellowship of Socialist Christians, he edited a quarterly, *Radical Religion,* which drew on advanced liberal and socialistic thought in its analysis of American life.[37] Much of Niebuhr's speaking and writing criticized as tinged with naïvete and utopianism the religious, social, and political opinions cherished by many American Christians, and demanded a realistic facing of the stubborn and often tragic facts of human existence. Just reaching his prime as World War II broke out in Europe, Niebuhr devoted much of his time and energy in the next few years to a critique of pacifist analyses of the world situation and to an exhortation to Christians to become responsibly involved in the tragic power struggles of the time. Many characteristic Niebuhrian themes appear in the following article, "Politics and the Christian Ethic," written early in 1940.

DOCUMENT

I

All life is an expression of power. Human life, as other life, must have power to exist. The relation of life to life is, therefore, a relation of power to power. This fact is not changed by the *spiritual* character of life, that is, by the fact that human life is capable of speech, ideas, passions, ideals, etc. This merely means that human centers of power transcend themselves as animals do not. Since they transcend themselves they are capable of an infinite variety of relationships, as animals are not. The latter are bound by the relations which nature imposes. Human communities may therefore grow in the intensity and extent of social cohesion, while animal communities remain static. But human communities also grow in the intensity and extent of imperialism, tyranny and social conflict.

There is no inherent moral advantage in the expression of spiritual power over physical power. The propagandist uses spiritual power and the general uses physical power. The propagandist seeks to establish his cause by impressing the minds of others with its justice. He seeks to prove that it

---

[36] D. B. Robertson, *Reinhold Niebuhr's Works: A Bibliography* (Berea, Ky., 1954).

[37] In 1940 the quarterly was renamed *Christianity and Society,* and in 1948 the organization became the Frontier Fellowship.

is not his cause, but a cause which deserves the allegiance of others. The general enforces obedience. The propagandist uses a cheaper and more lasting method than the general: but it is not morally better. Or were the priests who helped to fashion early empires "better" than the soldiers who were their subordinate allies? Means are not completely neutral, but on the whole they are judged not of themselves but in terms of the ends they serve.

There is a "power" element in all forms of spirituality as long as there is an egoistic element in them. The idea that purely spiritual weapons are good while physical weapons are evil is derived from the assumption that to be spiritual means to transcend the interest of the ego and to achieve some universal interest. But human spirituality is never as simply universal as rationalists assume. All truth is spoken from a perspective. It is, therefore, however subtle, a weapon of one ego, individual or collective, against another. It is a tool of conflict. This is the truth in the Marxist theory of ideology and, more profoundly, in the Christian doctrine of original sin.

We do not stop lying any more than we stop fighting, simply because we make up our minds to be good. We lie because we see the truth from our perspective and refuse to admit that it is from our perspective. Sometimes a long conference, a "meeting of minds," may convince us that our perspective is partial and needs to be revised. But if we refuse to be convinced, our opponent has no choice but to submit to our untruth or to resist it.

The idea that we have reduced the "power" element in life when we have spiritualized it is pure illusion. Every form of spiritualization increases the potencies of both good and evil in life. Spiritual power is a concentrated form of power. Through it one personality may impose itself on another more completely than through any form of physical power. But even if it were not more potent it would still be futile to separate the spiritual from the physical; because man is a unity of physical and psychical vitality.

II

Life is not in conflict merely when it is reduced to physical proportions; and it does not transcend conflict when raised to spiritual proportions. Life is in conflict with life because each life seeks as its own, something which is equally required by other life. The most common realm of conflict is in the realm of means of subsistence. Animals and humans share this realm of conflict. Human beings, however, may have conflict in many realms about which animals know nothing. They may fight for honor, and glory; and they may be prompted to conflict by ambition, envy, jealousy, etc. The spiritual nature of life increases the number of areas in which there may be conflict and it also increases the sharpness of the conflict. The memory of an ancient wrong is no cause for conflict with either children or primitive tribes, among whom the wrong of the moment leaves no marks in the memory. But stored up vindictiveness is a potent source of conflict among the civilized peoples who have become sufficiently "spiritual" to remember past wrongs.

The conflict of life with life is never purely individual. There are always some groups, from family to national community, in which the conflict of life is sublimated and restricted. It is not restricted merely by the force of the community, but also by natural impulses of sympathy of life for life. But these forces of sociality do not eliminate the element of conflict, though they may reduce them to a tension in which overt conflict is avoided. Love between parents and children does not eliminate tension between youth and age. Love between wife and husband does not eliminate tension between the sexes. Women have had to wait for the development of independent economic power to reduce the full measure of male autocracy.

III

There are many ways of avoiding and sublimating overt conflict. Pure egotism is suicidal. It is possible to help people to realize that their good includes the good of others and is not diametrically opposed to it. Intelligence may therefore restrict conflict. Sympathy may be extended from the limits it has in nature until it includes life beyond the limits of nature. Society may set up various forms of arbitration and adjudication to mediate between conflicting social forces. If the social dispute is fairly narrow with reference to the total communal force represented by the courts, its adjudications may be said to be impartial and its mediations are usually successful. But there is no perfectly impartial judicatory; and this becomes apparent when the social forces in conflict are very inclusive, particularly when a society is divided by two contending forces. At such time courts and governments are always revealed to have a particular social locus on one or the other side of the conflict. There is, therefore, no court which can absolutely guarantee the adjudication of critical disputes. In international affairs we have not yet risen to the place where a total international community can even pretend to have either an impartial perspective upon particular disputes, nor yet instruments for disciplining recalcitrant members of the community.

All forms of moral suasion, of arbitration and of mutual accommodation have their special limits. We may yield to an opponent because we have discovered his claim to be reasonable. We may yield because, though we regard his claim as unreasonable, we think it cheaper to yield than to resist; or we may hope that generous action may beguile him from his undue claims.

IV

If his claims are really unreasonable, or if we are certain that they are, and if we would rather risk the perils of conflict than accept the certainty of submission, conflict becomes unavoidable. In such moments it is quite irrelevant to declare that nothing is worse than war. Even if it should be true that nothing is worse than war (a dogmatic assertion which has not been proved and cannot be proved) we might find the evils of submission to tyranny in the present moment so intolerable that we are ready to run the perils of an uncertain future rather than submit to the certain evils of the present. Europe may not gain a new peace out of the present war. That is still a question. But there were nations in Europe which were certain that they could not tolerate further encroachments by Nazi tyranny. Between slavery and an uncertain future, they chose the uncertain future. Only nations which are not confronted with such a choice can stand aside and make wise and moralistic remarks about the wisdom of such a choice. It belongs to the inevitabilities, and perhaps to the tragedies of history.

The whole moralism which asks men to "disavow the war system" is beside the point. The war system is a part of the character of historic reality. It is not overcome by lifting life from the physical to the spiritual level. Human conflicts are more deadly than animal conflicts precisely because man is spiritual. This does not mean that a wise statesmanship will not seek to mitigate conflict, to divert and deflect contending forces, to beguile conflict and transmute it into a higher form of social tension. Only there is no statesmanship and no religion which can guarantee such results when irreconcilable social wills face each other.

V

Of course there is always one possibility to avoid conflict and that is to allow any injustice to be done rather than to resist an aggressor. This way of complete non-resistance is rightly understood by Christianity as standing on the edge of history and eternity and not in history. The Christ who reveals the character of God to us is completely powerless. There is no way of revealing the goodness of God (in whom alone goodness and power are perfectly united) but to be powerless in history. The Saviour dies upon the Cross. History is a balance of social forces and if life does not enter into that precarious balance to maintain itself, it is lost. Perfect love ends on the Cross. Quite rightly Christianity sees in this act on the Cross not only the revelation of the ultimate character of God, but of the essential character of man. Man ought not to live in conflict with his fellowman. It is sinful, and not normal, that history should be a conflict of competing egos. There will always be men (and there ought to be) in the Christian church who will declare that rather than assert their lives in this contest of forces they will prefer to sacrifice their lives. Such an act is not immediately relevant to history. It is indirectly relevant because history is something more than merely sinful conflict. It is touched by eternity.

The difficulty with this philosophy of pure non-resistance is that modern Christians, not recognizing the profundity of the problem of sin, do not regard an act of pure sacrifice as an act which transcends history and reaches into eternity. They try to make it into an act of historical policy. They persuade themselves that if one yields to the foe, the foe will ultimately be shamed into goodness. This may happen, but there is no certainty that it will. Jesus asked His disciples not to expect it. "Rejoice," He said, "not that the devils are subject unto you, but that your name is recorded in heaven." Or again, the policy of sacrifice is transmuted from the individual to the social sphere. A nation, culture and civilization is asked not to defend itself against the aggressor. Practically this means submission to tyranny; and all the efforts of modern pacifists to show that it does not mean this, prove that they do not understand the Cross as standing on the edge of, and not in history. The Cross is not an instrument of social policy. The reductio ad absurdum of the argument that the Cross is an instrument of social policy is given in Richard Gregg's book, "The Power of Non-Violence," in which Jesus is pictured as the initiator of a new movement of social life, who did not understand political techniques as well as Gandhi does, and therefore unfortunately ended His life upon the Cross. If He had perfectly understood He might have known that "non-violent techniques" are the best way of "breaking the morale of the enemy."

The whole effort to change the doctrine of non-resistance to one of non-violent resistance or to place the emphasis upon spiritual rather than physical resistance is nothing but the fruit of the confusion of liberal religion. There is no absolute line between physical and spiritual coercion, nor is there one between violent and non-violent resistance. There are tentative and pragmatic distinctions; but none of them can justify the assertion of their proponents that they have broken with the "war system." They would like to mitigate conflict. So would we. There is no decent person who will not exhaust the ingenuity of statecraft to mitigate conflict. The question is whether we are able to see that finally history is conflict. The Saviour who dies on the Cross reminds us that it is not natural that history should be like that. But that He dies on the Cross proves that it is inevitable that it should be like that. Perfect love may enter the world but only as suffering love. Any cheap philosophy which declares that it will be turned from suffering to triumphant love, if you only believe hard enough, understands little about history. This Christ will ultimately triumph; but not in history. Only at the end of history. Let our Christian moralists study the eschatology of the gospels a little more seriously.

The difficulty with the assumption that the "way of the Cross" is a simple alternative to the balance of power and the conflict of power, between which history alternates, is that it produces such loveless and pitiless criticisms of the people who are involved in overt conflict on the part of those who are not involved, even though freedom from involvement may be merely the fruit of an "uncovenanted mercy" such as a broad ocean. It is assumed that those involved could easily have chosen a different course, or if they could not have done so easily, they could nevertheless have done so. The only true pity and forgiveness possible to sinful men is possible to those who know themselves to be sinful men. The best chance of transcending social conflict is the chance of those who know themselves certainly to be in it, by reason of their own sin. If they imagine themselves actually to have transcended it by reason of some moral achievement on their part, they will merely take their favored social position, where the social struggle has not yet reached a crisis, for their own virtue.

This is what betrays the socially comfortable classes into such self-righteous criticisms of the socially desperate. This, also, betrays contemporary America, particularly Christian America, into such fatuous criticisms of Europe. The plight of Europe is tragic enough. If we cannot see it as a tragedy in which we are all involved, we merely add the cruelty of Pharisees to the cruelty of nationalistic pagans.

VI

There are, of course, many moral acts of "sacrifice," of concession, of one life yielding advantages to another life. Human history is never purely a contest of power. These deeds of sacrifice may be only casual and they may be more thoroughgoing. But it is very sentimental to identify them with the "way of the Cross." Most philanthropy, for instance, does not disturb the eminence of power which the giver holds; and generally it does not seriously restrict the privileges which flow from this power. "They gave," said Jesus, "of their superfluities." Preachers who preach glibly of the way of the Cross would do well to remember that their life does not usually end there, and that if there are preferments in the church they are quite anxious to have them. Deeds of sacrifice may, even if they fall short of the sacrifice of life, change the quality of history. Whenever they transcend all canons of prudence, they do not, however, justify themselves in terms of their historical consequences. They are done that we may be children of our Father in Heaven. This is the paradox of the relation of Eternity to history. That which is most influential in history is what is done not for history, but for eternity.

It is this fact which persuades some Christians to believe that the very character and texture of historical and social reality can be changed so that it will cease to contradict the Kingdom of God. But history remains continually in the same relation to the Kingdom of God. The perfect love of the Kingdom of God, revealed on the Cross, is on the one hand the fulfillment of all "community," of all loving relation of life with life "intended" in history. It is on the other hand a contradiction of the self-will and self-love of history; and when it is pressed through consistently enough, it ends history.

SOURCE: Reinhold Niebuhr, "Politics and the Christian Ethic," *Christianity and Society,* V (Spring, 1940), 24–8. Used by permission of *Christianity and Society* and the author.

173. Principles of a Durable Peace

The Department of International Justice and Goodwill of the Federal Council of Churches (later the Department of International Affairs of the National Council of Churches) served as an important center in Protestantism for thought and action about peace. During World War II, the Department established a Special Commission on a Just and Durable Peace, under the chairmanship of a Presbyterian layman, John Foster Dulles (1888–1959), later the Secretary of State. The Commission prepared a "Statement of Guiding Principles" to help shape Christian opinion on the problems of peace; it was adopted by the Federal Council itself in 1942. The Special Commission went on to frame a brief "Statement of Political Propositions" which became popularly known as the "Six Pillars of Peace." [38] The larger "Statement of Guiding Principles," here reprinted, gave clear direction to many churches and Christians as they thought about peace and international order. The Statement also figured strongly in Federal Council critiques of specific peace proposals as they were publicly discussed, and it gave significant direction to a National Study Conference on the Churches and a Just and Durable Peace held at Cleveland in 1945.[39]

DOCUMENT

Preamble

As members of the Christian Church, we seek to view all problems of world order in the light of the truth concerning God, man and God's purpose for the world made known in Jesus Christ. We believe that the eternal God revealed in Christ is the Ruler of men and of nations and that His purpose in history will be realized. For us He is the source of moral law and the power to make it effective.

From this faith Christians derive the ethical principles upon which world order must be based. These principles, however, seem to us to be among those which men of goodwill everywhere may be expected to recognize as part of the moral law. In this we rejoice. For peace will require the cooperation of men of all nations, races and creeds. We have therefore first set out (Points 1 to 9) those guiding principles which, it seems to us, Christians and non-Christians alike can accept.

We believe that a special responsibility rests upon the people of the United States. We accordingly (Point 10) express our thoughts in that regard.

[38] The Six Pillars, often circulated with much supplementary material prepared by the Commission, were not official statements of the Federal Council itself, but were authorized for publication.
[39] See *International Conciliation, Documents for the Year 1945* (N.Y., 1945), 129–77.

Above all, we are impressed by the supreme responsibility which rests upon Christians. Moral law may point the way to peace, but Christ, we believe, showed that way with greatest clarity. We therefore, in conclusion (Points 11 and 12) address ourselves to Christians.

Guiding Principles

1.

WE BELIEVE that moral law, no less than physical law, undergirds our world. There is a moral order which is fundamental and eternal, and which is relevant to the corporate life of men and the ordering of human society. If mankind is to escape chaos and recurrent war, social and political institutions must be brought into conformity with this moral order.

2.

WE BELIEVE that the sickness and suffering which afflict our present society are proof of indifference to, as well as direct violation of, the moral law. All share in responsibility for the present evils. There is none who does not need forgiveness. A mood of genuine penitence is therefore demanded of us—individuals and nations alike.

3.

WE BELIEVE that it is contrary to the moral order that nations in their dealings with one another should be motivated by a spirit of revenge and retaliation. Such attitudes will lead, as they always have led, to renewed conflict.

4.

WE BELIEVE that the principle of cooperation and mutual concern, implicit in the moral order and essential to a just and durable peace, calls for a true community of nations. The interdependent life of nations must be ordered by agencies having the duty and the power to promote and safeguard the general welfare of all peoples. Only thus can wrongs be righted and justice and security be achieved. A world of irresponsible, competing and unrestrained national sovereignties whether acting alone or in alliance or in coalition, is a world of international anarchy. It must make place for a higher and more inclusive authority.

5.

WE BELIEVE that economic security is no less essential than political security to a just and durable peace. Such security nationally and internationally involves among other things the use of material resources and the tools of production to raise the general standard of living. Nations are not economically self-sufficient, and the natural wealth of the world is not evenly distributed. Accordingly the possession of such natural resources should not be looked upon as an opportunity to promote national advantage or to enhance the prosperity of some at the expense of others. Rather such possession is a trust to be discharged in the general interest. This calls for more than an offer to sell to all on equal terms. Such an offer may be a futile gesture unless those in need can, through the selling of their own goods and services, acquire the means of buying. The solution of this problem, doubtless involving some international organization, must be accepted as a responsibility by those who possess natural resources needed by others.

6.

WE BELIEVE that international machinery is required to facilitate the easing of such economic and political tensions as are inevitably recurrent in a world which is living and therefore changing. Any attempt to freeze an order of society by inflexible treaty specifications is bound, in the long run, to jeopardize the peace of mankind. Nor must it be forgotten that refusal to assent to needed change may be as immoral as the attempt by violent means to force such change.

7.

WE BELIEVE that that government which derives its just powers from the consent of the governed is the truest expression of the rights and dignity of man. This requires that we seek autonomy for all subject and colonial peoples. Until that shall be realized, the task of colonial government is no longer one of exclusive national concern. It must be recognized as a common responsibility of mankind, to be carried out in the interests of the colonial peoples by the most appropriate form of organization. This would, in many cases, make colonial government a task of international collaboration for the benefit of colonial peoples who would, themselves, have a voice in their government. As the agencies for the promotion of world-wide political and economic security become effective, the moral, social and material welfare of colonial populations can be more fully realized.

8.

WE BELIEVE that military establishments should be internationally controlled and be made subject to law under the community of nations. For one or more nations to be forcibly deprived of their arms while other nations retain the right of maintaining or expanding their military establishments can only produce an uneasy peace for a limited period. Any initial arrangement which falls short of this must therefore be looked upon as temporary and provisional.

9.

WE BELIEVE that the right of all men to pursue work of their own choosing and to enjoy security from want and oppression is not limited by race, color or creed. The rights and liberties of racial and religious minorities in all lands should be recognized and safeguarded. Freedom of religious worship, of speech and assembly, of the press, and of scientific inquiry and teaching are fundamental to human development and in keeping with the moral order.

10.

WE BELIEVE that, in bringing international relations into conformity with the moral law, a very heavy responsibility devolves upon the United States. For at least a generation we have held preponderant economic power in the world, and with it the capacity to influence decisively the shaping of world events. It should be a matter of shame and humiliation to us that actually the influences shaping the world have largely been irresponsible forces. Our own positive influence has been impaired because of concentration on self and on our short-range material gains. Many of the major preconditions of a just and durable peace require changes of national policy on the part of the United States. Among such may be mentioned: equal access to natural resources, economic collaboration, equitable treatment of racial minorities, international control of tariffs, limitation of armaments, participation in world government. We must be ready to subordinate immediate and particular national interests to the welfare of all. If the future is to be other than a repetition of the past, the United States must accept the responsibility for constructive action commensurate with its power and opportunity.

11.

WE BELIEVE that, as Christian citizens, we must seek to translate our beliefs into practical realities and to create a public opinion which will insure that the United States shall play its full and essential part in the creation of a moral way of international living. We must strive within the life of our own nation for change which will result in the more adequate application here of the principles above enumerated as the basis for a just and durable world order.

12.

WE BELIEVE that a supreme responsibility rests with the Church. The Church, being a creation of God in Jesus Christ, is called to proclaim to all men everywhere the way of life. Moreover, the Church which is now in reality a world community, may be used of God to develop His spirit of righteousness and love in every race and nation and thus to make possible a just and durable peace. For this service Christians must now dedicate themselves, seeking forgiveness for their sins and the constant guidance and help of God, upheld by faith that the kingdoms of this world shall become the kingdom of Christ and that He shall reign for ever and ever.

> SOURCE: *A Just and Durable Peace. Statement of Guiding Principles Adopted by the Federal Council of Churches, December 11, 1942* (N.Y., n.d.). Used by permission of the National Council of the Churches of Christ.

174. *Planning for a Just Peace*

In November of 1945, the year that had seen victory over Germany in the spring and over Japan in the late summer, one hundred and ten members of the hierarchy of the Roman Catholic Church in the United States met for their annual meeting in Washington, D.C. Conscious of the importance of their church in American life and mindful of the role played by it in the war just ended, the bishops felt the time was appropriate to release a formal statement concerning America's foreign policy. Troubled because earlier hopes for a sound and permanent peace were already dimming, the bishops spoke frankly and forcefully in their statement, "Between War and Peace," reprinted here in full. They did not hesitate to criticize the weaknesses of the newly formed United Nations, even while endorsing the nation's membership in that organization. The document was signed in the name of all the bishops and archbishops by the Administrative Board of the National Catholic Welfare Conference, and given wide coverage in the press.

DOCUMENT

The war is over but there is no peace in the world. In the Atlantic Charter we were given the broad outline of the peace for which we fought and bled and, at an incalculable price, won a great martial victory. It was that ideal of peace which sustained us through the war, which inspired the heroic defense of liberty by millions driven underground in enslaved countries. It made small, oppressed nations confide in us as the trustee of their freedoms. It was the broad outline of a good peace. Are we going to give up this ideal of peace? If, under the pretext of a false realism, we do so, then we shall stand face to face with the awful catastrophe of atomic war.

Since the Moscow Conference of 1943, the United States, Great Britain and Russia have undertaken to shape gradually the peace which they are imposing on the nations. From the conferences of these victorious powers there is emerging slowly their pattern for the peace. It is disappointing in the extreme. Assurances are given us in the announced peace principles of our country but so far results do not square with these principles. We are in perhaps the greatest crisis of human history. Our country has the power.

the right and the responsibility to demand a genuine peace, based on justice which will answer the cry in the hearts of men across the world.

We want to work in unity with other nations for the making of a good peace. During the war perhaps, it may have been necessary for strategic reasons to postpone final decisions on many questions mooted at the conferences of the three great powers. Now we must face the facts. There are profound differences of thought and policy between Russia and the western democracies. Russia has acted unilaterally on many important settlements. It has sought to establish its sphere of influence in eastern and southeastern Europe, not on the basis of sound regional agreements in which sovereignties and rights are respected, but by the imposition of its sovereignty and by ruthlessly setting up helpless puppet states. Its Asiatic policy, so important for the peace of the world, is an enigma.

The totalitarian dictators promised benefits to the masses through an omnipotent police-state which extends its authority to all human relations and recognizes no innate freedoms. Their theories, moreover, look to the realization of world well-being as ultimately to be secured by the inclusion of all countries in their system. Sometimes Russia uses our vocabulary and talks of democracy and rights but it attaches distorted meanings to the words. We think in terms of our historic culture. We see God-given, inviolable human rights in every person and we know democracy as the free collaboration under law of citizens in a free country.

There is a clash of ideologies. The frank recognition of these differences is preliminary to any sincere effort in realistic world cooperation for peace. The basis of this cooperation must be mutual adherence to justice. It would be unjust for us to be an accomplice in violating the rights of nations, groups and individuals anywhere in the world.

A first step toward effective negotiation for peace is to have a plan. A good plan states principles in terms of all the specific questions at issue. Instead, so far we have compromised and sought to make mere piece-meal settlements. Instead of honest, promising discussion even on diverging plans, we are witnessing a return of the tragedy of power politics and the danger of balance of power arrangements which, with the substitution of mere expediency for justice have begotten war after war. We must indeed aim at collaborating with all of our allies in the making of a good peace. There are, however, concessions which we dare not make because they are immoral and destructive of genuine peace.

Our peace program envisions a world organization of nations. The Charter which emerged from the San Francisco Conference, while undoubtedly an improvement on the Dumbarton Oaks proposals, does not provide for a sound, institutional organization of the international society.[40]

[40] The Dumbarton Oaks Conference in Washington, D.C., in 1944, prepared drafts for the charter of the United Nations. The Yalta Conference early in 1945 reached further agreements which made possible other modifications and the signing of the charter at San Francisco later that year.

The Security Council provisions make it no more than a virtual alliance of the great powers for the maintenance of peace. These nations are given a status above the law. Nevertheless, our country acted wisely in deciding to participate in this world organization. It is better than world chaos. From the provision in the Charter for calling a Constituent Assembly in the future, there comes the hope that in time the defects may be eliminated and we may have a sound, institutional organization of the international community which will develop, not through mere voluntary concessions of the nations, but from the recognition of the rights and duties of international society.

While peace is in the making, there are urgent issues which we can no longer evade. At Yalta we gave a pledge to the Polish people and assumed responsibility before the world that they would be unhampered in setting up their own independent, democratic government. Are we working to the fulfillment of that pledge in the full measure of our responsibility and our power? What apology can be offered for the failure of the protagonists of democracy to protest the absorption by force and artifice of the Baltic countries into the Union of Soviet Republics? We are shocked by the news which is leaking out from Slovakia, Croatia, Slovenia and other southeastern European countries. Religious persecution which is both brutal and cunning rages in many lands. No reason of policy justifies our silence. What is happening behind the blackout of eastern and southeastern Europe is a stark contradiction to the high ideals which inspired our fighting to save the world from totalitarian aggression.

No one can fail to see the importance of a reconstructed, revitalized Europe which is the cradle of western culture. We deplore the tragic indifference to the plight of the Italian people who threw off the chains of a Fascist regime, who fought side by side with us in ardent loyalty. For over two long years of agony the friends of democracy in that country have had to stand by in impotence while we have toyed with the vital problems of relief and rehabilitation and deferred the fulfillment of our own solemn promises.

Our own national interest, as well as the cause of world peace, and the fate of Christian culture are at stake in Italy. Today it is an outpost of western civilization. We are fully confident that the Italian people, if we save them from despair by our helpful interest, will stand fast against the deceitful appeal of alien and subversive ideologies and shape their future in the spirit of their own noble Christian tradition.

We cannot be unconcerned about the future of Germany, Austria and Hungary. Whatever period of probation must be imposed on the vanquished nations, we must help them to take their rightful place in the family of nations. To treat them in a spirit of vengeance is neither right nor politic. Justice demands the punishment of the guilty and reasonable reparations of damage done. But we cannot forget, or allow our representatives to forget, that our traditional system of punitive justice is anchored to the concept of individual responsibility. The inhumanities which now mark the mass transference of populations, the systematized use of slave labor and the cruel treatment of prisoners of war should have no place in our civilization.

Acute suffering is the daily lot of whole populations in many war-torn lands. Every report indicates that unless heroic measures are taken at once, millions will die from starvation and exposure during the coming winter. The feeding and clothing and sheltering of these suffering people is not a work which can be left to some future convenient date. Our country, because of our greater resources, must do the major part of this work of relief. In it we have the right and duty to insist on the leadership which corresponds to our sacrifices and contributions. It is imperative that Congress make adequate appropriations for this work from the public treasury.

It is equally imperative that private relief agencies be given a full opportunity to carry on their beneficent work among all suffering peoples. And relief must envision something larger than merely feeding the starving and sheltering the homeless. Help must be given to people whose economies are ruined. They have the right to assistance in getting back to normal economic life. Neither the prosperity of the greater nations nor their might will prevent war unless conditions are removed in which poor, helpless peoples are denied the opportunity of a decent living standard. The world is one only insofar as men live together as brothers under God.

Ours is a grave responsibility. The heart and hand of America are called upon in a way that is unique, not only in the history of our country but even in the annals of mankind. We know that democracy is as capable of solving the admittedly difficult problems of peace as it has shown itself in war. We must be true to ourselves. We must hold fast to our own free institutions. We must resolutely oppose the few amongst us who are trying to sabotage them. We may well pity those who in their half-veiled sympathy for totalitarianism are playing with the thought that perhaps in this great emergency its day is at hand. On bended knees let us ask God in His Blessed Providence to help us to be the vigorous champion of democratic freedom and the generous friend of the needy and oppressed throughout the world.

> SOURCE: "Between War and Peace," *Catholic Action*, XXVII (December, 1945), 27–8. Used by permission of National Catholic Welfare Conference.

175. The Threat of Mass Destruction

The perplexity of Christians with modern war was intensified by the terrible success of the atomic bombing of Hiroshima and Nagasaki during the summer of 1945. Representatives of many traditions had come to see the warfare of the atomic age as a tragic demonstration of human sinfulness. To help Christians think their way through the fateful issues raised by the threat of atomic destruction, the Federal Council of Churches early in 1950 appointed a Special Commission to study the moral problems involved. Bishop Angus Dun (1892—) of the Protestant Episcopal Church was named chairman of the Commission. Among its twenty members were such distinguished thinkers as John C. Bennett (1902—), Reinhold Niebuhr (1892—), and Paul J. Tillich (1886—) of Union Theological Seminary; Robert L. Calhoun (1896—) and Theodore M. Greene (1897—) of Yale University; Walter M. Horton (1895—) of Oberlin, and Benjamin E. Mays (1895—) of Morehouse College. The Commission found that most Christians, though aware of the terrible dangers, could see no way of avoiding the dreadful responsibilities of conflict in taking necessary collective action against aggression within the framework of the United Nations.

The Commission's report, *The Christian Conscience and Weapons of Mass Destruction,* was cast in two main parts: "War and the Weapons of Mass Destruction," and "Peace and a Positive Strategy." The first section, largely reproduced herewith, continued the debate between pacifist and nonpacifist Christians. Many of the members of the Commission had belonged to a previous one which, under the chairmanship of Calhoun, had prepared a report on "The Relation of the Church to the War in the Light of the Christian Faith" (1944). This earlier report had indicated a clear division of opinion between a majority who affirmed that Christian duty was more adequately conceived by those Christians who voluntarily supported the military campaign of the United Nations against the Axis powers, and a minority who believed that those who chose conscientious objection in time of war judged more accurately the meaning of Christian duty. These differences of opinion were reflected in the controversial first section of the new Commission's report. Not all the members could sign it. Calhoun indicated his hearty accord with much of the statement, but protested that it seemed to assign to Christian conscience only the negative, inhibitory role of suggesting "restraint" on destructive procedures. "But the norm for practically effective inhibitions turns out to be, after all, military decisiveness; and beyond ruling out wanton destruction, Christian conscience in wartime seems to have chiefly the effect (certainly important but scarcely decisive) of making Christians do reluctantly what military necessity requires." [41] Georgia E. Harkness (1891—) of the Pacific School of Religion also dissented from the section, finding that it lacked such distinctive moral guidance from the Christian gospel as was possible and necessary for the times. The debate within the Commission showed how difficult were the issues posed by atomic destruction for Christians in America at mid-century. [42]

[41] *The Christian Conscience and Weapons of Mass Destruction* (N.Y., 1950), 23.

[42] For a later critique of this and allied documents, see Paul Ramsey, *War and the Christian Conscience: How Shall Modern War Be Conducted Justly?* (Durham, N.C., 1961), 141–7.

What are the decisions open to us?

The clearest and least ambiguous alternative is that urged upon us by our most uncompromising pacifist fellow-Christians. They believe that the refusal of all kinds of military service and an unqualified witness against war and for peace is for them the will of God. They would summon all Christian people and all Churches to unite with them in this witness. For them the infinitely heightened destructiveness and the morally catastrophic character of modern war confirm their conviction that followers of Christ can make no compromise with so great an evil. They find themselves called to follow the way of love and reconciliation at whatever cost and to accept the historical consequences of a repudiation of armaments and of war. For those who make this radical decision need for debate as to the choice of weapons is ruled out by a repudiation of all weapons.

Pacifist and non-pacifist Christians can probably agree that, as men are, responsible political leaders could not take the pacifist position and continue to hold positions of effective political leadership. But that fact does not relieve those of us who are Christians from making our own decisions in the sight of God and urging what we believe to be right Christian decisions on those who govern as our representatives.

The large majority of professing Christians are not pacifists. But Christian non-pacifists share with their pacifist brethren abhorrence of war and with them see in it a sign of man's Godlessness. They agree that in all human conflicts the most righteous side is never so righteous as it thinks it is. They acknowledge that whatever good may ever come out of war, incalculable evil always comes out of it, too. We believe that God calls some men to take the way of non-violence as a special and high vocation in order to give a clearer witness to the way of love than those can give who accept responsibility for the coercions in civil society. We rejoice that God has called some of our brethren in the universal Christian fellowship to bear this witness and are humbled by the faithfulness of many in bearing it. Without minimizing the moral heroism it can require, we are even envious of the greater inner simplicity of that non-violent way.

But most of us find ourselves called to follow a course which is less simple and which appears to us more responsible because more directly relevant to the hard realities of our situation. And we believe it is the way in which most Christians must go.

There can be no justice for men and no responsible freedom without law and order. When men confront one another with their contending egotisms, without moral or spiritual bonds, they take the law into their own hands and work what is at best a very crude justice. They reach beyond that only when they have achieved some substantial moral community and a sovereign law rooted in moral community. This we have reached, however imperfectly, where we find ordered society. Even then the law which gives any just order must be sustained by power, and, when necessary, by coercive power.

The world we live in, the world of states and of great masses of men struggling up towards nationhood, is without strong uniting moral or spiritual bonds. It possesses no overruling law and in the United Nations an institution which marks only the beginnings of common order. In large measure our world is a "frontier" of self-regarding, mutually distrustful human masses. God's will for justice and for mercy broods over this disorder in which we find ourselves. We Christians believe that we are called to be the servants of His justice and His mercy. But can we be just to men if we do not struggle to maintain for them and for ourselves some order of justice in which good faith and freedom and truth can find a dwelling place? And can we extend the beginnings of this order in the United Nations, if we do not undergird it with effective power?

So most Christians, faced with the lawlessness of our world of nations, see no way of serving the righteousness of God in the presence of brutal and irresponsible violence save by taking responsible collective action against aggression within the framework of the United Nations. That we must do in fear and trembling, as those who know how our own self-interest blinds us. We must take upon ourselves the dreadful responsibilities of conflict, if we are to accept even the imperfect justice and freedom which others have painfully won and for which others fight and die even now. In the last resort we are in conscience bound to turn to force in defense of justice even though we know that the destruction of human life is evil. There are times when this can be the lesser of two evils, forced upon us by our common human failure to achieve a better relationship.

The deep disorder within men and among men, which Christian faith calls sin, leads to both brutal dominion and conflict. Today, two great dangers threaten mankind, the danger that totalitarian tyranny may be extended over the world and the danger of global war. Many of us believe that the policies most likely to avoid both dangers inevitably carry the risk of war.

Does this mean that for those who take this position the love of God and the judgments of God and the commandments of God cease to have meaning? We know that Christ died for our enemies as well as for us. We know that we are bidden to pray for our enemies as for ourselves. We know that we stand with them in need of forgiveness. We know that our failure to find another way of dealing with our deep differences and conflicts of interest and distrust of one another is a judgment on us and our forefathers as well as on them. But this does not extricate us from the hard realities of our situation.

We cannot lightly assume that a victory for our own nation, or a victory for the United Nations, is in itself a victory for God and His righteousness. Even in war we cannot rejoice that more of the enemy are killed than of our own people. Even in victory we can rejoice only if, from the sacrifices of so much life, some little gain is made for order and freedom, and renewed opportunity is found for mercy and reconciliation.

Concepts of Total War

Christians who have decided that in the last resort they may be compelled to accept the terrible responsibilities of warfare are now confronted with these questions: Does that mean warfare without any limits? Does that mean warfare with any weapons which man's ingenuity can provide?

War has developed rapidly in the direction of "total war" in two meanings, which it is important to distinguish.

In the first meaning total war refers to the fact that in a conflict between highly industrialized nations all human and material resources are mobilized for war purposes. The traditional distinction between combatants and non-combatants is far less clear. Only small children and the helpless sick and aged stand outside the war effort. It is practically impossible to distinguish between guilty and innocent. Certainly men who are drafted into uniform may be among the least guilty. Total war, in this sense of the involvement of the whole nation in it, cannot be avoided if we have a major war at all.

Total war, in the second sense, means war in which all moral restraints are thrown aside and all the purposes of the community are fully controlled by sheer military expediency. We must recognize that the greater the threat to national existence the greater will be the temptation to subordinate everything, all civil rights, the liberty of conscience, all moral judgments regarding the means to be used, and all consideration of postwar international relations, to the single aim of military victory.

Christians and Christian Churches, if they admit that occasions can arise when the use of military force by a nation or a group of nations may be less evil than surrender to some malignant power, cannot deny that total war in the first sense may be inescapable.

But Christians and Christian Churches can never consent to total war in the second sense. The only possible justification for war is that it offers a possibility of achieving a moral result, however imperfect, to prevent an overwhelming moral evil and to offer a new opportunity for men to live in freedom and decency and in just and merciful relationships. . . .

The Weapons of Mass Destruction

What then of the weapons we shall or shall not be prepared to use?

Can we find some absolute line we can draw? Can we say that Christians can approve of using swords and spears, but not guns; conventional bombs or jellied fire, but not atomic bombs; uranium bombs, but not hydrogen bombs? Can we say that Christians must pledge themselves or seek to pledge their nations not to stock this or that weapon, even though the enemy stocks them; or not to use some weapons, even though the enemy uses them?

We find no "clean" methods of fighting, but some methods are dirtier than others. Some cause more pain and maiming without commensurate military decisiveness. Some are more indiscriminate.

We have no more—nor any less—right to kill with a rifle or a bazooka than with an A-bomb or an H-bomb. In the sight of Him, "to whom all hearts are open," the inner quality of an act is to be distinguished from its consequences. There may be more hatred and less penitence in the heart of a man who kills one enemy with a rifle, or in the heart of a frenzied super-patriot in his armchair, than in the heart of an airman who devastates a city with a bomb. Sin in its inward meaning cannot be measured by the number of people who are affected. But a reckoning of consequences is also a part of a Christian's decision. It is more dreadful to kill a thousand men than one man, even if both are done in the service of justice and order. We cannot, therefore, be released from the responsibility for doing no more hurt than must be.

Here a distinction can be drawn between precision weapons, which can be directed with reasonable control at primary military objectives, and weapons of mass destruction. But we are compelled to recognize that the increasing distance from which bombs or projectiles are released and the speed of planes and guided missiles are likely to offset all gains in precision. If, as we have felt bound to acknowledge, certain key industrial targets are inescapably involved in modern war, we find no moral distinction between destroying them by tons of T.N.T. or by fire as compared with an atomic bomb, save as greater precision is possible in one as compared with others. But this recognition that we cannot isolate the atomic bomb or even the projected H-bomb as belonging to an absolutely different moral category must not blind us to the terrible dimensions of the moral problem they present.

With a single atomic bomb, destruction is produced that is as great as that from a large fleet of airplanes dropping conventional explosives. If the H-bomb is made, it will be destructive on a still more horrible scale. If such weapons are used generally upon centers of population, we may doubt whether enough will remain to rebuild decent human society.

But the abandonment of atomic weapons would not eliminate mass destruction. Conventional or new weapons may produce comparable destruction. The real moral line between what may be done and what may not be done by the Christian lies not in the realm of the distinction between weapons but in the realm of the motives for using and the consequences of using all kinds of weapons. Some measures corrupt the users, and destroy the humanity of the victims. Some may further the victory but impair the peace. There are certainly things which Christians should not do to save self, or family, or nation, or free civilization. There seems to us, however, no certain way to draw this moral line in advance, apart from all the actual circumstances. What may or may not be done under God can be known only in relation to the whole, concrete situation by those responsibly involved in it. We can find no moral security, or moral hiding place, in legalistic definitions. The terrible burden of decision is the Christian man's responsibility, standing where he does before God.

Nevertheless, real distinctions can be made to illumine and help the conscience in its trouble. The destruction of life clearly incidental to the destruction of decisive military objectives, for example, is radically different from mass destruction which is aimed primarily at the lives of civilians, their morale, or the sources of their livelihood. In the event of war, Christian conscience guides us to restraint from destruction not essential to our total objectives, to a continual weighing of the human values that may be won against those lost in the fighting, and to the avoidance of needless human suffering.

Unhappily we see little hope at this time of a trustworthy international agreement that would effectively prevent the manufacture or use of weapons of mass destruction by any nation. This should not deter us from the search for such an agreement, perhaps as a part of a general disarmament program, and for a restoration of mutual confidence that would make an agreement possible and effective.

As long as the existing situation holds, for the United States to abandon its atomic weapons, or to give the impression that they would not be used, would leave the non-communist world with totally inadequate defense. For Christians to advocate such a policy would be for them to share responsibility for the world-wide tyranny that might result. We believe that American military strength, which must include atomic weapons as long as any other nation may possess them, is an essential factor in the possibility of preventing both world war and tyranny. If atomic weapons or other weapons of parallel destructiveness are used against us or our friends in Europe or Asia, we believe that it could be justifiable for our government to use them with all possible restraint to prevent the triumph of an aggressor. We come to this conclusion with troubled spirits but any other conclusion would leave our own people and the people of other nations open to continuing devastating attack and to probable defeat. Even if as individuals we would choose rather to be destroyed than to destroy in such measure, we do not believe it would be right for us to urge policies on our government which would expose others to such a fate.

Having taken the position that no absolute line can be drawn we are especially concerned to emphasize checks on every step towards the increased destructiveness of war.

To engage in reckless and uncontrolled violence against the people of any other nation is to reduce the possibilities of peace and justice and freedom after the war's end and even to destroy the foundation of ordered society. Military judgment must not yield to the vengefulness that too often possesses civilians in wartime; nor must the national government yield to the military its own responsibility for the immediate and the postwar consequences of the conduct of the war.

We have recognized that indiscriminate mass destruction may be caused by atomic bombs or by a fleet of armored tanks or by a ruthless army laying waste cities and countryside. We have found no moral distinction between these instruments of warfare, apart from the ends they serve and the consequences of their use. We would, however, call attention to the fact that the first use of atomic weapons in another war, even if limited to sharply defined military targets, would open the way for their use in retaliation. Because of the very power of these weapons, it would be difficult to prevent their use from extending to military targets that would involve also the destruction of non-combatants on a massive scale. If the United States should use atomic weapons, it would expose its allies to similar attack. The nation that uses atomic weapons first, therefore, bears a special burden of responsibility for the almost inevitable development of extensive mass destruction with all its desolation and horror.

Even more fundamental, the dreadful prospect of devastation that must result from any major war illuminates with special clarity the immorality of those in any country who initiate an aggression against which the only effective means of defense may be the resort to atomic weapons, and which may thus be expected to lead to an atomic war. If general war comes it will probably be a war for survival, not only for the survival of a free civilization, but for the physical survival of peoples. In such a war the temptation will be tremendous to forget all other considerations and to use every available means of destruction. If this happens, physical survival may be bought at the price of the nation's soul, of the moral values which make the civilization worth saving.

> SOURCE: *The Christian Conscience and Weapons of Mass Destruction; Report of a Special Commission Appointed by the Federal Council of the Churches of Christ in America* (N.Y., 1950), 8–10, 12–5. Used by permission of National Council of Churches.

176. The Catholic Church in a Democratic State

Traditional interpretations of Roman Catholic teaching on church-state relations often appeared to run counter to the American heritage of democracy and religious freedom.[43] This charge was made by certain critics of Catholicism, especially by Paul Blanshard in a book published in 1949, *American Freedom and Catholic Power*. Blanshard was more secular than

---

[43] E.g., see the widely used textbook by John A. Ryan and Francis J. Boland, *Catholic Principles of Politics* (rev. ed., N.Y., 1950), 311–21.

Protestant in tone, and his spirit more that of prosecutor than judge,[44] but his book did press Catholics toward that "fresh formulation of the Catholic position" [45] which was already implicit in the situation.

One of the most conspicuous among those who sought to harmonize Catholic tradition and American democracy was the Rev. John Courtney Murray, S. J. (1904—). Educated at Boston College, Woodstock College, and the Gregorian University in Rome, he became professor of theology at Woodstock in 1937. He has been influential as editor of *Theological Studies*. Believing that basal conflict between the claims of church and state creates tensions in the conscience of the individual and must therefore be resolved, he has addressed himself in many writings to the statement of a dynamic view of church-state relations as against more popular static views.[46] In an article entitled "The Problem of State Religion," here reproduced in part,[47] Murray contended that the concept of religious freedom as generally held in democratic America is more rational and more Christian than the medieval concept of the state church. It remained to be seen, however, whether the church would endorse a dynamic view of church-state relations, though that position was apparently gaining ground in the later 1950's.

DOCUMENT

What therefore the Church must seek, and has sought, in every age is such a vital application of her principles, such an institutional embodiment of them, as will make them operative in particular temporal contexts towards the permanent ends, human and supernatural, which she has always in view. The history of Church-State relations is the history of this manner of adaptive application. It records many compromises, but no ideal realizations.

The legal institution known as the state-church, and the later embodiment in the written constitutional law of territorial states of the concept of Catholicism as "the religion of the state," represent an application of Catholic principles (and of the medieval tradition, itself an adaptation) to the complex political, social, religious, and cultural conditions prevailing in the modern state, as it appeared on the dissolution of medieval Christendom, took form in the era of political absolutism, flourished in the era of "confessional absolutism" (to use Eder's phrase) under the royal governments in the "Catholic nations" of post-Reformation Europe, and sought

[44] John C. Bennett, "A Protestant View of Roman Catholic Power," *Christianity and Crisis,* XVIII (1958–59), 115.

[45] Gustave Weigel, S.J., "The Church and the Democratic State," *Thought,* XXVII (1952), 169.

[46] Many of his essays on this theme were reprinted in his *We Hold These Truths: Catholic Reflections on the American Proposition* (N.Y., 1960). See Thomas G. Sanders, "A Comparison of Two Current American Roman Catholic Theories of the American Political System with Particular Reference to the Problems of Religious Liberty" (typed Ph.D. dissertation, Columbia University and Union Theological Seminary, 1958).

[47] Several long footnotes and the author's serial enumeration of sections have been omitted.

reinstatement in the monarchic restorations of the nineteenth century. As a necessary adaptation of principle this legal institution was at first tolerated by the Church; later, in the circumstances of fixed religious divisions, it became the object of more positive acquiescence; still later, in the circumstances created by the French Revolution, it was defended against the laicizing monism of Continental Liberalism, which destroyed the institution of the state-church in consequence of its denial of the Catholic thesis of juridical and social dualism under the primacy of the spiritual, of which the institution was, however defectively, an expression. In the course of this defense the application of the thesis was identified with the thesis itself—an identification that was never canonized by the Church.

Since the institution of the state-church was an adaptation to a particular historical context, it does not represent a permanent and unalterable exigence of Catholic principles, to be realized in any and all historical situations in which there is verified the general hypothesis of a "Catholic population." This legal institution need not be defended by Catholics as a sort of transtemporal "ideal," the single and only institutionalized form of Church-State relationships which can claim the support of principles, the unique "thesis" beside which all other solutions to the Church-State problem must be regarded as "hypothesis," provisional concessions to *force majeure.*

Where the conditions of its origin still more or less prevail, the institution of the state-church is still the object of defense.[48] But the long history of the Church's adaptation of her permanent principles to perpetually changing political realities has not come to a climax and an end with this institution, in such wise that the only valid present effort must be in the direction of a restoration of what existed in a particular epoch of the past—the national state-church by law established, with legal disabilities for dissenters.

On the contrary, the Church can, if she will (and if Catholic thinkers clarify the way for her), consent to other institutionalizations of Church-

---

[48] However, I should like to except from this whole discussion the special question of Spain, because it seems to have become impossible rationally to discuss it. Perhaps the reason is that for the Spaniard the question fundamentally involves a matter of prestige—the prestige associated with the assertion, "Spain is a Catholic nation." You touch a neuralgic spot when you presume to suggest that the religio-political structure of Spain, traditional since Ferdinand and Isabella, may possibly be more intimately related to the peculia. political and historical experience of Spain than to any abstract Catholic principles. In saying this you are implying that Spanish politics and history may perhaps be something less than Catholic—and that implication seems to be intolerable. Again, there is the special meaning of the Spanish axiom, title of a famous book, "Liberalismo es pecado." The specialty of the meaning can be seen, for instance, in the fate met by M. Maritain's books in Spain and South America. If you make an argument in favor of the method of freedom in political and economic life, you are immediately convicted of the sin of Liberalism and invited to enter, not further argument but the confessional. In these circumstances argument is discouraging. Besides, one has no wish further to wound religious and national susceptibilities already exacerbated by much unjust criticism. [Murray]

State relationships and regard them as *aequo iure* valid, vital, and necessary adaptations of principle to legitimate political and social developments.

Such a development is presented by the democratic state. The term does not designate the special type of state which issued from French Revolutionary ideology and Continental Liberalism, which was merely another form of the absolutist state. The term refers to the political idea of the state derived from "the liberal tradition" of the West, which has been best preserved, though not guarded in its purity, in the Anglo-Saxon democratic tradition. Continental Liberalism was a deformation of the liberal tradition; it was in effect simply another form of absolutist state-monism, to which the liberal tradition stands in opposition.

Democracy today presents itself with all the force of an idea whose time has come. And there are two reasons why the present task of Catholics is to work toward the purification of the liberal tradition (which is their own real tradition) and of the democratic form of state in which it finds expression, by restoring both the idea and the institutions of democracy to their proper Christian foundations. First, this form of state is presently man's best, and possibly last, hope of human freedom. Secondly, this form of state presently offers to the Church as a spiritual power as good a hope of freedom as she has ever had; it offers to the Church as the Christian people a means, through its free political institutions, of achieving harmony between law and social organization and the demands of their Christian conscience; finally, by reason of its aspirations towards an order of personal and associational freedom, political equality, civic friendship, social justice, and cultural advancement, it offers to the Church the kind of cooperation which she presently needs, and it merits in turn her cooperation in the realization of its own aspirations.

Consequently, the theological task of the moment is not simply to carry on the polemic against Continental Liberalism. It is also to explore, under the guidance of the Church, the possibilities of a vital adaptation of Church-State doctrine to the constitutional structure, the political institutions, and the ethos of freedom characteristic of the democratic state. To this task the theologian is urged by Pius XII's affirmation of the validity of the democratic development and the new concept of "the people" that it has brought into being. The concept of "the people" is the crucial one in this present day, as it was in the past age that saw the birth of the institution of the state-church, which was itself based on a particular concept of "the people." The political teaching of Pius XII (and of Pius XI) represents considerable progress over the political teaching of Leo XIII,[49] and this progress invites

[49] Leo XIII was primarily the theorist of the political relationship insofar as it asserts that political authority is ultimately of divine origin and that the citizen is subject to it; this aspect of the matter was to the fore in the heyday of the "sovereignty of the people" in the rationalist sense, anarchism, and political and social unrest. But this is not yet a total theory of the political relationship. There are the further aspects of citizenship, namely, active par-

to a commensurate development of the theory of Church-State relations. In order that this development may be organic in the Catholic sense, a work of discernment has to be done on tradition—the rational political tradition of the West, the Church's theological tradition, and her tradition of practical conduct in the face of the changing realities of the political order.

It is not a matter of debating the "thesis" versus the "hypothesis"; these categories are related to a particular and predominantly polemic state of the question. The doctrinal problem is to discern in their purity the principles that are at the heart of tradition. The categories of discussion are "principle" and "application of principle," or (what comes to the same) "ideas" and "institutions."

Certainly in the conditions of the twentieth century, when a new revolutionary movement has violently altered the nineteenth-century state of the question, it would be an abdication of the theological task, if the theologian were to remain simply the literal exegete of Leo XIII, as if somehow the total doctrine and practice of Church-State relations had reached their definitive and ultimate stage of development in the Leonine *corpus*. Such an abrupt closure of development would be altogether untraditional. It would be to repeat the mistake of the fourteenth- and fifteenth-century canonists who supposed that with the "traditional" theory of society expressed in the Bull *Unam Sanctam* and with the "traditional" canonical doctrine of the direct power Catholic tradition had received in every respect its permanent and unalterable statement. Leo XIII did not fall into this mistake; if he had, *Immortale Dei* would never have been written.

Concretely, the present problem concerns the provision guaranteeing "the free exercise of religion" that has become characteristic of the democratic state constitution. At least, this is usually conceived to be the major aspect of the problem. In fuller form the problem may be stated as follows: can the Church accept, as a valid adaptation of principle to the legitimate idea of democratic government and to the historically developed idea of "the people" (to which democratic government appeals for its legitimacy), a constitutional system of Church-State relations with these three characteristics: (1) the freedom of the Church is guaranteed in a guarantee to the people of the free exercise of religion; (2) the harmony of law and social

---

ticipation in the institutional organization of civil society (Pius XI's emphasis) and in the political process itself whereby the state functions (Pius XII's orientation). In his social theory Leo XIII did indeed urge Christian democracy in the sense of beneficent action on behalf of the people; but in his political theory he never really answered the great question, raised for the first time in the nineteenth century, "Who are the people?" Actually, the first great historic answer to the question was given in the United States; but the din raised by the conflict with Continental Liberalism was too great to permit the voice of America (ironically, a deist and Protestant voice giving a Catholic answer) to be heard in European canon-law classrooms. In fact, to this day European authors of textbooks *de iure publico* seem unaware that there is any difference between Jacobin democracy and Anglo-Saxon democracy, or between "the sovereignty of the people" in the sense of '89 and "government of the people, for the people, and by the people" in the sense of Lincoln. *Hinc illae lacrimae*, spilled by an American on reading books *de iure publico*. [Murray]

institutions with the demands of the Christian conscience is to be effected by the people themselves through the medium of free political institutions and freedom of association; (3) the cooperation between Church and state takes these three forms: (*a*) constitutional protection of the freedom of the Church and all her institutional activities; (*b*) the effort of the state to perform its own function of justice, social welfare, and the favoring within society of those conditions of order and freedom necessary for human development; (*c*) the effort of the Church, through the action of a laity conscious of its Christian and civic responsibilities, to effect that christianization of society in all its dimensions which will enable and oblige the state, as the instrument of society, to function in a Christian sense.

This lengthy question is not to be transformed into a brief tendentious one: Can the Church at last come to terms with Continental Liberalism? The answer to that nineteenth-century question is still the nineteenth-century answer: No. But when the nineteenth-century question has been given its nineteenth-century answer, the twentieth-century question still remains unanswered. To it, as put, I am inclined to answer in the affirmative. The Church can, if she wishes, permit her principles of freedom, harmony, and cooperation thus to be applied to the political reality of the democratic state. The application of each of the three principles (freedom, harmony, cooperation) can be justified in terms of traditional Catholic thought, political and theological.

The resulting system would not indeed be some "ideal" realization of Church-State relations, some sort of "new thesis." The point is that no "ideal" realizations are possible in history; no application of principle can claim to be a "thesis." For instance, in the series of Concordats beginning with the Council of Constance (1418) and ending with the Concordat with Francis I (1516) the Church first undertook to assume an historical attitude to the emerging modern state; in these Concordats were likewise laid the juridical foundations for the institution of the state-church in the *ancien régime*. Yet no one would say that the system of Church-State relationships set forth in these Concordats, and the institutions through which the system operated, represented some "ideal" realization of principle—least of all an ideal realization of the principle of the freedom of the Church. In every respect principle was adapted to political reality—to a political reality, it should be added, that was much less justifiably rational, because absolutist, than is the contemporary democracy of the liberal tradition. One should therefore expect the Church's attitude toward democracy to be only what her attitude towards absolute monarchy was—a valid and vital, because purposeful, application of principle. Not an "ideal," not a "thesis."

With regard to the special problem of religious freedom one remark may be made. There would seem to be a valid analogy between the constitutional provision for religious freedom in the democratic state and the legal institution of the state-church in the post-Reformation monarchic states, in the sense that both represent an analogical adaptation to analogous situations. The latter institution was an adaptation to two facts: (1) the emergence of the modern state as a "person," as autonomous, with an autonomy that extended to state determination of the religion of the people; with this fact is allied the concept of "the people" as purely passive in the face of government, whose purposes are determined apart from consultation of the people; (2) the religious division of universal Christian society into separate and autonomous Catholic and Protestant nations and states. The former institution is an adaptation to two analogous facts: (1) the emergence of "the people" into active self-consciousness, into a spiritual autonomy that extends to a rejection of governmental determination or even tutelage of their religion; with this fact is allied the concept of "the state" as the instrument of the people for limited purposes sanctioned by the people; (2) the religious divisions within territorial states between persons of different religions. When they are viewed in this historical perspective, it is difficult to see why one institution is any less, or more, an adaptation of principle than the other, why one should be considered more valid and vital than the other, why one has a greater right to claim the support of principle than the other.

Actually, from the standpoint of principle the crucial point is not the fact of religious unity or disunity, with the former basing a "thesis" and the latter an "hypothesis"; for both situations are predicated on a disruption of Catholic unity in the proper sense. The crucial question is whether the concept of the state and the concept of the people that undergirds the legal institution of the state-church is any more rational than the concept of the state and the concept of the people that undergirds the legal institution of religious freedom. The answer would seem to be that the latter concepts are certainly more rational and better founded in Christian thought.

The foregoing propositions set forth, simply in outline, the major points of a theory of Church-State relationships which may, I think, be considered tenable in the light of the full Catholic tradition of thought and practice in the matter.

> SOURCE: John Courtney Murray, S. J., "The Problem of State Religion," *Theological Studies,* XII (1951), 160–7. Used by permission of *Theological Studies* and the author.

177. The Churches and Segregation

The national and regional assemblies of many denominations and of various interdenominational bodies often took clear stands favoring desegregation in the churches and in society. In the Protestant world, the councils of churches often served both as centers for discussion of racial matters and as channels of action toward desegregation. The Federal Council of the Churches of Christ in America (1908–50) had been especially active in this field since World War I. Taking leadership in the struggle against segregation in church life, it approved an official statement on "The Church and Race Relations" at a special meeting in Columbus, Ohio, in 1946. The heart of the declaration was the following:

> The Federal Council of the Churches of Christ in America hereby renounces the pattern of segregation in race relations as unnecessary and undesirable and a violation of the Gospel of love and human brotherhood. Having taken this action, the Federal Council requests its constituent communions to do likewise. As proof of their sincerity in this renunciation they will work for a non-segregated Church and a non-segregated society.[50]

The National Council of the Churches of Christ in America continued to provide leadership in this area. In 1952, its General Board adopted as an official statement and resolution "The Churches and Segregation," here reprinted in part. It was a revision of the earlier document.

The National Council soon had occasion to follow up its statement concretely, for shortly after the Supreme Court decision of May 17, 1954, calling for desegregation in the public schools, it summoned the churches to exert their influence in helping the authorized agencies in the communities to bring about compliance with the decision. When the Court issued its decree of May 31, 1955, for the implementation of its decision, placing responsibility on local authorities, the Council's Department of Racial and Cultural Relations speedily issued "Suggestions for Action" that Christians might be helped to contribute to the acceptance of the decision.

DOCUMENT

Introduction

As Christian disciples work together, their redemptive power in society is heightened. That power is released most transformingly when, in motive and method, it flows directly from the mandates of our Lord. In this statement, the National Council of the Churches of Christ in the U.S.A. sets forth some of the clear implications of Christ's command, "Thou shalt love thy neighbor as thyself."

1. The Pattern of Segregation

Segregation is the externally imposed separation or division of individual persons or groups, based on race, color or national origin. It is practiced, with some difference of emphasis, in all sections of the country. In many places, segregation is established and supported by law. In others, it is almost as rigidly enforced by social custom and economic practices.

Segregation is an expression of the superiority-inferiority attitudes concerning race, color or national origin held tenaciously by vast numbers of

[50] *The Church and Race Relations* (N.Y., 1946), 5.

Americans. Segregation is not only the expression of an attitude; it is also the means by which that attitude is transmitted from one generation to another. Children in our society, observing minorities as we segregate them, cannot easily escape the inference that such minorities are inferior.

Moreover, segregation as practiced in the United States probably has more effect on the attitudes of the young than the formal teachings of the schools about democracy or of the churches about Christian brotherhood.

Segregation subjects sections of our population to constant humiliation and forces upon them moral and psychological handicaps in every relation of life. Still more devastating is the moral and spiritual effect upon the majority.

Segregation has meant inferior services to the minority segregated. The theory of "separate but equal" services does not work out in practice; segregation is always discriminatory. Discrimination sets apart those discriminated against so that in effect, they are segregated spiritually and psychologically, if not always physically.

Segregation as applied to our economic system denies to millions of our people free access to the means of making a living and sets for them insurmountable obstacles in their efforts to achieve freedom from want.

At all times and particularly in great crises, segregation makes it impossible to utilize fully large sections of our manpower. It seriously limits the contributions of racial and cultural minority groups to the ongoing life of our people in every aspect of our national existence.

Segregation handicaps our Nation in international relationships. At a time when the United States has come to play a leading role among the nations of the free world, our racial practices which are publicized abroad are made the basis of charges of hypocrisy against the Nation. These charges reverberate throughout the world in a period when the largely submerged non-white groups are becoming self-conscious, striving for recognition of their dignity, for autonomy and equal opportunity. The world community which we are seeking to build must rest on genuine respect for the worth of persons who are created equally the sons of God.

Large numbers of our citizens are being disfranchised and discriminated against as a result of the fears and mutual suspicions engendered by the pattern of segregation. These cause unnecessary confusion in dealing with important public issues, create unreal political divisions and give rise to a type of political appeal that threatens our democracy and democratic institutions.

Segregation increases and accentuates racial tension. It is worth noting that race riots in this country have seldom occurred in neighborhoods with a racially mixed population. Our worst riots have broken out along the edges of and in rigidly segregated areas.

Above all, the principle of segregation is a denial of the Christian faith and ethic which stems from the basic premise taught by our Lord that all men are created the children of God. The pattern of segregation is diametrically opposed to what Christians believe about the worth of persons and if we are to be true to the Christian faith we must take our stand against it.

II. The Churches and The Pattern of Segregation

The pattern of segregation in the United States is given moral sanction by the fact that churches and church institutions, as a result of insensitiveness and social pressure, have so largely accepted this pattern in their own life and practice.

A. Segregation in Church Practice

While the pattern of segregation is too common in our public education at all levels, it is even more general in the churches in worship and fellowship. There are large areas of the public education field where racial separation is not practiced and only a relatively few churches which are racially inclusive in practice.[51] Furthermore, the pattern of segregation in public education appears to be changing more rapidly than in the churches.

While there are some exceptions among the communions and in certain interdenominational agencies, notably councils of churches, nevertheless, religious bodies are generally divided on a racial basis, in national organizations, in regional bodies and in local congregations. The acceptance by the churches of this pattern of segregation is so prevalent that fellowship between white and non-white Christians in the United States is frequently awkward and unsatisfactory.

It should be noted, however, that the communions have expressed an increasing concern for the elimination of segregation from the churches and society. Since the statement titled "The Church and Race Relations" was adopted by the Federal Council of Churches in 1946, the national bodies of twenty communions have issued statements that sanction the practice of an inclusive ministry to all people without regard to race, color or national origin. Nine of these national church bodies have renounced the pattern of segregation both in their own fellowship and in society; two have placed emphasis on the elimination of discrimination; and nine have indicated their concern for justice and opportunity for all people. In addition to defining denominational policy, these statements have served as a basis for launching denominational programs for the improvement of racial and cultural relations.

While members of racial groups other than the one to which a majority of the congregation belongs are not absolutely barred by a rule from attend-

---

[51] At this point in the text is a long footnote, here omitted, which provides facts about segregation in the churches. It is pointed out that according to estimates made in the 1940's, only one-half of one per cent of the Negro Protestant Christians of the United States worshiped regularly in churches with fellow Christians of another race.

ance, in many local churches the self-consciousness which their presence arouses bars them from freedom to worship in fellowship, and even from the initial contact.

At the level of the local church there are some encouraging examples of pastors, church officers and congregations who have come to grips with the dilemma of the segregated church. There are congregations and especially Sunday church schools and vacation church schools which are racially inclusive, and there are other church groups in the process of becoming so. These efforts need to be more widely known and the methods employed shared more fully with others.

A church located in a community in which the population is changing has a responsibility to serve the people of that community without regard to race, color or national origin. National and regional denominational bodies as well as councils of churches should encourage local congregations to consider this responsibility and cooperate with them in achieving this type of service.

However, the local church faces the difficult, although not insurmountable, obstacle of segregated housing in both the city and the suburbs. When a church is located in a community where segregated housing limits the population to one racial or cultural group, the people whom the church serves will tend to be limited to that racial or cultural group. Churches and councils of churches should, therefore, take definite steps to help create unsegregated residential communities where normal day-to-day relationships will develop among people of all races, colors, creeds and national origins. . . .

F. The Responsibility of the Churches to Eliminate Segregation

Christians in the United States, more than ever before, honestly desire that quality of Christian fellowship which brings to the total Church the gifts of all for the spiritual enrichment of each. Efforts directed toward such spiritual enrichment are frequently confused and ineffectual because of the pattern of segregation which defeats goodwill. Many persons find themselves frustrated when they attempt to live out their Christian impulses within a racially segregated society.

The Church, when true to its higher destiny, has always understood that its gospel of good news has a two-fold function, namely:

To create new men with new motives;
To create a new society wherein such men will find a favorable environment within which to live their Christian convictions.

The churches in the United States, while earnestly striving to nurture and develop individuals of goodwill, have not dealt adequately with the fundamental pattern of segregation in our society which thwarts their efforts. This must be corrected. The churches should continue to emphasize the first function. In addition, they must launch a more comprehensive program of action in fulfillment of the second function. This is imperative now.

III. The National Council and Segregation

The communions and the interdenominational agencies have faced this question and taken action on it. A number of the interdenominational agencies which merged to form the National Council of Churches had renounced the pattern of segregation based on race, color or national origin as unnecessary and undesirable and a violation of basic Christian principles. A number of the communions have adopted the 1946 statement of the Federal Council of Churches and others have adopted statements of their own on this question.

The National Council of the Churches of Christ in the U.S.A. in its organizational structure and operation, renounces and earnestly recommends to its member churches that they renounce the pattern of segregation based on race, color or national origin as unnecessary and undesirable and a violation of the Gospel of love and human brotherhood. While recognizing that historical and social factors make it more difficult for some churches than for others to realize the Christian ideal of non-segregation, the Council urges all of its constituent members to work steadily and progressively towards a non-segregated church as the goal which is set forth in the faith and practice of the early Christian community and inherent in the New Testament idea of the Church of Christ. As proof of our sincerity in this renunciation, the National Council of Churches will work for a non-segregated church and a non-segregated community.

IV. The Churches Should Ascertain The Facts About Their Own Practices

We urge that in studying their own practices, the churches use the following statement of principles as a standard of measurement:

A. Membership

All persons who accept Christ as Lord and Master and the doctrinal standards of the communion ought to be invited and welcomed into membership of our communion's parish churches.

B. Fellowship

Christian fellowship means that all who accept Christ as Lord and Master are united by bonds of brotherhood which transcend race, color or national origin.

C. Worship

Worship opportunities inclusive of all groups ought to be available both regularly and frequently, so as to make such worship a normal expression of our common worship of God without self-consciousness or embarrassment.

D. Outreach of the Minister

The outreach of the minister should be inclusive. This means that his services ought to be available to persons of all groups in the community without discrimination.

E. Educational and Welfare Services

Church-related schools, colleges, hospitals, homes for children and the aged and other institutions have a responsibility to serve persons who are members of their communion without regard to race, color or national origin.

Church camps, conferences and projects conducted for the purpose of training persons for leadership or participation in the program and activities of the churches have a responsibility to serve the churches and their members without regard to race, color or national origin.

F. Employment

Christian churches demonstrate belief in the essential worth of persons because they are the children of God when they provide full opportunities for the employment at all levels and on the same basis of character and ability, of all persons found in the membership of their communion, including those from racial and cultural minorities. . . .

V. The Churches Should Help to Relieve Community Tensions

Churches, having chosen to renounce the pattern of segregation as a violation of the Gospel of love which is committed unto them, and having outlined steps by which that pattern shall be eliminated from their own practices, should at the same time direct their attention to the community, at the national, state and local levels.

In order that the community may sense the transforming power of organized religion in relieving community tensions arising from the pattern of segregation, the churches should assume responsibility for dealing with such questions as discrimination in employment, housing, education, health and leisure-time activities. We should cooperate with other organizations in the formulation and execution of a community-wide plan of action to eliminate patterns of segregation and to change the policies and practices that create tensions.

Our Hope and Strength

We thank God, especially in a time when so many men are estranged from Him and from one another, that He has created us "of one blood" and through Christ has brought Christians into one family. It was by God's power that Christ's disciples lived and worked in love. This faith that Christians are "one body in Christ," commits us inevitably to the task of transcending barriers of race, color and nationality in our churches and in our communities until we may, by His Grace, one day demonstrate our faith that "we are members one of another."

SOURCE: *The Churches and Segregation: An Official Statement and Resolution Adopted by the General Board of the National Council of Churches in the U.S.A. in Chicago, Illinois, June 11, 1952* (N.Y., n.d.). Used by permission of the National Council of Churches.

178. The Majesty of Truth

The spread of communism in the 1940's and 1950's profoundly disturbed the majority of American citizens. Distrustful of collectivism, most Americans were determined to preserve democratic freedom. But in the atmosphere generated by the fear of communism, certain Congressional committees of inquiry began to resort to methods which many Americans felt to be inconsistent with the nation's heritage of freedom. There was a growing body of opinion that in some quarters dissent was being misunderstood as treason, nonconformity as disloyalty. The role of Senator Joseph R. McCarthy (1908–57) as chairman of the Senate Permanent Subcommittee on Investigations was considered by many to be domineering and inquisitorial. A new word, "McCarthyism," entered common usage. Government employees and many others feared being held guilty by reason of incidental association with communists or with persons whose loyalty had even been questioned.

In the early 1950's, the mood of suspicion was at its height. At this point, the General Council of the Presbyterian Church in the United States of America unanimously adopted and issued on October 21, 1953, "A Letter to Presbyterians, Concerning the Present Situation in Our Country and in the World." The man chiefly responsible for the letter was the moderator of the church and chairman of the Council, John A. Mackay (1889—), then President of Princeton Theological Seminary.

The forceful letter immediately attracted national and international attention. The full text was reproduced not only by such American papers as the *New York Times,* but also by overseas papers, for example *Le Monde* of Paris. It was the first clear evidence that many Europeans had of internal dissent against irresponsible anti-communism. Many commended it, but a few sharply attacked it. In the April 24, 1954 issue of the *Saturday Evening Post,* Daniel A. Poling (1884—), popular preacher and editor of the *Christian Herald,* observed that the exact sentiment and the exact language of certain passages in the communist *Cominform Journal* were mirrored in the letter. He declared that the sinister character of communist infiltration was to be found in this official statement. Mackay denied even knowing of the existence of the publication referred to by Poling.[52] When the General Assembly of the Presbyterian Church met in May of 1954, it adopted almost unanimously as its own the statement which had been issued by the General Council.[53] The full text of this important letter follows. It contributed significantly to the clarification of points of view on Congressional inquiries in the churches and in the nation, and urged calm, face-to-face negotiations with our opponents at the conference table.[54]

DOCUMENT

DEAR FELLOW PRESBYTERIANS:

The General Council of the Presbyterian Church in the United States of America is instructed under the constitution of the Church, "to cultivate and promote the spiritual welfare of the whole church," and "to correspond with and advise the General Councils of Presbyteries . . ."

Profoundly concerned about the present situation in our country and the world, the Council addresses itself to fellow-Presbyterians through the Presbyteries and the ministers and officers of the congregations. In doing so it is guided by the historic witness of our Church and the deliverances of successive General Assemblies. The Council hopes that the following statement may help to clarify certain important problems and at the same time initiate a process of thought by which our Church can contribute toward their solution.

The 165th General Assembly made the following pronouncement for the guidance of Presbyterians: "All human life should be lived in accordance with the principles established by God for the life of men and of nations. This is a tenet of Biblical religion. It is also a basic emphasis in our Presbyterian heritage of faith.

"As individuals and as a group, Christians are responsible for adjusting their thought and behavior to those everlasting principles of righteousness which God has revealed in Holy Scripture. It is no less their responsibility as citizens of their nation, to seek as far as their influence may extend, to bring national life and all the institutions of society into conformity with the moral government of God, and into harmony with the spirit of Jesus Christ."

In full accordance with this deliverance, the General Council would share with our Church constituency the following thoughts:

---

[52] *Presbyterian Life*, VII (May 29, 1954), 19. For discussions of the Poling charges, see "Dr. Daniel A. Poling Answers!" *Christian Herald*, LXXVII (August, 1954), 4, 75, and Edward A. Dowey, Jr., "Poling and the Presbyterian Letter," *Christianity and Crisis*, XIV (1954–55), 124–7.

[53] "The Presbyterian Letter: A Vote of Confidence," *Presbyterian Life*, VII (June 12, 1954), 12–3; *Minutes of the General Assembly of the Presbyterian Church in the United States of America*, Fifth Series, Vol. III (Philadelphia, 1954), 28, 119–20.

[54] The letter was cited by Justice William O. Douglas, *An Almanac of Liberty* (Garden City, N.Y., 1954), 116, entry for October 21, 1953.

Things are happening in our national life and in the international sphere which should give us deep concern. Serious thought needs to be given to the menace of Communism in the world of today and to the undoubted aim on the part of its leaders to subvert the thought and life of the United States. Everlasting vigilance is also needed, and appropriate precautions should be constantly taken, to forestall the insidious intervention of a foreign power in the internal affairs of our country. In this connection Congressional committees, which are an important expression of democracy in action, have rendered some valuable services to the nation.

At the same time the citizens of this country, and those in particular who are Protestant Christians, have reason to take a grave view of the situation which is being created by the almost exclusive concentration of the American mind upon the problem of the threat of Communism.

Under the plea that the structure of American society is in imminent peril of being shattered by a satanic conspiracy, dangerous developments are taking place in our national life. Favored by an atmosphere of intense disquiet and suspicion, a subtle but potent assault upon basic human rights is now in progress. Some Congressional inquiries have revealed a distinct tendency to become inquisitions. These inquisitions, which find their historic pattern in medieval Spain and in the tribunals of modern totalitarian states, begin to constitute a threat to freedom of thought in this country. Treason and dissent are being confused. The shrine of conscience and private judgment, which God alone has a right to enter, is being invaded. Un-American attitudes toward ideas and books are becoming current. Attacks are being made upon citizens of integrity and social passion which are utterly alien to our democratic tradition. They are particularly alien to the Protestant religious tradition which has been a main source of the freedoms which the people of the United States enjoy.

There is something still more serious. A great many people, within and without our government, approach the problem of Communism in a purely negative way. Communism, which is at bottom a secular religious faith of great vitality, is thus being dealt with as an exclusively police problem. As a result of this there is growing up over against Communism a fanatical negativism. Totally devoid of a constructive program of action, this negativism is in danger of leading the American mind into a spiritual vacuum. Our national house, cleansed of one demon, would invite by its very emptiness, the entrance of seven others. In the case of a national crisis this emptiness could, in the high sounding name of security, be occupied with ease by a Fascist tyranny.

We suggest, therefore, that all Presbyterians give earnest consideration to the following three basic principles and their implications for our thought and life.

I.

The Christian Church has a prophetic function to fulfill in every society and in every age.

Whatever concerns man and his welfare is a concern of the Church and its ministers. Religion has to do with life in its wholeness. While being patriotically loyal to the country within whose bounds it lives and works, the Church does not derive its authority from the nation but from Jesus Christ. Its supreme and ultimate allegiance is to Christ, its sole Head, and to His Kingdom, and not to any nation or race, to any class or culture. It is, therefore, under obligation to consider the life of man in the light of God's purpose in Christ for the world. While it is not the role of the Christian church to present blueprints for the organization of society and the conduct of government, the Church owes it to its own members and to men in general, to draw attention to violations of those spiritual bases of human relationship which have been established by God. It has the obligation also to proclaim those principles, and to instill that spirit, which are essential for social health, and which form the indispensable foundation of sound and stable policies in the affairs of state.

II.

The majesty of truth must be preserved at all times and at all costs.

Loyalty to truth is the common basis of true religion and true culture. Despite the lofty idealism of many of our national leaders, truth is being subtly and silently dethroned by prominent public figures from the position it has occupied hitherto in our American tradition. The state of strife known as "cold war," in which our own and other nations, as well as groups within nations, are now engaged, is producing startling phenomena and sinister personalities. In this form of warfare, falsehood is frequently preferred to fact if it can be shown to have greater propaganda value. In the interests of propaganda, truth is deliberately distorted or remains unspoken. The demagogue, who lives by propaganda, is coming into his own on a national scale. According to the new philosophy, if what is true "gives aid and comfort" to our enemies, it must be suppressed. Truth is thus a captive in the land of the free. At the same time, and for the same reason, great words like "love," "peace," "justice," and "mercy," and the ideas which underlie them, are becoming suspect.

Communism, as we know to our sorrow, is committed on principle to a philosophy of lying; democracy, in fighting Communism, is in danger of succumbing, through fear and in the name of expediency, to the self-same philosophy. It is being assumed, in effect, that, in view of the magnitude of the issues at stake, the end justifies the means. Whatever the outcome of such a war, the moral consequences will be terrifying. People will become accustomed to going through life with no regard for rules or sanctities.

A painful illustration of this development is that men and women should be publicly condemned upon the uncorroborated word of former Communists. Many of these witnesses have done no more, as we know, than transfer their allegiance from one authoritarian system to another. Nothing is easier for people, as contemporary history has shown, than to make the transition from one totalitarianism to another, carrying their basic attitudes along with them. As a matter of fact, the lands that have suffered most from Communism, or that are most menaced by it today, Russia and Italy, for example, are lands which have been traditionally authoritarian in their political or their religious life. And yet the ex-Communists to whose word Congressional committees apparently give unqualified credence are in very many instances people whose basic philosophy authorizes them now, as in the past, to believe that a lie in a good cause is thoroughly justified.

III.

God's sovereign rule is the controlling factor in history.

We speak of "This nation under God." Nothing is more needed today than to explore afresh and to apply to all the problems of thought and life in our generation, what it means to take God seriously in national life. There is an order of God. Even in these days of flux and nihilism, of relativism and expediency, God reigns. The American-born poet, T. S. Eliot, has written these prophetic words:

> Those who put their faith in worldly order
> Not controlled by the order of God,
> In confident ignorance, but arrest disorder,
> Make it fast, breed fatal disease,
> Degrade what they exalt.

Any attempt to impose upon society, or the course of history, a purely man-made order, however lofty the aims, can have no more than temporary success. Social disorder and false political philosophies cannot be adequately met by police measures, but only by a sincere attempt to organize society in accordance with the everlasting principles of God's moral government of the world. It is, therefore, of paramount importance that individuals, groups and nations should adjust themselves to the order of God. God's character and God's way with man provide the pattern for man's way with his fellow man.

That we have the obligation to make our nation as secure as possible, no one can dispute. But there is no absolute security in human affairs, nor is security the ultimate human obligation. A still greater obligation, as well as a more strategic procedure, is to make sure that what we mean by security, and the methods we employ to achieve it, are in accordance with the will of God. Otherwise, any human attempt to establish a form of world order which does no more than exalt the interest of a class, a culture, a race, or a nation, above God and the interests of the whole human family, is fore-doomed to disaster. Ideas are on the march, forces are abroad, whose time has come. They cannot be repressed and they will bring unjust orders to an end. In the world of today all forms of feudalism, for example, are fore-doomed. So too are all types of imperialism. The real question is how to solve the problems presented by these two forms of outmoded society in such a way that the transition to a better order will be gradual and construc-tive.

Let us frankly recognize that many of the revolutionary forces of our time are in great part the judgment of God upon human selfishness and complacency, and upon man's forgetfulness of man. That does not make these forces right; it does, however, compel us to consider how their driving power can be channeled into forms of creative thought and work. History, moreover, makes it abundantly clear that wherever a religion, a political system or a social order, does not interest itself in the common people, violent revolt eventually takes place.

On the other hand, just because God rules in the affairs of men, Com-munism as a solution of the human problem is foredoomed to failure. No political order can prevail which deliberately leaves God out of account. Despite its pretention to be striving after "liberation," Communism enslaves in the name of freedom. It does not know that evil cannot be eradicated from human life by simply changing a social structure. Man, moreover, has deep spiritual longings which Communism cannot satisfy. The com-munistic order will eventually be shattered upon the bedrock of human nature, that is, upon the basic sins, and the abysmal needs, of man and society. For that reason Communism has an approaching rendezvous with God and the moral order.

Nevertheless, Communists, Communist nations and Communist-ruled peoples, should be our concern. In hating a system let us not allow ourselves to hate individuals or whole nations. History and experience teach us that persons and peoples do change. Let us ever be on the lookout for the evi-dence of change in the Communist world, for the effects of disillusionment, and for the presence of a God-implanted hunger. Such disillusionment and hunger can be met only by a sympathetic approach and a disposition to listen and confer.

There is clear evidence that a post-Communist mood is actually being created in many parts of Europe and Asia. Let us seek to deepen that mood. Let us explore afresh the meaning of mercy and forgiveness and recognize that both can have social and political significance when they are sincerely and opportunely applied.

Let us always be ready to meet around a conference table with the rulers of Communist countries. There should be, therefore, no reluctance to em-ploy the conference method to the full in the settling of disputes with our country's enemies. Let us beware of the cynical attitude which prevails in certain official circles to regard as a forlorn hope any negotiated solution of the major issues which divide mankind.

In human conflicts there can be no substitute for negotiation. Direct personal conference has been God's way with man from the beginning. "Come, now, and let us reason together," was the word of God to Israel through the Prophet Isaiah. We must take the risk, and even the initiative, of seeking face-to-face encounter with our enemies. We should meet them officially, whatever their ignominious record, and regardless of the suffering they may have caused us. We too have reasons for penitence and stand in need of forgiveness. In any case, talk, unhurried talk, talk which does not rule out in advance the possibility of success, talk which takes place in private, and not before reporters or microphones or television, is the only kind of approach which can lead to sanity and fruitful understanding. Let the process of conference be private, but let its conclusions, its complete conclusions, be made public.

In this connection such an organization as the United Nations is in harmony with the principles of God's moral government. American Presbyterians should remember with pride that it is the successor of a former organization which was the creation of a great American who was also a great Presbyterian. While the United Nations organization is very far from perfection and it functions today under great handicaps, it is yet the natural and best available agent for international cooperation and the settlement of disputes among nations. It is imperative, therefore, that it be given the utmost support. It stands between us and war.

While we take all wise precautions for defense, both within and outside our borders, the present situation demands spiritual calm, historical perspective, religious faith, and an adventurous spirit. Loyalty to great principles of truth and justice has made our nation great; such loyalty alone can keep it great and ensure its destiny.

May God give us the wisdom and courage to think and act in accordance with His Will.

With fraternal greetings,

THE GENERAL COUNCIL
OF THE PRESBYTERIAN CHURCH
IN THE U.S.A.

John A. Mackay, Chairman
Glenn W. Moore, Secretary

October 21, 1953

SOURCE: *A Letter to Presbyterians Concerning the Present Situation in Our Country and In the World, Unanimously Adopted by the General Council of the General Assembly of the Presbyterian Church In the United States of America, October 21, 1953* (Phila., n.d.), 2–8. Used by permission of The United Presbyterian Church.

179. Nonviolence and Social Change

In 1956 the Negro community of Montgomery, Alabama, won a long struggle against segregation in public buses. It was a major victory for those who had long suffered from segregation, and it had been accomplished by nonviolent means. Called to the leadership of the movement of Montgomery Negroes to boycott the buses as long as they were forced to take rear seats was the young pastor of the Dexter Avenue Baptist Church, Martin Luther King, Jr. Born in Atlanta in 1929, King was educated at Morehouse College, Crozer Theological Seminary, and Boston University, from which institution he received the Ph.D. degree in 1955. In 1957, following the Montgomery achievement, King became the first president of the Southern Christian Leadership Conference, founded to extend the integration drive throughout the South. The young leader became a nationally known figure; he was the center of much concern when he was almost assassinated in New York City in September, 1958, by a woman who appeared to be demented.

King was invited by the editors of *The Christian Century* to contribute to its series of articles, "How My Mind Has Changed." His response, entitled "Pilgrimage to Nonviolence," traced his intellectual and spiritual growth to his position of conspicuous leadership in the Negro American's struggle for dignity. In Part I, he gave an account of the modifications of his earlier theological liberalism. Parts II and III of the article, dealing with the development of his social and pacifist convictions, are here reprinted.[55]

DOCUMENT

II.

Not until I entered theological seminary, however, did I begin a serious intellectual quest for a method to eliminate social evil. I was immediately influenced by the social gospel. In the early '50s I read Rauschenbusch's *Christianity and the Social Crisis,* a book which left an indelible imprint on my thinking. Of course there were points at which I differed with Rauschenbusch. I felt that he had fallen victim to the 19th-century "cult of inevitable progress," which led him to an unwarranted optimism concerning human nature. Moreover, he came perilously close to identifying the kingdom of God with a particular social and economic system—a temptation which the church should never give in to. But in spite of these shortcomings Rauschenbusch gave to American Protestantism a sense of social responsibility that it should never lose. The gospel at its best deals with the whole man, not only his soul but his body, not only his spiritual well-

[55] See King, *Stride ⎯ward Freedom: The Montgomery Story* (N.Y., 1958), and also consult L. D. Reddick, *Crusader Without Violence: A Biography of Martin Luther King, Jr.* (N.Y., 1959).

being, but his material well-being. Any religion that professes to be concerned about the souls of men and is not concerned about the slums that damn them, the economic conditions that strangle them and the social conditions that cripple them is a spiritually moribund religion awaiting burial.

After reading Rauschenbusch I turned to a serious study of the social and ethical theories of the great philosophers. During this period I had almost despaired of the power of love in solving social problems. The "turn the other cheek" philosophy and the "love your enemies" philosophy are only valid, I felt, when individuals are in conflict with other individuals; when racial groups and nations are in conflict a more realistic approach is necessary. Then I came upon the life and teachings of Mahatma Gandhi. As I read his works I became deeply fascinated by his campaigns of nonviolent resistance. The whole Gandhian concept of *satyagraha* (*satya* is truth which equals love, and *graha* is force; *satyagraha* thus means truthforce or love-force) was profoundly significant to me. As I delved deeper into the philosophy of Gandhi my skepticism concerning the power of love gradually diminished, and I came to see for the first time that the Christian doctrine of love operating through the Gandhian method of nonviolence was one of the most potent weapons available to oppressed people in their struggle for freedom. At this time, however, I had a merely intellectual understanding and appreciation of the position, with no firm determination to organize it in a socially effective situation.

When I went to Montgomery, Alabama, as a pastor in 1954, I had not the slightest idea that I would later become involved in a crisis in which nonviolent resistance would be applicable. After I had lived in the community about a year, the bus boycott began. The Negro people of Montgomery, exhausted by the humiliating experiences that they had constantly faced on the buses, expressed in a massive act of noncooperation their determination to be free. They came to see that it was ultimately more honorable to walk the streets in dignity than to ride the buses in humiliation. At the beginning of the protest the people called on me to serve as their spokesman. In accepting this responsibility my mind, consciously or unconsciously, was driven back to the Sermon on the Mount and the Gandhian method of nonviolent resistance. This principle became the guiding light of our movement. Christ furnished the spirit and motivation while Gandhi furnished the method.

The experience in Montgomery did more to clarify my thinking on the question of nonviolence than all of the books that I had read. As the days unfolded I became more and more convinced of the power of nonviolence. Living through the actual experience of the protest, nonviolence became more than a method to which I gave intellectual assent; it became a commitment to a way of life. Many issues I had not cleared up intellectually concerning nonviolence were now solved in the sphere of practical action.

A few months ago I had the privilege of traveling to India. The trip had a great impact on me personally and left me even more convinced of the power of nonviolence. It was a marvelous thing to see the amazing results of a nonviolent struggle. India won her independence, but without violence on the part of Indians. The aftermath of hatred and bitterness that usually follows a violent campaign is found nowhere in India. Today a mutual friendship based on complete equality exists between the Indian and British people within the commonwealth.

I do not want to give the impression that nonviolence will work miracles overnight. Men are not easily moved from their mental ruts or purged of their prejudiced and irrational feelings. When the underprivileged demand freedom, the privileged first react with bitterness and resistance. Even when the demands are couched in nonviolent terms, the initial response is the same. I am sure that many of our white brothers in Montgomery and across the south are still bitter toward Negro leaders, even though these leaders have sought to follow a way of love and nonviolence. So the nonviolent approach does not immediately change the heart of the oppressor. It first does something to the hearts and souls of those committed to it. It gives them new self-respect; it calls up resources of strength and courage that they did not know they had. Finally, it reaches the opponent and so stirs his conscience that reconciliation becomes a reality.

III.

During recent months I have come to see more and more the need for the method of nonviolence in international relations. While I was convinced during my student days of the power of nonviolence in group conflicts within nations, I was not yet convinced of its efficacy in conflicts between nations. I felt that while war could never be a positive or absolute good, it could serve as a negative good in the sense of preventing the spread and growth of an evil force. War, I felt, horrible as it is, might be preferable to surrender to a totalitarian system. But more and more I have come to the conclusion that the potential destructiveness of modern weapons of war totally rules out the possibility of war ever serving again as a negative good. If we assume that mankind has a right to survive then we must find an alternative to war and destruction. In a day when sputniks dash through outer space and guided ballistic missiles are carving highways of death through the stratosphere, nobody can win a war. The choice today is no longer between violence and nonviolence. It is either nonviolence or nonexistence.

I am no doctrinaire pacifist. I have tried to embrace a realistic pacifism. Moreover, I see the pacifist position not as sinless but as the lesser evil in the circumstances. Therefore I do not claim to be free from the moral dilemmas that the Christian nonpacifist confronts. But I am convinced that the church cannot remain silent while mankind faces the threat of being plunged into the abyss of nuclear annihilation. If the church is true to its mission it must call for an end to the arms race.

In recent months I have also become more and more convinced of the reality of a personal God. True, I have always believed in the personality of God. But in past years the idea of a personal God was little more than a metaphysical category which I found theologically and philosophically satisfying. Now it is a living reality that has been validated in the experiences of everyday life. Perhaps the suffering, frustration and agonizing moments which I have had to undergo occasionally as a result of my involvement in a difficult struggle have drawn me closer to God. Whatever the cause, God has been profoundly real to me in recent months. In the midst of outer dangers I have felt an inner calm and known resources of strength that only God could give. In many instances I have felt the power of God transforming the fatigue of despair into the buoyancy of hope. I am convinced that the universe is under the control of a loving purpose and that in the struggle for righteousness man has cosmic companionship. Behind the harsh appearances of the world there is a benign power. To say God is personal is not to make him an object among other objects or attribute to him the finiteness and limitations of human personality; it is to take what is finest and noblest in our consciousness and affirm its perfect existence in him. It is certainly true that human personality is limited, but personality as such involves no necessary limitations. It simply means self-consciousness and self-direction. So in the truest sense of the word, God is a living God. In him there is feeling and will, responsive to the deepest yearnings of the human heart: this God both evokes and answers prayers.

The past decade has been a most exciting one. In spite of the tensions and uncertainties of our age something profoundly meaningful has begun. Old systems of exploitation and oppression are passing away and new systems of justice and equality are being born. In a real sense ours is a great time in which to be alive. Therefore I am not yet discouraged about the future. Granted that the easygoing optimism of yesterday is impossible. Granted that we face a world crisis which often leaves us standing amid the surging murmur of life's restless sea. But every crisis has both its dangers and its opportunities. Each can spell either salvation or doom. In a dark, confused world the spirit of God may yet reign supreme.

> SOURCE: Martin Luther King, Jr., "Pilgrimage to Nonviolence,"
> *The Christian Century*, LXXVII (April 13, 1960), 439–
> 41. Copyright 1960 Christian Century Foundation. Reprinted by permission of *The Christian Century*.

LITERATURE

That the Protestant social gospel was undergoing transformation in the 1930's and 1940's was early perceived from within the movement itself. Charles Clayton Morrison published his Rauschenbusch lectures at Rochester as *The Social Gospel and the Christian Cultus* (N.Y., 1933), in which he argued that the social gospel could not be simply grafted onto evangelicalism but demanded a revolution, another Reformation, in the entire cultus of the church. H. Richard Niebuhr took an opposite position in a brief but significant article, "The Attack Upon the Social Gospel," *Religion in Life,* V (Spring, 1936), 176–81, arguing that the social gospel rested on a false analysis of the social situation, and therefore followed a false strategy. F. Ernest Johnson wrote *The Social Gospel Re-examined* (N.Y., 1940) to show that there was no necessary incongruity between the social gospel and the basic concerns of Christian faith. Since World War II, a number of younger scholars have probed into the question of what had happened to the social gospel in the years between the wars. J. Neal Hughley vigorously criticizes the social thought of the liberal social-gospel leaders while defending the "dialectical theological socialism" of Reinhold Niebuhr in *Trends in Protestant Social Idealism* (N.Y., 1948). Robert M. Miller's *American Protestantism and Social Issues, 1919–1939* (Chapel Hill, N.C., 1958) draws heavily on periodical literature and denominational reports in describing the major trends in Protestant thought and action with respect to the social order, civil liberties, labor, race, and war. Paul A. Carter, *The Decline and Revival of the Social Gospel: Social and Political Liberalism in American Protestant Churches, 1920–1940* (Ithaca, N.Y., 1954), also utilizes periodical material extensively in defense of the thesis that the social gospel declined under fire in the 1920's but was vigorously reassertive in the depression. Donald B. Meyer's *The Protestant Search for Political Realism, 1919–1941* (Berkeley, Calif., 1960) focuses on the main leaders in discerning a metamorphosis of Protestant social concern from a criticism of society to a criticism of religion under the pressure of politics. A central figure in these books is Reinhold Niebuhr; in addition to his own many writings, consult Charles W. Kegley and Robert W. Bretall, eds., *Reinhold Niebuhr: His Religious, Social, and Political Thought* (N.Y., 1956); Gordon Harland, *The Thought of Reinhold Niebuhr* (N.Y., 1960); John A. Hutchison, ed., *Christian Faith and Social Action* (N.Y., 1953), especially the editor's own essay, "Two Decades of Social Christianity"; and D. B. Robertson, *Reinhold Niebuhr's Works: A Bibliography* (Berea, Ky., 1954). The emergence of extremist trends in Protestant social thought has caused much controversy in this period; on these matters see the carefully documented works by Ralph L. Roy, *Apostles of Discord: A Study of Organized Bigotry and Disruption on the Fringes of Protestantism* (Boston, 1953), and *Communism and the Churches* (N.Y., 1960).

The overall story of social action trends in American Roman Catholicism from the viewpoint of a sympathetic Catholic historian has been told by Aaron I. Abell, *American Catholicism and Social Action: A Search for Social Justice, 1865–1950* (Garden City, N.Y., 1960). A symposium which gives vivid impressions of Catholic social action is Leo R. Ward, ed., *The American Apostolate: American Catholics in the Twentieth Century* (Westminster, Md., 1952). Another symposium which contains informative essays is *The Catholic Church, U.S.A.,* ed. Louis J. Putz (Chicago, 1956). The impact of Pope Pius XI's important encyclical *Quadragesimo anno* was mediated to the American scene through many channels; see especially Joseph Husslein, *The Christian Social Manifesto: An Interpretative Study of the Encyclicals Rerum Novarum and Quadragesimo Anno of Pope Leo XIII and Pope Pius XI* (Milwaukee, 1931), and Virgil Michel, *Chris-*

tian Social Reconstruction: Some Fundamentals of the Quadragesimo Anno (Milwaukee, 1937). The way in which the American hierarchy dealt with social issues can be traced in *Our Bishops Speak: National Pastorals and Annual Statements of the Hierarchy of the United States . . . 1919–1951* (Milwaukee, 1952).

There has been much discussion of the relationship of religion and ethics to economic and industrial life since 1925. See the multi-volume series, "The Ethics and Economics of Society," prepared under the leadership of the Department of Church and Economic Life of the National Council of Churches, especially A. Dudley Ward, ed., *Goals of Economic Life* (N.Y., 1953), and John C. Bennett, *et al., Christian Values and Economic Life* (N.Y., 1954). A nontechnical interpretation of this massive study was prepared by Marquis W. Childs and Douglass Cater, *Ethics in a Business Society* (N.Y., 1954). Walter G. Muelder's *Religion and Economic Responsibility* (N.Y., 1953) was written from the viewpoint of personalistic social ethics and makes use of the results of socio-economic research. A thoughtful study by a leader in the Lutheran Church—Missouri Synod is John Daniel, *Labor, Industry and the Church: A Study of the Interrelationships involving the Church, Labor, and Management* (St. Louis, 1957). Roman Catholic views on economics and industry are well summarized by John F. Cronin, *Social Principles and Economic Life* (Milwaukee, 1959). The Catholic interest in industry councils is discussed by Mary L. Eberdt and Gerald J. Schnepp, *Industrialism and the Popes* (N.Y., 1953).

Works which include informative discussions of the racial situation in American church life and have helpful bibliographies are Kyle Haselden, *The Racial Problem in Christian Perspective* (N.Y., 1959); John La Farge, *The Catholic Viewpoint on Race Relations* (Garden City, N.Y., 1956); Liston Pope, *The Kingdom Beyond Caste* (N.Y., 1957); and Paul Ramsey, *Christian Ethics and the Sit-In* (N.Y., 1961).

The last three chapters of Roland H. Bainton's useful *Christian Attitudes to War and Peace: A Historical Survey and Critical Re-evaluation* (N.Y., 1960) deal with the period since 1918, compactly summarizing and commenting on the main developments in this field. A scholarly study of the Thomistic ethic of war and its relevance to twentieth-century warfare is John K. Ryan, *Modern War and Basic Ethics* (Washington, 1933). Trends in pacifist thought can be discerned in part by tracing the successive editions of Richard B. Gregg, *The Power of Nonviolence* (2nd rev. ed., Nyack, N.Y., 1959). Published originally in 1934, it was revised ten years later, and published again in 1959 with much additional material, a foreword by Martin Luther King, Jr., and bibliographical helps. A book which reflects the Protestant realist approach to the issues of war and peace is Kenneth W. Thompson, *Christian Ethics and the Dilemmas of Foreign Policy* (Durham, N.C., 1959); see also Reinhold Niebuhr, *Christian Realism and Political Problems* (N.Y., 1953).

Much recent Christian social interest has focused on political thought and political problems. John C. Bennett in *Christians and the State* (N.Y., 1958) competently surveys alternate viewpoints concerning the Christian understanding of the state in presenting his own conclusions, which show the influence of liberal, Niebuhrian, and ecumenical contributions. Heinrich A. Rommen's massive *The State in Catholic Thought: A Treatise in Political Philosophy* (St. Louis, 1945) is a general treatment but with many references to the American scene.

Essays by William L. Miller, Dayton D. McKean and R. Morton Darrow in James W. Smith and A. Leland Jamison, eds., *Religion in American Life*, vol. II: *Religious Perspectives in American Culture* (Princeton, 1961), deal perceptively with various aspects of religion and politics. Luke E. Ebersole, *Church Lobbying at the Nation's Capitol* (N.Y., 1951), summarizes the nature and methods of religious lobbies in Washington, dealing chiefly with the 1940's. Peter H. Odegard, ed., *Religion and Politics* (New Brunswick, N.J., 1960), is a collection of sources focused on the Catholic-Protestant tension in American political life. For a discussion of this on the local level, see Kenneth W. Underwood, *Protestant and Catholic: Religious and Social Interaction in an Industrial Community* (Boston, 1957).

Extensive and valuable bibliographical material on the topics covered in this chapter may be found in Nelson R. Burr, *A Critical Bibliography of Religion in America*, in Smith and Jamison, eds., *Religion in American Life*, Vol. IV (Princeton, 1961), Part III: "Religion and Society," 545-750.

CHAPTER XXII

The Ecumenical Awakening

THE ecumenical movement, which seeks to discover, express and further Christian unity throughout the world, became one of the major forces in American Christian life from 1930 to 1960. Though there had already been some significant developments in co-operative Christianity, it was in this period that the impact of the Christian unity movement was strong enough to produce an ecumenical awakening. In this chapter the background for ecumenicity before 1930 will be briefly treated, followed by a discussion of the major aspects of unitive Christianity in America since then.

Though the nineteenth century is often remembered for its theological controversies and denominational schisms, it was not without some important co-operative developments. The Plan of Union of 1801 [1] was finally frustrated by the divisive tendencies of the nineteenth century, but not before a half-century of united work by two denominations on the frontier had been accomplished. Some of the new American denominations—for example, the Disciples of Christ—had been born in the hope of providing a pattern for Christian unity, and though the hope was frustrated, the concern for union continued. Many of the national voluntary benevolence societies which had been formed in the early nineteenth century drew their memberships from Christians of various denominations, thus not only providing channels for co-operation but also stimulating interest in fuller Christian unity. The longing for wider union among Protestants was articulated with prophetic power by several prominent churchmen. For example, Samuel S. Schmucker (1799–1873), a Lutheran seminary professor and president, published in 1838 a *Fraternal Appeal to the American Churches: With a Plan for Catholic Union, on Apostolic Principles*. The times were not propitious for his plan for federal union, but his work contributed to the quest for unity.[2] German-born Philip Schaff (1819–93) was another scholarly prophet of Christian union. From the publication of his inaugural address as professor at the Theological Seminary of the German Reformed Church at Mercersburg, Pa., on *The Principle of Protestantism* (1845), to his inspiring address on "The Reunion of Christendom" at the World's Parliament of Religions in Chicago in the last few weeks of his life (1893), Schaff contributed significantly to the movement for Christian

---

[1] See *American Christianity*, I, 523, 545–7.

[2] For a discussion of this and other appeals, see Donald H. Yoder, "Christian Unity in Nineteenth-Century America," in Ruth Rouse and Stephen C. Neill, eds., *A History of the Ecumenical Movement, 1517–1948* (Phila., 1954), 221–59.

unity, most permanently through his studies in church history and symbolics, but also through effective service in the American branch of the Evangelical Alliance.[3] A contribution of lasting importance in the quest for Christian unity was made by an Episcopal clergyman, William R. Huntington (1838–1918). His book, *The Church Idea: An Essay Toward Unity* (1870), suggested a platform of essentials on which churches could unite. Revised and adopted by his own church (1886) and two years later by a world conference of Anglican bishops, the "Chicago-Lambeth Quadrilateral" named as essential to the restoration of unity: (1) the Holy Scriptures as the rule and ultimate standard of faith; (2) the Apostles' and the Nicene creeds as the sufficient statement of the Christian faith; (3) the two Sacraments ordained by Christ himself, Baptism and the Supper of the Lord; and (4) the Historic Episcopate.[4]

In the later nineteenth century, the movement for increased official co-operation among the churches began to bear fruit. It proved easier to work out formal arrangements first between church boards and societies than between the churches themselves. These achievements helped to pave the way for direct denominational participation in councils of churches. In 1893, official delegates from many foreign mission boards met to confer on common problems and to plan for co-ordinated efforts on the missionary frontiers. From this important beginning grew the Foreign Missions Conference of North America. The home-missions leaders felt the need for a similar co-operative agency, and after some preliminary experiments, early in 1908 they formed the Home Missions Council. By that year plans for an interchurch council had been carefully worked out, and in December the Federal Council of the Churches of Christ in America came into being.[5] The constituency of the Federal Council varied somewhat through the years, but approximately thirty denominations, including many but not all of the major bodies, were full members. The major purposes of the Federal Council were to express the fellowship and "catholic unity" of the Christian church, and to bring the Christian bodies of America into united service for Christ and the world.

Co-operation in Christian education and Sunday school work had been important in preparing an atmosphere in which movements for church unity could develop. Ever since the institution of the American Sunday School Union (1824), there had been much co-operative effort across denominational lines in the field of religious education. The interdenomina-

---

[3] David S. Schaff, *The Life of Philip Schaff, in Part Autobiographical* (N.Y., 1897). In his *Romanticism in American Theology: Nevin and Schaff at Mercersburg* (Chicago, 1961), James H. Nichols has called attention to the sources of Schaff's churchly and unitive interests (see Chap. 3, and the Epilogue).

[4] For the various revisions in the Quadrilateral, see Rouse and Neill, eds., *A History of the Ecumenical Movement*, 250, 264–5, 446–7.

[5] Elias B. Sanford, *Origin and History of the Federal Council of the Churches of Christ in America* (Hartford, Conn., 1916).

tional aspects of church-school leadership were especially emphasized in the influential work of the International Sunday School conventions, which have met regularly beginning in 1875. The organization of the International Sunday School Council of Religious Education (1922), soon renamed the International Council of Religious Education, represented an attempt to find a balance between denominational and nondenominational approaches. Through these various channels, millions of American Protestants had opportunity to work with members of other communions, often thus gaining their first significant contacts across denominational boundaries.

At the same time that these many movements for Christian co-operation were influencing the religious scene in America, unitive forces were also appearing on the world Christian scene. These developments were not unrelated, but mutually enhanced each other. The growth of the world movement for Christian unity can be traced along four major lines to twentieth-century embodiments.

Unitive interests have been of serious concern to Protestants ever since the Reformation.[6] But the rise of the modern ecumenical movement was intimately related to the great missionary thrust which began at the close of the eighteenth century, touched off by the inspiration and example of William Carey (1761–1834) and others. The missionaries soon discovered that competitive denominationalism presented serious obstacles to the advancement of their cause. Many of the early missionary societies, such as the American Board of Commissioners for Foreign Missions (1810),[7] drew support across denominational lines. On the missionary frontiers themselves, it was soon found advisable for Christian workers to meet on occasion for fellowship and discussion. In 1854, missionary leaders from various parts of the world gathered for significant sessions in New York and London. These world affairs were sufficiently fruitful to be continued; the famous World Missionary Conference at Edinburgh, 1910, recognized as the major turning-point in ecumenical history, was the eighth in the series.[8] At this meeting, differing from its predecessors in that most of the delegates had been officially appointed by the missionary agencies of their churches and were not simply attending as interested individuals, many of the representatives caught a vision of Christian co-operation and unity which was to guide them for the rest of their lives. From Edinburgh ran many streams which were to nourish the growing ecumenical movement.

The conference was followed up by a continuation committee which

[6] John T. McNeill, *Unitive Protestantism* (N.Y., 1930); see also his essay, "The Ecumenical Idea and Efforts to Realize It, 1517–1618," in Rouse and Neill, eds., *A History of the Ecumenical Movement*, 27–69.

[7] See *American Christianity*, I, 523, 547–52.

[8] Henry P. Van Dusen, *World Christianity: Yesterday-Today-Tomorrow* (N.Y., 1947), 87. In his *One Great Ground of Hope: Christian Missions and Christian Unity* (Phila., 1961), Van Dusen persuasively argued that "the Christian world mission has been both the precursor and the progenitor of the effort after Christian unity."

matured into the International Missionary Council (1921). In 1928, the I.M.C. conducted an important world-missionary conference at Jerusalem. One of the major achievements of this conference was the preparation of a statement on "The Christian Message." The task was a difficult one, for two distinct schools of thought were in conflict. One of these, in the words of William R. Hogg,

> emphasized exclusively the gospel's uniqueness, maintaining that the convert must renounce completely his former system of religious belief and any practice associated with it. The other, appealing to the comparative study of religions, saw elements of value in non-Christian religions and viewed Christianity as the fulfillment of some truths already possessed in part by other faiths.[9]

But largely through the skill of an American Presbyterian, Robert E. Speer (1867–1947), and an Anglican bishop, William Temple (1881–1944), the gap was bridged, and the statement won the full consent of the gathering. A central paragraph in "The Christian Message," conveying something of its spirit and content, declared:

> Our message is Jesus Christ. He is the revelation of what God is and of what man through Him may become. In Him we come face to face with the Ultimate Reality of the universe; He makes known to us God as our Father, perfect and infinite in love and in righteousness; for in Him we find God incarnate, the final, yet ever-unfolding, revelation of the God in whom we live and move and have our being.[10]

Such statements as this, backed by the growing weight of the maturing ecumenical movement, gave encouragement and direction to the thrust for Christian unity in America and in other lands.

The second major line of ecumenical development was that of youth work. The Young Men's Christian Association, founded in London by George Williams (1821–1905) in 1844, provided opportunities for religious activity among youth on a nondenominational basis. The Young Women's Christian Association was established in 1855. Both associations soon had branches throughout the world.[11] In 1886, a youth movement with a

[9] *Ecumenical Foundations: A History of the International Missionary Council and Its Nineteenth-Century Background* (N.Y., 1952), 247.
[10] *The Jerusalem Meeting of the International Missionary Council* (8 vols., N.Y., 1928), I, 402.
[11] See Clarence P. Shedd, *et al., History of the World's Alliance of the Young Men's Christian Associations* (London, 1955); Kenneth S. Latourette, *World Service: A History of the Foreign Work and World Service of the Young Men's Christian Associations of the United States and Canada* (N.Y., 1957); C. Howard Hopkins, *History of the Y.M.C.A. in North America* (N.Y., 1951); Elizabeth Wilson, *Fifty Years of Work Among Young Women, 1866–1916: A History of the Young Women's Christian Associations in the United States of America* (N.Y., 1916).

distinctive missionary focus was formed at one of Dwight L. Moody's conferences at Mt. Hermon, Mass.: the Student Volunteer Movement for Foreign Missions. A Methodist layman, John R. Mott (1865–1955), served as its organizer and chairman for many years. Student Christian movements arose in many lands; under Mott's leadership the World's Student Christian Federation was founded in Sweden in 1895. The non-denominational youth organizations were often marked by a seriousness of purpose and a prophetic willingness to experiment.[12] Many of the men who later became prominent ecumenical leaders first learned to know and to trust Christians of other communions through their work in student Christian affairs. Mott himself, for example, presided at the missionary conferences at Edinburgh and Jerusalem.

A third line of ecumenical development was that of federation for Christian service and ethical action, often called "Life and Work." The Evangelical Alliance, founded in London in 1846, in general followed this line, being especially active in defending religious liberty. Josiah Strong (1847–1916), a Congregational minister, served as secretary of the Alliance's American Branch (founded 1867) for a dozen years, using its influence to press for closer co-operation on the part of the major communions, in order that their witness in the social order might be more effective. In 1898 he resigned in order to work more directly toward the formation of the Federal Council of Churches, an American manifestation of the Life and Work approach. Many American Christians were especially committed to this way, believing that "dogma divides, service unites." The leading exponent of the federative approach on the world scene was Nathan Söderblom (1866–1931), Swedish Lutheran Archbishop of Uppsala. Under his leadership the first Universal Christian Conference on Life and Work was held at Stockholm in 1925.[13] A continuation committee became in 1930 the Universal Christian Council for Life and Work.

The fourth line of ecumenical growth has been in many ways the most difficult, for the "Faith and Order" movement calls for the frank facing of the most crucial theological differences between the churches. The original Protestant unity discussions in the sixteenth century had broken down at the doctrinal points which serious discussion of faith and order would inevitably raise again. There was much hesitation lest the theological approach should disrupt such harmony as had been achieved in church co-operation. At Edinburgh in 1910, however, Charles Henry Brent (1862–1929), then missionary bishop of the Protestant Episcopal Church in the United States of America to the Philippine Islands, was inspired to initiate a movement for renewed doctrinal discussion among churches. He urged

[12] Clarence P. Shedd, *Two Centuries of Student Christian Movements* (N.Y., 1934); John R. Mott, *The World's Student Christian Federation: Origin, Achievements, Forecast* (N.Y., 1920).

[13] G. K. A. Bell, ed., *The Stockholm Conference, 1925* (London, 1926).

his own communion to take the lead, but it took many years of hard work before the First World Conference on Faith and Order could meet in Lausanne, Switzerland, in 1927. Over one hundred denominations, including some Eastern Orthodox and Old Catholic churches, were represented. A surprisingly large measure of agreement on many important theological issues was reached, and a continuation committee was entrusted with carrying on the movement.

By 1930, therefore, there had already been much thought and action toward Christian unity in America, while on the world scene the four main lines of ecumenical development had come of age. In the period presently under consideration, the movement for Christian unity at home, stimulated directly by encounter with the unitive currents in the churches around the world, brought an ecumenical awakening to American churches. The ecumenical movement continued to grow impressively. A Roman Catholic observer declared that it "is undoubtedly the most striking ecclesiological event since the sixteenth-century Reformation." [14] This impressive ecumenical advance meant that the thought and action of Christians in other lands had come to have a more immediate and direct significance in American Protestantism than had been the case for nearly two centuries. In an ecumenical era, it is increasingly difficult to discuss the church history of a given nation without continual awareness of events in other places. Thus the formation of the World Council of Churches has perhaps been as important to the ecumenical awakening in America as has been the organization of the National Council of Churches. And the discussion of the other major topics related to Christian unity in America for this period—issues dividing churches, church unions and reunions, criticism of ecumenical endeavor, world denominational fellowships, and Roman Catholic ecumenism—cannot be carried on without continual reference to movements and events in the larger Christian world.

The major event in ecumenical history in this period was the formation of the World Council of Churches at Amsterdam in 1948. In 1937, the second world conferences of both Life and Work (Oxford) and Faith and Order (Edinburgh) were held, and at such times that it was convenient for delegates to attend both gatherings. Each conference voted to merge with the other, and at Utrecht the next year (1938) a provisional structure for the World Council of Churches was prepared. The basis of the Council was as follows: "The World Council of Churches is a fellowship of Churches which accept our Lord Jesus Christ as God and Saviour." During the difficult war years the World Council, although still in process of formation, did notable work in assisting refugees, aiding prisoners of war, and providing for "orphaned" missions. When the World Council was finally formally

[14] Gustave Weigel, S.J., *A Catholic Primer on the Ecumenical Movement* (Westminster, Md., 1957), ix.

constituted, one hundred and forty-seven churches from forty-four countries became members. Twenty-nine of these churches were American. The Second Assembly of the World Council met at Evanston, Illinois, in 1954, the first of the major ecumenical gatherings to be held in this country. It did much to heighten ecumenical awareness in America. The World Council represented the convergence of three of the main lines of ecumenical history: Life and Work, Faith and Order, and youth work. It maintained a close association with the International Missionary Council. The full merger of the two Councils took place at the Third Assembly at New Delhi, India, in 1961. At this time the basis of the Council was revised.

The various lines of co-operative Christianity in America also converged in this period in the formation of the National Council of Churches. As the work of the Foreign Missions Conference, the Home Missions Council, the Federal Council, and the International Council of Religion Education prospered, these agencies found their work overlapping more and more. The necessity of "co-ordinating the co-ordinators" was increasingly felt, for there was much duplication of effort. In 1941, a significant meeting to outline plans for their merger was held at Atlantic City. Nine years later, in Cleveland, Ohio, in November, 1950, eight major Protestant interdenominational agencies[15] merged to form the National Council of the Churches of Christ in the United States of America. The Council was responsible to the member churches, originally twenty-nine in number, twenty-five Protestant and four Orthodox. The National Council continued the major functions of the merging agencies and developed new ones of its own. The Federal Council, for example, had done outstanding work in the field of social thought and action; this interest was continued in appropriate ways by the National Council, especially through its Division of Christian Life and Work.

As Christian churches became better acquainted through serving together in ecumenical endeavor, it became increasingly clear that the range of doctrinal differences among them was far narrower than had been believed. At the very first world Faith and Order conference, a climactic moment came when a statement on "The Church's Message to the World—the Gospel" was received without dissent by the whole conference, including the Eastern Orthodox delegates.[16] At the second conference, a comprehensive theological statement on "The Grace of our Lord Jesus Christ" won unanimous consent. In view of the theological conflicts of the sixteenth century on this doctrine, it was remarkable that the delegates could declare that "we agree on the following statement and recognise that there is in

[15] The four just mentioned, plus the Missionary Education Movement of the United States and Canada (1902), the National Protestant Council on Higher Education (1911), the United Council of Church Women (1941), and the United Stewardship Council (1920).

[16] H. N. Bate, ed., *Faith and Order: Proceedings of the World Conference, Lausanne* (N.Y., 1927), 461-3.

connection with this subject no ground for maintaining division between Churches." [17] But though the *range* of differences was far narrower than had been suspected, the *depth* of the differences, focused largely on questions concerning the nature of the church, was found to be very great indeed. The fundamental disagreements in the doctrine of the church showed themselves in many ways in interchurch discussion. Efforts were often made to state the differences in terms of cleavage between "catholic" and "protestant" concepts of the church, but they were too deeply embedded and revealed themselves at too many points to be easily described.[18] The tensions appeared with greatest force at two particular points: the nature of the ministry, and the theory and practice of the sacraments.[19] As the ecumenical movement matured, these differences emerged as the real stumbling blocks to fuller unity. The Faith and Order movement, which for several decades had focused on comparative ecclesiology, redirected its study program at the third world conference at Lund in 1952. On the one hand, greater emphasis was given to Christology, in the hope that as Christians were drawn nearer to the center of their faith, they might be drawn closer to each other. On the other hand, attention was called to the importance of tradition in the life of the churches, and to the importance of nondoctrinal and institutional factors in movements of unity and disunity.[20] It was shown that cultural, ethnic, and national barriers play important, often decisive, roles in perpetuating Christian divisions, and that the movements for unity themselves have sociological as well as theological roots.[21]

The issues of ecclesiology which had emerged with special clarity in the world conferences seemed somewhat remote to most active Christians, and perhaps particularly to American Protestants, whose acceptance of the faith was often in practical and activistic terms. It was recognized that if the cause of Christian unity were really to be advanced, these issues would need to be understood far more widely among Christians. Accordingly, it was decided to launch faith and order discussions at regional and national levels. The first such conference was held in the United States: the North

---

[17] Leonard Hodgson, ed., *The Second World Conference on Faith and Order* (N.Y., 1928), 224.

[18] See R. Newton Flew, ed., *The Nature of the Church* (London, 1952); J. Robert Nelson, *The Realm of Redemption: Studies in the Doctrine of the Nature of the Church in Contemporary Protestant Theology* (Greenwich, Conn., 1951); and Lesslie Newbigin, *The Household of God* (N.Y., 1954).

[19] Henry P. Van Dusen, "The Issues of Christian Unity," *Christendom*, XI (1946), 327–40.

[20] See Oliver S. Tomkins, ed., *The Third World Conference on Faith and Order, Held at Lund . . . 1952* (London, 1953), and Anders Nygren, *Christ and the Church*, tr. Alan Carlsten (Phila., 1956). For treatment of these issues with particular attention to the American scene, see Albert C. Outler, *The Christian Tradition and the Unity We Seek* (N.Y., 1957).

[21] C. H. Dodd, G. R. Cragg, and J. Ellul, *More Than Doctrine Divides the Churches: Social and Cultural Factors in Church Divisions* (N.Y., 1952); Robert Lee, *The Social Sources of Church Unity: An Interpretation of Unitive Movements in American Protestantism* (N.Y., 1960).

American Conference on Faith and Order. Meeting on the campus of Oberlin College in September, 1957, the conference focused on the theme, "The Nature of the Unity We Seek." For two years prior to the gathering, representative study groups in various parts of the continent dealt with aspects of the theme, introducing ecumenical theological debate at local levels. It was required that participating communions send representatives of their youth, their laymen and laywomen as well as of their clergy. Eastern Orthodox churches were represented at the conference; as had been the case in some of the world conferences, they felt obliged to make clear their distinctive views concerning the church and the ministry in a formal statement.

An important area of ecumenical concern is that of specific church unions. Interchurch agencies have not been responsible for the active promotion of the reunion or the merger of churches, but have left the actual initiation, development, and consummation of unions to the interested bodies, which alone are competent in the areas of their own jurisdiction. American church life before the dawn of the ecumenical era had been marked by several significant unions within denominational families. For example, Old and New School Presbyterians merged in 1869–70 to form the Presbyterian Church in the United States of America, and in 1918, three Lutheran synods merged as the United Lutheran Church in America. In the period since 1930, more mergers of this type continued. In 1930, three synods (not involved in the 1918 merger) united to form the American Lutheran Church; in 1939, three churches united as The Methodist Church; in 1946, two evangelical bodies of German background combined as the Evangelical United Brethren Church; in 1958, two Presbyterian churches merged into the United Presbyterian Church in the United States of America. But especial interest attaches to church unions across denominational lines, for here the difficult theological issues concerning the nature of church, ministry and sacraments must be faced in a realistic way. The example of the Church of South India, a union consummated in 1947 in which churches of congregational, presbyterian and episcopal polities were merged, was widely heralded. In the United States, the initiation of the United Church of Christ in 1957 related four denominational traditions (Congregational, Christian, Lutheran, Reformed) and two polities (congregational, presbyterian) into one church.

From its early days, the ecumenical movement has had its critics. Some of them have come from the ranks of the liberals, who have believed ecumenical theology to be too traditional and church union to involve too much centralization. Others have spoken on behalf of denominations where the understanding of the nature of the church does not permit unqualified recognition of other Christian bodies as true churches, and therefore, as they see it, does not allow them to participate in ecumenical endeavor— both Southern Baptists and Missouri Synod Lutherans have reflected such views from their quite different perspectives. The most vigorous criticism, however, has come from the ranks of the fundamentalists, who have often seen the Federal, National, and World councils as instruments of the "modernists," and have been very suspicious of them and their activities, particularly their social action. In 1941, the American Council of Christian Churches was formed, with some small and very conservative denominations as members. The next year, a larger National Association of Evangelicals was launched; at its constitutional convention in Chicago in 1943 it adopted a Statement of Faith affirming belief in the Bible as the inspired and only infallible, authoritative Word of God.[22] Both of these organizations were instrumental in forming small world interdenominational fellowships of fundamentalist nature (in 1948 and 1951, respectively).

A side of world Christianity which often appears to be working at cross-purposes with the main ecumenical movement has been the rise of world denominational fellowships. The roots of many of the global denominational associations lie in the nineteenth century. The Lambeth Conference of Anglican Bishops, which met initially in 1867, was in many respects the first such movement. As a meeting of bishops only, including of course the bishops of the American Protestant Episcopal Church, it has a somewhat distinctive character. In 1875 the Alliance of Reformed Churches throughout the World holding the Presbyterian System brought together in a fraternal relation many churches of Calvinist heritage. The World Methodist Council was formed in 1891; the Baptist World Alliance in 1905. The Lutheran World Convention, later renamed the Lutheran World Federation, was organized in 1923. In 1930 were instituted the World Convention of the Churches of Christ (Disciples), and the International Association for Liberal Christianity and Religious Freedom. In 1937 the Friends [Quaker] World Committee for Consultation first met; in 1947 the first Pentecostal World Conference was held. Most of these world denominational bodies have entered into a consultative relationship with the World Council of Churches. Many leaders in the denominational fellowships are prominent also in ecumenical activities. Most of the American denominations belong to their appropriate world denominational fellowships.

As the ecumenical movement was gathering headway early in the twentieth century, there was considerable hope that Roman Catholics might be included in ecumenical discussion and action. Many Catholics were deeply interested in the reunion of Christendom. A formal invitation for Roman Catholic participation in the World Conference on Faith and Order at Lausanne was issued, but courteously declined. The dogmatic position of the Roman Catholic Church—that unity already exists, and that she is the center and source of it—prevented any participation. In 1928, following Lausanne, Pope Pius XI issued the encyclical *Mortalium animos,* on "Foster-

[22] H. Shelton Smith, "Conflicting Interchurch Movements in American Protestantism," *Christendom,* XII (1947), 165–76.

ing True Religious Unity." The encyclical declared that "the Apostolic See can by no means take part in these assemblies, nor is it in any way lawful for Catholics to give to such enterprises their encouragement or support. If they did so, they would be giving countenance to a false Christianity quite alien to the one Church of Christ." The encyclical further ruled out any distinction between "fundamental" and "non-fundamental" articles of faith: "All true followers of Christ, therefore, will believe the dogma of the Immaculate Conception of the Mother of God with the same faith as they believe the mystery of the august Trinity, the infallibility of the Roman Pontiff in the sense defined by the Oecumenical Vatican Council with the same faith as they believe the Incarnation of our Lord." [23]

The longing among Catholics for the reunion of all Christians in the One Church, to be fulfilled in keeping with the dogmatic position of the Roman Church, increased in the 1940's and 1950's as various books, journals, and movements within the church bore witness to "Catholic Ecumenism." The need for an authoritative statement to set the limits and point the direction of this trend was felt, and in 1949 the Sacred Congregation of the Holy Office issued an "Instruction on the Ecumenical Movement." Affirming the teaching of *Mortalium animos* and allied documents, the Instruction encouraged and safeguarded a distinctive Catholic ecumenism. Though Roman Catholics may not participate formally in ecumenical and World Council activities, nevertheless, in Father Weigel's words, this "does not in the Roman mind mean that there is no recognition of the Council or that she cannot in a completely neutral but friendly way have unofficial observers at the meetings, if the occasion favors such an action." [24] Thus unofficial but accredited Roman Catholic observers were present at Lund in 1952 and at Oberlin in 1957—Father Weigel himself at the latter. A number of Catholic scholars have devoted considerable attention to the ecumenical movement, while participation in the distinctive Catholic Ecumenism was growing in the 1950's. Toward the end of that decade, a new stage in Protestant-Catholic relations developed, with new openness and interest in the other on the part of both.[25] The appointment by Rome in 1960 of a Secretariat for Promoting Christian Unity contributed to a deepening encounter. The election of a Roman Catholic as president of the country in 1960 was one sign of a deeper change of attitude, though the older views on both sides found many spokesmen.

In this period, then, the ecumenical movement became an effective force in the life of American churches. The documents that follow provide some glimpse into the ecumenical awakening as it shaped fresh organizational channels, focused theological thought on the issues of Christian unity, and

[23] From *Mortalium animos,* as translated in Sir James Marchant, ed., *The Reunion of Christendom* (N.Y., 1929), 18–9, 22.
[24] *A Catholic Primer on the Ecumenical Movement,* 45.
[25] Robert M. Brown and Gustave Weigel, S.J., *An American Dialogue: A Protestant Looks at Catholicism and a Catholic Looks at Protestantism* (Garden City, N.Y., 1960).

stimulated church unions and reunions. At the close of the period, several new denominational mergers were soon to be consummated, while others were under serious discussion. General interest in ecumenicity was high, though an undercurrent of criticism persisted, and though there were those who believed that stubborn issues, both theological and nontheological, would keep the ecumenical awakening from transforming fundamentally the existing denominational-conciliar pattern of American Christian life.

180. Methodist Union

The union of three branches of Methodism in 1939 brought into being the largest single Protestant denomination in America. The separations had been of long standing. The Methodist Protestant Church had been organized by those who withdrew from the main body of Methodism in 1828 in protest when the latter denied a petition asking that presiding elders be elected rather than appointed and that lay representatives be admitted to conferences. The division of the parent church into northern and southern branches because of differences in attitude toward slavery took place in 1844. Following the break, there was a long period of bitterness between the Methodist Episcopal Church and the Methodist Episcopal Church, South. With the meeting of commissions appointed by the two churches in 1876, a new period of fraternity was entered; and thereafter fraternal delegations were exchanged frequently. In 1894 and 1896, commissions on federation were named by the two bodies, and some co-operative missionary and publishing work was undertaken. But federation did little to ease the serious problems of overlapping and duplication between the two churches, and it became widely recognized that organic union was the preferred solution.

Beginning in 1908, with representatives of the Methodist Protestant Church also participating, steps were taken toward eventual full union of the three bodies. Some opposed the prospective union because they feared the new church would be too large or its authority too centralized. Others opposed it because of different understandings of Methodist polity, particularly with respect to the role of the bishop (of which the Methodist Protestant Church had none). Then there was considerable unhappiness over the theological and social liberalism of the northern church. But the most difficult issue was the status of the Negro members of the united church. Some southern Methodists, believing in the principle of the separation of the races, argued for the setting apart of Negro Methodists in an autonomous church in fraternal relations with the reunited (white) church. Relatively few northerners were zealous for mixed congregations, but they did object to the exclusion of Negroes from the merger. Certain prominent Negro Methodist leaders were willing to go along with a plan to put the Negro congregations under a separate "jurisdiction" of the church. A plan of 1920 provided for a series of geographical jurisdictions for the white membership, and a separate one for all Negro work. The plan failed for lack of support; an alternate plan to divide the reunited church into a northern and a southern jurisdiction, Negro membership to belong to the former, did not receive the necessary three-fourths affirmative vote from the southern conferences, and also failed in 1925. In the 1930's, negotiations were reopened again. This resulted in the preparation of a Plan of Union which returned to the jurisdictional principle, with five Regional Jurisdictions and one Central Jurisdiction, the latter encompassing Negro conferences and missions. Many were dissatisfied with the compromise, but it cleared the way for the union. The Methodist Protestant Church accepted the episcopacy, and in turn Methodists from the other two bodies consented to having lay delegates from each pastoral charge at annual conferences.[26] The Plan of Union was approved in each church by large majorities, and the union was consummated at a Uniting Conference in Kansas City, Missouri, April 26–May 10, 1939. At the conference, an Episcopal Address to The Methodist Church was delivered, from which the section entitled "A Glance at History" is here reprinted.

DOCUMENT

These three Churches, remembering today their origins and the conditions that gave them existence, have only pride in the capabilities and the achievements of their ecclesiastical ancestors. Stalwart men of noble purpose and eminent ability differed in principles and convictions and took divergent ways to build a Methodism that accorded with their consciences and their judgment. Their voices rang clear for what to them was right. By their molds, their ecclesiastical posterity have wrought faithfully and well for a century and have produced Methodism of distinction and power. We give reverent praise to the men who established the ways of our going and made possible the Churches through which we have lived, moved, and had our being. But from the high level of their characters and attainments we are able today to press across and above the lines of cleavage for the building of a greater and finer Methodism to the glory of God and the establishment of Christ's Kingdom on Earth.

The separations in Methodism brought neither disaster nor decadence. That of 1828 which resulted in the organization of the Methodist Protestant Church dramatized the importance of lay representation in the councils of the Church; and lay representation has long been a fundamental principle in our several branches, and is such in the Plan of Union. Without the separation of 1844 Methodism would have been a house of contention and condemnation from two sides; but with separation it won honorable stand-

[26] For the history of the negotiations, see Paul N. Garber, *The Methodists Are One People* (Nashville, 1939); John M. Moore, *The Long Road to Methodist Union* (N.Y., 1943); and James H. Straughn, *Inside Methodist Union* (Nashville, 1958).

ing, steadfast sympathy, and unfailing support from both sections of a divided people. The tragic era of the nation seriously affected the mind and spirit of the great ecclesiastical bodies; but the people continued increasingly loyal to their respective Methodist Churches, which never receded from each other in doctrinal beliefs nor in essential elements of governmental polity. While Methodists have been distressingly divided, Methodism has continued inherently one. Its faith, its polity, its thought, its life, whatever the realm, never failed its founders. Methodism has had a basal unity, central, elemental, and enduring. No divisions of men could destroy that deeper harmony which is ever the primary basis for governmental oneness.

Faith and order are fundamental for real union in Church life and structure. The Church itself as an instrument for stabilizing the Kingdom of God has become more and more central in all Ecumenical thinking. Before its parts can be co-ordinated those parts must show integrity, and the valid and intrinsic elements of the whole. Any proposal for any Church union must take cognizance of the order involved. Without unity of thought and polity only federation may be possible. Councils may effect co-operation in life and labor, but only kinship can furnish the true and enduring basis of a united Church. Religious faiths go in families, and the normal procedure for union is along family lines. This procedure Methodism has adopted. When families have healed their own separations they will be in position to consider and accept the larger unities.

The problem of Methodist Union has not been solely ecclesiastical, but largely social and human. It has not been really a Methodist problem, but an American problem, the problem of restoring to two great peoples on opposite sides of a chasmic line the mutual good will, the respect, the esteem, and the confidence which had been disrupted by a great political upheaval. For fifty years the suggestion of union received little sympathetic response. Fraternal messages, however felicitous and forceful, were largely formal. The prevailing attitudes, sentiments, and even normal prejudices on both sides had first to be recognized, appraised, and appeased. There was the need for the show of consideration, of understanding, of Christian virtues as prerequisites to any merger. Following the first fifty years of unyielding separateness were two decades, from 1894 to 1914, during which joint Commissions on Federation tempered the winds, softened the atmosphere, and brought in a new climate of springtime and hope. In that period the old family love began to come back; the grandchildren sought fellowship with their unknown but worthy kin; and family gatherings and homecomings gradually increased. Where contacts were most numerous and associations most frequent, respect and confidence most rapidly returned. Union is here today because good will, genuine respect, mutual confidence, and Christian love widely and substantially prevail among the Methodists of the country. Union in American Methodism has been and is a matter of American life. Its consummation is linked with national understanding and national solidarity. This union of ours performs a triple service: It restores unity, harmony, and love to its own religious family; it creates a mighty bond among the great sections of this country; it sets before the religious forces of Christendom an example which is both appealing and challenging. With the consciousness of this duty performed, Methodism again faces the world in faith, hope, and love.

> SOURCE: Lud H. Estes, *et al.,* eds., *Journal of the Uniting Conference of the Methodist Episcopal Church, Methodist Episcopal Church, South, Methodist Protestant Church* (N.Y., 1939), 150–2.

181. *"We Intend to Stay Together"*

The First Assembly of the World Council of Churches at Amsterdam in 1948 was a momentous occasion in church history, and it was only appropriate that the representatives from churches around the world should address a suitable message to the churches. A Message Committee was appointed to prepare the draft of such a statement for the consideration of the gathering. Eivind Berggrav (1884–1959), Lutheran Bishop of Oslo, was named chairman; John A. Mackay (1889—), then President of Princeton Theological Seminary, was the vice-chairman. It was a distinguished Committee, including such well-known names in ecumenical life as Bell, Nygren, Hromadka, Florovsky, Niemöller, Niles, Kraemer, Schlink, Reinhold Niebuhr, Dahlberg, Newbigin, and Neill. The task of finding a common Christian mind was difficult, although it was hoped that the Committee's work would win the endorsement of the entire Assembly. As a news sheet prepared at the conference observed, "To build a message which shall carry the support and enthusiasm of some four hundred men and women from all parts of the world most of whom have never met before, and who are under the compulsion of different theological and sociological allegiances is a prime feat of drafting architecture." [27] But so thoughtfully did the Committee discharge its responsibility, that when the Message, after preliminary reading and discussion, was presented in final form, "It was unanimously adopted, and there was a period of silence followed by a prayer thanking God that He had led His servants to this moment, and beseeching Him to accept these humble words and bless them, and to forgive their imperfections." [28] The full text of "The Message of the Assembly" follows.

DOCUMENT

The World Council of Churches, meeting at Amsterdam, sends this message of greeting to all who are in Christ, and to all who are willing to hear.

---

[27] World Council of Churches, *Assembly News* (September 2, 1948), 1.
[28] W. A. Visser 't Hooft, ed., *The First Assembly of the World Council of Churches* (London, 1949), 44.

We bless God our Father, and our Lord Jesus Christ, Who gathers together in one the children of God that are scattered abroad. He has brought us here together at Amsterdam. We are one in acknowledging Him as our God and Saviour. We are divided from one another not only in matters of faith, order and tradition, but also by pride of nation, class and race. But Christ has made us His own, and He is not divided. In seeking Him we find one another. Here at Amsterdam we have committed ourselves afresh to Him, and have covenanted with one another in constituting this World Council of Churches. We intend to stay together. We call upon Christian congregations everywhere to endorse and fulfil this covenant in their relations one with another. In thankfulness to God we commit the future to Him.

When we look to Christ, we see the world as it is—His world, to which He came and for which He died. It is filled both with great hopes and also with disillusionment and despair. Some nations are rejoicing in new freedom and power, some are bitter because freedom is denied them, some are paralysed by division, and everywhere there is an undertone of fear. There are millions who are hungry, millions who have no home, no country and no hope. Over all mankind hangs the peril of total war. We have to accept God's judgment upon us for our share in the world's guilt. Often we have tried to serve God and mammon, put other loyalties before loyalty to Christ, confused the Gospel with our own economic or national or racial interests, and feared war more than we have hated it. As we have talked with each other here, we have begun to understand how our separation has prevented us from receiving correction from one another in Christ. And because we lacked this correction, the world has often heard from us not the Word of God but the words of men.

But there is a word of God for our world. It is that the world is in the hands of the living God, Whose will for it is wholly good; that in Christ Jesus, His incarnate Word, Who lived and died and rose from the dead, God has broken the power of evil once for all, and opened for everyone the gate into freedom and joy in the Holy Spirit; that the final judgment on all human history and on every human deed is the judgment of the merciful Christ; and that the end of history will be the triumph of His Kingdom, where alone we shall understand how much God has loved the world. This is God's unchanging word to the world. Millions of our fellow-men have never heard it. As we are met here from many lands, we pray God to stir up His whole Church to make this Gospel known to the whole world, and to call on all men to believe in Christ, to live in His love and to hope for His coming.

Our coming together to form a World Council will be vain unless Christians and Christian congregations everywhere commit themselves to the Lord of the Church in a new effort to seek together, where they live, to be His witnesses and servants among their neighbours. We have to remind ourselves and all men that God has put down the mighty from their seats and exalted the humble and the meek. We have to learn afresh together to speak boldly in Christ's name both to those in power and to the people, to oppose terror, cruelty and race discrimination, to stand by the outcast, the prisoner and the refugee. We have to make of the Church in every place a voice for those who have no voice, and a home where every man will be at home. We have to learn afresh together what is the duty of the Christian man or woman in industry, in agriculture, in politics, in the professions and in the home. We have to ask God to teach us together to say "No" and to say "Yes" in truth. "No," to all that flouts the love of Christ, to every system, every programme and every person that treats any man as though he were an irresponsible thing or a means of profit, to the defenders of injustice in the name of order, to those who sow the seeds of war or urge war as inevitable; "Yes," to all that conforms to the love of Christ, to all who seek for justice, to the peacemakers, to all who hope, fight and suffer for the cause of man, to all who—even without knowing it —look for new heavens and a new earth wherein dwelleth righteousness.

It is not in man's power to banish sin and death from the earth, to create the unity of the Holy Catholic Church, to conquer the hosts of Satan. But it is within the power of God. He has given us at Easter the certainty that His purpose will be accomplished. But, by our acts of obedience and faith, we can on earth set up signs which point to the coming victory. Till the day of that victory our lives are hid with Christ in God, and no earthly disillusion or distress or power of hell can separate us from Him. As those who wait in confidence and joy for their deliverance, let us give ourselves to those tasks which lie to our hands, and so set up signs that men may see.

Now unto Him that is able to do exceeding abundantly above all that we ask or think, according to the power that worketh in us, unto Him be glory in the Church by Christ Jesus, throughout all ages, world without end.

> SOURCE: "The Message of the Assembly," in W. A. Visser 't Hooft, ed., *The First Assembly of the World Council of Churches* (London, 1949), 9–11. Used by permission of World Council of Churches.

182. Catholic Instruction on Ecumenics

The rapid progress of the ecumenical movement, so clearly expressed in the formation of the World Council of Churches in 1948, stimulated a need among Roman Catholics for definite guidance in the ecumenical field. The "Instruction on the Ecumenical Movement," issued by the Sacred Congregation of the Holy Office in Rome on December 20, 1949, carefully defined the way in which certain properly qualified Roman Catholics may participate in interchurch discussion. The document explains that "Catholic

Ecumenism" means the return of non-Catholics to the Roman Church.

The Instruction, as issued in translation in America by the National Office of the Chair of Unity Octave, is here reprinted. The Octave of Prayer for Christian Unity was founded by Father Paul James Francis (Lewis Thomas Wattson, 1863–1940). While still an Anglican priest, Father Paul formed the Society of the Atonement, which was received with its founder into the Roman Catholic Church in 1909. From its center, Graymoor, in Garrison, N.Y., the Society actively encourages the observation of the Octave of Prayer (January 18–25) each year.[29] At Graymoor also the American edition of *Unitas,* an international quarterly review and organ of the Unitas Association of Rome, is published, and other aspects of Catholic Ecumenism encouraged.

DOCUMENT

The Catholic Church takes no actual part in "ecumenical" conventions and other assemblies of a similar character. Yet, as numerous pontifical documents show, she has, despite this fact, never ceased, nor will she ever cease to pursue with deepest concern and promote with assiduous prayers to God every endeavour to bring about what was so close to the Heart of Christ the Lord, viz. that all who believe in Him, "may be made perfect in one." [30] Indeed she embraces with truly maternal affection all who return to her as the only true Church of Christ. Hence any plans and enterprises, which with the consent of the ecclesiastical authority, have been undertaken and are being carried out to enlighten converts properly in the Faith or to impart a more thorough instruction to those already in the Church, can never be sufficiently approved or given too much encouragement.

At this time in many parts of the world, owing partly to various external events and changes of mental attitude, but, under the inspiring grace of God, due chiefly to the common prayers of the faithful, a desire has awakened and is growing daily in the hearts of many, who are separated from the Catholic Church, that a reunion be accomplished among all who believe in Christ the Lord. Assuredly to the children of the true Church this is a source of holy joy in the Lord as well as an inducement to lend their assistance to all, who are sincerely seeking the truth, by entreating light and strength for them from God in fervent prayer.

Certain attempts, that are being designated by diverse names in different countries, have hitherto been made by various persons, either individually or in groups, to effect a reconciliation of dissident christians with the Catholic Church. Such initiatives, however, do not always rest upon correct principles, although inspired by the best of intentions, and even when sprung from sound principles, they do not avoid besetting particular dangers, as past experience has shown. For this reason this Supreme Sacred Congrega-

[29] Weigel, *Catholic Primer on the Ecumenical Movement,* 29.
[30] John, XVII, 23. [*Catholic Instruction*]

tion, which has been charged with the care of defending and preserving intact the deposit of faith, has seen fit to call to mind and enjoin what is here set forth.

I.

The work of "reunion" belongs above all to the office and charge of the Church. Hence it behooves Bishops, whom "the Holy Ghost hath placed to rule the Church of God," [31] to bestow upon it their special attention. They should therefore not only carefully and efficaciously keep this movement under vigilant observation, but also prudently foster and guide it unto the twofold end of assisting those, who are in search of the truth and the true Church, and of shielding the faithful from the perils which readily follow in the tread of the movement.

Consequently they shall first of all thoroughly acquaint themselves with what has been accomplished and is actually being done under cover of this movement in their dioceses. For this purpose let them appoint suitable priests, who, in accordance with the teaching and the directions of the Holy See, as found, for example, in the Encyclical Letters *"Satis Cognitum"* [32] *"Mortalium Animos"* [33] and *"Mystici Corporis Christi,"* [34] shall give close attention to all that concerns the movement and make a report about it at the time and in the manner prescribed.

With special care shall they exercise their vigilance and urge the observance of the sacred canons "on previous censorship and prohibition of books" (can. 1384 ff) with regard to the publications, which are edited by Catholics in any form whatsoever concerning this matter. The same holds good with reference to non-Catholic publications on this subject, insofar as these are intended to be edited, read or sold by Catholics.

Likewise they will diligently provide what may be serviceable for non-Catholics who are seeking to know the Catholic faith. They will appoint persons and set up offices that non-Catholics may visit and consult, and yet more will they be intent upon making provision, that converts may have within easy reach the ways and means of obtaining a more basic and complete instruction in the Catholic faith and of carrying their religion into actual life, especially by means of seasonable meetings and study circles, spiritual retreats and other exercises of piety.

II.

As to the manner and method of procedure in this work, let the Bishops themselves prescribe what is to be done and what to be omitted, and take measures that the ordinances are observed by all. They will also be on their

[31] Acts, XX, 28. [*Catholic Instruction*]
[32] Acta Leonis XIII, vol. XVI, a. 1897, pag. 157 ff. [*Catholic Instruction*]
[33] Acta Ap. Sedis, vol. XX, a. 1928, page 5 ff. [*Catholic Instruction*]
[34] Acta Ap. Sedis, vol. XXXV, a. 1943, pag. 193 ff.[*Catholic Instruction*]

guard, lest, under some false pretence, for instance by stressing things on which we agree rather than those on which we disagree, a dangerous indifferentism be fomented, particularly amongst those who are less thoroughly grounded in matters theological and not so well trained in their religious practice. For they must beware, lest, from a spirit of "irenicism," as it is called nowadays, Catholic tenets, be they dogmas or questions connected therewith, in a process of comparative study and from a delusive design of attaining a certain progressive assimilation and approximation among the various professions of faith, are so whittled down and somehow made to conform to heterodox teaching as to jeopardize the purity of Catholic doctrine or obscure its clear and genuine meaning.

Furthermore Bishops will not allow recourse to a perilous mode of speaking which engenders false notions and raises deceitful hopes that can never be fulfilled. Such would be, for example, the allegation that what is taught in the Encyclical Letters of the Roman Pontiffs about the return of dissidents to the Church, or about the constitution of the Church, or about the Mystical Body of Christ, need not be so rigorously taken, inasmuch as not all things are of faith, or, what is worse still, in matters of dogma not even the Catholic Church is already in possession of the fullness of Christ and hence others are still in a position of contributing towards its perfection. They should scrupulously take precautions and firmly insist that, in rehearsing the history of the Reformation or the Reformers, the faults and foibles of Catholics are not overemphasized, whilst the blame and defects of the Reformers are dissimulated; nor that rather accidental circumstances be placed in such a light that the main fact, consisting in the defection from the Catholic Faith, is allowed to dwindle from sight and mind. Finally they will take care, lest, by an excessive and misleading extrinsic display and imprudence, or by clamorous methods of procedure and treatment, more harm than good may result in reaching the end desired.

The whole and entire body of Catholic doctrine is therefore to be proposed and explained. Nothing embraced in the Catholic truth concerning the true nature and means of justification, the constitution of the Church, the Roman Pontiff's primacy of jurisdiction and the only real union effectuated by a return of the dissidents to the one true Church of Christ, must be passed over in silence or cloaked under ambiguous language. Non-Catholics may certainly be told that, in returning to the Church, they will forfeit none of the good that the grace of God had hitherto wrought in their souls, but that the return will bring this to its perfection and final consummation. Yet this must not be represented in such a fashion as to create in them the impression that by their return they were making a contribution to the Church of something essential that she lacked in the past. All this must be truly set forth clearly and intelligibly for the double reason that they are really seeking the truth and that outside of the truth no true union can ever be attained.

III.

Ordinaries will need to employ altogether exceptional watchfulness and control as regards mixed conventions and meetings held between Catholics and non-Catholics, which in recent times have come into vogue in many places to foster "reunion" in the Faith. If in truth these offer a desirable occasion for spreading a knowledge of Catholic doctrine with which generally non-Catholics are not sufficiently conversant, on the other hand they also readily conjure up no slight danger of indifferentism to Catholics. Where some hopes of good results appear, the Ordinary will be solicitous to secure their proper direction by designating for them priests, who are best fitted for such gatherings and show ability to expound and defend Catholic doctrine in a suitable and competent manner. The faithful, however, shall not assist at such assemblies without a special permission from the ecclesiastical authority, which should be given only to those who are known to be well instructed and firmly established in the Faith. Where no prospects of good results are apparent, or if for some reason special perils are to be feared, the faithful shall be prudently kept away and the meetings themselves shall be suspended in due time or gradually brought to a close. Larger common assemblies may not be permitted except upon most careful scrutiny, since experience bears out the fact that such conversations are wont to be fraught with dangers and produce but little fruit.

For colloquies engaged in between Catholic and non-Catholic theologians, priests only may be sent and these must have proven themselves truly qualified to take part by their knowledge of theology and staunch adherence to the principles and norms laid down by the Church in this matter.

IV.

All such conferences and conventions, whether public or otherwise, small or large, are subject to the prescriptions of the Church, which were called to mind in the Monitum, *"Cum compertum,"* issued by this Sacred Congregation on June 5, 1948.[35] The supposition is that they were organized as a result of previous agreement to have the parties, both Catholics and non-Catholics alike, on a basis of perfect equality, treat matters of faith and morals and give an exposition of the teaching proper to their religious creed for the sake of discussion. Mixed gatherings are not then forbidden outright, but they are not to be held without the previous sanction of the competent ecclesiastical authority. Not subject to the Monitum just mentioned are catechetical instructions, even when imparted to several persons simultaneously; nor conferences in which the Catholic doctrine is explained to prospective converts. This holds good even if on such occasions the listeners also expound the teaching of their church for the purpose of ascertaining clearly and accurately in what it agrees and disagrees with Catholic truth.

[35] Acta Ap. Sedis, vol. XI, a. 1948, pag. 257. [*Catholic Instruction*]

Nor does the same Monitum refer to mixed assemblies of Catholics and non-Catholics, in which nothing touching faith and morals is under consideration, but discussions are held to take counsel as to the advisable ways and means of defending, by concerted action, the fundamental principles of the natural law and the Christian religion against the enemies leagued together against God; or of reestablishing the social order, or of dealing with and settling questions of a similar nature.

Even in these assemblies, as is evident, Catholics are not allowed to approve or concede anything that is not in accord with Divine revelation and with the Church's teaching, including her teaching on the social question.

Concerning local *conferences* and *conventions,* which, according to the directions specified in the foregoing, fall within the purview of the Monitum, local Ordinaries are empowered with faculties for a period of three years from the date of publication of this Instruction to grant the requisite previous authorization of the Holy See on condition that:

    1. all communication in sacred rites be utterly eschewed;

    2. the discussions and proceedings be duly supervised and directed;

    3. at the end of each year a report be made to this Supreme Sacred Congregation, specifying the place where such assemblies were held and what experiences were gathered from them.

As to *theological colloquies,* which were mentioned above, the same faculty for an equal period of time is extended to the Ordinary of the diocese, where the conversations are held, or to that Bishop whom the other Ordinaries have appointed by common consent to assume the direction. The conditions remain the same, as particularized above, plus the further provision that in the annual report to this Sacred Congregation mention be made what questions were treated, who were present and who were the participants and speakers on both sides.

For convoking interdiocesan, national and international conferences and conventions a previous consent, to be procured specially from the Holy See for each individual case, is necessary. The petition for the permission must set forth what questions and issues are to be discussed and who the speakers will be at the proceedings. Before this permit has been obtained no one is allowed to initiate preliminary external preparations for such conventions, nor to collaborate with non-Catholics who are engaged in designing similar plans.

V.

Every species of communication in sacred rites is forbidden at all conventions and assemblies of this kind, as has already been stated. Yet it is not discountenanced to open and close the meetings with a common recitation of the Lord's prayer or some other prayer approved by the Catholic Church.

VI.

Each individual Ordinary has the right and duty to study, favor and preside at this work in his diocese. Nevertheless, the cooperation of several Bishops may be timely and even necessary in setting up the offices and organs to observe, examine and guide the whole activity in this field. Consequently upon Ordinaries rests the responsibility, after having taken counsel mutually, to decide in what way suitable uniformity and well concerted action can be attained.

VII.

It is incumbent upon religious superiors to give heed and take measures that their subjects strictly and conscientiously abide by the regulations laid down upon this matter by the Holy See and local Ordinaries.

This excellent work of "reunion" of all Christians in the one true Faith and Church should daily become more integrated as a distinguished portion in the universal pastoral charge and be made an object of concern that the whole Catholic people take to heart and recommend to God in fervent supplications. Much progress will be made, if the faithful are appropriately enlightened, for example by means of Pastoral Letters, about these questions and issues as well as the measures taken with regard to them by the Church and the reasons prompting them. All indeed, but mainly priests and religious, must be admonished and encouraged to seek to fecundate and promote the work by their prayers and sacrifices. Finally all must be made conscious of the fact that, for those wandering outside the fold, there is no more efficacious means of preparing the way to embrace the truth and the Church than the Faith of the Catholics associated with a good moral conduct and an edifying life.

Given at the Palace of the Holy Office, in Rome, the 20th day of December, 1949.

FRANCIS CARD. MARCHETTI-SELVAGGIANI,
Secretary

ALFRED OTTAVIANI,
Assessor

> SOURCE: National Office, Chair of Unity Apostolate, *Unity Studies Number One. Instruction on the Ecumenical Movement, by the Sacred Congregation of the Holy Office* (Graymoor, Garrison, N.Y., n.d.). Used by permission of the Chair of Unity Apostolate.

183. The National Council of Churches

The merger of eight major interdenominational agencies to form the National Council of Churches of Christ in the United States of America on

November 29, 1950, was a major event in American church history. The delegates, representing a constituency of more than thirty million Christians, felt that it was fitting to address a message "To the People of the Nation," reprinted herewith. The Committee on Message was made up of one representative from each member-communion of the new National Council, twenty-nine in all. The chairman was Douglas Horton (1891—), then minister of the General Council of the Congregational Christian Churches and later Dean of Harvard Divinity School.

During the discussion of the Message by the General Assembly of the new Council, attention was directed to the phrase "Jesus Christ as divine Lord and Saviour," taken from the Preamble of the Constitution of the Council. It was wondered if the formula should be revised to read "Jesus Christ as God and Saviour." This would of course make it analogous to the "Basis" of the World Council of Churches. The matter was referred to the General Board of the Council.[36] After minor revisions, the Assembly then approved the statement, which strongly reflected the American Christian concern for freedom, the co-operative bent of modern Protestantism, and the spread of ecumenical thought among the religious leaders of the United States.

DOCUMENT

To the People of the Nation

The NATIONAL COUNCIL OF THE CHURCHES OF CHRIST IN THE UNITED STATES OF AMERICA

Sends Greetings:

This Council has been constituted by twenty-nine Churches for the glory of God and the well-being of humanity. It manifests our oneness in Jesus Christ as divine Lord and Saviour; his is the mandate we obey and his the power upon which we rely. It is designed to be an instrument of the Holy Spirit for such ministries of evangelism, education, and relief as are better achieved through Christian cooperation than by the labors of separated groups. It coordinates and continues the work of eight interdenominational agencies ministering in as many fields of Christian usefulness.

The Council is linked in spirit with the world-wide ecumenical organizations which provide for interdenominational cooperation at the international level. It is likewise similar in purpose to the federations of churches in state, county and city through which the several communions do their common work in our land. So it becomes the national unit of a system of unified Christian enterprise which circles the inhabited earth.

For the denominations which compose it the Council opens an avenue for mutual confidence, a widening way along which potential controversy among them may be wrought into concord, and unhappy competition into

[36] National Council of Churches, *Christian Faith in Action* (N.Y., 1951), 261. A constitutional change on this matter was not made.

emulation in pursuit of whatsoever things are true, honest, just, pure, lovely, and of good report.

The Council itself, however, is not a denomination, not a Church above the Churches. The autonomy of each communion is assured by constitutional provision. The Council is an agency of cooperation—not more but magnificently not less.

The Functions of the Council

In behalf of the denominations the Council continues and develops many services. It assists in the preparation of materials for the Church School, and through its scholars it is making ready for the world the Revised Standard Version of the Bible; it serves as a clearing house for full reports and statistics bearing upon church membership, denominational organizations and programs, and social trends of interest to Christians; it seeks to aid the Churches in undergirding and coordinating their home and foreign missions; it searches out and trains leadership for Christian undertakings; it lifts up its voice in behalf of the Christian way of life in messages to the people of the country; it provides a single inclusive agency through which, if they wish, the denominations may nominate and support chaplains and minister to the men and women of the armed forces of the United States; it offers a means of approach to agencies governmental and civil in matters of justice and goodwill; it devotes itself to the presentation of Christian ideals through radio, television and motion pictures; it is an organ of evangelism both specifically and broadly conceived, standing ready to serve the cause of Christ in every area as need arises, to the end that the entire country may be permeated by the blessings of His Gospel. Through these and other means it gives help to the churches, bringing the experience of all to the service of each.

The Spirit of the Council

The Council has nothing to fear from the times, though it has much to desire of them. Being the servant of One who holds in His hand all the nations, and the isles, as a very little thing, it is free from the apprehensions of those who, taking counsel of men alone forget that no age is isolated from God's ageless purpose. We call our fellow citizens to Christian faith: this will defend them from groundless social dreads and lift them to concerns worthy and productive.

The Council stands as a guardian of democratic freedom. The revolutionary truth that men are created free follows from the revelation of God in Jesus Christ, and no person who knows that God as Father has given him all the rights of sonship is likely to remain content under a government which deprives him of basic human rights and fundamental freedoms. The nation may expect in the National Council a sturdy ally of the forces of liberty.

The Council stands for liberty with the richest content. It stands for the freedom of men to be as the Lord God meant them to be. It stands for Christian freedom—including the freedom to pursue happiness and with justice and sympathy to create conditions of happiness for others. It therefore stands against the misuse of freedom. The nation may expect from the National Council, in the name of One who suffered death upon a cross, an unrelenting, open-eyed hostility, as studious as it is deeply passionate, to all of man's inhumanity to man.

The Council opposes materialism as an end in itself. It is the foe of every political system that is nourished on materialism, and of every way of living that follows from it. From that smug idealism which is a form of selfishness, the Council prays to be protected; but danger on this hand does not lessen the necessity it feels to fight a constant fight against all kinds of secular materialism which demolish the slowly built edifice of Christian morality and fair dealing.

Through the Council the churches, as they are dedicated to the doing of God's will, must increasingly become a source of spiritual power to the nation. The American Churches, of which the Council is one of the visible symbols, are in their true estate the soul of the nation. When those Churches take their true course, they draw their standards not from the world around but from the guiding mind of Christ. The Church is not the religious phase of the civilization in which it finds itself; it is the living center out of which lasting civilizations take life and form. In this sense the Council will be an organ through which the will of God may become effective as an animating, creative and unifying force within our national society.

The Council gives thanks to God for all those forces which make for harmony in our society. When, for example, science employs its ingenuity to knit the world together in bonds of communication, when business and industry make a like contribution through the life-bringing mutuality of commerce, when the arts depict the beauty and the tragedy of our existence which draw us into unity with one another, when the many professions and occupations recognize themselves as callings to human usefulness, then the Council salutes and supports them. By word and deed and in the name of Christ who gave his life for all mankind it affirms the brotherhood of men and seeks by every rightful means to arrest those forces of division which rend the nation along racial lines and stay its growth toward unity.

The Present Crisis

Because this message is sent at a moment when clouds arising from the war in Korea threaten to darken the entire sky, the time is big with peril and with opportunity.

To the leaders we have set in authority in our government is committed the solemn and momentous task of making necessary choices in the political and military spheres.

We who are the people of the country, however, have a part to play as well. The call of Christ to us all seems clear, that we play it with calmness, self-control, courage, and high purpose, as becomes those whose lives are in the hands of God. Without hysteria, without hatred, without pride, without undue impatience, without making national interest our chief end, but shaping our own policies in the light of the aims of the United Nations, without relaxing our positive services to the other peoples of the world, and in complete repudiation of the lying dogma that war is inevitable, let us live and, if need be, die as loyal members of the world community to which Christ summons us and to which we of the Council are dedicated.

The Larger Significance of the Council

We of the National Council of the Churches of Christ in the U.S.A. begin our work in humility as we see the magnitude of the task ahead. We are not unconscious of our own shortcomings. Knowing that men too often dream in marble and then build with straw, we whose very human lives are not separate from sin and ignorance can make no boast of past or future excellence.

But this we have done: by God's grace we have forged an implement for cooperation such as America has never seen before. Into it have been poured the thoughts of wise and noble men and women, the prayers and consecration of the faithful, and the longing of all the participating Churches to serve the spiritual needs of all the people. The Council is our Churches in their highest common effort for mankind.

Our hope is in Jesus Christ. In Him we see the solution of the world's ills, for as human hearts are drawn near to him, they are drawn near in sympathy and understanding to each other. The Council itself is a demonstration of his power to unite his followers in joyous cooperation. Let nation and nation, race and race, class and class unite their aims in his broad purposes for man, and out of that unitedness there will arise new strength like that of which we ourselves already feel the first sure intimations.

In this hope we commend you, our fellow citizens, to God's mercy, grace and peace.

> SOURCE: *Christian Faith in Action: Commemorative Volume, The Founding of the National Council of the Churches of Christ in the United States of America* (N.Y., 1951), 150–3. Used by permission of National Council of Churches.

184. Union Across Denominational Lines

The formation of the United Church of Christ brought together churches from four denominational traditions. The Congregational Christian Churches resulted from a union in 1931 of the Congregational Churches with a smaller group of Christian Churches. The latter were one of the denominational outcomes of the movement for a simple, evangelical Christianity in the late eighteenth and early nineteenth centuries which also led to the emergence of the Disciples of Christ.[37]

Three years later another merger brought two other denominational heritages together. The Reformed Church in the United States was of German and Swiss Calvinist background; it was organized as a fully independent church in 1792. The Evangelical Synod of North America can be traced back organizationally to 1840, when in the West groups of pietistic German-speaking immigrants of Lutheran and Reformed backgrounds began to associate together. The two churches commenced merger talks in 1922, and completed the union as the Evangelical and Reformed Church in 1934.

In 1942, representatives of these two "enlarged" denominations began to discuss a still larger union. The Basis of Union went through many revisions; certain Interpretations were added. By 1949 the Basis of Union had been given approval by both denominations, but a small minority of Congregationalists firmly opposed the union. Court action blocked the union for some years, but in June, 1957, the United Church of Christ came into formal existence. Some Congregational churches vigorously resisted the union, and the practical implementation of the formal action was slow. In 1961 the union was finally consummated. Only a very few congregations refused to enter the union.

The Basis of Union gives considerable insight into the complicated matters that arise in such church union movements. This one has special interest, because two polities—congregational and presbyterian—were involved. The first three articles of the eleven-article Basis are reproduced here, with footnotes omitted since they were explanatory only and were not a part of the Basis of Union.

DOCUMENT

Preamble

We, the regularly constituted representatives of the Congregational Christian Churches and of the Evangelical and Reformed Church, moved by the conviction that we are united in spirit and purpose and are in agreement on the substance of the Christian faith and the essential character of the Christian life;

Affirming our devotion to one God, the Father of our Lord Jesus Christ, and our membership in the holy catholic Church, which is greater than any single Church and than all the Churches together;

Believing that denominations exist not for themselves but as parts of that Church, within which each denomination is to live and labor and, if need be, die; and

[37] See *American Christianity*, I, 563, 578–86.

Confronting the divisions and hostilities of our world, and hearing with a deepened sense of responsibility the prayer of our Lord "that they all may be one";

Do now declare ourselves to be one body, and do set forth the following articles of agreement as the basis of our life, fellowship, witness, and proclamation of the Gospel to all nations.

I. Name

The name of the Church formed by this union shall be UNITED CHURCH OF CHRIST.

This name expresses a fact: it stands for the accomplished union of two church bodies each of which has arisen from a similar union of two church bodies. It also expresses a hope: that in time soon to come, by further union between this Church and other bodies, there shall arise a more inclusive United Church.

II. Faith

The faith which unites us and to which we bear witness is that faith in God which the Scriptures of the Old and New Testaments set forth, which the ancient Church expressed in the ecumenical creeds, to which our own spiritual fathers gave utterance in the evangelical confessions of the Reformation, and which we are in duty bound to express in the words of our time as God Himself gives us light. In all our expressions of that faith we seek to preserve unity of heart and spirit with those who have gone before us as well as those who now labor with us.

In token of that faith we unite in the following confession, as embodying those things most surely believed and taught among us:

We believe in God the Father Almighty, Creator and Sustainer of heaven and earth and in Jesus Christ, His Son, our Lord and Saviour, who for us and our salvation lived and died and rose again and lives for evermore; and in the Holy Spirit, who takes of the things of Christ and shows them to us, renewing, comforting, and inspiring the souls of men.

We acknowledge one holy catholic Church, the innumerable company of those who, in every age and nation, are united by the Holy Spirit to God in Christ, are one body in Christ, and have communion with Him and with one another.

We acknowledge as part of this universal fellowship all throughout the world who profess this faith in Jesus Christ and follow Him as Lord and Saviour.

We hold the Church to be established for calling men to repentance and faith, for the public worship of God, for the confession of His name by word and deed, for the administration of the sacraments, for witnessing to the saving grace of God in Christ, for the upbuilding of the saints, and for the universal propagation of the Gospel; and in the power of the love of God in Christ we labor for the progress of knowledge, the promotion of justice, the reign of peace, and the realization of human brotherhood.

Depending, as did our fathers, upon the continued guidance of the Holy Spirit to lead us into all truth, we work and pray for the consummation of the Kingdom of God; and we look with faith for the triumph of righteousness and for the life everlasting.

III. Practice

A. The basic unit of organization of the United Church of Christ is the Congregation; that is, the local church.

B. The Congregations, through their ministers and through delegates elected from their membership, may organize Associations for fellowship, mutual encouragement, inspiration, and such other functions as may be desired.

C. The Congregations, through their ministers and through delegates elected from their membership, constitute Conferences for fellowship, counsel, and cooperation in all matters of common concern. The Conferences exist to make cooperation effective (a) among their Congregations and (b) between their Congregations and the General Synod, the Boards, commissions, agencies, and instrumentalities of the Church.

D. The Conferences, through delegates elected by them from the membership and ministers of the Congregations located within their respective bounds, constitute the General Synod.

E. Officers, Boards, councils, commissions, committees, departments, agencies, and instrumentalities are responsible to the bodies that elect them.

F. The government of the United Church is exercised through Congregations, Associations, Conferences, and the General Synod in such wise that the autonomy of each is respected in its own sphere, each having its own rights and responsibilities. This Basis of Union defines those rights and responsibilities in principle and the constitution which will be drafted after the consummation of the union shall further define them but shall in no wise abridge the rights now enjoyed by Congregations.

G. Individual communicants have the right of appeal, complaint, or reference to their Congregations, Associations, Conferences, and ultimately to the General Synod. Ministers, Congregations, Associations, and Conferences have similar rights of appeal, complaint, or reference. Decisions rendered in consequence of such appeals, complaints, or references, are advisory, not mandatory.

H. Each Congregation, Association, and Conference has the right of retaining or adopting its own charter, constitution, by-laws, and other regulations which it deems essential and proper to its own welfare. This right includes the holding and operation of its own property.

I. The freedom of worship and of education at present enjoyed by the Congregations of the negotiating communions will be preserved in the

United Church. Other freedoms at present enjoyed are not hereby abridged.

J. Men and women enjoy the same rights and privileges in the United Church. It is recommended that at least one third of the members of the national administrative bodies be women.

K. Baptism and the Lord's Supper are the recognized sacraments of the Church.

> SOURCE: *The Basis of Union of the Congregational Christian Churches and The Evangelical and Reformed Church with the Interpretations* (n.p., n.d.). Used by permission of United Church of Christ.

185. Unity in Christ

During much of American history, the Lutheran churches were largely isolated by ethnic, language, and confessional barriers from the rest of Protestantism. In the twentieth century, a significant reversal began. As the nationality differences receded, Lutherans were freer to respond to the testimony to unity in their own confessional statements. As they became fully at home on the American scene, Lutherans found that they had much to learn from other churches, as well as much to contribute to them, and they began to play larger roles in councils of churches.

Franklin Clark Fry (1900—) illustrated these tendencies to unity and ecumenicity in this period. Born in Bethlehem, Pa., educated at Hamilton College and the Philadelphia Lutheran Seminary, Fry was elected President of the United Lutheran Church in America in 1944. He has occupied responsible positions in the National Council of Churches, the Lutheran World Federation, and the World Council of Churches; he was elected Chairman of the Central and Executive Committees of the latter in 1954.

At the 1956 biennial convention of the ULCA, Fry focused his presidential report on the theme of Christian unity. Slightly revised, it was published in *The Lutheran World,* the organ of the Lutheran World Federation. The sections of the statement dealing with the principles underlying the unity of the church are reproduced here; other parts of the document dealt with wrong reasons for church union, with equally mistaken objections to church union, and with the implications of all this for Lutherans.

DOCUMENT

No one will dispute that church cooperation and unity are in the air. That is plainly to be seen wherever we turn our eyes, on every level of action and thought. Our own church, the United Lutheran Church in America (ULCA), belongs to the World Council of Churches, the National Council of the Churches of Christ in the United States of America, the Lutheran World Federation, the National Lutheran Council and the Canadian Lutheran Council and is in friendly association with the Canadian Council of Churches. That is impressive in itself and reveals the temper of the times. The growth of Christian partnership is in many ways the most conspicuous development in church life today, and we have our share in it. On a deeper plane, a truly historic event has occurred within the past biennium. The Augustana Church has joined our ULCA in inviting all the Lutherans of America to enter into organic union as an act of loyalty to the Christ whom we confess with one voice.[38]

In the mind-life of the church this accent is equally clear and all-pervasive. The Minneapolis Assembly of the Lutheran World Federation in 1957 will center around "Christ Frees and Unites," with its chief stress, we hope and expect, on the latter verb. One week later the evangelical churches of nearly all confessions in North America are to grapple with "The Nature of the Unity We Seek" at the first Faith and Order conference on this continent. This meeting will be a radical innovation on our side of the Atlantic, where doctrinal studies have been slighted in the past in interchurch activities, and so highly welcome to Lutherans.

All of these stirrings focus on Christian unity. Sound principles need to be laid down and reverently thought through. That is the aspiration that inspires these lines. I hope and pray that it will not prove to be presumptuous.

In candor I must confess at the outset that the analysis that follows makes no pretense to a high degree of originality. No startling new depths will be plumbed. I have gleaned in many fields. The best I can say for this document is that it reflects a conscientious effort to weigh and absorb into my own thinking the truths I have found. In addition to ingestion, there has been prolonged digestion, as you will see from numerous applications of the root ideas to the current situation. The ultimate norm, after all and over all, is the Holy Scriptures! The standard according to which every judgment must stand or fail is, Does it rightly interpret the Word of God? And what I have to say here must also ultimately be measured by this norm.

Five Basic Presuppositions

Unity is a gift from God. We do not create or achieve it. Here is the most fundamental fact of all, a truth which we need to understand clearly with our minds and hold firmly and obediently in our hearts. Like all the undergirding axioms of the Bible and of life itself, it is very simple. It is so simple that Christians often fall into irretrievable error by overlooking it; by not realizing that unity is as directly his gift as life, strength, love, joy, hope, yes even forgiveness. God is its source. Unity is a reflection of his nature. Whatever else the often used and sometimes abused text from John 17 means, it teaches that! When our Saviour prayed, "That they also may be

---

[38] The American Evangelical Lutheran Church, of Danish background, and the Finnish Evangelical Lutheran Church (Suomi Synod) agreed to enter the negotiations with the ULCA and the Augustana Church. The constitution for the merged body, The Lutheran Church in America, was prepared and approved by the four bodies to go into effect in 1962.

one; as thou, Father, art in me, and I in thee, that they also may be one in us," he spoke not only of the standard of unity, nor of its goal, but equally of its origin.

Since God gives it, unity exists. It is not full and perfect in today's world; that is obvious. God himself would be the first to disclaim any such thing. Indeed, the present unity of Christ's church is pitifully fragmentary, both inwardly and outwardly. But one thing we cannot say—that the impediment is in God. He does not willfully withhold this blessing or any other. We can be sure, because we know him, that God stands ready to give more and more.

Man's role, we have said, is not to manufacture or devise or scheme out unity. Our peril is that we may not discern God's gift; our pride, and even our busy-ness, can stand in the way. A still more sobering and warning thought is that even after we have had a glimpse of the unity he offers, we may not accept it. It is the same with faith and pardon. To our sorrow, we know that human nature can reject and turn away from both. Unity is no exception. Our calling is to manifest all the unity that he has given.

Unity is in Christ and, reciprocally, through Christ being in us. St. Paul's haunting phrase "in Christ" is as practical as it is mystical. In it the secret of the unity of the church is unfolded a vital step further. All true oneness among Christians not only goes back to him; it flows from him. It is because we have one Lord that we also have one faith and one baptism. Every syllable in his classic declaration, "I will build my church," is heavy with meaning, but the first person singular looms high over all. The living, the being, and the unity of the church are all in the "I."

One of the favorite dictums of Martin Luther was, "The Word constitutes the church." That is only another way of saying that Christ is its unitive principle. He is the one who is in the Word, and is its perfect embodiment. He makes the Lord's Supper a sacrament by being really present in it. As he sends life coursing out from himself to all the members of his body, he binds them together. Well St. Paul exclaims, "The bread which we break, is it not the communion of the body of Christ? For as it is one bread, so we being many, are one body, for we are all partakers of that one bread." To be in Christ is to be caught up by him into the new redeemed humanity, of which he is the head. It is to be with many brethren in the community of his resurrection.

Conversely, when Christ comes into each one's individual heart, he also draws his own to one another. He is the great reconciler; how often our estrangements offend and go counter to him! The wonder is that all of us have not driven him away with our harsh judgments and antagonisms. If he remains, the uniting Christ will inevitably show himself in our affections and attitudes. He will ignite in us his zeal for the unity of his people.

What is true of Christians as single persons, is also true of Christ's church. His desires and his power are the same for both. The only business churches have to associate with one another is "to manifest oneness in Jesus Christ as divine Lord and Savior." When they can do so without equivocation, they have no right to refuse. When they are deeply one in faith and confession, "What God hath joined together, let not man put asunder."

Leading into Unity, as well as into Truth, is the work of the Holy Spirit. We Lutherans have tended to emphasize truth; sometimes we place such exclusive stress upon it that the other pole of the Spirit's magnetism has been obscured. Insistence upon agreement in doctrine as a pre-condition for church fellowship is the distinguishing mark of Lutherans among all Protestants, and should never be relaxed. Allegiance to Christ as the Truth rules out indifference, or even a casual attitude, to the truths about him that have been revealed. Here we stand and we shall not renounce our conviction.

At the same time, we Lutherans need to remember two things. One is that this virtue can be carried to excess. A danger lies at our doorstep; it is the danger of intellectual pride. A man, even an earnest Christian, can get to the point of loving theological refinements just for their own sake, of allowing the thing (faith) that ought to unite to become unnecessarily divisive. At the worst, as a specially accusing irony for Lutherans, our very doctrinal rectitude of which we are so proud can be twisted into good works.

Furthermore, never forget that the Spirit still leads on. We do wrong to the dynamic Holy Ghost to try [to] make him static. His leading into truth is not exhausted; we must continue to be wide open in mind and spirit to it. Granted that the Scriptures are a sufficient and unalterable revelation, the possibility of our being guided into a deeper and truer understanding of what they teach is not at an end. With humility and with gratitude, we have experienced such growth in our generation, not the least in the new weight with which the cause of the unity of the church has been laid on our souls.

The Spirit, with equal dynamism, leads to the church. It is no coincidence that at the very hour when he descended, the church began; a Christian community was born, which because it was a community had unity as one of its inherent features. It is more than an accident of language that the word "church" appears in the New Testament in only two meanings, denoting the local congregation and a single universal church of God. The many, separated "churches" of today do not fit in the New Testament vocabulary, not only because they did not come into existence until a later period of history; the very idea of them would have been a jar to the apostles and evangelists who wrote as they were inspired by the Holy Ghost. "Is Christ divided?" was an absurdity to the mind of St. Paul. The dividedness of the church does violence to the Holy Ghost who lives in it.

This does not mean that the Spirit never consents to divisions. We believe and testify that he, and not Luther or Melanchthon or any of their colleagues, was the moving force in the Protestant Reformation, the widest and deepest split of all. What it does mean is that the Holy Ghost, from all we know about him, does not bless divisiveness in itself. He is not content with its results nor does he exonerate us for sitting down and complacently accepting them. In his eyes, we can be certain, division is an evil to be tolerated only until a greater evil has been overcome. The burden of proof is on those who would perpetuate it. They have to show continuously that loyalty to the Word, which is Christ, compels them to remain separate from their fellow-believers.

He who affirms unity must also desire union. Is not all of this stated too strongly? some will ask. Isn't unity an affair, an attribute, of the "invisible" church, and shouldn't you speak only of that? The reply is, No. Bishop Anders Nygren refers in the book *This is the Church* to the negative consequences to Christ himself of such a contention. If we limit Christ to being the head of the "invisible" church, we come dangerously close to separating him from human life as it is actually lived on earth. The inmost nature of our Lord was fulfilled by his entering into our tangible world, by his becoming flesh and dwelling among us so that men beheld his glory. Just so, he is the Lord of the church that we see as well as of the mystical church that is beyond our sight. He is in the Word that we hear from our earthly pulpits and in the sacraments that we receive at fonts and altars of wood and stone.

So, too, the church that the Holy Spirit formed on Pentecost was "visible." Living men were pricked in their hearts by the Gospel and exclaimed, "What shall we do?" They were baptized by other human beings, the apostles, and a church that was in plain view of the people of Jerusalem, and could even be measured by statistics, came into being. The Spirit, who lives among us and in us here on earth, is in the church that we know.

All of this has an important word to say about the contrast between "unity" and "union" that is often drawn nowadays, particularly among Lutherans. You might think that there is an antithesis, almost an antagonism, between those two terms. "Unity" is a mark of the "invisible" church and is from God; "union" has to do with the church in this world and can be negotiated and, if desired, postponed by men. To sharpen the opposition between these two ideas even more, some go so far as to fall into the error of belittling the "visible" church and end up by thinking that it is exclusively their own affair to do with as they choose. That is a pitfall from which a proper reverence for the Spirit and a right understanding of the church should enable all of us to stay clear. Union for the sake of expediency is evil, because the church is the Lord's. For the same reason, unity without union cannot be condoned.

Since the Holy Spirit is omnipotent God, no one can set limits on what he can do. It is wrong to say dogmatically, This far we can go and never any further. Shouldering off the issue of unity on future years, and then shaking our shoulders in relief because we have transferred the burden, will not do. We, in our own generation, must beware of quenching the Spirit.

Thanks to him, praise God, a church like ours that yearns for unity is never justified in having a defeatist attitude. God the Holy Ghost is able to bring his will to pass, leading into a vista whose end we cannot see. . . .

Unity, as a concept, is glorious. There is a reflection of God in it and a vital principle for his church. A matching, equally important, value in it that we must not overlook is in what it does. Unity is not an ethereal, platonic idea that floats high in the air; it has a practical mission in this world. God never gives any of his blessings simply for our own enjoyment, merely for us to keep to ourselves. Health is not for idleness but for productive work. Forgiveness is not to enable us to relax in a glowing feeling that we are the sons of God but to send us out to be little Christs to our neighbors. The peace in our hearts is to radiate out to all mankind. When nations containing many Christians with God's peace in them are not peaceful, unbelievers do not know what to make of it. They keenly sense the inconsistency and point the finger of shame. To be grateful and obedient, Christians must act on their gifts.

Just so it is with unity. Dr. T. N. Hasselquist, the first president of the Augustana Synod, saw this almost ninety years ago when he wrote, "The Church of God, according to the Word of God, should be united in one communion *in order that* its unity might contribute to the strength of its influence both within itself and in its external witness." Another unimpeachable Lutheran voice, that of Professor Edmund Schlink of Heidelberg University, goes a step further in our own times: "If we do not manifest the unity which has been given to us, this act of God's grace will become an accusation."

Far more authoritative than either of them is the clear testimony of the Bible itself. "Ye are a royal priesthood," St. Peter exclaimed in his first Epistle, and then went on to say why: "that ye should show forth the praises of him who hath called you out of darkness into his marvelous light." Even God's old Chosen People, unlike the other nations of antiquity, did not think of him as only a tribal deity, but recognized that the promised Messiah was to rule over all of humanity. All peoples would catch hold of their cloaks in order to ascend into the mountain of the Lord. Above the whole orchestra of the Holy Scriptures sounds Christ's own high priestly prayer: "That they all may be one . . . *that the world may believe.*"

The unnecessary divisions of the Christian church are a *scandalon* in non-Christian lands. They are a handicap for the Holy Spirit as he sends out the rays of the Gospel and a sinful deterrent to the Good Shepherd gathering new sheep. Unnecessary divisions confuse and deter many who are otherwise ready to become believers. Worst of all, they are a misleading, and even false, witness to the one Lord.

We are grateful that the Lutheran family within the Christian church is rapidly uprooting this cause of offense in Asia and Africa, where united churches of our confession are springing up almost everywhere. With all our hearts we wish it could be so in North America too! Every vestige of competition, with its wastage of men and means, accuses us. Every hesitation to act on the deep unity of faith that God has given us shows unthankfulness to the Giver. Every stride in comity, of which the activities of the Regional Home Mission Committees of the National Lutheran Council are an encouraging example, has powerfully aided in spreading the Good News and, as a corollary, in the growth of our still separate churches. Who can justify being content with half-measures? A divine imperative, like the command at the Red Sea, calls on us to go forward, under his leadership, as one people of God.

Unity is not an end in itself. Through it, at its best, God gives new life to Christians, a new glow to the Gospel, a new flowering to the church, and a new and clearer witness to his Son.

> SOURCE: Franklin Clark Fry, "The Unity of the Church," *Lutheran World,* III (1956–57), 322–8. Used by permission of the author.

186. Eastern Orthodoxy and Ecumenicity

Though most of the major Eastern Orthodox communions in America belong officially to local, national, and world councils of churches, their differences in ecclesiology and liturgy from the Protestant majorities in those councils serve to push them into the role of a self-conscious minority at ecumenical gatherings. At the Faith and Order Conference at Edinburgh in 1937, for example, the Orthodox delegates presented a statement indicating their own particular viewpoint on some of the issues under consideration.[39] On the American scene, Orthodox Christians often felt even more keenly their differences with their Protestant brothers in conciliar activity. Even as they engaged in co-operative efforts, they have wished to make their own distinctive positions clear.

At the North American Faith and Order Conference at Oberlin, 1957, the ten representatives of the four Eastern churches formally participating in the conference prepared a statement setting forth their understanding of the Orthodox role in theological discussion. Entitled "Christian Unity as Viewed by the Eastern Orthodox Church," the text, reprinted here in full, was read to the conference in plenary session by Archbishop Athenagoras of the Greek Archdiocese of North and South America.

DOCUMENT

We are glad to take part in a study conference devoted to such a basic need of the Christian world as unity. All Christians should seek unity. On the other hand, we feel that the whole program of the forthcoming discussion has been framed from a point of view which we cannot conscien-

[39] Leonard Hodgson, ed., *The Second World Conference on Faith and Order,* 116.

tiously admit. "The unity we seek" is for us a *given* unity which has never been lost, and, as a Divine gift and an essential mark of Christian existence, could not have been lost. This unity in the Church of Christ is for us a unity in the historical Church, in the fulness of faith, in the fulness of continuous sacramental life. For us, this unity is embodied in the Orthodox Church, which kept, *catholikos* and *anelleipos,* both the integrity of the apostolic faith and the integrity of the apostolic order.

Our share in the study of Christian unity is determined by our firm conviction that this unity can be found only in the fellowship of the historical Church, preserving faithfully the catholic tradition, both in doctrine and in order. We cannot commit ourselves to any discussion of these basic assumptions, as if they were but hypothetical or problematic. We begin with a clear conception of the Church's unity, which we believe has been embodied and realized in the age-long history of the Orthodox Church, without any change or break since the times when the visible unity of Christendom was an obvious fact and was attested and witnessed to by an ecumenical unanimity, in the age of the Ecumenical Councils.

We admit, of course, that the unity of Christendom has been disrupted, that the unity of faith and the integrity of order have been sorely broken. But we do not admit that the unity of the Church, and precisely of the "visible" and historical Church, has ever been broken or lost, so as to now be a problem of search and discovery. The problem of unity is for us, therefore, the problem of the return to the fulness of faith and order, in full faithfulness to the message of Scripture and Tradition and in the obedience to the will of God: *"that all may be one."*

Long before the breakup of the unity of Western Christendom, the Orthodox Church has had a keen sense of the essential importance of the oneness of Christian believers and from her very inception she has deplored divisions within the Christian world. As in the past, so in the present, she laments disunity among those who claim to be followers of Jesus Christ whose purpose in the world was to unite all believers into one Body. The Orthodox Church feels that, since she has been unassociated with the events related to the breakdown of religious unity in the West, she bears a special responsibility to contribute toward the restoration of the Christian unity which alone can render the message of the Gospel effective in a world troubled by threats of world conflict and general uncertainty over the future.

It is with humility that we voice the conviction that the Orthodox Church can make a special contribution to the cause of Christian unity, because since Pentecost she has possessed the true unity intended by Christ. It is with this conviction that the Orthodox Church is always prepared to meet with Christians of other communions in interconfessional deliberations. She rejoices over the fact that she is able to join those of other denominations in ecumenical conversations that aim at removing the barriers to Christian unity. However, we feel compelled in all honesty, as representatives of the

Orthodox Church, to confess that we must qualify our participation, as necessitated by the historic faith and practice of our Church, and also state the general position that must be taken at this interdenominational conference.

In considering firstly "the nature of the unity we seek," we wish to begin by making clear that our approach is at variance with that usually advocated and ordinarily expected by participating representatives. The Orthodox Church teaches that the unity of the Church has not been lost, because she is the Body of Christ, and, as such, can never be divided. It is Christ as her head and the indwelling of the Holy Spirit that secure the unity of the Church throughout the ages.

The presence of human imperfection among her members is powerless to obliterate the unity, for Christ himself promised that the "gates of hell shall not prevail against the Church." Satan has always sown tares in the field of the Lord and the forces of disunity have often threatened but have never actually succeeded in dividing the Church. No power can be mightier than the omnipotent will of Christ who founded one Church only in order to bring men into unity with God. Oneness is an essential mark of the Church.

If it be true that Christ founded the Church as a means of unifying men divided by sin, then it must naturally follow that the unity of the Church was preserved by his divine omnipotence. Unity, therefore, is not just a promise, or a potentiality, but belongs to the very nature of the Church. It is not something which has been lost and which should be recovered, but rather it is a permanent character of the structure of the Church.

Christian love impels us to speak candidly of our conviction that the Orthodox Church has not lost the unity of the Church intended by Christ, for she represents the oneness which in Western Christendom has only been a potentiality. The Orthodox Church teaches that she has no need to search for a "lost unity," because her historic consciousness dictates that she is the *Una Sancta* and that all Christian groups outside the Orthodox Church can recover their unity only by entering into the bosom of that Church which preserved its identity with early Christianity.

These are claims that arise not from presumptuousness, but from an inner historical awareness of the Orthodox Church. Indeed, this is the special message of Eastern Orthodoxy to a divided Western Christendom.

The Orthodox Church, true to her historical consciousness, declares that she has maintained an unbroken continuity with the church of Pentecost by preserving the apostolic faith and polity unadulterated. She has kept the "faith once delivered unto the saints" free from the distortions of human innovations. Man-made doctrines have never found their way into the Orthodox Church, since she has no necessary association in history with the name of one single father or theologian. She owes the fulness and the guarantee of unity and infallibility to the operation of the Holy Spirit and not to the service of one individual. It is for this reason that she has never felt the need for what is known as "a return to the purity of the apostolic faith." She maintains the necessary balance between freedom and authority and thus avoids the extremes of absolutism and individualism both of which have done violence to Christian unity.

We reassert that which was declared at Evanston and which has been made known in the past at all interdenominational conferences attended by delegates of the Orthodox Church. It is not due to our personal merit, but to divine condescension that we represent the Orthodox Church and are able to give expression to her claims. We are bound in conscience to state explicitly what is logically inferred; that all other bodies have been directly or indirectly separated from the Orthodox Church. Unity from the Orthodox standpoint means a return of the separated bodies to the historical Orthodox, One Holy Catholic and Apostolic Church.

The unity which Orthodoxy represents rests on identity of faith, order, and worship. All three aspects of the life of the Church are outwardly safeguarded by the reality of the unbroken succession of bishops which is the assurance of the Church's uninterrupted continuity with apostolic origins. This means that the uncompromised fulness of the Church requires the preservation of both its episcopal structure and sacramental life. Adhering tenaciously to her apostolic heritage, the Orthodox Church holds that no true unity is possible where episcopacy and sacraments are absent, and grieves over the fact that both institutions have either been discarded or distorted in certain quarters of Christendom. Any agreement on faith must rest on the authority of the enactments of the seven Ecumenical Councils which represent the mind of the one undivided Church of antiquity and the subsequent tradition as safeguarded in the life of the Orthodox Church.

We regret that the most vital problem of ministry and that of the apostolic succession, without which to our mind there is neither unity, nor Church, were not included in the program of the conference. All problems of order seem to be missing in the program. These, in our opinion, are basic for any study of unity.

Visible unity expressed in organizational union does not destroy the centrality of the Spirit among believers, but rather testifies to the reality of the oneness of the Spirit. Where there is the fulness of the Spirit, there too will outward unity be found. From apostolic times the unity of Christian believers was manifested by a visible, organizational structure. It is the unity in the Holy Spirit that is expressed in a unified visible organization.

The Holy Eucharist, as the chief act of worship, is the outward affirmation of the inner relation rising from unity in the Holy Spirit. But this unity involves a consensus of faith among those participating. Intercommunion, therefore, is possible only when there is agreement of faith. Common worship in every case must presuppose a common faith. The Orthodox Church maintains that worship of any nature cannot be sincere unless there is oneness of faith among those participating. It is with this belief that the Orthodox hesitate to share in joint prayer services and strictly refrain from attending interdenominational Communion services.

A common faith and a common worship are inseparable in the historical continuity of the Orthodox Church. However, in isolation neither can be preserved integral and intact. Both must be kept in organic and inner relationship with each other. It is for this reason that Christian unity cannot be realized merely by determining what articles of faith or what creed should be regarded as constituting the basis of unity. In addition to subscribing to certain doctrines of faith, it is necessary to achieve the experience of a common tradition or *communis sensus fidelium* preserved through common worship within the historic framework of the Orthodox Church. There can be no true unanimity of faith unless that faith remains within the life and sacred tradition of the Church which is identical throughout the ages. It is in the experience of worship that we affirm the true faith, and conversely, it is in the recognition of a common faith that we secure the reality of worship in spirit and in truth.

Thus the Orthodox Church in each locality insists on agreement of faith and worship before it will consider sharing in any interdenominational activity. Doctrinal differences constitute an obstacle in the way of unrestricted participation in such activities. In order to safeguard the purity of the faith and the integrity of the liturgical and spiritual life of the Orthodox Church, abstinence from interdenominational activities is encouraged on a local level. There is no phase of the Church's life unrelated to her faith. Intercommunion with another church must be grounded on a consensus of faith and a common understanding of the sacramental life. The Holy Eucharist especially must be the liturgical demonstration of the unity of faith.

We are fully aware of deep divergences which separate Christian denominations from each other, in all fields of Christian life and existence, in the understanding of faith, in the shaping of life, in the habits of worship. We are seeking, accordingly, a unanimity in faith, an identity of order, a fellowship in prayer. But for us all the three are organically linked together. Communion in worship is only possible in the unity of faith. Communion presupposes unity. Therefore, the term "intercommunion" seems to us an epitome of that conception which we are compelled to reject. An "intercommunion" presupposes the existence of several separate and separated denominations, which join occasionally in certain common acts or actions. In the true unity of Christ's Church there is no room for several "denominations." There is, therefore, no room for "intercommunion." When all are truly united in the apostolic faith and order, there will be all-inclusive communion and fellowship in all things.

It has been stated by the Orthodox delegates already in Edinburgh, in 1937, that many problems are presented at Faith and Order conferences in a manner and in a setting which are utterly uncongenial to the Orthodox. We again must repeat the same statement now. But again, as years ago at

Edinburgh, we want to testify our readiness and willingness to participate in study, in order that the truth of the Gospel and the fulness of the apostolic tradition may be brought to the knowledge of all who truly, unselfishly, and devotedly seek unity in Our Blessed Lord and His Holy Church, One, Catholic, and Apostolic.

> SOURCE: Paul S. Minear, ed., *The Nature of the Unity We Seek: Official Report of the North American Conference on Faith and Order, September 3–10, 1957, Oberlin, Ohio* (St. Louis, 1958), 159–63. Used by permission of The Bethany Press.

187. The Lord's Supper

The main work of the 1957 Oberlin Faith and Order Conference was done in the meetings of the twelve sections. One of the most delicate issues in ecumenical discussion is that of the sacrament of the Lord's Supper. Section Four of the conference addressed itself to this theme. Its report, "The Table of the Lord," reproduced below, has been widely hailed as making fresh contributions to difficult matters in Christian theology and in liturgical practice. Meeting under the chairmanship of James I. McCord (1919—), then Dean of Austin Presbyterian Theological Seminary and now President of Princeton Theological Seminary, the section made good use of an orientation paper which had been prepared by a study group working under his leadership in Austin, Texas. That this statement on the Eucharist could contain such significant agreements among representatives of churches of widely diverse historical backgrounds was itself indicative of the progress of the ecumenical movement in America.

DOCUMENT

Part I—Preamble

In faith, hope, and love we have met at Oberlin, discovering anew what Christians have discovered before, the richness and depth of our unity as brethren in Christ. Yet all of us are painfully aware that it is at the table of the Lord, given to us as the continuing sacrament of unity, that Christians in history have been divided from each other and continue to be separated. In our present situation we face a distressing predicament; on the one hand we recognize the long history of controversy which has surrounded the Holy Communion, obliging each one of us to adopt positions and hold convictions which conform with the confessions and traditions of our churches; on the other hand we acknowledge a heightened awareness of the judgment upon our separate tables and our inability to join with each other in celebration of the Supper of the Lord.

We rejoice, therefore, that in such a dilemma we have been able to converse with one another meaningfully about the Eucharist. Our ability to speak and to listen to one another is, we believe, the result of the guidance of the Holy Spirit of God Who has not ceased to speak to the Church and to lead her into all truth. We would, however, record our belief that this leading of the Holy Spirit has been mediated to us in several ways.

a) In the tragic situation of man in our time, we who believe in the reconciling power of the Gospel of Jesus Christ, the central fact proclaimed at his table, have been forced to listen anew to what Christ would say to his Church.

b) In the liturgical movements present in all our churches with their renewed interest in the worship of the triune God by his redeemed community, we see evidences of a return of all the churches to deeper concern with the Lord's table.

c) Above all, in the Church's reading and rereading of the Bible in our ecumenical situation and in the many new areas of insight gained into the life of the apostolic Church we acknowledge the prompting of the Spirit of Christ.

In this new situation we believe that all who consider the Holy Communion in its relation to unity share these common concerns:

1. A concern that our eucharistic faith and practice should in the deepest sense of the word be biblical; not in the sense of using the Scriptures as an arsenal of texts to support our points of view, but in the sense of seeking a fuller understanding of the sacramental life of the apostolic Church; in this common concern we all read the Scriptures freely and freshly as a shared book;

2. A concern that the table of the Lord should have its unique place in the common life of the Church, both in her internal strengthening and upbuilding in Christ and in her external mission on the geographical, social, and ideological frontiers of the faith;

3. A concern that we shall see in the Eucharist primarily what God in Christ is doing for our redemption as we look back in faith to what he has done and forward in hope to what he shall do.

Impelled by these motivations, sharing these concerns, and above all in obedience to the Lord of the Church, we who have been together at Oberlin present our agreements regarding the table of the Lord.

Part II—Agreements

1. At the table of the Lord the Church remembers in thanksgiving and gratitude the life, death and resurrection of Jesus Christ (1 Cor. 11:24). What is meant by this commemoration is more than mere recollection of a past event. Our agreement is based on a fresh understanding of the biblical doctrine of God and history. The God of the Bible has not only acted decisively in the past through Christ's atoning death and resurrection; he continues to act in the present; he will continue to act in the future. Therefore, the faithful commemoration of what Christ has done for us is at the same time an action in which Christ mediates himself to us in the present

moment. This is the same Christ who will in the last day share with his church the victorious completion of his purpose (Heb. 13:8).

2. Jesus Christ on the night in which he was betrayed chose bread and wine as the elements for the first Eucharist at the Last Supper. Rejecting any one-sided preoccupation with the elements in isolation, we agree that in the entire eucharistic action the whole Christ is personally present as both subject and object, *i.e.*, as the One who is at the same time the Giver and the Gift.

3. In view of our belief in Christ's active presence in the whole eucharistic action, we agree that this action is our participation in his risen life and the fulfillment of his promise to his church.

4. Christ's presence at his table follows from his promise and command. It is only in repentance and faith that the believer as an "empty vessel" receives the fruits of redemption, including the forgiveness of sins, justification, sanctification, newness of life and communion with his brethren. The Holy Spirit bears witness in the present to the reality of these fruits and directs our hope to their realization in the consummation of God's purpose (Romans 8:16–17). The Holy Communion is a means of placing us in the presence of Christ in a total way. In his presence we are judged as well as forgiven (1 Cor. 11:17–34).

5. The indispensable quality of the Eucharist derives from the once-for-all character of the atoning death and resurrection of Jesus Christ as it was prophetically and proleptically set forth in the Last Supper and remembered by and represented in the Christian community. "This do in remembrance of me" (1 Cor. 11:24–25; cf. Luke 22:19) calls us to the table where he has covenanted to meet us. As a consequence of our meeting him at his table we are made aware that he confronts us in other situations where we must respond in faith and love.

6. The Eucharist is therefore in the center of the response of the worshiping church to God's gracious activity in Christ. That which is offered and received in the Eucharist is central to the Christian life. It is important that all elements of proclamation—worship, service, obedience, and mission—be understood in their unity (2 Cor. 9:12–13). Liturgy in the narrow sense is not enough; the service of God by his people in their witness in the world and in winning others to Christ is inextricably bound up with their eucharistic life. The preached word of God is not to be set over against the Supper of the Lord. Both are commanded by Christ; both are involved in his work of redemption.

7. There is a growing realization of the eschatological nature of the Eucharist. "You proclaim the Lord's death until he comes" (1 Cor. 11:26) points unmistakably to the relation between the Supper and the Parousia. Our communion with Christ at the table of the Lord is thus both a present participation in his risen life (1 Cor. 10:16) and a foretaste of the messianic Feast (Mark 14:25; Rev. 19:7–9).

8. In the Eucharist God's covenant with man is renewed as revealed

and sealed in Jesus' sacrificial surrender of his life to God and for man. It points continually both to the constancy of God's faithfulness to his covenant people and to the relationship maintained by the renewal of the life of faithful obedience through the power of the Holy Spirit. The new age has broken through; God in Christ makes all things new. It is to this covenant life that we, as heirs of God and joint heirs with Christ (Rom. 8:17) are called and come in the Holy Communion. We are "a royal priesthood, a holy nation" (1 Peter 2:9), called to offer to God our sacrifice of praise and thanksgiving, ourselves, our souls and bodies. By personal participation in the body and blood of the One Lord Jesus Christ, we are strengthened for life in the corporate community of the new covenant and enabled to discern our oneness with each other. The blessings we receive at the Lord's table empower us for our witness and work in the world into which we are sent.

Part III—An Appeal to The Churches

All that we have gained from our discussions at Oberlin is only a preface to the larger task which still confronts the churches in their eucharistic life. This task, put in its simplest terms, is the heightening or, in some cases, a recovery of an utter seriousness toward the Eucharist as the sacrament of communion between Christ and his Body and the sacrament of unity in the Body. We are convinced that this task can be greatly aided by the process of ecumenical study, the process, that is of surveying our respective traditions, of facing seriously the crucial problem of intercommunion, of taking upon ourselves the pain of our division at the table of the Lord, of searching and finding new agreements in our understanding of the gracious mystery of Christ's act and promise in Holy Communion. The new situation, to which we have referred, and the progress in consensus which we ourselves have experienced, persuades us that all our churches should join with us in this study process, on the broadest possible scale—that this is, indeed, imperative and possible. The benefits of such a sharing would be twofold—a greater vitality in understanding and fellowship in the whole realm of eucharistic action, and also a powerful impetus to seek the fullness of communion with all our fellow Christians. And from both these benefits would flow new power, new courage, new clarity for the church's mission and outreach in this distraught and broken world, for which Christ's Body was broken and his blood shed.

Professor Sittler spoke for us all when he said to us, "The celebration of the Supper of the Lord is indeed recollection, Eucharist, the seal of forgiveness of sins, and the gift and nurturing of life in the Lord of the feast. But it is something more; something immediate and poignant in the history of all the embattled 'little flocks' of the first century, known again in our day by millions in shattered and cut-off lives in cells, rubble, behind wire and behind curtains. It is the proclamation of engrafted membership in a kingdom not born of history, and therefore, not at the mercy of history's demonic tyrannies. The somber chalice of the table of the Lord has in our day again become a defiant sign uplifted, the believer's toast of terrible joy." [40] It can also become the gift of hope and anticipation to those whose hunger and thirst is for "the unity of the spirit in the bond of peace" (Eph. 4:3).

In all our discussions we have been acutely conscious of the difficult problems of order and ministry as these are related to the due administration of the sacraments. We recognize that these cannot be separated from the full meaning of the Eucharist or from the problems of Christian unity. But we have found it possible to express our common understanding and fellowship apart from and prior to agreement on all matters of order. It may be that the time is not yet ripe for a really fruitful exploration of these long-standing disagreements. But the time for that *is* coming and will be hastened as Christians in all the churches engage in some such enterprise as this one in which we have received so rich a blessing and such a sure token of our community in Christ's self-giving love.

It is our hope that all the churches will take up and carry forward some such process of study and search. We earnestly invite them to encourage critical and appreciative conversation between themselves and Christians of other traditions, to stimulate the reading *together* of that history of our salvation that judges all our separate histories, to bend every effort to the end that all Christians may come to share the imperative for the oneness which is ours by God's gift and by his will.

We commend to them the guides and materials that have shaped our own conversation, but we urge them to experiment for themselves in new ways of search and exploration in this great central area of our common Christian concern. And if we are faithful and serious in such a study, we can "grow up in every way into him who is the head, into Christ, from whom the whole body, joined and knit together by every joint with which it is supplied, when each part is working properly, makes bodily growth and upbuilds itself in love." (Eph. 4:15–16) [41]

> SOURCE: "The Table of the Lord," in Paul S. Minear, ed., *The Nature of the Unity We Seek: Official Report of the North American Conference on Faith and Order, September 3–10, 1957, Oberlin, Ohio* (St. Louis, 1958), 200–5. Used by permission of The Bethany Press.

[40] From: *The Shape of the Church's Response in Worship* by Joseph Sittler, address given September 6, 1957, Cf. p. 114. [Oberlin report]

[41] The following bracketed note follows the above report in the official record: "No members of the Society of Friends or the Salvation Army were present in the discussions of Section 4. The position of these groups involves a basic assumption which was not fully recognized by those who produced the report. We find great inspiration in the new depth of meaning which the report of Section 4 gives to the act of communion with our Lord. However, we wish to interpret this report in accordance with our belief in the non-necessity of the outward elements of bread and wine to mediate the living presence of Christ to the believer in the act of communion with him. Written by T. Canby Jones in consultation with all of the Quaker delegates and one of the Salvation Army delegates.

LITERATURE

There is a vast and growing body of literature on the many aspects of the ecumenical movement. Indispensable is Ruth Rouse and Stephen C. Neill, eds., *A History of the Ecumenical Movement, 1517–1948* (Phila., 1954). A massive work of over eight hundred pages, it is a somewhat uneven symposium but contains a wealth of information on the whole movement from the outbreak of the Reformation to the founding of the World Council of Churches. Ecumenical libraries and bibliographies are listed. The volume builds on earlier treatments of the ecumenical theme, such as John T. McNeill's *Unitive Protestantism* (N.Y., 1930), and Gaius J. Slosser's *Christian Unity: Its History and Challenge in All Communions, in All Lands* (N.Y., 1929). A good critical review article on the work, by James Hastings Nichols, may be found in *Church History,* XXIII (1954), 272–7. For the basic historical sources of the ecumenical movement of the present day, see G. K. A. Bell's useful *Documents on Christian Unity* (4 vols., London, 1924–58).

There have been many books introducing and interpreting the ecumenical movement for Americans, such as Robert S. Bilheimer, *The Quest for Christian Unity* (N.Y., 1952); William Adams Brown *Toward a United Church: Three Decades of Ecumenical Christianity* (N.Y., 1946); Norman Victor Hope, *One Christ, One World, One Church: A Short Introduction to the Ecumenical Movement* (Phila., 1953); Walter M. Horton, *Toward a Reborn Church: A Review and Forecast of the Ecumenical Movement* (N.Y., 1949); Charles S. Macfarland, *Steps Toward the World Council: Origin of the Ecumenical Movement as Expressed in the Universal Christian Council for Life and Work* (N.Y., 1948); O. F. Nolde, ed., *Toward World-Wide Christianity* (N.Y., 1946); Matthew Spinka, *The Quest for Christian Unity* (N.Y., 1960); and Henry P. Van Dusen, *World Christianity:Yesterday-Today-Tomorrow* (N.Y., 1947). On world missions and ecumenicity, see especially William R. Hogg, *Ecumenical Foundations: A History of the International Missionary Council and Its Nineteenth-Century Background* (N.Y., 1952), and Henry P. Van Dusen, *One Great Ground of Hope: Christian Missions and Christian Unity* (Phila., 1961). Certain aspects of ecumenical development, especially those relating to mission and evangelism, are discussed in Edward J. Jurji, ed., *The Ecumenical Era in Church and Society: A Symposium in Honor of John A. Mackay* (N.Y., 1959). See also Stephen C. Neill, ed., *Twentieth Century Christianity* (London, 1961).

Church union movements were surveyed by H. Paul Douglass' *A Decade of Objective Progress in Church Unity, 1927–1936* (N.Y., 1937). Stephen C. Neill continued the study in *Towards Church Union, 1937–1952: A Survey of Approaches to Closer Union Among the Churches* (London, 1952). *The Ecumenical Review* has regularly published supplementary surveys on this theme: VI (1953–54), 300–15; VIII (1955–56), 76–93; IX (1956–57), 284–302; XII (1959–60), 231–66; XIV (1961–62), 351–79.

A series of volumes was produced in connection with the Amsterdam Assembly of the World Council of Churches: W. A. Visser 't Hooft, ed., *Man's Disorder and God's Design: The Amsterdam Assembly Series* (5 vols., London, 1949), of which the fifth volume is the official report of the First Assembly of the

World Council. Visser 't Hooft also edited *The Evanston Report: The Second Assembly of the World Council of Churches, 1954* (London, 1955), while James Hastings Nichols provided an evaluative report in *Evanston: An Intepretation* (N.Y., 1954). G. K. A. Bell has written on the first six years of the World Council in *The Kingship of Christ: The Story of the World Council of Churches* (Harmondsworth, Middlesex, 1954); for the next period see World Council of Churches, *Evanston to New Delhi: 1954–1961* (Geneva, 1961). Paul G. Macy has covered the earlier period in a very readable way in *If It Be of God: The Story of the World Council of Churches* (St. Louis, 1960). Edward Duff has contributed a thoughtful study on *The Social Thought of the World Council of Churches* (N.Y., 1956).

A good deal of information on the specifically American developments occurs in many of the books that have been mentioned. Elias B. Sanford prepared *The Origin and History of the Federal Council of the Churches of Christ in America* (Hartford, Conn., 1916); John A. Hutchison wrote *We Are Not Divided: A Critical and Historical Study of the Federal Council of the Churches of Christ in America* (N.Y., 1941). H. Paul Douglass has written a number of books on church unity in America, especially *Protestant Cooperation in American Cities* (N.Y., 1930), and *Christian Unity Movements in the United States* (N.Y., 1934). The history of the Home Missions Council of North America has been told by Robert T. Handy, *We Witness Together: A History of Cooperative Home Missions* (N.Y., 1956). The record of the formation of the National Council of the Churches of Christ in the United States of America is preserved in an informative commemorative volume, *Christian Faith in Action* (N.Y., 1951). Robert Lee effectively utilized sociological analysis in discussing *The Social Sources of Church Unity: An Interpretation of Unitive Movements in American Protestantism* (N.Y., 1960). Ross W. Sanderson studied local and regional forms of cooperative effort in *Church Cooperation in the United States: The Nationwide Backgrounds and Ecumenical Significance of State and Local Councils of Churches in Their Historical Perspective* (N.Y., 1960). Concerning the North American Faith and Order Conference at Oberlin in 1957, Paul S. Minear has edited the official report, *The Nature of the Unity We Seek* (St. Louis, 1958); George L. Hunt has prepared a study book, *A Guide to Christian Unity* (St. Louis, 1958); and J. Robert Nelson has edited *Christian Unity in North America: A Symposium* (St. Louis, 1958). One of the major themes of Faith and Order since Lund, the importance of tradition, is discussed by Albert C. Outler, *The Christian Tradition and the Unity We Seek* (N.Y., 1957). Winfred Ernest Garrison is critical of the concern for theological consensus in ecumenical endeavor in *The Quest and Character of a United Church* (N.Y., 1957).

The story of co-operative efforts among neo-fundamentalists has been told by James DeForest Murch, *Cooperation without Compromise: A History of the National Association of Evangelicals* (Grand Rapids, Mich., 1956). See also H. Shelton Smith, "Conflicting Interchurch Movements in American Protestantism," *Christendom*, XII (1947), 165–76. The Association's criticisms of the National and World Councils of Churches can be found in Murch's pamphlets, *The Growing Superchurch: A Critique of the National Council of the Churches of Christ* (n.p., 1952) and *Evanston, 1954—The Coming Great Church: A Critique of the World Council of Churches* (n.p., 1955). For the American Council of Christian

Churches' attack on the World and National Councils see Carl McIntire, *Modern Tower of Babel* (Collingswood, N.J., 1955). For a critique of the American Council itself, see Ralph L. Roy, *Apostles of Discord: A Study of Organized Bigotry and Disruption on the Fringes of Protestantism* (Boston, 1953). A sharp critique of the social thought and action of co-operative and ecumenical agencies is Edgar C. Bundy, *Collectivism in the Churches: A Documented Account of the Political Activities of the Federal, National, and World Council of Churches* (Wheaton, Ill., 1958). Criticism of a different sort, arising from the fear that historic Congregationalism is threatened by ecumenical trends, is presented by Marion John Bradshaw, *Free Churches and Christian Unity: A Critical View of the Ecumenical Movement and the World Council of Churches* (Boston, 1954).

On Catholic ecumenism and the relationship of the Church of Rome to the ecumenical movement, see E. C. Messenger, *Rome and Reunion: A Collection of Papal Pronouncements* (London, 1934); Henry S. Leiper, *Relations Between the Ecumenical Movement and the Vatican in the Twentieth Century* (mimeographed memorandum; N.Y., n.d.); Christophe J. Dumont, *Approaches to Christian Unity: Doctrine and Prayer,* tr. Henry St. John (Baltimore, 1959); Edward Francis Hanahoe, *Catholic Ecumenism* (Washington, 1953); Bernard Leeming, *The Churches and the Church: A Study of Ecumenism* (Westminster, Md., 1960); George H. Tavard, *The Catholic Approach to Protestantism* (N.Y., 1955) and *Two Centuries of Ecumenism* (Notre Dame, Ind., 1960); John M. Todd, *Catholicism and the Ecumenical Movement* (London, 1956); Gustave Weigel, *A Catholic Primer on the Ecumenical Movement* (Westminster, Md., 1957), and Hans Küng, *The Council, Reform and Reunion* (N.Y., 1961).

Biographical material of particular importance can be found in Alexander C. Zabriskie, *Bishop Brent: Crusader for Christian Unity* (Phila., 1948); F. A. Iremonger, *William Temple, Archbishop of Canterbury, His Life and Letters* (London, 1948); Galen M. Fisher, *John R. Mott, Architect of Cooperation and Unity* (N.Y., 1952); *Addresses and Papers of John R. Mott* (6 vols., N.Y., 1946–47); Finis S. Idleman, *Peter Ainslie: Ambassador of Good Will* (Chicago, 1941); and Stephen C. Neill, *Brothers of the Faith* (N.Y., 1960).

INDEX

Index

A

Abbot, Francis Ellingwood, 224
Abbott, Lyman, 258n, 321, 415
Abel, Theodore, 366n, 415
Abell, Aaron I., 360n, 363n, 364n, 365n, 384n, 414-5, 513n, 560
Abolitionism, 16-7, 167-75, 186-200, 212; English influence upon, 171
Abrams, Ray H., 368n, 416, 420n
Adam, Karl, 435
Adams, Alice Dana, 167, 170n, 211
"Address to the Young Men of the United States on Temperance," 36-41
Adger, John B., 177n
Adler, Felix, 224-5, 253
Advent Christian Church, 18-9
Adventism, 18-9, 315, 422
Ahern, Patrick H., 415
Ahlstrom, Sydney E., 100n, 130n, 164, 311n, 427n, 428n
Ainslie, Peter, 611
Alcott, Bronson, 166
Allen, Joseph Henry, 223n
Alliance of Reformed Churches, 572
American Anti-Slavery Society, 16, 170-3, 186-90, 192, 195n, 198
American Bible Society, 52, 67n, 90
American Board of Commissioners for Foreign Missions, 53-4, 565
American Colonization Society, 170, 172, 181-2, 186, 191-2, 195, 197, 211
American Council of Christian Churches, 572, 610-1
American Home Missionary Society, 3, 52, 64, 89, 91
American Lutheran Church, 571
"American Lutheranism," 101, 118, 310-1
American Oriental Society, 160n
American Peace Society, 15, 59-60
American Society for the Promotion of Temperance, 36
American Sunday School Union, 67n, 90, 564
American Temperance Society, 15
American Tract Society, 28, 37, 41, 52, 67n, 90

American Unitarian Association, 130n
"Americanism" (Roman Catholic), 310, 336-41, 356, 363, 514
Ames, Edward Scribner, 223, 254, 372-3, 429
Anabaptism, 99
Anderson, Bernhard W., 431
Anderson, Charles A., 117
Andover House, 365
Andover Theological Seminary, 263-4, 266
Andrew, James Osgood, 374
Anglicans, see Episcopalians
Anselm, 262
Anti-Catholicism, 6, 19, 49-50, 56-7, 65, 93, 105-6, 317, 336
Anti-Saloon League, 366-7
Antislavery newspapers, 168, 170, 173-4
Antislavery societies, 16, 167-8, 170, 174, 186-98
Anti-Unitarianism, 24, 29
Appel, Theodore, 93n, 117
Aquinas, Thomas, 435, 497, 500-1
Archimedes, 143
Arianism, 128
Aristotle, 244
Arminianism, 105
Armstrong, Maurice W., 117
Arrington, Leonard J., 117
"As Deceivers, Yet True," 455-65
Assembly of God, 314
Association of Catholic Trade Unionists, 514
Athanasius, 402
Athenagoras, 599
Atkins, Gaius Glenn, 220
Atlantic Charter, 526
Atonement, doctrine of the, 127, 261-2, 270-5, 284-5
Aubrey, Edwin E., 254
Augsburg Confession, 70, 100-2, 311, 351
Augustine, 403, 500
Aulén, Gustaf, 427n
Authority of Holy Scripture, 276-9
Automation, 421

B

C

D

E

F

G

H

I

J

K

L

M

Millennialism, 12, 16, 18, 293, 314–5, 332–6, 357
Miller, Charles E., 496–502
Miller, Francis P., 443, 447
Miller, Kenneth B., 421n
Miller, Perry, 4, 5n, 66n, 116, 121n, 125n, 164–6
Miller, Robert M., 505, 511n, 560
Miller, Samuel, 70
Miller, William, 18, 315
Miller, William L., 562
Millerism, 55–6, 65
Mims, Edwin, 354n
Minear, Paul S., 431, 604, 608, 610
Ministry, doctrine of the, 75, 111–2, 157–9, 425, 489
Miracle, doctrine of, 123, 278, 316, 347
Missionary Education Movement of the United States and Canada, 569n
Missionary movements, 3–5, 64, 71, 73, 89, 91, 219, 221, 314, 354, 366–7, 422, 425, 506, 564–6
Missouri Compromise, 167, 183
Missouri Lutherans, 6, 311, 350–1, 358, 493, 571
Modernism, 223, 238–45, 310, 316, 341–6, 356, 438, 448–54, 483–4, 572
Mohammedanism, 163, 304, 467
Monism, 268–9, 538–9
Moody, Dwight L., 312–3, 320–4, 358, 475, 567
Moody, William R., 358

Moody Bible Institute, 313, 321
Moore, John M., 575n
Moore, Glenn W., 555
Morgan, John, 191
Mormonism, 69, 72, 80–4, 99, 116–7
Morrison, Charles Clayton, 436, 559
Morrow, Ralph E., 365n, 372n, 414
Morse, Samuel F. B., 6
Mortalium animos, 572–3, 581
Mortensen, A. Russell, 116
Mott, Frank L., 8n
Mott, John R., 567, 611
Moynihan, James H., 415
Muehl, William, 509n
Muelder, Walter G., 509n, 561
Mühlenberg, Henry M., 100
Muhlenberg, William A., 365
Mulder, William, 116
Muldoon, Peter J., 408
Mullins, Edgar Y., 357
Mundinger, Carl S., 358
Munger, Theodore T., 306–7
Munificentissimus Deus, 422n
Murch, James DeForest, 610
Murray, John Courtney, 424n, 514, 537–42
Murray, R. H., 317n
Muste, A. J., 512
Muzzey, David S., 253
Myrick, Luther, 13n
Mystical Presence, 94–100
Mystici Corporis Christi, 435, 581
Myth in religion, 457, 467

N

Nash, Arnold S., 425n, 502, 508n
Nash, Daniel, 13n
National Association of Evangelicals in the United States, 493, 572
National Catholic War Council, 219, 407–8
National Catholic Welfare Conference, 219, 364, 407–8, 513, 526
National Conference of Christians and Jews, 424–5
National Council of Churches, 422, 438, 493, 495, 510, 512, 522, 543–9, 561, 568–9, 572, 585–9, 593, 610
National Legion of Decency, 513
National Lutheran Council, 593, 599
National Organization for Decent Literature, 513
National Prohibition Party, 366
National Protestant Council on Higher Education, 569n
National Study Conference on the Churches and a Just and Durable Peace, 522

Nationalism, 8, 68, 216, 445–6, 521, 523–4
Nativism, 366
Natural and revealed religion, 123–4
Naturalism, 223, 245–9, 254, 259, 316, 346, 354, 356, 430, 448–9
Nature, doctrine of, 122, 135, 251, 268, 456–8, 461
Nature of the Unity We Seek, 599–608
Neander, August, 89, 93
Negroes, church life, 421, 545–9, 574–5; Communism among, 420; social conditions of, 167, 193–5, 211, 364–5, 511, 556
Neill, Stephen C., 563n, 564n, 565n, 577, 609, 611
Nelson, J. Robert, 436, 503, 570n, 610
Neo-fundamentalism, 422, 488–96, 610
Neo-liberalism, 472–8
Neo-orthodoxy, 422, 428, 437, 448, 502, 506; opposition to, 438, 471–4, 476, 488
Neo-Platonism, 120–1
Neo-Thomism, 427n

O

P

T

U

V

W